THE WOMEN OF
GENERAL MOTORS

A Century of Art and Engineering

CONSTANCE A. SMITH

GENERAL MOTORS

SCHIFFER
PUBLISHING

4880 Lower Valley Road • Atglen, PA 19310

To my dad, William R. Smith, who fought for my place in the all-male drafting class at my high school and allowed me to inherit his big oak-and-maple drafting table.

Edited by Karla Rosenbusch
Designed by Danielle Farmer / Chris Bower
Cover design by Ashley Millhouse
Type set in URW DIN & URW DIN Cond/Crimson

ISBN: 978-0-7643-6428-0
Printed in India

Published by Schiffer Publishing, Ltd.
4880 Lower Valley Road
Atglen, PA 19310
Phone: (610) 593-1777; Fax: (610) 593-2002
Email: Info@schifferbooks.com
Web: www.schifferbooks.com

For our complete selection of fine books on this and related subjects, please visit our website at www.schifferbooks.com. You may also write for a free catalog.

Schiffer Publishing's titles are available at special discounts for bulk purchases for sales promotions or premiums. Special editions, including personalized covers, corporate imprints, and excerpts, can be created in large quantities for special needs. For more information, contact the publisher.

We are always looking for people to write books on new and related subjects. If you have an idea for a book, please contact us at proposals@schifferbooks.com.

CONTENTS

FOREWORDS

ANNE ASENSIO
Design Influencer

Martin Christian

Women designers have long struggled to establish themselves in the design industry, a male-dominated world. Limited to a specific field or forced to work behind a man's shadow, they nevertheless contribute to the history of design. Today, women's careers in design are as varied as this field.

And automotive is the fiercest of design fields.

Male-dominated culture has overshadowed women's creativity and impact in the industry since its infancy: cultural bias and sexist assumptions have consolidated an unfair picture of Design Made by Women. The pioneers hid in the shadow of men, husbands or collaborators, or worse, were confined to certain areas of design. In the early twentieth century, the Bauhaus was assigning disciplines to men and women on the basis of a nineteenth-century philosophy of "separate spheres," allowing men to participate only in painting, molding, and designing classes. Crocheting was designated for women. It was later the case in automotive design, where women were directed toward upholstery, colors, and fabrics.

Automotive design systemically lacked a consistent narrative. Few have the opportunity to see the inside of a professional design studio, since secrecy is a necessary part of the process. When it comes to women in design, the issue gets worse. In turn, secrecy led to more invisibility for women designers. Women in design are the "forgotten" of design history. Many of them have atypical backgrounds and singular destinies, and very quickly, when their stories unfold, we realize that women have played a role both considerable and surprisingly neglected in the evolution of the discipline.

I am a woman designer, part of a very small group of women to have managed to establish themselves in a very masculine environment and make their way to the top of automotive design. All along my career, I have been a relentless supporter of women's evolution and promotion, yet the battle is far from over.

This is why I value this initiative aiming to shed a sincere and authentic light on women's creativity and impact, in industry, in society, and in our lives.

I met Constance about two decades ago, when I was the first woman design executive at GM. I worked with Wayne Cherry and then Ed Welburn as vice president and under Bob Lutz's stellar leadership. As a French woman, I was acutely aware that I was following the footsteps of GM's first woman designer hired by Harley Earl. Helene Rother had an incredible personality and independence and was inducted into the Automotive Hall of Fame this year. I came to GM with my European expertise of design, bringing what designers value the most: creativity, innovative thinking, and singularity. I never doubted I was made for the job. This may be the single most important common trait among women designers.

Constance immediately impressed me with her "constance," a French synonym for "pugnacity." Her book, her quest, is an incredible journey in design from a unique perspective, enabling a well-deserved recognition of women's huge contributions in automotive design history, a perspective everybody should draw from.

Highlighting the women's representation in the auto industry is not just a decent, fair, and necessary task: it is now a critical one as a key driver for this industry's future.

Successful innovation depends on good design. In the world of business, this is recognized, and the consumer wins. Today's stronger-than-ever consumer-focused business, the idea of developing new business models without a strong design input, would be anathema—especially in the highly competitive global economy.

The development of new aspects of mobility will greatly affect the automobile industry and the image of automobiles. The disruption of the traditional models of ownership will shift market preferences and attitudes. New challenges such as intensification of usage and changes in consumer responses mean that design innovation must stay as close as possible to the user's needs. A development system that lacks the imaginative and user-centered qualities of design is reducing its capacity for successful innovation. In tune with the importance of diversity, not only because they have social responsibility policies to address, companies and brands have to grasp its importance for business. Customers and services of these companies need to benefit from the diversity of teams, regardless of gender or origin, to compete effectively. Companies need to be bold with regard to design and hire more women designers to reshape a more ethical and sustainable automotive culture.

What we have learned from the past is that female designs are often symbols of progress, empathy emphasizing the creation of proposals designed for the user audience. These skills are now challenging the male predominance in exterior design and styling preferences. Shifting to user-centered design, the qualities women designers have displayed for decades would move to the forefront.

If the design sector still consists in average of 78 percent men and 22 percent women, even if it may seem a disheartening statistic, it is certainly a more promising percentage than in the past, and a clear sign that there is more room for talented women in the design world.

It would start by promoting women's design and women in design.

This is why Constance's book is so important.

Commonly said, to understand the present and prepare for the future, it is important to understand the past.

GM's midcentury women designers hired by Harley Earl in 1942 and in the 1950s have contributed to bridging the art world to mass production in the auto industry, and these modern business pioneers were an exception. This was right before the auto design profession would go on to become a global phenomenon called "the Modern Art of Industry."

They were the pioneers. Earl's business-driven patriarchal approach paved the road for women to enter design practice in the automotive industry. However, despite their skills, women had to continually fight to exist in design.

The greatest inputs and impacts women designers made in the last 100 years, the design stories around their modern and forward-thinking masterpieces, their dynamic artistic production, their innovative breakthroughs, and their user-centric, differentiated identity were simply missing or poorly reported in the vernacular automotive design culture. As for the biographies, Hall of Fame, and car design publications, designers and men are just synonyms.

Today, more than 50 percent of design school students are women. However, too few are selecting an automotive design career. On education programs, on corporate structures, and on design management, the absence of fair and critical discussions around gender issues in automotive design may prevent a renaissance of the industry. The quality, the elegance, the comfort, and the emotion that design arouses have nothing to do with the gender of its creator, but with its personality. We should eradicate the confusion between feminine design and design made by women. We hope in the future that gender will not be any more a decision-making factor in the choices of design actors.

The designer's practice proposes to meet several fields . . . and its ability to gather may be more compatible with female values. The designer of tomorrow may be less and less the one who "signs," and more than the one who unites; it will be less a design that appears and more a sensible design.

In the Age of Experience, design practice efficiency must be seen as a socio-anthropological system that aims for possible and desirable futures.

This is why more than ever, success resides on design's emphasis at large: "*We should never lose the focus on design,*" as Bob Lutz claims.

Amazing women designers are working and creating in design studios all around the world: to highlight them and to promote them as role models should motivate women working in the industry.

Women will continue to challenge in our male-dominated society.

Anne Asensio is a designer with global design experience that spans more than three decades. She held executive roles in design management and innovation strategy at Renault and General Motors and continues to serve Dassault Systèmes as its vice president of design.

Asensio led the design of numerous concept and production vehicles, including the revolutionary Renault Scenic concept car and the groundbreaking Volt concept, perhaps the most awarded automobile in GM's history. Asensio, working with GM, assisted in the founding of the Transportation Department at Lawrence Technological University and later built a vehicle design curriculum with DS's 3D at its core. At Dassault Systèmes (3D), Asensio continues to provide design and innovation counsel to car companies and automotive design studios. She founded the DESIGN Studio, a multidisciplinary design team in innovation strategy by design, design research, design management, and consultancy.

Asensio has won several design and innovation awards and plays an active role within the global-design community, and on strategic boards for companies, design schools, and institutions. She is a board member of the World Design Organization.

- Anne Asensio, August 25, 2020

MEI CAI
Engineering Leader

Many women are not aware of the range of opportunities available to them in the automotive industry, which remains male dominated. While most women gravitate toward human resources, marketing, accounting, communications, and legal, few work in design, manufacturing, and engineering.

Despite this, GM has many strong leaders, including engineers such as Mary Barra, GM chairman and chief executive officer, and Pam Fletcher, who served as vice president of global innovation.

While Barra may be the most decorated woman in the automotive industry in this century, Pam Fletcher, the former executive chief engineer for GM's electrification program, was charged with engineering the Volt HEV and Bolt EV and oversaw GM's technology-led business transformation.

GM engineers are always striving to find new ways to reinforce the safety of our products, as well as to improve the quality and performance of our vehicles. They are responsible for many industry firsts, such as the airbag, catalytic converter, shatterproof glass, vehicle-to-vehicle communications, and extended-range electric vehicles, which all are the result of GM teamwork. Today, innovations such as Teen Driver, OnStar Proactive Alerts, the CarbonPro pickup box and Super Cruise—GM's first partially automated driving system, now with lane change—are indicative of the vast number of the company's inventions that improve the lives of our customers.

GM has been making production electric vehicles for the last twenty-five years, dating back to EV1. GM recently revealed its all-new Ultium batteries and flexible modular platform, which will enable a multibrand, multisegment EV portfolio that will reach the market quickly.

Working in the automotive industry can be both challenging and rewarding. Automotive engineers must understand every area of the industry, from the look and feel of vehicles to the safety and performance. With more than a century of history, the automotive industry is now on a revolutionary journey. How we power and interact with our vehicles is fundamentally changing because of new technologies. Electric, self-driving-connected vehicles and shared mobility services will transform how we get around. Most importantly, what is possible today is just the beginning of what is possible.

Engineers generally work as part of a team responsible for vehicle design, development, manufacturing, and testing. Women play a significant role on this team.

Perhaps lacking the confidence of their male counterparts, women are also underrepresented in the engineering education programs as well as in the workforce. According to the Society of Women Engineers' 2019 Research Update, 20 percent of bachelor's degrees are awarded to women in engineering and computer science, but only 13 percent of engineers in the current workforce are women. Also, 61 percent of women engineers report that they have to prove themselves repeatedly to get the same level of respect and recognition as their male colleagues.

It is a well-known fact that women influence more than 80 percent of all new-car purchases. We need more female engineers who can have an impact on vehicle design and execution as well as incorporate the advanced features that OEMs are now offering.

Many studies have shown that men and women have different approaches to solving complex problems. Other studies have shown that men, on average, tend to display higher degrees of overconfidence and competitiveness than women, while women, on average, are more risk averse. In group situations, men may feel more comfortable shooting from the hip, while women may be less likely to take stands unless they feel they are on solid footing.

In engineering, there is a need for a balance between confidence and caution. Confidence is needed to try new things, and caution is necessary to execute them successfully. A better balance between men and women may be helpful in achieving these goals as well as advancing our business to the next evolutionary level.

One of the biggest choices we must make in our lives is our career path. If we are lucky, our career path can also be our passion. Choosing a field that is still male dominated has presented challenges, and there were times I had to make tough choices to balance work and family responsibilities.

Looking back now, my career has been one of the most rewarding experiences of my life. I am very fortunate to satisfy the technical side of my personality by working in the automotive engineering field, which has still provided me time with family and for my passions outside the office. I would never change my decision to become an engineer in the automotive field. I would certainly recommend our industry to any woman who has a passion for automobiles.

Constance Smith, who worked in the Advanced Studios at GM Design, opened our eyes with her first book—*Damsels in Design*. In *The Women of General Motors*, she has captured the in-depth stories of more than eighty women whose accomplishments have and will continue to improve our ability to communicate and advance in the business. These brave and strong women are mothers, daughters, and wives outside the workplace. They all have struggles, issues, and challenges in their lives, but they have chosen to follow their dreams. Their successes in one of the world's most male-dominated industries will, I hope, inspire more girls and young women to choose the engineering path and pave the way for even more to enter this rewarding profession.

There is much to gain from a team consisting equally of brilliant men and women of all ethnicities in the workplace. They can change our lives forever.

Dr. Mei Cai is a GM technical fellow and the manager of the Energy Storage Materials Group. She is responsible for technology innovations in advanced energy storage materials for future electric vehicles. Mei has far-reaching R&D experience, including extensive knowledge in novel materials processing. She has managed multi-million-dollar R&D projects in the development of low-cost and durable vehicular energy storage materials and systems. Mei was recognized as the 2018 Asian American Engineer of the Year for her contributions in fundamental research and technology development and was the recipient of the prestigious Kettering Award.

In 2016, Mei Cai was the recipient of the prestigious Kettering Award for "Industry Leading Integrated, Long Range, and Low Cost RESS." *Constance Smith*

PREFACE

Many of the over one hundred women designers and engineers profiled here were introduced to the automotive industry, more often than not, by male family members or mentors. My own father fought for my place in an all-male drafting class in high school. I won first place at a technical fair, only to find that someone had ripped my drawing off the wall and that my large blue ribbon lay on the floor. My drawing was never found. This was a valuable lesson I will never forget, since it prepared me for the kinds of challenges I would have to deal with as a woman in all aspects of the automotive industry for the rest of my life.

When I was preparing for college, my dad fashioned a handmade fiberglass-and-leather portfolio case for my interview at Pratt Institute. He quietly encouraged my ambitions. Many years later, I discovered that the scholarship that he described winning himself in 1933 in high school was the result of the model he built of a Fisher Body Napoleonic coach. He had tried to explain it. My mom and I knew what a car was, but had a hard time envisioning what a coach consisted of. It remained in the Glen Cove High School, New York, display case for years. No women participated in Craftsman's Guild events in the States; however, some photos were discovered abroad of models women had made.

Although I majored in sculpture and education in undergraduate school, I soon came across a series of showcases set up by the Industrial Design Department at school, where abstract models of a sewing machine and an automobile were on display. Liz Wetzel, who is later profiled, had a similar awakening after visiting the College of Creative Studies. It was time to so some research.

While the Werkbund married design education and manufacturing in Germany in 1907, the first industrial design programs were not introduced in America until the early to mid-1930s, many years after engineering schools flourished in the latter 1800s. I view industrial design as a marriage of engineering and art, since the curriculum included drafting and production methods courses. Intent on building things with my hands, I was later lured to the graduate Industrial Design Department, where I took some undergraduate courses gratis to catch up and received some funding via a partial scholarship.

When I proposed to write a study on women in industrial design for a master's thesis project, I was simply ignored while the other proposals entertained were discussed. Although most of the women in the auto industry graduated from my school, none of the men wanted to acknowledge them. At this time, there was one lady on the faculty who taught three-dimensional design: Rowena Reed Kostellow. Her husband, Alexander Kostellow, had assisted in founding the department. They later hired an accomplished ceramist who had escaped from wartime Europe. When I started my thesis project in the 1970s, "Design Capabilities with the Rotary Engine," I designed and made a model of a safety car inside and out and proposed an all-in-one heated/cooled glove box. Again, no one ever mentioned any women who had come before me in the auto industry at school. However, all but one of the six 1950s Damsels of Design graduated from my school, and most of the instructors and tenured professors must have known this.

Before graduation in the 1970s, the invitation to work as a GM designer remains one of the highlights of my career.

In this decade, I saw only six or seven women designers and engineers on staff at the Tech Center, and one was a GMI (General Motors Institute) co-op student. It took some time for me to discover that the women working in factories, some of them starting on the assembly lines, were participating in the GMI co-op program. Because of the diversity of my portfolio, I was the only female accepted into the advanced studio, but this was also after I flatly refused to work at Frigidaire designing appliances or a production interiors studio—where women who were likely viewed as interior designers belonged. In the early 1970s, I met Suzanne Vanderbilt, who I later discovered held a number of US patents—she designed the first industrial helmet while still in graduate school, and later the adjustable lumbar support for car seats. Vanderbilt was asked to assist me in settling in, and I was also introduced to Kathy Denek, who invited me to join some of the clubs she belonged to. It was rumored that two other women were hired about the same time as I was, but it took weeks before meeting either of them. In this era, the design studios were locked unless you had the code. Jan Tribbey left to marry a boyfriend in New York and joined the J. C. Penney design staff, and the other, Barbara Munger, decided to return home after losing a close family member. However, she did not make the decision to retire until after completing a twenty-year stint in GM's interiors studios.

To bolster my education and confidence, I also studied engineering in a GM management-training program at the Technical Center, automotive mechanics at MOTECH, and business in the Wayne State MBA program—all with much enthusiasm. I learned to design circuits and rebuild Hydramatic transmissions just before the dominance of front-wheel drive. With the help of seasoned colleagues Bill Porter and Ed Walter, I also honed my drawing and illustration skills.

Ten years ago, I decided to put women pioneers who designed interiors, exteriors, and safety components on the map in *Damsels in Design: Women Pioneers in the Automotive Industry, 1939–1959*. It took years to find these women, if they were still breathing, and in some cases their heirs were fighting dementia and dropping dead before I could get to them.

On another note, in the past two years I grieved the loss of another two of the six original 1950s Damsels of Design. Only one is still alive.

In 2019, following in the footsteps of archivist Lawrence R. Gustin—who has always inspired me—I received the 2018 AACA's McKean Award; I had not submitted my book, so it came as a surprise. McKean founded the AACA Research Library. I also received an Award of Distinction for books written in the English language from the predominately male Society of Automotive Historians. I felt I was competing against the whole bodies of work of the most-celebrated male authors in the world instead of my book against their last books.

After more than a decade of research, I look forward to adding some additional women pioneers and those from 1960 to the present into the automotive history books. Today, I cannot find a car in the GM portfolio that did not benefit from a woman's touch.

While in earlier times there were few women lifers, some women today are choosing to retire along with their male counterparts solely because of their advancing age and changes to their retirement plans.

Those who remain face another set of challenges. The more that things are supposed to change for women, the more that they remain the same. Whether women are welcomed or continue to be challenged in an industry that is still a male bastion, while women play catch-up, remains to be seen.

There is no question that as chair and CEO of GM, Mary T. Barra will continue to recruit and promote men and women of diversity. Barra continues to educate the world by what she advises and what she does. Her rise, tenure, and successes will always be celebrated by the over one million men and women who follow her online and everywhere else.

I am in awe of the brave women who are featured in this heavily researched history. Records, archival material, original drawings, US patents, heirs, colleagues, and the women themselves substantiate their contributions. Society can no longer hide or deny their accomplishments. Many have worked to improve and will continue to touch some facet of our lives.

ACKNOWLEDGMENTS

Meredith B. Jaffe with her late father, H. Roy Jaffe. *Meredith B. Jaffe*

I thank those who have encouraged and assisted me over the last ten years to promote my lifelong journey to add the contributions of women in the automotive industry—in this case, designers and engineers—to America's history books. With many of my profiles based on firsthand information, I am forever indebted to the women participating, their families—in some cases, heirs—and their colleagues for their contributions.

I give thanks to General Motors Media, the GM Archives, GM Legal, GM Design, GM Korea, Holden, and PATAC for their assistance. I also thank Kettering University archivists and librarians. I greatly appreciate the help of those at Opel Public Relations.

I also wish to thank Gina Peera, Kathleen Adelson, Kevin Kirbitz, Christo Datini, Angela Caligiuri, Brenda D. Eitelman, Monte Doran, Shelly Joseph, Larry Kinsel, and Tobias Suenner.

I give thanks to Nardina Mein, Melanie Bazil, Lief Rohwedder, Linda Pierce, Susan Skarsgard, Steve Wolken, Doug Didia, Julie Sabit, Matt Hocker, Werner Meier, Chris Ritter, Louis F. Fourie, Chris Shires, Bill Porter, Martha Fotopolis, Norm J. James, Dan Nelson, Lars Kneller, Robin Montgomery, Tyra Light, John and Deborah Curren Aquino, the Petersen family, the Linder family, Marion and Mark McAlpine, Stuart Sobek, Lynn and Leroy Barrett, John Jacobus, Jeannie West, Althea Travis, and others.

I give special thanks to Meredith B. Jaffe, who assisted with final research, edited early drafts before submission, and contributed images from the estate of her late father, H. Roy Jaffe, a designer under Harley Earl. I thank Karla Rosenbusch, who also assisted with the editing process before publication on behalf of Schiffer Books.

Having relied on a number of research facilities, I thank their archivists for their direction: the AACA Library, the Lawrence Technological University Design and Architecture Department, the Detroit Historical Society, the Detroit Public Library, the Gilmore Car Museum, the Cranbrook Art Museum and Archives, the University of Michigan Library, the Michigan State University Archives, the Hagley Library, the Benson Ford Research Center, the West Hempstead Public Library, the Nassau County Library System of New York, the University of Wisconsin Library, the Archipenko Foundation, the United States Holocaust Memorial Museum, the Catholic University of America Library, AP Wide World, and others.

I also thank those photographers, collectors, specialists, and car club members who assisted, including John S. Fackre (research), Keith Furino (collector), Brent Havekost (collector), Steve Fecht (photographer), Savanah Michel (artist), John Martin (photographer), James McCarty (collector), Stanley Rusinyajk (collector), and others.

GM Heritage Center. *Constance Smith*

Over 100 years ago, a strong and talented woman reported for work at the Fisher Body facility in Detroit, Michigan, where she would spend over twenty-five years at a drawing board before retiring. Not only was Bonnie Lemm GM's first female designer and design engineer, she was more than likely the first in the automotive industry. I am indebted to Richard P. Scharchburg, a GM historian, for having the foresight to collect and safeguard many of Lemm's original drawings, and Kevin Kirbitz, who headed GM's Archives and Media Division sometime later, to advise me of this donation. I photographed these rare remarkable drawings to share with readers. Helen Blair Barlett follows Lemm in this history. Utilizing a grant from AC Spark, she completed the requirements for her PhD in mineralogy in 1931 before joining the AC Ceramic Research Department. With the exception of an assignment on the Manhattan Project at MIT, Barlett also spent her entire engineering career at AC Spark and continued to share her knowledge with students after retirement.

Other daring women, some having to fight negative attitudes, unprofessional behaviors, and shenanigans poorly conceived by their male colleagues, followed Lemm and Barlett. Harley Earl recognized the enormous talent of Helene Rother Ackernecht, an émigré from Nazi-occupied Germany via France; she started work at the end of 1942 and completed her first full year in 1943. Amy Light, a California girl, arrived at the same time to assist with the design of the Train of Tomorrow. She was advised that she was the first woman designer at Styling, which was located in the Argonaut Building; however, she was a product designer and did not design automobiles.

MaryEllen Green also moved from Earl's California to New York to study industrial design. Green's father was heavily in-volved in the auto industry as an importer of Bantams—early small cars. She graduated from Pratt Institute with a certificate in industrial design around 1950. Green was likely the first women to complete the program.

The mid-1950s brought the Damsels of Design—the original six were joined by five others. Marketing created the phrase to attract attention, although one woman was already married and another would soon join her. By today's standards, this term is disparaging to some still alive. Most women were trained in art or industrial design, and two studied engineering at some point in their careers. While many left to accept other positions or raise families, some stayed on for a decade or more, and one spent the rest of her life there. The flight of those who left is attributed in part to the attitude of William L. Mitchell, who replaced Harley Earl as the vice president of design. One studio head felt that Bill

Mitchell was trying to protect the women from the men who used foul language in the exteriors studios, but most reasoned the opposite, since there were men assigned to all the studios.

Approximately six or seven designers were recruited by GM Design, and almost thirty women engineers followed Karen Morman Stewart at General Motors Institute, the first woman to arrive, in the 1960s. The designers included Catherine S. Denek—the lifer among them, Joan Klatil Creamer—an exterior designer, Joan Gatewood, Margaret Schroeder, Bernadette Mate, and Pamela Waters. A seventh might have been lost in a plane crash. In the case of the designers, the tenure of some or lack thereof was largely blamed again on the attitude of William L. Mitchell, the all-powerful vice president of design. However, some of the women designers confessed that they had enrolled in college to study something else—perhaps painting, graphics, fashion design—or even attended to find husband material.

Karen (Morman) Stewart graduated in 1970 in mechanical engineering from GMI and was their first female graduate. Sometime in the 1970s, three new designers joined the two already on staff. However, Elizabeth Burgess Griffith, who graduated in 1972, was part of the largest GMI class ever—fifty women. However, not all completed the program. Theresa Ullrich, who was married to a GMI graduate, worked in our department in 1973 and went on to join the engineering staff.

Barbara Perluke, a 1972 graduate of Pratt Institute, was trained in engineering and industrial design and assigned to the Frigidaire Studio. She left Design Staff for New York to marry and later joined IBM. Elizabeth Burgess went to work after graduating from GMI. Two other women arrived for assignments in the production interior studios. They were considered interior designers, and this is where some felt they logically belonged. Jan Tribbey left for New York to marry and joined J. C. Penney as a staff designer. Barbara Munger served at GM Design for twenty years before retiring.

Also in the 1970s, with a portfolio that included innovations and design work, the author was accepted into the Advanced Design Studio. On the first day of work, her drawing board sat in the center of a large room, with a vase of flowers on top. The men's cubicles hugged the outer walls.

In 1980, Mary Barra enrolled in the GMI co-op program and subsequently rose through the ranks. She has served as CEO since January 15, 2014, and chairman since January 4, 2016, and has inspired women and men around the world.

She was not alone. In the 1980s, the ranks of women appear to have become more diverse. Marietta Kearney, the first African

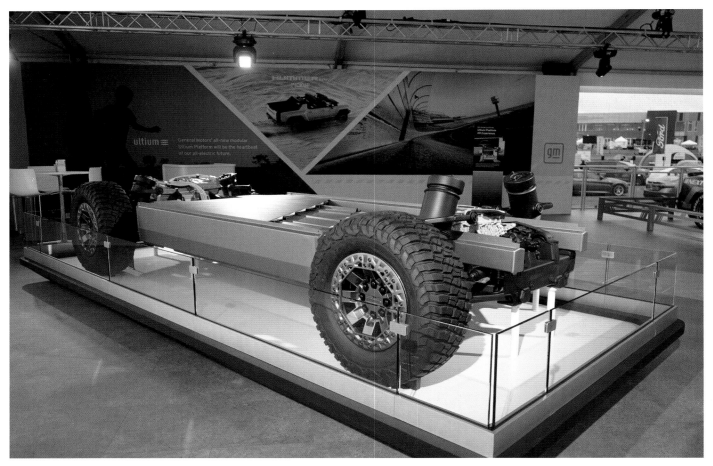

The wireless Ultium battery back sits below the passenger compartment in the Hummer. *Constance Smith*

American female designer, registered her talent. Mary Gustanski, a 1985 Kettering University graduate, began her climb. At this time, Elizabeth Wetzel, from a GM family right around the corner, also began her ascent. Diana Werrell and Grace Larrinua arrived full time from GMI.

Of course, GM's international locations employed women of all nationalities, but not many were to be found.

Women who started in the 1990s made a giant leap toward the glass ceiling, as evidenced by the careers of Renee Bryant, Mei Cai, Helen Emsley, Pam Fletcher, Marie Johnson, Brigid O'Kane, Kristy Rasbach, Katherine Sirvio, Susan Skarsgard, and Yan Huang. Sharon Gauci, an Australian, relocated to the United States in the 1990s. Some appear to have broken through it.

In 2000, many were given an opportunity to join GM and did; Anne Asensio, Alexandra Dymowska, Amanda Kalhous, Magdalena Kokoznska, Ven Lai, Christine Park, and Stephanie Thompson were among those who applied or were recruited. One Cadillac designer noted, "I didn't decide to enter auto; it just happened."

After 2010, the doors opened wider and an initiative to recruit women expanded.

This history records a cross section of women from around the world, and not all women. The ladies profiled here all have something in common. While they may have been born brilliant and talented, their work ethic has contributed to their success. Through the many products they have developed, they have both saved lives and continue to change the way we move.

PART I.

IN THE BEGINNING: THE ORIGINS OF GENERAL MOTORS

GENERAL MOTORS (GM), HEADQUARTERED IN DETROIT, MICHIGAN, is composed of numerous American and international entities. It was incorporated by W. C. Durant as the General Motors Company on September 16, 1908. After a subsequent name change, ultimately it reorganized and regained its original moniker. While Buick and Olds were part of GM in 1908, Oakland (Pontiac) and Cadillac were not added until 1909. Durant teamed up with Louis Chevrolet to found the Chevrolet Motor Company, and in 1918 GM acquired Chevrolet and the Guardian Frigerator Company. In 1909, GM would acquire 60 percent of Fisher Body. Although at least two dozen other acquisitions were made, Rapid Motor Vehicle Company and the Alliance Motor Truck Company were combined to create the Rapid Truck, which was absorbed by General Motors Truck Company in 1911. The subsequent acquisition of almost half of the McLaughlin Motor Car Company Ltd., of Canada, in 1916 would prove invaluable, and Buicks would be shipped internationally. Initially under the direction of W. C. Durant and later under a number of other leaders, the GM Company would endure a number of acquisitions, dispositions, mergers, and management turnovers and continues to divest and invest in properties today.

The original GM Building still stands in Detroit. General Motors

GENERAL MOTORS GAINS MOMENTUM

The motoring world served notice of its arrival when W. C. Durant, a prominent businessman, was called in to save Buick, a struggling car company in 1904. Durant, with partner Dallas Dort, had built perhaps the largest carriage company in the area. The founder of Buick, David Dunbar Buick, entered the automobile field from the plumbing industry and was most noted for developing a method for affixing porcelain to bathtubs. A clever inventor, he also mounted a sink on a tub to save space. Before Durant's arrival, Buick, even with affiliations with and sales of power trains and parts to McLaughlin of Canada, struggled to survive. Durant's success rested on his formation of a new company around Buick. He was praised for recognizing that there were a variety of consumers with different tastes and budgets in the marketplace. He also realized the tremendous savings that resulted from the integration of shared parts.

The former Durant-Dort carriage factory was refurbished to serve as a research facility in Flint. Constance Smith

This 1903 Cadillac was welcomed at the first Las Vegas Concours—the Helene Awards. *Constance Smith*

The 1940 LaSalle brings to mind Harley Earl, its originator. *Constance Smith*

Between 1908 and 1910, General Motors acquired approximately two dozen other companies, consisting of car manufacturers such as Marquette as well as parts and accessories manufacturers. Charles W. Nash, who had worked with W. C. Durant for years prior as a manager, took over the presidency of Buick in 1910 and General Motors in 1912. Walter P. Chrysler was hired in 1911. After being forced to step down from management in 1910, Mr. Durant later joined Louis Chevrolet to form the Chevrolet Motor Company in 1911 and offered it in exchange for GM stock. Around 1918, McLaughlin bought parts for McLaughlin-Buick, and the McLaughlin Motor Car Company was later renamed GM Canada.

Early on, Buick engineers Eugene Richard and Walter Marr perfected a valve-in-head engine that produced significantly more power than most competitive power plants. Sales skyrocketed.

OLDSMOBILE WAS FRONTRUNNER

While the Olds Motor Works was in existence and flourished well before Buick made its mark, it was not initially part of the newly formed General Motors. Pliny Fiske Olds, the father of Ransom E. Olds, built a machine shop in 1885. P. F. Olds and Son was initially owned by his father and older brother, Wallace. Ransom bought out Wallace. While Ransom's first steam car was not successful, he succeeded with a second one. He began manufacturing small gas internal-combustion engines and, in 1896, adapted one of these in a Clark Carriage and built four vehicles. Olds built the first automobile plant in Detroit in 1899. However, soon after, investors took control.

The R. E. Olds Transportation Museum in Lansing, Michigan, showcases its influence through a presentation of early power plants, starting with steam engines with their boilers for both marine and automotive use. In addition, a well-researched display outlines the company's history and references the noteworthy US patents awarded to its engineers.

With the success of the Curved Dash Oldsmobile at the turn of the century, Olds Motor Works continued to flourish. In the 1930s, the first female design engineer, Bonnie Lemm—later Walsh—would design interior and exterior components for Oldsmobile. There are many examples of her work affixed to the vehicles in the museum.

CADILLAC RECOGNIZED

Henry Martyn Leland, a machinist out of New England who worked in the Colt revolver factory and Brown & Sharpe Manufacturing, founded the Cadillac Motor Company. He initially established the Leland, Faulconer & Norton Company, later becoming a principal with the firm Leland & Faulconer Manufacturing Company. Accuracy of machine tools, including grinders and gear cutters, resulted in the production of precision machined castings. Cadillac, originally Leland & Faulconer, would not gain momentum until it began manufacturing transmission gears for the Olds one-cylinder, curved-dash runabout. In the early 1900s, Cadillac captured the Dewar Trophy in Europe for the brand's mechanical performance—in 1908 for interchangeable parts and in 1913 for its electrical systems.

At the first automobile show in Detroit, the Olds display contained two cars, one powered by Olds with a 3.0 hp engine and the second by Leland. Leland had developed a larger engine with 3.7 hp. With more accurate machining, the one-cylinder reached 10.25 hp, but Olds refused to make the change and use it in their cars because of the expense.

OAKLAND IS ACQUIRED

Oakland Motor Car Company, named for the county in which it was founded, had absorbed several floundering carriage companies. The largest of the acquired factories was the Pontiac Buggy Company, incorporated in 1893 by Edward M. Murphy, S. E. Beach, and Francis Emmendorf. Murphy, too, had formed other affiliations and made other purchases. In 1909, Durant purchased the Oakland Motor Car Company for his newly formed General Motors Company. It would take another twenty years before a female designer or engineer at Fisher Body would pen numerous designs for Oakland once it morphed into Pontiac; the designs made for the 1930s Pontiacs by a woman—Bonnie Lemm—were notable.

SMALLER COMPANIES LEAD TO GM TRUCK AND LATER GMC TRUCK

Another significant change was the incorporation of GM Truck Company in 1911 as a sales company to handle the products of the Rapid Motor Vehicle Company of Pontiac, Michigan, and the Reliance Motor Car Company of Detroit, Michigan.

CHEVROLET TAKES THE LEAD

In 1909, Louis Chevrolet was experimenting with a small six-cylinder car. With financial support from "Billy" Durant, he sharpened his driving skills. Louis and his younger brothers, Gaston and Arthur, drove for the Buick Racing Team, with several wins. But Louis, a risk taker, also had other ideas about automotive design. Having been dismissed by GM in 1910 for overextending its resources, Durant devoted his energies to backing Chevrolet. In 1911, the Chevrolet Motor Car Company was incorporated by Durant, Chevrolet, William H. Little, and Edwin R. Campbell.

Over the life of the company, businesses were added and subtracted, here and abroad. While important when war was imminent, scientific and technical research became a greater priority. In 1911, the Engineering Department became the GM Research Department. In 1920, GM took over the Dayton Engineering Laboratories Company (Delco), from which Charles F. Kettering would set up the GM Research Labs. In 1912, before it was associated with GM, Kettering made history when the first practical electric starter was introduced. In the next six years, engineers discovered the antiknock gasoline additive tetraethyl lead and mastered the application of cellulose lacquer to the finish on car bodies.

The year 1908 is also noteworthy for another reason. Fred Fisher, who had risen to the position of superintendent at the

C. R. Wilson Body Company—the largest firm in the horse-drawn carriage body business, which was starting to make inroads into automotive bodies—founded the Fisher Body Company with his brother Charles. By 1901, all seven Fisher brothers had arrived in Detroit from their Norwalk, Ohio, hometown. It would take some time before they realized that automobile bodies had to be stronger than carriage bodies to maintain a high quality of ride. Today, we are also more attuned to and measure NVH—noise, vibration, and harshness.

In 1905, out of the need to collaborate, the Society of Automotive Engineers was established. This led to the standardization and nomenclature of parts.

With the testing and research laboratories originally established in 1911, GM engineers analyzed painting techniques, lubrication, cutting-oil practices for the shaping of metal, and many other critical components. Each of the GM divisions had its own engineers. In 1920, the GM Research Corporation was reorganized as the GM Research Labs and headed by Charles P. Kettering.

The Fishers also sought to address the needs of women. The manufacture of closed cars and the electric starter changed the automotive industry forever. In 1910, as the Fisher Body Company, they received their first order for 150 closed bodies from Cadillac. By 1912, they had formed Fisher Body Company of Canada, Ltd., in Walkerville, Ontario, and the Fisher Body Corporation four years later. In 1919, the Fisher brothers sold 60 percent of the company to GM but remained to manage the company as Fisher Body Ohio. Perhaps they were prophetic when they invested $4 million in the National Plate Glass Company, which consisted of three factories. By 1927, GM acquired the remainder of Fisher Body, which became a full division of General Motors.

In 1916, William Durant also bought stock in the Frigidaire Corporation and completed the purchase in 1919. The name "Frigidaire" became synonymous with refrigerator across the land. Shortly after, GM's earliest female designer would contribute significantly to their new products.

The metal fittings used in Fisher Bodies and for other manufacturers were made by the Ternstedt Manufacturing Company. In 1920, Fisher had introduced the Ternstedt window regulator, the first concealed window control for closed cars. Fisher acquired Ternstedt and merged it with three complementary companies: the International Metal Stamping Company, the Shepard Art Metal Company, and the England Manufacturing Company of Detroit. For the first time in history, a complete staff of engineers, designers, artists, and modelers prepared to create body hardware and interior fittings that were strong, functional, and appealing.

In 1924, GM established its first outdoor testing facility in Milford, Michigan. The 1,125-acre GM Proving Ground was used to test cars under controlled conditions.

FIRST WOMAN DESIGNER-ENGINEER IN THE AUTOMOTIVE INDUSTRY JOINS TERNSTEDT'S ART & COLOR DIVISION

William Schnell headed the Art & Color section for Ternstedt in the Fisher facility. In 1926, a patent was finalized for a Pontiac mascot under his name, but he did supervise a team, and it has not been unusual for managers in the auto industry to take credit for the work of those reporting to them.

FIRST WOMAN NAMED ON AN AUTOMOTIVE PATENT

Bonnie Lemm was the first full-time female designer-engineer with a lifelong career in the automotive industry. Her first patent was finalized in 1929. It would take years for other women with similar responsibilities to be hired, and this took place elsewhere in the corporation.

It should be noted that Bonnie Lemm could have already joined General Motors prior to this time as a designer for Frigidaire and moved over; however, this assignment would have included the design of appliances and not automobiles.

ALFRED SLOAN AND HARLEY EARL

Early on, Durant hired Alfred Sloan, who came with the purchase of Hyatt Roller Bearing in 1916. Sloan was later selected to lead GM.

Sloan recognized the fact that all the cars were fundamentally equal when it came to engineering features, so appearance would now have to become the distinguisher. Sloan supported emphasizing styling and color—also referred to as art and color. More importantly, Alfred P. Sloan was the genius who promoted the initiatives of Harley Earl.

Young Harley Earl's talents were discovered at his father's factory, Earl Automotive Works, where they built customized automobiles and accessories for the movie stars of Hollywood. He was brought east in 1926 to design the 1927 LaSalle for Lawrence Fisher. The car's success led to Sloan's decision to start an art-and-color section with Earl at its helm.

As time progressed, GM established and sold properties on the basis of the needs of the company and its stockholders. GM has divested of and acquired a large number of assets since 1908, leading to its current structure.

By 1929, GM had a long-standing relationship with Greyhound and produced early GM buses that were initially powered by sleeve-valve engines—the earliest of these engines is credited to a female engineer by some—before being equipped with more-modern power plants.

GM worked through the Depression and welcomed recovery in the 1930s. Around 1939, GM was challenged to build diesels for streamliner trains. The engineers and stylists created the GM LaGrange. Later, commercial trucks benefited from the new streaming style created by stylists. Introduced at the New York World's Fair, the 1939 Silversides buses were a mainstay for Greyhound. Double-deckers appeared between 1936 and 1938. The Cruiser was an intercity bus.

By 1941, GM started receiving its first contracts for war materials—explosive shells, trucks, antiaircraft gun parts, engines, and similar. However, in 1940 and 1941, over a million Chevrolets rolled off assembly lines, and the Cadillac-LaSalle, Buick, Olds, Pontiac, and GMC were almost as popular. GM of Canada, Vauxhall, and Bedford did well. By 1941, the wartime production took over civilian needs. In the 1950s, styling is said to have taken the lead, while refinement and growth dominated the 1960s. The transition of performance to safety in the 1970s is notable; this topic is more important today than ever before. In the 1980s, GM joined Toyota to establish NUMMI (New Motor Manufacturing Inc.), a joint venture to share resources in the production of a small car relying on a Toyota power plant. There was an emphasis on J-cars, diverse X-cars, front-wheel drive, and transverse engines.

The Yellow Cab Company was founded in 1920 by John Hertz. GM took the controlling interest in 1925 and bought it in 1943, adding it to GMC. Hertz, the company, has also been owned by competing manufacturers and struggles to survive under the investment group that owns it as it came out of bankruptcy in 2020. The Yellow Coach was a subsidiary that manufactured traditional buses.

In Europe, where Alfred Sloan sought to establish an international presence, GM bought 80 percent of the German Adam Opel AG in 1929, completing the acquisition in 1931. In 2016, it was reported that outside North America and China, Opel-designed cars had outsold all other GM makes combined. They had also acquired the British Vauxhall Iron Works in 1925. Founded in 1857 as Alex Wilson and Company, Vauxhall, like Olds, originally manufactured steam engines. Through the years, Vauxhall held its own, sometimes even providing vehicles for other locations. In 2017, PSA Groupe bought Opel, Vauxhall and GM's lending division.

In the late 1950s until 1970, Canadian P-B-G dealers in Canada created the Envoy from Vauxhall models. Similarly, in the 1960s, the Epic, also a Vauxhall, was imported into Canada and sold by P-B-G stores as well as Chevrolet-Olds franchises. Sold from 1968 to 1979, the Ranger was a version of the Vauxhall Rekord. In the 1960s, the Acadian and later Beaumont were based on the Chevelle. From 1988 to 1991, the Canadian dealer also sold the Passport, which came from Europe or Asia.

GM Overseas is still an evolving organization that has negotiated numerous acquisitions and dispositions, only some which are highlighted here.

After forty years, in 1978, changes were made to the Overseas Group. In 1988, the GMOG became GM International Operations. GM acquired 50 percent of Saab Auto AB of Sweden. In 1999, GM invested in Fuji Heavy Industry to have access to Subaru, and later sold it.

GM's first undertaking involved Korea, as the GM Korea Co. began in 1972. It involved a fifty-fifty joint venture with Shinjin Motors Co., previously called Shinjin Eng. Co., which was founded in 1955 to produce Jeep-like vehicles. Another branch of the company was Saenara Motor Company, which started in 1937 under the name National Motor Co. Saenara was later acquired by Shinjin Industrial Company in 1965 after a bankruptcy. However, through many years, GM's partners would change; much of the time 50 percent of the company was held by the Korean Development Bank and various other investors, which included SAIC, Toyota, and even India. There was a time when GM held no interest at all. The liabilities of the company, at times called or owned by Daewoo, eclipsed its assets. With the assignation of Korea's president, politics prevailed. It took the Asian crisis of 1997 to topple Daewoo, giving GM the opportunity to invest far less expensively with far-reaching results. With the transitions of this asset, many GM cars were produced from 1972 forward. The Chevrolet 1700, based on the Holden Torano in the early 1970s, opened opportunity. While Korean women did not drive, many were chauffeured. Popular cars included the Maepsy and the Maepsyna. The Daewoo LeMans, which was based on the Opel Kadett and the design of the front, was credited to Pontiac's American designers. The Matiz was also designed in part by a woman, Yan Huang. In 2007, they sold the G2X—a rebadged Saturn Sky. It is significant that Korean designer Sangyeon Cho managed the exterior design team for the Chevrolet BOLT. GM Korea sold numerous notable vehicles.

In the 1970s, the BTV (Basic Terrain Vehicle) arrived and was sold under the Amigo, Andino, Cerito, Morina, Pinolero, Harabas, Plai Noi, Indino, Harriman, and other names.

While the Lotus name dates from 1948, when Colin Chapman was a student developing a race car in a garage, the Lotus Engineering Company, Ltd., was created in 1952 by engineer Chapman and Michael Allen. In 1986, GM acquired 58 percent of Group Lotus PLC. GM bought most of the remaining shares from Toyota. Taking full ownership in 1987 after Chapman died from a heart attack, Lotus took over Vauxhall's Old Millbrook Proving Ground until 1993, when GM sold Lotus to Romano Artioli of Bugatti. The Elise carries the name of his grandchild. During GM's ownership, the Lotus Elan was redesigned and restyled as a front-wheel-drive car. Lotus Engineering, a subsidiary of Group Lotus PLC, worked for outside clients too. Tony Rudd, the engineering manager, supervised the creation of heads for the ZR1 engine, and Lotus engineering contributed to Cadillac's luxurious ride.

GM has also purchased Canadian brands. In 1988, GM bought the Passport, which built cars in Asia and Europe. Unsuccessful, it was replaced by Asuna and subsequently closed.

From 1989 to 1997, GM investment in Isuzu, Suzuki, and Toyota enabled the establishment of GEO and the sale of Metros, Storms, and Trackers in Chevrolet franchises until 2004. In Canada, the Asuna was shipped from Asia and was sold at BPG dealerships.

GM worked with Toyota to establish the jointly owned NUMMI plant to learn Japanese manufacturing techniques. The reliable Chevrolet Nova/Prism used Toyota Corolla components, and the Pontiac Vibe shared components with the Matrix.

Saturn LLC was established by GM in 1985 and billed as "a new kind of car company." The well-engineered cars featured lightweight and well-engineered durable plastic body panels. While early product included coupes and sedans, the lineup went on to include station wagons, the Vue crossover, the Sky roadster, and the Relay minivan. The Vue crossover was selected for use in the EcoCar Program.

Robert Stempel, Owen Bieber, Roger Smith, and Richard Lefauve welcome the first Saturn off the line in 1990. *General Motors*

The GEO brand relied on imports. *General Motors*

Around 2007, the EV-1 electric was sold by Saturn dealers. While the car was way ahead of its time and signaled the future, availability ended in 2010.

In 1992, GM's HUMMER Division was created. The original models were AM General vehicles until GM bought the brand in 1998; it was discontinued in 2010 due to the bankruptcy. The new, remarkable Hummer EV PU and SUV are marketed as GMCs.

From 1996 to 2003, GM created the brand name EV-1 for its electric vehicle, presented more in depth in chapter 3.

By 1997, Shanghai GM, a fifty-fifty joint venture between GM and Shanghai Auto Industry Corp. (SAIC), was formed. Other joint ventures followed under GM (China) Investment Corp. The first locally produced Buick left the production line in 1998. By 2006, GM claimed market leadership in China. In 2002, SAIC-GM-Wuling Auto Co., Ltd., was jointly established by Shanghai Group Co., Ltd.; GM (China); and Liuzhou Wuling Auto Co., Ltd. In 2015, SAIC-GM-Wuling established an Indonesian subsidiary to address the needs of Southeast Asia.

In 2000, having been a 50 percent owner, GM completed its purchase of Saab and worked on alliances with Fiat—Alpha Romeo and Lancia—for parts. The Saab 9000 was a joint venture with Fiat. GM also exchanged engines with Fiat.

In 2002, the AUTOnomy concept utilized a fuel cell in a sealed chassis that would allow different cars to be built on top, much like the modern-day Ultium chassis. The Hy Wire was constructed above the skateboard and featured drive-by-wire technology.

However, GM would be restructured in 2009, and the new pared-down GM would consist of Buick, Cadillac, Chevrolet, Holden, Opel, Vauxhall, and the majority stake in Daewoo.

The EV-1 arrived as a production electric. *General Motors*

The new HUMMER, a state-of-the-art 1000 hp electric-powered pickup truck, turns heads while competitors begin to chase it. *General Motors*

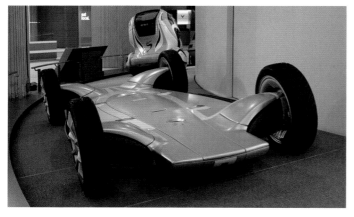

The chassis of the GM Autonomy concept led to the Ultium platform. *Constance Smith*

The Hy Wire concept featured drive-by-wire technology. *Constance Smith*

At this time, GM and its subsidiaries and its joint-venture entities sold vehicles under the Buick, Cadillac, Chevrolet, and GMC nameplates, as well as those of Baojun and Wuling. With the divesture of its European division in 2020, this global organization seems to consist of GM North America; GM Latin America, Africa, and Middle East; GM Asia Pacific; and other entities.

GM has recently shut down its Holden operations in Australia and New Zealand. It is likely that this could affect ventures in the Asia Pacific.

GM's newer brands focus on developing technologies and addressing the changing transportation needs of business, the military, and consumers.

In a humanitarian role, in 2020 GM began the manufacture of masks and ventilators rather than vehicles in some factories to address the urgent needs of those fighting coronavirus. It has shared its own processes for working during the COVID-19 pandemic with the business community.

GM's continued promotion of women and minorities during the last decade to leadership positions will ensure its success with the innovative redesign of staple commodities and the introduction of new technologies and stunning products.

In addition to the divisions above, in 2022 GM owned or had an interest in LG Energy Solutions, Cruise, and BrightDrop, and anticipated continued collaborations with NASA, Honda, AT&T, Microsoft, Navistar, Goldman Sachs / MasterCard, Walmart, Liebherr-Aerospace for Lockheed Martin, Wabtec Corporation for rail and freight, the US Postal Service, and other anticipated partners.

The stunning Cadillac Lyriq was unveiled in the domed auditorium at the GM Technical Center. *GM Book*

Some of—but not all of—the brands that have defined or now define GM, alone or with a partner, include Ultium batteries, Hydrotec, Charge 360,GM Financial, GM Lease, GM Defense, GM Marine, OnStar and OnStar Vehicle Insights, GM Ventures, GM Electro-Motive Power, AC Delco, Frigidaire, GM BuyPower, and so on.

GM currently owns or has an interest in Cruise and BrightDrop, and collaborates with Honda, Microsoft, Navistar, Goldman Sachs/MasterCard, Walmart, smaller companies, and the US Postal Service.

Nowadays, as in days past, GM continues to divest of selected properties, invest in new ones, and concentrate on research and improvement of its manufacturing capabilities. It leads in the development and introduction of electric and partially and fully autonomous vehicles, which will change the way we communicate, transport goods, ensure our safety, and promote our mobility.

The newer GM building towers over Detroit. *General Motors*

GM is the majority owner of Cruise, the originator of the autonomous Bolt and Cruise Origin, a driverless transport for ridesharing. *General Motors*

MARY T. BARRA

Chairman and CEO, General Motors Corporation

General Motors

Do what you're passionate about. You'll do it for a long time, and if you're passionate about it you'll have better results ... Do the work. Don't worry about what you can't control, control what you can, and put that energy in.

—Mary T. Barra (b. 1961)

CAREER HIGHLIGHTS

Mary Barra is chairman and chief executive officer of General Motors Company. She was elected chairman of the GM Board of Directors on January 4, 2016, and has served as CEO of GM since January 15, 2014.

Under Barra's leadership, GM envisions a world with zero crashes, so as to save lives; zero emissions, so future generations can inherit a healthier planet; and zero congestion, so customers can get back the precious commodity of time.

Focused on strengthening GM's core business of great cars, trucks, and crossovers, Barra is also working to lead the transformation of personal mobility through advanced technologies such as connectivity, electrification, autonomous driving, and car sharing. She has also established a strategic direction based on putting the customer at the center of everything the company does.

Prior to becoming CEO, Barra served as executive vice president, Global Product Development, Purchasing & Supply Chain, since August 2013, and as senior vice president, Global Product Development, since February 2011. In 2011, she was the highest-ranking woman in the automotive industry. In these roles, Barra and her teams were responsible for the design, engineering, and quality control of GM vehicle launches worldwide.

Previously, she served as vice president of global human resources, vice president of global manufacturing engineering, plant manager of the Detroit Hamtramck Assembly, and in several other executive engineering and staff positions.

Barra began her career with GM in 1980 as a General Motors Institute (now Kettering University) co-op student at the Pontiac Motor Division. She graduated with a bachelor of science degree in electrical engineering in 1985. In 1988, she started at Stanford and earned a master of business administration from the Graduate School of Business in 1990.

Barra serves on the board of directors of the Walt Disney Company, the Stanford University Board of Trustees, and the Detroit Economic Club. Notably, she is a member of the Business Council and an at-large board member of the Business Roundtable, where she also serves on the Social Issues Committee.

BIOGRAPHICAL NOTES

Mary T. Barra, née Mary Teresa Makela, was born in Royal Oak, Michigan. Royal Oak was a popular area for General Motors employees who worked at the GM Technical Center nearby. She and older brother, Paul, were born into a General Motors family.

Barra notes that her mom grew up on a farm during the Depression and believed in the American dream—hard work was the distinguisher. You could do anything if you worked hard. Barra's son, a Duke University alumnus, promoted this phrase on his jacket: "Hard work beats talent if talent doesn't work hard." Her daughter also chose to attend Duke with the other Blue Devils. Before Duke, her husband, Tony, and son put their talents together to rebuild a 1971 Pontiac Trans Am. Today, Barra and her husband lead others in contributing to and in raising funds for Duke.

Barra's mother, Eva (née Pyykkonen), was a bookkeeper who completed a two-year college program. Her father, Ray, was a journeyman diemaker who honed his skills on the job and obtained related training as he progressed. He was a member of the UAW and served GM for thirty-nine years.

This 1914 Leland engine was the last manufactured and is in the collection of the Swigart Museum in Huntingdon, Pennsylvania.
Constance Smith

Automotive historians are well aware of the significance of the accuracy of tooling to make both engine and body parts. A die is an accurate tool used in manufacturing to cut or shape, usually metal, using a press.

When it comes to tooling, Leland & Faulconer manufactured precision gears and engine parts made to the nearest 1,000th of an inch, for the first Cadillacs. Their work led to Cadillac's development of the first interchangeable parts. Cadillac was awarded the Dewar Trophy by the Royal Automobile Club in 1908 and 2013. European craftsmanship was considered by many far superior before this event. Charles F. Kettering was instrumental in developing electric starting, lighting, and ignition in 1911. In 2001, VP Bob Lutz was successful in encouraging workers to reduce or even the gaps in body panels.

Many of us got our hands dirty in our youth. Growing up, we watched our fathers and brothers repair their own cars and anything else that broke down, and followed suit as we grew older. We appreciated getting the first hand-me-down that needed some work on it. Mary was even luckier; sometimes her dad brought new Pontiacs home from the factory even before they reached the showroom. She had the opportunity to appreciate the new muscle cars that were destined to fly down the road, and the comfort of a Safari wagon with simulated wood sides in junior high school, before she could even legally get behind the wheel. In a September/October 2011 article in the *Stanford Magazine*, Barra noted that a cousin acquired a late 1960s red Camaro convertible with a white ragtop: "It was just a beautiful, beautiful vehicle—the first vehicle where I went, 'Wow, that's cool.'" Even today, one cannot pass a 1967 and 1968 Camaro or its sister Firebird without being tempted to record this collectible on our smartphone's camera. Welly sells accurate die-cast models in 1:24 scale with a GM code sticker affixed to the gas tank. Model kits are still marketed under the Monogram name, which was acquired some time ago by Odyssey from Mattel.

In 1980, Makela graduated from Waterford Mott High School. As a student she excelled, as evidenced by her membership in the National Honor Society and her 4.0 grade point average. Quite an organizer, Mary was coeditor of the school's yearbook,

The Camaro of yesteryear is an iconic collectible. *Constance Smith*

Polaris—named for the star and not the manufacturer of the Polaris Slingshot. Her mother valued education and made it known to her and her brother, who later graduated from the Wayne State Medical School. Her high school classmates voted Mary the girl most likely to succeed. While she obviously hit the books to attain a perfect average, she also found time to explore the ice cream parlors and skating rinks with others of her generation.

Initially intending to attend Michigan State University, Makela instead opted for General Motors Institute (GMI), now known as Kettering University. In 1910, Charles F. Kettering was the researcher who began experiments that led to the development of the car's entire electrical system. His design was standard on the 1912 Cadillac and relieved the driver from hand-cranking.

GMI was founded in 1919 as the School of Automotive Trades to train employees of the burgeoning automotive industry. The founder later sought to recruit management personnel, and, still later, engineers participated. In 1923, it became the Flint Institute of Technology, offering a distinctive four-year co-op program. The GM Corporation took over financial support in 1926, and it was renamed GMI. While Major Albert Sobey was the founder of the "West Point" of the automotive industry, other men played important roles—Harry Bassett, Alfred B. Sloan Jr., and Charles F. Kettering. Kettering was also a founder of Delco and a prolific inventor. Male and female engineers vie for the prestigious Kettering Award annually. In 1945, a fifth-year thesis requirement was added. When GM divested of ownership of GMI in 1982, the school was renamed GMI Engineering & Management Institute. Also in 1982, the institute began offering graduate programs. In 1998, the school adopted the name Kettering University in honor of Charles F. Kettering. In 2019, Kettering had their 100-year-anniversary celebration on the Flint campus.

Having enrolled in 1980, Makela experienced the change in ownership and moniker. Students found this upsetting. She later noted, "If you started at GMI, part of your affinity was GM, because you spent 50 percent of your time at GM. School and company were inextricably linked."

Makela was offered an opportunity in the co-op program, which initially enabled her to alternate study and work to pay tuition. Students were worried about their tuition. She noted, "One of the big draws for me to go to GMI had been the co-op program and the ability to pay my own way; because my dad retired when I was a senior in high school, the ability to work and pay for my own college was something that was very, very important to me." Each student was initially sponsored by a division of GM—it would not be a surprise that Pontiac stepped up. The students were put to work in a car plant and had two twelve-week breaks per year to pursue their college studies. After completing five years, they earned a degree in engineering or industrial administration, the latter of which was perceived as an easier path to which women gravitated. Of course, Mary chose electrical engineering, where the majority of students were male. Each year's class was divided into two sections so they could alternate between school and work. EE students might study communications, programming, manufacturing, chemistry, calculus, and so on. Graduation required the completion of 140 credits.

Barra notes, "I picked electrical engineering because a lot in the electrical world is based on math, and because my drafting skills weren't very good. Everything now is on computer, but back then you were drawing everything, and my drafting professor was not impressed by my line quality."

The first woman did not graduate from this GMI until 1971; enrollment has grown due to recent initiatives but was still under 20 percent in 2015. With her father's retirement and mother's part-time job, she was fortunate to have the opportunity to be able to pay for her education without being strapped by college loans for years.

With the co-op arrangement, Makela reported to a Pontiac plant to work on the line, where she checked hoods and fender panels for quality. While not a glamorous assignment, it would last only a short time, and she would learn how cars were assembled. Factories are noisy, and women were challenged in one way or another (and likely some still are today). No matter how insignificant it seemed to some men, having to fend off remarks and catcalls was and is degrading to women. In addition, it would become particularly difficult for student managers during times of layoffs when they had to supervise workers twice their age.

MARY MAKELA'S FIRST RIDES

While Makela had savings from a part-time job, she found that the price of a Firebird, the sister to the Camaro, was over her head, and she had to settle for a 1970 red Chevette without power accessories and lack of truck space for her needs. This model was designed and manufactured much faster than usual to meet the onslaught of cheap Japanese cars flooding into the United States. Arrogant American executives and even factory workers dismissed the threat, until it became real as the sale of entry-level American cars

declined rapidly. By junior year, Mary ditched the starter car for a black Fiero—a reasonably priced sports car that highlighted the tremendous achievements made by chemists in formulating plastics.

After graduating, she was retained as a control engineer and later became the engineer responsible for plant facilities and maintenance. The guys kept the plant clean and running. "It was the first time I ever supervised people," she noted. "We worked a lot on quality."

Now as Mary Barra—she married Anthony Barra in 1985—she wanted to experience innovation and applied for an assignment in the Pontiac Fiero plant. Fiero means "proud" in Italian and "wild" in Spanish.

From 1985 to 1988, Barra served as the senior plant engineer and general supervisor for the Fiero plant in Pontiac. GM is said to have followed some of the manufacturing methods Toyota used that were proposed by W. Edwards Deming at about this time; when GM set up NUMMI, the joint factory in California manufactured the Pontiac Vibe on the same line as a Toyota Matrix. Both used Corolla engines; however, sharp consumers realized that the Vibe had Pontiac's three-year warranty and the Toyota had only a two-year one.

The wedge-shaped Fiero, which debuted in 1984, was a revolutionary two-seat sports car—midengine like the C-8

Barra inspected the Pontiac Grand Prix's sheet metal that came down the line during assembly. *Constance Smith*

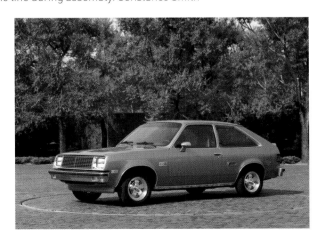

The Chevrolet Chevette, which competed with early Japanese imports, served as an entry-level car for many. *General Motors*

The student center at Kettering University. *Constance Smith*

The Fiero's instrument panel was penned by designer Dan Nelson under the direction of Ron Hill. *Constance Smith*`

This pristine 1985 Pontiac Fiero was featured at the 2020 AACA Fall Nationals. *Constance Smith*

Corvette of today. The cult that surrounded the Fiero still exists nationwide.

The construction of this two-door coupe was remarkable. The steel space frame sat below plastic panels: Enduraflex skins, SMC plastic panels, and SMC panels on horizontal surfaces. Because of the cost, it had not been easy for Pontiac to incorporate Endura on the front end of its first Firebirds either, but designers fought bean counters to get it done. It made a difference on the Fiero too. Reinforced, reaction-injected, molded urethane panels with high resistance were mounted in vulnerable areas such as the front fenders and doors.

The halogen headlamps retracted—reminiscent of the earlier Opel GT. Glass surfaces and rear taillamps were flush to the body; this also lowered the coefficient of drag.

The cars were equipped with the 2.5-liter engine. The manual transmission was always promoted ahead of the automatic. The highest of three models included the WS6 performance package with a luggage rack.

Inside, the clean instrument cluster was designed by the author's former colleague, Dan Nelson, in somewhat of a European style. Dan was initially hired to work with Jayne Van Alstyne, one of the earliest female designers. While Jayne loved her split window, Dan had his own collection of Corvettes. Coincidentally, John Cafaro, a colleague from the author's alma mater, Pratt Institute, worked on the Fiero's exterior design.

The 1985 Fiero was a bit fiercer, and some came with a rear spoiler. The 2.8-liter V-6 was optional on the SE model, but standard on the GT. The smoother body panels conveyed a meaner look. While the initial design might have been marketed toward women, there is no question that the 1985 would summon some testosterone. The Fiero served as a pace car for the Indy 500, and over 270,000 were made. There were some engine fires associated with the Fiero, and this led to a 1987 recall. Later models included a Formula package before the Fiero's reign ended; the last model was the 1988. When the plant finally ceased production and shut its doors, many workers set sail for the Saturn plant.

Looking back, it is indeed amazing that in 1985 Barra completed her co-op assignment, graduated from GMI (a.k.a. Kettering), took on the role of senior plant manager and general supervisor at the Fiero plant, and married Tony Barra, another Kettering graduate.

In 1988, she began studies at Stanford, utilizing a GM fellowship, and earned a master of business administration from the Graduate School of Business in 1990. While Wayne State offered an MBA program, it would prove advantageous to study with the elite whom Stanford attracted. Barra studied the usual courses and then selected electives. At Wayne State, she would have studied managerial and financial accounting, marketing, economics, and so on. Stanford's requirements were similar if not the same the first year. As time went on, there was more emphasis on the soft skills. MBA programs of today usually consist of three years of study.

From 1990 to 1995, Barra worked as a senior engineer and manager for operations and manufacturing. Her education, expected of an executive, put her on the fast track.

Barra got a ticket to the executive suite when Jack Smith, the chief executive officer of GM, summoned her by phone to offer her a position as his assistant. She was so surprised and consulted her boss to see if it was real. She ended up working for Smith and his deputy, Harry Pearce.

Sometime later, after Barra helped Gary Cowger with communications in factories, Rick Waggoner created a senior executive program for those with high potential and instituted MBA-like courses for the chosen to take. Harvard and Duke professors were brought in, and they traveled to view operations worldwide. The idea enabled a global team able to work together on any problem.

From 1990 to 1995, Barra served as senior engineer and manager for operations and manufacturing, from 1999 to 2001 as general director of communications, and from 2001 to 2003 as executive director of manufacturing engineering.

From 2003 to 2004, Barra managed the Hamtramck Assembly Plant. Barra is said to have implemented a more formal communications program in the plant and changed the line speed. This resulted in the plant winning awards for the first time.

From 2004 to 2008, she served as executive director of

A beguiling black Fiero, with its new nose and cladding, had an aggressive stance and aligns with other Pontiac performance models. *Constance Smith*

manufacturing engineering, and from 2008 to 2009 as vice president of global manufacturing engineering.

On June 1, 2009, GM filed for bankruptcy, after which Barra was promoted to the position of vice president of global human resources. While she herself could have bolted, perhaps she was perceived as the best person to handle the firings and resignations that resulted.

From 2013 to 2014, Barra took the wheel in February as GM's senior vice president for global product development and became the highest-ranking woman in the automotive industry. In charge of engineering, design, and quality control for the world's second-largest automaker (after Toyota), she has arrived just in time to lead GM's product line into a very uncertain future.

On January 15, 2014, Barra was appointed chief executive officer. This left only one step to reach the top; she was appointed chairman of the corporation in 2016.

In 2015 and 2017, Mary Barra became a household word once more. She placed first on the list of *Fortune Magazine*'s most powerful women and was the highest paid of the Big Three automotive executives. In 2020, she was recognized for the third time by *Automotive News* as one of the 100 leading women in the North American auto industry. This event is held every five years.

In March 2020, Barra tweeted, "A gender-equal world is an enabled world—where diversity of thought and experience sparks an innovative and collaborative culture. I look forward to the day when a woman CEO is the norm and not the exception."

It has not been easy road for Barra. She has had to make unpopular decisions to encourage early retirements, eliminate jobs, discontinue car models, sell Opel and Vauxhall, halt retail sales in South Africa and India, and put Holden on the chopping block to meet financial goals. Globally, GM has a smaller footprint than ever before. However, General Motors continues to expand on what they do well.

Barra has been described as a smart, tough, shrewd, and

strategic leader. The company continues to invest heavily in electric and autonomous technology, works closely with Cruise, and collaborates with Honda. GM has continued to add new partners in and out of the automotive industry—from LG Energy Solutions to POSCO Chemical and from Pure Watercraft to Liebherr Aerospace. New battery factories and facilities continue to open. The Wallace Battery Cell Innovation Center, scheduled to open in 2022, is located at the Technical Center. At the same time, GM strives to decarbonize its products. Barra is aware that GM needs to continue to make great cars and trucks.

The mission statement formulated for GM's future is clear and easily understood: "To earn customers for life by building brands that inspire passion and loyalty through not only breakthrough technologies but also by serving and improving the communities in which we live and work around the world." It is not enough to design impressive vehicles. Barra understands that the consumer must be at the center of everything the company does.

Barra overcame obstacles at the Hamtramck plant. After being turned around, it was highly awarded. This facility, which manufactured the first Volt, has been refurbished as Factory Zero, where electric vehicles will be assembled. *General Motors*

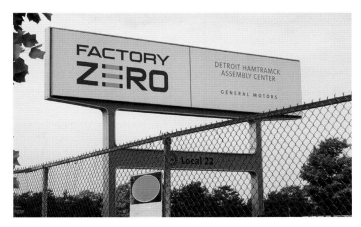

Constance Smith

"I am a results driven, strategic leader; I enjoy people leadership and technical challenges. Integrity is my overriding principal, and I'm committed to delivering excellent results with relentless tenacity. I am an automotive enthusiast working hard every day because the safety, reliability, and performance of the products we sell make lifelong customers, build our brands and lead to the company's success."

"It's a great honor to take on the role of GM Canada president and managing director at such as pivotal time for our company and our industry in Canada. I am passionate about innovation and can't wait to support our people and partners as we unleash our talent and ideas to drive the transformation of the automotive industry."

Marissa West posts 2021, 2022
1981 (Est.) to present

MARISSA WEST
Canada's Newest Leader

CAREER HIGHLIGHTS

In March of 2022, Marissa West was appointed to GM Canada President and Managing Director, as Scott Bell took the lead for Chevrolet as Vice President Global Chevrolet.

Marissa West previously served as the Chief Engineer of the GMC Sierra Heavy Duty and the Chevrolet Silverado Heavy Duty Truck programs. As Chief Engineer, West led the launch of GM's all new heavy duty pick-up trucks. With new power-trains, upgraded suspension, and a heavy measure of electronics, you can be sure that the development, testing and manufacture of these trucks required a diverse team of engineers.

West also served as the Director of the Global Noise & Vibration Center in 2016, and in 2018 the Vehicle Dynamics Center was added to her responsibilities. She subsequently led the transformation and merging of the N&V and Dynamics centers into an agile and lean organization before moving into her role as a Chief Engineer.

In 2015, West worked as the global business planning manager and, in 2016, as director of noise, vibration, and vehicle dynamics.

In 2013, West served as a lead driveline systems engineer and, in 2014, as the engineering group manager for chassis.

West spent approximately one year as an executive assistant before rising to hybrid safety design engineer in 2009. As a lead development engineer, she directed component design release engineers to ensure design and hardware were capable at a systems level of delivering vehicle needs.

West started as an intern in 2001 and joined GM full time in 2003, before circulating through a number of relevant positions preparing her for her current assignment and the innovative approach she would look to incorporate.

BIOGRAPHICAL NOTES

Marissa West grew up in southeast Michigan, about 60 miles from Detroit, and she was surrounded by engineers. Her father was a GM engineer, and both grandfathers worked in GM plants as did her great-grandfather. "There was never any question that I wanted to be in the automotive industry," she said. "And there was also no question that I wanted to work for General Motors."

West graduated with a Bachelor of Science in Mechanical Engineering in 2003 from the Michigan State University and a Master of Science in Mechanical Engineering in 2009 from the University of Michigan. After an internship at the Milford Proving Grounds, there was no doubt what her career would look like.

She has been at GM ever since, working in noise and vibration, chassis design, and hybrid powertrain technologies.

At GM's Noise and Vibration Center, West and her teams used laser vibrometers to identify the natural frequencies of various components and identify structure-borne noises. They employed chassis dynamometers to analyze propulsion noises, including those coming from the motors of electric cars. They also used sophisticated binaural noise acquisition systems (so-called AachenHeads) to capture sounds, and then apply software to analyze them. Once

they can identify such noises, they can get feedback on what needs to be fixed. "Our team is spending time defining customer expectations," West said. "And we're making sure that electric motors and other tonal noises are mitigated." In some cases, West added, they can use new technologies, such as noise cancellation, to remedy the problems that can no longer be fixed by adding mass.

To date, the results have been impressive. GM's Chevy Bolt has been praised for its noise and vibration performance, with Consumer Reports calling it "very quiet." "We're really proud of the Bolt," West said. "The road noise is extremely good and it's fun to drive. We're on a new frontier with electric vehicles. We're just beginning to understand what vehicles of the future will sound and feel like."

A series of videos feature West and the 2020 GMC Sierra HD. She was also responsible for the same features in the Chevrolet Silverado HD pickup. West notes that this truck is: "taller, longer, lighter, and has increased interior space". The trucks were tested extensively at maximum capacity while hauling heavy loads in order to prefect the design. While the 2020 has a lot to follow, the 2021 even add more.

Because of its trailering responsibilities, the Sierra 2020 came to market first. In addition to the 5.3 V8 now available with a ten-speed transmission, the truck is also available with a 3.0L Duramax in-line six turbo diesel with a 10-speed transmission. The truck is rated at 277 hp and 460 lb.-feet of torque goo for towing an incredible 35,500 lbs. Nothing in its class touches this. Innovative engineers developed a number of unheard of before features.

In 2020, the first Pro Grade Trailering package came with the first see-through or transparent trailer, a system incorporating 15 camera views so the driver can virtually see through the trailer as though it was not even there. Late in 2019, GMC introduced their Carbon Pro Edition with the 6.2L V8 with a carbon fiber bed. The 6 position Multi Pro tailgate was first offered here, with the majority of customers onboard. Of course, there is a camera to surveil the bed and data about the truck included. When it comes to West, there are numerous upgraded and new features.

Mechanical features on a high-end truck also usually include Magnetic Ride Control, an automatic locking differential, automatic load leveling, a trailer brake controller, a trailer sway bar, and a two-speed transfer case. Moving up to a Denali Package can add a power sunroof, electric retractable assist steps, 22" aluminum wheels and even wheel locks.

In 2021, a new Trailering Suite replaces Pro Grade trailering, adds a Jack-Knife Alert to monitor the position of the truck to the trailer, a length indicator, enhanced trailer view for backing up, enhanced side view and camera bed mirrors—now with zoom and hitch guidance.

With over fifty components listed on the window sticker on a GMC truck, West and her team had their work cut out for them for quite some time.

This Sierra Denali HD is heavily equipped for work and trailering. It was the first truck with the amazing, innovative see-through trailering feature.

MARISSA WEST TAKES THE LEAD

In March of 2022, Marissa West was promoted to the position of president and managing director of GM Canada likely fulfilling her life-long dream.

West's intentions are admirable, "Under Scott Bell's leadership, the team at GM Canada emerged from the pandemic with remarkable sales and business results, true community leadership and the announcement of transformational new investments in manufacturing, the EV battery supply chain and in engineering and R&D. I want to build on that leadership by ensuring our dealers and customers are supported and prepared to embrace connected services and our all electric future."

"With GM Canada manufacturing now growing quickly, another priority will be the launch of new vehicles including Canada's first full scale BrightDrop electric vehicle production at CAMI later this year. I can't wait to explore ways to leverage CTC as a hotbed of GM talent, innovation and the advancement of our new software enabled vehicles. And I plan to continue spending time on gender equity, diversity, and accessibility as a priority for people with disabilities, in the workplace and in our vehicles".

"My family and I could not be more excited to become part of this amazing country, culture and innovative community."

The Chevrolet Bolt presented at the 2020 Philadelphia Auto Show illustrated the complex array of components packed under the hood. General Motors; photo, *Constance Smith*

PAMELA FLETCHER

Global Innovation

What's exciting is the transformation that is happening in the industry that is occurring much more rapidly than anyone could've predicted. It brings the additional challenge of new technology and new technology on a very rapid timeline.

—Pamela Fletcher, 1966–present

CAREER HIGHLIGHTS

Pam Fletcher has served in a number of positions. As vice president of global innovation at General Motors, Pamela Fletcher oversaw the creation of new businesses that allowed GM to enter new markets, attract new customers, and diversify its revenue streams.

Pam continues to build on an established track record of bringing cutting-edge products and technologies to her role. For more than a decade, she has been in leadership roles guiding the development of GM's electric-vehicle and self-driving technologies.

Her teams were responsible for developing several of GM's most awarded vehicles, including the Chevrolet Volt and the Chevrolet Bolt EV, the industry's first mass-market, long-range, affordable electric vehicle. Her team also led the development of Super Cruise and Super Cruise with lane change, the industry's first hands-free highway driver assist system, and three generations of Cruise AVs.

Fletcher earned her bachelor's and master's degrees in engineering and serves as a corporate director of Coherent Inc. (COHR), a NASDAQ-listed company based in Silicon Valley. She graduated from the Executive Development Program at the Kellogg School of Management at Northwestern University, the Stanford Graduate School of Business Transformational Leadership Program, and the Harvard Women on Boards Program.

Fletcher was named to Motor Trend's 2018 and 2019 Power List of auto industry leaders and was one of Fast Company's "Most Creative People" of 2017. She serves on the Board of Advisors for the College of Engineering at the University of North Carolina, Charlotte. In 2022, Fletcher joined Delta Airlines as Chief Sustainability Officer.

ELECTRICITY DOMINATES AT THE TURN OF THE CENTURY

Historians believe that the scientists in the Netherlands and Germany invented electricity, although the Greeks exhibited an awareness of it, and the word "electricity" comes from the Greek word for amber—electron. In 1800, Luigi Galvani ran experiments and Alessandro Volta put together voltaic piles. Early electric cars competed with steam- and IC-engined vehicles. In 1900, electric technologies were far more advanced than the others. Early gasoline-powered cars, such as the Curved Dash Olds and the 1904 Buick, ran on single- or two-cylinder engines. However, it took some time to heat up water in boilers in steam cars.

THE ELECTROVAIR AND EV1

In 1912, GM engineers built 682 electric trucks with Edison lead-acid and nickel-iron batteries. Almost fifty years later, they partnered with Boeing to build vehicles for NASA's Apollo Program—the subcompact-sized cars are still on the moon. They built an Electrovan from hydrogen-oxygen fuel cells that ran up to 1,500 miles before needing a fill-up.

The modern-day Electrovair I and II that followed proved significant. The Electrovair I was built on a 1964 Corvair chassis, and the Electrovair II utilized 1966 Corvair components. The II weighed in at about 3,400 pounds, about 800 pounds more than the production vehicle on which it was based. Its power train accounted for 1,200 pounds. The driveline consisted of an induction motor that drove a quill shaft through a

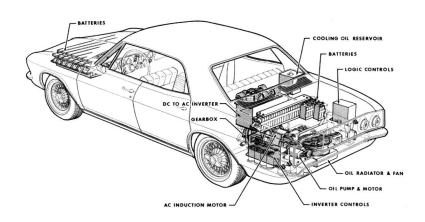

CUTAWAY VIEW OF GENERAL MOTORS ELECTROVAIR

The basic components for the Electrovair were illustrated. *Collection of Constance Smith; GM Public Relations*

The Electrovair, which relied on lead-acid batteries, was an experimental derivative of the Chevrolet Corvair. *General Motors*

The Electrovair had batteries front and rear. *General Motors*

differential carrier, pinion shaft, planetary gear set, and read axle pinion shaft in the differential assembly. In addition to a three-phase induction motor, the Corvair was also equipped with 286 costly silver-zinc cells, connected in series, which were spaced out in thirteen coated aluminum trays that were part plastic. A 530-volt battery pack occupied the front luggage and rear engine compartments. The power pack provided about 120 kW and a 530-open-volt source. The batteries would

withstand 100 cycles and were chargeable in six hours on household current.

A unit employing eighteen SCRs converted the batteries from DC to three-phase AC power and varied the voltage and frequency of the power. The inverter and capacitors were located beside the motor, and other logic circuits were mounted beside the wheel wells. Both oil and air were used to cool the electric components. The cooling assembly utilized a heat exchanger and a motor-driven fan 10 inches in diameter. Researchers concluded that future vehicles would need a lighter and smaller drive system, cheaper materials, a more refined motor control system, and longer-lasting batteries. Auxiliary power was needed for car heating and air-conditioning.

In 1969, GM assembled a state-of-the-art show—Progress of Power—at the Technical Center. Media on the GM website noted that the show included twenty-six special vehicles that were exhibited or demonstrated for the first time. This small fleet was powered by a number of unconventional engines, including turbine, steam hybrid, experimental piston engines designed for reduced emissions, and an electric motor.

Four experimental-purpose vehicles for limited urban transportation, the GM site notes, were demonstrated. Harry F. Barr, VP in charge of Engineering Staff at the time, described the cars as "engineering studies with actual vehicles of many shapes and sizes and various forms of power." Four cars were included in three categories. A three-car series of tall cars with small-diameter wheels was powered by gas, electric, and hybrid units. The fourth car, the 511, powered by a four-cylinder gas engine, rested on three wheels.

The electric XP 512E, an ancestor of the current-day Bolt, was a two-passenger electric urban vehicle. Just 86.3 inches in length and 56 inches wide, it was constructed of fiberglass atop a steel chassis and floor pan. Powered by a d-c

The 512 hybrid was the most complicated of the series. *Collection of Constance Smith; GM Public Relations*

The 512-E was a similar-sized concept. *Collection of Constance Smith; GM Public Relations*

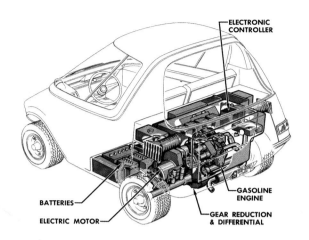

This 512 was the hybrid. *Collection of Constance Smith; GM Public Relations*

series Delco-Remy motor with solid-state controls, it relied on an 84-volt battery pack constructed of specially built lightweight cells. The charge was good for 58 miles of travel at 25 mph after a seven-hour charge. GM exhibited it at its "Progress of Power" event in 1969.

When describing the concept of hybrid gas-electric, an ancestor of sorts to the Chevrolet Volt, website marketers noted, "It was powered by a 12-cubic-inch gas engine coupled with a series DC electric motor through an electromagnetic clutch. The electric energy was produced by a 72-volt power battery pack. An added 12-volt accessory battery powered the accessories. The car operated in either all-electric or hybrid mode, and battery recharge was achieved with a built-in charging unit connected to a 115-volt household outlet. In the hybrid mode, the car was good for up to

35 mph. Its range in the electric mode at 30 mph was 5.2 miles. In the hybrid mode with 3 gallons of gas, it had a 150-mile range."

The 511 three-wheeled, gas-powered commuter vehicle measured 149 inches in length and had an 86-inch wheelbase and a rear tread of 54 inches, since the single wheel was up front. A 66-cubic-inch, four-cylinder gas engine was rated at 67 hp at 6,000 rpm. It was equipped with a three-speed automatic-torque-converter type of transmission. The power plant delivered a top speed of 80 mph.

In the late 1960s, the XP-883 commuter concept car appeared in a magazine. It was a plug-in hybrid vehicle with a fiberglass body.

The Electrovette was an urban electric vehicle powered by a 240-volt battery pack. The major components of the energy

The Electrovette was an experimental urban car powered by a 240-volt lead-acid battery pack. *General Motors*

The Electrovette was a modified Chevette. *General Motors*

The main components, including the onboard computer that functioned as a control signal processor, were under the hood. *General Motors*

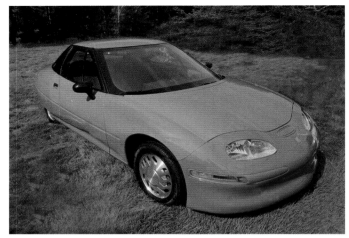

Although dismissed by critics, the EV-1 was a viable and significant vehicle in this era. *General Motors*

General Motors

system were under the hood and included an onboard computer that functioned as a control signal processor and the brain of the system. Batteries were also in the rear seat area.

In 1980, GMC Truck and Coach Division delivered fifteen electric vans to Michigan Bell in Detroit as part of the US Department of Energy demonstration project with American Telephone and Telegraph Company for installation and repair operations, powered by thirty-six Delco lead-acid batteries. GMC also had twenty electric vans in AT&T service in Culver City, California.

In 1990, the Impact made its debut at the Los Angeles Auto Show, and its systems were later tested in converted Geo Storms, Lumina APVs, Opel Astra Wagons, Chevrolet S-series pickups, and the HX-3 hybrid electric cars, according to a posting from the GM Heritage Center. These models were developed to reduce emissions and our dependency on fossil fuels. The Impact utilized some of the technology from the aerodynamic Sunraycer solar-powered electric race car and became the iconic EV1.

The EV-1, GM's first production electric car, produced in more than one version, was made from 1996 to 1999. Built on an aluminum space frame, it utilized plastic body panels and was leased through Saturn dealerships. Canceled and crushed because it was deemed unprofitable, it is rare but does exist in the collections

of the R. E. Olds Transportation Museum in Lansing, Michigan, and the Henry Ford Museum of American Innovation in Dearborn, Michigan. Early cars had three-phase induction motors and twenty-six lead-acid battery packs; the lead-acid battery is attributed to physicist Gaston Planet and dates from the 1850s. Carl Gessner of Germany is credited with invention of the dry-cell battery; Lewis Uri developed the alkaline battery in the mid-1950s. In the 1970s, nickel hydrogen was used for communication satellites. This led to consumer nickel metal hydride (NiMH) batteries. NiMH batteries are supplemental and not sufficient to power vehicles alone. Lithium was looked at as early as 1912 and marketed by the 1970s and was first used in a vehicle in 2003 and later would in part power the Volt.

THE EN-V AUTONOMOUS POD IN SHANGHAI FLEET

In 2010, GM designers introduced the EN-V, the two-seat urban mobility vehicle that is an autonomous car. It was developed under Dr. Chris Borroni-Bird, in collaboration with gyroscopic scooter maker Segway. Equipped with vehicle-based sensors and V2V technology inherited from the Chevy Tahoe, which placed first in 2007's DARPA Grand Challenge, its rechargeable batteries enabled it to travel 25 miles. Other EN-Vs were developed as time went on.

General Motors

SPARK EV

Revealed in 2012, the Spark EV was the first electric vehicle sold to the public. A pure electric minicar, it first arrived in California in 2014. Its development took place under Fletcher's direction. While the gasoline-powered Spark captured the entry-level buyer even before this time, the EV would muster excitement at a low price point with GM's support. The Spark required no gasoline, and GM Media posted an in-depth description of its technical stats. Improvements were made in subsequent years:

The Spark worldwide and the all-electric model were unveiled in 2012. *General Motors*

> *[The Spark's] GMC-built motor and drive unit deliver 400 lb.-ft. (542 Nm) of instant torque, a top speed of 90 mph and a 0–60 time of less than eight seconds. Storing that energy from the charging process and the vehicle's regenerative braking capability is a 21 kWh lithium-ion battery pack. When fully charged, Spark EV features a combined city/highway EPA-estimated range of 82 miles and an EPA-estimated city/highway 119 MPGe fuel economy equivalent, making it the most efficient U.S. retail electric vehicle on the market. Three available levels of recharging capability include the industry's first use of the recently approved SAE combo charger for DC fast charging, which charges 80 percent of the battery in just 20 minutes.*

The 2011 Volt included themes from the concept. *General Motors*

THE VOLT AND THE LITHIUM-ION BATTERY

In her 2015 *Automotive News* interview, Pamela noted that being named chief engineer for the Chevy Volt propulsion system was a big break for her—making the business of electrification make sense for customers and the business.

Combining award-winning style and engineering, the groundbreaking Chevrolet Volt was one of the most notable accomplishments in GM history. It was marketed and distributed internationally and was identified as the Holden Volt, Vauxhall Ampera, Opel Ampera, and Buick Velite 5. It was the groundwork of others that would launch the development.

China explored various configurations for the EN-V. *General Motors*

The hybrid vehicle became feasible only with the advancement of battery technologies. It was the work of John B. Goodenough, an American chemist working for Sony in the 1980s that advanced technology. He developed lithium-ion batteries for portable devices. GM's Denise Gray was tasked with finding batteries that could power the Volt and putting them together—they were later arranged in T packages. Gray, who attended General Motors Institute (a.k.a. Kettering University) and participated in the co-op program, graduated with a degree in electrical engineering and later served as GM's director of energy storage systems for twenty-nine years. She currently serves as the CEO and president of LG Chem Power. LG was a GM supplier and still is. GM engineer Tony Posawatz noted at the time that making a pure electric vehicle would have been a much-easier technological challenge. In 2006, notable concepts were presented in-house when Rick Wagoner gave a keynote speech introducing the Volt. Wagoner noted that what was ahead was "an unequaled opportunity to really reinvent the automobile with a transformation from horses to horsepower." He noted, "The key is energy diversity. We believe that the best way to power the automobile in the years to come is to do so with many sources of energy." To the surprise of the press, six weeks later, a model was unveiled in Detroit.

The first Volt concept was introduced in 2007. Its electric motor produced up to 121 kilowatts, the equivalent of about 161 horsepower. It produced 320 newton-meters, or about 236 foot-pounds, of torque. Electric motors offer more torque—the pulling power a car uses to accelerate—relative to their kilowatt or horsepower output than gasoline engines do.

GM News issued a letter in September 2008 about its launch of the production car that read, "GM launched its next 100 years today by unveiling its much anticipated production version of the Chevrolet Volt—a vehicle that delivers up to 40 miles of gas and emission-free electric driving; the extended range capability of hundreds of additional miles. For trips up to 40 miles, the Volt is powered only by electricity stored it its 16 kWh lithium-ion batteries. When the vehicle's energy is depleted, a gasoline/E85-powered generator seamlessly provides electricity to power the Volt's electric drive unit . . . for several hundred miles. The first-generation Volt was 177 inches in length, 70.8 inches wide, and 56.3 inches high. Its motor was rated 111 kW and at 150 hp with 273 lb.-ft. of torque. Perhaps, without the support of GM vice chairman Bob Lutz, the Volt would not have existed. The Chevrolet Volt has been described as an electric vehicle that uses its gasoline engine only to recharge its batteries and not to power its wheels. In one of his books, Bob Lutz emphasized that its sequential power train was very different from that of its Japanese competitor.

Ed Welburn, GM's VP of Design, and Anne Asensio, the advanced design chief, selected the exterior design of Jelani Aliyu as the basis for the Volt, but after numerous changes for various reasons, his aggressive styling transitioned to a more conservative design, perhaps to accommodate the manufacturing process and attract more consumers.

THE CONVERJ CONCEPT

In 2009, the stunning Cadillac Converj Concept was unveiled at the Detroit Auto Show. It also captured the prestigious EyesOn Design Award. This well-appointed two-door coupe, equipped with white synthetic suede and black leather accentuated by aluminum inside, is a derivative of the Chevrolet Volt. It was designed in GM's UK advanced design studios under the direction of Simon Cox and exemplifies the strong Art & Science design philosophy that perhaps continues to dictate the exterior-styling direction for the brand today. The "2 plus 2" layout accommodates four passengers.

For the most part, the Converj shares its mechanical components with the Chevrolet Volt. The lithium-ion battery consists of 288 prismatic cells assembled in a T configuration and powers the 120 Kw (161 hp) electric motor that provides power to the wheels.

When the battery capacity is low, the 1.4 L gasoline engine drives a generator to produce electric to power the car. It uses high voltage stored in its main battery as its primary source.

THE CADILLAC ELR

Pamela was the executive engineer for electrification when reporters speak about the Cadillac ELR—a production two-door, four-passenger luxury plug-in hybrid compact coupé introduced in January 2013 at the North American International Auto Show and marketed by Cadillac for model years 2014 and 2016—but not 2015 as the Cadillac-designed engineered upgrade for the 2016. In 2013, the stunning Cadillac ELR, following the lead of the Converj, captured the EyesOn Design Award by a small margin over the incredible new generation Corvette Stingray (the Converj, which greatly influenced the ELR, had captured the 2009 award).

Inside the ELR
Collection of Keith Furino Photo, *Constance Smith*

General Motors

When asked about the constant evolution of product for a Cadillac Spectrum article by Dan Grantham in winter 2015, Fletcher noted, "To me, that's the true beauty of my job; I have that opportunity to look at combining customer trends and technology trends, and advancing what I think are the world's greatest consumer products, cars and trucks that allow people the freedom of going where they want, when they want."

D-GEN VOLT

The second-generation 2016 Volt was a finalist in the World Car design awards, and it was more powerful and efficient than previous models. The 2016 is powered by a two-motor drive unit that is lighter than the original. Battery capacity had increased to 18.4 kWh, using 192 cells (six fewer than in the previous year, as well as 20 pounds lighter). The Regen feature allows the driver to control energy regeneration by using a paddle on the back of the steering wheel.

In 2107, the Volt won the *Motor Trend* Car of the Year Award.

In 2016, the Chevrolet Bolt joined the Chevrolet Spark EV and the Volt to create the industry's largest portfolio of electric vehicles.

While GM had decided to end Volt production in 2019, let us not forget that it was the recipient of the North American Car of the Year Award, the European Car of the Year Award, and three Green Car of the Year Awards, as well as being applauded by *Ward's*, *Popular Mechanics*, and *Popular Science*.

THE BOLT SETS THE NEW BENCHMARK

Fletcher led the team in developing the Chevrolet Bolt EV, as well as hammering out plans for future electric vehicles. The timely introduction of the groundbreaking Bolt put it well ahead of the competition, allowing it to carve out its own niche.

Designed on the exterior by Sungyeon Cho in Korea, the handsome 2017 Bolt EV set a benchmark and raised the bar in terms of design, engineering, and performance, promising a range of well over 238 miles.

Similar in nature to some of the EVs of the past, the Bolt utilizes a 60 kW permanent magnetic-drive motor rated at 200 mph / 150 kW—which supplies 201 horsepower—in this case with an offset gear configuration. Combined with a 7.05:1 final drive ratio, it helps propel the 3,580-pound Bolt EV from 0 to 60 mph in less than 6.5 seconds.

The battery system is further described as a 60 kWh

The Volt was redesigned and had a long tenure. *General Motors*

The exterior of the Volt was designed in Korea. *General Motors*

lithium-ion, rechargeable energy storage system aided by the 12-volt battery with rundown protection. The battery pack, which spans the entire floor, from the front foot well to the back of the rear seat, was developed with LG Electronics—GM's long-term Korean partner in developing the Volt. Mei Cai of GM's Research Labs has been influential in the development of batteries. With a 60 kWh rating, it consists of 288 lithium-ion cells weighing 960 pounds, divided into five sectors. The battery system has 160 kilowatts of peak power and 60 kilowatt hours of energy.

Under the hood, some of the major components are visible from above. The traction motor and gear reduction system sit centrally and are not visible. A heavy crossbeam sits atop the motor, and a number of modules, which can be seen, sit on top of it; there is a single power inverter module, a high power distribution module, an onboard charging module, and a step-down accessory power module. An added A/C compressor module drives the passenger A/C unit and cools the battery. A RESS sits in back of the motor—simply a battery coolant heater called the rechargeable energy storage system.

According to GM Media posting, the battery system is mated to a standard-equipment 7.2 kW onboard charger for regular overnight charging from a 240-volt wall box. A typical commute of 50 miles can be recharged in less than two hours. The Bolt EV also features an optional DC Fast Charging system, using the industry-standard SAE Combo connector. Using DC Fast Charging, the Bolt EV battery can be charged up to 90 miles of range in thirty minutes. Outside temperatures may affect charging times.

Regenerative braking has become more than just a tool to boost range; it has also transformed into a feature that can provide an improved EV driving experience. The Bolt EV features a new regenerative braking system that has the ability to provide one-pedal driving. Through a combination of increased regenerative deceleration and software controls, one-pedal driving enables the vehicle to slow down and come to a complete stop without using the brake pedal in certain driving conditions.

When operating the Bolt EV in "Low" mode, or by holding the Regen on Demand paddle located on the back of the steering wheel, the driver can bring the vehicle to a complete stop under most circumstances. Although the system does not relieve the need to use the brake pedal altogether, one may brake by simply lifting their foot off the accelerator.

OUR AUTONOMOUS FUTURE

In 2019, many felt that the Bolt was leading the race to produce a self-driving car. Contenders worldwide were still just playing catch-up.

Cruise Automation and Strobe were brought together to be able to deliver autonomous vehicles to the masses. GM acquired Cruise, founded by Kyle Vogt in 2013. In 2016, Strobe,

The Autonomous Bolt signaled the future. *General Motors*

which initially included only a dozen employees, was founded by Julie Schoenfeld in 2014 and acquired by GM in 2017. One of its board members and directors, Dr. John Bowers, is an engineering professor and researcher at UC in Santa Barbara. Bowers has spent years researching how to pack sensors onto a silicon chip. In a photograph posted online, Strobe's design is about the same length as a magic marker.

While we have available multiple technologies, ultrasound, radar, and LiDAR to maneuver our autonomous vehicles, the availability of LiDAR, because of its speed, has allowed GM to change the course of history. In very simple terms, LiDAR uses laser pulses to project beams that, when returned, calculate the distance of objects or people in a vehicle's path. While early LiDAR units cost $80,000, the key to success rested on reducing the cost.

LiDAR, short for light detection and ranging, made its appearance at MIT in 1962, was employed during the Apollo program, and was promoted by DARPA (Defense Advanced Research Projects Agency) challenges sponsored by the US Department of Defense. Most early systems incorporated a large roof sensor that swept the field around a vehicle. Davis Hall, of Velodyne, is said to have set an industry standard by his entrance in DARPA's third competition. He mounted an array of lasers on a spinning gimbal in order to collect distance data. However, in 2007, an autonomous Chevrolet Tahoe dubbed "Boss" won the third Grand Challenge. GM collaborated with Carnegie Mellon University.

The 2015 paper, emanating from Strobe researchers, titled "Fully Integrated Hybrid Silicon Two Dimensional Beam Scanner," describes MEMS-like scanning capabilities without using mechanical parts. (Note: arstechnica online 10/11/2017 Timothy B. Lee arstechnica.com/cars/2017.) Advances in Strobe's LiDAR are protected.

Writers in *Crain's Automotive Engineering* (August 2018) describe Flash LiDAR as consisting of flashes of infrared light being sent out and reflected off objects and read by a photosensitive chip. The chip is made of a grid that breaks light reflections into 3-D images.

MEMS LiDAR consists of a laser reflected off a moving

mirror. The mirror sends the laser beam in different directions. The laser beam scans a specific area, then the reflections are measured, forming a 3-D image.

Phased Array LiDAR consists of a beam through a grid, with each point of the array assigned a different light-beam direction. A 3-D image is formed when the beams are fired off, received, and measured.

A phased array is also described as a row of transmitters than can change the direction of electromagnetic beams by adjusting the relative phase of the signal from one to the next.

When it comes to the future, the infrared and LiDAR technologies continue to progress rapidly. Conferences are planned annually to explore the many facets of both. Infrared consists of examining the electromagnetic spectrum, spectral irradiance, night vision, and eye safety. The exploration of LiDAR begins with the examination of flash, scanning, wavelengths, detectors scanners, range and resolution calculations, and so forth.

In 2016, GM Media noted that on the heels of the signing of the SAVE Act legislation to support autonomous vehicle testing and deployment in Michigan, General Motors would immediately begin testing autonomous vehicles on public roads. GM also announced it would produce the next generation of its autonomous test vehicles at its Orion Township assembly plant beginning in early 2017.

In 2018, GM Media noted that General Motors filed a safety petition with the Department of Transportation for its fourth-generation self-driving Cruise AV, the first production-ready vehicle built from the start to operate safely on its own, with no driver, steering wheel, pedals, or manual controls.

In October 2020, Cruise obtained a permit from the California Department of Motor Vehicles that allows the company to have as many as five autonomous vehicles without human safety backups in its fleet.

In 2020, Dan Amman proudly announced that Cruise had started testing fully self-driving vehicles without driver monitors in San Francisco. GM, which is the majority owner of Cruise, with Cruise, Honda, and now Microsoft, looks forward to adding the Cruise Origin for usage both here and in Japan.

CADILLAC SUPER CRUISE

Fletcher played a key role in the development of innovative Super Cruise, which is marketed as the world's first true hands-free system for highway driving; however, smaller roads are now mapped and included. Super Cruise, a semiautonomous system, delivers comfort and convenience to the CT6 driver and will be available on all Cadillacs—if not now, then in the near future. While consumers might eventually buy into driving a fully autonomous car, they are more comfortable with a system like Super Cruise at the current

General Motors

Super Cruise is popular on Cadillacs products. *General Motors*

time. To add to its accuracy, Cadillac has mapped out all roads considered highways, and now even smaller roads in the United States, so that the system can take over reliably; no other manufacturer has gone to this extent.

Super Cruise is easy to engage. Once on the highway, an icon appears to signal that the system is available, and the driver pushes a button to activate it. A lighted green strip appears at the top of the steering wheel to indicate it is on. The system shuts off while the car is changing lanes, and the lighted strip turns blue. The system provides head-tracking software to track your eyes, which should remain on the road. If you are distracted, visual alerts and seat vibrations call your attention to it. LiDAR and advanced GPS monitor what lane you are in. Map curvature data and precision cameras track your position for up to 2,500 meters ahead.

In 2021, Cadillac added a lane change feature to Super Cruise. They have dubbed it "Enhanced Super Cruise." Drivers can now leave it to this technology to plan and make lane changes when it is safe.

The Malibu was also made in a hybrid. *General Motors*

HYBRIDS AND MILD HYBRIDS

Early on, GM added the word "hybrid" in the description of many vehicles. While some motors operate vehicles directly, others offer an assist.

The 2018 Malibu Hybrid offers everything in terms of a vehicle and power plant. It features what GM describes as Motor A, generating 55 kW, and Motor B, at 76 kW. Power comes from an eighty-cell lithium-ion battery pack. GM Media notes that the battery pack can power it up to 55 miles per hour before a gas power assist activates.

In September 2017, *Car and Driver*'s Joseph Capparella wrote an in-depth article about the CT6 Plug-In Hybrid, which he noted was introduced in 2016 and was scheduled to be assembled in Shanghai. The entirely new gas-electric was directed at the Chinese market. He noted that the CT6 features a 2 L engine and combines three power sources, including two motors in the transmission and a 18.4 kWh lithium-ion battery pack, which offers a combined output of 335 hp, 442 lb.-ft. of torque, and 31 miles of range using electric power. The 0–60 rating of 5.2 is phenomenal. In the all-electric mode, the motors can power it up to 78 mph, and the car will travel at least 31 miles, after which it switches between electric and gas. A regenerative system is accessed via steering wheel paddles. The CT6 was discontinued in the US in 2019.

The Lacrosse Hybrid. *General Motors*

The 2018 LaCrosse hybrid combines a four-cylinder motor and small electric motor that sources power from a 0.45 kWh lithium-ion battery pack. This is considered a mild hybrid and provides extra torque under acceleration and helps the start/stop system. The car also includes a regenerative system. The 2.5-liter with eAssist is standard on all versions except the AWD. This car is likely also called the Velite 6 in other countries where manufacture will continue after it is discontinued here.

LPG was desirable for the business partner. *General Motors*

GNG AND LPG

GM Fleet collaborated with Power Solutions International, Inc., to offer 6-liter V-8s that are LCD-hardened and LCD-compressed natural gas (CNG) and liquefied petroleum (LGP) capable, for Express and Savana vans, Silverados, Sierra HDs, and low cab forward models. Hardened valves and valve seats enable upfits.

Early in 2020, General Motors was reported to have twenty vehicles on the drawing board that will debut by 2023. When GM was founded, Charles "Boss" Kettering made the decision to buy or sell numerous other companies to move forward. His infinite wisdom led to the divestment of companies such as Marquette and the preservation of Buick. Today, GM is faced with similar challenges.

THE ULTIUM BATTERY

Having further produced and manufactured both hybrid and electric vehicles, sometime in 2019 GM chose to begin development of the electric vehicle over its gas-electric counterpart. The Detroit Hamtramck plant, renamed Factory ZERO, is producing vehicles for Cadillac, Chevrolet, and Hummer.

GM's Battery Lab, located at its Warren Tech Center, is the largest in North America. GM is in a joint venture with LG Chem of Korea to produce batteries named Ultium cell LLCs. These cells are configured in pouch form as opposed to cylindrical.

GM engineers have left the door open for continued improvements. While the Bolt batteries rely on nickel-manganese-cobalt cathode chemistry, researchers have discovered that the addition of aluminum to the mix would lower the cost per kWh. However, one must be mindful of the source of a chemical as it is added or subtracted. GM engineers believe that batteries in their sight could last for a million miles.

The stunning Lyriq has a very accessible charge port. *Lyriq Book*

THE LYRIQ, HUMMER, AND CELESIQ

In August 2020, the trendsetting, technology-laden Cadillac Lyriq EV was introduced virtually and also in the Design Staff auditorium at the GM Technical Center. It is available in FWD and AWD and was scheduled for production at the end of 2022.

The 1,000 hp Hummer truck unveiled in October 2020 is loaded with tech. An acceleration of 0–60 seconds for something the size of a half-ton truck is remarkable. Its inventive Crab Walk feature consists of four wheels that can turn in any direction, enabling diagonal movement on any terrain.

In January 2021, the GMC Pressroom announced a new multiyear sponsorship with Chip Ganassi Racing for the team's first electric racing venture in the inaugural Extreme E season in 2021. CGR's 550-horsepower electric SUV, which features a unique grille, graphics, and bodywork, was inspired by the GMC HUMMER EV, the world's first all-electric super truck.

At this time, Cadillac continues development on the Cadillac Celestiq—a full-size flagship that will feature roof panels that adjust color separately. Originally planned as a gas model, it now relies on one or more electric motors. The Obtiq and Symboliq names have been registered for future Cadillacs.

BRIGHTDROP, PAV, AND VTOL UNVEILED

In a video, Rachel Kuhn, director of BrightDrop Strategy, described the advantages of BrightDrop. BrightDrop is an ingenious system for the delivery of cargo from the warehouse to consumer, a valuable service particularly for business-to-business needs. In testing, the system reduced the time to deliver goods from warehouse to customer dramatically.

Cargo is loaded on e-pallets, which subsequently are efficiently moved and loaded into an electric light-commercial vehicle. This reduces the need for physical activity on behalf of the worker and reduces the time needed to load and deliver curbside. It is also beneficial to the public in the area of the activity. The progress of the delivery can be monitored.

PAV, a personal autonomous vehicle, presented by Candice Willetts at CES, is a concept created to explore comfort and convenience features as a result of the removal of a driver.

The e-VTOL concept is driven by electric power, operating four propellers created for single-person use.

GM and a partner are targeting the heavy-duty truck market with the fuel cell. *General Motors*

THE FUEL CELL

In 2021, the GM Press website noted the advancements and future of fuel cell technology: "GM is committed to fuel cells as a complement to battery-electric propulsion. We are fully engaged with our partner, Honda, to commercialize the world's best fuel cell technology for use by both companies across a range of applications. These fuel cells will be manufactured in Brownstown, Michigan, as previously announced. Our commercialization commitment and timing for fuel cells remains unchanged. In fact, we are currently installing the manufacturing equipment in our Brownstown facility … the timing of our fuel cell program has not been delayed due to the COVID-19 pandemic."

THE FLETCHER EFFECT

Pamela Fletcher led Innovation at General Motors, and her experience, talent, training, skills, and passion have and will continue to dictate our ability to navigate the road ahead while ensuring our safety.

PART II.
THE 1920s AND 1930s

Constance Smith

Early in the decade, engineering was king, and new technologies boosted the sale of vehicles. However, once all manufacturers delivered comparable features, the consumer looked further at styling. In the beginning, only small shops had the funds to offer customized automobiles. The design and quality of custom bodies of European makes exhibited in a New York hotel attracted the well-to-do, and the auto industry here took notice. As the emphasis shifted, manufacturers knew they had to rely on attractive physical design to sell cars, and they created separate styling departments to do so. In 1926, Lawrence Fisher arranged for Harley J. Earl, the head designer for the Earl Carriage Works, a custom body shop, to serve as a consultant to Cadillac.

ENGINEERING TAKES THE INITIATIVE

Immediately following World War I, GM Research Corporation was incorporated. Among the many notable engineering achievements were those features introduced by Chevrolet and Cadillac. Chevrolet saw the first window regulator come from Fisher Body's Ternstedt facility, enabling owners of closed-body cars to lower the windows. Cadillac engineers developed thermostatic control for carburetor air heat, and a compensated, inherently balanced V-8 crankshaft. Twisting the crank throws 90 degrees reduced vibration. In 1923, Duco lacquer, which replaced paint and varnish,

was used by Oakland. Buick's four-wheel brakes were manufactured in quantity. By 1923, GM had begun its overseas operations, and by 1925 GM began its acquisition of Vauxhall. Holden began bodying GM cars. In 1925, Fisher Body introduced the one-piece ventilating windshield, which eliminated the vision-robbing seal in the center of earlier ones of this era.

In addressing what we today call engine harshness, vibration, and noise (NVH), Pontiac and Buick discovered the suitability of rubber for engine mounts. Middecade, GMR (GM Research) developed the crankshaft harmonic balancer and a high-production dynamic-balancing machine, which it supplied to Buick—the machine located the imbalance by rotating the part and allowing the operator to drill out the area causing the imbalance. Other achievements included Durex bearings, engine-driven fuel pumps, hydraulic shock absorbers, V ventilation at the base of the windshield, adjustable front seats, and engine-driven fuel pumps.

As the decade ended, AC Spark developed the mechanical fuel pump, and Olds used chrome-plating in volume. In 1928, Cadillac introduced shatterproof safety glass in all of its windows, and by 1929 it was standard on Cadillacs and LaSalles. The same year they introduced the Syncho-Mesh transmission, which eliminated destructive shifting and encouraged women to take the wheel. Oakland brought out its foot dimmer switch, and Guide Lamp introduced its fixed-focus headlamp bulbs.

STYLING MADE THE DIFFERENCE

Styling came into its own after World War I. In design, the flush cowl would replace the ogee. The relationship between the hood and the body would change dramatically. The low, narrow hood and the wide body behind it were not aesthetically pleasing to style-conscious critics. The time came to raise the hood high enough to match the beltline and make it wider. Sports cars and touring cars would become low-slung and sleek. When it came to styling, Fisher Body's Ternstedt Division in Detroit housed the first Art and Colour Department. When Harley Earl arrived full time, he would found his own Art & Colour Department in the Argonaut Building, where artists would start to explore the development of three-dimensional forms and build clay models to this end. A full-size blackboard drawing or elaborate illustration does not always equate to a successful three-dimensional design. A full-size clay model would offer the opportunity to see the perfect design and still does today.

1930S OVERVIEW

Engineering and styling departments continued to create groundbreaking products with a new regard for safety. Around 1930, Cadillac took the lead by offering automatic valve lash adjusters with the V-16. The hydraulic valve lifter automatically maintained proper valve mechanism adjustment for each valve, eliminating the need for periodic manual adjustment. In 1930, GMR and AC developed resonance intake and exhaust silencers. By 1931, Olds introduced an automatic choke, while Delco-Remy introduced vacuum-operated spark control. In 1933, Engineering Staff designed independent front-wheel suspension, and Fisher Body developed No-Draft ventilation.

In 1933, the Century of Progress World's Fair in Chicago featured two diesel engines developed by Kettering at GM's Research Labs.

A significant advance of the era was the appearance of the turret top in 1934, designed by Fisher Body. As roofs became lower on the car, people could see the deterioration of fabrics and wear on the top—some were subject to drumming. The one-piece steel turret top was made possible by the availability of wider steel strips and allowed for large-scale production. The V-type windshield also appeared. Two years later came dual windshield wipers—how could we have ever lived without them?

The end-of-the-decade introductions were significant and included the four-speed semiautomatic transmission utilized by Buick and Olds. In 1937, Pontiac introduced a steering-column gearshift lever. Guide Lamp's introduction of the Sealed-Beam Headlamps was a notable safety improvement. A single unit, hermetically sealed, could focus more accurately and would be with us until 1955. In 1939, Buick announced rear directional signal lamps.

Other advances in the 1930s included inside sun visors, windshield washers and defrosters, directional signals, dual taillights and stoplights, headlamp beam indicators, dimmer switches, adjustable front seats, independent suspension, improved tires, and other similar advancements.

STYLING

The upright and vertical themes continued to fall by the wayside. Cars were lower and longer to suggest speed and power.

The stunning 1930 Cadillac, with its long hood, was powered by a V-16, with 453 cubic inches of displacement. A tall radiator with a brass-plated chrome heron mascot on top was offset by huge arched fenders and enormous separate headlamps. Spares were mounted on each side of the long hood. Fenders were more graceful, and the flying-wing design was always elegant. More-ornate wheels were sometimes eclipsed by balloon tires. In 1930, the REO-Royale Eight was more luxurious and featured handsome lines and rounded corners. As the decade progressed, elements of the Cadillac would filter down to Chevrolet and other divisions. By 1934, the LaSalle was praised. During this decade, Styling took on the responsibility of designing trucks and buses.

Designers made numerous changes during the Depression years, in 1933 and 1934, that changed car design forever. By 1934, the LaSalle's graceful vertical grille was praised both by consumers and the press. On many cars, customers could choose from a smooth back or trunk. We can't deny that the Buckminster Fuller Dymaxion concept was revolutionary, but it was not destined for production, nor was the Stout Scarab. In 1935, Buick's square form was more rounded, as if designers had already acknowledged streamlining, but in 1938, Cadillac forms were still described as rectilinear and desirable. In 1935, Opel's small cars appeared. The first Parade of Progress rolled out in 1936. This consisted of six vans with awnings and nine tractor trailers. All five automotive divisions were represented. In the 1940s, this dazzling traveling exhibit used Futurliners. Harley Earl's all-new Y-Job in 1938 was a milestone. Atop a Buick chassis, it was long and low and would set the direction of styling far into the future.

The newest production cars would feature one-piece bumpers with low leading front fenders and smaller aprons. Other features appearing included V-shaped radiators, more-slanted windshields, fender skirts, deep roof crowns, rear body extensions, and front fenders with a low leading edge.

BONNIE EVA LEMM
GM's and the World's First Female Automobile Designer and Engineer

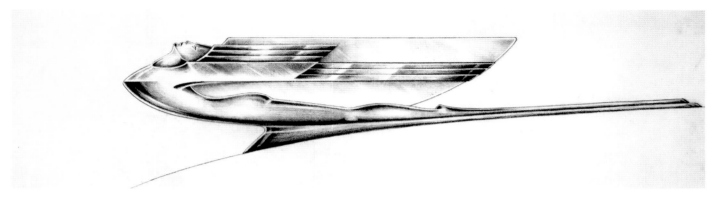

Bonnie Lemm's creativity is evident in this stunning drawing made for Chevrolet in 1939. *Courtesy of Kettering and GM; photo, Constance Smith*

CAREER HIGHLIGHTS

Original drawings and United States Patents secure Bonnie Eva Lemm's place in history as the first female career artist, designer and design engineer in the automotive industry.

To appreciate the contributions Bonnie Lemm made to the Fisher Body Division of GM for more than twenty-five years, one needs to revisit the founding of General Motors, since it acquired numerous other companies in its infancy. Lemm designed both appliances and automobiles. From 1916 to 1919, William Durant and General Motors bought stock in the Guardian Frigerator Company. The company, later rebadged as Frigidaire, would sell more electric refrigerators and appliances than anyone else in this time period. In modern times, the word "Frigidaire" became a household word for just about all refrigeration products. Some Frigidaire and automotive drawings made by Bonnie Lemm still exist today.

Early in her career, Bonnie Lemm served the Ternstedt Manufacturing Company, which was founded by Alvar K. Ternstedt in 1917 and was acquired by Fisher Body three years later.

William Schnell, who arrived around 1921, designed jigs for the factory and new automotive components. He received his first patent in 1923 for a decorative dome lamp and, in 1924, designed a complicated but artistic "Fixture For Auto Bodies," for which he received a 1935 patent. This multifunction part, which securely anchored to the back of the front seat, served as a handle to help someone enter the car, as a bracket for a rope rail, and also as a hook for an umbrella or cane. It is noted in the patent that it is an artistic design and pleasing to the eye.

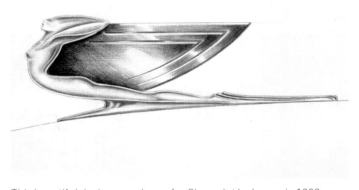

This beautiful design was drawn for Chevrolet by Lemm in 1938. *Courtesy of Kettering University and GM; photo, Constance Smith*

Fisher established a new Art & Color Department and the Die Sinker Department, which Schnell assisted with and was affiliated with until 1935. Ternstedt was GM's first styling studio and was located in a Detroit factory-style building. Ternstedt Art & Color appeared well before Lawrence Fisher found and hired Harley Earl. While Earl would later utilize clay for models, Joseph D. Thompson, who was on Cadillac's staff before Earl arrived, noted in an interview that Mullins Body Company offered a clay-sculpting service as early as 1912[2] and would make full-sized clay models over boxlike bucks, and clay was also used at Packard and Cadillac in 1916.

Later, Earl created his own styling department—the Art and Color Section of General Motors—which was located in the Argonaut Building near GM's mammoth Detroit headquarters. While most early cars consisted mainly of a chassis with parts bolted to them, Earl would rely heavily on using modeling clay to define form.

If Lemm was not already on staff to address Frigidaire's needs in 1917, she would have arrived at Fisher Body's Ternstedt Manufacturing Division shortly after the department head, Schnell. By 1925, at about thirty years old, Lemm was already a highly trained and experienced artist. While she was adept at creating realistic sculpture for hood ornaments with the best of European artists, many of her designs went far beyond the traditional.

Lemm's initial automotive assignments included a handle for a window regulator and hood ornament. This later led to her design of grilles, lights, outside door handles, and numerous radiator caps, which collectors affectionately term "mascots." An automotive-magazine writer mentioned that the first Ternstedt window regulator appeared in 1920 on a Chevrolet. It is not known if this was a concept or production automobile. The first patent was also applied for in 1920. While Ternstedt was acquired by GM in 1927, fittings were designed and manufactured throughout the industry before and after this time. More importantly, Lemm's first patent for a window regulator handle or similar is dated 1929. Lemm's design appeared on the 1933 Pierce Arrow Silver Arrow. Of the five cars manufactured, one of the perhaps only three left was part of the Thomas F. Derro Collection and recently sold at an RM auction for approximately $3.7 million. The 1929 patent also substantiates Lemm's place in our automotive-history books. Archival drawings exist for hundreds more components that Lemm designed, many of them reaching production. There was a time when the art deco style dominated design, and some mascots of this period reflect this. With the introduction of more-elaborate radiator caps, motometers, and mascots, Lemm's assignments even included these design components and the archer for 1931–1933 Pierce Arrows. This was the second in the series, with derivatives appearing until 1937. Recall that in the early days, Pierce Arrow was still owned by Studebaker, and it would take many years for them to become separate entities.

Lemm also designed Buick, Cadillac, Chevrolet, GM Truck, and REO (Oldsmobile) mascots and components. Lemm's drawing for a 1937 automobile grille still exists. She and just a handful of colleagues literally designed everything inside and outside automobiles with the exception of the mechanical underpinnings, which were simple and shared in the early days.

When it came to mascots, some were custom-made, but most came from the factory. Some parts departments offered alternatives, and outside accessory manufacturers offered others of varying quality—from inexpensive to the precious figures designed by Lalique.

Lemm pioneered the use of clear ¼-inch glass for GM mascots; they were integrated with GM's zinc, die-cast, chromed Goddesses. This added an ethereal dimension. During wartime, when metal was scarce, Pontiac Division capitalized on the new plastics, and all-plastic ornaments graced hoods.

While we all can picture the Spirit of Ecstasy that adorned the 1920 Rolls-Royce Silver Ghost, we are equally enamored with the iconic archer designed for Pierce Arrow in the early 1930s. We are also fascinated by the Cadillac Goddesses that followed. Enthusiasts still mount reproductions of 1941 Cadillac chrome-plated Goddesses on their 1970 cars. Mascots featuring women, and later projectiles, dominated the hoods of Buicks, Pontiacs, and Oldsmobiles, while Lemm provided Chevrolet with strong birds. During the art deco era, when streamlining reigned supreme, bullet-like or train-like ornaments, which looked fast, gained popularity. While some collectors commissioned artists to create individual works of art, just about every subject appeared on factory hoods at one time or another, and GM offered accessory ornaments in their parts departments.

CLOSE TO HOME

Bonnie Eva Lemm resided in Sandusky, Ohio, before relocating to Detroit. She was one of four children born to Adolph C. and Minnie Gertrude Wright Lemm on October 22, 1895. In an obituary from the *Sandusky Register*, published on January 26, 1943, it is noted that her father was a former Fremont carpenter. Bonnie was baptized in the United Evangelical Lutheran Church. She had two sisters and a brother and was closest to her younger sister, Nelle K. Lemm, also later living in Detroit. While it is not known which college she chose to attend, the Cleveland Institute of Art would have offered a strong industrial-design program, which emphasized ceramics and automotive design and was close to their home. In 1939, Elizabeth Thatcher Oros, Hudson's first female interior and exterior designer, graduated at the top of her class from Cleveland, as did her husband; Joe Oros designed Cadillacs and the first Mustang.

After moving to Detroit, Lemm resided at 1120 Campbell Avenue and a few other Detroit locations. She recorded her position as artist in the 1926 census. By this time, she was about thirty years old. Someone noted that Lemm smoked like a chimney and perhaps exhibited other masculine behaviors to fit in. Coincidentally, Lemm designed ashtrays for vehicles.

Lemm later married a manufacturing foreman at Ternstedt Manufacturing named William Walsh. It appears Walsh was initially a lodger in her parents' house. Records show that Lemm earned only two-thirds of what Walsh was paid. Lemm had no children of her own, and, after her death, she was survived by two nieces—Kathleen Zucker of Fremont and Norma Elminger of Huron.

From the original drawings in archival collections, one can conclude that Lemm was well trained in orthographic drawing, since she needed to provide drawings from many views for manufacture. However, her creative talent even exceeded her ability to capture three-dimensional designs accurately. Bonnie worked in Fisher's Ternstedt Art & Color Department full time.

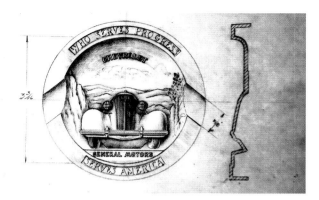

This ashtray was produced as a marketing piece for Ternstedt.
Courtesy of Kettering University and GM; photo, Constance Smith

THE TERNSTEDT MANUFACTURING COMPANY

In developing Ternstedt to its larger proportions, Fisher merged into it three companies: International Metal Stamping Company, Shepard Art Metal Company, and England Manufacturing Company. The head of Shepard was a degreed metallurgist with impressive credentials. Fisher gathered for the first time a complete staff of engineers, designers, artists, and modelers, prepared to fill the modern demand for artistic harmony of design in body hardware, interior fitting, and similar appointments.[3]

Alvar Ternstedt is credited with initiating the design for the first working concealed window regulator control for closed cars. A handful of Ternstedt patents show early directions, and the first regulator was said to have been available on a 1920–1921 Chevrolet. In 1920, Ternstedt had applied for a Canadian patent for a window regulator, with the assignee listed as W. Gates Louis. The patent was finalized in 1922. In the early 1920s, the Fisher brothers maintained their own Art & Color styling section to provide components that added individuality and appeal to cars. Even before the advent of the industrial design profession, these engineered designs were physically works of art. Grilles, lamps, door handles—inside and out, trunk hinges, radios, headlamp bezels, hinges, body side moldings, license plate holders, nameplates, ashtrays, and mirrors were highly stylized. Perhaps the biggest differentiator of cars in the 1920s and 1930s was the design of radiator caps, motometers, and mascots. These took many forms.

While motometers were initially measuring devices, later designs were decorative. At some point in time, hood ornaments were referred to as mascots, and they gained a life of their own as art form both on and off vehicles. When it came to General Motors, some mascots were standard fare while others were accessories.

Early on, Ternstedt designers at Fisher Body designed components for all manufacturers before focusing on GM's divisions. In 1921, Ternstedt hired William (born Wilhelm) Schnell, a German jewelry designer, silversmith, and diemaker. Schnell introduced a number of modeling processes for making intricate castings—the lost-wax technique was used by jewelry designers.

He also designed components and jigs for manufacturing. Schnell's good-sized staff consisted of artists, modelers, chasers, and foundry personnel; some were relocated from Germany and Scandinavia. The team received orders from all manufacturers before specializing in components for GM.[4] In addition to designing appliances and motor vehicles, at some point in time Ternstedt even designed for GM's aviation holdings. Drawings still exist for instruments designed for World War II airplanes.

Lemm was the first career female designer and design engineer in the automotive industry. Her first patent for the "handle of a window regulator or similar" was finalized in 1929. Lemm's design was made for Pierce Arrow. Lemm's door handle for the 1933 Pierce Arrow Silver Arrow is captured in the photograph of its interior taken at an RM Auction.

Fisher Body also designed products for Frigidaire, which was purchased by GM in 1916. It should be noted that Bonnie Lemm may have already worked there at this time as a designer and moved over to Ternstedt; however, this assignment would have included the design of appliances and not automobiles. Before concentrating on GM products, Ternstedt had contracts with others. Schnell and Ternstedt received a patent for the 1927 Marmon and 1928 DeSoto hood ornaments even before Ternstedt undertook the Studebaker-Pierce Arrow assignment.

Both 1925 and 1926 design patents exist for Schnell and Ternstedt. The 1926 design patent was finalized for an Indian head that he or their department designed. Schnell hired, or acquired, a highly talented Bonnie Lemm. It is possible that Lemm was retained to focus on products for Frigidaire. When it came to exploring three-dimensional space as an original style, Lemm was more creative than Schnell, who relied on the realistic designs found in Europe for inspiration. Her creative design work for Buick, Cadillac, Chevrolet, LaSalle, Olds, and Pontiac is striking.

Al Gonas, a colleague of Bonnie Lemm's, described an order from Pierce Arrow. In 1931, Ternstedt was commissioned to design an automotive mascot that turned out to be a new archer. Lemm received the assignment.[5] Pierce Arrow's earlier archer consisted of a slim-helmeted figure on the run with a bow and arrow. Lemm, a talented sculptress, had no problem creating complicated realistic figures. She designed the Pierce Arrow archers by using her colleague as a model. Al Gonas, who studied and modeled archery positions for her, noted that Lemm's drawing was selected from others. The archer Lemm drew was muscular, but the idea of using a separate arrow was not new—many are still missing.

While Lalique used this subject for a 1920s hood ornament, its mascot consisted only of a glass bas relief of an archer and not the intricate freestanding figure with a separate bow that Lemm perfected. In another communication, Frederick Guntinni was recognized for sculpting the archer from her drawing. Relatives of Lemm noted that Frederick Guntinni sculpted the figure in clay. As the live model, Al Gonas, a newly hired apprentice who

Lemm designed interior components and the mascot for the Silver Arrow Pierce Arrow. A US patent verifies her work. *Constance Smith*

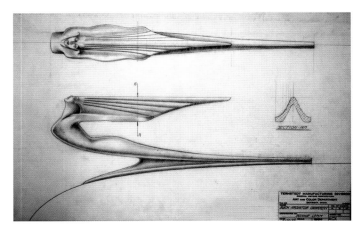

This exquisite double illustration was penned by Lemm. *Courtesy of Kettering University and GM; photo, Constance Smith*

This is one of many mascots made in 1937 for Buick. *Constance Smith*

would later rise to the manager's position, was asked to strip to the waist and pose for Lemm. Gonas thought Lemm was joking and refused to strip, but, after being persuaded, he enrolled in an archery school and learned how to hold a bow correctly so he could pose properly. In another conversation, Gonas described the drawings penned by Lemm leading to this assignment. Pierce Arrow approved the design, and Ternstedt produced the archer initially from 1931 to 1933 and continued versions of it until 1937.

In 1929, Lemm filed for a patent for a window regulator handle or the like for an automobile vehicle; the design patent was recorded in 1930.

THE LEMM PORTFOLIO

While collectors still search for motometers and mascots, the Lemm portfolio consists of hundreds of components designed both for inside and outside the vehicle. It should be emphasized that Lemm was assigned to create hood ornaments for almost all cars powered by eight-cylinder engines, with the exception of Chevrolets. When it came to Chevrolet, she designed components for cars powered by six-cylinder engines when no eights were manufactured. This included everything from mascots to grilles. The drawings, patents, and images featured here highlight the Lemm legacy.

BUICK CAME FIRST

Early Buick mascots (1927–1929) consisted of a chubby, winged goddess head credited to William Schnell and also distributed by the Irving Florman Company in New York City for use with and without a motometer. Smaller, frailer figures of

Mercury—designer unknown—followed (1929–1931). From 1931 to 1932, K. Forbes received a patent for a winged number eight. C. L. Sislo made small changes to this design for 1933. Sislo is credited with the design of a leaping lady introduced in 1933 or 1934.

While the above illustration was drawn for Buick, Bonnie Lemm designed a number of mascots during this time period for other divisions. Her figures for Oldsmobile are similar in nature; however, her figures are kneeling. Perhaps they were designed this way to add strength to the piece, since the 1933 Buick design, which attached to the hood with one foot, was fortified for 1934.

By the late 1930s, Buick and Chevrolet changed their mascots completely, incorporating streamlined styling influenced by locomotives. A versatile artist, Lemm was a master of form. Archival drawings for mascots and numerous components indicate that Lemm contributed significantly to the 1937 Buick and, in all likelihood, designed the hood ornament.

In addition, Lemm is credited with the design of its 1937 Buick's exterior door handles—for which she holds the patent—trunk hinges with the same motif, and inside controls.

THE CADILLAC PORTFOLIO

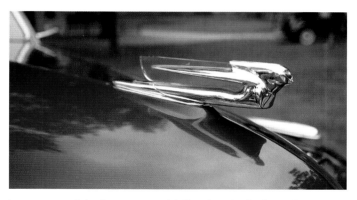

Lemm created the first mascot with flat glass for Cadillac. *Constance Smith*

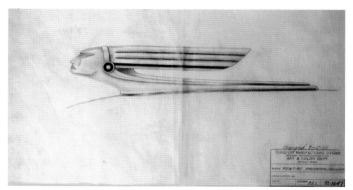

This modified Indian head hood ornament was used on production Pontiacs. *Kettering University General Motors. Constance Smith*

The 1936 Cadillac featured a simple chromed Goddess with her arms training behind her. No patent exists for this figure, but Bonnie Lemm more than likely designed or contributed to its design, which was similar to the 1937.

It is clear that the 1937–1938 zinc, die-cast, chromed Goddesses were Lemm's creations. This style of mascot was one of the first, if not the first, to incorporate a carefully shaped piece of ¼-inch glass that was positioned around the perimeter, with the back edge polished to hold the light. This direction is explored with numerous exquisite designs illustrated by Lemm. Furthermore, the 1939–1940, with its glass insert and V-8 engine, were also Lemm's stunning designs.

LEMM-DESIGNED COMPONENTS, GRILLES, AND ICONIC MASCOTS

Lemm made at least two grille designs for Chevrolet. Each design incorporated the Chevrolet bow tie and name in a sans serif typeface. The thin lines of this 1937 design are reminiscent of neon lights.

In terms of creativity, the mascots Lemm designed for the Chevrolet Division were remarkable, and they set it apart. In 1935, Chevrolet offered the Master Deluxe and Standard manufacturing over an astonishing half-million cars. Lemm's iconic chrome-plated Master Passenger mascot was simply styled with bold stripes. The Standard was based on the 1934 model, and the Master was new. These models were equipped with six-cylinder engines, delivering from 74 to 80 hp. While Lemm took a similar direction for the 1937–1938 Cadillac, with its glass element, the 1938 patent of the 1939 Master Deluxe proved significant. Lemm incorporated a ¼-inch glass insert decorated with stripes or grooves.

In 1941, Chevrolet offered the Master Deluxe and Special Deluxe equipped with six-cylinder engines. The mascot Lemm designed was similar to those she made for Cadillac and was die-cast, likely chrome plated, with a glass insert.

There is no question that Lemm's drawings and those of colleagues changed the face of the automobile from utilitarian to fashionable.

Not only did Lemm design decorative components, she also conceived of interior and exterior hardware for all divisions. At some point in time, she designed decorative inserts for window regulator handles that added beauty to a simple window crank.

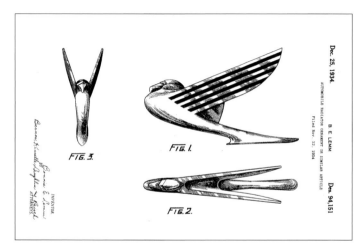

1934-35 Chevrolet (*US Patent and Trademark Office*)

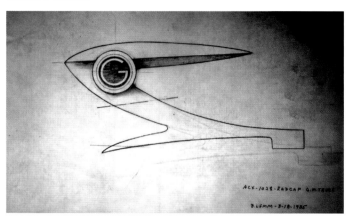

Lemm's mascot design for GM Truck took another direction. From the collections of Kettering University and GM. *Constance Smith*

GM TRUCK (GMC TRUCK)

The Rapid Motor Vehicle Company and the Reliance Motor Truck Company, early GM acquisitions, were combined to create the GM Truck Company. It was incorporated as a sales company in 1911.[6]

This gave Lemm the opportunity to propose hood ornaments for GMT. However, she did design other components put into production.

RANSOM E. OLDS

In 1933, Lemm's designs included a mascot for the Olds L33 model—a rare collectible today. The hood ornament consists of a female figure, head thrown back, with a scarf soaring behind. Most of the convertibles made, if not all, featured this figure. The 240-cubic-inch V-8 engine powering the L33 generated 90 hp at 3,350 rpm. The F-33 model, which featured a simple traditional Indian head in a circle, is attributed to Schnell and was installed in the six-cylinder version. It should be noted that Lemm was chosen to design mascots primarily for cars powered by eight-cylinder engines, with the exception of those for Chevrolet. However, this was an extra model added to utilize leftover motors.

Lemm also designed the mascot for both the 1933 and 1934 Oldsmobiles. She lifted the head of the lady upright. Lemm had an innate flair for three-dimensional design. This early Olds design was similar to but gentler than the one designed by a colleague for Buick.

LEMM'S CONTRIBUTIONS TO PONTIAC

Early Pontiac drawings were indicative of Lemm's talent and creativity, and a simple sketch for the 1937 model would later lead to the direction that Pontiac decor would take well into the future.

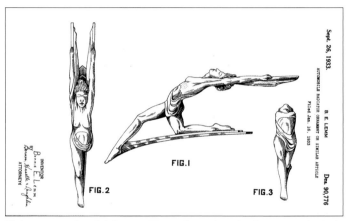

Olds was a major division, and Lemm's mademoiselle was protected. *Courtesy of the US Patent and Trademark Office*

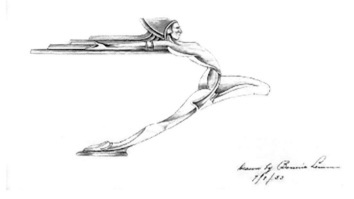

Lemm's 1933 drawing of an Indian was pure Pontiac. From the collections of Kettering University and GM. *Constance Smith*

While Schnell designed the mascot for the 1933 six-cylinder models, Lemm was brought in to create a different design when the corporation decided to add an eight-cylinder car. Schnell's Indian head surrounded by a circle was a reiteration of a 1932 design by W. R. Milner. Lemm, on the other hand, created a full-figured Indian lady in the art deco style. This was a challenging assignment, and not an easy design to manufacture. The unexpected eight outsold the six-cylinder.

While Lemm was clearly a talented draftsperson, sometimes a rough sketch is all that is needed to create something distinctive. Her 1937 Pontiac mascot was a simplified design of an earlier ornament as well.

This simple Lemm Pontiac drawing led to the mascot for the 1937 Pontiac-8. This hood ornament was a takeoff on an encircled Indian head designed by Frank Hershey in 1936; Hershey was a designer recruited by Harley Earl who created the new Styling Studio in the Argonaut Building. However, this simplified design set the stage for head ornaments far into the future, including the 1941 and 1943 plastic mascots. Features of the 1937 mascot still surfaced in 1953.

This drawing featuring a portrait with a stately headdress was far ahead of its time. Lemm included a small electric bulb to light the head. Similar Pontiac mascots would not appear until around 1950.

LEMM SETS THE STAGE FOR THE FUTURE

Lemm, hardly a temporary employee, worked at Fisher Body for over twenty-five years, designing many of our most memorable and iconic cars and trucks, inside and out.

It would take over twelve more years before other women designers were hired in a GM facility, and this took place elsewhere in the corporation, after the arrival of Harley Earl. In 1942, Helene Rother was retained to design and manage train and automotive interiors, and Amy Light designed products for "the Train of Tomorrow." Both worked in the newer Art & Color Division, which was part of the Styling section. The styling team was placed in the Argonaut Building, located in the vicinity of the massive GM Building, and was later donated to the College of Creative Studies. It opened as an educational center in 2009.

Portrait drawing by Constance Smith

HELEN BLAIR BARLETT

CAREER SUMMARY

Helen Blair Barlett, utilizing a grant from AC Spark, completed the requirements for her PhD in mineralogy in 1931 before joining the AC Ceramic Research Department. With the exception of an assignment on the Manhattan Project at MIT, Barlett spent her entire engineering career at AC Spark.

HISTORICAL NOTES[2]

The future of AC Spark was solidified a few years after other early GM affiliates and subsidiaries formed the new corporation. The AC Spark Company was founded by W. C. Durant and Albert Champion in Flint, Michigan, in 1908. Mr. Champion presided as its president. However, AC Spark became a subsidiary of General Motors when Mr. Durant sold his interest in it to the corporation in 1910–1911. Mr. Champion seemed to have a personal connection with the wheel. He was a trained mechanic and had raced foot-driven cycles, motorcycles, and automobiles. Champion won the world championship in bicycling and eighteen motorcar races in France.

When he returned to Boston from abroad in 1905, he began making spark plugs. He later relocating to Flint, and his products

She was an outstanding woman scientist. A pleasant smile showed her warm personality and her love for others and her profession. She had the respect of all who had the opportunity of know her.

—Karl Schwartzwalder, director of R&D, General Motors (1968), speaking about Helen Blair Barlett (December 14, 1901–August 25, 1969)

were also used in aircraft for the flight of Charles Lindbergh and others. His operation was set up in the corner of the Buick building, before a new two-story facility was erected. In 1917, he provided components for World War I. The Flint Faience Tile Company was organized in 1921 by AC because of the relationship of its products to the porcelain industry. It employed numerous designers working in the art deco and arts-and-crafts styles, ending production in 1933. In 1922, AC's speedometer also reached production. AC was the largest company of its kind anywhere, with plugs being made in St. Catharines in Ontario, Clichy in Paris, and Birmingham in England. Insulators were made in France from clay shipped from Flint.

HELEN BLAIR BARLETT'S JOURNEY

In 1927, Helen Blair Barlett received her BS degree in mineralogy from Ohio Wesleyan University in Delaware, Ohio, and pursued graduate studies at Ohio State University on an AC Spark Division fellowship. Barlett was granted the PhD in mineralogy in 1931. During summer months, while working on her doctorate, she

St. Catharines power train plant in Canada harnesses pure energy from water from the Welland Canal to cool processes in its operation. *General Motors*

served as petrographer in the Ceramic Laboratory at AC.[3] A classmate, Karl Schwartzwalder, was also completing the requirements for his master's degree at this time. Ceramic specialist Arthur S. Watts taught at Ohio State and would change the course of their lives forever.

Upon graduation, Helen joined the AC Ceramic Research Department as a mineralogist-geologist, as did Schwartzwalder. While Karl was promoted to director of research in 1955 and director of R&D in 1968, Helen became a ceramic research specialist in 1955 and was promoted to supervisor of ceramic research in 1956, and to ceramic scientist in 1959. Schwartzwalder noted in her memorial that she was the first woman to attain a top technical position in the General Motor Corporation.

As a mineralogist, she worked with various clay-based materials—which included porcelain—to develop ceramics resistant to electric current.

Memorial annotations published in 1971 were composed by Karl Schwartzwalder, who noted that early in her career, she became identified with alumina ceramics, having discovered that high-alumina melts containing about 0.35 percent lithium oxide precipitated zeta alumina, $Li_2O\ 5Al_2O_3$. Over the years, she became an authority on sintered alumina ceramic structures, particularly those relating to spark plug insulators. She wrote or cowrote a number of papers during the period 1931 to 1965 with Schwartzwalder, Fessler, and McDougal. Her ceramic interests, though, were wide and varied; she was issued seven patents from 1939 to 1968.[5]

Barlett's first patent, on April 4, 1939, was for a spark plug insulator.

Schwartzwalder also noted that during World War II, Barlett was granted a leave to assist with the Manhattan Project at MIT under Dr. John Chipman and received a citation for her contributions. It can be noted that the Manhattan Project was the code name for the atomic bomb. She returned to GM upon completing her assignment, which involved the development of a nonporous porcelain. GM's contributions to the war effort, which included personnel, components, and craft during this conflict, were unsurpassed.

In her spare time, Helen experimented with golf and assisted students at the Flint Science Fair.

During her retirement, Helen taught mineralogy to a group of young students and assisted at Campbell College in North Carolina. She was an influencing member of Flint's Zonata International and assisted with the Flint Science Fair. When we lost Helen in 1969, she was also memorialized by those at Campbell College and with the purchase of a mobile oxygen unit.

While these plugs were made for 1931-37 Buicks, they were also later used by Studebaker. Plugs from the author's collection. *Constance Smith*

PART III.
THE 1940s

In the early 1940s, designers and engineers joined together following an organizational plan formalized in 1935, bringing all
factors of the company together and paving the way for improvements in safety, performance, comfort, and appearance. Engineering
and designwise, Buick, Cadillac, and Fisher Body led the effort
pre–World War II.

GM Styling made a huge leap when it introduced a more
rounded body style, which was available in all divisions with the
exception of Chevrolet (1940). The 1940 Buick was praised for
its torpedo body for its Super and Roadmasters. The following
year, its new fastbacks and roadsters were well received. The
1941 Cadillac was a good example and, with its coffin-nosed hood
and horizontal tombstone grille, led the pack. Eggcrate inserts
would appear for years after. While the fenders of some cars
would trail into the front doors as the decade progressed, in 1942
a through-fendered Buick appeared. The front fenders would
reach to the rear fenders, and this first appeared on two coupes.
Later, four-door models relied on new hinges from Fisher body
for rear-hinged doors (1946).

In 1940, when it came to engineering, Buick introduced
front and rear directional signaling lamps with a self-canceling
switch. Both Chevrolet and GMC offered large stations wagons,
a.k.a. Surburbans and Carryalls. Oldsmobile introduced Hydramatic
Drive, a fully automatic transmission replacing the safety automatic. Pontiac created a see-though World's Fair and Golden
Gate car incorporating thermoformed plastic body panels. In
1941, Fisher Body introduced the safety-type door lock with a
freewheeling feature.

Emphasis shifted to war work, and GM made substantial
contributions. In 1940, Chevrolet had already received a contract
to make high-explosive shells, and Pontiac would manufacture
aircraft engines. As the US was pulled into the war after the attack
on Pearl Harbor on December 7, 1941, the production of all civilian autos and trucks ceased in early February 1942. After
January, chrome plating was allowed only on bumpers, if at all.
Metal trim was sometimes painted in contrasting colors.
Subsequently, Buick developed the step-on parking brake in
1942, and 1942 was also the first year of what would be dubbed
Buick's "toothy grilles." The stunning Cadillac Series 62, with its
streamlined body, was considered the most handsome of all
Cadillacs.

Civilian car and truck production resumed in late 1945, after
the war ended on VE-day (Europe) in June and VJ-day (Japan)
in August. Since manufacturers were fully focused on the war,
there was little time for new designs. Cars introduced right after
the war mainly consisted of 1942 designs with new grilles and
trim. The first new vehicle for Chevrolet was the redesigned
light-duty pickup, which would ride the waves until 1955.

The fish-mouth grille appeared on the 1946 Oldsmobile and
was refined in 1948. With its small fins, the 1948 Cadillac was
all new too, with the exception of the Fleetwood. The new Cadillac
and Oldsmobiles returned to yesteryear with rear fenders. Earl
and Andrade brought nuances of the P-38 Lightning fighter into
design, but only the fins stuck. The interior of the Cadillac featured a chrome ring on the steering wheel, and chrome on the
instrument panel cluster, radio surround, and numerous other
interior parts. The chosen fabric on some, brown and tan broadcloth, came in wool or cotton. Both Cadillac and Oldsmobile had
all-new bodies. For 1949 midyear, the Buick featured a toothy
grille, sweep spear, and portholes. Pontiac and Chevrolet had a
new look.

In 1947, Buick introduced the Dynaflow torque converter,
based on a design developed by Engineering Staff. In 1948, Olds
and Cadillac offered high-compression, short-stroke, V-8
engines.

In 1948–49, Cadillac introduced the curved windshield,
which would offer significant improvement to visibility and the
opportunity for stylists to design new models around it. The
wraparound rear window in 1949 was also groundbreaking.

On another note, the hardtop coupe developed by Fisher
Body in 1949 would change the look of many models.

While prewar models lingered after World War II, the new
introductions of Buick and Cadillac (1948) were here to compete.
The same year, Cadillac introduced power windows.

In 1949, Chevrolet would introduce a Powerglide transmission, incorporating an Engineering Staff design. At the same
time, Buick introduced E-Z Heat heat-absorbing glass.

Other styling changes included headlights that were integrated
into front fenders, and running boards that were either eliminated
or hidden behind doors.

From a budget standpoint, the grilles of some Chevrolets
and some Buicks were identical, with the exception of the fact
that the Buick's headlights were integrated into the front fenders
and mounted farther outboard. In only some divisions, front
fenders were being extended well into the doors.

HELENE ROTHER ACKERNECHT

The experiment of bringing a woman into this strictly male industry was shockingly radical. The lady might not last out the year. To forestall possible embarrassment for everyone, better to keep the whole matter hush, hush.

—Mary Morris, *Detroit News*, speaking about Helene Rother Ackernecht (1908–1999)

Rother portrait. *Collection of Constance Smith*

CAREER HIGHLIGHTS

In 2019, Helene Rother was the first woman designer nominated and selected for induction into the Automotive Hall of Fame by its prestigious board of directors; the ceremony was rescheduled for 2021. Rother, highly trained, was one of the most talented women of her generation. This award is being made posthumously.

Rother's design of fashioned interiors for General Motors and Nash, working alongside Harley Earl and Pinin Farina, inspired those who followed. While Earl led in the creation of sculpted exteriors, Rother chose, designed, or led in the design of fabrics, colors, and instrument panel decor, serving as an inspiration of today's designers. Rother also contributed to the design of comics for the Funnies, Inc. (which could supply art to Marvel), as well as to the design of children's books, magazine articles, radios, furniture, and silverware. Although her books were never published, the Advertising Club of St. Louis, Missouri, recognized Helene's work and presented the Brass Hat Award to her.

Before she emigrated from France in 1941, Rother established her own design business—the Contempo Studio—while working for Monocraft Products Company and others. Monocraft established its fashion jewelry line in 1929 before rebranding as Monet in 1937.

After arriving in New York City in 1941, Rother tried to market children's books she had written and illustrated, and she paid a Florida attorney to market two books. She would have been unable to support herself and her daughter even if she had been successful. Following a suggestion, she applied for work as an illustrator for the Funnies, Inc., a newspaper service studio creating comics on request for Marvel and others, and assisted other artists there until connecting with General Motors.

Rother was the first woman automobile designer hired by Harley Earl. At this time, a new Styling Section (formerly the Art and Color Section) was located in the Argonaut Building, near GM's Detroit headquarters. A newspaper recorded Rother's affiliation with GM in late 1942. Helene was retained to design vehicle interiors and would later assist Earl in managing the interiors studios; her first full year began in 1943. Amy Light later arrived from California to design products solely for the Train of Tomorrow. One of Rother's assignments consisted of the design of interior seating and wall coverings for the spectacular Train of Tomorrow, which toured the United States and southern Canada from May 1947 until October 1949.

Beginning with postwar offerings, Rother would go on to contribute to or influence the design of automobiles and trucks for all major GM Divisions—Cadillac, Buick, Chevrolet and Chevrolet Truck, and GMC, as well as Pontiac and Oldsmobile. Postwar models, such as the 1948 Series 61, 62, and Sixty Special Cadillacs and the 1948 Olds Futuramic 98, inspired other new offerings. Rother was photographed with an experimentally configured van.

Rother was the first woman to present at a Society of Automotive Engineers (SAE) conference. During this appearance, she explored and promoted automotive interior design.

During Rother's affiliation, a number of concept cars were prepared for introduction at Motoramas. These extravagant shows at the Waldorf Astoria in New York and other cities here and in Canada also featured future appliances and kitchen concepts. In 1949, at Transportation Unlimited Autorama, the Cadillac Caribbean, Embassy, and convertible with calfskin carpets were unveiled. In 1950, at the Mid-Century Motorama, the Cadillac Debutante convertible sported gold paint and leopard skin upholstery. In 1953, the Buick Wildcat, Buick XP-300 convertible, Cadillac Le Mans, Cadillac Orleans, Chevrolet Corvette, Buick LeSabre, Olds Starfire X-P Rocker, and Pontiac Parisienne were revealed. Other Motoramas—from 1954 to 1961—continued past her affiliation.

Rother established her own design office in the Fisher Building after reinforcing her association with American Motors in 1947; this assignment ended around 1955. In 1951, she still assisted Earl at that year's Paris Auto Show, and she maintained her association with GM as a consultant into the early 1950s. The image of Rother driving the LeSabre Concept in 1951 past thousands of men en route to the Paris Auto Show is perhaps the most notable of the era. No other woman had been entrusted to drive a running concept car, and Rother was not known for her driving abilities.

Working alongside Battista "Pinin" Farina at Nash-Kelvinator, Rother designed dozens of textiles for late 1940s and early 1950s Airflytes, which featured a controversial exterior design but relied on a GM transmission and other parts. She was photographed sharing the Jackson Award design for the Airflyte with Pinin Farina.

Inside the 1951 Paris Show, Rother was also photographed with the Nash elite and alongside the Nash-Healey Airflyte and sports car. Upon returning to Detroit, she wrote a significant article about the show for a local newspaper.

Intellectually brilliant, Rother created presentations for executives and conducted research behind the scenes for magazine writers. Besides being the first woman to address the SAE, she also addressed the Chicago advertisers, from which she received the Brass Hat Award. Rother prepared a nineteen-panel illustrated presentation for an unknown client that has survived. Noted for designing stained-glass windows for cathedrals in and near Detroit later in life, she also presented to groups of fine artists.

As part of her vocational range, Rother designed professional vehicles, which usually relied on GM frames. Her consultancy also designed for Spartan Radio, Mengel Furniture, and U.S. Rubber.

In 2019, at the first Las Vegas Concours d'Elegance, the Helene Awards was created by Stuart Sobek, in part to honor Rother. This is now a recurring charitable event, and the organizers recognize two vehicles and contributors to auto history with a trophy that is a stylized portrait head of Helene. In 2021, Peter Brock and Constance Smith were award recipients.

Rother's <u>complete</u> portfolio of artwork and additional photos are featured in *Damsels in Design: Women Pioneers in the Automotive Industry, 1939–1959* (Schiffer Books, 2018).

BIOGRAPHICAL PROFILE

Rother was born to German parents in 1908 in Leipzig and had an older brother. When it came to education, girls had their own schools and generally did not receive the same educational opportunities as boys.

Germany was a nation that entered the First World War in 1914 and suffered from the effects of surrender in 1918, around Helene's tenth birthday. The consequences of economic ruin and the threat of revolution opened the door for Nazism. In 1920, the National Social Workers Party was formed.

Rother's original résumé verifies the fact that she graduated from a crafts school, Kunstgewerbeschule, in Leipzig, around 1930, after five years of study with the equivalent of our master's degree. In 2020, after an early news article posted by the SAE was unearthed, it is now believed that she attended the State Academy of Graphics and Book Trades (a.k.a. the Leipzig Academy), which was in Wachterstraße. As a student or shortly afterward, Helene illustrated a book she titled *The Little Man* in watercolor or gouache.

Around 1929, Helene met Erwin Heinz Ackernecht, son of Dr. Erwin J. Ackernecht and Clara Pfitzer, in Leipzig. Erwin was born in 1906. Erwin's father was a librarian, professor, and library director. Erwin, like Helene, was a passionate artist and painter. However, his father found painting frivolous and encouraged Erwin to pursue a career in medicine. He studied at the University of Freiberg and later the University of Leipzig. Erwin later gained prominence as a scholar of medical history and ethnomedicine.

Erwin and Helene shared their love for painting and each other. Their daughter, Ina, was born in 1934.

Rother, the only woman to drive the LeSabre concept, was photographed in the car en route to the 1951 Paris Auto Show, in this rare photo likely shot by Harley Earl. *Constance Smith*

Erwin's political activism would change their lives. An early Trotskyist, Erwin later disassociated from the political theorist and politician because of philosophical differences. Erwin was also an active member of various groups and founded an anti-Nazi organization. Erwin vehemently opposed Nazism and rightism.

A marked man by the Nazis, Erwin was forced to go underground; he feared for his own life and family. However, it did not take long before he ignored the needs of his wife and daughter to spend time with other women. Erwin escaped to France in the mid-1930s and enrolled in the Sorbonne. After separating physically from her husband, Helene continued to associate with politically active people. She too was forced to flee, with her seven-year-old daughter in tow.

A very capable, confident young woman and now a single parent, Helene moved on to Paris, France, in an effort to escape from the Nazis, who she thought were tracking her. She spoke French perfectly and set up her own design office, the Contempora Studio, to develop designs for Haute Couturiers.

She created fashion accessories in metal, glass, leather, and plastics and designed textiles and table silverware—hollow and flatware.

MONOGRAM AND MONET

In 1929, while Helene finished her education, Jay and Michael Chernow founded the Monocraft Product Company to provide gold and silver monograms for women's handbags. As the company expanded to provide reasonably priced jewelry in hard times, it was renamed Monet in 1937. In the late 1930s, Rother reinforced her lifelong love for animals and began designing pendants. Monet initially questioned her design of a piece of jewelry using an animal. This silver pony became the first piece in their Menagerie Collection She also designed a greyhound. The Monet Collection grew to include eleven whimsical animals. Monet invited Rother to come to the United States when Paris was submerged by occupation forces.

Monet had invited Rother to join their staff, and she brought the invite with her in case it was needed to use in her escape. However, as the war spread, there was a hiring freeze at Monet. While considered costume jewelry, it is well made, fashionable, and affordable. As more women entered the workforce in the 1950s and 1960s, Monet flourished. Monet products continue to be distributed worldwide.

At some point in time, Helene is said to have lost her brother, who joined the French army, in the conflict. It appears that a nephew remained in France and established an architectural office and exhibited his own paintings in a gallery.

EVERY LIFE IS PRECIOUS; VARIAN FRY AND HIRAM BINGHAM SAVE REFUGEES

The fall of France in 1940 would change the course of history. Since the Russian Revolution, France had served as a haven for Europe's exiles. However, Hitler's invasion was said to have decimated the French army. A few weeks after the French defeat, the American Federation of Labor had persuaded the State Department to grant emergency visas to a list of European labor leaders and other refugees still in France.

When it was learned that the armistice between France and Germany contained a clause providing for the "surrender on demand" of German refugees, a group of Americans shocked by this violation formed the Emergency Rescue Committee to bring the political and intellectual refugees through and out of France before the Gestapo, OVRA, and Seguridad captured them. Varian Fry and Hiram Bingham IV assisted with this initiative, promoted by Eleanor Roosevelt herself.

As head of the Emergency Rescue Committee, Varian Fry, who resided in Marseilles from 1940 to 1941, saved hundreds of refugees from starvation and death in concentration camps. He was initially given a list of about two hundred, which included labor leaders, writers, and artists trapped in France, including Marc Chagall, Max Ernst, Franz Werfel, and Nobel Prize winner Otto Meyerhof.

This pony, designed in the 1930s, was Monet's first and started their Menagerie Collection. *Helene Rother*

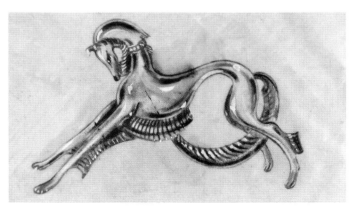

These beautiful illustrations were made for pins or pendants. *Constance Smith*

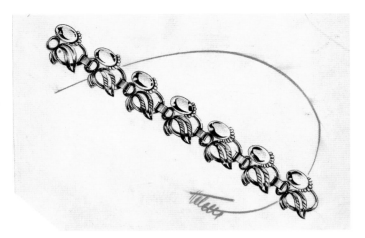

Constance Smith

Constance Smith

As a vice consul to the US consulate in Marseilles, "Harry" Bingham assisted by issuing visas and bogus passports to Jews and other refugees, and it is believed they were able to save almost 2,500 during their extended tenure. It is not known if Helene Rother Ackernecht and her daughter, Ina, were on the initial list of two hundred or were added to it. As a jewelry designer for Monet, she was an identified artist. Her daughter recalls that Helene also had an invitation to work for Monet in hand.

AN AFFIDAVIT SAVES HELENE'S AND INA'S LIVES

Erwin escaped and with money earned would assist in getting his family out. The American Committee sent Helene a letter, which still exists today, using an alias for her and informing her that she would be assisted by the committee and had been given $400 for her travel expenses—the money for passage appears to have been provided by Erwin. Helene and Ina would have to travel to Marseilles to escape; the city could be described as both a prison and an escape route.

Helene Ackernecht was issued an "affidavit in lieu of passport" signed by Hiram Bingham in May 1941. Surviving documents indicate Helene's ancestry. Although she was perfectly fluent in French, the investigator corrected the affidavit to record her nationality. She was German and never a French citizen.

The immigration document—the affidavit in lieu of passport—meant the difference between life and death for Helene Rother Ackernecht and Ina Ackernecht.

In a presentation, Helene noted in her own words that when she came to the United States in 1941, half of France was already taken over by the Germans. When the Gestapo had arrived searching for her estranged husband, Helene feared for her life. She went to the American consulate, seeking a visa. In a presentation some years later, Helene noted, "We left from Marseille [*sic*] but the English restricted French boats to cross Martinique and they found munitions hidden in the boat.

The trip ended and I instead had to go through Casablanca." There, they waited in a refugee camp to obtain the required paperwork to New York.

A letter exists in archives verifying her arrangements to travel on board the SS *Nyassa*. However, after they changed ships, Rother's daughter believed that they arrived on the *Britannia*, Cunard's first steamship.

After legally divorcing Helene in 1943 in the United States, Erwin later married two other women there.

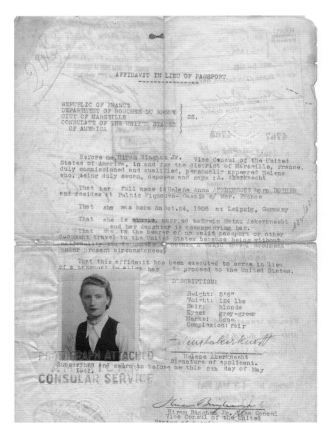

When the Nazis infiltrated France, this Affidavit of Immigration saved the lives of Helene and her daughter Ina. *Collection of Constance Smith*

Helene and Ina escaped from Nazi-occupied France. *Collection of the author*

Rother's drawing skill is evident even in these illustrations; early comics had no balloons. *Photo courtesy of Constance Smith*

There is no question that Helene was one of the most talented artists of her generation. While many of her colleagues emphasized engineering, Helene would marry color and style. She has been described as physically attractive. Blond, sophisticated, and strong, she was a young lady who rose above the devastation surrounding her. Already fluent in German and French, she mastered conversational English and much later proceeded to master the written word in order to write her own speeches and children's books.

Art deco, popular in the 1920s and 1930s, was dubbed "European style" by some. Rother did not rely on trends, and she had her own abstract style and handled representational subjects beautifully too. She was knowledgeable about weaving techniques, and her beautifully decorated copper cloisonné plates appear to have been created in an industrial oven.

In a 1950s interview, Helene noted that she was an admirer of the Bauhaus School in Weimar and of the French architect Le Corbusier, who conceived of the house "as a living machine." But Mrs. Rother herself believed that while "simplicity is a great quality—it does not of itself make style."

HELENE TACKLES NEW YORK CITY

Helene shared an apartment in New York with her Jewish companion and secretary from Paris. Helene's secretary's father was a physician who was imprisoned and murdered.

Helene enrolled her daughter in Public School 166, on the west side of Manhattan. While she had planned to work for the largest American jewelry company, Monet, the assistant's position was eliminated when the United States entered World War II in 1941. In the 1930s. Helene wrote and illustrated two additional children's books. Upon arrival in the United States, she offered one children's book to an agent or publisher, offering to give up half the proceeds. At the time, she provided black-and-white copies of her illustrations, which were less impressive than full-color art. However, the stipend offered by the publisher could not provide for her and Ina. A number of magnificent illustrations were later made for *Two Princesses* and another book as well. While the agent felt that the word "princesses" was too European, this book is very reminiscent of Cinderella. Rother's characters were creatively devised, and the illustrations included numerous figures. Although her books were never published, the Advertising Club of St. Louis, Missouri, recognized Helene's work and presented the Brass Hat Award to her; this consisted of a walnut plaque, an engraved plate, and a gilded top hat on top.

It was at this time that the publisher introduced her to cartoonists working at Marvel Comics, and she joined Funnies, Inc., a related entity, as an illustrator.

HELENE APPLIES FOR A POSITION WITH THE GENERAL

In 1927, Alfred Sloan obtained permission from the GM Board of Directors to establish a special department to study the art and color combinations of products. The job description also called for the candidate to assume a broader role, which included body design and research for the development of special car design. There was no doubt that the description was written for Harley Earl.

The LaSalle was so successful that Earl was hired to establish an Art & Color Section for General Motors in 1927 and was directed to find fifty people to "man" it. In 1942, Earl was approached or advertised for a designer, and Helene Rother forwarded her portfolio. Helene's daughter thought that General Motors placed an advertisement in the *New York Times* in 1941 or 1942 for a "Designer of Fashioned Interiors." Perhaps this advertisement appeared somewhere else; it has not been located in the *New York Times'* classified archives.

Helene was excited by this opportunity. Although she struggled with written English, she did not lack talent for training. Helene applied with a letter and followed up by mailing exquisite artwork from her professional portfolio.

Helene met Harley Earl, a tall man well over 6 feet who was GM's vice president of styling, and was offered a position in 1942, with a modest salary alluded to in a presentation she gave to a group of stained-glass artists: "I earned less than the men I supervised." Similarly, one of the other talented women, MaryEllen Green, hired in 1950, recalls receiving a secretarial salary after moving from California and paying steep tuition for a design education at Pratt Institute in New York.

In 1934, *Fortune* magazine reported that male designers with consultancies, such as Raymond Loewy (Hupp) and Henry Dreyfuss (Sears, Roebuck and Company), made thousands of dollars. Perhaps Helene's gain was exaggerated by a member of the press who recorded that she had hit the jackpot.

Helene established her own design office on the sixteenth floor of the Fisher Building, one of Detroit's iconic art deco skyscrapers, and registered her own business.

At this time, the women who could contribute to the war effort did. The departure of many men from GM during the war left the door open for female replacements. General Motors' contributions in winning the war in Europe and the Pacific would later be recorded by historians as one of its greatest achievements.

CONTRIBUTIONS WERE KEPT HUSH-HUSH

In 1942, according to her own writings, Helene was the first woman to venture into the field of automotive interior design at General Motors. She designed and updated the interiors for the Buick, Chevrolet, Cadillac, Olds, GMC, and Pontiac Divisions. As the war ended, manufacturing resumed in 1945. When she first eyed the drab interior fabrics, Helene thought, "Why not make cars beautiful?" Chevrolet increased the number of color offerings inside. Certainly, Helene would be pleased with the hues, exquisite fabrics, and leathers found on today's luxury car instrument panels, seats, and doors. Not only was she responsible for fabrics and colors, but also for lighting arrangements, instrument panel jewelry or hardware, and the seat design.

Rother needed no help to create or select fabrics. *Collection of Constance Smith*

WOMAN THREATENS THE STATUS QUO

Helene was seen as a pioneer, a dynamic talent, and a radical, and she likely was considered a threat by some of her male colleagues. Some felt that no one alive would even believe that she existed. Mary Morris, women's editor for the *Detroit News*, had a field day following Helene's career:

> GM officials insisted that designer Rother be kept under cover. The experiment of bringing a woman into this strictly masculine industry was shockingly radical, they explained. The lady might not last out the year. To forestall possible embarrassment for everyone, better to keep the whole matter hush-hush.

Unfortunately in this era, it should be noted that these attitudes reflected business as usual. In the early years and many to follow, it was the policy of most big companies to shroud design staffs in anonymity. In the auto industry, the manager is recognized for the work of those below him or her. All designs were credited to Harley Earl, the vice president of design in the earliest years.

Helene had described the interior designs of some of the cars of this era as simple, since GM continued most of the instrument panels from prewar models. However, the 1948 Cadillac, famous for its tail fins inspired by the P-38 Lightning aircraft, was likely the first all-new automobile from the "Big Three" post–World War II, and the interior was Helene's department. As the 1940s progressed, Buick extended its lines on the sides of its offerings, making cars appear sleeker, lower, and sportier.

CADILLAC LEADERSHIP

Around 1946, Harley Earl planned for a new Cadillac, and production likely began in 1947. As a manager, Helene would have contributed to the design of the 1948 production Cadillac interior under the personal direction of Harley Earl.

The Cadillac Series 61 and 62 and convertible were all new for 1948. The 61 was a GM B body, and the 62 a C body. The 61 featured a flared body over the rocker panels, and the 62 a slimmer body and venti-panes (vent windows) front and rear. This coupe, presented by Charlie Saganek, was exhibited at the EyesOn Design. *Constance Smith*

The new design was offered in Series 61 and 62 models, and a convertible on new B- and C-body platforms. The Series 61 cars were bullet-like from the front and bulged on the sides and had skirted rear wheel openings. The twin tail fins were reminiscent of the P-38. Behind the split windshield, the new instrument panel was assembled in four sections—an expensive affair made for only one year. It featured a central pod—an inverted Tucker-shaped cluster—and both cars were revealed simultaneously. The pod was dominated by a ribbed, stamped plate below the narrow san serif numbers of the speedometer, placed on an arc at the top. The needle began as a large circle in the center, narrowed as a thin line, and ended in an elongated arrow. Four gauges sat at the bottom, below a divider—the fanciful Cadillac insignia—just atop the steering column. The wheel, with simple chrome decoration and a chrome horn ring, was made of white plastic and featured a Cadillac dicrel in the center. The radio, with two chrome-plated, fashioned knobs, was encapsulated by a chrome-plated bezel in the center of the car. The clock, face to face with the passenger, was also surrounded by a double chrome frame. The door panel was simply divided and featured a Cadillac emblem just below the window glass. The channeled leather upholstery was devoid of imperfections, and the carpeting was luxurious. As usual, Harley Earl took credit for the designers for all cars.

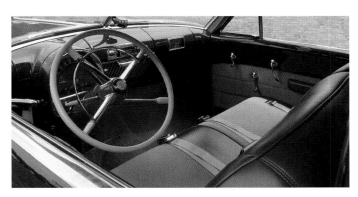

The sophisticated cluster of this 1948 Cadillac Club Coupe and the radio surround were jewellike. *Constance Smith*

Rother would later contribute to the design of professional cars—ambulances and hearses—offered by Miller and Flxible. Many ambulances rested on GM chassis.

THE TRAIN OF TOMORROW

In 1944, GM's Cyrus R. Osborn, who headed GM's Electo-Motive Division, made some sketches for a domed passenger train. While it was not an entirely new concept, the resulting project was one of the most elaborate in GM's history. The project was assigned to Harley Earl, who directed the Styling Division; he in turn selected George Jergenson, an ArtCenter graduate, to head the project.

Jergenson, in turn, would both assign stylists and hire new designers for this project. While Amy Light was recruited from California, Rother was already retained. Under the direction of designer Jergenson, his team made hundreds of sketches, and modelers spent over $100,000 to build a model to show train executives.

Rother appears to have made early designs for seating—a rough sketch discovered in the back of a 1940s sketchbook is reminiscent to seating in a lounge area. The wall covering in the dining car resembles some of the plants in Rother's children's book illustrations.

ROTHER AND PININ FARINA JOIN NASH

After a disagreement with Billy Durant, Charles Nash left General Motors. This ended a twenty-five-year relationship. In 1916, Nash, who had served as president of GM, joined James Storrow to purchase the Thomas B. Jeffrey Company, which was later renamed the Nash Motor Company. After an unusual merger, Nash-Kelvinator was born. George Mason eventually ran the company.

While Rother was retained by Nash in 1947 as a consultant, Pinin Farina was retained by Nash to design the Airflyte around 1950, the 1952–1954 Nash-Healey convertible, and the 1953–1954 Nash-Healey coupe. In 1954, Nash and Hudson formed the American Motors Company.

It is not certain how Helene arrived at Nash. It is possible that Helene met Italy's Pinin Farina while at General Motors and that they would become better acquainted at Nash, where he worked as a consultant from 1950 to 1956.

Pinin Farina wrote a letter to all Nash dealers, presenting his accomplishments. A signed archival copy and its envelope mailed from Italy to an Indiana dealership still exist. Rother designed hundreds of textiles, and swatch books are now in the possession of Nash collectors.

The late 1940s and early 1950s were significant for Nash. While the industry was plagued by work stoppages in 1948, a pent-up demand existed after World War II. There came a time, however, when Nash's prewar holdovers, the Nash 600 and Ambassador, became less appealing. A reintroduction of the convertible served to spark a renewed interest in the nameplate. Nash built a Suburban sedan—a woodie, which followed the lines of the fastback in 1946. The introduction of the 1949 Airflyte was even more significant. Nash marketers noted that these were "the world's first cars to apply the modern development of aviation to the building of an automobile." Nash offered Ambassador, Statesman, and Rambler models. Advertisements featured the 1953 Ambassador Statesman, which won the Jackson Award for design. Helene was pictured presenting new upholstery to Pinin Farina. The aerodynamic Statesman featured a smartly styled air intake, Sky-Flow rear fenders, and a racing-style teardrop tail. It was so different that some loved it and others questioned it. The 211-inch-long car, powered by an economical 235-cubic-inch overhead value six-cylinder engine, delivered 115 horsepower and featured an enormous 9.5-foot interior—larger than most. In 1951, Nash also offered a sporty Custom Convertible and America's lowest-priced Custom Station Wagon.

Helene designed folding seats, doors, and fabrics, and the aerodynamic 1951 Airflyte could be custom-tailored to the customer's taste, using her textiles. While early cars offered one or two colors for the interior, a choice of twenty-one interior color combinations, plus thoughtful appointments, made the car even more desirable. This created opportunities for Helene, who provided handwoven samples to the factory. The seating arrangement provided the best of worlds to travelers.

Swatch books are rare, and this one was shared by one of two collectors owning them. Brent Havekost Collection. *Photo courtesy of Constance Smith*

The right-hand front seat singly reclined, creating a daytime couch. Twin form-fitting mattresses transformed the interior, creating a private sleeping car. A screen package was created for the windows. The pictured Statesman is rare and was sold by Nash's Canadian Division.

Pinin Farina celebrates Nash-Healey. *Photo courtesy of Brent Havekost*

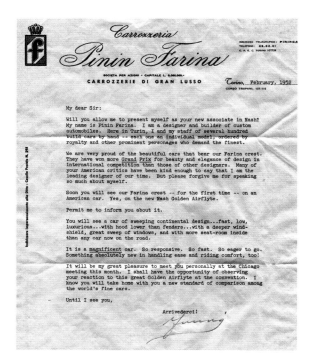

A letter was sent by Pinin Farina to an Indiana dealership to introduce himself to the American public. Pinin Farina was retained to design the Airflyte, 1952–54 Nash convertible, and 1953–54 Nash-Healey coup. *Courtesy of Brent Havekost and Nashparts*

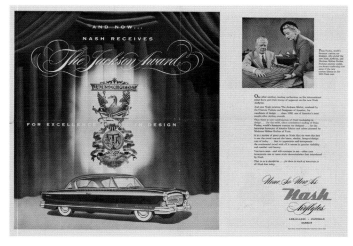

Pinin Farina and Rother celebrated a win and were captured with the Airflyte. *Collection of Constance Smith*

ROTHER PILOTS LESABRE ON ROUTE TO THE PARIS SHOW

In 1951, Rother would be invited to assist with the presentation of Harley Earl's LeSabre concept car in the 1951 Paris Auto Show. In a rare photo, she was photographed driving the car with a GM executive before crowds of gentlemen in Paris, France.

Rother would later tour the Paris show with Pinin Farina. Carrozzeria Pininfarina was founded in 1930, and Pinin Farina would be recognized as the father of coachwork and later of car design. In 1947, Pinin would build a small sedan with race car performance, marking a turning point in the history of design. He was recognized as the leading coach builder of his era. The Museum of Modern Art added the Cistalia Berlinetta to its permanent collection, which consists of just eight automobiles.

In 1951, after attending the Paris Auto Show with both Pinin Farina and Harley Earl, Rother wrote a lengthy article for a Detroit newspaper reviewing the exterior design of a number of notable automobiles.

By 1954, Rother was invited to make a presentation on automotive design and put together nineteen plates with simple illustrations.

ROTHER HORSE FARM

zHelene loved riding, and she purchased five or six racehorses with a partner—a college professor—and employed a trainer before excelling in this role herself. .She was quite successful, and her horses won a number of races. She would later be able to buy her partner's shares with her winnings.

While Helene would never return to Leipzig, her mother would remain a citizen for most of her life. When she was unable to care for herself, Rother had her flown to the United States.

After settling down, Helene, having worked on the interiors of cars of the latter '40s, was gifted a new Buick sedan. A well-constructed car, it was one she "did not roll" like the Nash she later bought. Records show that she borrowed funds due to an accident. As Helene's driving grew even more aggressive and dangerous, her daughter took over as her chauffeur.

Helene was invited to address the members of the Society of Automotive Engineers at their annual conference. She and George Walker gave presentations on automotive interiors at the Rackham Educational Memorial. At this time, she noted that she hoped engineers could provide better batteries to power gadgets—for heating baby bottles and canned soup, for cigarette lighters on springs, for umbrella holders, for safety belts, and so on. Some members of the press ignored CEOs to record excerpts of Rother's presentation and pose for photos with her.

Helene also submitted artwork to U.S. Rubber, International Harvester, Goodyear Tire and Rubber, and BF Goodrich. Helene could design just about anything, and she was later affiliated with

The LeSabre concept car was photographed from above at the Paris Auto Show by a GM photographer. *General Motors*

Mengel Furniture Company, Stromberg Carlson, Magnavox, Elgin Watch, and other companies.

Helene would never allow her career to end, and she returned to France to study the art of stained glass. Subsequently, she designed a number of stunning stained-glass windows for churches and cathedrals in and around Detroit. Helene addressed members of stained-glass organizations and left behind a typed presentation for one of these events. On January 12, 1969, the *Detroit News* ran a lengthy exposé with photos in their oversized magazine; Rother's designs went from the traditional to the contemporary, and she provided full-size drawings to Michele Mellini & Co. in Provincia di Firenze for constructions, which were later mailed back to her at her Fisher Building offices. When it came to contemporary design, she worked with Marcel Breuer on the construction of St. Francis de Sales in Muskegon, Michigan; he designed a church with parabolic walls, which opened in 1966. She signed a contact in 1966 for work on St. Lazarus Serbian Orthodox Cathedral, using 1-inch-thick glass; Rother also provided designs for Our Lady Queen of Peace Mission Church, a modern cathedral designed by Fleischman.

Helene died of natural causes in 1999 at age ninety-one. Her daughter, Ina Rother, MD, suffered from dementia and died in 2016.

Helene Rother was a pioneer, and her influence has and will continue to inspire men and women of past, present, and future generations.

she was GM's first female designer; however, she was not assigned to an automotive area. Instead, she designed products and textiles and was assigned to the Train of Tomorrow studio.

It is likely that Amy would have started work for the Train of Tomorrow shortly after the design was sketched by Cyrus R. Osborn from Electro-Motive Division (EMD). The concept was initiated to promote the sale of diesel locomotives by GM's Electro-Motive Division. The train consisted of a novel air suspension springing that incorporated rubber bellows. The four-car blue-green Train of Tomorrow was completed in 1947, with one of the cars featuring a domed roof oriented toward sightseers. Amy was entrusted with the design of silverware, plates, and upholstery, and carpeting for the dining areas.[2] After touring the United States and southern Canada for twenty-nine months, the "Blue Lady" was sold to Union Pacific.

While working for GM, Amy was selected by Harley Earl to design a futuristic trophy to be awarded to the best designer. She designed an automobile that was painted gold and sat on a base. Earl gave her the trophy, which she displayed for years.

Light later designed radios and refrigerators; however, is it unknown if these designs were made for Frigidaire and GM Delco or GE, but GE was not located in an area where she lived.

Amy's was selected for inclusion in *Damsels in Design: Women Pioneers in the Automotive Industry, 1939–1959* (Schiffer Books, 2018). This history also includes women from Ford, Lincoln, Nash, Studebaker, and Tucker.

AMY JEANETTE STANLEY (AMY LIGHT)

Her art teacher noted her natural ability and the quality of her drawings and advised Amy to take her portfolio over to Art Center in Southern California.[1]
—Tyra Light, speaking about her mother, Amy Light (1915–2006)

CAREER HIGHLIGHTS

Amy Light joined General Motors Styling after a recommendation from Vera and George Jergenson—George was a college cohort from the Art Center School (later the ArtCenter College of Design), in 1943 or early 1944. She was advised by Harley Earl, the first head of the Art and Color Section in the Argonaut Building, that

Amy often cared for her siblings when her mother was working. She is the tallest here. *Courtesy of Tyra Light*

BIOGRAPHICAL NOTES

Born in 1915, Amy Light was the eldest of five children. Amy's paternal grandfather worked as a contractor shoveling coal and assisted ranchers. Her maternal grandfather had worked as a mail carrier for the Pony Express and shoveled coal. Her father worked as a carpenter. Her mother was a housewife—that is, until the Great Depression, when she began designing catalogs for a wholesale sporting-goods company.

Amy spent her childhood in Pacific Grove, located adjacent to the well-known Carmel-by-the-Sea, in Monterey County, California. Carmel has been, and continues to be, home to a community of artists including painters, writers, poets, and actors.

Amy attended the Pacific Grove Elementary School, and around 1923 she entered Pacific Grove High School. Her siblings included three sisters, Jean, Phyllis, and Elizabeth, and a brother, Ty. After high school, Amy and her family, along with countless other American families, were financially compromised by the 1929 Wall Street market crash and later the Great Depression. During this time, her parents divorced. Her mother supported the family with a position as head housekeeper for the La Riviera Hotel in Carmel, and Amy, having to care for her younger siblings, lost part of her childhood. Her parents both eventually remarried.[3]

A brilliant student, Amy graduated from high school at sixteen, well ahead of her classmates.

Amy's impressionist-style self-portrait while still a high school student is remarkable. Her art teacher noted her natural ability and the quality of her drawings and advised Amy to take her portfolio over to the Art Center School in downtown Los Angeles. While her family continued to struggle financially due to the Depression, she received a full scholarship and room and board near the school.

The Art Center School opened in Los Angeles in 1930. The first class consisted of just eight students and twelve faculty members. Amy enrolled in 1934 and may have been the only female student. She was riding in the car, close to one of her instructors, when he stopped abruptly; she had just announced that she was only sixteen years old. At this point, he likely reconsidered his intentions. Amy completed four years of training; however, the school would not officially offer bachelor's degrees until 1949.

In 1965, it was renamed the ArtCenter College of Design, and the school expanded over time. ArtCenter is responsible for training some of the top automobile designers and illustrators in the world.

At the time Amy enrolled, streamlining, which originated with aerodynamic studies for warplanes and was purely decorative, seemed to dominate design. The look stemmed from the simple flow around an object by a stream of air. Streamlining transformed automobiles, giftware, and advertising design and glorified the mass-produced product.

From 1939 to 1940, the Golden Gate International Exposition

Tyra Light bears a strong resemblence to her mother. *Courtesy of Tyra Light*

was held in San Francisco. Light was commissioned to sculpt a replica of the Palace of Fine Arts, located in San Francisco, and accomplished this using papier-mâché.

In the 1940s, GM designers worked in a two-part building in Detroit; the Argonaut Building still stands but is now the Taubman Education Center. The refurbished building serves design students from the College of Creative Studies.

In 1936, GM's Caravan of Progress, conceived by Charles F. Kettering, had consisted of traveling exhibits. It was replaced by the Parade of Progress, which included twelve modern Futurliners and some new exhibits. The vehicles had clamshell sides that opened upon the cars' arrival. At this time, General Motors was also manufacturing the GMC forty-passenger bus, which would be the basis of a new project. The development of mass transportation for exhibits would spark other ideas.

Around this time, after graduation from the Art Center School, Amy qualified for an illustrator's position in the advertising art department of a San Francisco newspaper, the *Examiner*. However, Amy's Art Center classmates, George Jergenson and Harley Nelson, accepted positions at GM Styling and would invite her to come east. A friend or classmate, Vera, would also encourage Amy to seize this invitation. In the fall of 1943, Amy jumped at the opportunity to further her career

The Train of Tomorrow was the brainchild of Cyrus R. Osborn of EMD. The domes atop cars reminded some of the cockpit of an airplane. Styling, under the direction of Harley Earl, was later assigned to others. Amy Light was hired exclusively for this project. *General Motors*

Light's designs were used by diners. *General Motors*

and showcase her skills. She wanted to advance to the top of her field, and the salary was generous too. It is likely that she worked in the department headed by LeRoy Keifer, and reported to Jergenson. A snappy dresser, Amy frequented the Ritz department store and purchased designer clothes to stay up to date. Amy shared a three-bedroom apartment in Detroit with two other women and saved up enough money to buy her mother a home back in San Francisco.

THE TRAIN OF TOMORROW

Amy received assignments to design products and the interiors for a train. However, this train was far from a traditional model. In 1947, GM introduced the Train of Tomorrow Streamliner, and, in 1948, the EMD Diesel Electric Locomotive. Light's sister notes that Amy had a significant role in the design of products for the Train of Tomorrow, the experimental four-car concept built to promote the sale of diesel locomotives by its Electro-Motive Division.

The general manager of EMD, Cyrus R. Osborn, drafted his idea for domed passenger cars on a napkin at the Hotel Utah. This idea was shared with Harley Earl, GM's styling chief. Jergenson took numerous train rides to gather information on the design of cars. Historians note that nine designers were identified for the researchers. The designers, with the consideration of basic engineering requirements, were said to have penned 1,500 sketches in crayon, watercolor, or pencil.[4] At some point in time, designers and sculptors would assemble to impart form to the illustrations. In styling tradition, Earl's sculptors would build a small model and study related issues, including the history of observation cars, which appeared in various forms in the late 1800s. The GM press handout

stated, "Mr. Osborn had presented merely an idea. Mr. Earl and his staff had developed it into a practical and beautiful actuality."[5]

The Train of Tomorrow required the design of interiors, textiles, seating, and dinnerware. While all the cars required interior designs, the Sky View car required even more: table linen and tablecloths, place mats and napkins, silverware, dishes, coffeepots, creamers, chinaware, glassware, trays, menus, pencils, ashtrays, seat covers, uniforms, kitchen and pantry equipment, skillets, etc.

Amy was responsible for the pattern on the service plates, the upholstery pattern, and the original silverware. The silverware was a simple but handsome design and consisted of parallel ridges from the top to the bottom of each piece. Her daughter remembers her mother showing her the silverware she had designed in a department store. Light was probably called upon to create the china. Amy and her future husband, Dan, would travel from Detroit to the manufacturing facility in Ohio to check on the progress of the design project

At about this time, Amy was given an assignment by Harley Earl to design a plaque or trophy featuring a futuristic car to serve as an award for the best designers. On a gold base, it was also used as a centerpiece at a dinner hosted by Harley Earl. For her work, Earl gave a copy to Light. It would serve as the focus of her living-room table (sadly, it was lost in a fire many years later).

By 1946 or 1947, Earl decided that he would procure a Buick convertible coupe for her at cost; he gave her #5 off the assembly line. The shiny black Series 70 Roadmaster had a contrasting tan interior. The Roadmaster continued to provide comfort as Buick's full-size offering into the current era. Equipped with a Fireball 8 320 V-8 engine and manual transmission, the 4,520-pound automobile had a top speed of 69 mph. On a trip west, Amy totaled the car but was unscathed.

Earl helped out, allowing her to procure a second car; this one was tan. Amy would eventually drive the car on vacation from Detroit to San Francisco, California, with her younger sister in the passenger seat. Amy sold the car because she did not want to drive it back to Detroit. Instead she flew back to Detroit with the proceeds from the sale.

After a number of years at GM, Amy saved up a good amount of money and married in 1948.

She met her future husband, the 6-foot-3 Daniel Light, through George and Theda Jergenson at a party they attended. Although Dan had grown up on a farm in Lititz, Pennsylvania, he had a lucrative career as top salesman for Libbey-Owens-Ford (LOF) in Illinois. LOF also made windshields for war planes. As an employee of LOF, he sold glass to builders and architects. After Dan and Amy moved to California, he served Toledo Scales and a variety of other companies. Other positions he held addressed the horse and cattle trades.

Amy and Dan loved the water and served as crew members on their friend's yacht—the Blitzen—around the five Great Lakes.

In 1949, an article about inland sailing in *Life* overpowered large advertisements for the Nash Airflyte and Ford's British Anglia. The traditional concept of saltwater sailing was eclipsed by the phenomenal growth of pleasure yachting, and much of it took place in fresh water in and around the Great Lakes. Most of the bigger sailing boats, the kind over $100,000, were found in and around Detroit and Chicago.

Sailing clubs replaced the golf and tennis clubs frequented in other locales as social centers. At this time, the Detroit Yacht Club had 2,800 members. Some members were wealthy automobile executives. While not all members sailed, they paid annual membership dues of $125 to attend social events.

The Blitzen, on which Amy and Dan were crew members, was one of the best-known yachts on the Great Lakes. A 56-foot cutter, it cost $58,000 to build in 1938. By 1949, it had won twenty-six inland regattas over a five-year period and several ocean races, including the 1949 Miami–Nassau race.

When *Life* requested information about the Blitzen, they hired Amy, who likely contributed to the extensive article. The cover of *Life* featured a female sailor. Eight pages inside were devoted to the sport, with photos of the Blitzen.

After sailing on the Blitzen from the East Coast to California, Amy and Dan relocated to the Bay Area. Following in the footsteps of her grandfather, Amy built and upholstered a chair and a sofa. She also designed and built a playhouse for her three children, a doll cradle, and a toddler's rocking chair in the shape of a duck. She continued working in temporary positions after her children were born, preparing catalogs for publication. To Amy, this was the way to keep her fingers in the art world and to help support her family. She had two sons, Todd and Tobias, and a daughter, Tyra, who graduated with a degree in anthropology.

Tobias, the surfer, did not attend college, and Todd had no interest in it either.[6] When Amy was in her seventies, she and Dan decided on a change of pace, and the two moved to the mountains in Mendocino County in California with their son Todd, where they spent the rest of their lives together. Todd worked as a groundskeeper. He was injured in a motorcycle accident but still manages to get around. Todd recalls that his mother loved to find and negotiate for collectibles at local sales; she collected lots of cast-iron pans and paperweights. Dan predeceased Amy in 1994. She became ill and died in 2006. More recently, a fire demolished the interior of the home she shared with Todd, and little remains of her belongings. Tobias passed away from a heart attack a few years back.

It was some time before Amy, a caring grandmother, really retired—if she did at all.
Robin Montgomery

Mary Loring at home. *Courtesy of M. Loring*

MARY VIRGINIA LORING

Even though I knew I was not as gifted as Mary artistically, she taught me how to see and draw.[1]

—Martha Loring Fotopulos; now over eighty, she credits her much-older sister, Mary (1926–2013), with her own success as an abstract painter.

CAREER HIGHLIGHTS

Mary Loring worked primarily as an office designer at General Motors and subsequently served some of the most prestigious architectural firms across the country.

Unable to study architecture because she was a woman, Loring joined GM Styling after graduating with an art degree from Michigan State University.

In 1949, a press release announced plans to build the Technical Center. Loring was assigned to the Product and Exhibit Department under LeRoy Kiefer and designed offices for the proposed GM styling building, working with Eero Saarinen and the firm of Smith, Hinchman & Grylls.

After a year of two, she became uncomfortable with the attitudes of some of her male colleagues and left GM and joined the firm of Smith, Hinchman & Grylls as a designer and draftsperson. She continued to work on the development of the GM Technical Center. Sometime later, she resumed working for GM as a consultant before embarking on her own architectural career.

Loring joined Minoru Yamasaki, the designer of the original World Trade Center. She longed to work for the Skidmore, Owens & Merrill architectural firm; her dream would later become a reality.

Loring also earned a master's degree in art from Michigan State University, under the direction of noted fine artist Charles Pollock, a director of mural design for the WPA and eldest brother of Jackson Pollock. Charles was affiliated with MSU for twenty years. She was so talented that Pollock asked her to teach some of the courses he disliked—the first of these was calligraphy.

Later in life, she combined her educational experience and architectural knowledge and went on to teach at Cornell, San Jose State, and Montana State.

Mary Loring's expanded profile is featured in *Damsels in Design: Women Pioneers in the Automotive Industry, 1939–1959* (Schiffer Books, 2018).

BIOGRAPHICAL NOTES

Loring was one of three children; she had an older brother, Thomas Millard Loring, and a much-younger sister, Martha, to care for and mentor when her mother was ill. Her mother, Manila, died at forty-eight from what was believed to be cancer, but it was more likely that the rampant bacterial infections that were prevalent on Michigan's Upper Peninsula played a role.

Mary's father, Thomas W. Loring, was born in 1897. Tom sincerely believed that he could start his own automobile company. Having no related work or management experience like some others who had accomplished this feat, perhaps this was just a pipe dream. He proceeded to raise capital from two postmen who worked with his father. Before he could get the operation running, one of the partners stole everyone's money and disappeared. Perhaps things worked out for the better anyway.

Tom had joined the storied Oldsmobile Division of GM as a styling engineer. While he might have worked for a contractor to start, a former Olds designer, H. Roy Jaffe, recalls that Tom later served as a liaison between the Olds Division and the styling studios,[2] keeping the peace. Tom was a lifer and took pleasure in picking out a new Oldsmobile annually under the employee purchase plan. Mary's sister believes that he either designed or assisted with the design of the headlight dimmer. In 1952, Oldsmobile's Autotronic Eye automatically dimmed the headlamps when oncoming cars approached, as a courtesy. Before this invention, drivers dimmed the headlights with a foot pedal.

Early in his career, in 1926, Tom's life changed. The Olds Division was challenged by a newcomer—the Pontiac Division, which started as Oakland but quickly eclipsed Oakland in sales and popularity. Tom felt that Pontiac would draw sales away from Olds. Understandably, this made him uncomfortable. He denounced Pontiac at the dining-room table: "I hate Pontiacs." While Pontiac would outlast Olds, who would predict that neither would survive?

The very same year, the Lorings welcomed their daughter Mary. Her brother, Thomas, was born three years earlier; her much-younger sister, Martha, was born in 1939. Some would later note that Mary had as much artistic talent as her brother had engineering ability. Her likewise talented sister noted, "She was just born with it."[3]

Mary attended elementary school in the Lansing area. At just seven years old, she was a gifted artist. At West Junior High School, where she studied ceramics, Mary's handbuilt pieces were likely hidden by Mr. Hosner for samples and later used to motivate other students. Mary later served as his student teacher. However, when her younger sister, Martha, came through, the expectations were high.

The Motorama featured cars present and future. *General Motors*

One of their neighbors approached Martha and noted, "I see that your sister, Mary, taught you how to draw." Martha answered, "No, my sister taught me to see." The neighbor continued, "You are pretty, but your sister is beautiful inside and out." In fact, Mary was a model for Studebaker.

Tom was later reassigned to Trenton, New Jersey, to assist with war preparations and would have to spend part of the workweek there. Mary remained in Michigan, completed her senior year, and graduated from J. W. Sexton High School.

Mary loved architecture but realized that this field was just not open to women; she knew of no women architects. She longed to attend Pratt Institute, but her family could not afford to put her through a private school. Tom, who now struggled to support and educate three children, told her that they could afford to send her only to Michigan State University. She graduated with a baccalaureate in 1947 or 1948, after her brother, who studied engineering, and she later returned for a master's degree.

While her father was likely no judge of artistic ability and had little interest in the arts, he proceeded to introduce his daughter to LeRoy Kiefer who headed Product and Exhibit Design at GM under Harley Earl, GM's vice president of design. Kiefer, described as a brilliant man by his colleagues, was responsible for the extravagant Motoramas set up at the Waldorf Astoria Hotel in New York City. Mary was talented, educated, and attractive and had a pleasing personality as well. With all these attributes, she was invited to start work immediately.

While designing for Chevrolet, Mary had to stand up on a box to reach the top of the drawing board. It was hard enough to wear high heels all day, let alone stand on a box. This was amusing to the men around her. Finally, after falling off a number of times, other arrangements were made, and her colleagues proceeded to find other ways to amuse themselves. One of them decided to hang her drawing tools from the ceiling—she could not reach the dangling instruments.

In the mid-1940s, Earl's design team and shops grew too large for the Argonaut Building, which was located in downtown Detroit. The GM chairman, Alfred Sloan, commissioned the Finnish American architect Eero Saarinen, who had designed a number of buildings on the Cranbrook Academy of Art campus, where he headed the architecture department, to build a new technical center. Saarinen would employ the firm of Smith, Hinchman & Grylls, and Loring would design the executive offices for the Styling Building.

Loring found herself designing the executive offices. While Earl was satisfied with his digs, she reported that she designed a large desk for William Mitchell, the vice president of design, at his request. Mitchell took over after the retirement of Harley Earl.

After a year or two, Mary would leave GM and join Smith, Hinchman & Grylls as they continued work on the Technical Center.

The Tech Center would eventually occupy a 320-acre site in Warren, Michigan, between Van Dyke and Mound Roads.

On May 16, 1956, GM's Harlow H. Curtice dedicated the General Motors Technical Center alongside President Dwight David Eisenhower. Portions of this presentation are memorable:

We have gathered here for a momentous occasion. The dedication of the GM Technical Center has great significance for the welfare of our country and the world. ... No industry has contributed more to our nation's growth and development more than the automobile industry. Its products have completely changed the habits of all Americans. ... No industry has done more to raise the U.S. to a position of world strength and leadership. ... The improvement in product and process dominates the thinking of every automobile man worthy of the name.

Harley Earl's larger office was guarded by his secretary, Miss Hardin. *General Motors*

Mary Loring enjoyed golf as time permitted. *Courtesy of and photo by Martha Loring*

Over 5,000 dignitaries were invited; nary a woman is noted in photographs of the dedication.

In making this vision a reality, Mary was excited to work directly with Saarinen and designed executive offices, including one for Harley Earl and Bill Mitchell—Harley Earl's successor as vice president of design. While she started out with a tradition-al-sized desk, Mitchell demanded something larger. Perhaps the custom desk symbolized his immense power. A second large desk appears to the right, perpendicular to the first one, in another photograph. The design of Earl's office was similar.

When the Tech Center was completed, Loring would return to GM for a short time before resuming her architectural career with the top firms in the nation.

As the Technical Center neared completion, Kiefer's designers continued to work on Motorama exhibits.

After receiving an assignment in Frigidaire, Mary worked with Jane Van Alstyne, Tom Bradley, and Russ Dunbar to design the 1956 Kitchen of Tomorrow, one of GM's most popular Motorama exhibits. The display consisted of a collection of fu-turistic prototype appliances. Dunbar's cylindrical rotisserie oven topped with a Plexiglas dome visually dominated the design. A marble-topped range relied on induction coils to cook food without heating up. The glass-walled rotating refrigerator/freezer was dubbed the Roto-Storage Center. Other features included an electro recipe file and battery-operated serving carts. The H. B. Stubbs Company built entire rooms for the show.

Beginning in 1956, Mary bought her own cars—Chevrolets appeared in the driveway behind the Oldsmobile. Her father assisted with these purchases, he cringed at the thought of the VW Beetle her sister would bring home. However, it was recog-nized that it was underpowered and inexpensive compared to the American cars of the era that would monopolize the driveway.

At some point in time, Mary decided that there was no op-portunity for advancement for women, left GM Styling, and proceeded to earn a living in the offices of one of the most re-nowned architects in America. After joining Smith, Hinchman & Grylls, she worked side by side with Minoru Yamasaki (1912–1986). When Minoru set out on his own, Mary followed. Yamasaki, the designer of the McGregor Conference Center at Wayne State University, is perhaps best known for his design of the ill-fated Twin Towers of the World Trade Center in New York City.

Later Mary moved to California and provided drawings for Skidmore, Owens & Merrill. While in Skidmore's employ, she traveled to Australia to assist with the design of resort hotels and the Crocker Bank.

Later in her life, Mary joined the faculty of Cornell University, San José State University, and Montana State University with her colleague Jayne Van Alstyne. After surviving open-heart surgery in 2000, she returned to Michigan. Mary died at the Norlite Nursing Center in Marquette, Michigan, in 2013 at age eighty-seven.

PART IV.
THE 1950s

The iconic Damsels of Design photo was taken in 1957 and included (bottom, left to right) Sue Vanderbilt, Margarie Ford Pohlmann, Sandra Longyear Richardson and (top left to right) Ruth Glennie Petersen, VP Harley Earl, Jeanette Fioravera Linder, and Margaret Sauer. *General Motors*

General Motors engineers and designers made considerable contributions to appearance, safety, reliability, performance, comfort, and economy midcentury.

A number of significant engineering features were incorporated by one or more of the divisions, despite the sales drop from the Korean War.

In 1949–1950, Buick introduced heat-absorbing glass for windshields and windows, called E-Z-Eye Glass; it reduced glare and absorbed more than half of the sun's energy. It made it easier to air-condition the car and protected the occupants from solar heat.

By 1951, both the LeSabre concept, with tinted glass, and the Buick XP-300 concept arrived for review with their curved wraparound windshields. The LeSabre touted an all-aluminum 215-cubic-inch engine, magnesium body parts, and other aluminum parts sourced from Alcoa. The XP-300 convertible, which featured a 335-horsepower engine and shared some of its parts with the LeSabre, rode on a different suspension system and boasted its own low-slung design.

In 1952, Guide Lamp developed Autotronic Eye, an automatic-dimming device. Mounted to the instrument panel in the case of the 1952 Olds, this device dimmed your lights when approaching headlights were detected. It also was part of the Futurliner, a bus-like vehicle that was included in a traveling showcase. The Autotronic Eye remained on Cadillacs well into the 1980s.

GMC Truck & Coach announced air suspension for coaches in 1952. Air suspension was optional at some point on all 1950s cars from Chevrolet to Cadillac.

Buick's "Air Power" carburetor, also introduced in 1952, consisted of two dual carburetors back to back—the second unit kicked in at over 80 mph. Hydraulic steering also appeared on Buicks to make it easier to park.

In 1953, Buick introduced a Twin Turbine version of the Dynaflow, and in 1955 a Variable Pitch Dynaflow, which provided better performance. By 1958, another version of the Dynaflow transmission arrived, with three turbines and fully adjustable stator blades. The new air suspension came with a high-lift feature to navigate ramps and ruts.

The refinement of glass-reinforced plastic (GRP) led to the 1953 Chevrolet Corvette, which was unveiled at six Motoramas across the country titled "Motorythms and Fashion Firsts" in this year.

In 1954, GM tested the XP-21 Firebird Gas Turbine Car. This was the first gas turbine built in the US, under the direction of Research Lab's Charles L. McCuen, and was labeled "Whirlfire Turbo Power."

By 1955, Buick announced the variable-pitch Dynaflow transmission. Fisher Body developed a four-door hardtop sedan body.

The 1956 Firebird II concept was introduced at the Motorama. Powered by a gas turbine engine, it boasted numerous other features: titanium body, regenerative braking, all-wheel independent suspension, electric gear selector, and magnetic ignition key. In same year, Chevrolet introduced the Turboglide three-turbine transmission.

In 1957 and 1958, the Feminine Car Shows were held in the Styling auditorium, featuring beautiful new interiors and innovations—some of them groundbreaking—by female designers hired under Harley Earl. The inventions of Ruth Glennie, who incorporated retractable seat belts on a 1958 Corvette (the Fancy Free) and put reflectors and lights in Chevrolet's car doors, were far ahead of the time. Her drawing for the first heads-up display (HUD) in the late 1950s was incredible; some of her ideas did not arrive on production cars for decades. Peggy Sauer was already concerned about keeping the rear doors on a station wagon locked decades before power window and door lockout switches reached production. The attractive Jeanette Linder invented the first visor vanity mirror. It was a larger mirror with two powerful lights on the sides.

In 1957, Buick announced "Safety Minder," a preset speed-warning signal on production cars. In 1958, Buick announced aluminum-finned brake drums.

In 1958, the Firebird III concept was unveiled. Designed by Norm James, it influenced the design of the 1959 and 1961 Cadillacs. The same year, printed circuits were utilized in the Cadillac instrument panel for the first time.

In 1959, Chevrolet announced the Corvair, the first high-production American model to have a rear-mounted aluminum engine, transaxle, and four-wheel independent suspension. By the end of the decade, air suspension was available on all cars; it has never been abandoned.

STYLING NUANCES

With all the exhibitions, concept cars, and production cars, the day never ended for the designers at Styling.

Appearing early in 1951, the lower and longer Le Sabre concept and the XP-300 concept cars were extremely well received. Thousands of men gathered to get a peek at the LeSabre, busting with innovations such as a curved windshield, en route to the 1951 Paris Auto Show, to find that the car was being driven by the first female stylist retained by Harley Earl, Helene Rother, who was admitted into the into the Automotive Hall of Fame in 2020. The 300, with its 335-horsepower engine, featured a chro-

mium-molybdenum steel frame covered with aluminum skin.

Car models for the most part were visually heavy because of their massive bumpers and rounded body forms. These substantial cars with heavy seat bolsters were viewed as comfortable and safe.

BUICK

Buicks were offered in sedans, coupes, convertibles, and a hardtop—the Riviera—in the early '50s. Some automobiles of this era were still easily identified by their toothy grilles. Introduced on Buicks in 1942, they dominated until 1954. Teeth turned to meshes as the decade progressed. Chrome sweep spears appeared that made cars look sportier and longer, with rocker panel moldings. People dubbed Buick's ventiports portholes, and the number varied on the basis of the model or number of engine cylinders.

As the decade progressed, the hood, which was higher than the fenders, was gradually lowered, and the cars, which sat on X-type frames, acquired a longer look. Engines and transmissions were refined from year to year. Buick's "Air Power" carburetor consisted of two dual carburetors back to back—the second unit kicked in at over 80 mph.

As early as 1950, interiors featured herringbone-patterned cloth, door armrests, and a foldable center console in the rear. Door handles and window cranks were always as flawless as silverware, and as time went on, customers found comfort in the double-depth foam. Middecade trim included nylon, broadcloth, and leather. A gold-and-silver-woven fabric appeared. Inside and out, marketers touted a selection of fifteen colors.

CADILLAC

Following its new introduction in 1948, in 1950 Cadillac, under the direction of studio chief Bill Mitchell again for a short time, captured the luxury market and by 1952 delivered its Golden Anniversary Edition, equipped with a V-8 and 190 horsepower. Cars were wider and more significant looking. Large eggcrate grilles would become finer as the decade progressed. Rear fender bumps would sprout into bigger and bigger tail fins as the decade ended. Windshield dividers were removed and rear ones were on their way to popularity. Designers made numerous drawings of curved rear windows as they interfaced with the pillar. Some models had hooded headlights. The 1957 Eldorado Brougham was based on a 1954 Motorama Park Avenue. The iconic tall fins on the 1959 Cadillacs were equipped with bullet-style taillamps. The car also had exhaust-port backup lights. The grille up front was even more pronounced due to the flatter hood.

By 1952, the Series 62 sedan was upholstered in cord or broadcloth, and there were four two-tone color options that echoed on the doors. By 1958, a clock appeared on the instrument panel.

CHEVROLET

In the early 1950s, Chevrolet was slow to make changes, sometimes relying on the six-cylinder engines dating back to the 1920s. By 1953, the car picked up some chrome and a fender insert surrounded by chrome. Perhaps it saved all of its efforts for the Motorama and the introduction of the Corvette.

Chevrolet left it all on the table with the C1 Corvette (1953–1955), with its curved windshield—from the LeSabre concept—and jet pod taillight housings. Side coves in white or body color did not arrive until 1957 for the C2. Inside, the Vette features large, paneled, ribbed, red buckets with a hefty chrome-plated surround. A streamlined white instrument panel with two small arches passes under the top of the red dashboard. The first cars were white on the exterior, and the GM Archives appears to own car no. 2. A recent auction sale netted over $600K when a son sold a car he inherited. Changes to the 1956–57 Corvette were made by Bill Mitchell and studio chief Clare MacKichan, who also supervised the author's own Advanced Studio at GM in the 1970s. The fuel-injected V-8 arrived in 1957. Lots of nuances made the 1957 a success, including a strong chrome bumper, with ribbed aluminum quarter panels on the side included. MacKichan had also codesigned the Opel GT. The 1958 Corvette was easily identified by its quad headlamps and chrome strips on the rear deck.

In 1955, Clare MacKichan and Carl Renner, working under Harley Earl, were credited with the design of a sport wagon; the Nomad began as a Motorama Corvette concept and met with unheralded success.

On the basis of the previous model, MacKichan's team made the 1957 Chevrolet Belair Special.

OLDSMOBILE

In this era, Oldsmobile was the most predominant car division in the fold. However, early on, Oldsmobile jockeyed for position between Buick and Pontiac, and this affected sales. In 1951, they introduced a more advanced Deluxe 88 called the Super 88, which included a hardtop and convertible. Although popular, station wagons were discontinued. The heavy front grilles wrapped around the front corners of the cars and dominated the design. A number of identifiers, such as Oldsmobile's globe designs, hood ornaments above the grille, and chrome strips on the side, were secondary visually.

The extravagant 1950s exhibits, termed Motoramas, featured the Olds Delta in 1955 and Olds Golden Rocket in 1956. One of the most successful features arising from the Motoramas was the curved windshield, introduced from 1953 to 1955. A compound curved windshield appeared in 1959.

As the decade progressed, small-mouth grilles grew into heavy chrome elliptical grilles that wrapped to the sides. Grill members shrunk. Single headlights turned into dual headlights. In 1950 and then again in 1956, a coupe model of a wagon appeared. Families liked sporty too. Of course, hockey puck sides were created by chrome trim. By 1959, all GM cars had totally new skin.

PONTIAC

The 1950 line was similar to the 1949s. A significant new arrival, the Catalina, was Pontiac's first hardtop convertible. In 1952, the Korean War and a steel strike limited output. In 1953, the all-new Chieftain line captured sales. Optional power steering made Pontiacs easier to park. A plant fire in 1953 required Pontiac to equip cars with Chevrolet's Powerglide transmission. In 1954, after a facelift, the cars that followed were more luxurious.

The 1950s show cars included the 1954 Strato Streak—a pillarless four-door, a 1954 Bonneville—a Corvette-like two-seater, and the outrageous 1956 Club de Mer, with dual bubble windshields.

In 1955, the division's first OHV V-8 arrived. The 1955s were boxier but benefited from the wraparound windshield. From 1955 to 1957, stylists assigned to the Starchief two-door wagon followed the leadership of the Chevrolet Nomad design team. The Safari nameplate was later used for a four-door wagon. During a mild facelift in 1956, a four-door Catalina hardtop arrived, but because of lowered prices, Buick and Olds started to draw sales from Pontiac.

In 1956, Semon Knudsen (a.k.a. Bunkie) arrived and was the youngest GM ever. On a visit to the Feminine Show, Jeanette Linder, who was assigned as his tour guide, was photographed with him.

In 1958, an all-new lower body should have bolstered sales, but a recession limited them. The new styling featured a full-width grille, quad headlamps, and wider concave side spears.

By 1959, Knudsen had better control. New styling on the A-body, which had a split grille and modest twin-fin rear fenders, appeared, but the Tri-Power had reduced horsepower.

MARYELLEN GREEN (DOHRS)

I am not a "woman designer"; I am a designer who is a woman.[1]
—MaryEllen Green (Dohrs)
(1929-2022)

MaryEllen posed in the LeSabre Concept for a cover section of the Tribune. *General Motors*

CAREER HIGHLIGHTS

An accomplished illustrator, sculptress, and designer, MaryEllen Green—the first woman to complete Pratt Institute's certificate program in industrial design—has also raised a family.

Retained by GM Design in 1950, Green was the youngest designer hired under Harley Earl. Early on, she contributed to a luxurious red 1950 Anniversary Cadillac and later designed the interior of the custom Cadillac convertible for actor William Boyd, immortalized as cowboy Hopalong Cassidy. Following in the footsteps of her manager, Dick Teague, Green subsequently joined the consulting office of Sundberg-Ferar, where Teague served Packard Design. Green went on to contribute to the interior of the iconic 1955 tricolor Packard Caribbean, adding embellishments to the seating and doors. Green also designed a tricycle and a diverse range of other products.

Over the years, Green has developed a mastery of both two- and three-dimensional design.

She made a series of line drawings on a visit to Russia. She has also amassed a portfolio of sculpture and teaches students near her Florida residence. Her work has appeared in publications; an extensive array of her early drawings and sculpture are featured in *Damsels in Design: Women Pioneers in the Automotive Industry, 1939–1959*.

MARYELLEN'S JOURNEY

Who among you can say they knew exactly what they wanted to do for the rest of their life—when they were six years old? Green Dohrs was certain and determined that she would be an artist and would make things. Drawing was her consuming pastime, as well as building model ships and wind-up airplanes of balsa wood and tissue paper. At seven, she advanced to building furniture out of scrap wood and cups and bowls of mud. Anything useful was pursued. It did not matter that the cups would melt or that the tables were unstable. It was the desire to do it that counted. Of course, she got better at her craft, and, while other girls read *Nancy Drew*, she read *Popular Mechanics* and *Science Illustrated*. At home in Hollywood, California, she was fortunate to have her own little 8-by-10-foot shed behind the garage, which used to be the gardener's quarters during the Depression. This became her workshop, complete with workbench, a jigsaw, and a Philco cathedral radio. During junior high school, she designed and built a chicken coop and run for three copper-colored hens. These were the years of World War II and a time of conservation, rationing, and self-sufficiency.

Before that, the Depression still lingered on. Since no one had much money, ingenuity was needed to provide for a family. Her father, J. L. Green, an automobile salesman since he was twenty-two years of age, put a few borrowed dollars together and went to Vancouver, Canada, where he bought a tiny Austin 8. It boasted luxurious pleated-leather seats and a level of quality that cars in the United States did not have. He drove it nonstop to Los Angeles and negotiated a corner of a used-car lot on Figueroa Street, promising lots of action—all free. The newspapers were alerted and brought photographers. They wrote about the tiny "rare bird" of a car. The general public got a good laugh, but others were interested. Green Dohrs's father always said he catered to the "lunatic fringe." He took orders and "the game was on!" Green Dohrs notes, "My dad made his way to England and dealt directly with Lord Austin. He negotiated a deal and bought a few cars. But then came the war, and all shipping stopped. Immediately after the war, he renegotiated with Austin and got a sweeter deal with shipping as ships were 'dead heading' back to the U.S. With more profit and sales, he became the U.S. distributor for Austin, then Renault and Peugeot. With this expansion of his business, my dad took me to England, France and Switzerland during the summer of 1946. I saw, firsthand, the devastation of the bombings and remnants of war."[2] Certainly, this trip changed the outlook of the world for the teenaged MaryEllen forever.

Pratt Institute was her next step, and a good one at that. Alexander Kostellow and his wife, Rowena Reed, ran the Industrial Design program. After the obligatory foundation year of life drawing, color, and basic design principles, she narrowed her focus to industrial design, becoming the only girl in the class. Before she graduated, she was hired to work in the "Interiors Department" at General Motors Styling. Green notes, "Harley Earl and Kostellow had a connection in design, so when Earl asked for a female, I was it. Again, I became the only female designer in Styling."[3] Driving to Detroit in her graduation gift of a Renault 4CV, she entered GM at the age of twenty. There was one problem: personnel could not complete her contract until she turned twenty-one that September.

By this time, GM had introduced the 1950 Series 62 Cadillac. If was dramatically redesigned—longer, lower, wider, and faster than the 1948 design it replaced. The new one-piece windshield stood out, as did the eggcrate grille. The four-speed Hydramatic was new—but still no "Park." Approaching 60,000 sales, this redesign set a record for Cadillac. The car would serve as the basis of specialty cars, including the convertible with center glass designed for Hollywood star William Boyd.

Green Dohrs remembers, "That summer, while I was not an official employee, I designed the interior for a special black

The Hoppy Cadillac utilized Western motifs. *General Motors*

MaryEllen was mistaken for a secretary by the elevator operator in the Argonaut Building. Who knew? *ME Green Dohrs*

Cadillac convertible for Hopalong Cassidy (William Boyd). It had white pleated-leather seats and calf skin carpets. The door pads resembled steer heads with long horns and the decorative glitz provided by hob nails . . . very western."[4]

A surprise event occurred when she got the call to go up to the Photographic floor, where she encountered Earl's newest showpiece, the copper-colored LeSabre Concept. She notes, "Coincidentally, I had copper-colored hair. I was told to remove my shoes, walk across the black paper, climb over the belt line, and sit. Photos were taken from scaffolding and other ground-level pictures with Earl standing next to the car, because the car was so low and Earl was so tall. These were the official photos for newspapers and magazines."[5]

While at General Motors, Green worked under the direction of Richard "Dick" Teague. An ArtCenter College of Design graduate, he started his career with Northrup Aircraft in 1942 and moved to GM in 1948, where he spent three years in Oldsmobile and Cadillac. After leaving GM, he was named director of styling for Packard in 1953, which worked with Sundberg-Ferar. (Teague would end his career as VP of Styling after twenty-two years at American Motors, where he designed sporty and muscle cars such as the Javelin and AMX/3.)

After two and a half years of bench seats and door pads, MaryEllen interviewed with the independent industrial design consultancy Sundberg-Ferar and began her career in the product design world.

She was given "plum jobs" for IBM, Samsonite, Seeburg, and REO Motors because of her quick sketch-drawing skills, allowing her to solve problems and present ideas speedily.

In 1954, she was invited to design the interior for the 1955 Packard Caribbean.

Dick Teague was directed by J. N. Nash, president of Packard, "to get a good man to design an all-together new interior for this new 'top of the line' car, the Caribbean."[6] Green Dohrs's sketch was accepted "as is" and was reproduced for the 1955 and 1956 models. She reflects, "Funny thing; of the myriad of products I designed over the years and that have been relegated to the dustbin of progress, the iconic Caribbean lives on as vintage."

After marrying Dr. Fred E. Dohrs, professor of geography at Wayne State University, and having two children, Anne and Larry, her career shifted again into writing and illustrating. A talented sculptress, she taught in West Palm Beach, Florida before passing on in 2022.

Courtesy of Durga Garcia

RUTH GLENNIE (PETERSEN)

Ruth knew she was excellent at everything, but let her talent speak for itself.[1]

—Glennie family, regarding Ruth Glennie Petersen (1929–2018)

Courtesy of the Glennie family

CAREER HIGHLIGHTS

Designing far into the future, the gifted Ruth Glennie was the Steve Wozniak of her generation.

Glennie initially received a BS in commercial art from Skidmore College before studying industrial design at Pratt Institute. After joining Wheeler Electric as a street lighting designer, she registered for her first engineering courses in a Boston University program.

Glennie made significant contributions to Chevrolet and also contributed to Buick, Oldsmobile, and Pontiac. Her drawings set the design direction of concept and production cars, with an emphasis on instrument panels and interior design for the 1958–1960 Chevrolet Corvette. Components for the 1958 production Chevrolet Impala were based on her design drawings. She owned the 1958 Fancy Free Corvette Concept featured in the 1958 Feminine Show and later at the Gilmore Museum, the Chevrolet Impala, and numerous other products. Glennie was the first woman to work abroad and joined Vauxhall around 1960—GM's subsidiary in England.

While assigned to the Chevrolet Corvette studio, Ruth Glennie conceived of GM's first heads-up display (HUD) in 1957. In 1958, she designed the first retractable seat belts, also for Corvette, and the first door lights, which appeared as reflectors on the 1958 Impala.

After being passed over for a managerial position she deserved, Glennie chose marriage. She later served as a consultant to GTE Sylvania while raising two children.

RUTH'S JOURNEY

Ruth Glennie was born on August 31, 1929, during the era of the Wall Street crash and Great Depression. Her mother, Hazel Kent, was a homemaker who had studied nutrition at Framingham State College, and her father, George, was an engineer and son of a farmer who had emigrated from Scotland. Hazel and her forebears were educators who emphasized the importance of schooling—especially for women. George, an MIT graduate in mechanical engineering, made his living working in sales for insurance and steam companies. Ruth was one of three girls. Sisters Helen and Marion would later graduate from college and complete vocational training.

Glennie attended two elementary schools in Andover, Massachusetts; the latter was the Jackson School. She later attended Andover Junior High School and Punchard High School, graduating in 1946. Early on, she excelled in painting and particularly enjoyed working with watercolors.

Ruth and her sisters studied piano for about four years, relying on a spinet to practice since it did not take up as much space as a higher upright. Her sister Marion notes, "Perhaps we would have had been more interested if the teacher was not so crabby."[2] However, Ruth loved sports even more and was a good athlete. She was sought out by the boys in the neighborhood to join their teams. With her aunts and uncles owning properties on Cape Cod, she also developed an appreciation for the shore and nature.

Her mother, Hazel, would later note, "Ruth is just like a man; she can do anything. Ruth knew she was excellent at everything but let her talent speak for itself."

Her father's previous study of engineering and the activities he created while home were inspirational. Ruth was the son he never had.

George recognized Ruth's higher-level thinking skills and taught her to develop film negatives by using chemicals and to print her own photographs by using an enlarger. In addition, he taught Ruth about investment and family planning.

Upon her high school graduation in 1946, Glennie applied for college with an influx of GIs. It was difficult for women to get into coed schools at this time and, as a result, more difficult to gain entrance to women's colleges. Skidmore College, located near the Saratoga Racetrack in New York, was a pragmatic choice. During this time period, the 1948 Chevrolet Fleetmaster convertible—laden with graphics—served as the official pace car of the Indy 500 and turned heads; it still does today. Little did Glennie realize that after graduating from college, she too would make winning contributions to the largest division of General Motors.

School was never out for Glennie; she worked as a library assistant and counselor. The Skidmore Library attracted many an art and music student, since it offered reference materials and sheet music. While serving as a crafts counselor, Ruth acquired a thorough knowledge of metal crafts and ceramics. Glennie joined the *Andover Townsman* after graduation. As assistant to the advertising manager in 1950, Ruth provided typewritten to camera-ready copy—she prepared the layout and mechanicals necessary for publication.

A demanding student, Glennie always embraced education. She completed requirements for the bachelor of science program in commercial art at Skidmore. After graduating, she felt that she lacked practical skills, and enrolled in a program at Boston University where members of the Illuminating Engineering Society offered technical courses from 1950 to 1952. She completed Illuminating Engineering, Street Lighting, and other courses.

Glennie was offered a position as a draftsperson by a local lighting manufacturer—Wheeler Reflector Company—and from 1950 to 1952 served as assistant to the chief engineer, William Elmer. Wheeler Reflector opened in 1873 and closed its doors in 1962 and was noted for the manufacture of street, industrial, and commercial lighting that incorporated radial-wave incandescence. It was no surprise that she was not welcomed with open arms by all the others—drafts*men*. However, Elmer, realizing her potential, provided encouragement and was somewhat of a mentor. Ruth assisted the chief engineer in the development of layouts for mechanicals and electrical designs. The last existing Wheeler Reflector trade catalog, sixteen pages in length, was still in print in the midfifties and was titled *From Whale Oil Lamp to the Most Modern Lighting Fixtures*. Elmer would recommend Glennie for a position at Sylvania many years later.

Glennie's understanding of lighting would later lead to her design of groundbreaking automotive components in and outside the vehicle. Some of her designs would directly and positively affect our safety.

EDUCATIONAL MILESTONES

Already highly trained and talented, Glennie presented a portfolio of her work for entrance to the growing Industrial Design Department at Pratt Institute, located in Brooklyn, New York, in 1955. Glennie followed in the footsteps of MaryEllen Green, Pratt's first female student and a 1950 graduate. Pratt attempted to require Glennie to take liberal arts and more-basic art courses, but she had enough of them at Skidmore and wasn't going to pay hard-earned money to matriculate. She simply wanted to take advanced courses to supplement her commercial art education. Ruth paid $338 in September for term 5 in Industrial Design II-B and $219 in January 1955 for term 6 in ID III-B; no other receipts survive.

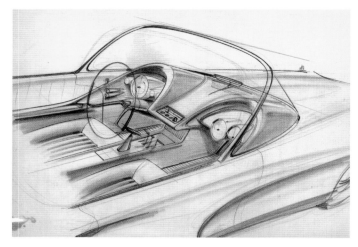

Glennie's illustration while assigned to the Corvette studio in the mid-1950s signaled what was ahead. *Glennie family*

The industrial design department was founded by Westinghouse's Donald Dohner and Alexander Kostellow, who arrived after teaching at Carnegie Institute of Technology. Kostellow and his wife, Professor Rowena Reed, from Kansas City Art Institute, worked together. Another notable graduate, Charles Pollock, noted, "Alexander made something from nothing."[3]

Industrial design students were required to study ceramics, and Ruth's work excelled. Eva Zeisel (Eva Polanyl Strictor), the noted ceramicist who joined the Pratt faculty, was born in 1906 in Budapest. Her career blossomed when she was recommended by Eliot Noyes, the design director at the Museum of Modern Art, to design a table service for Castleton China in 1938. In 1946, Eva had her first solo exhibit at the MoMA. She won a competition to design Museum Service dinnerware for the MoMA, and her work was on display in a 2014 exhibit there. A new book featuring her work was published around 2015.

After designing a new curriculum, Alexander Kostellow set up a learning laboratory for students to work hand in hand with industry. A very serious student highly trained in commercial art and engineering, Glennie completed two- and three-dimensional design assignments. At the end of the class, the students would pin up their work on a board for review. Kostellow would tear the papers off the wall and throw them on the floor in disgust but leave Ruth's work up as exemplary and praise it. She always sought more-demanding courses and professors and, at some point, put this request in writing.

At this time, representatives from General Motors came to recruit and were introduced to Ruth Glennie by Kostellow. Chance played a role in Ruth's future many times, and this was one of them: "I just happened to be there at the time." Ruth received the invitation below after applying for a position at GM Styling.

As an Oldsmobile designer, Glennie designed seats and door trim for the 1957 model. She contributed to Buick's 1957 custom cars, including the Boeing Electric—an experimental car. She also worked on the instrument panel of the 1958 Pontiac.

GLENNIE JOINS THE CORVETTE STUDIO

Ruth was assigned to the Chevrolet Corvette and a small car studio for approximately four years. She worked primarily in the Chevrolet interiors studio designing production cars—Corvettes and small cars. She specifically mentions her work on the 1957, 1958, 1959, and 1960 Corvettes. Ruth made sketches for the instrument panels, and her drawings set the direction for production.

GLENNIE DESIGNS THE FIRST HEADS-UP DISPLAY IN 1957 FOR THE CHEVROLET CORVETTE

In 1957, Glennie made a remarkable drawing of the first HUD in the auto industry. Glennie, both a designer and trained engineer working in the Corvette studio, proposed to project the speedometer on the windshield in front of the driver. This enables the driver to keep his or her eyes on the road ahead and is especially important for race car drivers. It would take twenty years for this feature to appear on aircraft. Further, it was not until 1989 that a team of GM designers published an SAE paper titled "The First Head Up Display Introduced by General Motors." This team consisted of M. Weihrauch, G. Melony, and T. Goesch.

In keeping with her assignment, Ruth was given a 1958 Chevrolet Corvette to upgrade for the Feminine Show of that year. However, some of her designs went far beyond the physical appearance. "Fancy Free" was one of ten cars created for the dome exhibit by female designers. The silver-olive exterior accentuated four different interior treatments—one for each season of the year. The green brushed-aluminum instruments featured white phosphorescent numbers and needles.

Ruth notes, "Originally, the stitch lines on the seat covers were vertical with molded outer edges and sides of white leather. There were 2-inch stripes of green inboard, and the central area of the seats was perforated green leather."

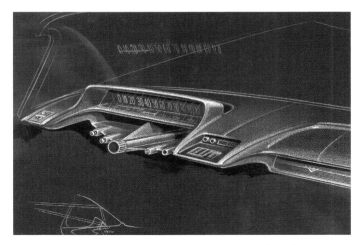

In 1957, Glennie proposed the first head-up display (HUD) in the auto industry for Corvette and was ignored. *Glennie family*

"We called that the spring mode. For summer, the central part of the sets could be covered with a yellow toweling fabric. For winter, there was a black fur cover, and for autumn an orange variegated tweed. Show cars didn't have to be practical."

Ruth's Fancy Free show car was the first to feature retractable seat belts. While they did not use today's familiar spring roller system, they utilized a pneumatic one instead. The standard reflectors at the base of the door were replaced by lamps that flashed when the door was open.

Werner Meier, a retired General Motors engineer and owner of Masterworks, restored Fancy Free to its original condition and added it to his own collection. In the past, he has also owned the personal cars of Bill Mitchell and Bunkie Knudsen. The car was on display at the Gilmore Museum in Michigan when German Heinz-Jergen purchased it.

The Fancy Free Corvette made its home at the Gilmore Museum before being sold to a German collector. *Constance Smith*

THE PRODUCTION IMPALAS

Glennie's contribution to the production Impala was fortuitous. After illustrating a series of doors with integrated lights and reflectors, designs similar to hers started to appear on production Chevrolets, including the 1958 Impala. A family member owns the illustrations.

She was a prolific designer of instrument panels, and it would not surprise anyone if she worked on the Impala's design too—alone or on a team. Her instrument panel drawings bear a strong resemblance to what went into production.

Glennie also designed Pontiac interiors before spending a year at Vauxhall in England. Although it is common today, she was the first woman to work abroad. She returned to GM after working at Vauxhall, as an expression of gratitude for letting her go. By this time, just working in the Pontiac studio was unsatisfying.

Because of the new administration, the managers had changed. Some no longer welcomed or tolerated women designers. It was apparent that as a woman, her chances for advancement had reached their limit. She observed that her superior was less qualified and less experienced than she was.

Glennie's lights or reflectors when it came to production were also handsome designs. *Courtesy of Glennie family*

FIRST WOMAN TO WORK ABROAD

After some years in Warren, Ruth was getting tired of the routine of having to churn out new designs annually for the sake of novelty. David Jones, the head of styling for Vauxhall, came for an extended visit to the Detroit area, accompanied by his daughter, Sonia. Sonia stayed on in the US and moved into the apartment Ruth shared with a couple of other women designers—they became close friends. It was through David Jones that Ruth got her foot in the door at Vauxhall. There was no precedent for GM workers to transfer to foreign subsidiaries—she had to arrange to be hired by Vauxhall temporarily. Special arrangements were made with GM's Overseas Division for her to be listed as an employee so that she could keep her continuous-employment status, even though she was essentially resigning from GM. She requested a leave for four months to travel throughout Europe and absorb the design culture from June through September 1959. She then joined Vauxhall from 1959 to September 1960, where she designed Victor interiors. She felt obliged to return to GM when her year at Vauxhall ended, but had her fill of the industry and left Pontiac after another year. While it is not unusual today for designers to work abroad, Glennie was the first woman to do so. The Vauxhall models were close in design to their American counterparts.

Vauxhall, acquired in 1935 at the direction of Alfred Sloan, offered a Detroit-like Victor from 1959 to 1962. The windshields of some models had a close resemblance to that of the 1957 Chevrolet. The wagon was introduced the last year. In 1962, the series FB offered international styling and more power. For a short time, the car was offered in Pontiac showrooms. While the car was a hit in Great Britain, it could not compete with Detroit's larger, more comfortable offerings in the same price range. Pontiac dealers preferred to offer the Tempest instead. Later, Vauxhall went on to share platforms with Opel.

After leaving GM in 1962, Glennie married Dr. E. Albert Petersen and arranged to work for GTE Sylvania full time. Her husband's father, Eugene Petersen, a talented designer, taught at Pratt Institute for about forty years, while Al worked as a dentist.

At GTE, she designed products, lighting, displays, and advertising for their plant. She resigned when her daughter was born in 1964. While raising two children, she kept herself busy and engaged with a variety of projects – designing and building furniture for their home, mask making, macramé, acrylic casting, making whirligigs, and raising saltwater fish. When her children reached school age, she returned to work part-time on special projects for Sylvania, including product design, displays, and interior design. She continued to work freelance for Sylvania into the 1990s, ultimately with the special-products engineering group.

Ruth Glennie utilized her knowledge of engineering and lighting to redesign the front end of an experimental Pontiac Firebird. The GTE concept incorporated four state-of-the-art headlamps. Because the lamps were unproven for automakers, Sylvania was never successful in selling them for production use. The idea of compact automotive lights is now commonplace, but at that time it was innovative. This was one of her later projects for the special-engineering division of GTE Sylvania. For several years, they tried to develop a compact headlight and sell it to one of the car companies. They bought stock cars—Firebirds and other sports cars—and remodeled the front end to fit the headlamps. These concept cars were presented at the annual automotive show in Detroit for at least three years running, each time with a new car painted some eye-catching custom color. Ruth was the only designer with the group, so she did the fixtures as well as the nose of the car and oversaw the bodywork and painting. She also designed auto show displays. The original series 3 Firebird was designed in GM's Pontiac Studio in 1982 by a team that included Roger Hughet, Bill Porter, and John Schinella. A series of facelifts led to the 1989 model.

FAMILY

Ruth had a lifelong bond with her two sisters, and they frequently traveled together. Observers would frequently ask, "Are you kin?"

She also frequently built canvas kayaks and canoes. When she served as a witness for the marriage of Carl and Sonia Olsen, the photographer caught Glennie and a home-built canoe in the photo.

Throughout her life, Ruth has engaged in a variety of activities and persisted with photography the longest. She was an inveterate photographer, taking on weddings and family travelogues, and served as the unofficial photographer for the United Church in Medfield.

We lost Ruth in 2018; she was predeceased by her husband and is survived by her daughter—Christine is a physician—and son. Glenn Petersen holds a position at New York's Metropolitan Museum of Art and has contributed to the conservation of original drawings.

GERE KAVANAUGH

Someone asked Gere what she liked to design best, and with a typical mix of humor and bluntness she answered, "Anything I can get my hands on."[1]

—Gere Kavanaugh (b. 1929)

CAREER HIGHLIGHTS

Tennessee designer Gere Kavanaugh, with the requisite Cranbrook Academy of Art mindset, joined the Product and Exhibit Design Department at GM under LeRoy Kiefer, the architect of the General Motors Motorama. Extravagant Motorama exhibits, held at the Waldorf Astoria, featured new automotive concepts and kitchens of the future. The department also designed the exhibit space for the 1957 and 1958 Feminine Shows, as well as the exhibition for the Textile Show held in the Technical Center Auditorium (a.k.a. Styling Dome). Perhaps Kavanaugh was most noticed at GM for her design of a creative centerpiece for one of the Feminine Shows, which caught the eye of a local newspaper columnist. Kavanaugh would later join Victor Gruen to design malls and exhibits. After opening her own business, she completed a wide variety of projects for which she has been recognized both nationally and internationally.

BIOGRAPHICAL NOTES

Gere's own own childhood home sat directly across from the Memphis Zoo in Tennessee. At various points in time, animals and nature would serve as the inspiration for her drawings, sculptures, and prints.

Her father, a rare-book collector, imbued Gere with an appreciation for books and read her the requisite fairy tales. Gere noted in a presentation that she still believes in fairy tales—adult fairy tales—and was thrilled to find an original copy of the book *Grimm's Fairy Tales: Twenty Stories*, illustrated by Arthur Rackham, in the Los Angeles Library. She was also fascinated by the books on botany and flowers in her father's collection and would trace images with her hand.[2]

THE IMPORTANCE OF COLOR

Almost every student studying art realizes the importance of color—an Element of Art—taught in most public schools. Some car-buying decisions are even made on the basis of the exterior

General Motors

color of a car sitting in the showroom.

Even before attending school, Gere's mother's preoccupation with sewing would spark Gere's fascination with color. Gere notes, "I first learned about color at my mother's sewing machine, where I stacked up wood spools of thread—the best color combinations. She remarked on the best and not-so-good ones, so I knocked them down and started over."[3] At some point in time, Gere started collecting things; she has a string collection, cans, funnels, and other things that have caught her eye.

Gere notes in a Carnegie Mellon lecture that after observing her behavior around books, Gere's mom instructed her father to take her to the art school. He enrolled her in the Memphis Academy of Arts at just eight years old, stating, "I don't expect you to do anything with this, but I do expect your life to be enriched."

Around 1960, Gere would relocate to California and savor the colorful landscapes. It was the first time she saw purple and magenta hillsides. However, visits to Korea to design silks, the Southwest, and Ireland were also magical. Gere, who taught color courses at Otis, ArtCenter, and Siart, would later build a color library that housed books and samples. She made numerous paintings of her materials to record color. However, she found it necessary to return the collection of Navajo sands to its rightful owner after completing color studies. The sands were sacred.[4]

After visiting her uncle's home in northern Minnesota, Gere would develop an interest in barns. She would later incorporate the coloration of them in a store as a designer for Hallmark. She created the Seasonal Décor line, which contrasted a neutral background.

WHAT WILL CARRY YOU EVERYWHERE?

Gere had a teacher, Tiller Lewis, whom she described as a terrific gentleman in a lecture at the School of Design at Carnegie Mellon. In challenging students, Lewis asked them, "What is the most important thing you can have and learn about being an artist?" After receiving no responses, he said, "Curiosity—and it will carry you everywhere."[5]

Gere would later graduate with a BFA from Memphis College. However, her arrival at Cranbrook to study in the master's program in fine arts established by George Booth changed her life.

THE CRANBROOK EXPERIENCE

Around 1930, Booth envisioned a program that would incorporate four master artists in residence; he included an architect, a painter, a sculptor, and a designer. Ultimately, other departments were also added to the mix. In 1931, Saarinen noted this in a presentation to the AIA:

> It is not an art school in the ordinary meaning. It is a working place for creative art. The leading idea is to have artists ... live at Cranbrook and execute their work there. Those artists form a more or less permanent staff of the Art Council. Besides these artists we will have ... visiting artists from various parts of the country or from foreign countries [who] will bring freshness and new impulses to the Cranbrook art life and will help to a richer and closer understanding of the contemporary movement in various minds and in various countries.[6]

However, the idea was not meant to revive the idea of medieval craftsmanship, but to go forward. There were no traditional classes, just a studio system. Weekly visits were required.

When Eliel Saarinen retired in 1946, he was replaced by Zoltan Sepeshy as director of the Cranbrook Art Academy. The academy buildings provided space for classrooms, studios, and office and living quarters.

Cranbrook changed Kavanaugh's life. Gere notes that she viewed things differently after enrolling. A teacher, Zoltan, advised the students they should leave the next day if they did not know why they were there. This, of course, would invite even more dedication on the part of those who remained. This was not the only college, however, where students worked around the clock. Weekly visits to the studios of other students encouraged the students to explore all disciplines, including

painting, sculpture, and architecture. Gere notes that she learned things by osmosis. Gere recounts, "All the people from the Birmingham and Bloomfield Hills were always visiting the studios—including the Eero Saarinen office, which was down the back road from Cranbrook, and the students visited the office there frequently too. They hung out with the ES staff at the Bar-B-Que on Woodward Avenue."[7]

TAPESTRIES, TEXTILES, AND PRINTS

When it came to founder Booth, the Saarinen family, and Kavanaugh, textiles were a significant art form. Booth, a tapestry collector himself, would purchase art to hang in the museum and schools built on the campus. Weaver Maja Anderson Wirde was appointed to a studio in 1929, when design for a girls' school began. In 1931, Loja Saarinen designed rugs and textiles for a residence at the academy. Some of the huge tapestries combined the talents both of Eliel and Loja Saarinen. A huge Loja tapestry hangs over the fireplace in the Saarinen home next to the academy. In 1934, Lillian Holm taught weaving under Loja. In 1937, Marianne Strengell was appointed instructor of weaving and costume design, although Holms continued to teach weaving at the Kingswood School. When Loja closed her weaving school in 1942, Strengell took charge of the department. Later, when Eliel Saarinen died in 1950, an exhibit of the fabrics of Strengell was mounted. In 1944, Robert Sailors was appointed instructor under Strengell. At about this time, stenciling and silkscreening designs on fabric became a less expensive of method than weaving.

Following in the footsteps of Loja, Strengell, and even Jack Lenor Larson, an earlier Cranbrook graduate, Gere would fall in love with patterns and textiles and learn printing processes—which included silkscreening. She would start the designs on papers before progressing to silkscreen. Taking it a step further, the designs would later serve as a backdrop for other projects presented.

Gere notes that a handful of talented women also preceded her in the design department on the campus of Cranbrook, including Ray Eames, Florence Knoll, Carol Vasberg, and Ruth Adler Schnee—all prominent in their own right. GM's Margaret Sauer, who arrived well before Gere, studied fine arts. Jayne Van Alstyne was likely not even enrolled when she visited and worked at Cranbrook in ceramics just after high school.

A MULTIPART THESIS

Gere's requirement for graduation culminated in a series of designs submitted to Cranbrook. Her allegiance to diversity and importance of form as related to function is noted in the written part of the thesis:

When a person fears to explore a certain facet of design he automatically hurts himself this way. For working in other or different fields which outwardly are not related but basically are linked he widens his scope. ... A designer should have the scope of an architect, painter, sculptor all combined into one ... he should know form in all of its ramifications. Always keep in mind that it should be honest expression of function.

Gere Kavanaugh's presentation included a number of physical products as well.

ROME COLLABORATION

The first project presented was called the "Rome Collaboration." This assignment appears to be a takeoff on Saarinen's contract with General Motors to design a styling dome and surrounding walls for the GM Motors Technical Center. The domed auditorium, used for presentations, occupies an area south of the main entrance of the General Motors Styling building. Man-made lakes are located across from the domed auditorium and between the dome and Styling. On a breezy day, the mist and spray from the larger lake reach the street and sidewalk.

Gere's project included an illustration of the dome, very similar to the one designed by Saarinen for GM Styling, behind a decorative wall running in front of it. Gere designed a mosaic, which would have to survive the fluctuating climates of Michigan, for the wall. The front of her wall would hold the visually complicated nonrepresentational mosaic, and the rear would be included as part of the exhibit.

The GM domed auditorium that exists features walls in the front and on the side. In the real world, Cranbrook ceramicist Grotell finished each Saarinen wall off with a series of glazed decorative bricks—each one exploring the subtleties of color. Similar bricks were used for the Styling building.

Immediately following graduation, Gere joined General Motors in the Product and Exhibit Design Department, where she worked on interiors. This department was most noted for early extravagant Motoramas. In 1957 and 1958, GM mounted two feminine exhibits and the textile exhibit in the domed auditorium. Gere's department would establish a theme and set the decor. Women in each of the divisions designed automobile concepts based on existing production inventory. Chevrolets, Pontiacs, Buicks, and Oldsmobiles took center stage.

In 1958, when GM unveiled its interior automotive concepts created by the other damsels, Gere was called upon to dream up something special for the unveiling in the Styling Center dome. Gere would leave GM for a year to join Victor Gruen and later return to work with the remaining men. Gere agrees that Gruen is the architect of the shopping mall in the United States, and notes that A. Alfred Taubman came afterward. One of his earliest malls, the Northland Mall, is located near GM's Technical Center.

Women in the Exhibits group prepared the domed auditorium for exhibits such as this textile show. *General Motors*

In early times, a number of prominent artists sculpted pieces displayed inside the mall, which is now slated for demolition. Gere's own clock, designed for the Monroe Mall, incorporated puppets—a welcome sight to children of all ages.

After returning to GM, Gere set up the automobile exhibits. In the 1958 show, a reporter noted that she (Gere) tried to create the atmosphere of a French garden with numerous birds and flowers. Gere, on the other hand, notes that she was not designing around this theme at all. A local newspaper recorded this event as well as Gere's design for the ranch-style home of GM's VP of marketing, Anthony de Lorenzo.

The description of the Feminine exhibit is hard to fathom. Gere ordered builders to fabricate three cages out of netlike material used for drapes. Measuring 30 feet high and 2 feet, 10 inches in diameter, one was made of Swiss cotton net fastened like a dress, with hooks and eyes at the openings. A chain was hung down the center, with wooden dowels used as perches for the cage that would house ninety live canaries. Colored cellophane under the plastic floors of the cages provided a rainbow of colors. While the lights were turned on, the birds sang.

Gere also installed white hyacinths near tiled terraces that held the cars. Her use of nylon chiffon panels enhanced the atmosphere.

At the same time, Gere was invited to design the interior of the new ranch-style home of Anthony de Lorenzo, a GM VP in charge of public relations. It was noted that Gere incorporated geometric wallpaper provided by Girad as well as the furniture of Charles Eames and George Nelson to achieve a folksy feeling. Gere incorporated pearlescent Naughahyde—an automotive fabric—in a bathroom.

Later, perhaps her infatuation with animals attracted her to the work of Will Edmondson. The son of a Tennessee enslaved man, his creations would seem to inspire her Dove Bench. She was the first of ten artists in the city of Los Angeles to be recognized annually. A small hole at the front of the bench serves as the dove's eye and provides a telescope of sorts to curious children. She cherishes the book *Noah's Ark* to this day.

Gere would later collaborate on a project with Frank Gehry and Deborah Sussman. The market umbrella was an outgrowth of this assignment and has grown exponentially in popularity over time. Gehry, a noted Jewish American architect, distorts conventional shapes and skews volumes to create unusual buildings. His use of metal cladding on the surface of buildings is innovative. Gehry also designed cardboard furniture, which he offers for sale. Gehry has recently designed rings for jewelry manufacturer Tiffany & Co.

Before starting her own business, Gere Kavanaugh Designs, she shared space with others in California. She also rented space to Don Chadwick, Deborah Sussman, and a writer who developed screenplays.

While Gere has worked nationally and internationally, she notes that one of the interesting things about Detroit in the 1950s was that it was a hub of design because of the ideas bubbling up from the offices of Saarinen, Yamaski, Gruen, the Detroit Art Museum, Case Tech, and the University of Michigan.

DIVERSITY

At the beginning of her career, Gere designed Christmas and Chanukah cakes for Blum's in San Francisco, a very famous bakery and candy company.

It appears that no investigation and no job were too small or too large for her to explore. Her office's design of the interior, furniture, and related logos for the Richard Nixon Library & Birthplace (now the Richard Nixon Presidential Library and Museum) and gift shop in Yorba Linda, California, stands out. She received a historical NEA grant to cocurate the exhibition *Home Sweet Home*, a study of American domestic vernacular architecture, with Charles Moore for the Craft and Folk Art Museum in Los Angeles. She designed the exhibition installation. Gere's exploration and design of interiors, furniture, papers, textiles, cards, alphabets, and books continues. Her contributions have been recognized in *Art in America*, *Progressive Architecture*, and other well-known art-and-design publications, and her work has also appeared extensively in magazines and books.

DO WOMEN DESIGN DIFFERENTLY THAN MEN?

In an AWID newsletter published back in 1999, Gere would note, "With design projects, women approach a problem from all sides—not all women but most. My work does not have what I would describe as a feminine aspect. My work has vibrancy, a life force as a strong aspect. I am not a 'party line designer' where you are taught certain directions to go in and you do not draw from your own wealth of soul and personal experience; there is no vitality."

THE FUTURE

Gere is still active in the art scene and is proud of the recent publication of her own biography, titled *A Life in Color*, written largely with the assistance of her California peers.

In 1957 and '58, Feminine Shows were held in the styling auditorium. *General Motors*

JEANETTE KREBS (LAPINE)

Drawing the figure provided an analytic versus design challenge Jeannette hadn't revisited in years, as does study with any teacher who has their own agenda, mine being the expressive quality of line. Despite the progression of health challenges she experienced in her final years, Jeanette's tenacious drive to keep learning alive and creating to engage with fellow artists, use her senses to appreciate the beauty of this world, and express the joy in living through art is testimony to her great creative spirit and an inspiration to all who knew and loved her.[1]

—Marc Chabot, M.C. Fine Arts, talking about Jeanette Krebs (1933–2018)

Krebs Lapine serves as tour guide for Knudsen. *Courtesy of J. Lapine / Damsels in Design*

CAREER HIGHLIGHTS

Jeanette Krebs (Lapine) served as a designer for Chevrolet, Pontiac, and Overseas and Truck Studios before following her husband to Germany when he accepted a position at Opel, a subsidiary of General Motors at that time. Her husband, Anatole Lapine, subsequently worked as director of design for Porsche. After raising children and returning to Connecticut, Krebs Lapine devoted many hours to refining her skills in painting and drawing.

Jeanette's work is prominently featured in *Damsels in Design: Women Pioneers in the Automotive Industry, 1939–1959* (Schiffer Books, 2018).

BIOGRAPHICAL NOTES[2]

Jeanette Krebs was born in 1933 in Queens, New York. Herman and Bertha Krebs welcomed their second child, Jeanette, as the Century of Progress International Exposition in Chicago showcased modern design and technology. In Jeanette's eyes, later on, it was more important that Frances Perkins became the first woman appointed to the US cabinet as secretary of labor; she held the position from 1933 to 1945. At this time, the Krebs's first child, Herman, was five years old.

Jeanette noted that her father showcased his expertise providing upholstery and drapery to a star-studded clientele and would later own an interior-decorating business. His talents were diverse, since he was a natural musician and played several instruments. His wife and son would later assist with the business, which Herman would eventually inherit.

Although Jan, as she was called by some, lived on Long Island early on, the family moved to Waterbury, Connecticut, when she was barely two years old. She attended Bunker Hill Grammar School, where a wisp of a lady, credited as an art instructor, sporadically showed up to give drawing lessons to the class. It was always the same—the scary Halloween witches, the Santa Claus and his sleigh and reindeer, and George Washington chopping down the cherry tree. Seeking to learn a bit more, Jan eventually attended Saturday morning classes at the Mattatuck Museum in Waterbury, taking lessons in drawing and painting. Two years later, at the age of twelve, she would take home a first-prize award in painting.

After graduating from high school, Jan was determined to follow her passion in art and decided to move to Boston, where an aunt and uncle lived. She enrolled in the Vesper George School of Art, which was accredited and maintained an exemplary reputation. The school, incorporated in 1927, had become one of Boston's most distinguished coeducational and professional commercial art schools. It was located in the Back Bay sector, close to the Boston's Museum of Fine Arts, the Isabella Stewart Gardner Museum, and many advertising businesses. The school closed its doors in 1983.

At Vesper George, she studied the fundamentals and basic requirements for commercial art during the first year. Students would concentrate on the thought process in drawing, design and design principles, color dimensions, color theory, and scheme. Creative painting and form projects in various mediums, in addition to anatomy, art history, and lettering, rounded out the first-year basic course.

Jeanette was awarded a scholarship for her second year. However, at this time, she discovered an even more impressive art program at Pratt Institute in Brooklyn, New York. As we are already aware, entrance in 1952 required the completion of the home test, and she would likely have had to find a sewing machine to draw for the first assignment.

Krebs joined Sue Vanderbilt, Ruth Glennie, and Dagmar Arnold in the Industrial Design Department. Alexander and Rowena Reed Kostellow made a lasting impression, as did many of her instructors who helped build the confidence needed to face the workforce in the real world.

Krebs noted that in 1955, just before graduation, "General Motors swooped in and recruited Sue, Ruth, Dagmar, and me to work in the GM Styling Department." Her first stop was the Argonaut Building in Detroit, as the GM Technical Center neared completion. The refurbished Argonaut Building, with financial gifts from Taubman, GM, and Ford, now serves as an education facility for the College for Creative Studies. The General Motors display in the lobby features the iconic cars designed there.

Krebs was assigned for a short time to the Chevrolet Studio and then would report to the Pontiac Studio.

Clare MacKichan and Carl Renner, working under Harley Earl, are credited with the design of a 1955 Chevrolet sport wagon; the Nomad began as a Motorama Corvette concept and met with unheralded success. Krebs started in the interiors studio at this time.

In 1955, Pontiac had just introduced new bodies with bumpers split in the center, new chassis, and a more powerful 173-horsepower V-8 engine, in an effort to provide youth with performance and style. By lowering the floor and the seats, the cars were lower and longer. Thin metallic streaks were added to the hood. Swept-back Indians adorned Pontiac hoods since the 1930s, and some were designed by Bonnie Lemm. By 1955, the Indian heads sprouted wings on their sides to address the public's fascination with aircraft. Chevrolet eagles of this era also sprouted wings.

More importantly, the new two-tones offered for the exteriors of cars such as the Star Chief would greatly influence the interior designers. New and lighter colors for the interiors were promoted. Two-tones were introduced on seats, doors, and instrument panels. Some noted that this change was made to attract women customers. Jan, and later Sandra Longyear and Ruth Glennie, would become part of the Pontiac design team.

In 1957, the first of two Feminine Shows was mounted in the auditorium at the Tech Center. Having contributed much of the interior design for Pontiac, Jan appears in photos with the Pontiac Star Chief convertible, a black beauty, with an interior of black leather and emerald-green trim.

She was also invited to provide a tour for Semon "Bunkie" Knudsen, the Pontiac Division head at the time.

In 1958, designers were to produce an even-bolder design. The Bonneville's 370-cubic-inch V-8 equipped with three two-barrel carburetors had a horsepower rating of 300. While the exteriors wore a Tri-Power emblem, the interiors of some vehicles were tricolor.

After Pontiac, Krebs was transferred to the Truck and Overseas Studio. In late 1957, she left the corporation to marry Anatole Lapine, a talented GM engineer. In 1965, Tony was offered and accepted a position at Opel in Germany for a period of six months, along with his family; however, this assignment grew into four years. Because of his success there, he was invited to head Porsche Styling and did so for the next twenty years. The Lapines and their children, Klaus, Hans, and Ingre, settled in a suburb of Stuttgart. While Hans was affiliated with VW, Jeanette embarrassingly noted that she was provided with VWs to drive. Hans now works for a different car company; after leaving Germany during investigations, he joined Genesis here in the United States. Following Tony's retirement, Tony and Jan took up residence in Baden-Baden.

Anatole died in 2012. Subsequently, after living in Germany for thirty-one years, Jeanette Lapine returned home to Connecticut. Once settled in, she enrolled in a figure-drawing class, taught by Marc Chabot, and also painted. Chabot notes, "I remember seeing a painting she exhibited at the Washington Art Association [show]."

Jeanette Lapine died in July 2018 at St. Francis Hospital at the age of eighty-five.

Jeanette oversees operations. *General Motors*

MAJORIE FORD POHLMANN

CAREER SUMMARY

Marjorie Ford Pohlmann designed automobiles for Buick. Her designs for concept cars featured prominently in each of two Feminine Shows and led to new directions for Buick production vehicles. Buick featured the Alouette in 1957, and the Tampico, a four-door hardtop, in 1958.

Marjorie married Charles Pohlmann, who played a significant role in the design of the Q-Car, the basis for the 1963 Chevrolet Corvette. Marjorie and Chuck would later leave General Motors to found Sacred Design Associates in Minneapolis, Minnesota.

THE JOURNEY

Marjorie entered Pratt Institute in 1953 and graduated in 1957 alongside classmates Jeanette and Peter Linder, in pursuit of a degree in industrial design. The noted Damsels of Design, graduating in 1955, predated her class. She appeared with five others in the iconic Damsels of Design photo.

In 1952, Alexander Kostellow, the founder and chair of Pratt's Industrial Design Department, had created the Experimental Design Laboratory at Pratt so that representatives of major companies could work with students on projects. Design labs were set up for autos, furniture, kitchen appliances, displays, boats, tools, and kitchen utensils. Major companies set up offices around the labs and worked with students. Shops with tools for wood, plastic, and metal were available. Participation by GM would have a significant effect on the careers of Pratt students. At one point in time, GM sent out clay modelers to assist students in designing automobiles. Monsanto, Sears Roebuck, Shell Oil, Elgin Watch, Heritage Home Group (Henredon furniture), Owens-Corning Fiberglass, Hickok Manufacturing, and Gorham Silver would also contribute funds and expertise. The program was featured in a 1952 issue of *Business Week*.

Marjorie would go on to marry Charles Pohlmann, a Pratt classmate, after they joined General Motors in 1957.

On February 8, 1958, the *New York Times* carried the notice "Marjorie Ford to Wed: She Is Engaged to Charles F. Pohlmann—Both at G.M."

Pohlmann was assigned to the Buick Studio, which at the time manufactured the Special, Century, Super, and Roadmaster and at this time placed third or fourth industry wide. In 1957, production models were totally redesigned, and all featured more-powerful 365-cubic-inch engines with horsepower ratings of 250–300. Cars were distinguished by heavy chrome grills and four ventiports or simulated port holes on each fender.

Pohlmann designed the interior, truck area, exterior colors, and exterior ornament and hubcaps of the Buick Alouette, which

Majorie Ford had just arrived at GM when she was asked to redo a 1958 Buick Special Convertible based on a Special called the Tampico. Her cutting-edge use of color was appreciated. The alabaster exterior featured flaming orange accents. *General Motors*

was based on a Series 70 two-door hardtop that featured prominently in the 1957 Feminine Show. As the Buick representative, Pohlmann made notable changes to the production 1958 Buicks and was particularly creative with contrasting colors. The 1958 Buick Special convertible show car, dubbed the Tampico, featured a stunning alabaster exterior with flaming orange accents.

The interior of the Tampico featured seats with four cloth inserts surrounded by leather. *General Motors*

The bucket-seating arrangement behind a curved-glass windshield allowed her to design a center console to house binoculars, a camera, and a trademark removable Sportable transistor radio. A Sportable radio with a substantial chrome-plated front would later appear on production Pontiacs. The seats featured four cloth inserts surrounded by leather—two on top and two on the seat cushion. A light-colored, T-shaped strip of leather ran up the center of the seat and along the side of the door. The seat backs had storage compartments for magazines and were handsomely tailored.

Majorie was put to work designing a second car, the Buick Shalimar. The Shalimar was based on the existing four-door hardtop and featured a striking royal-purple exterior and black-and-purple inside. The glove box housed a swing-out Dictaphone—this feature, however, is usually attributed to colleague Sue Vanderbilt. The center console, a place for cosmetics and a mirror at this time, had a cover.

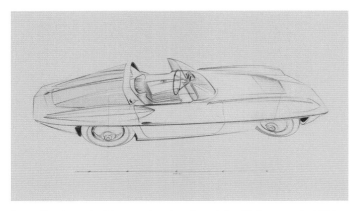

Peter Brook made this stunning drawing of the C3 Corvette in 1957. *Peter Brock Collection*

CHUCK POHLMANN AND THE CORVETTE STING RAY

In the book *A Century of Automotive Style* by Michael Lamm and Dave Holls (Lamm-Morada, 1996), the authors note, "In 1958, he [William Mitchell] paid $500 for the abandoned Corvette SS Mule (XP-87) that Fangio and Moss had tested at Sebring. Engineer Mauri Rose installed a prototype V-8 in 1954 and later installed the Duntov cam to extract more power. Smokey Yunick drove to a record setting 163 mph at GM's proving ground in Arizona."

Mitchell then announced a contest to design a new body for this car, reportedly based on a Ghia show car he had seen in Turin in 1957. Junior designer Peter Brock and Chuck Pohlmann in Bob McLean's special studio won the contest. Pohlmann put Mitchell's ideas into a little 8-by-10-inch pencil sketch, and he and Brock developed coupe and roadster versions. At that point, the project moved to the so-called hammer room.

Designer and car guy Peter Brock remembers his colleague:

Chuck Pohlmann was a good friend, a fellow designer with me in Research B under studio head Bob Veryzer (Bob McLean was the executive in charge of studios A and B but never came into B). This is where we developed the XP87 Sting Ray concept for Bill Mitchell (built on the SS frame). I did the coupe and Chuck did the roadster version after Mitchell determined there wasn't a budget to complete the coupe. The roadster was later detailed by Shinoda and Tony Lapine (who left soon after to go to Opel … and then Porsche).[1]

The Sting Ray was paraded by Mitchell from 1959 to 1960 and in 1960 won the national SCCA C-Modified class championship. In 1961, Mitchell retired the Sting Ray, converted it to street use, painted it silver, and unveiled it at the Chicago Auto Show as an idea car.

For unclear reasons, Charles Pohlmann would leave to go on to work for General Electric. His corporate positions, however, would end after nine or ten years. In 1966, he and Marjorie would establish Sacred Design Associates in Minneapolis. The consultancy assisted architects in modernizing church buildings and provided graphic design for Lutheran parishes. The Pohlmanns also designed and penned the weekly bulletins for churches and drafted collection envelopes and other items needed by the parishes.

In 1984, Charles received an Interior Design Award from the Minneapolis Society of the American Institute of Architects. He would later donate almost 2,800 photographs of churches, including stained-glass art, to a college archive. In addition, his work included shots of Rockefeller Center and buildings by Saarinen.

In 1986, Luther College, originally established to train Lutheran ministers, celebrated its 125th anniversary and commissioned Marjorie Ford Pohlmann to design and weave paraments for the altar and vestments for the pastors, with the overall theme of "a cloud of witnesses." Church apparel is redesigned for various occasions and holidays. For instance, white and gold are incorporated during joyous holidays, which traditionally include Christmas and Easter. In 2011, it would be noted that after twenty-five years of usage, the weaving remained as fresh as the day it was made. Her artwork appears in the book *Transformed by the Journey: 150 Years of Luther College in Word and Image.*

Mule car. *Constance Smith*

HELENE POLLINS

Sixty-three years later, I have evolved into a painter and to where ever it applies, I am still following the rule "Form Follows Function" espoused by my teacher [Alexander Kostellow headed the Industrial Design Department at Pratt Institute]. I use a sword brush to get beautiful line, washes, and rich color.[1] [In this situation, Pollins equates form with her tools.]

—Helene Pollins (b. 1933)

CAREER HIGHLIGHTS

Helene Pollins works in watercolor and acrylic and exhibits her fine arts. In 2019, she won a first-place award in the Mercer County Senior Citizen Art Show for her painting *White Water*.

Pollins retired a number of years ago from the New Jersey public school system, where she worked as a junior high school art teacher, a career that allowed her to stay in one place to raise a family.

Prior to joining the school system, she held positions with Frew & Squier, a design consultancy, and architects Skidmore, Owens & Merrill.

Before joining Frew & Squire, Pollins was recruited by General Motors from Pratt Institute (1955) with a group of women designers destined for the automobile studios; a group of six were later dubbed the Damsels of Design by GM marketing. However, she joined GM's Product and Exhibit Department. Her manager, Carl Benkert, reported to LeRoy Keifer—the genius who organized the Motorama exhibitions held across the US and Canada. At GM, Pollins designed displays, exhibits, kitchens, offices, planters, and decorative pieces. Her design for a textile show in the auditorium was notable.

Her contemporary design for a decorative kitchen named "The Mountain Retreat" was featured twice in newspapers in full color.

In 2018, Pollins's full portfolio and profile were featured in *Damsels in Design: Women Pioneers in the Automotive Industry, 1939–1959* (Schiffer Books, 2018). The book features women from all car companies.

Pollins continues to paint, teach painting to seniors, and win awards.

BIOGRAPHICAL NOTES

Helene Pollins, a.k.a. Polly, was born in 1933 in Edgewood, New York, to Sarah and Robert. Helene had an older brother, Harry. Pollins is proud of her Jewish heritage. Both her paternal and maternal grandparents started out as tailors. Her fraternal grandparents went on to set up and manage a large farm, complete with a still, in New Brunswick, enabling them to make donations of land in support of Rutgers University. Her father, an engineer, owned a tire store and worked for Grumman Aerospace as a manager. Her mother, an accomplished mezzo-soprano and pianist, appeared on stage at Carnegie Hall. Helene would attend performances at the Metropolitan Opera House. She studied piano at age seven, and her mother allowed her to do what she wanted—"mess around"—as long as she played by the rules. She was just one of the boys playing stickball and building things. Helene's parents would later move to Far Rockaway. Pollins studied at PS 106 under the influence of Mrs. Greenrose, her Italian third-grade teacher, who was a little rough with the children but got away with it back then.

Pollins met her mentor in ninth grade; Pollins enrolled in Far Rockaway High School, where she met Vivian Brickner, an art teacher. This relationship would later change her life. Bruckner, who had a good grasp of art occupations, introduced Helene to industrial design, a field that she said originated in the early 1930s.

To start the foundation year, required before selecting a major, Pollins commuted from home in Far Rockaway before deciding to move to a brownstone apartment near the Pratt campus.

Consisting of art courses, design courses, and an academic elective, foundation year was tough. The students frequently stayed up late to complete numerous assignments; students proudly announced their dedication by using the term "all-nighter" in preparation of judgment day. Some, not having as much talent or initiative as others, dropped out.

Helene was further challenged by Alexander Kostellow, the cofounder of Pratt's Industrial Design Department, who called her "Polly." The color class and Kostellow are memorable, due both to positive and negative memories.

Kostellow, the department head, would comment: "Women going out into this field should look as pretty as they can." It was not welcome then, nor is it now.[2]

Pollins studied life drawing with Calvin Albert, a notable painter and sculptor. Albert wrote the book *Figure Drawing Comes to Life*, published by Prentice Hall in 1987.

After foundation year, Pollins studied three-dimensional design with Rowena Reed Kostellow and Bob Kolli. She joined Eva Zeisel's ceramics class and studied literature with Professor Knowles. Miss Taylor also taught 2-D design. Pratt required Pollins to study painting on Saturday mornings—finally enabling her for once to wear jeans to class. Pollins worked summers typing in banks and as an arts-and-crafts counselor.

Upon graduation in 1955, with a bachelor's degree in industrial design, Pollins was invited to interview with General Motors Styling and met LeRoy Keifer and Carl Benkert. Earlier in his career, Keifer managed the iconic Motoramas staged at the Waldorf Astoria Hotel and throughout the US and Canada. Pollins directly reported to Benkert and joined the all-male Product and Exhibit Design Department, which included Wells Squier and Dave Maslan. She would later work in other studios with Sue Vanderbilt and Jayne Van Alstyne. Early on, she drove a loaner car to visit distributors of textiles and carpeting in the immediate area.

At some point, Pollins made illustrations of the division of office space.

Benkert's studio designed and coordinated the Textile Show mounted in the domed auditorium of the Styling Center. Pollins made illustrations for the overall design of the show, which was finalized with Benkert. Photos of her original exhibit design work featured here show ribbons of wool blends and tweeds manufactured by Knoll and Kroll above other displays. In one of the strips, Pollins blended pink and fuchsia. Pollins notes, as with other projects, that the shows held in the auditorium were made possible by a team of designers.

Pollins was later chosen, with three other colleagues, to design a decorative kitchen. This was a great honor. Each of four kitchens had a different theme. She created a "Mountain Retreat" that was featured in a color illustrated article in a Michigan newspaper.

The Mountain Retreat featured flop-down cooking units that sat on a weathered wood counter for simple meals. Chairs at the counter were manufactured by Thonet in Germany. The classic café chair was customized using black-and-white-striped padded cushions. Pollins notes, "Informality was most important to those engaged in hiking, fishing, swimming, hunting, and just relaxing. All the cooking units, the refrigerator, and the wall oven were made by GM's Frigidaire Division."

In other assignments, Pollins created decorative murals for use on the wall of the Styling building. She also designed chrome-plated planters to hold vases and Christmas decor.

Unable to find a husband with a similar background, and despite Benkert's invitation to stay with a salary increase, Pollins moved to Florida and worked for a design consultancy, Frew & Squier, set up by her GM colleague. After weathering some harassment, she returned to New York to Skidmore, Owings & Merrill, where she joined the team responsible for the design of the cafeteria for the Chase Manhattan Bank Building in New York City.

Helene met and married Edward Reed, an engineer. Ed's family had escaped the Nazis in Germany in 1934 as things heated up. An influential department store owner, Offin Falk, had worked with US senator Bohrer in the US to make the arrangements. This escape was reported to have cost $100,000.

Reed, an MIT graduate, held a position at Bristol Instrument. Pollins had two sons who became clinical psychologists. Both obtained undergraduate degrees from Rutgers, and graduate degrees—one studied at the University of Florida and the other at the University of Connecticut. As they grew older, Pollins returned to college in Montclair, New Jersey, to qualify for a teaching certificate and taught art to junior high students in New Jersey. After serving twenty-five years as a teacher, she retired at age sixty-five. Her older brother died at age seventy. Her son David passed away from complications of the flu at just fifty-three, leaving a wife and two sons behind.

Today, as a docent at Montclair State University, Pollins assists with the education of a new generation of artists and visitors. Pollins recently endured a move but still relishes family activities and creative endeavors. She notes, "After winning awards for my watercolor and acrylic painting, I get more satisfaction from the process of painting [than from the recognition]."[3]

Pollins's designs for contemporary kitchens were futuristic at this time. *Collection of Helene Pollins; photo, Constance Smith*

SANDRA LONGYEAR RICHARDSON

Luck came Sandra's way when she was selected to purchase a 1957 program car released by one of the executives at a greatly discounted price. The shiny black Corvette featured a stunning red-leather interior and a removable hardtop. Sandra notes, "This was a nice way to enter the design community."

S.L. Richardson

(b. 1933)

CAREER HIGHLIGHTS

Sandra Richardson, with two of her classmates, joined Harley Earl in the iconic Damsels of Design photograph. Richardson, *seated*, and Ruth Glennie showcased their pearl necklaces, a symbol of success.

Sandra attended Centenary Junior College before graduating from Pratt Institute in 1957. While her predecessors from Pratt graduated in 1955 and joined General Motors the same year, she did not arrive until 1957. Her cohorts included Majorie Ford Pohlmann, Jeanette Fioravera Linder, and Peter Linder.

Assigned to the Pontiac Division, the new graduate designed production and concept cars. While she did not participate in the 1957 Feminine Show, her work for the 1958 show included the 1958 Pontiac Starchief Bordeaux and Pontiac Bonneville Polaris. Selected as a tour guide for the show, Longyear was photographed with Edward Cole.

In 1958, Longyear married designer Deane Richardson. She notes that she left GM to help start RichardsonSmith with her husband. At this time, she held down three jobs—she was also a design translator for Columbus Coated Fabrics and an instructor at the Columbus College of Art and Design. RichardsonSmith was eventually one of the largest and most successful international design consultancies and research firms operating, with offices in the United States, London, and Japan.

In 2018, Sandra Richardson and her husband were the recipients of the prestigious Rowena Reed Kostellow Award from Pratt Institute. John Cafaro, a North American Global Chevrolet executive before his retirement, has also received this recognition.

Sandra Richardson's extended profile is featured in *Damsels in Design: Women Pioneers in the Automotive Industry, 1939–1959* (Schiffer Books, 2018).

General Motors

BIOGRAPHICAL NOTES

William Longyear, Sandra's father, was a Pratt Institute alumnus, and an accomplished designer who headed the Pratt's Advertising Art Department. A leader in his field, he was also an active member of the New York Packaging Design Council. His wife, Christine, was also a talented Pratt graduate.

Sandra arrived in 1933 with the Century of Progress—an exhibit was set up to create a sense of optimism by looking to the future. Visitors were delighted by the Cadillac V-16 Aerodynamic Coupe exhibited; however, the most radical car presented was the Dymaxion Car, created by Buckminster Fuller and Starling Burgess. The front-wheel-drive automobile had a third wheel in the rear, used to steer the car.

The Longyears resided in a home in Munsey Park, an affluent area of Manhasset on Long Island's north shore, about forty-five minutes to an hour away from Pratt's Brooklyn campus. William Longyear created a mural in the Munsey Park Elementary School that Sandra attended. In 1951, having expressed no great passion

Courtesy of the Richardsons

Sandra Richardson. *Courtesy of S. Richardson*

for art, Sandra graduated from Manhasset High School and enrolled in Centenary Junior College in Hackettstown, New Jersey. She remembers studying psychology. Upon graduation, she would review the offerings at Pratt Institute.

Although her father mentioned that "design is the tail of the dog," Sandra's acceptance at Pratt would not surprise anyone and would save the Longyears lots of money. A private college, Pratt was fairly expensive but free to the children of faculty members.

Upon graduation, Sandra was offered a position at GM Styling by Harley Earl. She would later be photographed with a group of elite women designers dubbed the Damsels of Design by GM photographers. Being able to work in a new technical center designed by Saarinen and dedicated by GM brass as well as President Dwight D. Eisenhower was particularly exciting. Sandra joined Fidele Bianco in the Pontiac interiors studio. Luck came Sandra's way when she was selected to purchase a 1957 program car released by one of the executives, at a greatly discounted price. The shiny black Corvette featured a stunning red-leather interior and a removable hardtop. Sandra notes, "This was a nice way to enter the design community."

Seating for the Bordeaux. *General Motors*

At GM, Sandra would later assist with the design of cars for the Feminine Shows. Her work for the 1958 show was particularly notable. She designed the substantially updated 1958 Pontiac Star Chief four-door.

The Bordeaux featured a heather-green interior and exterior. The front door panels were works of art and featured a striated leather panel, a fabric insert, and a Pontiac emblem. The seats also featured three panels with fanciful metallic rectangular cushions. Extras included slash pockets in the door panels, and leather pockets with straps to steady groceries in the trunk.

The Polaris convertible was blue with heavy chrome accents. Sandra chose black leather and intense-blue fabric for the seats, which were separated by a console in the front of the car. Way ahead of the times, the center console housed storage for picnic supplies, a thermos that matched the interior, and a Sportable radio that could be removed. A sliding lid covered the contents of the console. Touches of chrome on the doors matched the heavy chrome on the instrument panel.

Sandra was chosen to serve as the tour guide in the domed auditorium where the Feminine Show was held. Edward Cole intently listened to her presentation. By 1956, Cole was the general manager of Chevrolet; he was later promoted to the presidency of General Motors.

At this time, there was a large group of Pratt designers living and working in the Detroit area. Sandra met Deane Richardson and David Smith, 1956 graduates, working as industrial designers. They joined forces to start a design consulting firm in Columbus, Ohio. Deane and Sandra were married in 1958, and RichardsonSmith became their focus. Over a seven-year period, Sandra also taught three-dimensional design at the Columbus College of Art and Design; the syllabus was an outgrowth of the Pratt curriculum, and she served under Joe Canzani, the chair and another Pratt alumnus.

Over a forty-year period, RichardsonSmith became one of the largest design and research consulting firms, establishing offices in Boston and San Francisco in the United States and in Japan, Singapore, and London. Sandra played an integral role in the development of the firm. Through the 1990s, Sandra and Deane participated in ICSID (International Council of Societies of Industrial Design) seminars worldwide. Deane served as president, and the couple networked with design societies in more than fifty countries.

Sandra and Deane have three grown children: Mark and Christine in the New York City area, and Derek in the Denver area, with additional grandchildren. They chase good weather, spending half a year on the shore of Castine, Maine, and the other half on the barrier island of North Captiva in Florida. Together with David Smith, the Richardson family owns the wonderful "Design Farm" buildings that served as headquarters for RichardsonSmith.

Sandra loves sailing on their 39-foot Leaf, photographing her shell collection, and creating designs for needlepoint.

MARGARET ELIZABETH SAUER

Margaret Sauer was a highly trained industrial designer, educator, and entrepreneur; she also won numerous accolades for her fine arts—ceramics, sculpture, and jewelry design. However, Sauer is perhaps best remembered by her family, friends, and students for her generosity.

—Julie Sabit, speaking about Margaret Sauer (1925–1986)

CAREER HIGHLIGHTS

Margaret Sauer, a Wayne State graduate, designed exhibits and displays for B. Siegel Company, I. Himelhoch Company, and J. L. Hudson Company—all located in Detroit—before joining GM Styling in 1955 with five other women designers graduating from Pratt Institute in New York. Sauer, one of the earliest arrivals at Styling, was included in the group of six iconic women automobile designers labeled the Damsels of Design by GM marketers under Harley Earl.

In 1955, all women in auto received assignments in the divisional interior design studios. Sauer was placed with Oldsmobile and would later represent this division in designing production cars and a station wagon for the 1957 and 1958 Feminine Shows. In addition to selecting colors and fabrics, Sauer went on to suggest safety innovations that would not be suitably acknowledged for over fifty years. In 1958, she updated the Olds Carousel Wagon for the Feminine Car Show to include a remote window and door lockout system for the rear seat. It would take until 2004 for NHSTA to mandate this kind of device, and until a few years ago for car companies to add a warning device to signal a child left behind in the rear seat.

In late 1962, Sauer joined the Raymond Loewy/William Snaith consultancy, headquartered in New York, where clients included Formica, Home Components, and, last but not least, Studebaker. Sauer contributed to the interior of the early but iconic 1963 Avanti, while male colleagues rushed to design the exterior, for which Raymond Loewy would receive most of the credit anyway.

After leaving Loewy, Sauer worked for John Elmo Associates in New York and Dave Ellis Industrial Design Associates in Columbus, Ohio. Ellis is noted for their work on the Airstream trailer.

From 1953 to 1978, Sauer exhibited and sold her fine arts in exhibitions and galleries located in New York at the world-renowned Bertha Schaefer Gallery, and at the prominent Detroit Institute of Art. She also exhibited at other venues across the country.

Sauer also served as an instructor while still working, and later, just prior to retirement, sharing her knowledge and experience with the next generation of artists at area colleges, including the Columbus College of Art and Design, Highland Park Junior College, Macomb Community College, Henry Ford Community College, and CCS.

Julie Sabit

Margaret Sauer's corporate automotive portfolio and other pieces of fine arts are featured in *Damsels in Design: Women Pioneers in the Automotive Industry, 1939–1959* (Schiffer Books, 2018).

SAUER'S JOURNEY

Margaret Elizabeth "Peggy" Sauer was born on March 2, 1925, one of four children, to Kathleen and Joseph Sauer. She had three brothers—Donald, Richard, and Norbert.

Sauer grew up in Detroit, Michigan—better known as Motor City. The only girl in the household, she was very close to her mother, Kathleen. She attended more than one high school, but Southeastern High School stands out.

At some point in time, Sauer's father, Joseph, worked dredging the North Channel of Harsens Island in Lake St. Clair. While she was a small child, the family bought a cottage on the island, near the channel. Many fond family memories of stays on the island would prompt Sauer to buy a cottage of her own years later. Sadly, the cottage would turn out to be infested with termites and lead to heartache, and it was stressful for her to keep and maintain it.

Sauer still had a special bond and enjoyed just being on that island; her brother Richard would later inherit the cottage. After her father passed away, Sauer took special care of her mother, as many daughters do. They moved for a period of time to Columbus, Ohio, where Sauer became a professor at the Columbus College of Art and Design; both Peg Sauer and her mom became competitive in ceramics. It was a great mother-daughter bonding time until Kathleen passed away in 1974.

Growing up, Sauer bonded with an uncle, and she was made welcome in the garage out back, learning about machinery and tools. She would later prove to be quite masterful with the tools of her craft, which would include implements to work with wood, metal, stone, or clay—it did not matter.

SAUER JOINS SAMUEL CASHWAN

In 1933, the gallery of the Society of Arts and Crafts, in Detroit, according to a posting by the College for Creative Studies for the school, gained national attention as one of the first art institutions to recognize the automobile as an art form. Sauer would enroll at the Society of Arts and Crafts, later renamed the College of Creative Studies, in 1942.

Sauer would study under sculptor Sam Cashwan, a Jewish artist who emigrated from Russia, served in the army, and studied under sculptor Antoine Bourdelle at the École des Beau-Arts. While his figure sculpture was angular, to coincide with the architectural trends of the era, Sauer sought to develop her own style and explored three-dimensional design abstractly.

Cashwan joined General Motors as a designer following his service during World War II and remained until 1961. He would have been on hand to recommend and welcome Sauer in 1955. From 1944 to 1948, Sauer enrolled at Wayne State as an undergraduate in fine arts and later at the Cranbrook Academy of Art. She would later return to study in the graduate program at Wayne State. G. Alden Smith, professor emeritus at Wayne State, spent many hours with Sauer and described her work:

> The strength and forcefulness of Peg's work, her responsiveness to the inherent qualities of the material she chose, whether stone, wood, meal, or clay, are immediately, almost insistently apparent. ...

> The warmth and sensuous surfaces of wood are exploited as she shapes forms boldly, exposing inner surfaces of compelling subtlety while retaining the enfolding structural integrity of their outer surface. In contrast to the largely introspective nature of her wood forms, those in steel are aggressively dynamic growth-like forms that suggest the interplay of directional forces a wide range of ideas and symbols. Her forms in clay, both the tube-like forms as well as those more consciously modeled, express an almost timeless quality, occasionally archaic or primitive in feeling, yet at the same time strongly identifies with the sensitivity and the drama which are important components of today's modes of expression.

In 1946, Sauer sculpted *Bird* from limestone. While the majority of stone today would be cleared by using machine tools, early sculptresses would have used a hammer, chisels, rifflers, rasps, files, and sand papers. In 1947, she made an abstract wood sculpture by using lignum vitae, a hard, dense imported wood used for mallets. She also sculpted *Mother and Child* from the same material.

CRANBROOK BECKONS SAUER

In the same year that Sauer was born, George Booth, a Detroit newspaper baron and philanthropist, approached Eliel Saarinen, the Finnish architect teaching at the University of Michigan, with the intention of building an art academy. The result was the construction of a large complex on 319 acres in Bloomfield Hills, Michigan. The Academy of Art was officially recognized in 1932. The huge, woodsy campus, once a farm belonging to Booth, would later include numerous buildings, gardens, fountains, streams, row houses, and sculptures. There is no question that Margaret would later feel at home here.

While early design and architectural students assisted with the design of buildings and furniture for the campus, the BFA program was born out of the personal interests of Booth and Saarinen. Both were advocates of the Arts and Crafts movement in America and believed that craftsmanship could overpower the tasteless, mass-produced products being dumped on the American public.

By enrolling at Cranbrook after graduating from Wayne State, Sauer was given the opportunity to study under ceramics instructor Maija Grotell, sculptor William McVey, and designer Richard Thomas. She was also encouraged to spend one-day sessions with any faculty of her choosing, as long as she prepared and cleaned up her workspace. There is no doubt that she chose to spend some time with Marianne Strengell Hammarstrom.

With an avid interest in pottery, Sauer and many others gravitated to Grotell, a highly respected ceramicist. Grotell was invited to design the face of decorative bricks during Saarinen's contract to build the GM Technical Center. Carefully chosen coatings color the bricks outside buildings and the dome. At some point in time, Grotell hired McVey's wife to assist her. As a student of Grotell, Peggy would master the potter's wheel and develop glazes.

Sauer also studied sculpture with McVey. His campus sculpture of a group of birds in flight welcomes visitors to one of Cranbrook's lower schools.

Other well-qualified instructors guided Sauer. Richard Thomas, Peggy's silversmithing instructor, was born in Marion Center, Pennsylvania; received a degree in art education from Pennsylvania State College; and taught in the public schools before entering the US Army after Pearl Harbor. Thomas graduated with an MFA in 1948 and was invited to reestablish the metalsmithing

Raku ceramics, unknown date. *Collection of Julie Sabit; courtesy of Doug Didia*

department, which he headed from 1948 to 1984. Thomas later wrote a book titled *Metalsmithing for the Artist-Craftsman*, in which he introduced numerous tools and methods with photo illustrations. Throughout his career, his main interest involved the design and construction of liturgical elements for the college's church. While some students, including Suzanne Vanderbilt, went on to design and build religious objects, others favored sculpture and crafts.

Campus photos of this era capture a group of women behind an enormous loom and the ceramics studio of Grotell, who was a grandmother to her followers. Sculpture students could work in clay, stone, wood, and metal. Early on, Margaret would likely consider herself a sculptress or potter. Her work would later appear in exhibitions set up by the Detroit Institute of Arts, Wayne State University, and the Columbus Museum of Art.

At some point in time, Margaret would enroll in the master's degree program at Wayne State University; she likely attended in the evening after work, since GM was always happy to pick up the tab for additional education. She was the recipient of an MFA. Highly educated, and with a world of experience, Sauer would teach in a number of community colleges—Henry Ford Community College and Macomb among them. She also taught at the College of Creative Studies.

From 1953, before entering industry, until 1978, Sauer exhibited and sold her fine arts at the world-renowned Bertha Schaefer Gallery. Materials archived for Schaefer include letters written to her by Marcel Duchamp and Pablo Picasso. In 1962, Sauer entered the Morris Gallery, also in New York. Her work was also shown at the Detroit Institute of Art, Ohio State University, Wayne State, Henry Ford College, and Otterbein College in Westerville, Ohio.

GM STYLING'S ELITE: "DAMSELS OF DESIGN"

In 1955, Margaret received an offer of employment from General Motors Styling—perhaps with a referral from Sam Cashman, who worked there—and signed on with other women. She was the first of six women referred to as the Damsels of Design by GM marketing.

The most recognition of Sauer's industrial design abilities would come from the Feminine Shows of 1957 and 1958. In 1957, Sauer was invited to design a show car based on the Oldsmobile Ninety-Eight Holiday Coupe, named the Mona Lisa, and the Oldsmobile Chartreuse.

For the 1958 Feminine Show, Sauer redesigned the interior of the Oldsmobile Super 88 Convertible—the Rendezvous—and the Oldsmobile Carousel station wagon. In addition to the interior, women also created decorative trunks and matching suitcases. At this time, women proposed inventions that we would not see featured on cars for decades. New metallic colors, leathers, and custom-designed fabrics were incorporated. Sauer also used fabrics designed by Marianne Strengell Hammarstrom, a professor she met at the Cranbrook Academy of Art. A more in-depth study of theses show cars and their features appears in *Damsels of Design:*

The 1958 Oldsmobile Carousel Station wagon designed for the Feminine Show by Margaret Sauer featured an array of elastic bands and a magnetic seat back. Sauer also proposed a device to secure the rear openings to protect children from exiting the vehicle unexpectedly. *General Motors*

Women Pioneers in the Automotive Industry, 1939–1959.

A feature way ahead of its time, Sauer created a panel behind the front seats. The magnetized seat back featured elastic bands to hold toys. Bungee cords are even more ubiquitous today.

She also proposed a switch to shut off the power windows and doors in the back seat, to prevent children from exiting form the rear. It took until 1990 for NHTSA to create laws about this very invention.

In the late 1950s, Sauer also spent time in the Buick interiors studio. She likely contributed to the Buick Flamingo concept, based on a 1960 Invicta. Cars featuring decorative tops with patterns were designed and exhibited at a Motorama.

In 1958, an Oldsmobile magazine, *Olds Rocket Circle* (vol. 3, no. 2), featured an article titled "The Feminine Influence," introducing new color effects and new refinements. The article noted that designers can select colors from the 3,800 chips on display, and charts summarized the preferences of buyers.

SAUER MEETS RAYMOND LOEWY

The distinguished Raymond Loewy, who was recognized for his design of the Hupmobile, began his association with Studebaker in 1935.

There was no doubt that Loewy was drawn to the products of the Cadillac Division, of which Peggy would become a part of in the mid-1950s. While he found the inside and size of Cadillac cars attractive even for his own use, he hated the ostentatious fins and chrome that came with it. Regardless of his opinion, the iconic 1959 Cadillac is still a favorite of collectors today.

In 1943, even before Margaret joined the Cadillac studio, Loewy purchased a tan Cadillac convertible with a lush tan cowhide interior and rebuilt its body, utilizing a New York coach builder. Loewy replaced the heavy grillwork with a light aluminum panel in which he punched a large number of holes, which dominated the car visually from the front. On the front of the hood, he replaced a Frigidaire ornament with a gold-plated escutcheon in the center of a circle. The heavy front bumper, with a large bumper guard assembly and huge fog lights, completed the front. A circular ring about 5 inches in diameter affixed to the front of the side door, five louvers behind the front wheel well, and a rear wheel cover dominated visually from the side.

By 1959, Cadillac had introduced its largest tail fins ever, in an effort to stay ahead of the market. Having joined the Cadillac studio, Margaret was in the interior group at Cadillac at this time. Loewy was so annoyed by tail fins that he took a series of photographs of them as his toy poodle wandered in and out of sight. Loewy purchased a 1959 Cadillac that he shipped to France to use as a chauffeur-driven car for his daughter.

Detesting chrome and bulk, he proceeded to rip off the front and rear ends of the car, which he described as 150 pounds of junk, and redesigned the body. While it may have been inventive, after removing the bullet-like lights from the center of the large tail fins, he added them in grooves just behind and above the rear wheel wells.

This redesign created extra luggage compartments in the front and rear of the car. The tan interior remained intact.

In late 1962 or early 1963, Margaret joined Loewy in the Avanti Studio. Loewy's team, which consisted of John Epstein, Tom Kellogg, and Robert Andrews, designed the exterior of the 1963 Studebaker Avanti. Andrews also contributed to the 1948 Hudson and Willys Jeepster. Kellogg is credited with the design concept; however, Andrews sculpted the scale model and much of the full size—the clay is owned by the Smithsonian. The interior of the Avanti, like the exterior, was clean and perhaps straightforward.

Loewy contended that the vanity glove box was his idea and came out in 1951. We do not know which of his original artists designed it. If this is the case, Margaret would have upgraded it and contributed to or designed the seating and door panels.

Loewy has been criticized for taking credit for the designs of his staff and signing their drawings. Avanti drawings have been sold at auction and were labeled using the Loewy office stamp—a group of boxes in the corner used by most draftspeople.

After leaving the automobile industry, Sauer would pursue an educational career serving Columbus College of Art and Design, Highland Park Junior College, and Henry Ford Community College in Dearborn, Michigan.

A MENTOR AND TEACHER

Sauer's training was so diverse that she could teach just about anything, starting with an A for art or D for design or S for sculpture. Perhaps teachers learn most when both planning and executing lessons. At some point in time, Sauer noted that in order to keep her teaching skills sharp in the classroom, she needed to draw on the outside. While it is difficult to create a handsome new product, consider the skills called upon to capture the human figure in proper proportion and with proper foreshortening from a variety of angles.

From 1964 to 1967, Sauer taught Product Design, Life Drawing, and Sculpture at the Columbus College of Art and Design in Ohio.

From 1967 to 1968, she replaced a faculty member at Highland

Park Junior College on a sabbatical who taught Basic Design, Basic Drawing, and Art History.

In 1968, Sauer built the "GATES," a welded metal construction inspired by Marguerite "Peggy" Guggenheim. On one of Sauer's many trips to Europe, she visited Peggy Guggenheim at a small island in Venice. While there, Sauer took notes of the gates and was inspired to build her own creative version when she returned home to continue teaching.

From 1968 to 1982, the year of her retirement, she taught Basic Design I and II, Life Drawing, Sculpture, Art Appreciation, and Ancient Art History.

From 1983 to 1982, Sauer taught at Macomb Community College and the College for Creative Studies. Top professionals, who addressed the students vying for positions in the automotive industry or seeking to upgrade their skills, spent evenings here.

Former students appreciated her efforts on their behalf, Phyllis Walrad noted:

In her classes there was a wonderful student-teacher relationship, and as long as students were serious, there was no end to the lengths Peg would go to help them. Serious students sought her out and her classes were always full, and though she was not known as an easy teacher, she was always highly regarded. Thus hundreds of students have had their skills and talents developed and their lives enriched through the endeavors of Peg Sauer.

These were night classes in which students with a wide range of talents, ages, and interests were enrolled. It was great how well she could relate to and help each one. At one end of the spectrum were those like myself, just beginning and struggling, and at the other end were students with experience and talent, such as one I remember who was a medical illustrator with a New York agent and illustrating for major medical accounts. Peg was able to provide guidance to meet the range of our needs.

Margaret Sauer, who lost her battle with cancer at age sixty-one, left the art world way too early.

A retrospective featured the drawings, design work, and sculptures of Margaret Sauer. *Collection of Julie Sabit; courtesy of Doug Didia*

JEANETTE (FIORAVERA) LINDER ROBERTS

The day they were married, Jeanette and Peter were invited to join General Motors in Warren, Michigan. The bridegroom notes, "Jeanette did not even know how to drive, but there was a big public-relations effort, started by Harley Earl, to add to a group marketing dubbed 'The Damsels of Design.'"[1]

Peter Linder, speaking about his former wife, Jeanette Linder Roberts (1935-2022)

Jeanette designed the first lighted vanity mirror and this invention was ignored for years. Many of today's customers won't buy a vehicle today without one. *General Motors.*

CAREER HIGHLIGHTS

Jeanette Fioravera graduated from Pratt Institute in 1957 alongside Marjorie Pohlmann and her future husband, Peter Linder. She, Pohlmann, and four other women who graduated in 1955 composed GM's original Damsels of Design. Jeanette missed out on participating in the 1957 Feminine Show since she had not yet graduated.

Jeanette Linder designed the Impala Martinique for the 1958 Feminine Show and set the standard for Chevrolet color and trim for well into the future. She also proposed a large, lighted vanity mirror on both sides of the car. This technology would not arrive in the marketplace for years and was indispensable when it did.

Linder also worked on selecting or designing color and trim for production Buicks and Chevrolets.

Linder also designed a stunning one-off 1958 Buick Limited convertible called the Wells Fargo for western films and television personality Dale Robertson. Used by the actor for almost thirty years before his death, it has since been part of Bortz Auto collection, as well as in the stables of Wally Rank and Erich Traber. In 2018, RM Auctions valued the car at around $300,000.

A thorough presentation of Linder's artwork is included in *Damsels in Design: Women Pioneers in the Automotive Industry, 1939–1959* (Schiffer Books, 2018).

BIOGRAPHICAL NOTES[2]

Whereas Jeanette's parents were born in northern Italy, Jeanette and her identical twin sister, Jeanine, were born in the United States. The twins had an older sister, Elaine. At this time, Americans were recovering from the Great Depression and were promised relief in the second phase of President Roosevelt's New Deal.

Mother Jean had an eye for fashion and as a dress designer created patterns for a firm in the garment district in New York City. After visits to Bergdorf Goodman and other high-end stores, Jean would take note of the construction of clothing and create her own versions of these designs at her workplace. She would continue to work to assist with family expenses.

Jeanette's father, Jockamo Fiorentino Fioravera, would have some issues upon entering through Ellis Island. When the customs agents finally finished with his paperwork, they told him his name was now Jack. But things weren't that simple for a young Jeanette.

The Linder twins are identical.

The name Fioravera was hard to pronounce and harder for people to remember. After separating from her husband, Peter Linder, many years later, she appropriated her cousin's last name—Roberts—instead of reverting to her maiden name, which saved a lot of time for everyone. Jeanette's father was a cook and ran a restaurant.

The twin girls attended elementary, junior high, and high school in Leonia, New Jersey. The young pair would fashion clay figures and enjoy drawing even before registering for kindergarten. Jeanette's drawings would be featured in the newspaper at Leonia Elementary School. Enrolled in the usual art courses in high school, Jeanette mentioned enjoying capturing the outdoors in watercolor with her art teacher outside the school building. Fresh air seemed to invite freedom, which enhanced creativity.

The twins graduated from Leonia High School in 1952. While their sister studied at the Grand Central School of Art, the twins took note of Pratt Institute in Brooklyn, New York. It was ranked as a top school in the East. Jeanette worked as a typist for Robert Gair in New York City to raise money for tuition. Completing their first year in the workplace, the twins saved every penny they earned to be able to afford their first semester. Jeanette would later work summers in Catskill resorts and New Hampshire to afford the expensive tuition attached to a private-college education.

During the first two years, Jeanette and her sister commuted from their home in Leonia. Later moving to Brooklyn, the sisters found housing in one of the ubiquitous brownstones on Washington Avenue. They spent two years with a helpful Irish landlord who kept his eye on them. Jeanette's boyfriend, Peter, was housed in a dorm built in a park across from the school. It was really an old army barracks abandoned after the war.

In 1950, the Pratt Program had gone from a three-year certificate course to a four-year degree program. Alexander Kostellow, who headed the department, would add humanities courses, history courses, and economics studies to the curriculum.

In 1953, both sisters matriculated. Jeanette would learn about industrial design from a display of products in a lit showcase in the Main Building, while her sister was more interested in the illustrations on view. After considering the presentation, Jeanette recalls, "I thought these designs belonged in the Museum of Modern Art." Coincidentally, the Metropolitan Museum of Art exhibited the chair design of another Pratt student—Charles Pollock—at this time.

Jeanette would find Alexander Kostellow's first-year course in the auditorium fascinating, "He made the lectures come alive." She remembers a large roll of newsprint used for charcoal drawings. Designer and educator Bill Katavolos, recipient of the Rowena Reed Kostellow Award, would later note that the use of a roll of paper would enable designers to express themselves more fluently.

Peter notes, "During our years at Pratt we had little time for leisure. We were lucky to get to bed before 2:00 a.m. and sometimes were still awake in time to make a visit to the Fulton Fish Market to watch them unload their catch."

"When we finished the first year," Peter Linder adds, "Alexander Kostellow died prematurely while setting up a student program with GM one summer." Colleagues and students alike suffered through depressions. Kostellow's wife, Rowena Reed, who was devastated, would continue to spread his philosophies for a good fifty years.

In the second year, Jeanette was presented with convexity and concavity problems by Rowena Reed Kostellow. The concavity problem required students, who examined positive form in the convexity problem, to understand negative space in a form. The very sophisticated relationships in form were successfully examined by Peter Linder. Students today still struggle with these difficult assignments.

As a freshman or sophomore, Jeanette enjoyed putting together wire designs with a soldering gun. For this project, Rowena Reed Kostellow required students to differentiate between and use curves effectively to train the eye in creating a three-dimensional composition. Slow curves, fast curves, and independent curves were incorporated.

In the third or fourth year, Peter remembers sketching and designing products, including a slide projector. At this time, *Industrial Design Magazine* published its first issue.

Students also designed and illustrated interiors; Jeanette's sketches were outstanding.

Her contemporary design and model for a small toy vehicle, created in response to a Pratt assignment, was way ahead of its time visually, unlike the usual symmetrical toy. At some point, psychologists concluded that young children related to simple forms more than complicated ones, and pull toys were introduced in the 1950s. Fisher-Price's earliest ones were made of wood. Jeanette's modern-looking wood model was drilled out and painstakingly turned on the wood lathe with gouges in the basement of the engineering building. The design was so good that her teachers sent it to Japan to promote the industrial design program at Pratt.

As a junior, Jeanette explored a number of modern designs for the Open Kitchen project. The women arriving two years earlier designed chefless kitchens.

In 1960, GM featured more-modern kitchens in its Motorama Exhibit. It was evident that Frigidaire and others manufactured appliances on the basis of the exhibit, including the sliding cooktop stove. Today, another large company is manufacturing and selling cabinets using these enduring designs.

Alexander Kostellow had created the Experimental Design Laboratory at Pratt so that representatives of major companies could work with students on mutual projects. Monsanto, Sears Roebuck, Shell Oil, Elgin Watch, and Gorham Silver would also participate. While neither Peter nor Jeanette would directly participate in this program, General Motors participants could review the work of other students on display in the department. GM featured modern, even futuristic, kitchens in its spectacular Motorama Exhibits held through 1961.

The design department, however, was down the hall from the home economics department, which was kept impeccably clean. The plaster footprints, although they might look like flour on the carefully waxed floor, led to the industrial design department, and the designers were told that this could not continue.

CAREER AND MARRIAGE GO TOGETHER

The day they were married, Jeanette and Peter were invited to join General Motors in Warren, Michigan.

Peter Linder notes, "The newspapers, including the Detroit Free Press, featured our story, and Look magazine photographers packed our tiny apartment. We were the first married couple to work at General Motors. The reversal of roles was even more newsworthy. I was hired by Frigidaire to design kitchen appliances, and Jeanette was hired to design automobiles and assigned to Chevrolet."

He continues, "My wife did not know a Chrysler from a Chevrolet." However, we all realize that Jeanette was not expected to design mechanical parts. Furthermore, one can appreciate a beautiful form without identifying it by name. Chevrolet's new 1957 Belairs, easily recognized by a conservative fin with an aluminum side-ribbed insert, could not be manufactured fast enough. The iconic sedans, coupes hardtop, and Nomad wagon are sought after by collectors now more than ever.

Peter notes, "When we got out there, we were blown away by the GM Technical Center—a Saarinen masterpiece. The styling building and dome to the right of it were beautiful. The floating staircase in the lobby of Styling was exquisite." He continues, "There was a pale-green Russian olive tree against the bright-orange glazed-brick wall. Everything there was spotless and beautifully maintained."

Of course, there were some issues early on that had to be addressed. Peter notes, "Designers in the studios with a southern exposure complained about the heat buildup from the sun. In the winter, the humidity was kept very low, because the aluminum window mullions would freeze up. I couldn't believe they complained. They moved from a dumpy factory-like building in downtown Detroit."

While Peter joined three others in Frigidaire designing refrigerators, Jeanette was assigned to the Chevrolet studio under Bob Bartholomew.

INNOVATIONS TRANSFORM THE CHEVROLET IMPALA MARTINIQUE

This was an exciting era, and Chevrolet would develop a concept car based using the 1958 Chevrolet Impala to be included in the Feminine Show. It was dubbed the Chevrolet Impala Martinique. Jeanette would become responsible for designing the interior and trunk of the car.

Perhaps the most significant upgrade was Jeanette's innovative design for a lighted-visor vanity mirror. Most customers today still look for this feature and would not buy a car without it; manufacturers like to reduce the size of it to save production costs. Jeanette created a "large oval" turned on its side. Unlike the downsized mirrors used today, the curve at the top of the mirror captured the shape of a head. Jeanette notes that she worked closely with GM engineers creating the lights at the sides of the mirror. The large bulbs flooded the cabin with light.

TEXTILE DESIGN

Jeanette's textile design is featured in the front of six damsels with Harley Earl in the iconic 1958 photograph.

When it came to providing a suitable fabric for the seats, doors, and suitcases, Jeanette notes, "I was asked to design something that would just look nice—and be hospitable, you might say—something homey looking. I just like stripes; I thought they were maybe Italian looking since I am Italian as my parents were Italian. The stripes were beautiful."

STORAGE SYSTEMS

Jeanette notes that Chevrolet wanted her to make use of all the space in the car. While she designed containers inside, she also visited the trunk, which she equipped with side storage pockets and a container attached to the underside of the lid. Extra storage anywhere would be appreciated even more so if it were a convertible and the people were on their way to the shore. She covered expressly designed luggage with the interior fabric.

Linder covered a set of luggage with the same exquisite textile. *General Motors*

THE BUICK STUDIO

A year later, Jeanette was reassigned to the Buick Studio under the direction of George Moon: "I thought he was an excellent studio head. He never imposed his ideas on me. He was encouraging. Moon was quite a pleasant person, always smiling and nice to work for. He dressed beautifully. He was a handsome man too—nice looking."

THE WELLS FARGO BUICK

Dale Robertson was the star of NBC's popular series *Tales of Wells Fargo*, which was sponsored by Buick. One day, Robertson was invited to a Buick dealership. He arrived in an old truck and left in a stunning Glacier White 1958 Buick Limited custom convertible, complete with a curved windshield. Heavy walnut inserts on the exterior were emblazoned with the words "Wells Fargo" on both rear quarter panels of the car. A small longhorn

The Wells Fargo custom car for Robertson was based on a 1958 Buick convertible. *General Motors*

steer head was attached to the V emblem just above a massive chrome-plated grille. Powered by a 300 hp, 364-cubic-inch OHV V-8 and Flight Pitch Dynaflow automatic transmission, this car had ample power. It also featured Air Poise suspension and air-conditioning.

Linder completely transformed the interior. Bucket seats up front were upholstered in rich-brown, hand-tooled hides. Natural calfskin carpet covered the floor. The upper portion of the rear seats had ornate tooled designs in rectangles. The center console just below the instrumental panel was designed to accept two Winchester rifles with carved stocks—nonoperating—and there they sat. Small holsters at the bottom of each door housed Robertson's pearl-handled .38 Colt six-shooters.

Linder notes, "Robertson had sent me a little drawing. It was so complicated. It included a number of diamonds and sewing. When I finally finished, he did write to GM and said he liked it—it was nice to hear from him—but I had left by that time."

Robertson drove the Wells Fargo Buick cross-country on sponsored tours and continued to drive it for almost thirty years before he died. It has become a valuable collectable, fetching in the range of $300,000 at a 2018 RM auction.

GO HOME

In 1959, Bill Mitchell took over for Harley Earl, and things would never be the same. He is said to have stopped his predecessor's women's movement in its tracks. He further sought to ban women from the exterior designer studios and did so.

Jeanette saw the writing on the wall, became pregnant, and felt it would interfere with her being a professional. By the third month, she decided to leave, but they wanted her back after the baby was born. She never returned, since she felt it would be difficult to get suitable childcare. Today, she believes that there is much more evidence of good childcare, allowing mothers to work outside the home more readily. Her daughter, Andrea, was born, and she later graduated from the University of Michigan. Her son, Steven, following in his parents' footsteps, graduated from the College for Creative Studies, a school to which he is very loyal. He designs furniture for medical professionals. In 1986, Jeanette and Peter were divorced.

FINE ARTS

Always passionate about art, Jeanette continued to explore her creativity, primarily in oils.

Peter notes: "Jeanette's intelligence is appreciated and her free spirit loved by everyone. She's more interested in the big picture than the details."

MARTHA JAYNE VAN ALSTYNE

The Saarinens were young in spirit. Although different ages, the three of us were the same age when it came to creativity.[1]

M.J. Van Alstyne (1923–2015); Van Alstyne met the Saarinens, the architects who designed the GM Technical Center and the Cranbrook buildings, at the Cranbrook Academy of Art.

Jayne kept her eye on the Corvette studio. *Collection of author*

CAREER HIGHLIGHTS

M. Jayne Van Alstyne served in a number of positions following a diverse education that focused initially on ceramics and later industrial design.

Early in her career, she joined Gilbert Rohde Associates; Rohde also provided midcentury modern furniture design for Herman Miller.

Van Alstyne later taught in a number of colleges; she was instrumental in establishing the industrial design programs at Michigan State University and Montana State University.

In 1955, Van Alstyne joined General Motors Styling for a fourteen-year period, during which she designed innovative appliances that she received numerous patents for. A desirable stacked washer/dryer of her design was manufactured for small kitchens, and a rotating oven was well received. In 1958, she became studio head for the Frigidaire Research and Development Division and, in 1965, was promoted to assistant director of GM Styling, within the Safety and Human Performance Group. She resigned in 1969 when she was denied a promotion. She was not the first woman to take this route.

Later, after accepting a teaching position at Cornell University, Van Alstyne conducted research on the design of kitchens for the handicapped. In 1972, she accepted a position as head of the Industrial Design Department at Montana State University.

Van Alstyne received numerous awards for ceramics. Today, her works are in the collections of museums, galleries, and corporations, including the Detroit Art Museum, the Cranbrook Academy of Art, the Everson Museum of Art, the Stephens Art Center, and the GM Heritage Collection.

An extensive portfolio of Van Alstyne's design work and patents appears with her extended biography in *Damsels in Design: Women Pioneers in the Automotive Industry, 1939–1959*, the award-winning book published by Schiffer Books in 2018.

BIOGRAPHICAL NOTES

Jayne was born on April 11, 1923, in Delaware, Ohio. Her father was a basketball and golf coach for Michigan State, and her mother dabbled in real estate and interior design. When her father brought home a doll for her, she rejected it and told him she preferred a ball. Her mother rolled her eyes. In elementary school, Jayne noted, "I made a little chair out of wood—no problem for me." She added, "I made a pushcart and added a steering wheel to it so I could turn it and go down a hill. It was a little car just for me."[2] An avid skier, Jayne would continue to glide down hills for the rest of her life.

Jayne later noted, "My parents never had a daughter; they had a son."

In high school, Jayne developed a keen interest in ceramics. Dad was supportive, and Jayne purchased an electric motor, firebrick, and the chimney adhesive required for fabricating a kiln. She built her own ceramics studio at the rear of the garage and continued to master the formulas needed to mix glazes.

After her high school classes, Jayne would bike to the campus of the Cranbrook Art Museum and Academy of Art, some distance away. Her father eventually allowed her to use his car—a clunky Chevrolet sedan that was in sharp contrast to the coupes she would later acquire on her own. Jayne would ultimately enjoy driving a series of her own Corvettes. (Who wouldn't?)[3] Her first was a 1961 shiny black roadster. Her sale of this to a colleague enabled her to purchase a 1963 Daytona blue split-rear-window coupe.

As Jayne finished high school, in a kind of fortuitous decision, Eliel Saarinen, the noted architect and the director of Cranbrook's Art Academy, invited Maija Grotell to join the faculty as head of the ceramics department. As a teacher, Grotell emphasized the use of ceramics as a means of artistic expression. There is no question that she would serve as a role model for Jayne.

Jayne would note, "She was like having a grandmother. If anyone came around who had talent, she took them under her wing. I learned a lot from her. She was very good, intelligent. She knew her chemistry. She was smart, talented, and very kind."[4]

Grotell would experiment with glazes, some used on architectural bricks, for years. She discovered that she could use chromium and iron in place of uranium to produce a brilliant-orange glaze. Many of her students, Jayne included, were responsible for the establishment of ceramics programs at universities. Grotell held the chair position at Cranbrook from 1938 until her retirement in 1966. After attending Cranbrook (1941–1942) and Pratt Institute (1942–1945), Jayne would later complete studies at Alfred University.[5] It would take a lifetime of study and experimentation for Jayne to keep master the development in the ingredients of clays and decoration—glazes form a chemical bond among clays, silica, and oxides when a piece of ceramic is fired.

In 1949, Jayne taught a course in the summer school titled Raw Materials for Ceramics at Alfred University, and by 1950 she prepared an interior and industrial design program for Montana State University. While living in the Detroit area, she also taught at Oakland University and the Detroit Society of Arts and Crafts. In 1969, she served as an assistant professor at Cornell University, where she taught industrial design, human factors, and ceramics. She conducted research on kitchen design for use by people with disabilities. She would later return to Montana State University to manage the Department of Professional Design. It should be noted that she designed its nondenominational Danforth Chapel, including its furnishings and stained-glass windows.

18TH CERAMIC NATIONAL EXHIBITION

In 1954, Jayne submitted a 10-inch-high pot to the Jury of Selection and Awards for the Bozeman, Montana, area for inclusion in the prestigious 18th Ceramic National Exhibition in Syracuse, New York. This show was sponsored by the Syracuse Museum of Fine Arts (now the Everson Museum of Art); outside corporations provided prize monies. Her stoneware piece, which garnered an award, featured iron slip decoration. This honor was truly a highlight of her career. A guide to the show reads, "Has genuine spontaneity in its design of light gray swirls on brown, suggesting a living folk art at its best."[6] Jayne's pot is in the permanent collection of the museum.

Cranbrook attracted a host of other passionate artists and architects with whom Jayne would socialize and study. She was welcomed by Eliel Saarinen and his son, Eero, too: "The Saarinens were young in spirit. Although different ages, the three of us were the same age when it came to creativity. They took me under their wing. I audited their graduate and postgraduate courses beside the architects. The classes contained about a dozen students—they were small. Many of the architects were studying city planning. They brought models of multiple housing and factories. If I didn't show up, they would send someone looking for me. When I walked into a class that was doing something interesting, I helped out too."[6]

At some point in time, Jayne studied weaving. After Saarinen's wife, Loja, stepped down in 1937 as the first head of the Department of Weaving and Textile Design at Cranbrook, Marianne Strengell,

daughter of a Finnish architect, took over the program. Later in her career, Strengell was called upon to design the first textiles used by the Knoll Planning group, founded by Florence Knoll.

A German manufacturer, Hans Knoll, would visit the Saarinens on campus and fall in love with Florence Schust—sometimes referred to as a ward of the Saarinens. The couple would later take Knoll furniture to the top of the contract furniture industry. Even before the establishment of the planning group, Jayne worked with fabrics in the design of furniture for Knoll and would also assist Gilbert Rohde, the single designer who created furniture systems for Herman Miller in its infancy.

Jayne decided to relocate to New York City in 1942 to study in the Industrial Design Department at Pratt Institute; she audited some courses and registered for others, since Pratt did not offer bachelor's degrees until 1951. While at Pratt, Jayne studied with Alexander Kostellow and Rowena Reed Kostellow, as did most of the other Damsels of Design. After additional study from 1948 to 1950, she completed requirements for a BFA and MFA from the New York State College of Ceramics, Alfred University.

HOME APPLIANCES

Although Jayne had worked at J. W. Knapp Company, in charge of home planning, she joined GM Styling in 1955. Russ Dunbar likely headed Frigidaire at this time, and Mary Loring, who worked in the Exhibit Studio, was asked to assist Jayne in settling in. After sharing an apartment with Loring in Oak Park, they became lifelong friends, with Jayne outliving Loring. Jayne later found a two-story English Tudor, across from the golf course on Fourteen Mile Road.

Jayne started in the Frigidaire studios, where her contributions were significant. Colleague Dan Nelson noted that while experimenting with various handles for a refrigerator, she discovered that the handle should be large and firm for better control.

An early assignment required her to design a cooktop. Controls were roughed out and attached to the model. After six months, Jayne's work blossomed. Her design of a futuristic-style stove was perfect for the appliance show. Her advanced concepts group went on to create kitchen landscapes.

Martha Jane was selected to run the Advanced Frigidaire Studio. *Steve Wolken*

KITCHEN OF TOMORROW

Another significant project that debuted at a Motorama was dubbed the Kitchen of Tomorrow. The idea was to investigate and develop labor-saving, innovative appliances for homemakers. The kitchen layout included a number of devices run from two motor-driven central shafts. Standout innovations included mix and cooking centers, a sink and dishwasher island, a refrigerator center, and a planning center.

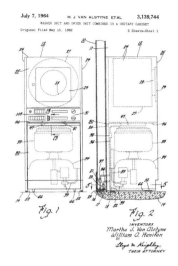

This side-by-side washer/ dryer was patented with many other appliances by designer Van Alstyne. *Courtesy of the US Patent and Trademark Office*

FUTURE PRODUCTS DIVISION

From 1960 to 1965, Jayne served as the studio head of Advanced Products for the Frigidaire Division of General Motors. At this time, Jayne recruited two designers for her team: Daniel Nelson, who graduated from Illinois Institute of Technology under the direction of Jay Doblin, and Keith Vreeland. It was noted that in 1957, Jayne had invented the "sheer look" as her designs hit the marketplace.

Her contributions were so far ahead of the times that they appear as though they were designed today. In many interviews, she described her philosophy. Kitchen appliances are like furniture and should be integrated within a household. She was against gaudy decoration and heavy chrome. Handles of appliances were light and elegant. Her integration of new technologies earned her numerous patents and awards.

At some point in time, a small publication titled *General Motors Presents Ideas for Living: A Display of Stimulating New Thoughts in Material and Methods for Home Decoration and Design* was produced. The display featured a refrigerator, an under-counter dishwasher, a food waste disposer, an automatic washer, the automatic dryer Delco-Heat, and other inventions.

However, the most-significant products included the Frigidaire Flair Range—Custom Imperial 40. The range highlighted a rollout cooktop, eye-height controls, see-level ovens, hand-high surface units, and the Flair automatic feature. This iconic product is still sought after today.

Another notable product was labeled the *Thermoelectric Refrigerator Study.* The designed unit would suffice for about 2 cubic feet of refrigeration. With this in mind, it was feasible to think of thermoelectric (TE) in terms of a mobile unit. Unit 1 consisted of an executive bar and refrigerator areas designed with some storage and an electrical outlet. It was styled like a piece of office furniture. Unit 2 consisted of a serving cart that included the refrigerator, warming trays, a hot plate, a work surface, and a tristorage area. Indoor and outdoor serving was explored.

On her résumé, Jayne listed eight more patents granted during her association with GM; these include the first stack-on washer dryer, the first portable dishwasher, a personal washer-dryer, a deep-well cooking system, a sink center, a thermoelectric refrigerator, a clean-up center, and an architectural panel system. Van Alstyne also designed an inventive rotatable oven that folded into an existing row of kitchen cabinets while not in use, leaving an empty countertop for the user.

JAYNE JOINS AUTO SAFETY AND HUMAN PERFORMANCE GROUP

From 1965 to 1969, Jayne served as the assistant director of styling within the safety and human performance group. Under her direction, designers explored the relationship of ergonomics to the driving task. This assignment would later lead to research in human factors for the Gallatin County of Health Department and Cornell's Gerontology Group, conducted in the 1970s and 1980s.

TITAN 90 TILT-CAB TRUCK

Around 1973, Chevrolet introduced the Titan 90, a continuation of a truck with a cab-over design. The entire cab pivoted forward in order to service the engine. Some of the units had steel tilt-cabs, and others aluminum tilt-cabs; some models were gas and others diesel. In terms of weight, the TW90, for example, had a GVW of 39,500 pounds. In the design of the driver's cockpit, Van Alystne's leadership was noticeable, and the brochure noted the improvements. The driver's environment was ahead of its time. Jayne and her group designed a wraparound console grouping instruments in modules, such as stoves, according to their function and frequency of use. From behind the adjustable-tilt steering column, the driver was able to monitor his rig with a minimum of eye movement. In additional to standard instruments, warning lights and buzzers indicated low air pressure, high coolant temperatures, and low coolant level.

In a career spanning over seventy years, Jayne also served as a consultant to William Lescaze (architect), Masonite Corporation, Simmons Furniture, Union Electric, and Lee Carpeting.

As noted earlier, Jayne received numerous honors for ceramics, and many of her works are housed in prominent collections. She sold her personal collection of ceramics by other artists, donating the proceeds to an animal shelter to memorialize her love of dogs.

The luxurious Cadillac Allegro was designed for the first Feminine Show in 1957. *General Motors*

SUZANNE E. VANDERBILT

Since there were other women willing to take a chance and drive out to General Motors in an old car and set up housekeeping, I decided, well, I'll try it. But, I think if I had to come alone, I would not have done it.

—Sue Vanderbilt (1933–1988), who drove out to Detroit with four other Pratt cohorts who would also be included in the group of six dubbed the Damsels of Design by GM marketers

CAREER HIGHLIGHTS

Suzanne Vanderbilt was a lifer. She joined General Motors Styling (later known as GM Design) one month after college graduation in 1955. The management seemed to feel that women had the potential to address every feature in an automobile that would appeal to women—color, fabric, and trim. Vanderbilt served as the first female head of an interiors studio in the automotive industry, leading the Chevrolet II Studio. Subsequently, as a coordinator across all studios, she worked with others to propose new products and new models and ensure the interchangeability of components.

After completing the Industrial Design Program at Pratt Institute, Vanderbilt headed to Detroit, Michigan, with a handful of other women classmates. Early on, Vanderbilt designed Chevrolet and Cadillac interiors. She designed a complete interior for the 1957 Chevrolet Belair Mademoiselle and contributed to the Belair Trieste, under the direction of H. D. Lauve, for the 1957 Feminine Show.

In 1957 and 1958, as the sole representative of Cadillac, she designed the 1957 Allegro and Elegante and 1958 Baroness and Saxony concepts; all were far more luxurious than the production models on which they were based.

Vanderbilt was granted a leave to be able to study in the Cranbrook Academy of Art's graduate program, majoring in silversmithing, but this would never lead to an assignment in an exterior design studio as she had hoped. Instead, William Mitchell demoted her when she returned to work. As an MFA student, she designed a number of silver implements used on the altar of a church. She also designed and patented a helmet for industrial workers. This led to her study of and interest in automobile accident crashes.

As designer and later as chair of the Human Factors group, Vanderbilt brought safety to the American worker, driver, and passenger.

When her early ideas for a safer automobile were developed and promoted, thousands of lives were saved. Modern versions of the LATCH (lower anchors and tethers for children) system and child safety seats similar to those proposed by Vanderbilt over fifty years ago are required by the National Highway Traffic Safety Administration (NHTSA) in all of today's vehicles. After consulting with a doctor and colleague, Vanderbilt also designed General Motors first driver's seat with lumbar adjustable controls to assist those with back conditions, and she holds the patent for it. Her designs for safer switches/knobs are also protected by patent.

During a lengthy career, Vanderbilt would go on to design or to manage the designers of the Vega, Monza, and Camaro/Firebird interiors. Produced in multiple styles, all of these award-winning products were mainstays for the Chevrolet Division.

We lost Vanderbilt prematurely at just fifty-five to breast cancer.

Vanderbilt's more detailed biography, with a fuller portfolio, is featured in *Damsels in Design: Women Pioneers in the Automotive Industry, 1939–1959* (Schiffer Books, 2018).

BIOGRAPHICAL NOTES

Suzanne Vanderbilt was born on August 23, 1933, in Mt. Vernon, New York, and was raised in Larchmont, an affluent village in Mamaroneck. She likely attended the Chatsworth Elementary School and expressed an early interest in the arts. Her mother sought to discourage her the best she could, but when a parent is against something, it makes it even more desirable. Drawing monopolized Suzanne's free time. Both she and her younger brother got a basic training on using a hammer and other basic tools in the basement from their dad. At some time during her childhood, Vanderbilt posed for a photograph in her Girl Scout uniform, and the image appeared in the newspaper; she was covered with merit badges signifying her mastery of skills.

When Vanderbilt reached Mamaroneck High School, she tried to pursue her interests—drawing and building. Like almost all of the other women after her, Vanderbilt was advised by administrators that the mechanical drawing and the auto mechanics classes were closed to her: "Women don't do that." This was a time when women wore skirts and dresses to school. Well into the 1960s, some women designers were forced to study these technical classes in evening programs; some fought their way into the drafting classes only with parental intervention.

Having no access to these male-oriented courses, Vanderbilt wondered why drafting was being taught by a woman at Mamaroneck High School. Suzanne studied Basic Lettering, in order to get the feel of using a T square and triangle. Her art teacher made some disparaging remarks at this time as well: "You'd better get married; don't go into art." She later added, "We'll give you a design project. Would you design a cutting board for me?" All of these comments led to hopelessness, and Vanderbilt did lots of posters, murals for student activities, and similar unclaimed projects. She graduated from high school in 1951 and explored her options.

The term "industrial design" was new to Vanderbilt. She notes that in the early fifties, she learned about it through a friend of her father's. She had told him that she had an interest in drawing and building things, from airplanes and boat models to scaled-down airports. Prior to researching the field, Vanderbilt thought that she might study medical illustration. Upon advice from her next-door neighbor, Rosalyn Frank, a Pratt alumna, Vanderbilt wrote a letter to the head of the art school, Mr. Boudreau, and submitted a "humble portfolio." The requirements for entrance also included the submission of a drawing of an iron, a piece of furniture, and the interior of your living room, and an illustration of an "exciting experience."

Vanderbilt noted the skills of her instructors, Alexander and Rowena Reed Kostellow: "They were very instrumental in keeping me interested because they were both excellent teachers, and Rowena urged me to go to GM." In order to show respect, most students addressed Rowena Kostellow by her maiden name—Miss Reed—for the rest of their lives.

In 1955, both Vanderbilt and the others entered a contest to design a chefless restaurant and made line illustrations in black ink. The designs were featured in a Mars outstanding-design series. After being selected as one of thirteen winners, Vanderbilt was contacted two years later by Geer, DuBois Inc., an advertising company that wished to publish her portrait.

About this time, Miss Reed engaged the women designers in a discussion. What ultimately convinced Vanderbilt to come to GM was this chat. Sue noted that Reed talked to about four or five of them and convinced them that this was a special opportunity.

In May 1955, GM launched their recruiters. Vanderbilt met Tom Christiansen from personnel and Dave Wheeler, a designer. She noted that the representatives were not young or old but had a rapport with students. Yet, they represented the biggest corporation in the country. Pratt did not have an automotive design or transportation department. However, after serving on a committee to establish a link with industry and attaining a high GPA, Suzanne received a scholarship in her junior year. Vanderbilt believed that companies were interested in the top industrial design graduates, and noted that it might have been because of the ideas that they had. The education was supportive of the creative spirit.

Perhaps a remark made by Miss Reed (Rowena Reed Kostellow) resonated and remained with all the female industrial design students: "Would you rather be designing silverware or polishing it?"

Suzanne noted, "Since there were other women willing to take a chance and drive out to General Motors in an old car and set up housekeeping, I decided, well, I'll try it. But, I think if I had had to come alone, I would not have done it. Christiansen and Wheeler said, 'Come on out. We have or might have something for you.'"

Vanderbilt was advised to report quickly, on July 5—one of the hottest days of the year—and drove out with Jan Krebs and Ruth Glennie; they were later joined by Dagmar Arnold. Along the way, Glennie would replace a shock absorber on the car, leaving it a little lopsided. The designers at this time still worked in the Argonaut Building, before Saarinen created the Technical Center on Van Dyke and Mound in Warren, Michigan.

Early on, some thought, "Well, this won't last." Vanderbilt was surrounded by accomplished illustrators, and she lacked the drawing training to express herself easily.

During this time, the female designers were looked upon as decorators by many. Some surmised that GM management viewed women as useful in designing features of interest to other women—car interiors. The men designed exteriors. It is unfortunate that the executives ignored the education of Pratt women, since they were highly trained in three-dimensional design, and some were even as good as or better than their male counterparts. It seems to have taken a number of years for the men to accept the competition, and in this era, some never did.

But there was a lot more than color trim in the interior of a vehicle. Designers learned from the ground up how to put a car together, with an emphasis on the seats and doors. Designers toured the plant responsible for assembling the iconic 1957 Chevrolet Belair—the exterior was designed under Claire Mackichan, who utilized the same chassis for a third year and ultimately created an iconic design.

Vanderbilt's elaborate interior for this car contrasted the simple one chosen for production.

In the studio, prototypes were made from sketches and quarter-scale drawings. Designers were not relegated to selecting just seats and doors, as some reporters seem to think. Vanderbilt did not have the opportunity to design instrument panels, but she did design components for them. However, her colleague Ruth Glennie was delegated the design of complete instrument panels. With cost objectives in mind, Suzanne designed components and suggested colors, new fabrics, leathers, and carpeting.

Vanderbilt was entrusted with the design of production cars, government cars for the US Army and Navy, and show cars at this time. Even George Moon, who headed the interiors area, noted that talented men and women had equal abilities to design automobiles.

While some designers worked in an orientation studio first, others did not. Vanderbilt received her orientation downtown in the Argonaut Building before moving to the new Technical Center in 1956. In an interview, she noted that she started out in the Chevrolet Studio under Henry de Ségur Lauve.

While the production 1957 Chevrolet was likely already on the market by 1956, the 1957 Bel Air Mademoiselle concept was photographed in May 1957 before the Feminine Show. Vanderbilt was in the Chevrolet Studio at this time, and it is more than likely that she contributed to the interior of this car and the Bel Air Trieste show car before reporting to Cadillac.

After a year, Vanderbilt was moved to Cadillac under Robert Scheelk, who had designed the famed spinner hubcap for the Olds Fiesta. When Scheelk was involved in an automobile accident, Vanderbilt assumed the duties as an assistant manager.

In 1957 and 1958, the executives at GM Styling invited the women in the building to participate in two Feminine Shows mounted in the dome exhibit center. To start, each lady was assigned a division for which to design show cars, but sometimes two women contributed to a car. Women were also involved in designing the exhibit space. While Vanderbilt, who had an early assignment in the Chevrolet Studio, contributed to the 1957 Belair, she was later the sole representative for Cadillac.

Vanderbilt was invited to meet with Eleanor Roosevelt shortly after the Tech Center was completed. *General Motors*

FEMININE SHOW CARS

In 1957, after completing the interior of the Chevrolet Belair Mademoiselle and contributing to the Trieste, Vanderbilt was assigned to Cadillac. Vanderbilt's 1957 Cadillac Allegro show car made its way to the lobby of the Styling Center for all to admire, and the Elegante exuded luxury.

In 1958, Vanderbilt's assignment included the design of new interiors for the Baroness and Saxony concepts. The exteriors of the production cars were exquisite to begin with. Vanderbilt continued to push the envelope. Vanderbilt's Baroness interior was subdued to let the passengers flaunt their own attributes, and featured black mouton carpet, a phone, and a pillow and lap robe in seal for rear seat passengers. In addition to luxurious styling, the Saxony also featured a secret compartment for an umbrella in the door panel.

J. M. Roche, the GM of Cadillac, was so impressed by the Baroness and Saxony that he wrote a letter calling the cars magnificent, and congratulating Vanderbilt.

Colleague Norm James and Vanderbilt formed their own photography club; both graduated from Pratt, where they developed an appreciation for photography. James designed the exterior of the Firebird III, and Jim Ewen the interior. Vanderbilt was later brought into the studio, but the concept car was already completed.

For the most part, James and Vanderbilt photographed nature when not in the studios. When Norm James finally left to diversity his career sometime later, Sue sent him a letter, which he still holds dear.

After serving GM for a few years, Suzanne took a leave of absence and registered in Cranbrook's graduate program to study silversmithing in 1963. Perhaps Vanderbilt felt that with an advanced knowledge of metalworking she could transfer to an exteriors studio. Eventually she realized that this was an impossible aim. One of the male designers noted that perhaps women should not be subjected to the foul language. It is rumored that Bill Mitchell, who replaced Earl as vice president of design, hated her leaving, thought he would never see her again, and demoted her when she returned. However, he both praised and distributed her written thesis.

The Cranbrook campus was and still is located in Bloomfield Hills, an affluent suburb near GM that is largely inhabited by automotive executives.

MASTER OF FINE ARTS

Requirements for the MFA in metalworking at Cranbrook would require a written thesis and the production of several objects related to a theme.

In her thesis document, Vanderbilt noted: "The purpose of this paper is to first briefly and simply re-examine the most basic elements of design observed in nature and man's world—examples

Vanderbilt designed and supervised the construction of the first substantial child seat over fifty years ago, in an effort to stabilize a child during an accident. It featured a shell, a seat belt system, a LATCH system, and even a seat protector. *Collection of the Cranbrook Art Museum; photo, Constance Smith*

of the order that can be seen by the naked eye. One needs to look, see, feel, read."

The thesis was broken down into four parts which included a package problem, a study of hand tools, the production of works in metalsmithing, and a study of Christian symbolism in liturgical art, emphasizing the Christian cross.

SAFETY HELMET PATENT

In 1968, Vanderbilt received a patent for a safety helmet designed for the American Safety Equipment Corporation. This idea was likely an outgrowth of her studies at Cranbrook. Helmet designers today continue to address rotational acceleration and the differing needs of football and motocross. Many modern bicycle helmets are constructed in the same way as the one she designed, and some of them even resemble her design.

Following graduation in 1965, Vanderbilt returned to work at General Motors. At an early age, she rose to senior designer, assistant chief designer, and finally chief designer, which meant she served as a studio head. She was the first woman to assume most of if not all of these positions. In addition to her work in production interiors, her most-notable designs included her early exploration of ergonomics and safety.

CHEVROLET PRODUCTION

As time progressed, Suzanne moved to the production Chevrolet studios, where she was promoted to studio chief in Chevrolet Interiors 2. She was the first woman to assume a position as a

chief designer in the American automobile industry. In this assignment, she would later make a lasting impact on Chevrolet automobiles. Vanderbilt would also brainstorm with other department heads for new products.

Vanderbilt's drawings, made in 1964 and 1965 for the F-Car Program—Camaro and Firebird, include designs for seats, doors, and the center console.

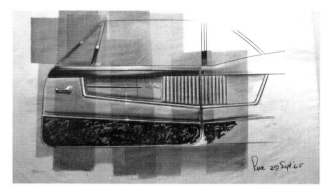

This stunning door illustration was for a car then titled Panther (later renamed Camaro). *General Motors; collection of the Cranbrook Art Museum; photo, Constance Smith*

CHEVROLET PANTHER OR CHEVROLET CAMARO: WHICH DO YOU PREFER?

In 1965, General Motors sought to offer a variant to the Corvair and Chevy II that could compete with the Ford Mustang. The object was to enter the race with another muscle car. It was initially named Panther or sometimes just referred to as the F-body, but by 1967, it was renamed Camaro.

A number of design drawings made by Vanderbilt bear the name "Panther."

Chevy's chief engineer Ed Cole was instrumental in getting the COPO (Central Office Production Order) Camaro project off the ground. Initially, the engine size was limited so that it did not compete with the Corvette. However, it would not be long until dealers such as Yenko, Gibb, and Nickey packed 427 V-8s in the engine compartment. This eventually led to the COPO Camaro, which could be ordered already equipped with a large engine. In ordering the car, COPO was submitted instead of the regular production order. These are extremely valuable today when found at auction.

Sometime later, Chevrolet received *Motor Trend*'s Car of the Year Award for its 1975 Monza. In Michigan, the Monza 2+2 hatchback coupe came with a 262-cubic-inch V-8. One had to live in California in order to get the 5.7 V-8 with an extra 15 horsepower. Chevrolet also offered the Towne Coupe. As Vanderbilt noted, the interior shared some features, such as the armrest, with the Vega and even the Camaro.

In a central management position, Vanderbilt would coordinate and integrate components across the line. The lineup included

Camaro, Vega, Monza, and others. Chevrolet received the Car of the Year Award for its design of the Chevrolet Vega. The first Vega was so well received that performance variations followed.

SIGNIFICANT SAFETY FEATURES

Vanderbilt worked in Human Factors and, at some point in time, was appointed the chair of the Human Factors group under the direction of P. Kyropoulis.

Vanderbilt's 1958 drawings set the direction for GM's first child safety seat. She can also be credited with designing the first complete LATCH system, to stabilize a child seat in a car. Later, she designed the first automotive seat with a lumbar adjustment. Lastly, she designed a series of components to reduce injury during a collision. While some of these inventions were patented, others were not.

Suzanne Vanderbilt designed General Motors' first seat with a lumbar adjustment for automobiles. This invention, which relied on a series of segmented inflatable air pockets and components to inflate and deinflate them, was the predecessor to all the lumbar adjustments provided today by vehicle manufacturers. This invention was primarily designed to provide varying degrees of support for the lumbar region of the back to users with back problems, but it also served to accommodate customers of various shapes and sizes. In addition, users could inflate just one pocket or many at one time. It has become an indispensable part of most vehicles.

To most, there is no one more important to us than our family members. A Corvette owner, Suzanne was well aware of the positive and negative effects of speed. Throughout the years, one could attend Stapp seminars on crashes, and the scenes presented were memorable.

Early child seats were booster cushions used to raise the height of children so that they could be seen by their parents.

In 1958, Vanderbilt designed a series of child safety seats fitted with various types of belts. However, it was not until after the three-point seat belt for adults became standard that manufacturers recognized the need to offer child safety seats. Vanderbilt designed built-in seats for vehicles. As time went on, manufacturers offered seats that folded into the standard back seat as an option. Today, there is a preference for removable child safety seats.

This design work led to our first seat restraints as well as laws requiring the use of infant and child safety seats.

In 1965, Suzanne Vanderbilt, L. Gelfand, and GM received a patent, "Safety Switch for Automotive Instrument Panel." It was noted that a number of protrusions on automotive instrument panels could inflict injury upon an occupant if the person were thrown forward upon rapid deceleration. Controls for window washers, radios, and lights protrude from the instrument panel; Vanderbilt proposed safer components.

Vanderbilt purchased a condo with a garage that was also home to her Corvette, which Zora Arkus-Duntov, the father of Corvette Engineering, had blueprinted. Arkus-Duntov also designed the first Corvette race car—a controversial form. Suzanne confessed in secrecy that the upgraded suspension gave the car a hard ride.

At some point in time, the author's studio manager, W. Larry Faloon, informed her that Suzanne was receiving chemotherapy for breast cancer and would have to cut back her work schedule or leave work altogether. The doctor she visited initially failed to detect her health problems. Her delayed diagnosis by another physician proved fatal, and she died prematurely at age fifty-five. However, the legacy of Vanderbilt's innovations continues to address our physical differences and save our lives on the road.

Suzanne Vanderbilt was the first woman designer in GM history to spend her entire career at Styling/Design under Harley Earl and William Mitchell. There have been only a handful of such "lifers" since.

The Chevrolet Vega caught the eye of the author after having lunched with Vanderbilt. *Marker illustration, Constance Smith*

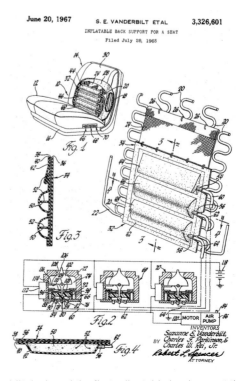

Vanderbilt designed the first adjustable lumbar seat that was patented. *Courtesy of the US Patent and Trademark Office*

DAGMAR ARNOLD-WAHLFORSS

Talent and education, not gender, shape the sequence in which you think about things, your orientation, and your methodology. Designers don't have to be part of a user set as long as they make the effort to understand that set. All of us too often assume we are the typical user, rather than just one user. Women have a great future in design—if they go after it.[1]

—Dagmar Arnold-Wahlforss (ca. 1934–1995), *Industrial Design Magazine* interview, September 1986

Dagmar Arnold (far left) joins a group which also includes Harley Earl and women exhibit and kitchen designers. *General Motors.*

CAREER HIGHLIGHTS

Arnold joined the Frigidaire studio of General Motors Styling in 1955. Her team created what was labeled the "Kitchen of Tomorrow," and this environment vied for attention at the extravagant Motoramas, which featured revolutionary automotive concepts. While most were shown in this country, the Kitchen of Tomorrow was also exhibited at the Brussels World's Fair in 1958 and included technologically advanced appliances and a communications center.

The kitchen communications center included a television, a telephone, and other devices. In the 1950s, the Kitchen of Tomorrow also featured the first nanny cam—a supervisory TV monitor that could be focused on the baby's crib, play areas, and entry doors. This was the predecessor of today's popular surveillance systems.

Awarded a Fulbright Scholarship, Arnold later moved to Germany and attended the Hochschule für Gestaltung Ulm defined by the Bauhaus pedagogy at the time. The school's curriculum underscored science and technology. Dagmar married Henrik Wahlforss and they subsequently founded Product Program AB in Stockholm, Sweden. The pair designed medical equipment, large household appliances, and products.

Returning to the US, Arnold joined the industrial design department at IBM's Developmental Laboratory in January 1960. Even before Arnold arrived, IBM had been recognized for the diversity of its staff. This inclusion was later most pronounced under the modern leadership of Ginni Rometty.

It could be said the Dagmar introduced the field of industrial design, and its many facets, to the greater IBM community.

Arnold was the first woman at IBM to be awarded a US patent; the patent protected the design of a disk-type data storage device. She also designed numerous other products for which she received patents, including keyboards and teller systems. After spending twenty-five years with IBM, Arnold was still passionate about computer design.

In 1994, Arnold was invited to partake in a show called *Goddess in the Details: Product Design by Women*—organized by the Association of Women Industrial Designers, a group affiliated with Pratt Institute. She exhibited her work at and attended the event, which was held at the Pratt Manhattan Gallery in New York City. A second show was mounted on the campus of Pratt Institute at the Rubelle and Norman Schafler Gallery in Brooklyn, New York.

Note: Arnold's US IBM patent drawings and additional images are featured in *Damsels in Design: Women Pioneers in the Automotive Industry, 1939–1959* (Schiffer Books, 2018). *Damsels in Design* also profiles seventeen other pioneering women from all car companies.

BIOGRAPHICAL NOTES

Arnold grew up in suburban Nassau County on Long Island, not far from Brooklyn. With the exception of Suzanne Vanderbilt, most of the men and women enrolling at Pratt Institute in Brooklyn, New York, planned to study something other than industrial design, a field that was still evolving. Dagmar Arnold was attracted to graphics and architecture. All students were required to complete a foundation year curriculum, and that entailed studying with Alexander Kostellow, Rowena Reed Kostellow, and others before choosing a major. Norm James, a classmate and designer of the Firebird III, noted that Arnold belonged at the head of the class since she was the best one in it.[2]

At the end of the first year, students chose a major, or department heads recruited the best students in their fields. In 1951, for some reason, the Industrial Design Department employed two women professors and was flooded with female applicants. It would take decades before this ever happened again. Rowena Reed Kostellow and ceramicist Eva Zeisel were skilled teachers. Rowena was married to Alexander Kostellow, who was instrumental in setting up the ID department at Pratt; she would continue to teach 3-D Design for over fifty years. Arnold was correct in concluding that there was an opportunity for women to succeed in this area.[3] After graduating in 1955, Dagmar was recruited by General Motors with other members of her class. She was invited to join the Frigidaire Studio at GM Styling. Since its inception in 1919, Frigidaire under Ternstedt had come a long before the word "Frigidaire" became a household term for refrigerator. Arriving at the Fisher Body Division of GM in the 1920s, Bonnie Lemm was Frigidaire's first female designer at their Ternstedt facility.

FRIGIDAIRE

Starting out as the Guardian Frigerator Company in Fort Wayne, Indiana, Frigidaire was purchased by Will Durant along with numerous other companies, mainly for use in the manufacture of automobiles. Frigidaire would diversify and thrive with the introduction of fridges and air-conditioning in Oldsmobiles, while also manufacturing washing machines, a stacked washer-dryer unit, flip-top Flair stoves, and other devices to make home chores easier. Frigidaire took part in all the elaborate Motorama exhibitions taking place throughout the United States and Canada. While the concept cars and entertainers were there mainly for the men, the "Kitchen of the Future" or "Kitchen of Tomorrow" displayed by Frigidaire was considered a draw for the women in attendance.

The GM Style Book, a marketing publication, featured the Kitchen of Tomorrow. *General Motors*

This optical scanner (medical notebook) was designed for IBM. *Sketch by Constance Smith*

In the 1950s, Harley Earl, GM's Styling chief, noted that the field of industrial design was oriented toward making useful things beautiful. He observed that elements such as form and surface quality all blended together to create visual beauty. To market the future, management proposed a number of experimental vehicles and a project called the Kitchen of Tomorrow. The idea was to create a kitchen of the future and feature the exhibit in the 1956 Motorama. With its outside dining area and planning center, this became one of the most popular displays, especially for the women in attendance.

The 1956 Motorama extravaganza monopolized the rooms of the Waldorf Astoria in New York City. This exhibition consisted of sixty-three exhibits and twenty-six production cars. Buick's Centurion show car was one of the most memorable. Its fins were tamed and more integrated compared to the 1957 Belair. It utilized an aircraft-style canopy—the clear roof was quite a technical accomplishment but would benefit from the tinting appearing on the forthcoming Cadillac Celestiq. Chevrolet's Impala, Olds' Golden Rocket, and Cadillac's Eldorado Brougham were perhaps eclipsed by the Firebird II turbine car. However, Frigidaire, perhaps oriented toward the women in tow, would also play a leading role here. While most people couldn't come to New York City or gain entrance to the show, GM decided to make the experience available to all in the form of a musical film advertisement, *Design for Dreaming*, which featured leading lady Thelma "Tad" Tadlock awakened by a handsome masked gentleman, Marc Breaux. Tad is then taken on a virtual ride by the stranger through the Motorama, over the heads of throngs of attendees, before being driven away in the Firebird II along the "road of tomorrow."

HOME HUB

Dagmar Arnold contributed to a communications center that included a phone and supervisory television that could be focused on a baby's crib, play areas, and even entry doors. The telephone included a PA system that could be used anywhere in the room without going near the receiver. Designers added an answering system and recording device that took over whenever the absent homeowner needed it.

The inventions didn't end there. Designers created prototype appliances that could be used both indoors and out. There was a marble-topped stove that remained cool since it cooked by induction, a battery-controlled serving cart, and a freestanding rotisserie-styled oven covered with a plastic dome at the end of a large island. The Roto-Storage Center consisted of a rotating refrigerator freezer.

In recognition of her outstanding design work, Arnold was selected for a Fulbright Scholarship and moved to Germany. She attended the Hochschule für Gestaltung Ulm, a school that emphasized technology and science in its curriculum. Once in Germany, she married and then founded Product Design Program AB with her husband in Stockholm. It is not surprising that the firm designed appliances, inclusive design products, and medical equipment. It is interesting that GM sold Frigidaire in 1979, and it was later purchased by AB Electrolux. After completing her year of studies, she attended the International Design Conference in Stockholm.

A PERFECT FIT FOR IBM

Upon returning to the US, Arnold chose to settle in California, where she found many creative souls. She had invites to speak at Cal and Stanford, but no time to do so. Arnold joined the industrial design department at IBM's Developmental Laboratory in January 1960.[4] After just one month, she was promoted to senior industrial designer.[5] She likely also worked in design offices in North Carolina and New York, gradually advancing to the position of advisory planner.

At IBM, she noted, "Design is a revolt against the abuse of materials." She thought that early designs resembled other objects, and early autos looked like carriages: "Even early IBM designs looked like sewing machines or china closets. But the development of business machines today is so rapid there is not an evolutionary pattern. New concepts and functions must be coordinated with the designer, which can take any form.[6] Manufacturers must consider volume, materials, resonance and vibrations; access to machine parts; the psychology of human factors; the layout for an operator; controls and displays; and so on. Longevity and future derivatives are also of prime importance.

In the early 1960s, Arnold was featured in IBM's *San Jose News* in an article titled "Two Get Special Awards, Woman Joins Ranks of Inventors."[7] In March 1963, an article in IBM's *Research News* included the following: "Dagmar L. Arnold, an IBM industrial designer, at the San Jose Plant, became the first woman to receive a U.S. Patent."

Arnold designed parts of the IBM 1301 Disk Storage Unit used with the 7000 series of IBM mainframe computers and was the first woman to receive an IBM patent. As many as five of these units could be attached to a computer system to provide a storage capacity of 280 million characters for the 7000 series and 250 million for the 1410. She also received additional patents; one in 1976 protected her design for a teller station. She designed numerous other products, including keyboards, a handheld scanner, a terminal and story unit, and systems,

After Arnold's career was covered by *Mademoiselle* magazine in their June 1961 issue, IBM's *San Jose News* editor followed with his own version:

Behind the attractive styling and the compatibility of today's IBM equipment lies a wealth of skill and effort in a new and growing field—industrial design. In this field of styling it would only seem natural to find a creative young woman like Miss Dagmar Arnold. The fact is though that Miss Arnold is somewhat of a rarity in her profession. The whole field of industrial design is so new that most of its members around the world are still on a first-named basis, and precious few of them are women. This puts Arnold among the trailblazers both in advancing a new type of work and opening a new avenue of endeavor for her sex.[8]

OTHER INTERESTS

When she was not at work, Dagmar divided her time as best she could between reading, Chinese cooking, visiting museums, and working out with the Alto Dance Co-op. Like her former colleagues at GM, she also valued the best ski resorts. However, while her friends loved their Corvettes, after returning from school in Germany she chose a different ride—a Karmann Ghia.

Arnold spent twenty-five years at IBM before retiring, and she passed away in 1995.

Dagmar L. Arnold held the patent on the 1301 Disk Storage Unit, and her manager, Jack Stringer, who headed the plant's production design and packaging department, was recognized for the design of the input terminal of the 357 data collection system. *Courtesy of International Business Machines Corporation, © International Business Machines Corporation*

PART V.
THE 1960s

General Motor's strong leadership came partly from the engineers that led it in the 1960s. James Roche served as president in 1965 and CEO in 1967. The landscape changed again when Ed Cole, another engineer, took the reins in 1967; under Cole, other like-minded engineering managers were also at the helm. The engineering innovations appearing were nothing short of amazing, and GM continued to capture the majority of the market share.

In the 1960s, Styling was under the direction of William L. Mitchell, the VP of Design who followed Harley Earl. The Corvair, which appeared in late 1959, led up to the Chevy II and Camaro/Firebird. In 1961, GM Styling would unveil numerous other cars of note, including the Pontiac Tempest, the Buick Special, and the Oldsmobile F-85. During this decade, Bill Mitchell would also take well-deserved credit for the development of the Buick Riviera, iconic 1963 Chevrolet Corvette, Oldsmobile Toronado, and Cadillac Eldorado.

By this time, GM owned or was affiliated with a number of other car companies, including Opel.

THE STANDARD-BEARERS

While only a four-door was ready in 1959, the decade kicked off with the introduction of the 1960 Chevrolet Corvair, equipped with a rear-mounted, air-cooled, aluminum, horizontally opposed, flat-six engine reminding some of a Porsche power train. Early engines required dual carburetors, and later models were equipped with turbochargers. When it arrived, the Corvair was considered by many to have the first modern unibody.

The Corvair styling was groundbreaking. While it lacked a grille, it featured quad headlamps, and its form was refined by a slight crease running down the hood, giving it a tailored look. Some reporters raved about the design. The belt-line bulge, which continued around the front and rear of the car, was imitated by some European manufacturers. Inside the car, the instrument panel was nearly symmetrical on Gen I cars, featuring a separate instrument cluster dropped in a surround on the driver's side, and a form with a similar feel on the passenger side. Base vinyl seats featured neatly arranged parallel lines. On Gen II cars, a sportier interior arrived. The Corvair 95 Rampside (the name was based on the size of the wheelbase) was an innovative truck variant. With the engine just forward of the rear bumper, the Rampside featured a side door behind the cab. Additionally, the Stinger, with 220 hp, was created for road course racing by Don Yenko.

Because of its flat floor and low body, a number of concept cars were built on the Corvair chassis. In 1967, the Electrovair I (based on a 1964 model) and Electrovair II (using components from a 1966 model) concepts debuted. The cars, which relied on induction motors, were built to evaluate new power plants and controls. It was decided that while these cars were feasible,

the power source was expensive, with the power pack adding 800 pounds to the curb weight. Stunning other Corvair derivatives included the Monza GT, Monza SS (with four carburetors), Astro I and II, and jet-powered Astro III—a triwheeler that was a hit at Chicago's 1971 Auto Show.

In 1961, GM continued to fend off the imports and introduced a second wave of compact cars. The Pontiac Tempest was GM's first four-cylinder in the US; in this case they relied on a slant four (1961–1963).

In an effort to design a smaller car, Pontiac designers desired to mate a rear-mounted transmission to a front-mounted engine, a situation that was cleverly addressed by engineers in order to be able to seat six passengers, DeLorean, who worked in Pontiac, created a so-called rope shaft. The transmission was moved to the rear (a transaxle), and a new flexible driveshaft that could twist while it turned eliminated the need for universal joints. DeLorean designed a low-profile, flexible driveshaft made from a bar of SAE triple-alloy steel, ball-peened and coated, which transmitted power to the rear wheels. This design eliminated the need for universal joints. Some dubbed the device a rope shaft. In an effort to save money, some parts came off Oldsmobile and other divisional shelves. The Tempest won the *Motor Trend* Car of the Year Award, which boded well for Bunkie Knudsen, but perhaps only for a short time.

In contrast, the Buick Special and the oddly named Olds F-85 were powered by V-8s. The cars incorporated some of the styling nuances of their larger brethren, and the Buick Special outsold the others.

When the Camaro was introduced, some saw it as an extension of the second-generation Corvair, but with a side Coke-bottle theme. Hood stripes and bumblebee-style stripes would also add the impression of improved performance to some cars.

In 1961, the 1962 Chevrolet II was introduced to capture sales. As the decade neared completion, the names Nova and Chevelle would follow.

A significant number of power plants were unveiled, tested, or added to production cars in this era. From 1961 to 1963, Pontiac introduced a new four-cylinder engine in the Tempest. The other divisions went their own way. Buick answered with an all-aluminum engine and a Fireball V-6. Bill Porter ran the exterior studio, and Joan Gatewood was assigned to the interior design studio. In 1961, road ability had improved for the Corvette. The 1963 Corvette, which features a split rear window, has always been and will always be an icon. GM also added four-wheel independent suspension to it, while four-wheel disc brakes did not arrive for Corvette until 1965.

On the engineering front, in 1961 a Society of Automotive Engineers presentation was made that was titled "Uses of Radioisotopes at GM."

In 1962, Pontiac stylists took a chance designing a split grille, and a deluxe hardtop called the Grand Prix was introduced. The quad headlights moved from a horizontal placement to a vertical one. This put even more emphasis on the small form in the center of the split grille. Sales increased; the changes were successful.

Buick hit a home run with the introduction of the 1963 Riviera, a hardtop featuring forms with sharp edges developed by the talented Ned Nickles. In this decade, the second-generation Riviera was made from 1966 to 1970. Bill Mitchell, GM's VP of Design, was so enamored with the design that he had three customized for his own use. The stunning Silver Arrow I had a chopped top and is now in the collection of and occasionally displayed by the Sloan Museum in Flint, Michigan.

Around 1962, GM engineers also made a presentation describing GM's catalytic converter, which was soon to appear on 1964 models. In 1966, they reviewed the needs for energy-absorbing steering columns. In 1963, front seat belts became standard in all cars, and rear seat belts followed in 1965.

In the midsixties, Pontiac, under the direction of John DeLorean, had to catch up with Chevrolet and the Camaro when it came to the Firebird. One of the models for the Firebird was referred to as the Panther, and this designation appeared on the interior drawings made by Suzanne Vanderbilt.

In 1961, road ability had improved for the Corvette. GM added four-wheel independent suspension to it to give it a better ride, while four-wheel disc brakes did not arrive for Corvette until 1965.

The groundbreaking front-wheel-drive Oldsmobile Toronado, lauded for its beautiful design, was introduced in 1966 and was followed by the 1967 Cadillac Eldorado, another designer's favorite. These front-wheel-drive sedans maximized passenger space, provided an almost vibration-free ride, and had exceptional directional stability.

In 1967, a fuel-cell-powered Electro-van was evaluated.

In 1968, Warren Fitzgerald devised the flexible Endura bumper to meet the needs of Pontiac GTO designers, and Pontiac created the Banshee II show car, powered by a 400-horsepower V-8 and covered by fiberglass skins. The Trans Am of 1969 would lead to more variations in the 1970s from the exterior studio and interior studio.

Looking abroad, Opel introduced its three-speed automatic, which spoke to more women than men, and in 1962, power-assisted steering. From 1959 to 1963, the revised PII model of the Opel Kapitan put the factory in Russelsheim to its limit; it churned out over 350,000 cars and over 19,000 lorries (large trucks). Later, a luxury version, the Admiral, was added. A Kapitan A arrived in 1964. There was also a Diplomat, which relied on a 190 hp, 4.7-liter V-8, from Chevrolet. In 1960, its brand-new Rekord P2 arrived with a new body—its bestselling midsized car. Before long, a four-speed gearbox was added to compete with competitors. In 1962, the Kadett took on competitors with great success, and in 1967, Commodores reigned.

By 1969, the Stir-Lec I concept hybrid was tested. It consisted of a 1968 Opel Kadett body with a variable-speed AC electric motor.

With all the new technology and stunning designs, the cars of the 1960s will live in our heads and hearts forever.

JOAN (ERHARDT) GATEWOOD

Classic design that is functional takes on a life of its own and lives forever.

—Joan Gatewood (b. 1944)

Courtesy of Joan Gatewood.

CAREER HIGHLIGHTS

Joan Gatewood, a color and trim designer, served Oldsmobile beginning in 1965 and Pontiac as the decade ended. Her design work would have been incorporated on the 1968 and 1969 Cutlass (A Model), Delta 88 (B), Luxury Sedan (C), and early 1970 Pontiacs.

BIOGRAPHICAL NOTES

Joan Gatewood was a native of Detroit, Michigan, and her paternal grandfather served as a tool- and diemaker for the Ford Motor Company. Her father worked as a civil engineer for the Wayne County Road Commission. After marrying, her mother remained home; needless to say, times have changed.

Gatewood and her sister, two years behind her, attended Ann Arbor Trail Elementary School and McClain Elementary School after a family move. From grades 6 to 8, she studied at the Vetal Elementary School. Perhaps her career began when she gained entrance to Cass Technical High School, which employed seasoned professionals.

While she was attracted to costume illustration, she also went on to study watercolor, freehand drawing, pen and ink drawing, and figure drawing. Her mastery of watercolor earned her a college scholarship from *Scholastic Magazine*, and she chose to attend Traphagen School of Fashion in New York City, a school not to be underestimated. It was founded by award-winning designer Ethel Traphagen, from Brooklyn, who desired to free America from Europe's dominance over fashion. Traphagen's alumni include the likes of Anne Klein, Jeffrey Beene, and numerous other dignitaries in fashion. After relocating to 1680 Broadway in New York City, it housed an enormous library and even a museum. The first program centered on design and illustration, while construction, theater design, and millinery were later added. The scholarship covered Gatewood's study of fashion illustration the first year. However, the study of clothing and construction required tuition, for which she received her parents' support. Ethel Traphagen and her staff educated hundreds before she passed away in 1963, when Gatewood finished her studies.

Gatewood was offered a position in Louise Frocks Dress Shop, which made basic communion dresses to which women added trim. There was no way she could keep up with the assembly line workers. She had never used a cutter before to get through a huge pile of fabric, and she became discouraged when she was required to fold and package veils to send to stores. They finally let her design dresses before she quit in 1964. Perhaps all they wanted were her designs in the first place.

Her father decided to help. His assistant was a neighbor of Milo McNaughton, who ultimately invited her to interview at GM. Roger Martin, who headed human resources for the design staff, would later review her portfolio. Because it was devoid of automotive work, he asked her to create some designs that would relate to the auto industry. It was no problem to design relevant trim and fabric at home. When she returned, he offered her a design position. She did not ever have any gasoline in her veins, but she loved fashion.

In August 1964, she joined the Development Studio, under the guidance of Bill Porter, with some others who were summer interns from the Society of Arts and Crafts—the predecessor of the College for Creative Studies. She remembers Jerry Palmer being part of the school group.

Gatewood was adept at designing luxury cars. *Jane Gatewood*

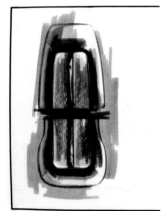

These designs were made for performance products. *Jane Gatewood*

After a few months, she was welcomed into the Oldsmobile Studio under the direction of Edward Donaldson. Ed's wife, Lora, worked as an assistant in the Color Studio and made an appearance from time to time. Gatewood was also greeted by Walter Gierschick, the assistant studio manager. This was a desirable assignment in the 1960s, since the Olds Division placed high in total sales industry wide and, by 1969, would deliver just short of 700,000 cars.

In 1965, the team likely projected ahead to 1968 for the redesign of many midsized cars and the upgrading of others. Gatewood notes that new designs were in store for the Cutlass (on the A platform), the Delta 88 (B), and the Luxury sedan (C). When it came to the 4-4-2 (four-barrel carburetor, four-speed manual transmission, and dual exhausts), the Hurst/Olds, equipped with 350 hp and the Hurst dual gate shifter, was hard to catch. The Toronado, the newsmaker from 1966 as the first front-wheel drive, would require a minimal facelift. It turned out that Gatewood would enjoy designing for the Luxury.

While living at home, Gatewood was able to purchase a brand-new 1966 Olds Cutlass convertible. The standard V-8 engine delivered a good 315 hp. This deep-blue car, which she fell in love with, was outfitted with a black power roof and was not cheap—the car was priced at about $3,400 before options, and Gatewood thinks it might have cost her $5,000. For the performance minded, with an optional 4-4-2, the Cutlass completed against the popular Pontiac GTO of the same year. Later the 4-4-2 was sold on its own.

In 1967, while dining in the second-floor cafeteria, Joan was approached by Jerry Palmer, who proceeded to introduce her to Charles Gatewood, an exterior designer. Not long afterward, they were married, and Palmer served as best man.

As things progressed, Gatewood was assigned to the Pontiac Studio. Around 1970, she received a stunning black-and-white pants suit as a gift and wondered how this would be perceived if she wore it to work with other designers, who were professionally dressed. She took a deep breath and walked into the studio. All eyes were on her. The men stood up and gave her a round of applause. She was likely the first woman to wear pants at General Motors Design.

By this time, Pontiac had dominated with numerous muscle cars. Gatewood would have been assigned to the 1973 and 1974 models.

However, she was soon teamed with Suzanne Vanderbilt on the project dubbed "Branching Out." Perhaps this was the most exciting assignment. With the latest colors, fabrics, and trim, she explored all the possibilities for the future. She loved the soft velvets and heavily embroidered fabrics. Alas, designers have to be practical and adhere to budgets.

At some point in time, Sue Vanderbilt was experiencing a twinge under her arm, which her physician seemed to ignore. A malignancy was diagnosed by another doctor, but chemotherapy came too late.

After resigning from GM, Gatewood discovered she was pregnant, and she went on to have two children. Andrew works as a computer systems engineer, and Jane is the vice provost for global engagement for the University of Rochester.

After fifty years of marriage, Joan granted Charles a divorce, and when he tried to return a short time later, he was turned down. It was time for Joan to celebrate her newfound freedom.

Joan distributes gifts on holiday. *Jane Gatewood*

The ladies in the family vacation together. *Jane Gatewood*

Jane and Joan revisit history on a vacation. *Jane Gatewood*

MARGARET ANNA SCHROEDER

CAREER HIGHLIGHTS

Margaret Schroeder began her career at General Motors in 1961, joining the Pontiac interiors studio after a four-month orientation. In 1963, she married exterior body designer Theodore Schroeder, who worked in Cadillac. In 1966, she was the first woman to receive an assignment in Australia's GM-Holden. This was a remarkable time in Holden's history, as the company prepared to change design directors, designed their own engine, and manufactured notable products such as the Monaro that were well received. Additionally, for the first time, Holden designers produced and built two concept vehicles—one of fiberglass. Schroeder was later transferred to the Cadillac studio, which was under the direction of George Moon, an accomplished and respected interiors manager.

Spending almost a decade with the General Motors, Margaret also gave presentations on behalf of the company, speaking about the process of designing for automobiles.

BIOGRAPHICAL NOTES

Margaret Schroeder notes that her maternal grandfather worked as a coal miner in Wilkes-Barre, Pennsylvania, and her father ran a roof-contracting business. Her mother, like most of her era, was a homemaker but also artistically talented. Margaret was one of four children, with a brother ten years her senior and two sisters. The oldest sister served as a teacher, and the youngest an accountant

Her studies began at Washington Elementary School in Northampton, Pennsylvania, and continued at Northampton Junior and Senior High Schools. She notes that early on, her art and pottery teacher, Melvin Klepinger, was a profound influence.

While most of the other women designers in this era graduated from Pratt Institute, Margaret was a graduate of the Philadelphia College of Art, which later merged along with the Philadelphia College of the Performing Arts into the University of the Arts. She holds a BFA degree. She studied painting, drafting, and other basic courses for two years and spent the last two years majoring in industrial design. She was in the class of 1948 with only one other woman, who went on to work for FMC.

In 1961, she was invited for an interview by Miles McNaughton at the new GM Technical Center on Mound Road in Warren, Michigan. She was placed in an orientation studio under Don Hoag for about four months. From 1961 to 1966, she served in the Pontiac Studio under the direction of Fidele Bianco and Ken Markum.

General Motors

From 1955 to 1975, customers and press alluded to Pontiac's muscle-car performance. In the early 1960s, GM's "Wide Track" dominated NASCAR's Grand National stock car race circuit before factory-supported racing ceased and the division concentrated on cars for the streets.

When Margaret arrived in 1961, Pontiac offered Catalinas, Venturas, Star Chiefs, Bonnevilles, and Tempests, mostly with 389 V-8s, and an off-road Catalina with 421 CID. There were four-cylinder Tempests and, later, eight-cylinder models. In 1962, almost 205,000 Catalinas alone were built. Pontiac's first Grand Prix, like the GTO of the future, was identifiable by its blacked-out grille. In the fast track were the sixteen 421 Super Duty Grand Prix hardtops, offering race car performance in a classy package.

Hundreds of paint chips and textiles were stored in a separate color studio. *General Motors*

The Monaro was introduced in July 1968. *General Motors*

On the interior, cars such as the Grand Prix were equipped with bucket seats and a center console and the preferred four-speed stick shift. Cars were built with a large standard tachometer. Margaret notes that she designed components such as knobs and seating. Some Super Duty 421s appeared in 1963, and some came without radios. By 1963, top brass, perhaps acting responsibly, put an end to the model. All of this hoopla stopped in 1964, when the Pontiac Division ushered in the A-body. In 1966 there was a Tempest GTO, and in 1967 a Firebird series. By 1968, the GTO was no longer just a Tempest, and by 1968, Firebirds with HO

(high output) packages turned heads. However, for Margaret, in 1966 there was a change of assignment.

When Margaret and Ted arrived at Holden in 1966, designers were completing work on the Monaro, which came out in July 1968 and proved significant. This was the only coupe equipped with a pillarless hardtop. It was an instant success. It did not hurt that it was equipped with a straight-six or 307 V-8 engine, and later the GTS 327 V-8 provided 125 hp, which resulted in 0–60 mph in 9.6 seconds. While most engines came from Chevrolet, for the first time Holden built its own V-8.

In 1968, Holden also introduced two new body styles—a coupe and longer sedan. For the first time in history, you could order a V-8 with power windows and A/C. Following the mindset of American marketers, customers were offered a wide variety of options on everything—even transmissions. A Torano range (HVB and LC) added complexity, and a utility and panel van were added to the offerings. Attractive Belmont and Kingswood trim packages were also available.

Holden also came out with two new body styles for the HK, introduced in 1968. In 1969, excited designers created the Hurricane concept car RD001, with an Aussie-made midengine V-8, or bent-eight. The two-seater featured a clamshell roof, doors, and windshield. A closed-circuit TV screen was incorporated to make up for the absence of rear vision—a precursor to today's rearview cameras. Its digital instrument panel also foretold automotive technology.

The next special project began in 1969 and was code-named GTR-X. Don Reharsh is credited with most of the exterior, made of fiberglass, under the direction of Joe Schemansky. Mechanical components came from the Torana UX-1, but a stronger chassis was made to stabilize the fiberglass body, which came from Reinforced Plastics of Clayton. The GTR Torana UX-1 was introduced in 1971 with front and rear spoilers and decals; it was considered a sports road car. Of the four car bodies made, it is likely that two with running gear have survived. The project was canceled since it was slated to be reviewed at the same times as the Opel GT. Further, fiberglass was an unproven material in Australia—no Corvettes were exported, and there was some rough terrain.

The HT model was introduced in 1969, and the HG model in 1970.

Upon returning to Warren, Margaret joined the Cadillac Studio and worked with the public-relations team, making presentations to the public. This included an appearance at the 1969 Society of Automotive Engineers convention, where she spoke about the processes for designing automobiles. Little did she realize that she was following in the footsteps of Helene Rother, who addressed the SAE more than twenty-five years earlier.

After retiring from industry, Margaret raised three children.

Like some of the other early women designers, Margaret had a bout with cancer. She was fortunate to beat it and looks forward to the future.

The Hurricane Concept car was prepared for the track. *General Motors*

JOAN KLATIL (CREAMER)

I sign my sketches J. Klatil because I don't want the fact that I'm a woman designer to influence the judgment of my work.[1]

—Joan Klatil Creamer (b. ca. 1943)

Joan attended Vision Honored to pay respects to designer and futurist Syd Mead before he passed. *Constance Smith*

CAREER HIGHLIGHTS

Joan Creamer honed her design skills upon joining GM Design Staff at the Technical Center. A.k.a. Joan Klatil, she was perhaps the most talented student in her class and was chosen to participate in the GM summer program as an intern following her fourth year (1965) of studies at the Cleveland Institute of Art. Klatil joined General Motors full time in June 1966, after graduating from Cleveland's five-year program with a BFA, with a major in industrial design. After a required stint in the Design Development Program, Klatil joined the Cadillac exteriors studio and was later transferred to the Oldsmobile interiors studio before returning to Advanced Buick Exteriors.

While Lemm was hired in the 1920s by William Schnell in the Fisher Body Division of General Motors and was the first female interior and exterior designer in the automotive industry, Klatil Creamer was the first female exterior designer under William Mitchell at General Motors Design. (Existing drawings substantiate the fact that Cleveland's Betty Thatcher Oros, who graduated in 1939, designed both interiors and exteriors for Hudson; the University of Michigan's Audrey Hodges—a Studebaker and Tucker designer—designed both interiors and exteriors between 1939 and 1948.)

Toppling the gender barrier was not so simple. Bill Mitchell, GM's vice president of Design, who had replaced Harley Earl, planned to remove Klatil from the exterior studios, where some men could be tagged for their use of bad language or perhaps other unwelcome behaviors. Why a single woman with men in the interior studios was different is puzzling. In the 1950s, Mitchell made it clear to the talented and highly trained Suzanne Vanderbilt that women were not welcome in the exterior design studios at Styling. She was demoted after receiving a master's degree with an emphasis on silversmithing. When Vanderbilt returned from school, Mitchell distributed and praised her thesis project. Other women pioneers jumped ship because of Bill Mitchell's attitudes. Susan Skarsgard, head of GM's Archives, noted in an interview that this set women at GM back ten years.

After spending a short time in the Oldsmobile interiors studio, Klatil was moved into the Advanced Buick Exteriors studio. Always wondering when Bill Mitchell would move the situation again, she moved on to the GE Corporation. Before opening her own consultancy about eight years later, Klatil also served as a staff designer and product manager for Textron and design director for Burnes of Boston.

An entrepreneur in more fields than one, Klatil Creamer continues to write and beautifully illustrate children's books and still welcomes freelance work.

IN THE BEGINNING

Joan Klatil was born in Cleveland, Ohio, an only child of Czechoslovakian parents. Both were first generation born in America and believed in a work ethic; they were driven perfectionists and wanted their daughter to do her best. Joseph Klatil was logical and relied on commonsense skills, while Mary Klatil had a creative flare. Although neither went to college, both were innovative. Dad was always fixing or innovating to make life easier and better. Mom did crafting, sewing, doll making, and so on. She added the aesthetic, colorful

This remote control model was sold in the 1950s. *Constance Smith*

part—also a perfect combination for an industrial designer; Joan inherited these abilities. Dad worked as an exterminator, and Mom added income as a secretary.

As a child, Joan enjoyed playing with small metal cars on the carpet border for hours, then later built ubiquitous Revell kits. Her father, who treated her like a son, bought her a small, battery-powered Studebaker electric model car with a cord for hand maneuvering it. Her parents provided an environment with cars and dolls, and when it came to making a decision, she naturally chose cars.

HIGH SCHOOL AND COLLEGE

Joan's Brooklyn, Ohio, high school art teacher, Mr. C. F. Carroll, must have seen potential and encouraged her to practice drawing. In grades 9 through 12, his constant reminder was "draw, draw, and draw." C. F. Carroll was also an entrepreneur, hunter, and fisherman—a man's man making his own fishing lures and hunting with bow and arrow. He designed and patented many unique crossbows.

With constant encouragement from C. F. Carroll, Joan joined the summer and Saturday classes at the Cleveland Institute of Art while still in high school. Living nearby, it was natural for her to matriculate full time after graduating. Her parents were accepting of her path, as long as her journey ended with a college degree. CIA became accredited after the end of its fifth year, 1969, and is now a four-year accredited college.

Cleveland's art program was founded in 1882. While it did not have a program solely devoted to automotive design, make no mistake that Cleveland Institute of Art was a major player in the automotive industry. Ford and GM recruiters visited frequently scouting out talent. The contributions of Cleveland automotive designers are as old as its Industrial Design Department, founded in the early 1930s by Viktor Schreckengost (Viktor attended the school of art from 1925 to 1929). Viktor's own design work is the subject of several books: *Viktor Schreckengost and 20th-Century Design* (Cleveland Museum of Art), *Viktor Schreckengost: American Da Vinci* (Tide-Mark Press), and *Viktor Schreckengost: Designs in Dinnerware* (Schiffer Publishing).

Viktor, who early on worked extensively for the White Motor Company, invented the cab-over-engine truck—advertised as "the Greatest Development in Truck Transportation." Placing the cab over the engine reduced the overall length of the vehicle, making it even more desirable for commercial users. However, Viktor is most widely known for his work at the Murray Ohio Manufacturing Company, where he made groundbreaking designs and incorporated new manufacturing processes for the production of bicycles, lawn mowers, and pedal cars. Viktor incorporated powerful motorcycle forms in his first bicycle—the 1939 Murray—to promote sales. It was no longer a child's toy or just transportation. After connecting

with Sears, he invented a supersonic-looking bike and incorporated streamlining. He would later create banana seat bikes with smaller front wheels. On the other end of the spectrum, Viktor—with his brother Paul Gruber Schreckengost—was a major designer at American Limoges and the Salem China Company. His skills led him to design the famous Jazz Bowl in 1931. He later discovered that his art deco design was destined for use by Eleanor Roosevelt.

While Viktor chaired the department, Roy Hess and Hugh Greenlee also added their expertise. Both Hess and Greenlee made significant contributions to George Walker's design team in the 1940s. Greenlee taught Product Design and Hess taught Engineering Drawing, Materials, and Processes. Perhaps Walker's greatest contribution was the appearance of the popular 1949 Ford, to which Joe Oros, another Cleveland graduate, contributed. Oros, who started his career at Cadillac, is credited with the first Mustang.

From 1930 to 1966, before Klatil would graduate, twelve Cleveland alumni made their mark at the General Motors Corporation. Klatil's contemporaries include William Davis, Stan Denek, and Jerry Hirshberg. After perfecting his skills in the Pontiac and Buick studios, Hirshberg went on to found and run Nissan Design America in 1988 and wrote a book about his experiences titled *The Creative Priority*. Other notable significant GM designers paving the way for Klatil included Elizabeth Thatcher Oros and Joe Oros (1939); George Lawson, Paul Meyer, and James Shipley (1930–40); Bill Balla, Adelbert Coombes, and Bill Lang (1941–50); and Russ Bolt, Drew Hare, Don Hronek, Don Lasky, Robert Lattin, and John Shettler (1951–60). Barbara Munger (1970s) and Phil Zak came later.

Given this history, it would appear that the Industrial Design Department last graduated a female interiors and exterior designer, Betty Thatcher Oros, in 1939.

During Klatil's three years in the industrial design major, Mr. Mankowitz taught engineering, drafting, and interior design. William McDermott was Joan's graphic design and packaging instructor. Courses in the two foundation years were taught by William Edward Ward, a gifted calligrapher who worked at the Cleveland Museum of Art; Joan appreciates him even more today. Kenneth Bates taught freshman design and was known for his enameling work worldwide. Life drawing was taught all five years by Frances Meyers and Clarence Van Duzer. Joan notes, "My theory is if you can draw the figure and the automobile . . . you can draw anything! Perhaps it was CIA's motto too."

The first two years consisted of art and design courses and a handful of liberal-arts selections. After the second year, the student had a better idea of his or her talents and interests. Professors and students then chose a major, which lasted the next three years. When another student, Peter Zorn, saw Joan's work in gouache in the CIA lobby, he started telling her about industrial design (ID). He told her, "You could do it." She loved challenges, so she submitted a portfolio for entrance into the Industrial Design Department. After her second year with much difficulty, John Paul Miller, who taught sophomore design theory and had a knack for knowing what "major" students should choose, advised her against studying ID. He thought she should pursue illustration. But Joan persisted and was sure the industrial design instructors were a bit leery since it had been a long time since a woman selected an ID major. They gave her a chance, and she was on probation for six weeks to see if she could handle the courses. Industrial design students studied product design, graphics, packaging, and manufacturing and were enrolled in a shop class. Assignments become more and more difficult with the progression of time. Students were also taught that if you couldn't make a deadline, don't even start the assignment. The day came when students would have to present their solutions to the instructors with concept renderings, explain the product, describe its production, and relate which materials would be used. Presentation day required students to "dress" the part; after pulling all-nighters, presenting concepts in a dress and heels (guys in suits and ties) was rough with the deprivation of sleep, but terrific practice for the real world.

Joan emphasized that her instructors were outstanding. The wisdom of Viktor Schreckengost, the team of Hugh Greenlee and Roy Hess (all CIA graduates), and others will always be useful to many industrial design majors. They taught differently, as quoted from Jerry Hirshberg's book *The Creative Priority: Putting Innovation to Work in Your Business*: "The instructors (all practicing artists and designers) at the Cleveland Institute of Art knew better than to try to externally motivate creativity. What they knew instinctively was how to get out of its way, how to get *behind* it."

Joan appreciated the fact that Schreckengost, Greenlee, and Hess never treated her any differently from the men. Whether shop time or modeling, she had to do exactly the same projects except for one—she preferred to design a sewing machine instead of a lathe.

SUMMER INTERN

In the fourth and fifth years, students were given a transportation assignment plus more product design projects, redesigning items ranging from a chair, dinnerware, or stemware to a water sprinkler. They were introduced to automotive industry practices, including the drawing of full-size elevations and production of one-fifth-scale models. In 1965, Joan was chosen to attend the GM Summer Internship, which included a total of nine students from colleges across America. Bob Veryzer, a Pratt graduate, headed up this program in 1965, and a professor from another institution assisted. Dave Rosse, chief model maker, was an exceptional designer himself who could make anything look great from student drawings. Joan notes that students were given the task of designing an automobile of their choice for the future. She chose a "Shopping" concept car. Everything was provided, from model makers to the finishing of clay models in the paint shop, art supplies, airbrush, fiberglass … anything desired. Confidential files were made available for research. It was a dream come true!

Klatil's "Shopping" concept model. *Joan Klatil*

Joan started sketches with the seating arrangement; this gave her concept a totally new look. She placed one seat in the center, the other three behind—this was a shopping car, not a long riding auto. Entrance was through the front center door, which opened upward, with a side door for children and passengers. Because of the front entrance, the area behind the front wheel was wide enough to house groceries that were refrigerated. Joan put a kickplate on the outside to open this compartment. Inside could also be accessed for the refrigerated area. The working woman was able to shop during her lunch hour, store her foods, and be home for dinner, eliminating the grocery shopping after work. Six openings on each front inside fender had small lights to spread the beam (LED lights were not invented yet). The engine was in the rear and slid out from under the rear window for easy accessibility.

At the end of the summer, students presented their concepts to GM's styling decision makers, Bill Mitchell and Chuck Jordan. Designs were exhibited in the domed auditorium at the GM Tech Center so that other designers could leisurely look at the nine concepts.

Joan notes that GM sent the drawings, elevations, and scale models back to their schools after a month to share. Two students were hired after graduation from the group, one of whom was Peter Maier, a Pratt graduate. (Maier, a senior designer for Cadillac, Pontiac, and Chevrolet, quit the automotive industry around 1980 to become a prominent painter; as a fine artist he would later paint a photorealistic painting of the Duntov race car and a mural for the Harley Davidson facilities. He is represented by a NYC gallery.) Joan was also selected and represented CIA.

During Joan's fifth year at the institute, she was required to design a camper van, inside and out. Joan noted that this was pure industrial design. The outside styling was aerodynamically functional and aesthetically pleasing.

EXPERIENCES IN THE DEVELOPMENTAL DESIGN STUDIO

After being hired, all new designers in this era started in Design Development (DD). David North (a Toronado and Oldsmobile

Bill Mitchell, the VP of Design, assessed Klatil's first model. *Joan Klatil*

designer) replaced Bill Porter (a studio head for Buick and Pontiac) in 1966. Tom Hale, Charlie Gatewood, John Holihan, Bill Michalak. Peter Maier, and Joan were included in the group of newly hired designers that year. They all started that summer after graduating. Jerry Palmer was already on staff and was assigned to a studio about a week later. David North gave the green peas the freedom to design and learn GM's techniques. It took from three to eight months to determine which studio you would fit into, using the concept drawings you generated in the DD studio. The chief studio heads and the executives would look at the end products to provide the next challenge.

KLATIL JOINS CADILLAC

From the Developmental Design Studio, Klatil was placed into production Cadillac Exteriors and would perfect both her design and illustration skills. At this point in time, designers relied on markers, Prisma colored pencils, and black tape to create full-size drawings. A modeler made scale clay models from designers' drawings. Joan notes, "The modeler could make or break you."

Stan Parker served as the studio chief, and Wayne Kady was the helpful assistant chief of Cadillac (later studio chief of production for Cadillac, Buick #2). They would have a tremendous influence on Joan's development. Wayne gave her a small model of the 1967 Eldorado. "Look at the light, the way it hits it, and what happens to the reflections; just study it."[2] She still has that scale model. After observing Wayne's renderings, she noted that he would add complicated backgrounds to his illustrations, and Joan would later also make this a priority too. This studio also included Charlie Steward, John Perkins, Don McElfish, and Charlie Gatewood—all excelled.

One day, Bill Mitchell came back from Europe, and the next day Joan was transferred to Oldsmobile Interiors. She was dismayed and questioned why, only to find out years later that Bill Mitchell was uncomfortable with women in the exterior studios and had

banned them. After only three months in Oldsmobile Interiors, Joan returned to Jerry Hirshberg's Advanced Buick studio. Joan was there only six months when General Electric called to offer her a position. Realizing that Bill Mitchell was far from retirement, it was time to decide what she would do for the rest of her life. After her departure, the next female exterior designer, Carol Perelli, did not enter the picture for years following Mitchell's retirement.

Klatil's design drawing for Cadillac was right on target. *Joan Klatil*

GENERAL ELECTRIC

After Joan left GM in 1969, GE used their only woman industrial designer to work designing consumer electronics in Syracuse, New York. On the second day on the job, she flew to NYC to meet with Peter Max—the iconic pop artist of the '60s—to collaborate and place his art on GE's consumer products. She also worked with Disney and other licensing companies within the GE brand. She was transferred to the Appliance Park in Louisville, Kentucky, to design ranges, refrigerates, washers, dryers, etc., again being the only woman industrial designer. GE then needed someone at Wiring Devices for a GE chime project in Rhode Island as well as night "Lites," receptacle cover designs, etc. Joan continued working there until she started her own freelance business, Joan Creamer Design. By that time, she had divorced after twelve years of marriage but kept the Creamer name, since it was easier to remember in the design freelance business.

A MASTER DESIGNER AND ILLUSTRATOR

From 1987 until the present, it was an exciting time to be at GM with the "muscle" car guys during the '60s! The career path after GM has also been an empowering and learning experience. It has led Joan to many diversified companies, products, and countries around the world.

OTHER EMPLOYERS

Joan enjoyed working in the gift and tabletop business designing crystal for top manufacturers. She also designed collectibles and religious objects.

BOOKS AND ILLUSTRATIONS

When the product industry dried up around 2006, Joan saw the product managers, who were providing her with freelance work, being let go, and knew she had to act. She decided to work on a totally different creation that would be her own. It was a gamble and scary for her to write and illustrate children's books. She notes, "Designers design for a need." So the burning question (for all ages) has been, "How does Santa get into your home if there is no chimney?"[3] Her drawing ability could tell a story better than words alone as she conveyed a logical answer to this ageless question of Santa. He comes in through the keyhole, but . . . he needed more magic. A magic scepter with special powers was the solution for Santa to deliver gifts clandestinely. The first book, *The Legend of Blue Santa Claus*, was well received; it's been reprinted four times. An additional five books were released in the Magic Sceptre series. In essence, these creative stories empower their young readers with approaches to resolve common concerns of childhood. A complementary coloring book "draws" the child into creating pictures in an additional story. There is also a screenplay that may provide the foundation for a movie.

As a GM designer, Joan learned how to make her drawings more dramatic by using bird's-eye-view and worm's-eye-view perspectives. These viewpoints enhance each concept. These methods of illustrating books ensure that the viewer is not bored

Klatil penned this stunning Duesenberg for a Retired Designers show.

with a continuous eye-level view. Joan's drawings have always conveyed the story easier than words have. Redesigning the "North Express" train for the CeCie book brought her right back to her GM days.

PHILOSOPHY OF DESIGN AND OTHER DESIGNERS THAT INFLUENCE

Joan observes, "I've had many mentors, starting with my high school teacher. The list is very long. While attending college, I heard about Jerry Hirshberg's career in industrial design. He was on his way to GM by the time I selected my major—industrial design. I decided to take every class and elective he had taken, as I wanted to pursue his goal. I minored in portraiture with Paul Travis, took photography and sculpture with John Clague. Jerry didn't know he was my mentor, and it's so ironic that I was transferred into his Advanced Buick Studio and started to learn even more from him when GE called again and decided I had to take their offer—it was so difficult to leave."[4]

The design philosophy Joan has followed is to "be" the person you are designing for. That is, put yourself in their shoes by using it, reading it, learning it, touching it, and experiencing it. Feel the emotions of that person that the product is for. When Joan is absorbed with creating a children's book, she notices her voice gets even higher. If it's a toy, Joan goes to the level and pretends she's the child playing with it; the concepts that will roll onto the drawing board or computer will be welcome surprises.

LEAGUE OF RETIRED AUTOMOBILE DESIGNERS

Joan is still a very active member of the League of Retired Automotive Designers and notes, "I've come full circle in my automobile exterior design career. In 2008, I was asked to join the League of Retired Automotive Designers. It is an informal group of mostly retired automobile designers whose ability has been honed by years of experience and who still have the creativity, passion, enthusiasm, energy, and ambition to design cars and trucks for the fun of it." Joan notes that each year, members are given a past-to-present automobile to "retro." They display their concepts annually at the EyesOn Design automobile show on the Edsel Ford Estate. Joan said, "It is incredible to see what beautiful works of art and concepts would be if the 'muscle car' designers were still working."[5]

She adds, "The men accept my work and I sign my full name most of the time." Joan's signature now reads "Joan Klatil Creamer."

PART VI.
THE 1970s

After rolling out fierce muscle cars in the early 1970s, the demise of the performance car as we knew it was in sight. By 1971, those on the outside would strive to dictate how cars performed and what they looked like. Safety and environmental experts would pose questions about safety and emissions and force government agencies to set more-stringent regulations. In 1971, a decision was made that all GM cars use unleaded gasoline, and catalytic converters would become standard by 1975.

By 1974, we faced a severe energy crisis. Car companies would eventually have to start thinking about CAFE (Corporate Average Fuel Economy) more than they would have liked. On another note, manufacturers would have to meet the onslaught of small Japanese products already addressing the size and safety equation. We would begin to rely more on Vegas and Chevettes and X-cars. The Chevrolet Citation made its debut in 1979 to address fuel economy. Its divisional counterparts would follow.

Beginning in 1970, each division aside from Cadillac offered big-block engines made for performance. Perhaps the letters SS represented the attitude of the times. There was an SS package available on the 1970 Camaro, new Monte Carlo, and even a special Nova SS 396. When it came to Pontiac, many of the performance features were standard. The Trans-Am was equipped with a 400-cubic-inch, Ram Air V-8 with 330 hp out of the gate. And let us not forget the Olds 4-4-2, with a choice of two 455-cubic-inch V-8s. To this day, these cars raise the bar at collectible car auctions, sometimes even generating the highest bid of the day.

In 1970, Vauxhall built an innovative experimental car; the Special Research Vehicle was designed to test engines, suspensions, and aerodynamics.

When it came to styling, all full-size Chevrolets were redesigned, including the Biscayne, Belair, Impala, and Caprice. Cars featured longer hoods and slimmer pillars, and the 1970 Caprice and Impala Deluxe had concave rear glass. Pickup trucks, Chevrolets and GMCs, were offered in step sides, fleet sides, and chassis cabs—six cylinders and eights. As time went on, to insure safety, metal elements—including the instrument panel—were padded.

By 1971, the compact Vega, and subsequently Vega GT and Kammback wagon, made their marks and featured the newest spot-welded construction. In 1971, Oldsmobile began manufacturing parts from sheet molding compound (SMC) as plastic replaced steel. Vauxhall celebrated the manufacture of its millionth Viva built in England. Holden of Australia introduced a station wagon. In 1971, Buick unveiled its iconic boat tail styling but discontinued it in 1974. GM's Holden introduced the HQ. At this time, General Motors Institute presented plans to establish a mobile emissions lab.

By 1972, the Urban Vehicle Design contest was opened to sixty-two universities, and sixty-six vehicle designs were evaluated against set criteria. The jury was looking for 5 mph bumpers, drunk-test devices, antitheft systems, lower levels of emissions, and the integration of systems. To create a safer vehicle, a handful of experimental safety vehicles (ESVs) built by aerospace companies and others entered into contracts with government.

GM's extensive testing of the Wankel rotary engine led to a midengine four-rotor. After research was completed, the car was converted to the V-8 powered Aerovette, still a beautiful form.

In 1972, all GM cars were equipped with 5 mph bumpers up front and 2.5 mph bumpers in the rear. Some bumpers were made thicker, and others were reinforced.

In 1972, the 26-foot GM Motorhome was designed, with four interior packages for different uses, from the ground up. Unlike the boxy rolling homes of the times, the slightly rounded form, with large windows radiused at the corners, was enhanced with wide decorative stripes associated with the packages. While still in production the Advanced Studio was called upon to design and integrate a new A/C system for it. One was fascinated by the fiberglass construction during a visit to the local factory that had been commandeered from previous users.

In 1972, Opel designed the Opel Rekordwagen, using an Opel GT chassis to test diesel engines.

The LUV pickup, made by Isuzu, also arrived in 1972.

Olds and Cadillac celebrated their anniversaries, the seventy-fifth and seventieth, and the 500-cubic-inch Eldorado documented record sales for the division. In 1972, Olds worked with Hurst to install a 455 hp V-8, and the Cadillac Eldorado was selected to pace the Indy 500 in 1973. There came a time when all cars were equipped with catalytic converters.

At this time, GM was involved in negotiating the rights to use the Wankel engine, and designers created stunning cars around it—one Corvette derivative was initially equipped with a four-rotor engine and sat in the lobby of the Design staff building to invigorate all who entered.

In 1973, new bumper laws would change the way cars looked and performed. An oil embargo and gasoline shortage would begin to dictate the size and shape of cars, and wind tunnels could evaluate the drag coefficient (Cd). Fairchild and AMF, among others, would be contracted and paid to develop an ESV. Other teams would need to design and build car models that were safer than ever before. In 1973, new bumpers were designed to store or dissipate energy.

Also in 1973, the Monte Carlo and the Gran Am offered new options. The Olds Cutlass sold well and won over *Car and Driver* readers for the best family car. Nova sales were impressive, and the El Camino, a friendly truck-like vehicle, gained followers. In 1974, the popular Trans Am had a beefed-up engine.

The 1975 Monza coupe was offered with various power trains depending on where you lived. It was puzzling that if you lived in Michigan, only a 262-cubic-inch V-8 was available; however, if you were a California resident, would have been able to order the 350 V-8. Either way, you needed a special tool just to change the plugs. The Monza coupe was recognized with a Car of the Year award, although other body styles were also offered. In 1975, Holden offered their SL/R 5000 with a 5-liter V-8.

GM's first response to the fuel crisis of 1974 was the Chevrolet Chevette. Cadillac introduced its smaller Seville in 1975. This was also the year when all GM cars were equipped with catalytic converters, and to accommodate the change, unleaded gas was required. GM also presented their driver air-cushioning restraint system. In an effort to improve fuel economy in 1977, Chevrolet introduced 3.3-liter, 90-degree V-6, with small cars in mind. In 1976, Buick's Skyhawk hatchback arrived, based on the 1975 Chevrolet Monza.

In 1976, the last Cadillac convertible of the decade was built, and it would take some time for soft-tops to come back in the '80s. The smaller Seville would come to market.

Perhaps the most noticeable car of the year was the fuel-efficient 1976 Chevette, with its 1.4-liter, four-cylinder engine ready to take on the Japanese product invasion. In 1978, an Electrovette coupe, a derivative, was powered by an electric motor and equipped with a heavy battery pack. However, in 1976, Olds was still making a killing with its Cutlass as the also-popular Grand Prix sought to keep up.

In 1977, the Toronado helped push Oldsmobile sales to over a million units. Weight was removed from the successful Impala and Caprice to improve fuel mileage. The freshened Corvette featured a new console inside.

In 1977, Irvin Ribicki would replace Bill Mitchell as VP of Design. While some predicted this selection, others thought the position belonged to Charles Jordan, but Jordan would have to wait his turn.

In 1977, a GMC transit bus, powered by a new diesel engine, made its debut. Chevrolet introduced a new Corvette with an upgraded interior.

By 1978, GMC introduced its RTS (Rapid Transit Series) bus, with a self-contained-climate air-conditioning system and a fuel-efficient turbocharged diesel engine.

The stately Opel Senator arrived in 1978 and was later joined by the Opel Monza and Vauxhall Royale Coupe derivatives.

By the end of the decade, one car after another, with the exception of Cadillac, was designed using the front-wheel-drive X-chassis to improve fuel economy. Opel introduced the Manta for its eightieth birthday. A shorter and smaller Malibu was offered with a 3.3-liter V-6. The Regal Sport and Le Sabre Sport Coupe made their entrance.

In 1978, the Special Edition gold Trans Am with T-top roof panels would generate record sales, and the 1978 Corvette paced the Indy 500.

The roomy Chevrolet Citation, made in 1979, would later lead the pack. For 1979, the lighter Olds' Toronado and Eldorado and Buick's fifth-generation Riviera continued to impress. The Senator was the flagship for Opel. As the decade ended, the front-wheel-drive configuration monopolized the future.

JACQUELINE "JACQUI" (DRURY) DEDO

I don't know if people understand how amazing it is to walk from an engineering office into a factory and to see the theoretical being applied to make a difference in people's lives and in communities. When you look at the level of technological sophistication in product and process and the level of GDP that it creates for our nations, it's a very exciting place to be for any discipline of study.[1]

—Jacqueline Dedo (2014)

(b. 1961)

Recognitions: 2005, 2010: "100 Leading Women in the North American Auto Industry" (*Automotive News*), US patents

CAREER HIGHLIGHTS

Jacqueline has served the automotive industry for over forty years. She began her engineering career in 1979 as a co-op student and spent seven years serving Cadillac as a co-op student and then as a validation engineer. In 1986, she joined Robert Bosch as a sales engineer and worked her way up to the president of the Ford Value Team, including a two-year assignment in Germany. After this fourteen-year stint, she joined Motorola in 2000, serving as its corporate vice president. In 2004, she joined Timken as president of the Global Automotive Group.

In 2008, she joined the Dana Corporation as its chief strategy and supply chain officer.

By 2014, Jacqueline was appointed president of Piston Group. In 2016, she cofounded Aware Mobility LLC. In 2018, she began her service on the Board of Directors of the Cadillac Products Auto Company, and in 2020 on the board of Workhorse Truck Group.

GROWING UP

Since she was little, Jacqueline was fascinated by how things worked and were put together. Jacqueline notes the influence her dad played in her life as a child: "It was a combination of my fascination with science projects and working on things that I could build with my dad. My father introduced me to different people at GM and used to talk to me about how General Motors is one of the most innovative manufacturing companies in the world, and the impact that they have on society."[2]

"My father was in the Commerce Department as assistant deputy secretary of strategic resources under Secretary Malcolm Baldrige. I met Pete Estes, and some of his staff, working around my dad, as well as longtime friend Neil DeKoker, recommended I look at Kettering even though I was from the East Coast."[3]

Jacqueline attended W. T. Woodson High school in Virginia and in 1977 was a National Merit Scholarship Corporation semifinalist.[4] In addition to high marks on a test, administrators in her school would have also attested to her high academic standing. She graduated in 1979.

Kettering University was called GMI (General Motors Institute) at the time Dedo began studies there in 1979. It was founded in 1919 and acquired by GM in 1926. GMI offered a cooperative education model not unlike the services—the Naval and Air Force Academies come to mind. Students applied to various divisions of General Motors, and these entities sponsored them. In actuality, they were hired as employees and were paid for the work they performed in a car plant or other

Albert Sobey was a leader in technical education. *Constance Smith*

facility. During two twelve-week breaks, they received their formal education and graduated in either engineering or administration after five years. While women may have surfaced during World War II while the men served, women hadn't been recruited until around 1970. Women were common in administration and rarer in engineering. GM changed its relationship with the school around 1982.

Coincidentally, Jacqueline serves on the board of Kettering University and continues to be active in alumni affairs.

In 1979, as an employee of Cadillac, Jacqueline was assigned to the Clark Street Plant in Detroit. She started in the paint shop and then worked on the line. As a sophomore, she was invited to work in the engineering departments.[5] In 1984, Jacqueline was one of the few women who graduated with a bachelor of science degree in electrical engineering.

Jacqueline would continue to work with GM until 1986 before moving on to Robert Bosch Corporation–Automotive Group, which designs, manufactures, and sells automotive components, subsystems, and systems for all types of vehicles globally.

Her fourteen years at Bosch confirmed her passion for technology and advanced development, being exposed to a company continually focused on future improvement through technology.

In 2016, Jacqui cofounded Aware Mobility, which focuses on the emerging ecosystem born from the blending of the network economy and the transportation industry and market-valued products in electrification. Aware primarily develops, integrates, and consults on mobility connectivity, electrification, and electrified propulsion.

This 1983 Cadillac was exhibited in a show held at Sarant Cadillac. *Constance Smith*

ELIZABETH GRIFFITH

Do not live a life of regrets and I-should-haves—
but a life of I will, and I did.
We are bulldogs![1]
—Elizabeth Griffith (b. 1953), offering advice at Kettering
    University's 2019 centennial commencement

CAREER HIGHLIGHTS

Griffith's career in the automotive industry, spanning over forty-five years, has been diverse. In her role as the director of engineering and program quality for Faurecia Interior Systems, Griffith supported a team of fourteen people on the GM Global account. Some of her responsibilities included growing the business and developing customer relationships; achieving GM and Faurecia safety, quality, and cost objectives; and understanding the complex customer product systems to ensure that the product, processes, and people are focused on success over the product execution timeline.[1]

Before coming out of retirement to join Faurecia in 2010, Griffith held various positions, among them vice president of advanced engineering and program management at Magna International Automotive from 2001 to 2007. Prior to that, Griffith held the position of vice president of engineering and program management at Peregrine Incorporated, as well as serving as a plant manager.

By 2015, Griffith served as director of engineering, product development, GM Global, for Faurecia. This was the second time she was recognized by inclusion in *Automotive News* as one of the "100 Leading Women in the North American Auto Industry."

Griffith currently serves as director of program management for HFI, a supplier of interior components for the automotive industry.

Griffith also participates in a number of women's automotive groups, inspiring women to explore STEM occupations. She is cochair of AutomotiveNEXT, which looks to inspire women in the future.

THE JOURNEY WITH A SURPRISE ENDING

Elizabeth was the only girl of four children born to her parents. She believes that being socialized with wolves might have made her bossy and led to her lack of emotions. She is direct, like a man or today's strong woman. She grew up in the inner city of Detroit, so her plans to study music and library science at the University of Michigan on a full scholarship were normal

Elizabeth Griffith

for a young lady her age until her brother, a student at General Motors Institute (now Kettering University), submitted her name at school because GM was looking for "smart women." After an interview at GM's Fort Street Plant in 1971, she was offered a position by a GM sponsor on the spot. Perhaps the fact that her family struggled financially helped her make the right decision. This opportunity was unheard of, but her mother wisely allowed her to make her own decision: "Do whatever you want to do." These events, which Griffith terms an accident, changed her life.

Griffith was likely intimidated by Bob Dieber, superintendent of process engineering at the Fort Street plant, to which she was assigned. He was described as tough, mean, and perfectionistic, and this scared her. However, Griffith achieved great success here. She rose to exceed the challenge. Thus, her career began at General Motors, where she was part of the first large class of women to go through the General Motors Institute program.

Griffith holds a bachelor of science degree in mechanical engineering from General Motors Institute in Flint, Michigan. After graduating from the program in 1977, she held various positions within General Motors—her first as an industrial engineer recording time and delay studies on the factory floor at Fisher Body in 1977. She also served as a manufacturing general supervisor, platform program manager, and chief manufacturing engineer for mechanical components and interiors.

Opportunity came when John "Jack" Smith Jr., who served as a GM president, and J. T. Battenberg III were in the office setting up Delphi. In an effort to establish GM in eastern Europe, they set up a program with the Polish government. Elizabeth was put in charge as all the divisions of Delphi as they sought to up-fit and westernize a Polish vehicle for sale. They added an automatic liftgate and created a fresh interior and presented it to Smith and other GM executives. This was truly a breakthrough. Although it would later become more the norm, Elizabeth was transferred to a new position every eighteen to twenty-four months.

Beyond her professional accolades, Griffith was named one of the "100 Leading Women in Automotive" by *Automotive News* in both 2005 and 2015.

Griffith champions various women in automotive groups that inspire women to join STEM fields and careers. It is time for the women to pursue engineering without being baited. She believes that girls need mentoring at an early age. They need to turn on to math and science and be apprised of the opportunities.

She is the cochair of AutomotiveNEXT, inspiring and supporting the next generation of automotive leaders. Her organization is an Inforum industry group that provides a network and support community for automotive women to empower them to achieve their full potential and make a lasting impact on the industry.

In 2017, Griffith was recognized by the Kettering University Alumni for Management Achievement group and joined the Kettering University Engineering Board.

Elizabeth Griffith enjoys spending time with her husband and reading—she is a fan of science fiction—and looks forward to a time when she can sit back and relax. That time-out is not now.

Kettering University recently celebrated their one hundredth anniversary. *Constance Smith*

GRACE (LARRINUA) LIEBLEIN

I have always been slightly hesitant when somebody wants to give me a new job. There's always the voice in the back of your head saying, "You don't have experience in that," or "I'm not sure you can do that,'" she said. "I've had to get over that."[1]

—Grace Lieblein (b. 1960)

Courtesy of General Motors

CAREER HIGHLIGHTS

Grace Lieblein served General Motors for thirty-five years. In 2015, prior to her end-of-year retirement, she held the position of vice president of global quality and was GM's highest-ranking Hispanic woman. During her rise, Lieblein had also served as president of GM Brazil and GM Mexico.

In 2015, Lieblein was named to the *Automotive News* register of the "Top 100 Leading Women in the North American Auto Industry." She was also among *Fortune*'s "10 Most Powerful Women in Automotive" in 2013.

During the course of her career, Lieblein has served a number of charities and also supported STEM activities to encourage young women to pursue engineering careers. Today, Lieblein serves on the Board of Directors of Honeywell International, American Tower, and Southwest Airlines.

BIOGRAPHICAL NOTES

Grace Lieblein was raised in Los Angeles. Her father came here from Cuba, and her mother from Nicaragua. Mr. Larrinua was an autoworker at GM's South Gate Assembly plant in Los Angeles. Her mother assured her daughter that she could do anything she set her mind and heart to do. In an interview, Grace noted, "He brought home that love of vehicles and cars and the company. When I decided to go into engineering, he kind of pointed me toward GMI."[2] She was sponsored by her father's plant.[3]

Lieblein met her husband, Tom, at General Motors Institute (now Kettering University). She married when she was still in college, working toward her bachelor of science in industrial engineering. Subsequently, she completed requirements for an MBA in materials and logistics management from Michigan State University. In 1998, she received a certificate from the Thunderbird School of Global Management.

In 1978, Grace left California and headed for Flint, Michigan, to join other early women students in the co-op program at General Motors Institute (GMI) in Flint, Michigan. The draw for most was the guarantee of free tuition and a salary. At GMI, she was influenced by the leadership of John Lorenz: "John was a professor of industrial engineering, then he became the head of engineering and eventually provost, but he was my fifth-year advisor. He was one of those remarkable teachers, like Reg Bell, but quite the character. He truly loved teaching, loved students, and was super supportive. He was an incredible guy."[4]

When she first arrived at GMI, there was a hectic six-week-on and six-week-off schedule; students were relieved when intervals moved to twelve weeks on and twelve weeks off.

Lieblein's first postcollege assignment was with Oldsmobile in Lansing, Michigan, where she received an assignment in ergonomics and served as first line supervisor and manager of die engineering. She notes, "I started the ergonomics program at what was then Oldsmobile in Lansing, Michigan. At GMI, I did my thesis on ergonomics. At that time (around 1983), people didn't know what ergonomics was. I worked with the medical department in the plant to look at medical records to see what jobs were injuring people. It was a cool job."[5]

Grace Lieblein experienced a new culture with each assignment.
General Motors

By 1996, Lieblein served as an engineering director. In 2004, she was elevated to chief engineer of Lambda crossovers (Chevy Traverse, Buick Enclave, GMC Acadia). Lieblein relocated to Mexico when she moved from engineering director to managing director. She felt like she was running her own company, with responsibility for planning and logistics.

"I was fortunate," she continues. "I had a couple of leaders who pushed me out of my comfort zone. I remember, while I was chief engineer, the vice president of engineering wanted me to take an assignment, and my first instinct was just what I was referring to. I didn't think I had the right experience for it." But her vice president insisted. "I just remember being told, 'You can do this and you will do this, and you're going to do a great job.' And it turned out great," she laughs.[6]

Two stretch assignments took her career international. In January 2009, Ms. Lieblein was named president of GM Mexico, making her the first woman ever to lead that operation. For three years, she led an operation with $2 billion in revenue and 11,000 employees, bringing GM Mexico back to profitability in the process. But it was not without its challenges, especially outside the workplace.[7]

As the president of GM do Brasil in Sao Paulo in 2011, Lieblein's oversight included total planning-and-logistics responsibility, with $12 billion in revenues. Her operation consisted of some 25,000 employees producing and selling over 600,000 vehicles a year. Her initial challenge focused on transforming the business unit into a sustainably profitable entity. Grace developed a three-year road map and provided the strategic guidance to improve financial operations, reduce costs, and capitalize on the organization's core competencies.[8]

Her successes in Brazil preceded her assignment as the vice president of global purchasing and supply chain (2014–2015), a position that made her the highest-ranking Hispanic American woman in the auto industry. Without qualifying her success or her talent, she credits General Motors with one thing over everything else: opportunity. "I have been blessed with an incredible career, and I can't thank General Motors enough for giving me great opportunities at every level," she says. "Without opportunities to begin with, then you don't even get the chance to succeed, right?"[9]

Lieblein's husband, Tom, has always been supportive and cared for their high-school-aged daughter when Grace had an overseas assignment. Formerly a group engineering manager, Tom retired before Grace. Their daughter, Amy, followed in her footsteps to Kettering University and MSU and is an engineer. The Liebleins reside in San Clemente, California, and relax at their lake house in Michigan.

BARBARA MUNGER

John Paul Miller at the Cleveland Institute of Art made a lasting impression on me. He prized innovation. More importantly, he taught me to value my own work. He made it clear that you don't have to change your designs to satisfy others.

—Barbara Munger (b. 1947)

Courtesy of Barbara Munger

CAREER HIGHLIGHTS

After graduating from the Cleveland Institute of Art, Barbara Munger accepted a position at Black & Decker in Maryland. After a short period of time, she learned of a position at GM Design in an interior design studio for a woman, from the head of the industrial design area at Cleveland. Initially, Munger designed mainly seats and doors for Buick, Chevrolet, Pontiac, and Saturn. When it came to Chevrolet, she contributed to the Celebrity, Impala, Lumina, and Monte Carlo. However, when it came to the Lumina, her design for an instrument panel was selected for production. Munger's affiliation with GM lasted for over twenty years.

BIOGRAPHICAL NOTES

Kentucky born and raised, Barbara Munger is the youngest of three artistic sisters. Both parents were educators. Her father taught high school mathematics and was subsequently selected to serve as the school principal. Her mother, already schooled in home economics, retrained to qualify as an elementary school teacher. Mother loved the little ones to whom she taught reading readiness. Despite her father's death while she was a young teen, the family moved to Cleveland, where Barbara studied with a series of teachers that recognized her passion for art and provided encouragement and extra training.

As a student at the Park Hills Elementary School, Barbara was recognized for her creativity and talent. Following in the footsteps of both her sisters, she qualified for a free program provided by the Baker Hunt Foundation—the classes offered were financed by a wealthy benefactress to advance the arts. She was impressed with Miss Kunnie, an avant-garde art teacher with a neat bun. Kunnie's 7-inch-wide leather belt, with diamond-shaped holes stamped in it, left an impression on her. While a student at Oak Hills High School, Barbara later qualified for another free program at Kansas University. Her high school teacher, Louis Koenig, encouraged and assisted her in finding this opportunity.[1]

By this time, her sister Julia mastered plein air painting, and her sister Charlotte rounded out her art skills.

Barbara would later quality for a scholarship to the Cleveland Institute of Art. The Western Reserve School of Design was established in 1882 before gaining its own separate identity as the Cleveland School of Art, and later as the Cleveland Institute of Art. It has been described as one of the nation's leading independent colleges of art and design.

During the first two years, Barbara completed a range of art courses. She subsequently fell in love with industrial design. In the seventies, industrial designers emphasized aesthetics. As time went on, designers were more concerned with ergonomics, marketing, brand development, and sales. The industrial design department at Cleveland was founded by Viktor Schreckengost. Viktor had already received praise for his design of the Jazz Bowl for Eleanor Roosevelt. He also designed bicycles for Murray and Sears, Roebuck and Co. Working alongside Ray Spiller, Viktor designed the first cab-over-engine truck—this design is still offered today.[2]

When it came to the automobile industry, Viktor recognized and promoted talent and knew what was required. A number of his most talented students built reputations in the automotive industry, including Joe and Betty Oros and Jerry Hirshberg.[3] Starting his career at Cadillac, Joe Oros later headed the design team responsible for the iconic 1964–65 Ford Mustang. Betty Thatcher Oros was Hudson's first female designer.[4] Jerry Hirshberg, also a degreed engineer, left his position at Pontiac and Buick to found Nissan in America and serve as president of Nissan Design International (NDI).[5] Hirschberg's team designed the first

Pathfinder, Altima, and Maxima and additionally worked for Apple, Motorola, and other notable corporations. Hirshberg served on Cleveland's board of directors and the National Endowment for the Arts design committee. Barbara admired the work of these Cleveland graduates. More importantly, Barbara loved and respected Viktor. He was larger than life.

With just two other young ladies, Munger enrolled in Viktor's industrial design program. Other professors also admired her work.

Munger's silversmithing instructor would also make a lasting impression on her. John Paul Miller introduced her to organic form and granulations, a technique in which he encrusted small silver or gold balls on top of an abstract surface. Munger still values the ring she made forty-four years ago. Munger believes he could have created this technique.

In 1971, Barbara graduated into the real world of work and dragged her portfolio everywhere in a weak economy until landing at Black & Decker in Towson, Maryland. She notes that the executives at B&D were paying attention when their studies indicated that women selected and used most garden tools. Her initial assignment included designing graphics and molded cases for power tools. However, the design of cases did not thrill her. After about nine months, she received a call from Viktor. A representative from General Motors Design had contacted the Cleveland Institute of Art, looking to hire a female graduate. Viktor contacted her immediately. Yes, she was very interested.

There is no question that a large number of women were introduced to the automotive industry by their college professors. Viktor had excelled in the automotive industry himself, trained top automobile designers, and maintained close relationships with corporate recruiters.

MUNGER INTERVIEWS

Immediately following the recommendation by Viktor Schreckengost, Barbara Munger was interviewed by Roger Martin, General Motors' personnel manager. At the initial interview, Barbara was informed that no women were allowed to work in the exterior design studios. She notes, "If you told a recent graduate they could not work in the exteriors studio, she would think you have two heads."[6] She was subsequently interviewed by Don Schwarz, area head of Chevrolet, Pontiac, and GMC, and offered a position in one of the two Chevrolet Interiors Studios. There was no question that Barbara had big high heels to fill. Ruth Glennie and Sue Vanderbilt had built enormous reputations at Chevrolet, as far back as 1955.[7]

During an affiliation lasting over nineteen years, Barbara contributed to the design of interiors for the Chevrolet, Buick, Pontiac, and Saturn Divisions. Although she worked on the design of Monte Carlos and Impalas, Barbara is perhaps best noted for her work as the lead designer for the first-generation Chevrolet Lumina, which was built on the W-body platform in 1989. The Lumina family included a sedan, coupe, and APV (minivan).

Barbara designed dozens of doors and seats. She remembers working on the Monte Carlo, Celebrity, and Impala. After passing though the Pontiac, Buick, and Saturn Studios, she would later return to Chevrolet—this time as lead designer for the Chevrolet Lumina.

However, she notes that this time it wasn't just seats and doors; she was given the responsibility for the instrument panel. After penning a series of sketches, she gravitated to the wall and mounted a huge sheet of grid paper on a sliding panel. Although designers used pencil, marker, and tape to explore designs, full-size airbrush illustrations of the instrument panel were completed on the wall in two views. Later the studio engineer and clay modeler would study the drawings before producing a clay model for the seating buck for the W-body Lumina, complete with its 60/40 seat.

The new Lumina was built in the Oshawa, Ontario, Canada, plant starting in 1989; this facility later received the J. D. Power and Associates Founder's Award.

Lumina also became the nameplate that Chevrolet used in NASCAR. The Lumina and Lumina Euro were offered as

A touch of wood completed the interior of the Chevy 1993 Lumina. *Constance Smith*

1993 Lumina. *General Motors*

General Motors

two-door notchback coupes and four-door sedans. The sporty Euro was offered with a 3.1-liter six-cylinder and upgraded interior. The 2.5-liter engine featured throttle body injection, and the 3.2-liter had multiport fuel injection. In 1991, the Z34 four-door coupe featured a 3.4-liter twin-cam V-6 and 210 hp.[8]

In this period in time, the Lumina addressed consumers' interests in safety and accident avoidance, since this was very much a family car. As lead designer, Barbara designed an innovative instrument panel that ran the better part of the width of the car; GM would later emphasize the fact that the energy-absorbing instrument panel would soften the impact in the event of a frontal collision. The illuminated entry system automatically lit the instrument panel control when the driver closed the door. Traditional gauges in the base model were clear and easily read. On the 1993 model, a gauge package included a tachometer and trip odometer on the Z34 coupe and Euro 3.4 sedan. A Delco AM/FM radio, with a cassette or compact disk player on higher models, was located centrally to the right of the driver. The radio included a Delco-Loc II theft-deterrent system. An optional 80-watt Delco-Bose Silver Series Music System with four Bose speakers filled the interior with natural sound. At this time, air-conditioning was an expensive option for some families.

As was customary, the designers made numerous sketches and renderings of seats. With the assistance of the studio engineer and clay modeler, full-size drawings later led to the construction of a seating buck. The production seats were straightforward and comfortable and included a split-back bench and 60/40 split with wide headrests. In contrast to the full foam conventional designs, the seats relied on steel spring suspension. They were offered in beige, dark blue, gray, and garnet red both in stock cloth and custom cloth to complement ten exterior colors.

In terms of safety, the Lumina also featured a unitized body/frame, shatter-resistant windshield glass, and side-guard door beams. Chevrolet touted their ABS VI, halogen headlamps, independent front and rear suspension, and four-wheel power disc brakes.

Occasionally, the vice president of Design, Bill Mitchell, would invite the designers into the auditorium, and Barbara joined her colleagues. At this time, Mr. Mitchell gave a presentation of some product advertisements and noted that "to be a good automobile designer, gas has to run in your veins." It never did for Barbara. She relished what she was doing despite this unwelcome comment.

In 1990, *Family Circle* magazine named the Lumina sedan its Car of the Year. In the movie *Days of Thunder,* Tom Cruise, who portrayed USAC/NASCAR driver Cole Trickle, piloted a specially designed Lumina race car. In 1991, the Z34, a high-performance version complete with spoiler, was added. In 1992, the new Euro 3.4 sedan was powered by a twin dual-cam engine. At the time, this engine was the most advanced regular production V-6 in Chevrolet history. With a 9.25:1 compression ratio, it featured pent roof combustion chambers, centrally located plugs, and computerized spark timing. Production continued through 1995.[9]

By the time the last year of production ended in 2005, Chevrolet had sold over one million of various Lumina models.

Never marrying, Barbara later retired after a twenty-year stint after being questioned by a new male manager. However, in 2009 her age group of colleagues was encouraged or forced to retire.

She rejoined her family back home.

CAROL PERELLI

A car is like a human being. It should have human qualities; I feel like it's partially human and is an extension of the human body.[1]

On January 30, 1994, Roger Worthington wrote a piece for the Chicago Tribune recognizing three women designers in "The New Breed Enters the Male World of Cars by Design." At the time of the interview, Perelli notes, "To me a vehicle is not just transportation, it's a piece of moving sculpture, one of the biggest pieces of moving sculpture, and for that reason it should be beautiful."

—Carol Perelli (b. 1942)

CAREER HIGHLIGHTS

After being awarded a bachelor's degree from Wayne State University, Carol Perelli was retained by a design office, where she took a major responsibility in designing the building for an Arabic school. Her colleagues were so impressed that they convinced her to seek further education, and she enrolled in the design program at the College for Creative Studies (CCS) in the evening.

Perelli, who spent twenty-three years with GM, started her automotive career in 1979. From 1981 to 1989, she received assignments in the Pontiac, Oldsmobile, Buick II, and Advanced II Corvette Studios. She made notable contributions to the 1984 production Buick Regal Coupe.

In 1997, just prior to retirement, she worked in the Engineer Center Group with others from across the corporation. Perelli retired in 2003.

PERELLI'S JOURNEY[2]

While we were engaged in the deadliest war in our history, Carol Perelli was born in 1942 at St. John's Hospital in Detroit, Michigan. Her sister, Sherry, is slightly younger. After emigrating from northern Italy, her grandfather worked the coal mines in Illinois to support four children; he would later suffer the consequences of tuberculosis. Her father, Hector, was a tool- and diemaker for the Ford Motor Company. He was handsome, 5 foot 11, and made sure his daughters followed the rules or they faced the consequences. An avid gardener, he loved to work with his hands and constructed a huge stone wall near the house and harvested plenty of fresh vegetables in the hot summer months. Carol's mother, with light-brown hair and blue eyes, was pretty and average in height. Both her grandmother and mother kept the house in order and cared for the children.

With the war underway, Carol's father developed an active interest in aviation and proceeded to purchase aircraft kits. A ¾-scale Lockheed Hudson Bomber from a gasoline kit manufactured by the Cleveland Model & Supply Company was found at an estate sale. Carol's dad also made pencil and pen-and-ink-drawings of the airplanes he modeled, and later some automobiles as she watched.

As the war wound down, the family moved to Royal Oak, and Carol was enrolled in the Benjamin Franklin Elementary School. She attended junior high school nearby and later Dondero High School. She admired and grew close to her government teacher, Mrs. Miller. Carol was fascinated by Miller's view of the world: "Look at the opportunities around the world. China is a silent giant." Carol would later enroll in a college course at Oakland University to learn more about China and visit Hong Kong and Gansu—a Communist area—on a vacation.

One summer, Carol's dad decided he could fashion an electric lawn mower by mating a push mower with a small gasoline engine. Although there were some dangerous connections, he taught both Carol and her sister to mow the lawn, and they "lived to tell about it."

In 1960, Carol applied to Wayne State University and later met her future husband, who attended Michigan State before "flunking out"; however, he ultimately earned his degree at Wayne State. Rick's Polish parents were Lutheran and cared little for Carol—an Italian Catholic—and expressed it. Rick would not stand for it and knew what he wanted. Carol was about nineteen when they were married by a justice of the peace, in a civil ceremony witnessed by a couple of people dragged in from a nearby office of the building. In the early stages of a difficult marriage, Carol worked to help support them both. She took every job she could get, including service and sales jobs at Michigan Bell, Hudson's, and Sears, where she rose to assistant manager. The bottom line in business was simple—success was based on profit, and she excelled at making money for her employers.

One summer, she was retained by a design office where she took a major responsibility in designing the building for an Arabic school. One of her male colleagues was so impressed with her ability that he encouraged her to enroll in CCS, which offered an evening program in design to further her education. It would be years before she would follow through with his recommendation, but the stage was set.

Because her husband, Rick, feared he would be drafted, he insisted that Carol have a child, and she bore a son. She took four years off from studies and graduated with a BA in fine arts in 1977. Around this time, she worked part-time as a coordinator for Junior Achievement and met the officer of a local bank; he offered to procure an educational loan for her to supplement her education as she was working. Excited and hopeful, she applied for entrance to the College for Creative Studies, which was nearby.

COLLEGE OF CREATIVE STUDIES

The Society of Arts & Crafts was founded in 1906 and offered informal art classes. At the turn of the century, it is likely the founders sought to promote handmade articles made popular by the Arts and Crafts movement, established in England. Early offerings included design, drawing, and woodworking. After attracting an outstanding faculty from the automobile companies around it, the school made headlines after recognizing the automobile as an art form in 1933. Shortly after, courses were offered in both industrial design and commercial art. Carol attended the school in the evening in a building behind the Detroit Institute of Arts. By 1975, the school took on a new name, the Center for Creative Studies (CCS), College of Art and Design. She met three professors in the evening program. Two of them, Homer LaGassey and Dennis Hugley, were car guys. LaGassey, a graduate of Pratt Institute, continued his career at GM Styling shortly after serving in World War II. Homer made the illustration below in the Oldsmobile Studio in 1950. After also serving Chrysler and Ford, he has won numerous awards, including the prestigious EyesOn Design award.

LaGassey, who was saluted by numerous students and colleagues, passed away in a nursing facility in 2014.

Carol was one of just two female students enrolled at CCS in her major from 1978 to 1979; her classmate's father worked as an executive for Ford, and she too would join Ford after graduation.

Carol learned to make the first of many tape drawings to delineate the exterior of a car and use an Iwata airbrush. While the male students usually concentrated on the design of performance cars, she chose to develop a minivan and sculpted a wonderful clay model of it. The design was significant. LaGassey was honest—he noted that the designers at Ford were also investigating the same direction. He gave her a separate room to continue work on it. He was impressed by her talent and work ethic. Sometime later, either Homer or Dennis Hugley, a former GM designer, introduced her to the decision makers at both Ford and GM. Each company bargained for her; Carol accepted a position at GM Design in 1979. Now a single mother, she had a son to care for alone, and Warren, Michigan, was physically much closer than Dearborn. LaGassey did his best to bring her to Ford; her father was likely disappointed.

At GM, only two female exterior designers—Bonnie Lemm (1920s) and Joan Klatil Creamer (1960s)—came before Perelli. While Lemm spent over twenty years on the job, Klatil grew disenfranchised after a year and a half when it was suggested she move to an interiors studio. Carol Perelli, who started her automotive career at age thirty-two, had her work cut out for her. While some events in the news were music to her ears, they also likely annoyed a few of her male colleagues. Fans followed the career of Janet Guthrie, the first woman to quality for the Indy 500, in the 1970s. By 1981, Sandra Day O'Connor was sworn in as the first female judge of the Supreme Court, and in 1983, Sally Ride was the first woman in space. Anita Hill, who brought charges of sexual harassment against Clarence Thomas, captured numerous headlines. While all knew this behavior existed for years in the workplace, way before the Me Too movement, Hill brought it to the attention of an entire country. Mary Beth Vander Schaaf and her colleague published the Project XX survey in *Automotive News* in 2017, in which men in various industries were called out for sexual harassment. While sometimes difficult and time consuming to verify in court, these events seemed to persist in some workplaces.

While some of her male colleagues supported and assisted her, others made, in Carol's opinion, unwelcome remarks or deliberate efforts to ignore her. She felt that they also failed to acknowledge the quality of her design work. The fact that her designs were chosen by consumers in design clinics made matters even worse, since the results of the clinics were often hidden from her and dismissed as insignificant. Some of the older men felt that she belonged in fashion, the color studio, or the interior design studio; the industrial and automobile design fields should be reserved for men. She was older than many of her colleagues, and some of the newest recruits—all male—called her "Mom."

After an unhappy marriage and subsequent divorce, Carol still loved design and had a son to support and educate to the best of her ability, and she was determined to do so no matter what anyone said or did. In accordance with policy, Carol was placed in various exterior design studios to begin a lengthy career. It is hard to believe that in this era she was still a pioneer.

The 1984 Buick Regal coupe was notable. *General Motors*

At first, she received assignments in two advanced design studios; one was run by Dick Ruzzin. By 1981, she served in a Pontiac studio and in the mid-1980s joined the group in the Buick II Studio under the direction of Dave Clark. Exterior designers are rated on the number of cars they initiate. Early assignments required the design of wheel covers and wheels; later assignments led to car exteriors. Around 1982, she developed a scale model alongside Dave North and Ed Welburn in Olds. Welburn would later retire after serving as vice president of Design. In 1984, Carol made a drawing of a Buick Regal Coupe, but this design was developed and manufactured boxier than she wished.

In 1988, as a part of the Buick II Studio, she contributed to the design of the Skylark, Century, Regal, Park Avenue facelift, and Reatta convertible under the direction of Wayne Kady. She was praised for her ability to mock up wheel covers, grilles, and the sail panel for what became the 1991 and 1992 Roadmaster.

By 1989, Carol finally received a welcome transfer. She was directed to report to the Advanced II Corvette Studio under the direction of Tom Peters.

Carol developed a very successful scale model with Anthony Campagne, a top sculptor. While it was initially included in a Styling Dome exhibit, Carol felt that it was prematurely removed from competition for no apparent reason, since no others were removed. Although it adhered to the specs, the division people never saw it. To this day, she wonders who hid her design.

Carol worked for Tom Peters. While some credit him with the design of the Pontiac Aztec, originally penned by Brigid O'Kane, he headed the 2014 Corvette exterior design team after her retirement. The Corvette was voted North American Car of the Year.

Sometime later, Tom Peters was asked to head the Advanced Concepts Center (ACC) in Newbury Park, California, and invited Carol to join him. She loved Peter's philosophy—JUST DO IT! The assistant studio director was Frank Saucedo. Carol also worked on the design and scale model for the new electric car. Carol's design received the best aerodynamics numbers of all designs. She also worked on accessories and the interior of the GMT800.

Perelli received two assignments in California. While working on the development of the GMT800 truck, she proposed a sliding tailgate, a collapsible bed cover, and some removable bed packages. The tailgate was later advanced by an engineer, who added electricity.

She also worked on the development of a version of an earlier electric vehicle. This six-month assignment lasted three years after Carol requested an extension. It was later closed by Jerry Palmer and someone else in an effort to save money.

Carol's experience and knowledge about retail remained with her, and at some point in time, she wrote a letter to Wayne Cherry, the VP of Design, about GM's loss of market share and how to address it. Later, in 1996, Cherry created a plaque that honored her extraordinary achievements in design.

Upon her return to the Warren Technical Center in 1997, she worked with an engineering center group with a diverse range of expertise under the direction of John Taylor. While one member came from R&D, another—Gail Trendler—came from a factory position. Together they tackled research projects. While Tom Peters was supposed to head the group, he was needed to lead another project.

While Carol believed that honesty of communication was needed for progress, others did not. Before retiring in 2003, she would publicly challenge the questionable behavior of one colleague toward her and her work.

At the time of my Perelli visit, Carol was retired and devoting her energies to spending time with her son's family and serving as a caretaker for a friend.

1992 Roadmaster: the Buick Roadmaster was reintroduced in 1991, and this body style was manufactured through 1996. *Collection of Marc Alssid*

VIRGINIA (GINNI) ROMETTY

No matter where you are in your career, work on something you're passionate about. And work on something bigger than yourself. You have great opportunities in front of you if you seize them.[1]
—Ginni Rometty (b. 1957)

© *International Business Machines Corporation*

CAREER HIGHLIGHTS

As a systems engineer, Virginia M. (Ginni) Rometty worked on General Motors trucks and buses at the start of her career.

Rometty became chairman, president, and chief executive officer of IBM in 2012 and retired from the company as executive chairman on December 31, 2020.

Joining IBM as a systems engineer in 1981, Ginni rose through the ranks, gathering a wealth of information by tackling diverse positions during her thirty-nine-year-long tenure. IBM has contributed significantly to the journey of digital transformation. Under her leadership, early on the Watson project incorporated the integration of AI for healthcare and cancer patients. The Watson initiative continues to expand.

During Ginni's tenure, IBM completed fifty-six acquisitions, including open-source companies. The company has continued to expand with its move into the cloud and into blockchain, which "will do for trusted transactions what the internet did for information," according to Rometty.[2] Red Hat is a fairly recent investment and runs on many platforms.

Rometty also worked on a program titled Pathway to Technology (P-Tech) and Open P-Tech, which were designed to create universal STEM degrees and train, mentor, and ultimately hire youth worldwide It has expanded and now functions in twenty-four countries. IBM has attained record results in diversity and inclusion under Ginni's leadership.

Ginni has given a number of keynote speeches internationally. In 2019, she spoke at the International Automobile Exhibition in Frankfurt, Germany; VivaTech 2019 in Paris, France; and Think 2019 in San Francisco, California.

Ginni is currently cochairman of OneTen. From 2018 to 2020, she served as cochair of the Cyber Group, and in 2018, she served as cochairman of the World Economic Forum.

Ginni Rometty was the recipient of honorary degrees from Rensselaer Polytechnic Institute (2014) and North Carolina State (2019).

She serves on the Council on Foreign Relations, the Board of Trustees of Northwestern University, where she is a vice chair, the Board of Trustees of Memorial Sloan-Kettering Cancer Center, and the Board of Directors of JPMorgan Chase. Ginni is also a member of the advisory board of Tsinghua University School of Economics and Management, the Singapore Economic Development Board International Advisory Council, and the BDT Capital Advisory Board.[3]

In a recent endeavor, Ginni interviewed Mary Barra, whom Rometty described as authentic.

A LONG JOURNEY

Born in the Chicago area, Ginni was the eldest of four children and is of Italian descent. When her parents' marriage ended in divorce, her mother was left with the responsibility of addressing the financial needs of the family and had to work multiple jobs in order to keep afloat. Despite her family's struggles, Rometty graduated with high honors at school and was awarded bachelor's degrees in both electrical engineering and computer science from the Robert R. McCormick School of Engineering and Applied Science at Northwestern University in 1979.

Rometty described her college experiences and her decision to join and leave GM and report to IBM in an interview:

GM had at the time back when I went to university—and I went to Northwestern University, and I was putting myself through school, back in those days ... GM offered me a scholarship with no strings attached; nobody does that anymore ... help me with school if I would just work in the summers. I felt a great obligation then to try what I learned, what I thought was at a really young age at the time. I learned the importance of passion about what you did, and it isn't (wasn't) this ... I say to Mary

Barra—I like helping you, but I wasn't in love; I was working on trucks and buses, and it taught me something—that I probably didn't crystallize until later in life, that was the importance of being passionate about what you do, and I guess it's easy to say you're doing something now you like or will do; oh boy, life is too short, so you've got to keep moving until you find what it is. I am not even sure if I knew what it was at that time; I knew what it wasn't, and that is what made me move.[4]

In 1979, Virginia Marie Nicosia married Mark Anthony Rometty.

After joining IBM, Ginni moved away from engineering, holding positions in sales, research, and finance. She noted, "I feel like I have had a number of careers; I did a consulting company and I did a tech company and you know—all within one place.[5] At another time, Rometty affirms that IBM stands for passion, purpose, and inclusion.

In 2018, Rometty proclaimed in a presentation that "data will be our next natural resource."[6]

DIVERSITY AND INCLUSION

IBM achieved record results in diversity and inclusion under Ginni's leadership. This included extending parental leave and making it easier for women to return to the workforce through a "returnships" program with hands-on work experience in emerging technologies. General Motors initiated and offers a similar program to bring women back into the workplace. IBM's

Courtesy of Brigid O'Kane

pioneering work was recognized in 2018, when it captured the prestigious Catalyst Award for advancing diversity and women's initiatives. IBM is the only tech company to have earned this recognition in the past twenty years, and the only company ever to be honored four times.[7]

INTERNATIONAL AUTOMOBILE EXHIBITION

In 2019, Ginni spoke about digital reinvention in her keynote speech on the road to mobility, in Frankfurt, Germany. When we think about IBM's earlier products, hardware dominated; it now constitutes only 10 percent of IBM's revenue, which in 2019 was estimated at $80 billion a year. According to IBM's report—*Automotive 2030*, half of all auto execs believe they must take a journey that includes innovation and reinvention for the companies to survive and thrive. Companies must embrace an open digital platform determined by experience and that defines software. Software can address anything from real-time traffic to concierge services. Software has to provide frequent updates. While companies can incorporate digital data they already use in communicating with the public, this may not leave an open back end to match today's rate of change. Red Hat, their recent acquisition, provides an open digital platform. Companies may need to build something now, then run it anywhere, on any cloud, on or off premises. In a short time, 100 percent of jobs will be changed by AI in some way. And companies will need to focus on training, with an emphasis on customer service.

Among the initiatives Ginni introduced, the Watson project—which initially incorporated the integration of AI for healthcare—was remarkable and especially valuable to the international health community, which included China and India. Researchers captured big data to improve cancer treatments. I think Rometty called this one of her moonshots.

Watson currently consists of three parts: Discovery, NLU, and Watson Analyze. GM Financial uses IBM Watson Assistant to develop a secure and powerful AI assistant.

GM's Bob Beatty recorded his work with IBM in 2020: "At GM Financial, it's my job to drive remarkable customer experiences. Answering customers' questions quickly and accurately is a big part of that. These days, much of our customer care comes in the form of live messages on our customer service app. People text us about things like the status of their remaining loan balances, or to confirm that we received their most recent payment. We made the strategic decision a few years ago to use a chatbot solution to answer these straightforward questions. GM chose IBM Watson Assistant on IBM Cloud for a few key reasons. First, IBM has a great reputation in the financial services industry. Customer privacy is paramount for us, and IBM's commitment to cybersecurity and regulatory compliance allows us to rest easy, knowing that our customer data is in good hands.[8]

"IBM has also proven to be quite flexible as we continue to develop our solution. Technology is important to us at GM Financial, but it is not our core competency. AI is a whole new endeavor for us, but the IBM team has worked hard to educate us and make us comfortable with this approach. When getting started we worked with IBM Garage in an Enterprise Design Thinking Workshop. We collaborated with users and IBM experts to create a road map for the project and a minimum viable product.

"With the effects of the [COVID-19] pandemic, the time for right to incorporate AI Assistant."

Ginni promoted design thinking and established a large staff—as many as 100,000 were devoted to it. IBM has contributed to the journey of digital transformation. During Ginni's tenure, IBM took the opportunity to make a number of acquisitions, including open-source companies. The company has continued its move into the cloud and into blockchain, which "will do for trusted transactions what the internet did for information," according to Rometty.[9]

She reinvented more than 50 percent of IBM's portfolio, built a $21 billion hybrid cloud business, and established IBM's leadership in AI, quantum computing and blockchain, while divesting nearly $10 billion in annual revenue to focus the portfolio on IBM's high-value, integrated offerings.[10]

She noted her support for AI, which augments what man does. However, it has to be introduced in an orderly way, and that should include purpose, transparency, explain-ability, ownership, and training.

CRYPTOGRAPHY

IT systems have been plagued by cyberattacks, and in 2018 IBM Fellow Gosia Steinder delivered a presentation introducing IBM's plan to provide better security. Steinder outlined advances in confidential computing, quantum-safe cryptography, and fully homomorphic encryption. The company became the first producer to offer confidential computer for use in its products.

Today, IBM delivers confidential computing capabilities via IBM Cloud Hyper Protect Services, and it is embedded into the IBM Cloud for Financial Services.[12]

To improve customer service, GM Financial replaced their basic chatbot with Watson Assistant, automating responses to customer inquiries and enabling agents to focus on more-complex work.[13]

GIVING BACK

Pathway to Technology, introduced in 2011, was a viral idea. With the rapid change of technologies, IBM's P-Tech program is more important than ever. IBM introduced a universal STEM degree to give all youth new opportunities. It now includes 600 industry partners, over 240 school partners, and operates in twenty-eight countries.[14] IBM describes the program online:

"P–TECH is a public-education model that provides high school students from underserved backgrounds with the academic, technical, and professional skills and credentials they need for competitive STEM jobs. P–TECH schools enable students to earn both their high school diploma and a two–year associate degree linked to growing, competitive STEM fields.

"Each P–TECH school is a partnership between a high school, a community college, and an industry partner or partners, all working together to ensure students have the supports required to graduate college—and career ready. The model combines rigorous coursework with workplace experiences that include industry mentoring, worksite visits, paid internships, and first in line for job considerations with a school's company partner. P-TECH schools are no cost to students and their families and open enrollment, with no testing or grade requirements. Free, digital learning is also available through Open P-TECH, which introduces students and educators to the tech skills of tomorrow, from emerging technologies such as artificial intelligence, cloud computing, and cybersecurity, to new ways of working such as agile and design thinking."[15]

In support of STEM, GM was a sponsor of the youth Wakanda Design Challenge at CBC, in which P-TECH students participated, and has organized numerous other activities.

Ginni Rometty was one of five founders of OneTen in 2020. The organization consists of a coalition of thirty-seven CEOs from US companies in an effort to upskill, hire, and provide one million Black Americans over the next decade with jobs with opportunities for advancement.

Dominic Peluso

CONSTANCE SMITH

While we salute the designers in our past, we do not know what form the transportation of the future will look like, but that it will change the world we live in.

Charles F. Kettering notes, "The Wright brothers flew right through the smoke screen of impossibility," and the women of General Motors followed.

—Constance Smith

CAREER HIGHLIGHTS

Constance Smith joined the workforce fifty years ago. After graduating with a BFA from Pratt Institute, she worked full time as a professional sculptress before studying industrial design. As a graduate degree candidate, she cotaught a course called Engineering Science 400 (a.k.a. Transportation Design) in Pratt Institute's engineering school. As an industrial designer, she has designed components and vehicles in General Motors' Advanced Studios, designed cars and other toys for Ideal, and partnered with the late Charles Pollock to design furniture.

An educator like many of the Damsels of Design, she has also held teaching and administrative positions for the public schools in New York City, Glen Cove (New York), and Valley Stream (New York) as well as in private schools, including the undergraduate and graduate industrial design programs at the University of Bridgeport and Pratt Institute.

In the mid-1980s, Smith was the recipient of a National Endowment for the Arts (NEA) Individual Award in Design Arts. She used the stipend to conduct research and design electronic components, which were way ahead of their time, for drivers with rheumatoid arthritis.

When her full-time, K–12 position as coordinator of humanities was eliminated in Glen Cove in 1990, she rejoined the automotive community, working as an automobile and truck salesperson or sales manager (or both concurrently) at area GM franchises, including Chevrolet, Buick, Pontiac, and GMC—the latter three referred to as BPG. She also worked in Chrysler-Dodge, VW, BMW, Mazda, and Hertz operations.

In 2010, Smith began writing *Damsels in Design: Women Pioneers in the Automotive Industry, 1939–1959*. She submitted it for publication in late 2014; however, it did not arrive in bookstores until 2018. In 2017, well past retirement age, Smith joined the Dealertrack Division of Cox Automotive, a software developer and supplier to the auto industry, in part to fund research, travel, and the purchase of images for *The Women of General Motors*. Dealertrack's company president, Sandy Schwartz, who serves on the board of the Automotive Hall of Fame, celebrated publication of *Damsels in Design* and supported Helene Rother's candidacy for the AHF; Rother, who is profiled both in *Damsels in Design* and this book, has since been admitted to the Automotive Hall of Fame.

In addition to the NEA award, Smith was the recipient of GM's Mark of Excellence Award annually for sales achievement and customer satisfaction, and Chrysler's Gold, Silver, and Bronze Awards. She has a choice of corporate rings to wear, but the GM ring she was awarded was designed for women.

Her developmental work in automotive innovations has appeared in *Popular Science*, *Motor Trend*, and *Industrial Design Magazine*. Articles she has written have appeared in other publications, including *Classic Sixties Magazine*. Reviews of her book have appeared in *Automotive News* and *Hemmings Motor News*, as well as in English and Italian publications.

In 2019, Smith was delighted to have been selected to receive the Thomas McKean Memorial Cup from the Antique Automobile Club of America (AACA), following in the footsteps of Lawrence L. Gustin, a GM archivist and author she has always admired. She also received the Award of Distinction from the Society of Automotive Historians for *Damsels in Design: Women Pioneers in the Automotive Industry, 1939–1959*.

In 2021, Smith was the recipient of the Helene Award at the second annual Las Vegas Concours for her contributions to automotive history. She also served as a judge at this event.

As a volunteer, Smith annually assists with Vision Honored as a helper and EyesOn Design judge; VH is part of the EyesOn Design charitable series of events designed to raise money for the Detroit Institute of Ophthalmology. She also serves frequently as a judge at AACA shows, including the Hershey National and Gettysburg events. In 2020, she judged Corvettes. Smith also adjudicates for the Greater New York Region of the AACA.

BIOGRAPHICAL NOTES

Constance Smith and her older brother, Bill, were born and raised on Long Island in West Hempstead, New York. Her fraternal grandfather, who later worked as a motorcycle police officer, fell in love with and married his high school teacher.

Her brother followed in the footsteps of her uncle on her mother's side; Dan was a Grumman engineer who contributed to the design of the lunar module. Bill worked for Grumman, Sperry, and Pan Am. When Uncle Dan moved up to a Buick, he gave her brother his black 1957 Chevrolet Belair, which Bill spent hours cleaning. Today, he wonders why he sold this icon. Coincidently, the head of Constance's department at GM, Claire MacKichan, designed this car.

Having dropped out of school for a semester to build a Napoleonic coach for the Fisher Body contest in 1933, her father, William R. Smith, won the award for New York State and four years of college scholarships. However, he sold the scholarships to a wealthy classmate (this was arranged by the school principal with the other student's father) because he had no interest in college. At age sixteen, he started flying lessons with the newly found money. His A&E license and his work as both an auto and aircraft mechanic would keep him at home during World War II, and he would be recognized for an invention he had made to repair warplanes. Smith's mother ran an optometrist's office before having children.

While Smith's father drove a 1952 Chevrolet early on, he also purchased a gray 1953 Pontiac with an Indian chief on the hood. One evening, before she even reached kindergarten, he took his daughter by the hand and walked her up to the front of the car to see the Indian chief, which was lit up. Smith is still delighted to see this mascot at car shows.

Childhood memories abound and created a basis for future paths. In second grade, Smith's elementary school teacher took her class to the library to borrow their first books. She was attracted to a book on a big display rack with a white Cord 810 on the cover, only to find only one other photo of the car inside, since it was merely a novel. This is still her favorite early classic car.

The following year, her dad gave her a pile of balsa wood and some plans to build a plane from scratch—she was dumbfounded until she received instructions from her older brother. She remembers sanding forever and the lump of clay she fashioned.

In fourth grade, she saw a tin gas station with rooftop parking on a top shelf at a toy store and begged for it. While her mother reviewed the expensive purchases, she found it under the Christmas tree.

As a high school student, her dad fought for a place for her in an all-male drafting course, since no women were allowed in before this time, and it was not meant for college-bound students.

Smith was naturally talented in drafting, and she started a small business doing complicated homework drawings for the men in higher-level classes. She met them a couple of blocks from the high school to deliver the drawings every morning. Smith still has a message for other women: "When I won first place in a technical arts fair in high school, someone ripped my drawing and large blue ribbon off the wall—it was never found. It was a valuable lesson that I'll never forget, since it prepared me for the kinds of obstacles I would have to deal with for the rest of my life as a woman in the automotive industry."

When it came to college, she applied to Pratt Institute, where her uncle had studied engineering. She took almost the same home test as the Damsels of Design who preceded her, and would study with most of the same teachers.

After qualifying for a bachelor of fine arts with majors in education and sculpture, Smith found a job before graduation as a professional sculptress, bringing Avon Products decanters to life from rough sketches. Three-dimensional forms were created using clay and casting materials, jewelry wax, and milling machines. Avon sold thousands of Sea Trophy decanters she sculpted—she created a large sailfish jumping out of the water.

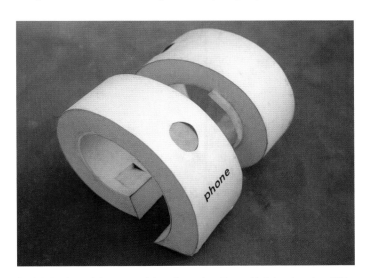

Smith designed these modular phone booths, which her teacher Bill Fogler praised, since the other students used rectilinear forms. *Constance Smith*

Before she could enter the master of industrial design program, she had to audit three courses with her normal workload and certainly was not expected to sleep. Her 3-D professor, Bill Fogler, was delighted by her spiraling modular phone booths, which tapered when viewed from above, while other students created rectilinear designs. Her model of a sewing machine was equally creative.

In 1972, Smith was a member of Pratt's Urban Vehicle Design team. She and the captain of the team, Rick Doherty, approached the president of the school—Richardson Pratt Jr.—for funds to buy a vehicle. With the $2,500, they procured a used Subaru. This FWD prototype was aimed at the needs and problems of personal transport in the city. It addressed safety, a reduction of exhaust emissions, and a reduction in noise. Features included a TV rear camera system way ahead of its time, a Drunkometer, a digital instrument panel, 5 mph bumpers, upgraded emissions, a padded roll cage, side bumpers, a crush-resistant battery, and high lighting. The car was driven to the GM Proving Ground in Milford, Michigan, from New York to be tested.

As a graduate student, Smith was invited to study with Rowena Reed Kostellow, a task master noted for her expertise in 3-D design.

Before graduation, she also studied gross anatomy alongside her professor at Columbia University's College of Physicians and Surgeons; her mentor and teacher, Arthur Bruce Hoheb, was also the head of the Sculpture Department at the Metropolitan Museum of Art and working on the King Tut exhibit. She received her master's degree in industrial design in 1973 as one of the two women in the program—the other lady designed clear plastic clothing for walking in the woods.

Smith was invited to coteach a course called Engineering Science 400 (a.k.a. Transportation Design) in Pratt's Engineering School. Students worked with a Peugeot and a Chrysler taxi from the NYC fleet. The team worked with the head of the NYC Taxi Commission, Steve Wilder, to address all facets of taxi design, which included seating, intercom, solid-state taxi meter, emission control, anticollision Doppler radar devices, coin boxes, tire tests, Lexan ballistics tests, taxi industry surveys, and so on. The report generated was titled *Modern Taxi Research: Design and Development*.

After designing and building a model inside and out of an experimental safety vehicle utilizing the somewhat early rotary engine for her graduate thesis, Smith also designed an all-in-one heated/cooled glove box and a space-saving sliding door.

In her spare time, she spun car wheels and made an RTV mold to produce sets of them. She then sculpted fairly large clay models of other cars. Again, with the exception of the safety car, she viewed the automobile as a piece of sculpture.

After GM's Charles Jordan visited campus, she was invited to interviews at the GM Technical Center. Upon arriving for work, she found that she was the only woman who had gained entrance in this era into the Advanced Interiors Studio, where her colleagues, W. Lawrence Faloon and Press Bruning, sometimes tackled other interior and exterior projects, including the XP 898 concept and a people mover.

The other four women designed production interiors. It was later made clear by Bill Mitchell that women were not allowed in production or the advanced exteriors in the 1970s.

Constance will always remember her first day on the job: all the men had their desks lined up against the outer wall, and there was one desk in the middle of the room with a vase of artificial flowers on it—hers. During her time at GM, she designed or designed around electronic displays and air bags, instrument panels, and seats.

Her group, working with the physics lab, also designed and

A professional sculptor, Smith made a series of clay models to explore form for her thesis project. *Photo, Constance Smith*

installed the first twisted nematic liquid-crystal displays in a Monte Carlo; these displays were later used for computer monitors. It would take seven years for AC Spark, however, to be able to build this technology for a production car.

LCDs gave designers the ability to incorporate new shapes and bars into the cluster. The first displays appeared in 1983 on the 1984 Corvette, an Opel, and later a Cadillac. While LCDs are common today, in part the press and public just did not appreciate them in 1984.

Something in the environment made her ill, and while she was recovering at her parents' home in New York, Smith was recruited by the director of design at Ideal Toys, who appeared at their door by way of a headhunter. She stayed in New York and went on to design exteriors of cars and logos

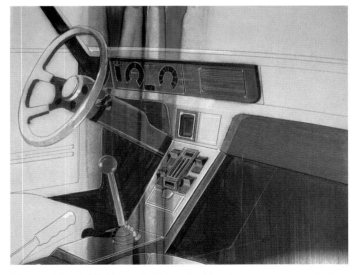

After arriving in Michigan, Smith worked hard to learn new rendering techniques from colleague Edward P. Walter. This one incorporated ink. *Constance Smith*

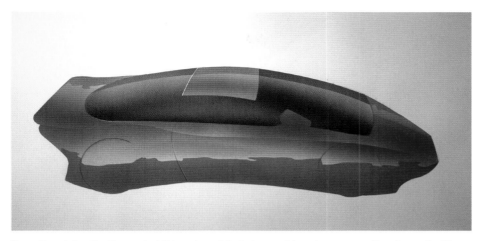

Sometime later, Smith created this automobile to learn airbrush nuances. *Constance Smith*

for Ideal's TCR (Total Control Racing) toys and doll accessories and suggested the first electronic handheld baseball game—this was in the late 1970s. However, the company apologized for not being able to manufacture it in their factory, which relied on molding plastic. It would take years for such handheld devices to appear.

Smith, who was on a waiting list for years to be hired by the New York City school system, would finally be called in. While she worked there, it was strenuous without the necessary supplies, and she got a second job at a local Chevy dealer evenings after reading about training programs for minorities to purchase dealerships. She continued to work both jobs for years to save money but could not qualify to take a loan from GM Motors Holding before the bottom fell out.

After leaving the NYC Department of Education, she designed and ran a gifted program for the Valley Stream Union

This rendering acknowledged the capabilities that instrument designers would have in the future, and the transmissive LCD technology was introduced first on the 1984 Corvette. *Collection of Constance Smith*

Free School District (UFSD), which was eliminated even though her students won the Ranatra Fusca Creativity Award and the Nassau County OM champion-ships. The Odyssey of the Mind, a.k.a. the Olympics of the Mind, was sponsored by IBM to promote research. The gifted program was eliminated by a new su-perintendent under the guise of saving money. She subsequently taught full time at the University of Bridgeport and part time in the Pratt Graduate Program in the evening (Connie has held two jobs at a time for most of her life). She re-members GM's Scott Wassell, who was enrolled in her Senior Product Design class at UB but spent most of his time drawing cars instead of designing products. His talent and hard work outside the classroom have proved fruitful. Most recently, Scott was assigned to Hummer PU exterior design team.

As the recipient of an individual NEA award with a stipend in 1985, Smith was enabled to design vehicle components for drivers limited by rheumatoid arthritis. A number of devices would be refined and found to be useful far into the future. In addition, she devised new steering wheels, touch controls, and a remote control that could be mounted anywhere in the vehicle for the driver or passenger to operate.

The true test of GM's commitment to safety innovations came when Smith was involved in a serious accident during a severe snowstorm while returning home to Long Island from the University of Bridgeport. The school should have been closed. Her Chevrolet Monza coupe, with its 262-cubic-inch V-8 up front, saved her life when she hit a cement divider on Interstate 95.

Smith would also join forces with Charles Pollock, of in-ternational fame, to design furniture before his untimely accidental death in the studio due to a fire.

Well after retirement age, Smith joined the Dealertrack Division of Cox Automotive, which creates and supplies auto-motive software to over 18,000 dealerships

Smith has witnessed all sorts of unprofessional behaviors and attitudes toward women—some in corporations, many in dealerships—and when male managers are questioned about them, the phrase "There is employment at will here; there's the door" is a popular one. Hence, she has always advocated that women be afforded the same respect and dignity as their male colleagues.

Women have worked hard in the auto industry, and Constance Smith is pleased to acknowledge them and their accomplishments. Her first book, *Damsels in Design: Women Pioneers in the Automotive Industry, 1939–1959*, recognized the earliest ladies.

In 2012, Smith designed this electric car with solar panels. *Constance Smith*

Before entering the graduate ID Design program, Smith designed and built this model of a chair for thermoforming. She had done some bodywork on cars and used fiberglass. *Constance Smith*

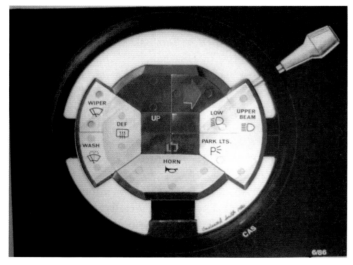

In 1985, utilizing a grant from the NEA, Smith designed instruments to ease driving for a physically limited user. This steering wheel made the operation of automobiles easier. *Illustration by Constance Smith*

After Smith designed an electronic instrument panel, doors, and seats, this buck was generated. *Constance Smith*

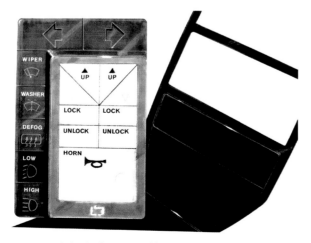

This remote module designed in 1985 could be mounted anywhere in the car for use by the driver or health aide. *Illustration by Constance Smith*

Smith worked with colleagues to add A/C to the production fiberglass GMC Motorhome. *Constance Smith*

JULIE (BEAUCHAMP) TONIETTO

Even during the time of changing social values, there were always people in our families and at work saying, "You can't do that" (be an engineer) or "You took a job that a boy wanted" or "You shouldn't pursue a professional career because you will only quit when you get married."

—Julie Tonietto (b. May 9, 1956)

Julie Tonietto has relied on teamwork to ensure success. Due to changing laws, culture and opinions, she has been at the leading edge of positive change for women.

Courtesy of Joseph Tonietto

CAREER HIGHLIGHTS

Julie (Beauchamp) Tonietto began her career in 1974 as a General Motors Institute co-op student sponsored by Pontiac Motor Division. She spent thirty-four years implementing continuous improvement and common processes. Her early successes included implementing statistical process control under the guidance of Dr. Edward Deming. Later, her jobs focused on lean engineering to develop and implement work standards as GM began consolidation and globalization. Tonietto received many special awards and was part of a cross-disciplinary team that received a maximum award for a successful, major cost-reduction idea.

Outside of work, Tonietto worked with her local Girl Scouts troop as the cookie mom and coached Little League softball for several years. She was the recipient of GM's Corporate Volunteer of the Year Award.

AUTOBIOGRAPHICAL NOTES

Julie was born and raised in southeastern Michigan. Her father, Charles Beauchamp, was a skilled tradesman with Chevrolet in Warren before joining GM Hydramatic. Her mother, Mary, worked part time in a number of pink-collar jobs. Her grandfather, also named Charles Beauchamp, worked in the toolroom at one of the GM plants in Detroit. He retired from the Fisher Body Division as a master craftsman and was proud of having worked without being laid off throughout the Depression. Julie grew up in a loyal GM family where being a GM employee meant job security, good pay, excellent benefits, and a guarantee of a comfortable retirement for the employee and their spouse.

Julie has an older sister who holds a doctorate in nursing and is a professor at a private university in Michigan. She also has two younger brothers, one of whom is also a GMI industrial-engineering

graduate who received an International Fellowship and bachelor's and master's degrees from Purdue University. The other is a CPA with an international corporation.

Due to changing laws and societal norms and views, Tonietto has been at the leading edge of positive change for women. She has frequently noted that there was a generation gap between her sister, of high school class of 1971, and herself in 1974 with regard to women's expectations and opportunities. Title IX, mandating girls' varsity athletics, was implemented her senior year in public high school, where she received three varsity letters. When the male athletes told her that "girls couldn't wear a varsity jacket," she bought one anyway and proudly wore it for the remainder of her senior year. Girls were required to wear skirts or dresses until her sophomore year in high school. During junior high school, only boys took drafting and shop classes, while the girls had cooking and sewing classes.

During her senior year, Tonietto attended many presentations by college recruiters. She had been leaning toward being a science or history teacher and coaching girls' sports when she heard about engineering as a career for people proficient in math and science. When she told her parents that she wanted to be an engineer, her father mentioned GMI since he was aware of the program at work. He brought home an application that he got from his union representative. She applied for and was awarded a small scholarship from her father's UAW local. It was the end of the slide rule era; the scholarship covered the cost of her first electronic calculator.

Tonietto was the first student at her high school to apply to General Motors Institute. GMI accepted numerous applicants every year, and the earnings from the co-op sponsorship assignments allowed students to cover the cost of their degrees. She selected Pontiac Motor Division because it was near home and it offered the opportunity to study marketing, product engineering, and manufacturing operations. Pontiac Motor Division designed and built large rear-wheel-drive cars with V-8 engines like her parents' Bonneville and Catalina. It also produced fast cars targeting young men, including the GTO and Firebird. At that time, GMI was the primary feeder college for engineers and managers in GM.

Tonietto could not know that 1974 would be the pinnacle of GM's US market share. She did not fully realize that the automobile industry was in a recession due to the increased cost of gasoline and foreign competition and was starting to convert to more-fuel-efficient, less polluting, and safer vehicles. The Pontiac site built the type of vehicles and engines that used some of the manufacturing processes that had to change due to shifting customer expectations and government regulations.

Tonietto notes that for her and her female classmates, there were always people in our families and at work saying, "Girls can't be an engineer" or "You took a job that a boy wanted" or "You shouldn't pursue a professional career because you will only quit when you have children." She always referred those people as "Uncle Archie and we all had at least one detractor that we wanted to prove wrong!"

"TI or HP?" followed by "Where are you sponsored?" and "What are you taking?" were the most-common opening lines heard during Freshman 1, week 1, at GMI. She felt she scored zero points with her off-brand calculator but drew envy when she said she worked in engineering at Pontiac Motor Division, where planning to be an electrical engineer or mechanical engineer was typical. She would quickly learn that the majority of her classmates were sponsored by a number of small manufacturing sites in the Midwest that sponsored very few students. Their careers would begin as production supervisors in the plant, while hers would be as a product engineer in the office.

Early on, Tonietto knew she lacked the required preparation for her freshman year. "GMI was hard. I quickly learned that many of my classmates had already had calculus, physics, programming, and drafting in high school. With the help of the tutors in the dorm, my friends, and hard work, I got through freshman and sophomore year with average grades." My friend Steve K. used to say, "School section is school section, and work section is work section." Tonietto could not completely separate the two and had to study while on work section.

Tonietto remembers, "At work, the most common question in engineering was 'What do you drive?' Responding with 'a used, brown, four-door, black cloth interior' was not a good answer. I found saying, 'A '71 Chevy Malibu with a 350, four-barrel, modified with a flipped air cleaner cover for better breathing' was a better answer but was still missing the lingo the car guys wanted to know. The men in product engineering were helpful and suggested that I read popular car magazines to gain a better understanding. They took the time to answer my questions and explain what the test and outcomes meant."

The product engineers were known to race their personal and test cars on Woodward Avenue outside work, as well as the Milford Proving Ground, as part of their job. Tonietto went along a few times, and it was fun and informative. She adds, "I had assignments in engine test, chassis test, emissions test, and A/C. I worked with many people I later read about in car magazines or who would go on to leadership positions at GM. My favorite assignments involved driving the cars. While in the emissions test labs, I drove vehicles both in the test booth and on the road. Some nights, we drove the cars on local roads over a set path at predefined speeds. Fortunately, I never got a ticket. Another assignment involved conducting heater testing on the all-new 1978 'A' body cars (Chevrolet Malibu, Olds Cutlass, Buick Century, and Pontiac LeMans) at Kapuskasing, Ontario, in the winter. My job on the test drives was to record data on how long it took to clear the windshield while driving down the road and while each of us in the car quit shivering."

Tonietto notes, "At the end of my sophomore year, I decided to make a change to find a better match for my skills and interests. I selected to study industrial engineering and was reassigned to the Industrial Engineering Department in Manufacturing Operations at Pontiac. I excelled in the IE curriculum at school and thoroughly enjoyed my work assignments. GMI professor John Mariotti once asked me why I was 'only doing average' in his class. I told him it was because I had to pass all of my classes, and scoring a 100 in his classes and flunking something else was not good."

Tonietto felt she was lucky to be sponsored at the Pontiac site because "it was exciting to be able to walk the process of building an automobile. I could start in the foundry and see cupolas pouring metal to make engine castings, watch the engine machining and assembly operations, and then see the same engine be loaded into a car in the assembly plant. I could also start with rolls of coil steel and watch hoods and fenders being stamped and welded. Then I could watch them get painted and loaded to the car. In the car assembly plant, I could watch as thousands of parts and subassemblies were brought to the line and hundreds of people add them to the cars moving down the line. The final thrill was watching the cars drive off the assembly line and into railcars." She had assignments in all of the plants, doing the full industrial-engineering job, including estimating, plant layout, simulation, ergonomics, simulation, work standards (common processes), and statistics. In 1976 there were still quite a few "Uncle Archies" in the plants and offices. Tonietto tried not to let the wolf whistles, cigar smoke during meetings, or crude calendars or magazine pictures intimidate her. She notes, "I was careful and focused on doing my job."

While a student at GMI, Julie met and married her husband, Joseph Tonietto. He was also a 1979 industrial engineer sponsored at GM of Canada's Windsor Trim Plant. Julie joined the Alpha

Courtesy of Joseph Tonietto

Sigma Alpha sorority. There were fraternity parties every Friday and Saturday night. Girls could attend any fraternity party, but the boys generally stuck to their own fraternity. GMI had a strong intermural sports program. Julie played and coached basketball, volleyball, and softball, first on her dorm team and then her sorority team. It could be hard to get enough players at times. Julie notes, "One softball game, our sorority team had to pull Connie G. off the bleacher to play by promising her that she didn't have to do anything. She was wearing platform sandals and a tube top. Of course, she hit the ball when at bat and had to field more balls than right field usually had to. We weren't good, but it was fun!"

After graduation, the Toniettos evaluated which country to live in. Julie interviewed with GM of Canada's Transmission Plant while Joe interviewed at the Fisher Body headquarters in Warren. They decided that they would both be better off serving GM in Michigan than Windsor, Ontario.

Julie's first big assignments after graduation were to quote installation costs and labor, be responsible for installation, and then be responsible to ensure throughput and cost for the production of 1,200 "J"-Car trailing axles per day. The 1982 J-car was an all-new corporate front-wheel-drive small car. She still remembers that the standard hours—the amount of labor budgeted for the production of each axle—was 0.12183 standard hour . . . and they never made it. She notes, "I always enjoyed working with my manufacturing team, applying Dr. Deming's statistical process control tools. One time when I was speaking with Dr. Deming about the details of my effort on the trailing-axle machining quality, our conversation was delaying our project status presentation to Pontiac's general manager and his staff. Dr. Deming told the general manager, 'You have to wait; don't you agree that her project is more important?'" Tonietto's job was to improve throughput and quality while reducing cost. She accomplished this with industrial-engineering tools and working with cross-disciplinary teams, which later would be called synchronous or lean engineering.

In 1982, Tonietto requested working part time after the birth of her daughter. She reminded her manager that she was just the first engineer to be pregnant. She was allowed to work reduced hours for twelve months, but at the end she had to quit or return to full time. She quit, knowing that she was pregnant again. In the spring of 1985, she was called by a former manager from Pontiac, offering a flexible-service position to work on the GM80 (Camaro/Firebird) program, which was later canceled. In the fall of 1989, with her youngest in kindergarten, she went back to work full time as a supervisor in Industrial Engineering. Tonietto is proud that she may have been the person that caused GM to develop official, sanctioned flexible-service positions. Years later, her director, Roy Goetz, told her that she was able to carry a full load and perform very well even though she worked fewer hours than her peers. As a manager and mentor, Tonietto recommended flexible service rather than quitting to women who were concerned about working after childbirth.

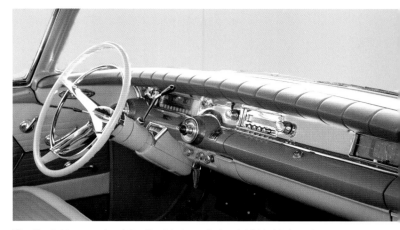

The Toniettos received the Zenith Award, the AACA's highest honor, for their Buick Century Caballero in Gettysburg. *Constance Smith*

Tonietto notes, "One negative of going to GMI is that you could get pigeonholed in the wrong location based on where you were sponsored as a freshman. When that occurred, your choices were to stick it out, try to transfer, or quit GM. With downsizing, many sites were closed or the business unit sold. Joe went from GM of Canada to Fisher Body to Delphi to an outside supplier always working with interior parts. I had enjoyed working at Pontiac Motor Division, but by 1991 there was no future for me there due to downsizing."

Julie Tonietto transferred to the GM Tech Center as a superintendent in manufacturing engineering, working in systems engineering. She held several other management positions in engineering, including product assembly document group manager and design group manager. As GM continued to consolidate and globalize, Tonietto focused on her industrial-engineering skills with synchronous and lean engineering tools, as well as teamwork to help develop common processes and systems. She received many special-recognition awards. One cross-departmental team wrote a group suggestion for a process change, since no one person on the team could implement it alone. The team was rewarded with a team maximum award. Tonietto enjoyed working with her global partners implementing a new global system. Every summer, Tonietto took her 1971 Pontiac GTO to the GM Tech Center Employee Car Show, knowing that this performance car would stand out. She retired in 2008 before GM declared bankruptcy.

Tonietto hasn't forgotten what she learned in industrial engineering about applying the right metrics now for life rather than business, and adds, "Joe and I were lucky to retire healthy and financially secure at fifty years old. We owned a small business for four years, manufacturing exhaust systems for vintage vehicles. Joe thoroughly enjoyed being in the restoration industry, but I thought the effort exceeded the benefit."

In summarizing the Toniettos' enjoyment of cars and their current lives, Julie shares, "Joe always enjoyed vintage vehicles and bought his first car in 1982, a 1957 Corvette that he restored. We have always owned GM cars, including several GTOs and Firebirds. We currently own four driving and two WIP vintage cars besides our daily drivers. Joe recently received national recognition for a recent effort on a 1958 Buick Caballero."

PART VII.
THE 1980s; SHARING THE ROAD WITH MARY BARRA

At this time in our history, we tried to hang on to old standards, and we did until some models lost sales volume, but small- and medium-sized entries more easily met government standards for safety and fuel mileage. GM created the all-new transverse V-6, the 1980 front-wheel-drive X-body cars thrived, and the 1982 J-car provided Cadillac with a smaller entry. However, a simple-minded reporter noted that all the J-cars, although originating from different divisions, looked almost the same, and a visual comparison of them appeared in *Fortune Magazine*. This was absurd but was quickly addressed. Once the price of gas stabilized, there was a renewed interest in full-sized cars.

In 1983, Delco offered a full array both of electronically and mechanically tuned receivers for cars in all five divisions. At the high end, the sophisticated Delco/BOSE sound system was available in 1983 on the Cadillac Seville and Eldorado, Buick Riviera, and Olds Toronado.

When it came to concept cars, in 1982, Opel had its Tech I. In 1985, the Buick Wildcat with a McLaren V-6 sent power to all four wheels at Sema.

In 1983, Chevrolet started its joint venture with Toyota in its NUMMI facility, which produced the Nova in 1986.

In 1984, GM acquired Electronic Data Systems (EDS), and in 1985, Hughes Aircraft Company. EDS was the world's largest and most technically advanced computer services company, expert in developing the software that controls automated manufacturing systems. GMHE, a new wholly owned subsidiary, held the holding company that owned both Hughes and the newly formed Delco Electronics Corporation. Hughes expertise included the integration of satellite communications in microelectronics and in systems engineering.

Saturn Corporation, added to the GM lineup as a new operating unit in 1985, prepared to begin construction of its Spring Hill, Tennessee, plant.

In 1985, the all-new or completely redesigned models included the Chevrolet Nova; Pontiac Grand Am sedan; Olds Toronado, Delta 88, and Calais sedan; Buick Riviera, LeSabre, and Skylark sedan; and Cadillac Seville and Eldorado. The top-selling car in the nation this year was the Chevrolet Cavalier.

In 1986, the Kevlar and carbon-fiber midengine Corvette Indy made its debut. These pricey materials would find a place much later down the road. In 1987, Dow Chemicals worked on an idea car with PMD. In 1988, the smooth Olds Aerotech, designed with short and long tails, set speed and endurance records. In 1988, we were also introduced to the California Camaro, Pontiac Banshee, and Cadillac Voyage; the streamlined Cadillac Solitaire, a two-door version, arrived in 1989. William Mitchell was so enamored with the Banshee that he configured a Banshee motorcycle for his own personal use. It took until 1989 for the beachcombing Pontiac Stinger, designed in part by Marietta Kearney, to appear. There was also a two-passenger commuter, a seventy-fifth-anniversary Citation 4, an Aero X, and a Buick

General Motors

Holden, Lotus, Isuzu, Saab, Daewoo, and other partners—even Toyota and Nissan.

Perhaps the Sunraycer signaled the future in 1987. The solar-powered vehicle, designed by Advanced Engineering, Hughes Aircraft, and aeroVironment, won the first International Solar Car Challenge. But we all realized that solar energy alone cannot power a production car.

Buick began the decade with the Skyhawk, Skylark, Century, Regal, LeSabre, Electra, and Riviera, adding the Reatta and Estate Wagon in 1988. While large cars hardly changed, small and midsized ones gained in popularity. Rear-wheel-drive cars were dropped for front-wheel-drive replacements as the decade progressed. The Skylark—an X-body FWD like the Citation—the Century, and the Riviera were popular. The Riviera was available in a coupe, a T-top configuration, and the first convertible debuted in 1982, but the conversion by an outside contractor did not lead to many sales since it was light on power; it disappeared by 1986. In 1984, sporty T-tops were added to all cars except the Electra. The Grand National commanded respect. Coupes disappeared when a separate Park Avenue was introduced. When the 1986 downsizing of the Riviera caused a dip in sales, it returned as a larger vehicle at the end of the decade. In 1987, the Regal came in three versions: the Regal, Regal Limited, and Regal Grand National, which benefited from its turbocharged, intercooled engine and sequential port fuel injection. The all-black Grand National is still sought after today. The most desirable Grand National, the 1987 GNX Limited Edition, was built by ASC Corporation during Pamela Fletcher's affiliation with ASC. In 1988, the Reatta coupe, described as smooth and rounded by some, arrived on a rebodied Riviera chassis.

Buick celebrated its eighty-fifth anniversary in 1989. After extensively restyling its Riviera and Century, midcentury it introduced its most luxurious model yet—the Park Avenue Ultra. However, when it came down to it, the car would have to compete in price with entry-level Cadillacs, and that wasn't easy when it came to leasing.

In the early 1980s, Cadillac relied on its sale of the new Eldorado, new Seville, DeVille coupe and sedan, Fleetwood Brougham, limo, and entry-level Cimarron to raise the bar. The Seville came with a diesel V-8. One of the innovative engineering contributions was the V-8-6-4, an optional engine on the 1981 Seville, to help with the CAFE stats; however, the electromechanical system was complex.

In 1984, the Biarritz convertible later returned, and in 1985 the DeVille was downsized to a C-body, which improved sales. In 1985, a stately neoclassic, bustle-back Seville featured a steeply raked rear window that was compared to a Rolls-Royce by some and was controversial. By 1986, the bustle back was discontinued and a new Eldorado appeared—an E-body.

By 1987, the Allante coupe arrived for the well healed. The car was designed by Sergio Pininfarina in Italy, and his firm was also contracted for the bodywork; a PF plant was set up in Turin. Management thought the Pininfarina nameplate from Europe would generate sales, but they were less than expected. In 1987, we saw the Fleetwood Sixty Special and d'Elegance arrive. Throughout the decade, the DeVille dominated sales, with the sedan numbers higher than those for the coupe, and the Eldorado placed second.

When it came to Chevrolet styling, with the exception of Corvette, hoods were lowered, decks were higher, and designers started replacing wraparound back lights with flat panels, but emphasis remained on small and midsized offerings. In 1980, Chevrolet also began production of its Kodiak, a medium HD truck.

The 1980 Chevette hit the mark—there was even a diesel later—and was joined by the 1980 Citation (an X-car), Camaro, Malibu, Monte Carlo, and full-side Chevrolet. The Camaro Z-28 was equipped with functional hood air intakes and fender parts. By 1982, the Cavalier replaced the Monza and the Celebrity was unveiled; there was a waiting list for its Eurosport edition. By 1984, most cars were smaller and lighter. Although the base Camaro could be ordered with a four-cylinder or six-cylinder engine, later in the decade the third-gen Camaro came in a Z28 IROC Z and the Belinetta featured sophisticated electronic instrumentation. In the second half of the decade, the Citation II, Corsica and Beretta (the L-body), and Nova had arrived, as the Caprice held its own. A Monte Carlo SS was introduced in 1983—this time around, a full-size chassis replaced the original one.

As the decade progressed, some substantial changes were made for Corvette. In 1980, engineers were losing performance in order to meet stricter emissions standards. At the start of the decade, Chevrolet could manage only 180 net horsepower for automatics equipped with the 305-cubic-inch-displacement (cid) engine. In 1981, a Computer Command Control Emissions system and fiberglass leaf springs debuted. In 1982, production moved from St. Louis to a more modern plant in Bowling Green, Kentucky. In 1982, a handsome Collector's Edition was offered.

Thankfully by 1982, with the first applications of fuel injection, numbers rose slightly to 200 hp. Engineers would track back pressure caused by the catalytic converter, although other GM cars could be used to maintain an acceptable CAFE (corporate average fuel economy).

While there was no 1983 except a few made by mistake, the new 1984 Corvette was likely initially destined to arrive in 1983. The Corvette was leaner, without the pronounced fender bulges of the past, with a new acute window rake of 64 degrees. A large fastback rear window replaced the tunneled roof. The Gen 6 also featured uniframe construction to improve rigidity and optimized the use of forged aluminum for suspension parts. A one-piece Targa top replaced the T-tops—a managerial decision. While the initial display plates for the instrument cluster were constructed by the physics department, the transmissive LCD display would be built by the AC Spark Plug Division and could now incorporate color masks. Somewhere along the line, an antireflective lens was missing on the backup, which caused some to criticize the design. By 1985, the Corvette Roadster returned for its adoring fans. By 1989, horsepower was recorded as 245, but the introduction of the ZR1 package would end any power complaints.

In 1983, Chevrolet entered into a joint agreement with Toyota (NUMMI: New United Motor Manufacturing Inc.). In 1986, the joint venture with Toyota produced the Nova; the Nova and Toyota Corolla shared parts. The first-generation S-10 Blazer and S-10 pickup arrived in 1982. The Yenko Blazer is a sought-after collectible. In 1984, Chevrolet exhibited the Citation IV concept, and, in 1987, the Blazer XT-1 Concept.

Oldsmobile began the 1980s with the Starfire (1980 only), the Omega, various Cutlasses, the Delta 88, the Ninety Eight, and the Toronado. By 1982, the Firenza a Cutlass Ciera made its entry. In 1986, the Cutlass Calais and Custom Cruiser were added. As the decade ended, other Cutlass Supremes were added. Of courses, there was also a fifteenth-anniversary Hurst Olds in 1983 and another revised in 1984. In 1986, Olds offered the trimmer Toronado Trofeo, outfitted with leather. In 1988, an international series was added to the Ciera.

Three muscle cars would interest collectors for years to come, all based on the rear-drive Supreme coupe. The first was the 1983 fifteenth-anniversary Hurst/Olds, the second a similar 1984, and the reborn 4-4-2 option package added from 1985 to 1987. All boasted a special four-barrel, 180 hp version of Olds' 307-cubic-inch small-block V-8.

The 1988 Calais coupes and sedans featured the first twin-cam sixteen-valve, four-cylinder engine in American production—the Quad 4.

In the 1980s, under the direction of William Hoglund and later J. Michael Losh as the general manager, Pontiac focused on size, weight reduction, and aerodynamics for its larger cars, in an effort to reduce fuel consumption.

At the start of the decade, Pontiac manufactured the Sunbird (dropped in 1981), Phoenix, Firebird, LeMans, Catalina, Bonneville, and Grand Prix. By 1982, the new small and intermediate cars arrived, including the T1000, J2000, 6000, 1000, and 2000.

The redesign of the LeMans in 1981 brought PMD (Pontiac Motor Division) back into racing. In 1982, Richard Petty, Cale Yarborough, and other drivers drove modified LeMans, Grand Prix, Firebirds, and other Pontiacs in races, including those sponsored by NASCAR, IMSA, NHRA, and IHRA. Petty won his two hundredth race in his STP Grand Prix.[1]

The Firebird was completely redesigned, gaining a more raked windshield and large rear glass in 1982. There were numerous models throughout the decade relying on four-, six-, and eight-cylinder engines. Perhaps the most memorable are the ASC convertibles, Formulas, and Trans Ams, and a GTA offered with a notchback rear.

While the Sunbird and Phoenix set their own sales record, there were a lot of firsts for Pontiac. The Phoenix FWD model was the first domestic car with a transverse engine and entered 1980 unchanged. A new lockup torque converter automatic transmission was shared with other divisions. GM built their 2.5-liter, four-cylinder engines for their own use and sold others to AMC. By 1982, all Pontiacs relied on Computer Command Control to regulate the air/fuel mixture. In 1982, the Bonneville replaced the traditional LeMans, but by 1987 the LeMans from Korea replaced the 1000 as a 1988 model.

In 1984, with chief engineer John J. Wetzel, the Saturn engineering founder, behind it, the Fiero relied on numerous engineering plastics for its exterior: Enduraflex, SMC, and RRIM urethane atop a space frame. The Fiero GT, powered by a 2.8-liter V-6 engine, would be based on a Fiero Indy pace car.

In 1985, the new Grand Am, in its third iteration as an N-car, would soon place as one of America's top-ten models. Its good looks relied on the usual split grille; ribbed wraparound facias and heavy-ribbed side moldings were both substantial and sporty. The Grand Am's optional 2.3 DOHC (dual overhead cam), sixteen-valve Quad Four was new for 1988, and in 1989, safety was improved with the introduction of three-point seat belts when the extra shoulder harness was added. In 1989, the Grand Am was America's ninth-best-selling car.

PMD teamed with Dow Chemical in 1987 to design an idea car that utilized its materials, which included a 3-liter turbocharged four rated at 313 hp at 550 rpm, built with magnesium block. Dow plastics and fluids appeared inside and out.[2]

In 1983, GM entered into an agreement with Toyota that resulted in the formation of NUMMI (New United Motor Manufacturing, Inc.). The Chevrolet Nova was based on the Toyota Corolla. As NUMMI progressed, they started research for the creation of Saturn, and in 1985, Saturn was announced as a wholly owned subsidiary of GM; however, cars did not reach the marketplace unit 1990.

In 1987 the LeMans, imported from Korea, replaced the entry-level 1000. The earlier 1000 (similar to a Chevette) lost sales to imports. An all-new FWD Bonneville, powered by the 3.8 V-6 with SFI, also arrived.

In 1989, Pontiac was the first division to offer AWD on its popular STE. The FWD 6000 was available in base, LE, and S/E levels; 1989 was Pontiac's second-best year. This year, Marietta Kearney contributed to the Pontiac Stinger concept car.

By the 1980s, the original GM Truck Division was renamed GMC Truck and Coach Division. GMC introduced its Top Kick medium HD truck. Early on, they produced heavy vehicles such as the 1983 Aero Astro, an HD tractor with a fold-down rooftop and air dam. In 1985, they signed an agreement with Volvo allowing Volvo to take over the manufacturing and marketing of an HD truck, and GMC produced a school bus chassis. But what stands out is their production of sister car lines, including Chevy's vans and pickups. While Chevrolet had the A-10 Blazer in 1982, GMC had the Jimmy. The safari was GMC's version of the Astrovan. When it came to pickups, the GMC had the option for the Heavy-Hauler or Sport. By 1990, the Safari would be offered in four-wheel drive.

When it came to Opel in Germany, the Ascona and Manta B carried over from the 1970s. In 1978 the Commodore version of the Rekord E featured a 2.5-liter L-6. Opel sold over two million Kadetts by 1983 (the Kadett C was a Vauxhall Chevette, and a diesel was more economical). In 1981, the Commodore Voyage station wagon appeared at the Geneva Auto Show. The Ascona, made until 1988, featured the first Opel with a catalytic converter and fuel injection. The Senator and Monza Sport coupe were also popular offerings. Customers could buy an AWD Senator up-fitted by Erich Bitter, somewhat through the back door. A new Corsa, designed in Germany but built in Spain, arrived in 1982. When the new Rekord came in 1983, the Commodore was let go. In 1986, the Rekords were superseded by the Omega, and the Ascona by the Vector, while the Kadett became the Astra and the Manta was replaced by the Calibra.

The 1980s Holden offerings included work with Detroit as well as with other suppliers, which included Isuzu, and manufactured the T-car or Gemini—a *Wheels* Car of the Year (1977–1985). Other offerings included the Camira and the VB, VC, VH (Commodore), and WB. Variations on these lines continued, and Jakaroo 4 (a rebadged Isuzu Trooper) arrived in 1982. The Rover was added in 1985, and the Piazza in 1986. The LE (Nova) was added in 1989.

Let us not forget the contributions made by other affiliates such as the Electro-Motive Division, GM of Canada and its diesel division, Vauxhall, Bedford, GM do Brazil, GM de Mexico, and GM South Africa. On top of this, GM owned part of other companies and worked with still other companies, including Lotus, Isuzu, Saab, and Daewoo.

Courtesy of Carla Bailo; photo by Thomas Cooper

CARLA (DIBROW) BAILO

CAREER HIGHLIGHTS

Carla Bailo has spent over forty years in the automotive in-

In my career, I had no "official" mentors; however, I took every opportunity to learn from my management, ask questions, and listen to their advice of how to consistently improve my performance.[1]

—Carla Dibrow Bailo (b. ca. 1960)

---

dustry. Following in the footsteps of David Cole and Jay Baron, she currently heads the esteemed Center for Automotive Research, although Baron still chairs the organization. She started her career at General Motors and over a ten-year period served in a number of roles in product development, program management, quality, product planning, and profitability. Bailo also spent a large part of her career serving Nissan, where she rose to the position of senior vice president, addressing assignments internationally.

In 1983, before graduating with a bachelor of science degree in materials engineering from General Motors Institute (later Kettering University), Bailo navigated numerous assignments in General Motors labs and factories that would help her prepare both mentally and physically for the challenges unfolding around and before her.

From 2009 to 2014, Bailo served Nissan North America directing various departments until rising to the position of senior VP of Honda R&D Americas and TCS—the acronym for Total Customer Satisfaction. In 2015, Bailo connected with AVP / Ohio State University, where she conducted research and business development. In this position, she notes in her book (*cited below*) that she implemented the university's sustainable mobility and transportation innovation, while integrating related research and education across Ohio State's academic departments. Ohio State also participated in Smart Columbus, a transportation initiative. In 2014, Bailo served as president and CEO of ECOS Consulting, and from 2016 to 2018 as the vice president of Society of Automotive Engineers International, on the automotive side.

In 2017, Bailo was invited to join the Center for Automotive Research as its president and CEO. In an online post, the center's representatives note that under Carla's leadership, CAR continues to be a preeminent resource of objective and unbiased research, analysis, and information regarding the North American automotive industry.

Bailo also serves on the National Academy Committee on Assessment of Technologies for Improving Fuel Economy of Light Duty Vehicle for the National Academies Board on Energy and Environmental Systems. An independent director of SM Energy, she also served on the boards of numerous nonprofit organizations.

In 2018, Bailo published a study with five colleagues titled *The Great Divide: What Consumers Are Buying vs. the Investments Automakers & Suppliers Are Making in Future Technologies, Products & Business Models.*

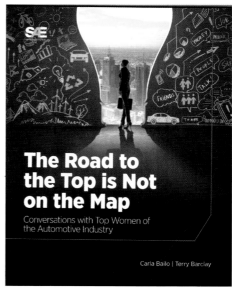

Courtesy of SAE International

In 2020, the SAE published her book, coauthored with Terry Barclay, titled *The Road to the Top Is Not on the Map: Conversations with Top Women of the Automotive Industry.*

BIOGRAPHICAL NOTES

Like some of the others profiled, Bailo was born and raised in Detroit and appears to have inherited her dad's interest in as well as his passion for automobiles. GM's VP of Design in the 1970s, Bill Mitchell, used to say, "To work here, you have to have gasoline in your blood," and most of us filled the bill. Perhaps the father of GM's chair and CEO, Mary Barra, comes to mind when Bailo notes that her father was in the tool-and-die business.

The editor in chief of *Her Highway*, Christina Seltzer, posted part of the script of Bailo's NAIAS interview online in 2020. Bailo's comments bring to mind some of the events in the lives that influenced other women in auto; namely, encouragement by a mentor in their family or school. She notes, "The one person who drove me to a career in engineering was my high school chemistry teacher (a female), who had two children in the engineering program at General Motors Institute. She recognized my skills and discussed [this] with me in earnest—she was right. In my career, I had no 'official' mentors, however, I took every opportunity to learn from my management, ask questions, and listen to their advice of how to consistently improve my performance."[2]

It was no surprise that Bailo would apply for and enroll in GMI's cooperative education program around 1978, when students earned a good amount of pay for working in between periods of study. After meeting expenses, there was enough left over to put down payment on a car.

Bailo noted that in her very first co-op assignment, she was in the test group doing durability working in the lab; she was just assisting in analyzing results. Later, she did everything from manufacturing engineering to PR to shows and exhibits to design engineering to working in the blueprint room. Bailo remembers well her most difficult assignment: "My hardest job was working over the grates, ten hours a day, filling rear axles with oil. I was bleeding brakes; that was my job every two and a half minutes on the grates, sliding around in oil. After the first two days, my calves hurt so badly I could hardly walk … my mother made me leave all my clothes in the garage after work. I got tougher as I was out there, but it was really illuminating. Great experience!"[3]

GMI helped Bailo see all the different roles and the group. She learned about design engineering—the elite place where everyone wanted to be—and had the sense that test engineers were just the people trying to break something that they designed, and that manufacturing people were just supposed to be quiet and build the stuff because the designs were perfect. After working in different roles around the plant, she didn't feel elitist because she had more opportunity than others. In the end, she realized that they were all in one group. She was seeing it from all the different viewpoints and understanding how all the roles really needed to come together to create the best product at the end of the day.[4]

On March 11, 1982, everything changed for the privileged students at GMI. A press release advised that the GM Corporation would be withdrawing a large part of its financial backing for the sixty-three-year-old GMI over the next three years, and that the school would become a private college beginning that summer. Last year, Bailo assisted with the school's centennial and responded to this change: "My last year, GM pulled out. We all knew GM was having significant financial issues. It was the era of Roger Smith, who was a bean counter. I think we heard rumors about it, but we felt it was such a good pipeline for so many executives. … When it was announced, they said nothing is going to change except that we were going to start increasing tuition, but gradually year over year. They said it would reduce our pain to do it that way."[5] Mary Barra was also enrolled during this period of time.

Bailo began her automotive career with General Motors' Truck & Bus division, where she was in charge of truck durability testing and test development.

Bailo joined Nissan in 1989 as a vehicle-testing engineer at the Nissan Technical Center North America (NTCNA) in Farmington Hills, Michigan. In 2003, she was promoted to director of vehicle program management, where she oversaw all of NTCNA's engineering development projects, as well as cost, quality, and delivery metrics. Also in 2003, she served as the assistant chief vehicle engineer for the Nissan Sentra and Nissan Quest. Later, Bailo was transferred to Nissan's global headquarters in Japan as vehicle program director, with responsibility for the profitability and product presence of Nissan's SUVs worldwide. She was also recovery program director through the financial crisis, reporting directly to the chief recovery officer, and supported measures to offset financial risks of economic business plans during fiscal year 2009.[6]

Carla Bailo rose to the position of senior vice president, Research & Development, Nissan Americas. In this role, Bailo was responsible for all of Nissan's vehicle engineering and development operations in Michigan, Arizona, Mexico, and Brazil. She was also a member of Nissan's MC-A, the company's highest-ranking decision-making body in the Americas region.[7]

In 2017, Bailo was invited to join the Center for Automotive Research as its president and CEO.

More recently, Bailo and Terry Barclay put together a book titled *The Road to the Top Is Not on the Map: Conversations with Top Women of the Automotive Industry*, which was published by the SAE in 2020. The duo explores the careers and opinions of women auto executives via short summaries and a series of six questions.

Courtesy of Lisa Benedict

LISA (CHILDS) BENEDICT

CAREER HIGHLIGHTS

Lisa Benedict, lead of Color and Trim Appearance Definition, began her career in 1983 as an illustrator for engine engineering with Ford Motor Company (FMC).

Sometimes the smallest step in the right direction ends up being the biggest step of your life. Tiptoe if you must. but take the step.[1]

—Lisa Benedict (b. 1962)

She left Ford to seek opportunities within General Motors. In 1984, she joined the Pontiac Motors team as an illustration PAD (portable application description) document artist.

She has since worked in many facets within General Motors, including product design, geometric dimensioning and tolerancing, illustration, and color and trim.

One of Lisa Benedict's career highlights that has had the

most impact took place in 2015, when a project that she was working on received GM recognition leading to a "Transformer Award," and her published professional paper titled "Grain Development & Grain Repair on a 7XXX Series Aluminum" was released in October 2015 at the SPE/TPO conference. Lisa has also been very involved with the Detroit Colour Council throughout her career.

In addition, she has volunteered as a mentor with the School-to-Work program in Macomb County and FIRST Robotics.

BIOGRAPHICAL NOTES

Lisa Benedict's paternal grandfather served as the chief librarian of the Library of Congress from 1925 to 1971. Her father served in the US Air Force after attending the University of Maryland's engineering school. He was later employed as an engine and electrical engineer for the FMC; after thirty years of fruitful employment, her father retired. Mr. Childs was never the type of man to sit at home, so he found employment as a pioneer for alternative fuel systems in a California-based engineering firm. He served there for approximately ten years before moving back to Michigan with his family as an engine engineer for Oldsmobile. Her mother was busy raising seven children and serving as the PTA treasurer.

Benedict and her six siblings—two older brothers, an older sister, a younger sister, and two younger brothers—attended Roosevelt Elementary School in Livonia, Michigan. From grades 7 to 9, she attended Riley Junior High School, where she began to accelerate in the arts. Upon entering Bentley High School, Benedict's paintings and pencil drawings were entered in several local competitions; she was awarded a $500 award from the Livonia mayor in her senior year.

While Lisa was attracted to automotive and residential illustration, she went on to study architectural design at Eastern Michigan University. Within a few months into her second semester, she began to investigate a program offered through Northwood Institute in residential and commercial design and management. Intrigued by this program, she transferred the following fall. While studying at Northwood, the program administrator offered the students several opportunities to compete locally in design challenges. This is where Benedict excelled—the challenge offered was to create the new home interior for the senior executive of Dow Chemical. Benedict won the competition with a very convincing storyboard, which afforded her a position with a local Midland, Michigan, firm as a residential and commercial design consultant. Benedict graduated with a dual associate of arts degree both in residential commercial design management and interior marketing and merchandising in 1983. She went on to complete her requirements for a bachelor's degree in business management and administration from what is now Northwood University.

After her associate degree, Benedict was offered a position

with the Midland Paper Company, where she designed offices both for Dow Chemical and the Midland Hospital. She soon left the Midland area to pursue an opportunity in Birmingham, Michigan, with Ben Pupko's Interiors. While this was a very creative environment, there was something lacking. Benedict began to explore the opportunities within the automotive industry.

Her father decided to help. With his influence within Ford, he was able to introduce her to the illustration senior manager in the engine design group, who recommended her to join his team. Lisa was employed as a contract employee within Ford Motor for a little over year.

In July 1984, she joined the illustration team under the guidance of Bruce Benter at Pontiac Motors as a contract employee. She began to take courses through Macomb Community College in the automotive design program, where, through the assistance of Captain Paul Gould, she was able to interview for a direct position within the engine and power-train design team of Chevrolet Engineering.

Lisa worked within that team for approximately four years before taking on a new challenge within the geometric design and tolerancing team for the newly organized midsize-car group in Warren, Michigan, focusing on the Pontiac F-body platform designs. She had held this position for three years when the next adventure in design took her to Saturn Engineering, located in Troy, Michigan. While stationed at Saturn, she worked to resolve the issues with the exterior door team. There were many long days and plenty of personal rewards while employed with this team. The successes led to a promotion back with midsize design, working with the B-car-platform Chevrolet Caprice program. Throughout this program there were several hands-on opportunities afforded where she learned spot welding and assembly structure methods.

In 1993, Benedict joined the Appearance Engineering team, led by Jim Welton. This was the liaison team among the studio design, color and trim, materials-engineering, and program release teams. The responsibilities were broad and entailed program management for the entire vehicle's appearance attributes.

The texturing and tooling of components intrigued her. Here she was able to improve on the aesthetics of each component through the injection-molding process. This involvement with the engineering team led her to a new opportunity with the Design Quality and Verification team, led by Mark Griffin. It is here that she became the subject matter expert in texturing with a range of tools.

Benedict was promoted to senior project engineer and became very involved with a team whose focus was to develop a method to enable less expensive tooling utilizing aluminum materials.

In 2012, Benedict was invited to join the R&D team that worked with Alcoa and their subcontractors. They were on a mission to replace P20 steel tooling for injection molding with aluminum, possibly mixed with various alloys for low-, medium-,

and high-volume usage. The aim was to reduce tooling costs. They also examined the grain patterns added to tooling, and the repair options should it be damaged in the manufacturing process.

Benedict and her team were the recipients of the prestigious "Transformer Award" in 2015. With this award the team was also recognized through the Society of Plastic Engineers and published their findings at the SPE/TPO Automotive Engineered Polyolefins Conference on October 5, 2015. This process made it possible for General Motors to reduce tool costs, and allowed the cycle time to be reduced by one-third, thus increasing part manufacturing.

Today, Lisa is employed with the color and trim group, led by Jennifer Widrick, under the direction of Sharon Gauci. She works in the Performance Studio under the direction of Rich Scheer, Kirk Bennion, and Chris Fusco, directly working for the color and trim manager, Brett Golliff. Her responsibilities entail managing the appearance attributes of the performance vehicles and ensuring that components are released correctly by validating through virtual builds prior to the vehicles going into production.

Her most recent program involved the Corvette C8, which has received several awards, including recognition as one of 2020's "10 Best Interiors" from *Wards Auto*.

The C8 has garnered numerous awards. *Constance Smith*

While working closely with the performance design team, Benedict was able to spec out her own 2019 Camaro 2SS with the assistance of Adam Barry, senior designer responsible for the Gen 6 Camaro design. This vehicle has been a dream come true, a one of a kind, built for her by the engineering and manufacturing teams at the Lansing Grand River Assembly facility.

In 2017, as an active member for the Detroit Colour Council since 2006, Benedict was voted in as president. The Detroit Colour Council is actively involved with color education within the industries of automotive and architectural design. During her tenure as president, Benedict has written several scholarships for

This is a concept sketch drawn by Adam Barry of the 2019 Spring Special—the only one of these cars that was ever produced from the factory. It is owned by Lisa Benedict. *Courtesy of Adam Barry; photo, Lisa Benedict; General Motors*

undergraduates at Kendall College of Art and Design, Northwood University, Lawrence Technological University, and the College for Creative Studies. In 2019, a grant was written by Benedict, through the Detroit Colour Council, to ensure that the education of the arts was maintained in Greenfield Union Elementary-Middle School, one of Detroit's public schools.

Throughout her career, she has been actively involved with the community; she has served as an active member of the School-to-Work program with Macomb County as a mentor for high school students interested in automotive design and engineering. Benedict was recognized by the governor of Michigan in 1997 as Mentor of the Year and was invited to a special ceremony in Lansing.

As a caveat to Lisa's extensive career within the automotive industry, she has been an active member of a mastermind team. Within this team of like-minded individuals, her goal has been to touch one soul every day through a positive message sent out to over a thousand people daily, titled "The Thought for the Day."

Lisa Benedict married her longtime friend and colleague Gavin Benedict in 2011. They have a beautiful blended family of three amazing children. Her older son, Jordan, is a recent graduate of Norwich University in Vermont; he commissioned on May 3, 2020, as a naval officer and will be reporting to Charleston, South Carolina, in the fall to study nuclear propulsion and engineering. Her daughter, Jillian, and her younger son, Bryan, graduated from Walled Lake Western High School in May 2020. Jillian will be attending the preveterinarian program through Oakland Community College and plans to transfer later to Northern Michigan University to obtain her degree as a veterinarian. Her twin brother, Bryan, will be starting an apprenticeship program through Kalitta Air in late August 2020 and studying to receive his certification in jet engine mechanics and airframe design.

The fox and snowy owl were drawn by Benedict—also a fine artist. *Courtesy of Lisa Benedict*

Off to the races for Benedict's blended family. *Left to right*: Lisa Benedict, Jordan Czarnecki, Gavin Benedict, Bryan Czarnecki, and Jillian Czarnecki. *Lisa Benedict*

HELEN EMSLEY

There are many reasons for success. They include having knowledge of your work, a passion for your job, and the ability to build a team that shares your goals.[1]

—Helen Emsley (b. 1965)

Due to the efforts of Emsley, the GMC 2500 and 3500 Sierras continue to exude strength.

CAREER HIGHLIGHTS

Having spent over thirty years with General Motors, Helen Emsley currently serves as the global executive director of GMC and Buick Design.

Helen Emsley started her career in 1989, at the Opel Division in Germany. At this time, she contributed to the Astra F, Omega, Catera, and Calibra. The Opel Astra F was the successor to the Kadett E.

Emsley accepted a position offered by Ed Welburn, the vice president of Design in the United States, in 1998. She has held numerous Color and Trim design and management positions. She is credited with the interior design of the award-winning 2014 C7 Corvette Stingray. Later, her responsibilities included the design of the GMC Sierra and Cadillac Escalade.

Both the Corvette and GMC Sierra Denali made WardsAuto's 2014 top-ten list of "Best Interiors."

In 2020, as the public gravitates toward highly equipped models, the 2020 Sierra HD was all new. Emsley introduced the 2021 Envision and 2021 GMC trucks and SUVs. By 2022, an AT4 subbrand will be offered across the GMC lineup.

In 2015, Helen Emsley was recognized as one of *Automotive News*' "100 Leading Women in the North American Auto Industry." In 2016 and 2018, she was the recipient of a design award from *Autocar* recognizing British women in the automotive industry.

BIOGRAPHICAL NOTES

Helen Emsley grew up in Yorkshire, a former mining village outside Doncaster. She notes, "My father worked on the railways, so we went everywhere by train."[2] She recalls that the family owned a Vauxhall Viva. While the deputy head at her school dismissed the value of the arts, her father supported her. She studied textiles at Birmingham and competed in a contest to design fabrics for the Ford Escort.

In the 1980s, Emsley was the recipient of a bachelor of arts degree from Birmingham Polytechnic College. She later received a master's degree in Transport Design from the prestigious Royal College of Art. While at the Royal College of Art, she met Wayne Cherry, who headed Opel at the time. He offered her a job at GM's Opel Division in Russelsheim, Germany, in 1989.[3]

OPEL

Adam Opel opened his business in Russelsheim in 1862 to manufacture sewing machines; he later manufactured bicycles before

The Calibra was offered from 1989 to 1997. At this time, Opel held the majority of the market share in Germany. *General Motors*

selling this part of the company. In 1929, GM acquired 80 percent of the business; however, Opel plants were badly damaged by Allied forces in the midforties. Early models included the Rekord and Commodore. Marketers created the saying "Only flying is better" to advertise the Opel GT sports coupe in 1968; the stylish coupe with its retractable headlamps was offered for sale in the United States, and the saying caught on in Germany. By 1972, Opel was Germany's largest automobile company, and in 1988 the Opel Vectra—a dynamic midsized model also offered in AWD—became an immediate bestseller.

In 1989, Opel introduced its first catalytic converter, and Helen Emsley reported to work as an automobile designer. Emsley contributed to the interior design of the Astra F, Omega, Catera, and Calibra. The Opel Astra F, the successor to the Kadett E, was offered for sale from 1991 to 1998. This small family car powered by an in-line four was manufactured in a variety of styles, including three-door and five-door hatchbacks, a sedan, and a wagon. Bertone designed a cabriolet. Astra was voted "Car of the Year" in South Africa, and its production also continued in other countries after its discontinuation in Germany.

The Opel Omega A, the replacement for the Rekord, was a full-sized family sedan built in the Rüsselsheim plant from 1986 to 1987. Several variations were made worldwide, and the car was marketed as the Cadillac Catera in the United States. Unable to compete with larger, more-opulent models, it was phased out. The Omega was offered with LS, GL, GLS, and CD interiors. Emsley contributed to the trim for this model.

In 2000, Emsley noted, "Leadership positions, especially in Germany, are usually dominated by males. The challenges that face women in industry are great. The positive side of this is that you work harder to prove yourself. You are more aware and more sensitive to your environment and the people with whom you work."[4]

Emsley's outstanding design work for Opel attracted the attention of GM's seasoned vice president of Design, Edward Welburn. Following Wayne Cherry, Emsley accepted his invitation to join GM's forces in the United States in 1998. Helen rose through the ranks of America's largest carmaker at this time to make her mark on Chevrolet's fastest marque. She served as assistant chief designer of Color and Trim and later lead designer of Color and Trim.[5] In 1994, she was appointed assistant chief designer of Color and Trim. She was subsequently appointed the global director of Color and Trim.

Perhaps her most-notable responsibilities include her leadership in the design of performance cars for the Chevrolet Motor Division, and the design of trucks such as the GMC Sierra and Cadillac Escalade.

In 2013, Chevrolet dominated the field on and off the track. The collection of winning automobiles was displayed at auto shows here and abroad. The Corvette coupe and convertible Stingray were later described as "it" cars and exotic rides by excited fans. Yet, one could not ignore the Z/28 Camaro, powered by an LS7 V-8, and the Chevrolet SS, a car baptized at the fifty-fifth Daytona 500 race and prepared for future sprint car competitions. In 2013, Chevrolet provided the winning ride for Jimmie Johnson and sponsored Danica Patrick—the first woman to win the pole position. Johnson also took home the Harley J. Earl Trophy, named for GM's first vice president of Design.

Emsley took responsibility for the interior of the C7 and contributed to the C8 Corvette as well. *Constance Smith*

Emsley led the interior design teams for the related production automobiles. The most remarkable introduction was the 2014 Corvette coupe and convertible, unveiled at auto shows in 2013. This seventh-generation model is called the Stingray—a significant designation. The original Sting Ray[6] was an open race car secretly designed under the direction of Bill Mitchell, GM's second vice president of Design. Mitchell bought a Chevrolet mule car from the company for one dollar when Chevrolet was banned from racing. Mitchell had to rebody the car at his own expense. Studio engineers had an idea that the car would hug the road better as an inverted airfoil—engineer Zora Arkus-Duntov viewed it an aerodynamic headache.[7] After sketching it like an inverted airfoil, the Corvette SS mule was renamed the "Sting Ray."

Coincidentally, in 1956, Arkus-Duntov was said to have brought a three-driver team to Daytona Beach, looking to set speed records. He drove the mule car with some 1956 panels added, and Betty Skelton and John Fitch drove two 1956 cars. While Fitch won, Skelton placed second. Being the US female aerobatics champion for three years, she also thrived on speed.

In 1963, Chevrolet introduced another Stingray that featured a controversial split rear window that would have to face Ford's AC Cobras on the track. While the car guys and gals among us would likely choose to get locked down in the competitive-style sports car seat, a GT magnesium seat is also strikingly beautiful.

In 2104, Chevrolet owed its newest awards solely to Emsley. As noted, both the Corvette and GMC Sierra Denali made WardsAuto's top-ten list of "Best Interiors" in 2014. A writer for WardsAuto simply stated what has become obvious to many: "The interior was competitive with more expensive rivals such as Porsche and Jaguar—securing its status as a sports car for the ages."

In January 2014, the 2015 Chevrolet Z06 Coupe, which delivered upward of 625 horsepower, was unveiled in Detroit, Michigan. This world-class performer, equipped with an all-new supercharged engine and an eight-speed paddle-shift automatic or seven-speed manual transmission, was introduced with a track-focused Z07 performance package outperforming even the 2013 ZR1. The engine delivers upward of 625 horsepower.

While many of the exterior design changes were made to accommodate larger tires, Emsley refreshed the interior as well. Unique color schemes emphasize the wraparound cockpit and accentuate the unique flat-bottomed steering wheel. Like the Stingray driver, the Z06 customer has a choice of two seats. The GT seat was designed for comfort, and the Competition seat has added side bolstering. The magnesium frames for both are lighter and more rigid than comparable steel seats. The interior continues to feature a grab bar, carbon fiber, suede-like microfiber, and Napa leather.

While the Chevrolet truck captured the North American Truck of the Year award in 2014, the WardsAuto jury put the interior of the all-new Sierra Denali in its top ten—right alongside the 2014 Corvette Stingray. The Denali model occupies the top spot when it comes to what GMC marketers call "Professional Grade" vehicles. On the outside, the extravagant chrome grille and 20-inch wheels add to a refined profile. Projector headlamps with LEDs are all the rage. The inside appointments truly set it apart from its predecessors.

Thanks to Emsley, this work tool is one of the most luxurious trucks to hit the road. The interior is defined by its comfort, high quality, and quiet ride, and attention to detail and technological conveniences put it on top.

GM literature took the description further. Perforated nuance-leather-appointed seating, heated and cooled driver and front passenger twelve-way adjustable buckets, a heated leather steering wheel, and aluminum—metal, not plastic—touches throughout the cabin make it easy on the eye and comfortable on an extended trip. GMC engineers created the quiet ride with the addition of triple door seals, shear body mounts, aerodynamic mirrors, and a valved exhaust system. The Bose symphonic sound system, with seven speakers, is a mainstay.

The bold center console dominates the instrument panel and is a virtual hub of technology—standard and customizable. There is an available Color Touch radio, natural language command, Bluetooth, phone integrations, and access to Pandora and HD radio, for starters. The large rear-vision camera is crystal clear and a must for some. The standard power-sliding rear window, also offered by a rival, is a convenience some drivers

expect. OnStar Directions and Connections are standard, as is Turn-by-Turn Navigation.

Yes, engineers added a host of safety features to this truck, earning a five-star rating from the National Highway Traffic Safety Administration—auto crash response, roadside assistance, an emergency services link, and a remote door unlock.

On November 9, 2015, Emsley, along with GM's first female CEO, Mary Barra, was recognized as one of *Automotive News'* "100 Leading Women in the North American Auto Industry." We look forward to many other great designs reaching the market under the direction of Helen Emsley.

The 2021 Encore GX continued to attract. *Courtesy of Bob and Penny Tetmeyer*

NEW PRODUCTS FOR BUICK

The 2021 Envision joined the 2020 Encore GX—a compact SUV—in the Buick lineup. Helen Emsley, the executive director of Global Buick and GMC Design, managed the design team that made the Envision lower and wider and sportier. Envision is powered by a 2-liter, turbocharged, four-cylinder engine.

Buick's popular premium Avenir trim was available on the 2021 Envision for the first time.

The 2016 Envision interior was strong. *General Motors*

Designers of the HD Sierra nailed it, adding an invisible trailer camera to the mix.

SIERRA HD FROM GMC

The GMC HD Sierra was also all new in 2020. The low-end work truck that featured vinyl seats stood in stark contrast to the high-end Sierra HD Denali, which dominated sales in the previous year. For those looking to take refined capability off-road, GMC fortified the new AT4 brand with an all-new Sierra AT4 Heavy Duty, available for Crew Cab configurations as both a 2500 and 3500 single-rear-wheel-drive offering.

While interiors are similar in nature depending on version, the distinct exteriors compete, with some observers commenting that the grill on the GMC had a more rugged appearance. Somewhere along the line, Helen Emsley, GMC's design director, noted that once someone on the road saw your GMC truck in their rearview mirror, it would leave an impression—and this was important. Accommodating the same payload, offering the same power train, and providing the same hauling capabilities, the HD Silverado and Sierras are considered mechanically identical.

However, the first year out, GMC offered one more option that Chevrolet buyers might not be able to resist: the world's first six-function MultiPro tailgate was available on all trims and standard on SLT, AT4, and Denali. The six functions are described as the primary tailgate, the primary gate load stop, easy access, full-width step, inner gate load stop, and inner gate with work surface. Of course, it was only a matter of time until Chevrolet offered this option.

The tweaks for 2021 included the AT4 Precision Plus and Denali Black Diamond Edition, which includes the trailer camera.

By 2022, an AT4 subbrand will be offered across the GMC lineup. Under Emsley's leadership, we look forward to the production 2021 off-road Terrain, 2022 GMC Hummer EV, Canyon AT4, and other new products.

The 2022 Hummer EV pickup, somewhat reminiscent in design to Hummers of yesteryear—especially in size—is loaded with features and oriented toward off-road use. Inside, the designers incorporate state-of-the-art displays and details acknowledging lunar typography. Crab walk seems to enable infinite movement in any direction; three electric motors and an Ultium battery pack propel this heavy truck from 0 to 60 mph in just three seconds. Rated at about 1,000 hp, with 11,500 foot-pounds of torque, a charge is good for 350 miles. The removable roof panels stow in the rear. Every detail, down to the logo, is notable.

FAMILY TIES

Helen Emsley's family is still in England. Her dad has retired from the railway. Her husband, David, works as a shop supervisor in her building, and her son, Connor, was eighteen when this was composed.

The GMC Hummer, described as the most capable truck on the planet, was powered by three electric motors and rated at about 1000 horsepower on arrival. *General Motors*

JANET GOINGS

People are complex, but technology shouldn't be—at least using it shouldn't be. My education as an electrical engineer has allowed me to discover opportunities and solutions where emerging technology meets the people who interact with it. It's a totally amazing space that offers new challenges on a continuous basis.

—Janet Goings (b. 1959)

Courtesy Janet Goings

CAREER SUMMARY

Janet Goings was awarded bachelor's and master's degrees in electrical engineering from Purdue University in 1982 and the University of Michigan in 1987, respectively. Throughout her career, she led GM's efforts in the use of design thinking to drive innovation across the industry, with a specific focus on new technologies and scientific breakthroughs. Using deep customer insights to drive the prioritization and development of new technologies, she directed resources on to innovations with the highest customer value.

In addition to her work in user-centered design, her assignments involved the development of advanced automotive control systems, new vehicle concepts, OnStar, strategic planning, and research and development. She holds more than ten patents and has been recognized for her work in technology and innovation.

Janet has also been active in GM's campus relations at Purdue for over thirty years. She was engaged in the creation of employee resource groups (ERGs) at General Motors, serving on the boards of the Women's ERG and GM PLUS (People Like Us), an LGBTQ ERG.

As part of the Purdue University Relations Team, Janet served on advisory boards for the College of Electrical and Computer Engineering, Women in Engineering Programs, and the Office of Professional Practice, bringing numerous programs to generations of Purdue engineering students to expose them to the importance of knowing how your work affects other people's lives for the better. In addition to identifying the next generation of GM engineers, she also has engaged with students globally through GM's PACE initiative, for which she led the customer insight portion of the global design competition.

In February 2020, after nearly forty years with General Motors and having risen to the position of senior manager, Janet took advantage of an early retirement opportunity. Having seen so many up and downs and business cycles over the years, she felt that the strategic vision of the company was solidly on track to value innovation that works for the customer, and that so many talented people were in place to make that innovation happen.

Goings is proud of the awards she has received, notably the Purdue University Office of Professional Practice Co-op Hall of Fame (2014) and the Purdue College of Engineering Alumni Loyalty Award (2018).

As a GM engineer, she contributed to the OnStar Product Launch (1996) and the Integrated Instrument Panel Project. She has been granted patents for a reconfigurable sunvisor, a gesture control key fob, and a console assembly, among others.

In an entertaining and informative presentation of the future of transportation, Goings appeared in an episode of NASA's *Sci Files* show titled "The Case of the Radical Ride," which aired on PBS.

BIOGRAPHICAL NOTES

Janet was born in Logansport, Indiana, to Carl and Dortha Saunders. She enjoyed camping across the country with her family in her early years and was active in student leadership, speech and drama programs, and tennis at Logansport High School. She chose engineering as her career path after a neighbor invited her to shadow

2004 Aztec. *General Motors*

him for a day at Delco Electronics, and she never looked back. She married her Purdue sweetheart, Scott, and is the proud mother of a second-generation Boilermaker, Alex (BSME '17).

Janet notes, "My brother and I are the first generation in our family to go to college. My mom was a homemaker, and my dad was a WWII hero, motorcycle cop, and insurance adjuster—nothing science or engineering related, just great parents. My brother, who is six years older than me, studied forestry at Michigan Tech. In K–12, I was the classic overachieving kid, involved in everything, and did make a volcano for a science fair once but never demonstrated any original thought . . . lol."

As a freshman at Purdue University in 1979, Jane entered its co-op program and received an assignment with Delco Electronics. She completed co-op assignments in ten work areas, including Design, Manufacturing Development, Service, and Sales.

Her projects have included development of advanced automotive control systems such as active suspensions and four-wheel steering, new vehicle concept development and portfolio entry, the OnStar launch, growth market strategy, marketing, recruiting, and diversity programs.

Janet reflects on the assignment that preceded the controversial Pontiac Aztek:

Where do new vehicles come from? This was the question the Advanced Portfolio Exploration team was asked to answer in 1995. We were a small team of engineers, designers, and analysts who wanted to use societal and technology trends as a way to look at what new vehicles could make a big impact in the market.

By starting with a very broad funnel that narrowed in scope based on customer, business, and technology filters, we felt we could systematically find high-value market opportunities. But first, we needed to understand how new vehicle programs came to be—the process side of the company. As it turned out, there wasn't a formal process. When times were good, if a senior leader liked a concept car, it might get the green light to be produced. When times were not so good, it was a moot point as nothing new would get funding. That didn't seem like a very strategic way to run a business, so after we showed the (dare I say somewhat random) process, the green light was given to do a pilot on a trends-driven approach to new vehicle concepting. Hurrah! We knew that the best way to invent something new is to actually do it, rather than just planning it, so we chose some trends that were already very much in evidence as the starting point for our pilot. From societal perspective, life was getting more complicated—ever busier. People wanted what they wanted, when they wanted it, with fewer compromises. On the technology side, we were learning to manufacture with lighter materials, connectivity was just beginning to have meaning, and Moore's law was showing no signs of abating. Looking at the portfolio as it existed at that time, we had cars and we had trucks and we had minivans. Trucks were less than 50 percent of the market. Minivans were already kind of a necessary evil—functional, but not fun. Combining the trends we were observing with the automotive landscape, we identified the opportunity for a class of vehicles that were in between these traditional definitions—hybrids, but not in the power

The 2001 Aztek was sourced to do just about everything. *General Motors*

train sense—a car and a truck, a car and a minivan, a minivan and a truck. This may not seem like rocket science in retrospect, but at the time, even suggesting these alternatives got us a lot of weird looks. From the APEx side, we felt that we needed to choose a pilot that focused on future opportunities that weren't really all that futuristic—if the market opportunity was too far in the future, it would be hard to value and hard to convince leadership that the market would be there when the vehicle was introduced. (Kind of like soccer players need to learn to go where the ball will be, rather than chasing it.) So crossovers became the target, and we defined three—one for each of the crossover categories. The names of the concepts were Ursa (car-truck), Joaquin (car-minivan), and Trango (minivan-truck). As the team socialized the idea of a new vehicle development process with these pilot concepts of crossover vehicles, the buy-in gained momentum quickly. The catch phrase for the car-truck crossover was "what do you get when you put a Camaro and a Blazer in a blender? An Unconventional, Recreational, Sport Alternative URSA. People got it and asked us to keep going to develop the alternative paths for the vehicle to get to market. Market research, engineering, and manufacturing alternatives all got underway, expanding the team to lots of other departments globally, and everyone was enthusiastic about contributing. Through months of study, design, engineering, and analysis the alternatives emerged and were readied for presentation to the strategy board—the people who ultimately decided what vehicle programs would be funded. They held the checkbook to fund dots (shorthand for a portfolio entry) or stop them. While

the other alternatives continued development, and other new concepts were discovered, I took the lead on URSA. I was the one who assembled the pitch deck, who went through all the pre-reviews that were required before getting to the strategy board. On the day of the review, I wore a polka dot blouse—my secret "dot" message to the board—and I was really nervous to be presenting to the top of the company. However, my job was to share the data that the whole team had assembled, which would allow them to make their decision. The pitch went well; the decision to move forward with URSA was made. A program team was formed, but no one from the APEx concepting team was included—we were the idea people, not the executers. In making the innumerable program decisions and trade-offs that are required, the spirit of URSA was lost. The vehicle that emerged as the Pontiac Aztek is not was the APEx team proposed. There are elements that can be seen if you squint—the functionality, the cooler, the tent. . . . So I learned a valuable lesson about keeping the true customer squarely in your sights, guiding your priorities at each step of a project. That lesson has stayed with me to this day, and I have worked hard to share it with as many others as possible!"

Thus, Janet expresses the call to satisfy the transportation needs of the public with foresight and innovation. Working across a multitude of engineering perspectives during an impressive career at General Motors, Janet Goings has raised the bar for advancing the possibilities of Human-Machine Interaction.

General Motors

DENISE GRAY

If you do the right thing, good things will come to you. We are where we are by the grace of God and the goodness in our heart to give back.[1]

—Denise Gray (b. 1965)

CAREER HIGHLIGHTS

Denise Gray, CEO of LG Chem's North American subsidiary, spent three decades serving General Motors. She led its efforts to develop battery technology for the Chevrolet Volt.

Denise joined GM as a full-time engineer after graduating from the GMI Co-op program. An early assignment included software development for the 1997 Corvette. This was the start of her thirty-year career at GM, and she continues communication even after leaving. Gray worked in vehicle electrical systems, in electric controls, and with propulsion system software that managed complex electronics. In the 1990s, Gray assembled an in-house team for the development of the Volt. When Gray's position was announced, GM had already built the hybrid Saturn Vue. Gray went on to manage the battery development testing program at the onset of the Chevrolet Volt project. She likely secured her pension before moving to other companies. Gray left GM in 2010 to work for Atieva in Silicon Valley. This battery pack supplier would later be renamed Lucid. From March 2013 to September 2015, she was vice president of power train electrification at AVL in Graz, Austria, and North America.

Gray is currently listed as president and chief executive officer of LG Chem Power, Inc., a company focused on bringing lithium-ion polymer battery technology to North America for applications in the automotive and commercial markets as of September 2015. LG Chem Power is the US side of the large Korean company that supplies cells and battery packs to dozen of OEMs worldwide. In addition, Gray has served as the president of LG Chem Michigan, Inc., since March 2018.

Gray has also contributed to various charitable organizations. From 2016 to 2018, she served a chair for the March of Dimes at NAIAS, Detroit's North American auto show. In 2017, Gray was honored with the 2017 Women of Color Technologist of the Year Award, which recognizes women who work in science, technology, engineering, and math (STEM) as it applies to industries including space, surveillance, military defense, and automotive.

GRAY'S JOURNEY

Denise Gray's mother's family of fourteen left a farm in tiny LaGrange, Arkansas, to replace cotton picking with assembly line work. She notes in an interview: "They came to the Detroit area because Detroit offered the possibility of having a job, a job where you could earn a good living for a family. That's what Detroit means for me. It means an opportunity for earning a decent living."[2] Her mother attended a one-room schoolhouse. Her father, a Georgia native, served in the US Air Force and worked construction. "Mom and Dad divorced when I was five, I think," Gray said. "It was a tough time." At first, Gray's mother worked as a waitress and in a laundromat.[3]

"It was low wages, but we never knew we were in that type of income. We always felt very blessed," Gray noted. "We had warmth and support from aunts and uncles and cousins. My mother would take us to the restaurant or tell us about the job at the forge being very hot and hard work and not being as respected as you'd want."[4]

Gray grew up in and went to school in Detroit; her mom still resides there. Her family of believers has attended the Shady

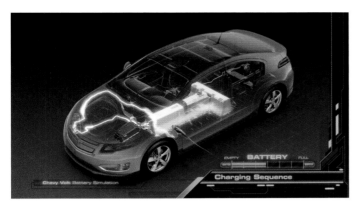

General Motors

hydride to lithium ion. Gray believes that the lithium batteries of today will be around another decade due to three advantages: they are lightweight, high capacity, and chargeable. GM was committed to making the Volt a reality—it was determined and never veered from the objective. General Motors opened doors for everyone.

She would go on to tap everyone at GM with the passion and the ability to contribute to the Volt project.

After resigning from GM, Gray spent three years in Silicon Valley for the company Atieva, better known today as Lucid.

As president and CEO of LG Chem, Gray now works for everyone. When asked about the Asian market, she notes that Europeans and Americans want finely tuned vehicles; the needs of the Chinese and their budgets are different. While starter vehicles are for teens here, there is a concentration on the low end in China.

After spending thirty years at GM, Gray looked for more opportunity to advance to a higher position and left GM. At this point in time, her retirement benefits were ensured. Some of her colleagues would bail out when GM altered the retirement plan. After leaving, things fell into place for her. She hit the jackpot, or perhaps LG did, as she has solidified their stake in the auto-motive industry at a time when it is was most beneficial.

Today, Gray lives in Farmington, not far from her childhood Detroit home. She notes that "work-life integration has always been a work in progress for me ... throughout a thirty-one-year marriage, two adult sons, extended family, community involve-ment, and a thirty-three-year career. It is only possible due to determination to have it all and a supportive husband, available family members, and a gratifying career."[7]

Grove Missionary Baptist Church in Detroit with their church family for most of their lives.

A seventh-grade math teacher, Mr. Oliver, recognized Gray's mastery of math and science early on. He took five or six students aside and advised them he was going to give them accelerated work. Gray notes, "He was a giving person; we all need to do that."[5]

Today, she and her colleagues volunteer at the Detroit Science Center, the YMCA, and wherever else they can. Mr. Oliver explained what engineering is—she and her mother had no idea—and encouraged her to study it. When she got to Cass Tech, he told her to choose electronics from the course list. Gray had planned to teach math or science, since even this would have been a challenging path for a young lady.

Cass Tech had numerous part-time teachers, fully established and active in their own careers who provided training for the real world. Denise notes that she was one of two girls in a class of thirty-five.[6]

Gray, like many of her GM colleagues, entered the co-op program at General Motor Institute (or Kettering University, depending on when she started). Gray also attended Rensselaer Polytechnic Institute from 1996 to 2000, earning a master's degree in engineering management. Gray found the strate-gic-thinking course she took in graduate school beneficial for advancing her career.

At GM, her assignment for the Volt project would change her life. She was appointed global director for batteries. She notes, "This was an amazing expe-rience." Gray leveraged twenty-five people from R&D and others from wherever she could find them. It was important to chase down the designers of the EV-1 at the start and not repeat their mistakes. She had to bring everyone together. In assessing battery technologies, we have moved from the lead acid to nickel metal

Theresa Priebe, who reported to Tim Grieg, was the lead interior designer. *General Motors*

Drawing by Constance Smith

MARY GUSTANSKI

When I was a freshman, our general manager was the guest speaker, and he made a very strong point that sticks with me today: "You can never have enough education and take every opportunity offered, even if it's not on your short list of choices."[1]

—Mary Gustanski (b. ca. 1962)

CAREER HIGHLIGHTS

Mary Gustanski was appointed senior vice president and chief technical officer of Delphi Technologies in 2017. The company's website notes that she was challenged to ensure the flawless execution of global engineering and to share Delphi Technologies' work product value proposition for propulsion systems. Delphi is more than just a company that builds parts for IC engines; it is moving toward hybrid, fully electric, connected, and autonomous vehicles, a transition that will take years because of the infrastructure and customer expectations. Delphi is the volume manufacturer of a leading 800-volt SiC inverter, designed to cut EV charging time in half. The inverter is one of the key components of highly efficient next-generation electric and hybrid vehicles. It enables electrical systems up to 800 volts, extending EV range and halving charging times when compared to today's state-of-the-art chargers in 400-volt systems. Gustanski retired at the end of 2019, prior to Delphi's anticipated merger with BorgWarner.

Gustanski was recognized as one of the "100 Leading Women in the NA Auto Industry" by *Automotive News* in 2010 and 2015. She was also ranked forty-second on *Motor Trend*'s Power List.

BIOGRAPHICAL NOTES

Gustanski was one of three children. Both brothers were younger and would follow in her footsteps instead of vice versa. Her mom, who did not have the opportunity to finish college, took care of the children, as was expected back then. Her dad traveled and was absent much of the time; his company made automation equipment.

The second time she was selected as one of the "100 Leading Women in the Auto Industry in NA" by *Automotive News*, in 2015, she noted, "My mother—she never finished her college education, but she ended up with motherhood and having kids at home. My dad traveled; he made automation equipment. Sometimes he was gone months at a time. . . . I was the oldest, so she (Mom) would say, "Mary, you're good at this stuff. You can do this; you can fix it." I can tell you stories from the time I was probably eight of taking the toilet bowl apart."[2]

Gustanski earned a bachelor's degree in mechanical engineering as well as a master's degree in manufacturing management. She was hired full time as an associate manufacturing engineer in April 1985.

Gustanski, who graduated from Kettering University in 1985, began her career as a General Motors Institute cooperative education student at the former AC Spark Plug facility. In 1909, AC Spark was acquired as a division of GM, and in 1974 it merged with GM's Delco-Remy Division. She was hired full time as an associate manufacturing engineer in April 1985 and went on to hold several positions in engineering and manufacturing. These included senior manufacturing project engineer, senior project engineer, and production superintendent, prior to being promoted to divisional plant quality manager in 1997. Gustanski became chief engineer for generators in 1998 and was promoted in 2001 to Technical Center director. In 2003, she was named global director of manufacturing engineering.[3]

In 2006, Ms. Gustanski was appointed as a member of the Powertrain Systems executive staff as the divisional director of engineering, customer satisfaction, and program management. She was named Delphi Powertrain's vice president of engineering, operations, and customer satisfaction in 2012 and, in August 2014, was appointed to the corporate engineering team as vice president of Engineering and Program Management.[4] After joining Delphi, she was promoted to CTO and senior VP. Gustanski retired at the end of 2019, prior to Delphi's anticipated merger with BorgWarner.

The student center at Kettering University houses some exhibits. *Constance Smith*

MARIETTA L. KEARNEY (ELLIS)

I owe my success first to God and then to my family.

Being able to see a car evolve from my sketches is very exciting … to start off with a two-dimensional sketch and end up with a three-dimensional model that runs on the road is amazing to see. It's almost like watching it (the car) being born.[1]

—Marietta "May" Kearney (b. 1961)

General Motors

CAREER HIGHLIGHTS

In addition to serving as an automobile designer and Buick design manager, Kearney is married—to a Ford guy—with children. She has held positions as a teacher, adjunct assistant professor, community activist, and entrepreneur. She could serve as a mentor to women everywhere and has guided many boys and girls through the years.

Kearney, likely the nation's and GM's first African American female automobile designer, contributed to a large array of notable concept and production vehicles. In 1983, she tackled interior design for the 1987 and later the 1991 Chevrolet Beretta and Corsica. She contributed to the interiors of the 1994 Pontiac Grand Prix, 1994 Buick Roadmaster, and 1998 Oldsmobile Intrigue. Later, she contributed to the design of the Olds Alero and 1997 Buick LeSabre. Kearney was called upon to design interiors for two concept cars: the futuristic 1998 Chevrolet Venture automobile and the youth-oriented 1989 Pontiac Stinger. In 1995, she rose to the position of assistant design manager for Buick.

After overcoming her own health issues and leaving General Motors to care for family members, Kearney founded her own consulting business, Sketch Whims & Design. She provides product, graphic, web, and interior designers for commercial and residential users. She notes that she is also a painter and sculptress and sometimes employs these skills.

THE JOURNEY

Born in Baltimore, Maryland, Kearney is the middle child of three raised by their mother, Delores Kearney. Her mother attained nursing and business skills to provide for her children, encouraging them to be the best they could be. Marietta was close to her grandparents; grandmother Lorraine Johnson inspired her to pursue art. She was extremely proud that her granddaughter joined GM, knowing her grandfather would have been proud

too. Her family, notably her mother, her older sister, Drusella Lewis, and her younger brother, Walter Kearney, are close and support each other. Kearney attended schools in Maryland, Michigan, and Indiana. From age eight onward, she remembers feeling content sitting and drawing. Her elementary art teacher cultivated what she saw as a gift, and asked her to create large cartoons for the wall of the school.

Kearney continued to gravitate toward art as a student at Detroit's Cass Technical High School. Through the years, Cass Tech has relied on experienced instructors to provide professional-level training. Early students participated in work study opportunities. Even before Kearney arrived at Cass Tech, General Motors hired Cass Tech graduate Tom Bradley, who later studied industrial design at Pratt Institute. Bradley designed the exhibit for GM's popular Futurama (1964 New York World's Fair) and GM's corporate identity program, providing signage for all car dealers. Bradley went on to hire Teckla Rhoads, a graduate of the Center for Creative Studies. Rhoads worked her way up from a lettering designer to director of global industrial design.[2]

Kearney notes that Irving Berg, head of the art department, encouraged her to perfect her skills. In an interview, she confided that she was very quiet, and he pushed her into entering contests. Contests at Cass Tech meant money and led to many scholarships and grants. It took her teacher to convince her parents that an art or industrial design could lead to a career. Case in point: Kearney attended the College for Creative Studies on a Ford Motor Company scholarship. She studied drawing and graphics, and, as she pursued studies as a sculpture and clay-modeling student, she found that she was more attracted to industrial design—it was more exciting. She received a BFA, majoring in industrial design, from the college in 1982. She later enrolled in the graduate business administration program at Central Michigan University and was awarded an MSA. Kearney also studied at the Kellogg University School of Management after embarking on a career in automotive design.

When it comes to automobile design, Kearney feels that it is difficult to predict what features will appeal to customers, and that the process to go from sketch to production involves many people and could take years.

CHEVROLET BERETTA AND CORSICA

"In 1983," Kearney notes, "I got involved with designing the Chevrolet Corsica and the Beretta. I started the cars as a student and was involved with the project from day one and worked on them from the ground up. To be able to get a car so quick[ly] (to actually have a car on the road) was very surprising to me, I think my bosses were also surprised to see that I was able to produce so quickly." (Marietta Kearny, *City Magazine*, March 1988, 18–20)

Chevrolet offered the family-oriented Corsica from 1988 to 1996 and the two-door sporty Beretta coupe from 1988 to

General Motors

In 1987, the 1988 Beretta, a two door coupe, and Corsica, were introduced. Chevrolet Public Relations. *Collection of the author*

1993. Kearny is credited for design work on the 1987, 1989, and 1991 editions. Both models contributed to the ongoing popularity of Chevrolet products. Early Corsicas and Berettas both were powered by 2-liter, four-cylinder and 2.8-liter, V-6 engines; 2.2s and the 3.1-liter V-6 later appeared, as did GTs and GTZs, and even a convertible touched down for a very short time. These cars and power plants continued to be a mainstay for GM across the board for years.

Other assignments included the interiors of the 1994 Pontiac Grand Prix and Buick Roadmaster. As the 1990s drew to a close, her assignments included interior designs for the tried-and-true Buick LeSabre, the higher-powered Regal, and the elegant Park Avenue.

IMAGE CARS

In 1988, GM produced a series of futuristic concept cars for a special exhibition—*Teamwork and Technology for Today and Tomorrow*—to perpetuate the thematic image of each division. With the Motoramas of old in mind, the cars were exhibited in the ballrooms of the Waldorf Astoria, and a diverse audience was invited to share the glory. In addition to the divisional concept cars, a two-seat sporty SRV-1 was set up in a separate room from the production car concepts as a design in progress to illustrate the design process. Half the clay model for the SRV-1 was completed, and the other half was being created by sculptors on-site. This model of an advanced sports car was designed under the direction of Clark Lincoln, chief designer of the Advanced 2 Studio. The flowing, curvaceous form, also referred to as the Stealth behind the scenes by designers, incorporated every advanced technology of the present and future—a heads-up display, ABS, night vision, navigation, and a rear vision video camera sometimes attributed to Charles Jordan. In lieu of a traditional steering wheel, the car was controlled by two sticks.

The concept cars for the production studios were a bit more tame, but futuristic as well. These included the elegant Cadillac Voyage; the upscale, powerful Buick Lucerne-Sceptre; the we-build-excitement Pontiac Banshee; the Olds Division's sleek Aerotech; the versatile GMC Centaur; and, last but not least, the Heartbeat-of-America Chevrolet Venture. Chevrolet designers, which included Kearney, were challenged to design an entry-level automobile with upscale features (Chevrolet later gave the Venture name to a minivan).

Don Lasky, the chief designer in the Chevrolet 1 Exterior Studio, designed the exterior for this family sedan slightly smaller than a Caprice. Lasky noted, in Crain's *Automotive News* in 1988, "The other part of our mission statement is to make sure we don't do any boring cars, that whatever we do is exciting and youthful."

Marietta Kearney was selected to work on the design of the interior of the Venture. In describing the inside, Lasky noted that

The Cadillac Voyage concept explored the future. *General Motors*

the roof consisted of removable glass, the panel featured high-tech instrumentation with voice-activated controls, and the car had touch switches instead of door handles. The flowing but modern-looking instrument panel consisted of a lengthy dark-

The Stinger would have been a popular entry but was only a concept. *General Motors*

ened-out display that wrapped across the breadth of the car into the door panels. This visually negative area, filled with advanced instrumentation, flowed down into the center console. It was noted that the car would accommodate four-wheel drive.

PONTIAC STINGER

It was time for Pontiac to recognize both the performance and recreational needs of its millennial customers. In 1989, Kearney

noted that she designed the Stinger to meet the "lifestyles of the young working person who wanted sophisticated transportation during the week and a fun car on the weekends."

The 1989 "We Build Excitement" Pontiac Stinger concept brings to mind the go-karts and dune buggies of yesteryear but predates the Pontiac Aztek and Vibe (note that this bears no relation to the 2018 KIA Stinger). A clay model led to a full-size model incorporating polystyrene panels. Make no mistake—in the end, this handsome all-wheel-drive carbon-fiber concept atop a steel frame was also a road car for all terrains and all seasons. The design provided seating for four adults with a storage area. At almost 165 inches in length, the Stinger relied on a variation of the Iron Duke Tech 4—a 3-liter, sixteen-valve, four-cylinder engine to deliver a meaty 170 horsepower. The driver could set the suspension to either a hard of soft ride via the pneumatic active suspension system. From beach to highway, the Stinger could conquer all terrains.

Bill Bowman further describes the Stinger concept in a Pontiac newsletter originating from the Public Relations Department on January 4, 1989.

Many things make this car remarkable. It was equipped with, except for the windshield, removable glass panels. Bowman noted, "The body can be transformed from two-door closed transportation to open-air fun, adaptable to a number of different activities. A roof light bar, adjustable rear spoiler, and removable glass roof panels complete the exterior transformation from a workday mode of transportation to weekend fun. Even the glass in the lower portion of the door can be removed and substituted with a panel containing a beverage holder and storage box for convenience." It was also noted that the Stinger featured a six-way power memory seat with an inflatable bladder system in the front. When the car was parked, the open roof allowed the rear seats to be raised 15 inches (38 cm) electrically to provide rear seat passenger with a unique view over the roof light bar.

While Dave Ross more than likely penned the exterior sketch for the initiation of this concept, Marietta Kearney was tapped to assist with the rest of the design. The gray-green color scheme on the outside was carried to the interior. The attractive, modern-looking instrument panel was equipped with an electric tilt wheel and steering column (both with memory), manual tilt gauges, a compass, and an attitude-gyro-recording vehicle tilt. The green-and-black contoured seats were complete with a racing-style harness. The removable built-in front passenger utility seat was designed for camping. All seats folded flat for resting or sleeping.

Bowman notes that the console featured a sport-styled shifter, a control switch for a soft or hard ride, a compact disc player, and a newly styled radio.

While two removable carrying cases stowed in the door, most of the other accessories added were paradigms of practicality: a pullout radio with a carrying case (an upgrade to the one found in a 1958 Feminine Show car), a portable vacuum, an extension cord, a tool box, a flashlight, a first-aid kit, an umbrella, tote bags, a sewing kit, a dustpan, and a flashlight. Add to this a picnic table and a camper stove, and you have a well-equipped apartment.

KEARNEY: TEACHER AND MENTOR

Kearney has also served as an art instructor for Henry Ford Elementary School, where she taught grade K–5 art and design. She notes, "Scholars study cultural arts, transportation design, 2-D (dimensional), and 3-D design. They explore design terms and industry techniques."

As an assistant professor at Wayne State University, Kearney not only taught industrial design but served as a career coach. Kearny notes, "I teach students about basic drawing, how to come up with ideas, and rendering techniques. I invite guests from other companies to discuss their areas of expertise, so that the students can talk to people who are actually working in the fields, and to ensure that student have some idea of what the demands of the market are, and what the various jobs entail. I enjoy teaching and find it very satisfying. I feel as if I am giving something back and sharing that which I have learned."

THE MOVE

Kearny left GM for California to address her daughters' health needs. Her husband's company transferred him. Once reaching California, her children were largely homeschooled.

SKETCH WHIMS

In 2009, Kearney started Sketch Whims & Design to broaden the awareness of design—a noble goal. She provides visuals, graphic design, web design, product design, and so on to individuals and companies. Her clients include the Dellew Corporation, iTramopline Hawaii, and the Pacific Revival Center.

MENTORING

In the late 1980s, Kearney joined colleagues in a group called IDEA, formed to motivate young people to pursue careers in automotive and industrial design.

A community leader, Kearney has contributed her time to Anointed Hands, South Bay United Pentecostal.

In the late 1980s, Kearney credited her success to her strong faith and a supportive family: "My parents were always there for us—even when we slipped or messed up. We are a close-knit family, and they have always been an inspiration to me. I owe my success first to God and then my family."

Kearney joined colleagues working on the Stinger concept car. *General Motors*

ELIZABETH PILIBOSIAN

During my automotive career, I have had a unique opportunity to see growth and expertise enabling us to move to a more efficient, reliable, and safe-vehicle portfolio—ultimately taking us to our goal of zero crashes, zero emissions, and zero congestion. I am excited about our new steps toward electrification, enabled by the best technical talent from around the world!

—Elizabeth Pilibosian (b. 1959)

Original photo by Michael Pilibosian

CAREER HIGHLIGHTS

Serving as the vehicle chief engineer from 2009 to 2012 for the compact SUV line, Elizabeth Pilibosian led her team to build the most-successful, most-competitive vehicles in the automotive industry.

Prior to this assignment, she served as director of electrical validation and supervised the EMC and Vehicle Performance Laboratory, housing both vertical bench test systems and A frames. Early in 2009, she worked on a Special Assignment Viability Plan; she assisted with the compilation of data for the US government on GM's behalf during bankruptcy proceedings.

From 2005 to 2009, Pilibosian held the position of vehicle chief engineer for the Cadillac CTS and managed complex vehicles with new and emerging technology, from advanced design to production.

Pilibosian has been recognized professionally for many contributions.

As chief engineer, Pilibosian led her team in the development of the second-generation, all-new 2008 Cadillac CTS sedan, coupe, and wagon. The CTS was recognized as the 2008 *Motor Trend* Car of the Year and the International Insurance for Highway Safety (IIHS) Top Safety Pick. Pilibosian was named to *Motor Trend*'s 2008 Power List of the automobile industry's Top 50 Influencers; she was number 38.

As a volunteer and mentor on behalf of General Motors, Pilibosian contributed to the training of future generations of engineers for well over fifteen years. She developed and conducted workshops for mentoring strategies and diversity training on behalf of entry-level engineers. She also has participated in volunteer activities organized by the company to assist local communities. In addition, Pilibosian also served as a Michigan Technological University Board member from 2014 to 2020.

ELIZABETH'S JOURNEY

Elizabeth (Liz) Pilibosian grew up in Michigan, in a family of six children. Her father, an industrial engineer, retired from Chrysler, and her mother was a special-education teacher for elementary, middle, and high school children. Her parents were extremely supportive of their children and nurtured each of them to develop their passions. They served as loving examples that hard work and perseverance pay off as one aspires to reach one's goals.

Liz graduated from Oakland University in Rochester, Michigan, with a bachelor of science in mechanical engineering. During that time, she had a summer internship at Fisher Body as a draftsperson in the seating group, an engineering co-op assignment at Bendix Supercharger, and an "off co-op session" stint as a supercharger dyno technician. These positions helped her gain valuable work experience and pay for school.

Upon graduating from Oakland University, she began her career at Pontiac Motor Division. She was hired into the computer-aided-design group (emerging technology), where she designed Fiero chassis components. Her next assignments walked her through structural engineering, noise and vibration, and vibration testing and validation projects.

In 1984, with the reorganization to "Large/Mid/Small" cars, she was assigned as the lead engineer for the GM10 Platform, where she performed vehicle environmental testing and validation at the Mesa Desert Proving Ground, performed noise and vibration testing, and recommended vehicle improvements. This assignment ultimately gave Liz the opportunity to be the lead engineer of the Chevrolet Lumina vehicle line, where she developed the chassis tuning (tire, shock, stabilizer bar/bushings, spring rates, etc.) for this vehicle offering. After assisting in the successful launch of the Chevrolet Lumina sedan and coupe in Oshawa, Ontario,

Canada, and introduction to the press in Stowe, Vermont, she moved on to position of lead development engineer for the CFIV (Camaro/Firebird, 1990–1993), where she helped with budget, vehicle planning, vehicle builds and development logistics.

After this vehicle launch in Sainte-Therese, Quebec, and introducing the vehicle to the press in Sainte-Sauver, Quebec, she moved to her next assignment to Pontiac Marketing.

While in Pontiac Marketing, she had the assignment as the assistant product manager for the Pontiac Montana minivan. This assignment as the liaison and platform representative between Marketing and Engineering was to ensure that engineering understood and implemented marketing and customer requirements. This was an exciting assignment, which exposed Liz to a different world of marketing. Ultimately, the Pontiac Montana exceeded its projected sales the first year.

After completing the launch of the Pontiac Montana, built in Doraville Assembly Plant in Atlanta and introduced to the press in Kalispell, Montana, she moved back to engineering to become the engineering group manager for the Mid-Size closures team. From 1998 to 2001, she led the team that designed developed and implemented doors, hoods, and liftgates on midsize vehicles. This was another position where components are key to the success of the customer experience. The driver and passenger use this part every time they enter and exit their vehicle, which is key to safety and interior comfort and convenience.

From 2001 to 2005, Pilibosian was given an opportunity to manage the Noise and Vibration team in the Milford Proving Ground as director. Here she was responsible for a team of over two hundred engineers, who worked diligently on vehicles going to market, ensuring they met requirements for interior and exterior noise levels. Squeak and rattle, power train noise and vibration, wind noise, articulation index, seat comfort, tire noise, and exhaust noise all were addressed.

In 2005, Liz took on the role of assistant chief engineer and ultimately vehicle chief engineer for the second-generation Cadillac CTS (sedan, coupe, station wagon, and V Series). Here she honed her global skills, since this vehicle was designed for a global market;

This 1993 Camaro pace car was spotted at the AACA's National event. *Constance Smith*

for right-hand drive and left-hand drive; and for China, Japan, and Europe, as well as North America. As noted earlier, this vehicle received many awards, including 2008 *Motor Trend*'s Car of the year and an IIHS Top Safety Pick. Liz, too, received accolades by being recognized as one of *Motor Trend*'s 2008 Power List of the Top 50 players in the automobile industry. She traveled to China and Europe to promote the family of vehicles.

In 2009, during bankruptcy, Liz took on the assignments of director of electrical validation, and a special assignment to assist with compiling data for the US government during bankruptcy. From 2010 to 2012, she took over the launch of the Cadillac SRX and SAAB 9-4X out of Ramos Arizpe, Mexico, as the vehicle chief engineer.

In the years spanning from 2012 to 2020, she continued as vehicle chief engineer for the Chevrolet Equinox and Captiva, GMC Terrain, and Buick Envision. Her career was planned and executed by her thoughtful mentors, who saw her potential to become a chief engineer. They ensured that Liz had the right background, right experiences, and right interactions to make her successful for her team and ultimately for General Motors.

FAMILY MATTERS

Pilibosian is married; she and Michael have two daughters, one an automotive purchasing manager and one a project engineer. Over a seventeen-year period, she served as a coleader and mentor for the Girl Scouts of the USA. She and Michael enjoy traveling, hiking, and spending time with family and their grandson. Without the support of her husband, parents, and extended family, she would have never been able to travel and perform her responsibilities for each of her assignments.

The 2008 Cadillac CTS captured the *Motor Trend* Car of the Year Award. *General Motors*

DIANA (WERRELL) TREMBLAY

My father worked for GM for twenty years at the Janesville [Wisconsin] and Lordstown [Ohio] assembly plants. I loved the cars he exposed me to, and I loved the stories he would tell about factory life.[1]

—Diana (Werrell) Tremblay (b. August 1959)

Jim Winslet; courtesy of Diana Tremblay

CAREER HIGHLIGHTS

Since 2017, Diana Tremblay has served as CEO of Riverhawk Consulting, LLC. Tremblay is also the independent board director of the Itron Company.

Tremblay retired from General Motors in September 2017, where she held a range of positions in engineering, manufacturing, and labor relations, including direct operational responsibility for over 50,000 employees. From July 2013 until her retirement, Tremblay served as vice president of global business services, where she was charged with streamlining administrative processes around the world to improve service quality, reduce complexity, and achieve cost efficiencies in such areas as finance, human resources, real estate, purchasing, asset management, and master data.[2] Prior to that, she was the VP of North American Manufacturing. From 2009 to 2012, Tremblay held the position of VP of Global Manufacturing. From 2006 to 2009, Tremblay served as vice president of manufacturing and labor relations. She started her career as a co-op student in 1977 and held various manufacturing positions from 1977 to 2006.[3]

From 2016 to 2018, Tremblay has served as a chair of the Board of Trustees at Kettering University. Tremblay also was affiliated with Inforum: A Professional Women's Alliance, Medical Advantage Group, and Focus Hope.

BIOGRAPHICAL NOTES

Diana Dawn Werrell Tremblay, like a number of her esteemed colleagues, followed in her father's footsteps right into automotive manufacturing; she credits her parents for their encouragement: "Every night when I was growing up, we had coffee time. I got to listen to my dad's counsel on how he handled things at work, and my mom's counsel on how he should have handled them. He had expert knowledge, but she had her own thoughts on how to lead people. And they both felt I should go out and do whatever it was I wanted to do."[4]

When it came to applying for college, Diana noted, "My parents had four kids and told us they would pay one year of tuition for each of us, and then we were on our own. So for me, the free education was the main thing. GM paid your tuition, and, if you managed your living costs, you had no debts."[5]

As a co-op student at General Motors Institute (GMI), Werrell Tremblay would be affected positively by changes in the structure of the university made by Dr. William Cottington, the dean who took office in 1975, not long before Werrell matriculated, and finished a major overhaul by 1982. By 1981, eleven departments were whittled down to just three, and the curricula were better defined. In an about-face, the administration had to feature its similarity to other universities and downplay its corporate affiliations in order to make sure the school was accredited by the ECPD (Engineers' Council for Professional Development), allowing students to receive PE (professional engineer) licenses. Cottington also upgraded facilities, including the library.

Diana had to be happy when in her sophomore year the six-week-on and six-week-off schedule for work versus study was revamped to more livable twelve-week sessions. She noted, "With a twelve-week term, you could actually finish classes . . . and work products.[6]

She finished the co-op program in 1982, right before the institute gained its independence from GM and was renamed GMI Engineering and Management Institute (now Kettering

University). Tremblay would later note, "With GM pulling out, the question was how much the school would now cost." The decision to separate the school from GM after fifty-six years was based on business changes, and the school was given title to its facilities. Mary Makela Barra, however, would remain to finish the program and weather this financial change.[7]

Werrell remembers her first automotive position: "I worked as a co-op student in Defiance [Ohio] in our iron-casting operations. I was a fill-in production supervisor."[8]

Werrell was the recipient of a bachelor of science in industrial administration from GMI in 1982. In an interview she described the break that enabled her to complete her master of science in management from MIT's Sloan School of Management: "It came when I was working with skilled trade unions as superintendent of advanced manufacturing engineering in Saginaw [Michigan]. We decided we were going to work as a team, and

we made enough business improvements that I came to the attention of the top management of the division. They selected me to go to MIT on a fellowship."[9]

During her years with GM, Tremblay moved about thirteen times, with the support and help of her husband, Daniel, in raising their daughter, to garner diverse experience. She described an unusual assignment: "One of the assignments I had in Luton [England] was to shut down an assembly plant that had been in operation for almost 100 years. We worked together as a team—union and management—and did the best we could through the run-out of the plant. But it was personally challenging. You hate to do anything like that."

After serving General Motors for forty years, she continues to provide leadership for other companies and, more importantly, remains active on Kettering University's Board of Directors to help navigate the future.

Tremblay is a staunch supporter of Kettering University. *Constance Smith*

ELIZABETH WETZEL

Not many women do what we do—and it's been a dream job for me.

—Liz Wetzel (Designing Women, Edge Magazine, GM Sales and O'Brien's Agency, Inc., March 2005)

As the leader of the creative design team, I contribute my part with passion. I proactively look for inspiration, innovation, and ways to accomplish great design in faster, more efficient ways while maintaining a high standard of [high] quality executions.

Design is more than skin deep. To embrace design is to embrace a creative way of thinking in terms of product innovation, marketing creativity, and even process improvements. I believe that innovations and creativity are invaluable to any company that strives to stay relevant. Tapping into your creative-design department can propel your company forward in product ideas, marketing, and customer interface. These can occur only in an environment where creativity is embraced. My passion as a product designer is to improve the life of the customer by offering high-quality, innovative design solutions that surprise, delight, simplify their lives, and connect them on an emotional level.

—Elizabeth Wetzel (b. 1964)

General Motors

CAREER HIGHLIGHTS

Elizabeth Wetzel, a.k.a. Liz, started her automotive career at GM in 1983 as a summer intern for GM's Truck and Bus Group, where she drew technical illustrations of truck assemblies to earn her way through college. She was focusing on getting an industrial design degree and designing products upon graduation. Her father, then GM head of Pontiac Engineering, arranged to get her into the Design Center for a tour to show her automotive design, since she had never previously stepped foot into an auto design studio. She started in the Pontiac Exterior Design Studio and met John Schinella, the chief designer, and then met Bill Scott, chief of the Pontiac Interior Studio. This was a pivotal moment, and Wetzel recalls being totally captivated by the full-size renderings of future products on the walls and the corresponding full-size clay models on the floor. Even the smell of the clay was enticing and added to the creative art studio ambiance. It was at that point she realized her dream was to get into the automotive design business.

In 1986 she graduated from the University of Michigan School of Art and Design with a BFA in industrial design and was hired by GM's Advanced Engineering Group. Her first job was as an associate engineer on an off-site "skunkworks" project called Chev 200, where she was responsible for designing innovative and cost-effective interior design solutions. It was there she worked with and caught the attention of Ed Donaldson, an interior design manager from GM's Design staff, who recommended to Chuck Jordan, Dave Holls, and Jerry Palmer that she transfer to Design.

In 1988, Wetzel transferred to GM Design and worked on several interior and exterior designs as she rotated through the design studios. During those rotations she worked on the interior of the Cadillac Aurora and Olds Silhouette concepts before settling into her first permanent assignment in the Cadillac Interior Studio in 1990. It was here that her craft developed and her drive and enthusiasm got her noticed. She became assistant chief designer for Cadillac Interiors in 1993, and both her interior designs for the 1996 and 1997 Cadillac Seville received Luxury Interior Design of the Year Awards from *Inside Automotive Magazine*. Her assignments also included the 1996 STS and Eldorado and the 2000 DeVille DTS.

The year 1997 marked a milestone for Wetzel and for GM Design as she became the first woman in GM's history to become a vehicle chief designer—responsible both for the interior and exterior of the 2002 Buick Rendezvous Crossover. Upon introduction to the public, it was named "Truck of the Year" by the *Detroit Free Press*.

In 2001, GM Design recognized a need to create an Interior Design Organization with executive support and a focus on creating experts in that area of design. It was then that Wetzel was given the position of director of all car interior design (her counterpart, Dave Lyon, had all truck interiors). In this assignment she led the teams that created the award-winning Pontiac Solstice

The CXL and Ultra offered upgraded interiors. The Ultra was equipped with the 3.6 V6 rated at 345 hp like some Cadillacs. *General Motors*

General Motors

roadster, the sister Saturn Sky, the Saturn Aura (NAIAS Car of the Year), and the Chevrolet HHR interiors, to name a few.

In 2004, Wetzel served as exterior design director for International Joint Venture Programs, exploring the initial phases of design for the Camaro and GTO as well as the Pontiac Torrent and Pontiac Vibe production vehicle.

From 2005 to 2009, Wetzel was director of the Global Brand Studio, her first global assignment. She was recruited by Ed Welburn, vice president of GM Global Design, to create a studio to guide the brand design differentiation for all of GM's global brands. Wetzel and her team developed brand assets to guide the design studios as well as marketing and advertising, to further separate the brand's designs, essence, and reason for being.

Another landmark was reached in 2010, when she was appointed director of interior design for GM Europe for a three-year period. She was and still is the first woman to achieve this level in GM Europe Design. In this role she led the interior design of all Opel and Vauxhall products as well as the Chevrolet Cruze. This included the 2012 Cascada, the 2012 Adam, the 2012 Corsa, and the 2012 Astra.

From 2013 to 2016, Wetzel served as director of Buick Interior Design, NA, managing the interior design of the 2015 Buick Avenir concept and the 2016 Buick Avista show car.

Since 2016, she has served as director of user experience component design, GM Global Design.

Wetzel has received numerous awards. Following in the footsteps of her father, Jay, in 2018, she received an award for Young Leadership and Excellence from the Auto Hall of Fame, was featured in the "100 Leading Women in the NA Auto Industry" in *Automotive News* twice, and was featured in the Women's Museum in Dallas, Texas.

WETZEL'S JOURNEY

Elizabeth Wetzel's great-grandfather, Johan Wetzel, was an Austrian immigrant who came to America to start a new life at age eighteen with his seventeen-year-old pregnant wife, Anna. He became a tool- and diemaker for the Hudson Corporation.

Elizabeth's grandfather, John J. Wetzel, graduated from Cass Tech in 1931 and the University of Detroit in 1936, with a BSEE. In 1933, he joined Dodge as a co-op student, holding various

positions, including division manager of quality control. He led the engineering team that invented the gearing system for WWII radar devices and was promoted to the position of director of the Corporate Office of Quality Control of Chrysler. After retiring, he also assisted Almor Corp. as administrative VP and GM. John was also noted for his work with the US Power Squadron. He had two children, one of whom was John "Jay" Wetzel, Elizabeth's father.

Jay Wetzel, also an engineer, served as vice president and general manager for GM Technical Centers. It is significant that Jay also served as a cofounder of Saturn Corporation. Saturn was established as an experimental project begun in 1982, and an operating Saturn prototype was unveiled to the press on January 8, 1985, at the GM Technical Center in Warren, Michigan. GM, which planned to introduce both coupes and sedans, also announced the creation of Saturn as a separate subsidiary at this time.

Born to John Jay and Martha (Foote) Wetzel, Elizabeth Wetzel attended elementary school in Waterford Township, Michigan, and junior and high school in Birmingham, Michigan. Her early interests included sports, drama, and—not a surprise—art.

At a young age, Wetzel's parents realized her talent for art and enrolled her in classes at the Pontiac Creative Art Center. By junior high, she was further encouraged by her art teacher; Ms. Sanko helped her develop skills in many artistic mediums and encouraged her to further her education. The summer of her junior year in high school, Wetzel worked several jobs to save up enough money to attend the Art Foundation Program at Parsons School of Design in New York City. That experience exposed her to various art degrees and careers and gave her a clear vision of what to do with her talent. She was fascinated with product design for its combination of creativity and invention.

For her college path, she chose to attend the program at the University of Michigan School of Art and Design, with a focus on industrial design. She also studied engineering and marketing.

Wetzel notes, "In my senior year, my professor for industrial design, Allen Samuels, collaborated with the College of Business and the College of Engineering to create a class that enabled students of design, marketing, and engineering to be on a team and create a product. Together we identified a customer need, created a design solution, engineered the design, and created a marketing campaign. It was highly collaborative and reflected the way we would be working in the real world, working cross-functionally as a team to create, build, and sell consumer products."

When asked whom she admires, she notes, "I have always loved the designers associated with the midcentury modern, Bauhaus design era." Of course, Bertoia was affiliated with the Cranbrook Academy and the Saarinens, who were responsible for the GM Technical Center, and the Cranbrook properties were well known in Michigan. Wetzel notes:

Designers like Harry Bertoia, Mies Van Der Rohe, Eero Saarinen. Their designs are bold, yet beautifully simple, clean, modern, and timeless. Their designs can be described with three to four gestural lines. The Saarinen tulip table is one of my favorite product designs—serving a purpose and bringing beauty and emotional pleasure to such a simple, functional product. Of the more recent designers, Zaha Hadid was an inspiration to me, and I was very saddened by her recent death in 2016. Her daring and bold designs are iconic and dynamic.

Of the automobiles designer who inspired me, the Bill Mitchell designs of the '60s were to me the most beautiful pieces of art on wheels. What made them more attractive was that these cars were accessible to many people—unlike the exotic and exclusive designs coming out of Europe. The 1963 Corvette Stingray with the split window still looks amazing over fifty years later. Its deeply sculpted surfaces are dramatic, and its proportions are well balanced. It's truly sculpture on wheels.

While attending the University of Michigan, Wetzel was the president of her local Industrial Designers Society of America for the UMich student chapter. She arranged a field trip to New York City for the members—her ID classmates. They visited several industrial design firms, one of which was Walter Dorwin Teague Associates. Teague is credited with the Marmon and Kodak products early on, and his consultancy also executed Boeing aircraft interiors, Pringles packaging, and numerous other products.

Wetzel's industrial design professors, Allen Samuels and Alfredo Montalvo, were highly influential and taught her the skills required to become an industrial designer.

It was there she learned that design is not just an art; it is a medium to problem-solve and offer beautiful yet functional solutions to improve and enhance people's lives.

While attending the University of Michigan program, she worked during the summers with GM's Truck and Bus group, doing technical illustrations for vehicle assembly.

OLDS DESIGN AND THE CADILLAC AURORA AND SILHOUETTE CONCEPTS

Both these concepts were done during Wetzel's first-year studio rotations. She was working in the Advanced Design Studios under Jerry Palmer during that time. Chuck Jordan was the VP

The straight lines on the exterior visually gave the car length and importance. *General Motors*

of Design and would come into the studio and give the young designers great design insights. Jerry Palmer was the director of advanced design, working for Chuck. Jerry was an inspiring leader, full of personality, who gave us young designers with little experience big projects. He trusted us, was always positive, and encouraged young designers. Being around Jerry Palmer was always fun. Of course, he had high expectations, but his approach was positive and encouraging vs. critical and judgmental. Wetzel's confidence grew substantially under Jerry's leadership.

Wetzel was the only interior designer on the Cadillac Aurora concept. Wetzel notes, "We designed it in record time at an off-site job shop. The exterior design was done by Carlo Barba—a recently retired executive director of GM do Brazil Design Studio. At the time, he was on an international assignment from the Opel design studio in GM Europe. At the job shop was an engineer by the name of Jim Phillips. He was great to work with, and I found his enthusiasm and ingenuity invaluable on that project. Soon after, we hired him into GM directly, and we spent several years together working on Cadillac interiors. His 'Let's do this' spirit was key to many of my own accomplishments. While in the Cadillac Studio he gave me the nickname 'Air Wetzel' (based on the tag of the popular Air Jordan sneakers first released by Nike in 1985) because of how hard I was working, running around all over the Design Staff building."

The Olds Silhouette was a sports sedan concept. Its name was later attached to a minivan. Jerry Durkin and Karim Giordimaina, a summer intern, were also designers on the team.

Another notable person in Cadillac was John Schinella, who was the design director for all Cadillac design. John's enthusiasm was contagious, and he was someone who propelled Wetzel to take on more and more.

When it came to the Cadillac Aurora, John Zelenak was the designer for its interior. He is currently a design manager in the Buick Interior Studio.

BUICK: THE 2002 RENDEZVOUS

In 1999, preparations began for the midsized crossover later named "Rendezvous." Wetzel is credited with the design of this

Opel Adam. *Opel Autombile, GMBH*　　*Opel Autombile, GMBH*

crossover—both inside and out. There is no question that this was her most notable achievement to date, and that she could handle anything that came her way. The Rendezvous, introduced in late 2001, was a game changer for Buick. It established the fact that Buick could build a trendy ride; it led to the later introduction of the costlier Rainier and Terraza SUVs and first- and second-generation Enclaves. While Buick strived to attract a younger customer for years, the Rendezvous did just that. Sales were nearly double what was predicted; by 2003, over 72,000 units were burning gas. The Rendezvous was built in the Mexican factory with the Pontiac Aztek but attracted a different consumer. While the Aztek was described as a failure and ugly by critics, the Buick made up for its declining sales.

The "Value Priced" model was affordable to young families, and the luxury model attracted the more established. A customer could buy a base CX for just $15,200, and this was amazing. When it came to bang for the buck, it left the Lexus and Acura equivalents behind and later tackled the Toyota Highlander Ltd. and Honda Pilot EX. Buick's addition of a CX Plus and CXL Plus was captured a wide audience. By 2004, the chic Ultra model provided a DIC, 17-inch aluminum wheels, ultra-suede seating, and a theft deterrent system. By 2006, vehicles were powered by a 3.5-liter V-6 or 3.6-liter DOHC VVT engine generating 242 hp at 6,000 rpm and 232 lb.-ft. of torque @3,500 rpm. Also notable, it introduced OnStar, QuietTuning, Theft Deterrent, and Rear Park Assist—all standard. While 17-inch steel wheels were the standard, when the Ultra was dropped and a monochromatic exterior became the norm, the two-tone was optional, as was a choice of aluminum wheels associated with packages and models.

Perhaps the first to offer a third seat that provided seating for seven—captain's chairs were later available in the second row—Buick foretold the future. With removable seats and a flip-down third seat, one could stow a 4-by-8-foot sheet of building material inside. Of course, the women in the family were perhaps even more appreciative of the up to 108.9 cubic feet of cargo space, oversized mirrors (which captured more of the road), traction control, and the quartet of air bags.

When it comes to luxury, the shiny simulated-wood instrument panel and comfy leather-suede seating of the Ultra were more reminiscent of a Park Avenue—also offered as an Ultra. Today, perhaps we call this kind of upgrade "Avenir," and a new line is also called Avenir.

WETZEL HEADS PONTIAC

There is no question that the Pontiac G6 was a game changer for the division. The model gained publicity when 276 cars were given away to preselected audience members at the televised *Oprah Winfrey Show.* Unfortunately, some of the recipients had difficulty paying the taxes associated with the gift, valued at $28,500.

Inside and out, the G6 was a head turner. The cockpit featured

a racing-inspired instrument cluster with analog gauges with chrome surrounds. Red numerals jumped out. The automatic climate control and a driver information system matched in color and style.

The exterior was easily identified by its cat's-eye lamps and dual opening grille. The low profile, the heavily raked A pillar, and the rising beltline made the sedan read from afar as a two-door coupe. The rear track was wider than the front one, and the rims came in 16, 17, and 18 inches and were described as aluminum and not alloy.

In August 2004, Pontiac began producing the 2005 G6 Sedan and GT Sedan. In the summer of 2004, Kyle Given described the all-new G6 sedan in *Pontiac Performance*—a publication provided through dealers. In April 2005, production began on the GTP, equipped with a 3.9 HO V-6. The 2005 sedan would later deliver the right stuff and contribute to Pontiac's survival as Australian-manufactured Pontiacs such as the GTO, without the preferred sunroof, later slowly trickled into the US, and GM fought off impending bankruptcy.

Wetzel's role in the G6 was as the director of car interiors. In describing the team, she notes that Anne Asensio was the executive director of all interiors, and her boss. Wetzel's counterpart was Dave Lyon, who was the interior director of all truck interiors. Crystal Windham was working for her as the design manager. Jennifer Kraska was the lead designer for the interior. It was her theme that was used in the G6 show car interior that was then transformed into the production design. Jeff Perkins was the chief designer of the exterior and reported up the Exterior Design organization—he did not work for Wetzel.

The design had to appeal both to men and women. In addressing women, the interiors provided creative comforts, which included power-adjustable front foot pedals.

One would think that replacing the hot-selling Grand Am was an impossible feat. In a roundabout way, you could say that the G6 was GM's version of a European car built to compete against Europe's best. While there were five renditions of the Grand Am, Pontiac changed the name of its sixth derivative to G6. The G6 relied on Epsilon Global Architecture and was close in kin to the new Saab 9-3 and Opel Vectra. Perhaps it is notable that Fiat's Croma, a large wagon designed by Giugaro himself, was built on the same ubiquitous Epsilon platform. The Malibu, Aura, and Cadillac BLS are also described as family. With a 3.5-liter V-6 rated at 200 hp and lb.-ft. of torque, one model sought to leave the Audi A4 and BMW 3 in its rearview mirror. A 3.9-liter V-6 would gun for the Accord, Camry, and Mazda 6. The seamless automatic shifts added European flavor. The design blended build quality, responsiveness, durability, and performance in higher models.

The straightforward shape was described as taut, tense, and buff. Outside, chrome accents surrounded the black-mesh, twin-port, honeycomb grille long owned by the Pontiac Division; BMW has its own. The spokes of GT's 17-inch wheels gently blend into the rim.

Base models featured cloth, but the leather GT seats became

the responsibility of Faurecia, the company that has provided seating for BMW, VW, Audi, and MB. Be reminded that there are hundreds of parts in a seat set. The leather option featured the rather universal French stitching, which seems to have been a mainstay in this era and still is.

The remarkable four-panel UV glass panoramic roof—the first one sold in America—was created and installed by Webasto, a German company. This ingenious design was equipped with a water management system to divert the rain. With the turn of the overhead control, the front panel tilted up to block the wind, and each of the four panels slid back in order. The sunshade worked in unison if desired. When it came down to it, customers likely went on to report more issues with the retractable roof in the G6 coupe than with this four-panel extravaganza.

ASSIGNMENT: GM EUROPE

At GM Europe (Opel), Wetzel was the interior design director responsible for all interior design, design quality, component design, and color and trim between 2010 and 2013.

Mark Adams was, and is, the vice president of Design at Opel/Vauxhall. Mark is a huge force on the GM Europe leadership team. He has helped that brand transform its image through the product and also through the brand vision. When Wetzel arrived, the Insignia had been on the road for one year. Wetzel notes that that was the first "beautiful" car out of Opel in a long time. "Sculptural Artistry with German Precision was our design philosophy, started by Brian Nesbitt during his ISP to GME, and carried on and reinforced by Mark," recalls Wetzel. "I found the team at Opel to be passionate about the brand. The great thing about GME is that they all are focusing on one brand. And many of the people there are second- or third-generation employees, so they have Opel in their blood. That makes for a dedicated and loyal team."

Opel was the largest and most expansive assignment Wetzel has had in her GM career. She was responsible for a large team (about ninety people). The departments that she led were Interior Design, Color and Trim, Component Design, and Design Quality.

Malcolm Ward was Wetzel's counterpart on the production exterior design, and Friedhelm Engler was her other counterpart as director of Advanced Design. The three of them made a good team, and they each had each other's back. This was important, because while there, GM Europe was going through a financial crisis. GME was losing millions. Wetzel witnessed the entire senior leadership team turn over, with the exception of Mark Adams. It was an exciting yet turbulent time. Wetzel formed some amazing relationships with the talented and dedicated team of designers, engineers, and marketing people at Opel.

Wetzel remembers, "The best part was the opportunity to lead the design of some great products, as noted. My favorite was the Adam. That project was a designer's dream and actually

sprouted its existence out of a concept we created in the Global Brand Studio—to develop a small mini car to appeal to the millennial generation. We had research that revealed the desire for millennials to be connected and the desire to 'customize' their cars, just as they could customize their smartphones. Our color and trim department was enabled to create combinations of options that enabled our target customer to customize their vehicle with a count of up to 300,000 combinations with exterior paint, wheels, sunroof, headliner, interior color and trim, and seats."

Wetzel led the teams designing the interior of Opel Vauxhall products: 2012 Cascada, 2012 Adam (Red Dot Award, WardsAuto European Interior of the Year Award), 2012 Corsa, 2013 Astra (European Car of the Year), and 2014 Chevy Cruze (the interior was done in my studio in Europe; the exterior was done in North America).

2014 CHEVROLET CRUZE

In 2014, the Chevrolet Pressroom described the Cruise as the bestselling passenger car worldwide.

Most models were powered by Ecotec engines. Standard on LS models was the 138-horsepower (103 kW) Ecotec 1.8-liter, four-cylinder with continuously variable valve timing; EPA-estimated fuel economy was 25 mpg in the city and 36 mpg on the highway with the manual transmission, and 22 mpg city and 35 mpg highway with the automatic. Standard on LT, LTZ, and Eco models is an Ecotec 1.4-liter turbo. Its exhaust-driven turbocharger helps the engine perform like a larger engine when needed, but retains the efficiency of a small-displacement four-cylinder in most driving conditions.

For the 2014 model year, Chevrolet also offered Cruze's all-new, 2.0-liter, clean turbo-diesel-powered model, which achieved an EPA-estimated 46 mpg highway—better than any nonhybrid or gasoline passenger car in America. The Cruze diesel could travel 717 miles on a single tank, or about ten hours of highway driving.

Inside, the twin-cockpit motif was matched with high-quality interior materials and exceptional assembly tolerances. Grained, soft-touch components and low-gloss trim panels convey a level of quality uncommon in the segment. The instrument panel featured richly detailed instruments backlit with light-emitting diode (LED) technology. The integrated center stack houses the infotainment display, climate controls, and radio controls and blends harmoniously with the instrument panel.

The interior pillar and other moldings are color and grain-matched to the headliner, while the seat inserts are color-matched to the instrument panel accent trim, giving the cabin the detailed appearance of a larger, more upscale sedan.

BUICK CASCADA

The dynamic, stylish 2016 Buick Cascada convertible was the

The Cascada convertible was the first for Buick in years. *General Motors*

first Buick convertible in twenty-five years and was welcomed in 2015. On January 11, 2015, GM's Corporate Newsroom posted these details.

Duncan Aldred, vice president of Buick, noted, "It's a car that will delight customers with its fun spirit and help drive the momentum that's fueling Buick's success. Powered by a 200-horsepower turbocharged engine, the Cascada's 2+2 configuration offers room for four adults."

AVENIR DEBUTS

Debuting at the 2015 Detroit Show, the Buick Avenir combines the successes of the past with the vision of the future. Inside and out, the Buick Avenir launches the next-generation Buick styling and Buick packages named "Avenir," introduced on select models in 2016. The sweep spear, which is becoming more ubiquitous, and profile bring to mind the styling of the 1971–1973 Buick Riviera. The front grille is reminiscent of the 1954 Buick Wildcat. The exterior was penned by lead designer Warrack Leach.

The Avenir concept won awards for interior and exterior design. *General Motors*

The interior, designed under the direction of Wetzel, relies on cues from nature—water washing ashore and floating elements. GM Media highlights observations by Rebecca Waldmeir and Liz Wetzel on its site. Sharon Gauci, Jenny Morgan, and Rebecca Waldmeir accepted an award for its interior design.

"With Avenir's interior, we really wanted to select materials that would complement the surfaces within," noted Rebecca Waldmeir, Buick Color and Trim design manager. "Using a distinctive combination of premium leather, suede, wood, chrome, and acrylic, we were able to design elements that flow seamlessly throughout the interior." In describing the door panels, she says, "We've used open-pore wood in a modern way, much like what you'll find in high-end furniture. It's an oiled, low-gloss execution that contrasts beautifully with other interior decor."

Kari Nattrass of GM Media notes, "Avenir's sculptural instrument panel incorporates an acrylate panel, carved to replicate three-dimensional wavelike patterns but layered beneath a smooth, high-gloss outer layer."

Wetzel notes, "There's an almost three-dimensional or bas relief effect to the design motif that adds depth and heightens the sense of place. Layered and floating elements such as the center console enhance the perception of lightness, efficiency, and dynamism."

Waldmeir adds, "As you look at the transparent surface from different angles, you will notice that it has a lot of visual depth and movement. It's a motif we carried to other areas of Avenir, including the seat design, and to the head- and taillamps."

While Avenir's exterior color is a cooler tone, designers wanted to provide a warm, inviting sensation within. The lighter "Lyric" hue, found on most interior surfaces, helps achieve that feeling, while restrained use of a darker tone—"Coastal Myst"—on the instrument panel and armrests provides a natural transition to the exterior. To further create a tailored feel, most surfaces within the Avenir are wrapped in leather or suede and accentuated with stitching.

All in all, Avenir's interior materials were designed to work in harmony and provide an upscale environment that feels natural and holistic to all passengers.

"The first thing you'll notice when you open Avenir's doors is just how clean and pure its interior design is," said Liz Wetzel, Buick interior design director. "We've stripped it of superfluous, fussy details in order to rely on sculptural forms and harmonious surfaces. The result is a refreshing environment that provides a sense of well-being to anyone seated within."

The 2015 Buick Avenir concept interior won an EyesOn Design award for Innovative Use of Color, Graphics, or Materials at the 2015 North American International Auto Show (NAIAS). Composed of prominent members of the automotive design community, the EyesOn Design jury also praised Avenir's overall design with a Best Concept Vehicle trophy. "Avenir's global design team set out to make a striking design statement," said Holt Ware, Buick exterior design director. "The Avenir embraces Buick's rich design heritage of creating exquisite sculptures, precise in their design and beautifully proportioned."

The Buick Avista received the EyesOn Design Award. *General Motors*

AVISTA

Dan Amman, GM's president, unveiled the Avista at the 2016 NAIAS. The Avista is built atop the Alpha platform shared by the Cadillac ATS and CTS. The low-slung GT 2+2 in dark sapphire with a light-mist-gray interior delivers a very respectable 400 hp with its twin-turbo 3.0-liter V-6 and eight-speed transmission. In describing the Avista concept, Wetzel notes:

The objective of the Avista design was to create an interior experience that reflected the vision of where we wanted to take the Buick design aesthetic in the future. This was accomplished by keeping the graceful, flowing, sculptural design aesthetic of Buick, yet adding a clean, visually light, modern twist.

Simple flowing surfaces are contrasted by clean yet bold technology that seamlessly integrates into the forms. It was also an exercise to capture the attention of the millennial generation and appeal to their needs. Staying connected is important to these customers. To enable this while avoiding distractions, we added voice activation and the Augmented Reality Head Up Display to enable many tasks to be accomplished effortlessly. The Avista has set the vision for Buick's future design direction."

GM Media notes that the exposed carbon-fiber and aluminum inserts throughout reinforce the precision of the performance-oriented driving experience. The fading pattern of the seats, console, and door was inspired by waves receding at a beach's edge.

The Buick Avista received the EyesOn Design Award for Design Excellence—concept car and interior design—at NAIAS.

ENCLAVE AND ENCLAVE AVENIR

Having been given the responsibility to design Buick's first crossover, it is fitting that Wetzel leads the interior design team for the second-generation Enclave. The general description of the latest Enclave appears no different than the one used for the Rendezvous: new, versatile functionality; more spacious than the Acura MDX; more third-row space; improved towing; a combination of safety technologies; premium materials.

Like the Rendezvous of the past, the current Enclave is turning heads. Duncan Aldred, VP of Global Buick and GMC, notes, "Enclave was introduced as a game changer for the Buick brand and has since become one of our most successful and important vehicles. It set the tone for a more progressive Buick, helping change perception for us and serving as the standard-bearer of what our products stand for: smart, stylish luxury."

The interior, particularly the interior of the Avenir, sets it way apart from first-generation Enclaves.

There is no question that the newest Avenir offering has an amazing list of features inside that exude luxury and connectivity, including seventeen radar, camera, and ultrasonic sensors; heated and ventilated seats; heated second-row seats; a dual moon roof; the most cargo room ever; a rear camera mirror; embroidered headrests; chestnut-ebony interior with piping; a wood-accented steering wheel; Evonik Acrylite lighting technology; a hands-free programmable liftgate; and so on.

The exterior is both muscular and luxurious.

THE NEXT CHAPTER

Wetzel continues to volunteer as a judge for the EyesOn Design Automobile Show, held at the Ford Estate annually to raise money for charity.

On another note, those reaching fifty-five and older at GM were invited to participate in an early-retirement program, since changes that were being made to the existing one were not encouraging for the staff. Shortly leaving GM and settling down, Wetzel accepted a position offered by Lawrence Technological University. She currently serves as codirector of the Department of Architecture and Design.

FAMILY MATTERS

Aside from her numerous contributions to the automotive industry, Elizabeth has managed to raise a family. She is married to GM software engineer / controls strategist Brad and has two sons, Blake and Bryce. Brad held other similar corporate positions before joining GM.

PART VIII.
THE 1990s: TALENT AND TECH

General Motors' goal was to bring the company back to profitability after losing market share and money during the last decade due to a variety of issues. It made matters worse when Iraq invaded Kuwait, setting off the first Gulf War, driving oil prices sky-high and sending the economy into recession. Replacing Roger Smith, Robert Stempel, an accomplished engineer, took the helm as CEO and chairman. Lloyd Reuss replaced Stempel as president. However, an engineer was not needed at this time, and other changes in management would have to be implemented throughout the decade to restore profitability. Then there were new divisions, new alliances, new technologies, new cars, and upgraded cars introduced faster than before. In addition to traditional new models, Saturn, Geo, and Shanghai Auto Industry Corporation (SAIC) explored new territory.

Although the project was initiated by Roger Smith, the EV1 was the first mass-produced electric car manufactured in the modern era and was leased to consumers from 1996 to 1999.

In a brilliantly thought-out plan, GM sought to keep its customers from purchasing competitive vehicles and Japanese imports and met with success. The Geo arrived in most Chevrolet dealerships in 1991; cars came from around the world. The purpose of this approach was to bring cars and a small SUV into dealers to compete with the imports and vehicles that were particularly attractive to first-time buyers, import intenders, and retirees. In 1991, Geo had the most fuel-efficient line of cars and trucks in America. They were designed to run cleanly thanks to the use of advanced emission-control technology, including the

GM-developed catalytic converter. The Geo Metro was the cleanest of all vehicles that were tested for pollutants via their tailpipes in 1991.

The four vehicles in the GEO line were manufactured by affiliates partly owned by GM.

The Geo Tracker and the subcompact Metro, except for the Metro convertible, were designed by Suzuki and built in Canada by CAMI Automotive, which GM owned jointly with Suzuki. The convertible was built by Suzuki Motor Corporation in Japan. The Tracker, a mini SUV, was the only Geo to use body-on-frame construction; the others were unibodies. It featured a 1.6-liter L4 with fuel injection and was rated at 80 mph.

The two-door Geo Storm was built by Isuzu Motors in Japan; Isuzu was owned in part by GM. Debuting in 1990, it was the successor to the Spectrum. It was very popular with first-time buyers; however, young drivers sometimes needed a parent to step in to procure affordably priced insurance. In 1992, the 1.6 OHC engine was replaced with a 1.8-liter. By 1996, the Storm coupe had run its course.

The Geo Prizm, a four-door sedan aimed at families, was built in the NUMMI plant in Fremont, California, and was part of the joint venture between GM and Toyota Motor Corporation. It featured a 1.6-liter DOC and four valves per cylinder. In 1992, it was offered in a base, LSi sedan and GSi sedan.

When it came to power trains, in 1997 the third-generation 4T65E, an electronic, four-speed, automatic transaxle, was introduced.

PRODUCTION

In 1992, Buick introduced a new Skylark. The rectangular lights went missing for thinner ones aligning with the new grille. With a lower hood and thinner grille area, it registered more as a sports car than a family car. Inside, the instrument panel flowed seamlessly into the side doors. In 1992, Buick redesigned the LeSabre. A new, longer model was introduced with a reliable 3.8-liter V-6 and an electronically controlled four-speed automatic transmission. A Roadmaster sedan joined the Estate station wagon, introduced in 1991. In 1993, Buick celebrated its ninetieth anniversary with a special LeSabre Custom model. A redesigned Riviera, the sister car to the Olds Aurora, arrived in 1995. When it came to concept cars, a Bolero arrived in 1990, a Sceptre in 1992, the XP2000 in 1995, and the Cielo in 1999.

In 1992, Cadillac celebrated its ninetieth anniversary. The Eldorado coupe and the Seville sedan were redesigned. The new Allante convertible was introduced as a 1993 model with an optional aluminum hardtop but was soon discontinued due to poorer-than-expected sales. In 1993, Cadillac introduced the Northstar system, which included the thirty-two-valve V-8, road-sensing suspension, and speed-sensitive steering in the Allante, Seville STS, and Eldorado Touring and Sport Coupes. The DeVille, Fleetwood (which was redesigned), and Sixty Special rounded out the model line.

In addition to the Geo, Chevrolet continued to offer a dizzying array of models that started to overlap: Caprices, Cavaliers, Corsicas, Berettas, Luminas, Camaros, and Corvettes. In 1991, the Caprice was redesigned, and a custom SEMA car version was produced to generate interest. In 1992, Camaro was twenty-five years old. In 1994, the Impala SS—a sporty version of the Caprice—was resurrected.

A new base 5.7-liter V-8 (LT1) and traction control appeared on the base 1992 Corvette, and later the ZR1 returned with its Lotus-developed, 375 hp, twin-cam, turbocharged, 5.7-liter V-8 and ASR traction control from Bosch. In terms of SUVs and trucks, in 1990 the factory delivered sport trucks: the SS454 was equipped with a big block and high torque. The lineup included three new models: a 1996 Tahoe and two vans.

Chevrolet's 1992 trucks were identified as best buys in *Consumers Digest*'s annual buying guide. The highlight of the decade for some was probably the Camaro's twenty-fifth-anniversary Heritage Edition package.

Chevrolet has never lacked concept cars; the 1992 Sting Ray III coupe featured unusual angled headlamps. The same year, a Chevrolet Lumina APV Sizigi appeared. In 1994, the Camaro convertible returned.

In 1993, GMC offered a line similar to that of Chevy and celebrated their ninetieth anniversary by including an illustration of a 1903 model in its product folders.

When it came to Oldsmobile, whose future would be affected by sales and new products from other divisions, they introduced the FWD compact Achieva, with a recognizable signature waterfall grille and rocket emblem. While the 88 was redesigned, the high-end Toronado Trofeo came with leather seating, power-adjustable lumbar supports, and steering-wheel radio controls. Olds also offered the Aurora, a sleek model from the future with a steeply raked windshield. While Bill Porter worked on the design of the exterior, the interior was equipped with a navigation system with satellite positioning to calculate distance, and a synthetic voice to direct the driver.

In 1992, Pontiac unveiled a new Grand Am and Bonneville; the Grand Am was recognized as a Best Buy by *Consumers Digest*; 1992 also marked the thirty-fifth year for the Bonneville, which was redesigned; the original in 1957 was a limited-production convertible with a Tri-Power fuel injection option. The 1992 also had front fenders with dent and corrosion resistance. This year, Pontiac offered the Richard Petty–edition Grand Prix to honor the NASCAR driver; 1,000 were produced. Pontiac's other five lines continued with little change. However, the Salsa concept was a subcompact convertible with a removable rear section and a lower tailgate that opened like a drawer; this converted it to a mini pickup. Many of the manufacturers of the 1920s and 1930s had likewise offered business coupes with a slip-in truck bed once the trunk lid was removed.

Project Saturn was conceived by Roger Smith in 1982 to combat the onslaught of small Japanese products. John (a.k.a. J.) Wetzel is recognized as a founder of Saturn and served as chief engineer. The first prototype arrived in 1983. By 1985, Saturn was a subsidiary with its own plant. Cars were manufactured, consisting of steel and plastic parts on a space frame. Customers were lured by the fact that plastic did not rust or dent, there was a no-haggle price, and they were invited to do business near their homes, eliminating the need for shady dealer practices. While the first car was driven off the line in 1990, production started for the 1991 model year. Saturn had its own full line of sedans, coupes, and station wagons. While the S models arrived first, at the end of the decade, in 1999 the model LS, a larger Saturn, would arrive. It would take several more years for Saturn to feature a hybrid in its Vue, an SUV. Although initially destined to be part of Chevrolet, Saturn succeeded in recruiting its own dealers to open stores, and its reliability ranked with the top Japanese luxury brands.

In the 1990s, GM had other global divisions and affiliates, which included Holden, Opel, Vauxhall, GM Canada, Daewoo, Wuling, Baojun, Isuzu, Suzuki, Lotus, and so on. They formed partnerships to manufacture vehicles and expand their horizons.

RENEE BRYANT

I love giving back, and General Motors allows me to do this on the clock through various engineering and outreach programs in communities, schools, universities, and charitable organizations. One of the greatest senses of accomplishment for me has been when my daughter Simone told me that she wanted to go give something back and thus help someone else.

—Renee Bryant (b. 1964)

Constance Smith

CAREER HIGHLIGHTS

Despite the odds, Renee Bryant has served diverse entities in the corporation and the larger community. An exceptional engineer, she continues to share her subject knowledge with others and to serve as a role model for men and women in the automotive industry.

Over a thirty-year period, Bryant has served in several engineering positions at General Motors. She has contributed to design, production, and marketing for concept vehicles across production car and truck lines.

In 1990, Bryant validated and tested door components for the Chevrolet Cavalier and Pontiac Sunbird. She developed manufacturing technical specs for GM's small-car platforms in 1995. In 1998, she designed and released interior door trim and garnish for the Saturn LS and Oldsmobile Cutlass products. She led Passenger Compartment Integration teams for the Pontiac Grand Prix in 2001 and was the sole voice for Concept Vehicle Engineering in 2003 for the Buick Velite convertible, Saturn Sky Roadster, and Cadillac STS SAE 100 (a nod to the one hundredth anniversary of the Society of Automotive Engineers) concept vehicles. In 2005, Bryant switched over to managing engineering teams in the Specialty Vehicle Activities for Platinum Editions, Supers, and Professional Vehicles. In 2008, she started working with Upfitters (or vehicle converters in the field) as an engineering group manager for Upfitter Integration. While there, she was promoted to a senior engineering group manager and then transferred over to her current position as senior engineering group manager for the GM Accessories Vehicle System Engineers Team in 2018.

Renee is a devoted and proud mother, who in her spare time enjoys spending time with her daughter Simone and embracing life every day. Tomorrow is not promised to any of us, as she sadly learned with the untimely passing of her older daughter, Noelle, due to cancer at the age of six in 2001.

BRYANT'S JOURNEY

Born and raised in Detroit, Michigan, Renee is the seventh of twelve children born to James Robert and Rosia Mae Greer. Her father was an electrical technician with the US Post Service, and her mother was a drapery and bedding sales manager at Northland Center.

They had moved to Michigan from Memphis, Tennessee, and Sardis, Mississippi, with hopes of better job opportunities. With her dad controlling the remote for the big TV in the house, Renee and her siblings grew up watching and learning about every sport that existed. On one rare occasion, a very young Renee became interested in cars by "accident" while flipping through stations and stumbling upon *MotorWeek*, hosted by John Davis on PBS. She was intrigued by his enthusiasm for the products, how fast the cars were traveling on the tracks, and how great they looked. As she grew, she wanted to help people who had been injured in accidents (mainly from people driving too fast), and thus, she planned on becoming a biomedical engineer and developing artificial limbs.

Bryant studied at Renaissance High School, a top school in Detroit, Michigan, with a notable college prep program. Its motto is "A School for the Mind, a Mind for the Future."

The two-door Beretta shared its chassis with the four-door Corsica. *Chevrolet Public Relations; collection of the author*

Velite concept car. *General Motors*

She joined the Detroit Area Pre-College Engineering Program (DAPCEP) to explore her interest in engineering. Bryant participated in a high school summer internship program at Sinai Hospital and worked in their Biomedical Engineering Department. As she shadowed the engineers, she went into operating and emergency rooms. She soon found out that seeing blood constantly and smelling the pungent hospital aroma was not to her stomach's liking. Thus, she decided to concentrate on what she could do to reduce or eliminate injuries instead of trying to repair them.

Upon graduation from Renaissance, she attended the University of Michigan. Because of her gender and color, she stood out. She was one of the few African Americans and few females who enrolled in the School of Engineering. For statisticians, she was considered a double minority. At this time in our history, too many professors felt that women belonged back home in the kitchen, and one openly admitted it. She had a tough time there. To her credit, she persevered and graduated with a bachelor of science degree in mechanical engineering. During her summers, she interned with General Motors. Upon graduation in July 1990, she accepted full-time employment with the company.

Her first work assignment at GM was analyzing warranties for the Chevrolet Cavalier, Corsica, and Beretta; the Pontiac Sunbird and Grand Am; the Buick Skylark; and the Oldsmobile Calais. Bryant then worked on door testing as a validation engineer for the Cavalier, Sunbird, and Sunfire. This included side impact testing, door slams, and a number of other door hardware tests.

From there, she moved on to various engineering roles. She developed Global Manufacturing Technical Specifications (for which she received the NAO Manufacturing Center's Award of Excellence) as a manufacturing systems engineer. While serving as a design release engineer, she later designed and released interior door and garnish trim components for the Saturn LS and Oldsmobile Cutlass. She spent many nights supporting these products at the assembly plants since they ran three shifts around the clock.

Renee then ventured into the overall vehicle as lead compartment integration design engineer, vehicle architecture manager, and program manager for concept vehicles, among other positions. Two major career highlights were the successful 2004 Buick Velite convertible concept and the 2005 Cadillac STS SAE 100 technology vehicle.

Bryant spent seven months traveling back and forth to Turin, Italy, overseeing the engineering, design, and build of the Velite concept car at Stile Bertone. She took a crash course in Italian to communicate with the teams there and to ensure that the vehicle was built according to specifications. At this time, she relied on her past experience with languages to communicate. She had taken four years of French in high school and learned some Spanish when assigned to work with GM of Mexico. Thankfully, the polite and patient Italians gave her credit for attempting to speak their language. She had the opportunity to work directly with the great Anne Asensio, GM's Advanced Design director at the time, in the development of the Velite. Although engineering execution was challenging at times, Anne's vision of the vehicle was impeccable. The Velite was revealed at the 2004 New York Auto Show and caught the eyes of television celebrities, making a subsequent guest appearance on *Live! With Regis and Kelly*. Numerous styling cues designed for the Velite still appear on Buicks today.

The Cadillac STS SAE 100 was created for the opening of the one hundredth anniversary of the SAE World Congress in 2005 in Detroit, where GM was the host company and Jim Queen, GM's vice president of global engineering, was the general chairperson. Renee and her engineering team worked less than a year with thirty-eight suppliers to integrate fifty different technologies into the vehicle, ranging across safety, chassis, power train, electrical, and comfort and convenience categories. A lot of outside-the-box thinking came about with the creation of this vehicle as she tasked the team to put any idea on the table. Things remained up for consideration as long as they could meet timing and, of course, be functional. There were no mockup concept technologies here! From a cost standpoint, Bryant had a low budget, and thus she used some very good negotiating skills with suppliers to get them on board for this project. In return, they received plenty of credit and advertising. On the opening day of the conference, they were caught by press photographer and appeared on the front page of the *Detroit News* and the *Detroit Free Press*. Renee got in a sneak peek of herself as well. The vehicle was well received at the conference and ultimately served as a working laboratory for engineers in developing future GM production vehicles.

The STS SAE 100 was powered by a supercharged LS2 engine yielding 505 horsepower at 5,600 rpm and 520 lb-ft. of torque at 3,600 rpm. It was mated to GM Hydramatic's newly developed, longitudinal 6L90E six-speed transmission.

The numerous future technologies that are a part of the STS SAE 100 have and will continue to affect our lives forever. The one-of-a-kind 3-D navigation system utilized images taken by satellites, a sensor system monitored the condition of the oil, the lane departure system used vibration to alert the driver when the car was out of lane, a carbon-fiber wheel with magnesium spokes eliminated unsprung weight, and a capless gas tank made filling it easier for physically limited users. The list of innovations went on and on, and many of these ideas have already been incorporated in Cadillac products.

The STS was tested at the Milford Proving Ground and in Mesa, California.

Renee received a "You Make A Difference" Diversity Award for her continued support and demonstration of diversity and inclusion in the workplace, in addition to a number of other recognition awards throughout the years for her work ethic and performance. After the completion of the Saturn Sky Roadster concept vehicle, she moved on to become an engineering group manager for GM's Specialty Vehicle Activities, where she led her engineering team in the creation of specialty vehicles such as the Cadillac Platinum Editions, the Buick Supers, and the Cadillac

Professional Vehicles (e.g., limousine, hearse, and livery vehicles). Her electrical team members supported the high-security Cadillac Armored and Presidential Program vehicles as well. She also was instrumental in creating an all-female student engineering team to work on a Bonneville Salt Flats vehicle-racing project.

From there, Bryant managed the GM Upfitter Integration Team and worked with outside specialty vehicle modifier companies (or upfitters) to utilize GM Fleet and Chevrolet commercial vehicles (e.g., medium-duty trucks, full-size trucks, and full-size vans) by providing technical information and communicating upfitter requirements to GM Engineering, Sales, and Marketing. She represented GM at association trade shows such as the National Truck Equipment Association (NTEA) show. It was here that she finally was able to meet in person her inspiration for cars and trucks, John Davis, at the 2016 NTEA Work Truck Show in Indianapolis. She worked on several special assignments, including the Domino's DXP "ultimate pizza delivery vehicle," which has been in several commercial advertisements. In addition, Bryant orchestrated the conversion of two left-hand-drive products into right-hand-drives for the Australian market.

In May 2018, she became the Senior Engineering Group manager for GM Accessories vehicle system engineers. She has eight direct reports who engineer and manage all the vehicle accessories for GMNA products. These include components such as tonneau covers, assist steps, all-weather mats, grilles, spoilers, decals, luggage racks, rear-seat entertainment, and, of course, bigger wheels.

Over the years, Bryant has helped recruit numerous engineering students for General Motors as a recruitment engagement team leader at North Carolina Agricultural and Technical State University and became an honorary Aggie in the process. She has also worked to engage future engineering students through GM at the SAE's A World In Motion (AWIM), the Michigan Science Center's STEMinista Project for girls, and speaking at local elementary and high school career fairs. She unofficially mentors younger (and some older) GM employees so that their roads to success will be easier. She volunteers both through and outside the company with community events such as the Grow Cody Rouge neighborhood project, Gleaners Community Food Bank, Adopt a Child for Christmas, Detroit Goodfellows Doll Program, Meals on Wheels, and Make-A-Wish Foundation, just to name a few. In her spare time, she enjoys developing her spirituality, traveling to new destinations, spending high-quality time with her daughter Simone, and making the world a little more "accident" free.

General Motors

General Motors

MEI CAI

"I think logically, but when it comes to technology and innovation, my brain is wired differently; I am a risk taker inspired to transcend the constraints before me."

Mei Cai

CAREER HIGHLIGHTS

Dr. Mei Cai, the recipient of the prestigious Boss Kettering Award in 2016, is a highly trained and accomplished engineer. This prize, in the form of a trophy, is the company's highest technical honor. Born in Beijing, China, Cai completed her education in the United States and has set a high benchmark both for men and women throughout the automotive industry.

From the campus of Tsinghua University, where she resided as a child, to the sequestered laboratories of General Motors R&D, Mei Cai has made significant contributions to advancing the technologies that continue to move the company, the industry, and the world forward.

Before joining General Motors, Mei held a number of significant industry-wide positions that established her expertise. Over a twenty-five-year period, Mei has served as a valued member of GM's R&D staff. She is currently a General Motors technical fellow and manager of the Energy Storage Materials

Group, responsible for the technological innovations in advanced energy storage materials for vehicular applications. During her career at GM, Mei has made many important contributions in the area of advanced energy storage materials, including developments in lithium-ion and advanced battery chemistries, automotive-competitive proton-exchange membrane fuel cells, hydrogen and compressed natural-gas storage, and battery-charging and hydrogen production technologies. Mei was a key member of the team recognized in 2016 with GM's Boss Kettering Award for development of an industry-leading low-cost, high-volume, and structurally integrated high-energy-density battery pack, which is used in the new Chevrolet Bolt EV.

That same year, she was an *R&D Magazine* "100 Awards" finalist for development of high-performance lithium-ion anodes.

Mei's professional accomplishments include more than a hundred peer-reviewed journal publications, one hundred issued US patents, and over fifty pending patent applications. She has presented sixty invited talks. In 2017, she chaired GM's Senior Leadership Technical Council, which is charged with identifying disruptive future technologies and promoting cross-lab collaboration and development opportunities within the R&D organization.

She was recently recognized as the Asian American Engineer of the Year and serves to motivate those around her as well as inspire women entering the industry. By teaming up with researchers from Sandia National Laboratories, they also won the 2019 Federal Laboratory Consortium (FLC) Mid-Continent Region Notable Technology Development Award for Detergent-Assisted Fabrication of Multifunctional Nanomaterials. Detergent-assisted fabrication is a technology that enables the production of new multifunctional nanomaterials with more-uniform and more-reproducible properties, with the potential for manufacturing-costs reduction while improving manufacturability and minimizing environmental concerns.

Furthermore, while participating in professional organizations, Mei does volunteer work for the Oakland Youth Orchestra.

MEI'S JOURNEY

Mei's grandfather returned to China, where Mei was born, after completing his education in the United States. Liu-Sheng Tsai, who earned a PhD in chemistry at the University of Chicago, would inspire her throughout her early childhood. He taught her how to push boundaries—she uses the idiom "The sky's the limit," meaning there are no restrictions.

Her father graduated from Tsinghua University, which is the highest-ranked engineering school in all of China. He majored in mechanical engineering and later became a professor in the same department. Her mother, a medical doctor in Beijing, graduated from the Capital Medical University there. Mei, the oldest child in her family, grew up on the campus of Tsinghua University. Her primary and secondary schools located there were all part of Tsinghua University. She has a younger sister who moved to Germany in 1989 and is now working for a Chinese-owned real estate company in Hamburg. Mei is currently living in Michigan with her husband, Jie, and two sons, Allen and Jason. Jie holds dual PhDs in nuclear engineering and scientific computing from the University of Michigan. He is now also working for General Motors as manager of Advanced Analytics, having previously served Ford, FCA, JD Power, and Trilogy. Both Allen and Jason matriculated in the engineering school at the University of Michigan. Allen is currently working as a system engineer II in guidance navigation and controls at Raytheon, after receiving his master's degree in electrical engineering in May 2019. Jason is working toward his bachelor's degree in industrial and operations engineering.

Mei Cai was different.

Mei was never a follower, and her uncommon behavior started to appear in early childhood. In the traditional Chinese education system, only the children who obey their teachers and parents are defined as good students. With this in mind, she notes that she was not in the good students' category until fourth grade. She can still remember clearly when she was punished by being directed to stand against the classroom wall on her first day of elementary school. In the early days of China, young kids could walk to school on their own without their parents by their side. On the first day of school, Mei's attention was drawn to a cicada coming out of its shell on a willow tree on the way to school. She was amazed by the process and completely lost track of time. As a result, she was the only one late for school on the first day, and this was also the starting point of her being labeled a "bad" kid. Due to Mei's personality as a young child, she did not really care how others viewed her, and refused to make changes for them. She notes, "My life started to change when I got a new fourth-grade teacher—Shuhua Wang—who taught literature at the time. She saw my potential and made me the leader of a study group. Shuhua ignited a fire in me that changed my life." Within one year, Mei rose to the top 10 percent of academically ranked students and remained a top achiever thereafter.

In 1983, Mei was accepted by Tsinghua University to study chemical engineering. She received her bachelor of science in 1988 and joined the Engineering Design Institute in Beijing. As a junior product engineer, Mei's responsibility included the design and optimization of manufacturing processes, as well as the production equipment for various industrial plants. In 1991, she decided to move to the United States with her husband and pursue a higher education.

The US leg of her journey started in Columbus, Ohio, where her husband, Jie, was accepted as a PhD student in the Ohio State University Nuclear Engineering graduate program. After a year of study, Jie decided to transfer to the University of Michigan,

and they moved to Ann Arbor. While Jie continued studies toward his PhD in nuclear engineering at the University of Michigan, Mei also enrolled as a PhD student in chemical engineering at Wayne State University. Both of these institutions were training grounds for the automotive industry. Growing up, Mei always dreamed of becoming a medical doctor, but she was pushed toward the engineering field by her parents. She still had a passion for bioengineering and the biomedical field when she first enrolled at Wayne State University. She studied with Professor Steve Sally, who had a joint research program with Dr. J. Richard Spears, a cardiologist specializing in interventional cardiology. Mei worked at Dr. Spear's lab in the medical school at Wayne State University, dreaming of making an artificial heart someday. Perhaps the first artificial heart pump displayed in the showcase at the entrance of the Engineering Building lobby at GM in the 1970s would have caught her eye.

In 1993, Mei accepted a summer internship in the Health and Safety Department at the General Motors Technical Center. She assisted in the development of coating materials used in evaporator cores in air-conditioning units to control the microbial growth and reduce the cabin air odor in Cadillacs. Over the summer, she flew to Florida and Texas several times to conduct the fleet tests to evaluate the effectiveness of coating materials. Mei had no idea what the "Automotive Industry and GM R&D" consisted of at this time. She was educated and trained on the campus of the GM Technical Center by a group of GM engineers and researchers. Due to her excellent on-the-job performance, she was invited back the following year to complete the study.

Constructed under the direction of architect Eero Saarinen, the lobby at Research Labs features a spiral staircase fashioned from two intersecting cones made of steel rods, which also support granite steps. *General Motors*

CNG cargo van.. *General Motors*

Mei's career path experienced an unexpected turn in December 1994. She received a phone call from the head of the Health & Safety Department at General Motors R&D and was asked if she was interested in a full-time position. Apparently, there was a full-time research position posted in the same department where she completed the two internships. Mei was informed that seven candidates had already completed the interview process and that she would be the eighth candidate to be considered, and she was asked if she was interested. An opening existed for a PhD research engineer to develop a new binder system for the engine-casting process, and she needed to agree to two conditions before being considered: (1) complete the PhD program while working as a full-time employee, and (2) change her major from bioengineering to polymer materials. Both conditions presented significant challenges. To complete a degree program while working full time meant double the workload, and changing a major meant she would need to start from square one. It did not take long for Mei to accept the challenges. After two internships, she "fell in love" with the automotive industry and General Motors R&D. Finally, she joined GM as a permanent employee in February 1995.

The first five years working at GM were really hard—she juggled between work and school. To make matters more complicated, her eldest son was born in November 1996. As a working mother and a PhD student, Mei had little time to rest. Early in her career, Mei developed a new understanding of lost foam-casting materials and thermal degradation, which resulted in $12 million in annual savings for GM. She also made significant contributions to the GMBOND sand-core binder used in the aluminum-casting process, which produced royalty revenue of $10 million annually for the company.

In December 1999, Mei received her PhD in chemical engineering from Wayne State University; this was a significant milestone in her career. Shortly after, she was promoted to senior

research engineer and then staff researcher, starting a twelve-year journey of hydrogen fuel cell technology development within GM.

In the area of fuel cells, Mei has made contributions to electrocatalyst chemistry that have resulted in reduced fuel cell corrosion and cost and increased durability and performance. She was the principal investigator in the development of low-cost, steam-reforming hydrogen production technology. In 2009, Mei Cai received a Best Paper Award for a paper on "Development of a Renewable Hydrogen Economy: Optimization of Existing Technologies."

In 2007, Mei was promoted to the manager of Energy Storage Materials lab, leading a group of twenty-seven PhD-level professional researchers with an annual material budget of $2 million to develop and deploy innovative energy storage solutions with low-cost and high-energy density for GM's future vehicles.

Mei continues to lead researchers in the design of next-generation battery chemistries, novel nanostructured materials, and advanced energy storage systems—areas critical to GM's commitment to a future of electric and sustainable mobility.

Among her accomplishments, she and her team developed a low-pressure (50 bar) adsorption-based natural-gas (ANG) fuel storage system and an efficient on-demand natural-gas power train system. The ANG demo system was delivered to three vehicle platforms with a home refueling option that offers lower mass and cost compared to conventional 250-bar compressed-natural-gas (CNG) technology.

The on-demand natural-gas power train system was offered in the 2015 CNG Chevrolet Impala and the 2015 2500HD and 3500 Silverado truck, which is still desirable to fleet owners today. The vehicles are equipped with hardened valves and a separate gas tank. The gas economy is better, and, with two sources of fuel, the driving range is extended.

BOSS KETTERING AWARD

Working with the Global Propulsion Systems (GPS) team, Mei and the cross-functional team completed the development of a cost-effective, long-range, high-energy-density, structurally integrated, industry-leading RESS (rechargeable energy storage system) for the Chevrolet Bolt. This technology not only put GM in the industry-leading position for long-range-battery electric vehicle (BEV) development but also was a key enabler of affordable BEV for GM customers when compared to their competitors. Due to her contributions in the development of RESS for electrified vehicles, she and her team were awarded the 2016 Boss Kettering Award. The RESS for the Bolt EV is an industry-leading battery pack manufactured by General Motors.

During her GM career, Mei also managed the company's

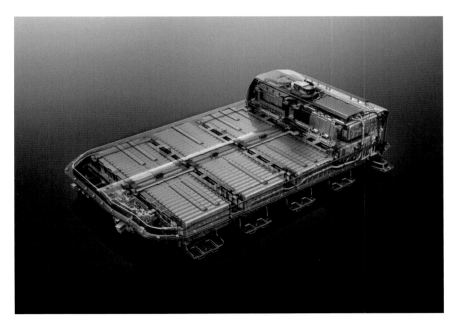

General Motors

collaboration with National Labs, universities, and other global partners in these areas. As a key member of the USCAR Hydrogen Storage Tech Team, she regularly reviews and provides guidance to the Department of Energy's Hydrogen and Fuel Cells Program. She is also a regular proposal and panel reviewer for the National Science Foundation and Department of Energy programs. She has successfully secured five DOE/DARPA-E contracts with multimillion-dollar government research funding coming to General Motors R&D.

In 2017, Mei chaired GM R&D's Senior Leadership Technical Council, which is charged with identifying disruptive future technologies and promoting cross-lab collaboration and development opportunities within the R&D organization. In addition, she has been involved in many professional society and community service activities, organizing seminars and other activities to promote culture diversity and partnership. She is a member of the American Institute of Chemical Engineers, the Materials Research Society, the Electrochemical Society, the International Society of Electrochemistry, the International Academy of Electrochemical Energy Science, and the Detroit Chinese Engineer Association.

ASIAN AMERICAN ENGINEER OF THE YEAR AWARD

In April 2018, Mei received the 2018 Asian American Engineer of the Year Award for original and sustained contributions to the development, understanding, and application of advanced energy storage materials while promoting industry–national lab–university collaborative research. She was recognized for her contributions in both fundamental research and technological development. The award is made by the Chinese Institute of Engineering to promote STEM and is supported by corporate America, academia, and US government entities.

AFTER WORK

Although not a musician herself, Mei is a longtime volunteer for the Oakland Youth Orchestras in Michigan. There is no question that her sons have sparked her interest in music. She proudly notes, "Both my boys are trained in music. Allen has played piano for twelve years and competed. As a high school senior, he won the first-place age achievement award in the American Guild of Music Great Lakes Regional contest. Jason played cello for eleven years. At age of thirteen, he participated in the Blue Lake International Exchange program's European tour and performed in seven communities in Europe. At age of fifteen, he performed at Carnegie Hall as part of the High School Honors Performance program."

The Boss Kettering Award. *Constance Smith*

GM Korea

SANGYEON CHO

Sangyeon Cho, who is currently a design director at GM Korea, served as the design manager for the exterior and interior of the handsome Chevrolet Bolt, a game-changing EV.

CAREER HIGHLIGHTS

Sangyeon Cho is currently one of two design directors at GM Korea. She runs a team of exterior, interior, and color and trim designers who are working on next-generation global products.

During her career, she led or contributed to the design of the Chevrolet Mini Triplet concept cars: the Beat, the Groove, and the Trax, which appeared in 2007. She also contributed to the design of the 2007 revised Chevrolet Spark, the 2012 Chevrolet Trax, and the game-changing 2017 Chevrolet Bolt EV.

In addition, the exterior and interior of Encore GX, the currently bestselling Buick product in US, was designed by Cho's team.

Cho also served as a judge in 2016 for the *Car Design News*

and GM Interactive Design Competition, seeking and exposing new talent. To that end, she participates in educational activities to encourage upcoming designers.

BIOGRAPHICAL NOTES

After earning bachelor's and master's degrees both in industrial design and car design at Hongik University, Cho joined Daewoo Motors in 1995, where she worked on interior and exterior programs for various production and concept cars.

For many years, Italdesign provided services to Daewoo. In 1995 they designed the Bucrane coupe, and in 1996 they ended their joint venture with GM.[1] In 1997, they introduced the d'Arts, an extravagant limited-production Matiz. The same year, they welcomed the Lanos and Leganza. Working in conjunction with Italdesign for several years helped Cho refine her global design skills. In 1992, Giorgetto Giugiaro of Italdesign designed the Lucciola concept car, a small subcompact that could still seat five passengers. This design served as the basis of the Daewoo Matiz.[2] Worldwide it has many other names: in the United States it is sold as the Chevrolet Spark. The first generation of the Matiz was made from 1998 to 2000. In 2002, the Kalos was born, a.k.a. the Chevrolet Aveo. In 2003, the Lacetti appeared—a world car.

After the sale of Daewoo Motors to General Motors in 2001, Cho worked on global advanced and production programs for various divisions, including Chevrolet, Buick, and Opel.

It is significant that the Bolt EV's exterior design made by Cho's team was selected for manufacture.

THREE MINI CARS

Chevrolet unveiled three minicar concepts at the 2007 New York International Auto Show—the Beat, Groove, and Trax—designed to meet the needs of active urban youth. All the concepts, even smaller than a Chevrolet Aveo, were designed and engineered in GM's South Korea facility. The Beat, a.k.a. Matiz in Korea, was the only running prototype. Attendees and readers of various magazines were asked to choose their favorite from these vehicles. Nearly a million people (more than 50 percent of the vote) selected the Beat, a vibrant-green three-door hatchback with a six-speaker sound system; it prevailed in this poll and a subsequent company study. It likely stood out against the orange-brown five-door Trax and the boxier five-door Groove. However, it is no surprise that these other concepts would resurface in some form in the future.

GM's previous VP of Design reviewed the results with *Automotive News*: "It was quite different than anything we've done in the past," recalled Ed Welburn. "It was a great way to have a positive dialogue with our consumers." While the Beat would go forward as the Spark, it took considerably longer for Chevrolet to introduce a utility vehicle under the Trax nameplate—it was unveiled here in 2013 and was recently refreshed. Neil Roland further noted the following in the *Automotive News* article: "The production Spark was unveiled at the Geneva auto show in March 2009. The Spark went on sale in the first quarter of 2010 in Europe, India, South Korea, and Turkey. In Europe it replaced the Matiz minicar. GM noted that 173,723 Sparks had been sold globally through August 2011"[3] ("Where Are Those Cute Chevy Minis?," *Automotive News*, October 31, 2011).

The Groove, a five-door retro wagon, could challenge the boxier Scion xB, introduced in 2000, and was a precursor of the HHR. It was rolled out at the 2007 New York Auto Show as one of the three triplets.

In 2013, the Spark was unveiled at the Greater NY Auto Show. *Constance Smith*

CHEVROLET TRAX

Exterior designer Sangyeon Cho suggests that this little four-door "brings a rational combination of SUV design, function, performance, and value to the consumer."[4]
GM's promotional material extolled the virtues of the Trax:

Chevrolet Trax is an urban front-wheel-drive crossover concept with a twist: This micro SUV has an electric limited-slip differential that features an independent battery pack and an electric motor to drive the rear wheels, providing a low-cost all-wheel-drive system.

Simple door lines make getting in and out easier, and fold-flat rear seats add functionality.

Other features that suit its dynamic and off-road character include a voluminous, single-unit bumper and fender in front and rear, a pronounced front wheel arch shape, dynamic side character lines, a rear-mounted spare tire, and roof rack.

"The Trax is a vehicle that you can show off anywhere, be it off-road or on the road," said Sangyeon Cho, manager of the minicar exterior design team at the GM Design Center in

Like the Encore before it, the Buick Encore GX is a best-seller. *Courtesy of Bob and Peggy Tetmeyer*

Inchon, South Korea. "It brings a rational combination of SUV design, function, performance, and value to the consumer."

After she led the development of the Chevrolet Mini Triplet concepts for the 2007 New York Auto Show, Cho was promoted to design manager in 2008.

The three Minis were voted on by attendees at the auto show. *General Motors*

GM KOREA

In 2016, Cho was appointed design director both of interior design and exterior design for GM Korea. She, along with Crystal Windham, director of Design for Cadillac Interiors, and Friedhelm Engler, design director, GME Design, were invited to judge a major competition sponsored by *Car Design News*.

BOLT: THE FRONTRUNNER

While the EV-1 of yesteryear took the back roads and the Chevrolet Volt came late to the party, the Bolt leads the pack.

Cho served as the design manager for the exterior of the timely Chevrolet Bolt. The handsome concept car was unveiled

The Bolt housed its batteries below the passenger compartment. *General Motors*

in 2015 at the North American International Auto Show, and the production model in 2016 at the Consumer Electronics Show by GM's CEO Mary Barra. Winning the 2017 North American Car of the Year Award made this event even more memorable for the Chevrolet team. Subsequent awards included *Motor Trend* Car of the Year, Green Car of the Year, and others. Perhaps the Bolt ultimately captured more awards than the Volt hybrid.

Bolt was the first production battery-electric to provide a range of 238 miles (EPA tested) at a price less than $40,000, to which a $7,500 incentive was applied in some localities. Its battery pack powers a 200 hp electric motor, and it has an EPA rating of 128/110 MPGe. This range is attributed to its new lithium-ion NMC battery chemistry ($LiNiMnCoO_2$) and a more efficient motor. The refinement of the concept car from wind tunnel testing kept the coefficient of drag at bay, contributing to the extended range.

Recently, Cruise has rolled out the amazing Autonomous Bolts, driverless cars, in San Francisco.

This ground-up vehicle project was a welcome sight to designers who spend much of their time on refreshers. Not so fast . . . under the direction of Cho, the Bolt's exterior stylists had to accommodate the large, flat battery pack beneath the floor—making the vehicle sit higher. A more spacious interior resulted from moving the wheels to the corners. While the central location of the vehicle's drive unit was likely a plus, designers were cognizant that an exterior design is a package; this was not the free-for-all that Harley Earl's designers from the 1950s would reminisce about.

Cho's vision, brought to reality, was described in part by the design team on the GM Media website. Chevrolet calls the resulting head-turning vehicle a crossover—perhaps it is classified as a small wagon by regulators. The front features a narrow-shaped trapezoidal grille—with a decorative golden bow tie in the center—and a larger hexagonal grille area underneath. The Bolt, unlike the Volt sequential hybrid, features a short front overhang due to the smaller space required by its power plant.

Fog lamp assemblies, wider rather than taller, on each side of the lower hexagon are loosely connected visually in depressions. Some automotive historians believe the hexagonal-shaped grille (which they also loosely refer to as trapezoidal) is a derivative of the early 1957 Aston Martin DB Mark. The Bolt shares its DNA with the Trax, the Camaro, and others that have similar fronts.

Front to back, the sculpted sides and rising beltline create an aggressive stance that leads to the taillights, lighted sculptures in their own right that dominate the rear. GM Media notes that the rear-window glass extends all the way to the license plate and integrates with LED taillamps on the liftgate. By integrating the taillamps into the full-width liftgate, the Bolt EV's architecture enables a wide opening that makes it easier to slide cargos in and out of the vehicle.

The flowing instrument panel surrounds the central 10.2-inch diagonal interactive tablet. In recent years, Chevrolet interior designers have very successfully explored interesting forms and lines to create a more visually exciting and spacious interior.

A Premier Package, compared to the base LT, provides a rear camera, surround vision utilizing four cameras, and leather-wrapped steering wheel. The machined 17-inch wheels, 1 inch bigger in the Premier package than on the LT, add to the Bolt's aggressive stance without dominating the form. A driver Confidence Package adds rear park assist, a rear cross-traffic alert, a side blind-zone alert, and a lane change alert. Heated seats and other options are available. GM Media notes that the large greenhouse offers a panoramic view from upright with SUV-like seating

With all its attributes, the 2017 Bolt delivers state-of-the-art technology in harmony with a modern design language. The subtlety of the fresh styling created by Cho and Chevrolet designers to address a global market will be valued over the long haul.

Today, in her position as the design director of GM Korea since 2015, Sangyeon Cho continues to lead interior and exterior designers for significant international entires.

ENCORE GX

In addition, the exterior and interior of Encore GX, the currently bestselling Buick product in US, was designed by Cho's team.

ALICIA BOLER-DAVIS

This recognition is a testament to your steadfast devotion to turning today's bold ideas into tomorrow's realities, something I have seen from you firsthand, and it is well beyond deserved. I hope you know how grateful I am for all you've done to help America dream up solutions and drive our nation forward on the path of progress.

—Barack Obama, forty-fourth president of the US

Alicia Boler-Davis (b. ca. 1969), executive vice president of Global Manufacturing and Labor Relations at General Motors in 2018, accepted the Black Engineer of the Year Award (BEYA) in Washington, DC. She was the sixth woman to receive this award and, during her honoring, was surprised by the above acknowledgement from President Barack Obama, sending his congratulatory praises.

Drawing by Constance Smith

of the GM Senior Leadership Team and reported to GM CEO and chairman Mary Barra.

For two years prior, Boler-Davis served as senior vice president of Global Connected Customer Experience. She led GM's global customer experience efforts to provide customers with the best overall service and experience in the industry, as well as market-leading connectivity and infotainment products and services. As senior VP, Boler-Davis led the company's response to consumers following the ignition switch affair.

CAREER HIGHLIGHTS

Alicia Boler-Davis currently serves as vice president of global customer fulfillment at Amazon, where she is responsible for centers across sixteen countries. She joined Amazon Operations in 2019 and is now a member of a handful of people in Amazon's inner circle. Keep in mind that Amazon also joined Cox Automotive and Ford to fund Rivian. It also invested in the self-driving tech company Aurora.

Prior to her current role, Boler-Davis was appointed to the position of executive vice president of Global Manufacturing and Labor Relations at GM, leading global manufacturing, manufacturing engineering, labor relations, facilities, and environmental strategies in June 2016. Under her leadership, General Motors built on its long manufacturing excellence to deliver on future technologies and transportation solutions with high quality, efficiency, and scale.

Boler-Davis oversaw GM's Global Manufacturing organization, which consisted of approximately 165,000 employees in more than 150 facilities in twenty countries worldwide. In 2017, GM built ten million vehicles, working collaboratively with more than forty union partners around the world. She was a member

GM's Orion plant has produced over 5.4 million vehicles, including Cadillacs, Oldsmobiles, and Buicks. Orion was chosen to build the all-electric Bolt EV and Cruise test vehicles, bringing jobs to the area. *General Motors*

The Pontiac Metal Center is also referred to as the Pontiac Stamping plant.
General Motors

Her scope included leading GM's twenty-year-old OnStar safety, security, and services business, which has passed one billion customer interactions. In this role, she was responsible for strategic planning, engineering, and P&L (profit and loss) management responsibility for OnStar. She also led GM's Urban Active team, which developed solutions to capitalize on the future of personal mobility, including car-sharing services through the Maven brand.

In 2007, Boler-Davis moved to Arlington, Texas, to become a plant manager and later moved back to Michigan to manage the Orion assembly plant and Pontiac stamping plant while also working as chief engineer for the Chevrolet Sonic.

In June 2012, Boler-Davis was appointed vice president of Global Quality and U.S. Customer Experience. Later that year, her role was expanded to senior vice president of Global Quality and Customer Experience.

Boler-Davis is a member of the Northwestern University McCormick Advisory Council and the General Mills Board of Directors. Around 2018, she provided a presentation at the Leading Ladies Conference sponsored by *Automotive News* in Detroit.

BIOGRAPHICAL NOTES

In an interview, Boler-Davis recalled her family's struggles: "I grew up in a single-parent home. My mom took care of four of us from the time I was five. She worked eleven-hour days. That forces you to have a level of independence and to figure things out on your own. You can't use it as an excuse for not achieving your goals."

In 1986, Boler-Davis participated in a high school program sponsored by Kettering University for aspiring engineers.[2]

She notes, "I grew up in Detroit, and I always liked cars. When I had an opportunity to come back home and to work in an industry that had a huge impact on my career and on me starting on my career and on me starting in engineering, I decided to take it."[3]

Boler-Davis graduated with a BS in chemical engineering from Northwestern University in 1991 and an MS in engineering science from Rensselaer Polytechnic Institute (RPI) in 1998. In 2015, she completed requirements for an MBA in the Kelley School of Business at Indiana University, and in 2018 she was awarded an honorary doctorate by RPI.

As a college student, Boler-Davis worked as a systems engineer for the Ford Motor Company.

Perhaps her first opportunity to prove herself in a management position arose in 2003, when she worked under Mary Barra, the manager who would overhaul the Hamtramck plant. In its heyday, Hamtramck had 3,400 workers on two shifts building six models for three divisions. Because of terrorist attacks in 2001, plants had to reduce staff to counter the loss in sales. Boler-Davis oversaw General Assembly at this time. This was the largest department, where workers attached most of the car's components to its body.[4] As a manager, it would have been her job to make a list of workers to be furloughed. Boler-Davis remembers Barra changing the content of line jobs to slow the line down. In referring to Barra she noted, "I learned a lot by watching her approach. She's humble, which makes people want to work for her. At the same time, she's pushing you to do more."[5]

It was Barra who suggested she leave this assignment in order to diversify her experience.

After serving as a plant manager in Lansing for just three months, Alicia Boler-Davis was called in to manage the Orion plant and Pontiac Stamping plant at the same time she was appointed chief engineer and vehicle line director on the Chevrolet Sonic.

The Orion plant required renovations to generate profit. This was a learning experience for which she would have to acquire a leadership style to meet diverse goals. She later described it as "the most rewarding assignment I have had."

Under her leadership, GM improved vehicle quality and fundamentally redefined customer care and its interaction with customers through social media channels and Customer Engagement Centers.

FAMILY MATTERS

Married to Fitzgerald Davis, Boler-Davis has two sons and a stepdaughter. Through the years, it was never easy juggling childcare and career. During her Leading Ladies presentation, she made it a point to mention how important the support of her husband and family were in advancing her career.

JENNIFER GOFORTH

Twenty years from now you will be more disappointed by the things that you didn't do than by the ones you did do. So … sail away from the safe harbor. Explore. Dream. Discover.
—Mark Twain

CAREER HIGHLIGHTS

Jennifer previously served as chief engineer for China Electrification. In 2022, she became Executive Director of Global Aftersales and Service Operations. Holding diverse engineering positions for over twenty years, she has shared her training and experience across GM's international community. With expertise in designing electric vehicles, there is no question that her contributions to General Motors have and will continue to have worldwide implications affecting our mobility. She is assigned to Pan Asia Technical Automotive Center (PATAC) in the Pudongxin District of Shanghai, China, where she is leading the engineering design of electric vehicles on General Motor's third-generation global EV platform (BEV3).

This quote has always resonated with me. Throughout my career and my personal life, I have been given opportunities to take on new and challenging assignments. And each time I have said "yes" … because I welcomed the challenge to do something outside my comfort zone, for it is there that I have grown the most professionally and personally.

As an individual, I strive to continuously learn and grow. I seek opportunities to try new things, to embrace change and take risks. I live a life rich in new experiences that help me better understand me and others. I love to surround myself with people who have diverse backgrounds and thoughts from my own.

Throughout my career, I have sought ways to gain unique experiences that aligned with my passions. Identifying strategic opportunities to expand my knowledge and grow as a leader. I was never discouraged when my path took me through lateral opportunities, as those were instrumental in building a strong foundation of experience to help me achieve my career goals. I enjoy the challenge of stretch assignments outside my comfort zone. Looking back, those are the experiences where I grew and contributed the most.

As a chief engineer, I strive to understand the customer and make engineering decisions to focus on what they need and want. I work with a team to bring the unique selling points to fruition that will differentiate the vehicle in the market and delight the customer.

General Motors

As a companion and mother, my husband and I strive to expose our daughter to diverse experiences and hope to inspire in her a similar passion for learning and growing.

—Jennifer Goforth b. 1972

Starting as components engineer at Mercury Marine's start-up Performance Craft Division in 1995, Jennifer engineered parts for a personal watercraft. In 1998, she moved to General Motors' Saturn division as an advanced manufacturing engineer, where she was responsible for the chassis and engine line processing and tooling. This was Jennifer's first experience working on a global program, the Saturn L Series, engineered by Opel and manufactured by Saturn. In 1999, Jennifer accepted her first international assignment and relocated to Germany to join Opel. She returned to Detroit in 2000, as manufacturing integration manager for Wilmington Assembly. After several years of advanced manufacturing work, she joined Pontiac Assembly Center as a production first-line supervisor, then was appointed business manager. In 2004, she worked on a special assignment as the project manager for SAE International's A World in Motion (AWIM) program, where she led GM volunteers to bring the engineering design experience to students in Detroit and our GM communities. She returned to engineering in 2006, taking on assignments in hybrid and electric vehicles in Detroit, Seoul, and Shanghai. In 2018, Jennifer was assigned the role of chief engineer for GM's third-generation global EV platform (BEV3).

Jennifer has recently returned to the US and serves as director of global after-sales, Mechanical Engineering, at GM.

BIOGRAPHICAL NOTES

Jennifer grew up alongside a small lake in rural Wisconsin with her parents, Kurt and Maureen, and three sisters, Theresa, Cori, and Karen. Her father was an orthopedic surgeon, while her mother was a community volunteer and full-time caregiver. She attended St. Kilian Catholic school, which graded both academic performance and effort. Her father always put the most focus on their "effort" grade. He said that he didn't expect them to be the smartest in the class, but he expected them to work hard to achieve their fullest potential.

Jennifer notes, "In a family of all girls, we did not have defined gender roles. With our father frequently on call, we had to step up and take care of whatever came up on a rural lake property. My relationship with my father was built on a healthy competitive connection. Whether swimming, sailing, or skiing, we were always competing against each other. After college, we even competed to see who could get the highest Professional Association of Diving Instructors (PADI) scuba certification level quickest. I certainly inherited my competitive nature from my father. We were raised to believe there was nothing we couldn't do. Jennifer's alma mater, Hartford Union High School, required all freshmen students to be certified in first aid and CPR. When Jennifer was sixteen, she called on her American Red Cross training in first aid to sustain the life of a boy who was involved in a boating accident. For her lifesaving action, Jennifer received the Certificate of Merit, the highest award given by the Red Cross to a person who saves a life by using skills and knowledge learned in an American Red Cross Training Services course. This life-altering event instilled in her the drive for continuous learning and courage in stepping forward.

During high school, her family began hosting international exchange students. She notes, "This was a way for my parents to introduce us to the world. We hosted nine students hailing from Austria, France, Italy, Japan, Mexico, Portugal, Spain, and Venezuela. We learned about new cultures and global perspectives of world history, and most importantly we learned that we are more similar than different. "I never took advantage of the opportunity to study abroad, so I promised my international siblings I would say 'yes' if I ever had the opportunity again."

"Our family activities focused on sailing. In the summer, we sailed four or five times each week, including races on weekends. Our family vacations took us to local and national regattas throughout the Midwest. To be successful in sailing, the skipper has to sweat the details—preparing the boat and rigging, reading the wind and waves, trimming the sails for maximum efficiency and speed, and keeping a keen eye on the competition. I learned that I can't win by following the pack. Sometimes taking calculated risks was necessary to break away from the pack to get ahead and win. Over the years, I earned national titles in the Butterfly class as Women's Single-Handed champion twice and qualified for the Inter-Collegiate Sailing Association (ICSA) Women's Regatta

in 1995. This attention to detail and thrill of competition continues to drive me."

Jennifer always loved math. During the summer, she enrolled in a local summer school where she continued learning math concepts during her break. Jennifer had two influential math teachers, John Grandin and Linda Hageman. They shared their love and passion for math, and both were instrumental in helping Jennifer find ways to apply it. As she progressed through high school, her parents set up a shadowing opportunity with a family friend, Mike Walter, who introduced her to engineering.

Her first engineering experience was during her studies at Marquette University, where she was a co-op engineer at Scott Paper Company in Oshkosh, Wisconsin. Jennifer took great satisfaction in her contributions to improving the efficiency of the production lines. She also enjoyed the challenges of a special assignment related to an Environmental Protection Agency (EPA) regulation for volatile organic compounds (VOCs). The assignment involved comprehending the regulatory requirements, meeting with local regulators, developing methods to track facility VOCs, and submitting annual documentation. This was her first exposure to government regulatory requirements, and she gained a better understanding of the impact that manufacturing can have on the environment.

During her junior and senior years at Marquette University, she joined the Society of Automotive Engineers (SAE) and participated in the SAE formula team. This was her first experience in vehicle development—designing a vehicle to specific requirements, building, testing, and performing at an annual race against other universities. She loved working on a team, the satisfaction of designing a vehicle from the ground up, and the thrill of racing. In 1995, Jennifer earned her bachelor of science in mechanical engineering.

After graduation, she learned about an opening for a components engineer at Mercury Marine's Performance Craft Division. This start-up division was in Oshkosh, Wisconsin, but would soon relocate to a manufacturing facility in her hometown of Hartford, Wisconsin. She engineered parts for two-passenger and three-passenger personal watercraft and a larger jet boat. She was one of the early engineers hired in this start-up division, which grew to more than one hundred. Like many start-ups, there was more work to do than people to do it. Job descriptions were ambiguous, and there were plenty of opportunities to stretch beyond our typical responsibilities. She notes, "We brainstormed and anticipated what needed to happen next, and with few people, we jumped in to get it done. The Performance Craft culture was an 'It's on me' culture." She helped develop a master timing plan for the programs, including validation and test cycles where the watercraft were tested in Placida, Florida. Working in a small team meant that she worked closely with creative designers, purchasing, quality, finance, manufacturing, validation, and production. Jennifer was responsible for a wide range of components, including seating, bumpers, and wiring. During her time at Mercury, she developed a love of the complexity of vehicle development. In late 1997, personal watercraft sales continued to decline, and the Brunswick Corporation dissolved the Mercury Performance Craft Division. Jennifer was offered a position to remain at Mercury Marine but instead took this opportunity to look for a new challenge.

In 1998, Jennifer joined the Saturn Corporation as an advanced manufacturing engineer for the chassis and engine on a team developing the Saturn L Series. This was her first experience working on a global team where the engineers at Opel International Technical Development Center (ITDC) reengineered the Opel Vectra to meet the US federal requirements. Within weeks of joining the team, she traveled to Wilmington Assembly in Delaware and Opel ITDC in Germany. She joined at the start of the Integration Vehicle Build. It was a hands-on learning experience as she learned the build process and design aspects of the chassis and power train. She learned to rely on the technical experts and the importance of asking, "Why?," about everything from component designs to system designs to build processes. Her contributions to the team were recognized, and she was offered her first international assignment in 1999. As a Product Development Team (PDT) assistant for chassis and power train engineering teams, she was responsible for ensuring quick resolution of production concerns and smooth transition of the engine and chassis parts to Saturn. Success in this role was largely based on her ability to see issues from different perspectives, find the common ground, and ensure timely implementation of the resolution.

Jennifer returned to Saturn in 2000, increasing her scope as a general assembly manufacturing integration manager for Wilmington Assembly. She led several advanced manufacturing planning studies, where she prepared the estimates for manufacturing tooling and investment for Current Product, Mid-Cycle Enhancements, and Future Vehicles. Jennifer spent multiple years representing production assembly plants and now sought an opportunity to work hands-on at a production plant. In 2002, she began as a first-line supervisor at Pontiac Assembly Center, learning the ins and outs of production throughput, first-time quality, and production assembly workers. She learned firsthand the direct impact a design or system had on their production line capability, and developed a keen sense of urgency because their performance was measured in real time. Using her experience as an advanced manufacturing engineer, she called on design release engineers to come to the production line to discuss design changes that would improve throughput, quality, or both. During this time, Jennifer went to school part time and graduated with her master of science in engineering from Purdue University in 2004.

In 2004, Jennifer accepted a special assignment as the GM program manager for SAE International's A World in Motion (AWIM). This was a program developed by the SAE International with financial support from the GM Foundation. Using her firsthand experience of developing standardized work, she led a team to develop a six-session classroom guide for GM volunteers to more efficiently bring AWIM into classrooms with minimal time commitment and streamlined training preparation. Her efforts in metro Detroit expanded beyond GM volunteers and included volunteers from many companies throughout southeastern Michigan. In Jennifer's prior assignment, she learned that the assembly plants looked for the opportunity to contribute to the communities where they lived and work, so she kicked off the GM Assembly Plant AWIM initiative, providing joint on-site training for volunteers and teachers. Jennifer also worked directly with the school districts to integrate AWIM into their school curriculums. She also created the GM Affinity Group AWIM initiative, recruiting and training volunteers from GM's diversity teams. During this time, she grew the GM volunteer base from about 200 to more than 750 nationwide.

Jennifer's involvement in SAE International's A World in Motion program was an opportunity to reengage with the SAE. She rejoined SAE International and served as the vice chair and a member of the Math & Science K–12 (kindergarten–grade 12) Committee from 2004 to 2006. Her involvement in the SAE Detroit Section continued even after her AWIM assignment ended. At the Detroit Section, Jennifer served on the Younger Members Committee (2007–2010) and the Section Governing Board (2005–2010 and 2014–2016). Jennifer's involvement in the Detroit Section exposed her to more opportunities to get involved in SAE International. She served as the chair of the Pre-College Education Committee (2009–2011), the Education Board (2010–2012), the Membership Board (2015–2017), the AWIM Awards Committee (2014–present), the Fellows Nominating Committee (2017–present), the SAE Foundation through the Women's Giving Circle (2010–2014), and the Sustainer's Club (2007–present) and is funding a STEM scholarship in her name recognizing Excellence in Engineering Education and Service to Others.

In 2006, Jennifer returned to engineering as the Issue Resolution Team (IRT) cochair for the Electrical Subject Matter Team (SMT). While she was formally trained as a mechanical engineer, many of the electrical challenges faced were related to mechanical or system integration issues. Her mentor encouraged her to take on the stretch assignment where she could use her prior knowledge of integration, manufacturing, and problem-solving. This was her first experience working with high-voltage systems on the full-size truck and utility 2-Mode Hybrid vehicles.

In 2008, Jennifer had an opportunity to join the Vehicle Dynamics Center as a handling specialist at GM's Milford Proving Ground. In this role, she worked with the GM-Korea team in completing correlation studies on the Chevrolet Orlando. This involved completing and sharing test data with the GM-Korea team as they brought their new Cheongna Proving Ground (CPG) on board.

In late 2008, GM began growing their high-energy storage

systems team. Jennifer had experience with high voltage from the 2-Mode Hybrid, so they asked her to join the team. She worked closely with the Volt battery team on reconfigurations for other vehicle applications. She contributed to the development and documentation of pack-level wiring standards and designs, including the low-voltage signal wiring to the high-voltage bus bars and battery disconnect unit.

This was about the time of the economic downturn. The automotive industry and southeastern Michigan were going through a difficult time, and many people found themselves unemployed. Jennifer was approached by Terry Woychowski to actualize a concept. Terry proposed we retrain laid-off engineers in a growth area—advanced propulsion—through a trilateral partnership with General Motors, Michigan Technological University, and the Engineering Society of Detroit. On December 23, 2008, Jennifer led the first cross-functional team meeting, where they laid out the plan to create a three-credit course for the spring 2009 semester, covering many aspects of advanced propulsion, from energy storage systems, power train controls, and various hybrid systems to the hands-on use of development and calibration tools and methods. Michigan Technological University provided full scholarships to forty students (all unemployed engineers in southeastern Michigan), the Engineering Society of Detroit donated the use of its new training facility in Southfield for lectures, and General Motors provided a hands-on laboratory experience for the students at the Milford Proving Ground and at the Road Load Simulator in Pontiac. The first class was held on February 5, introducing students to these new technologies and, more importantly, giving them hope. Many of the participants found employment in this emerging field and still cite this course as a turning point for their careers. In fall 2009, Michigan Tech expanded the course by offering a multicourse certification for both on- and off-campus students and now offers a comprehensive Hybrid Electric Vehicle (HEV) curriculum.

In late 2009, Jennifer was offered a special assignment in the office of the vice chairman. She was responsible for working with speechwriters, ensuring the technical accuracy of all internal and external written and verbal communications. In this assignment, Jennifer led the coordination of technical fact-checking to support the Investor Relations team responsible for the initial public offering (IPO) following GM's bankruptcy. She was one of few GM employees recognized for their contributions to GM's successful IPO.

In 2011, Jennifer's special assignment ended, and she was ready for a new challenge. She was offered the opportunity to move to Seoul, South Korea, as the vehicle line director for the Spark EV (Battery Electric Vehicle Gen 1), which was GM's reentry into the electric-vehicle market. In this role, it was her responsibility to ensure that the program achieved customer and market requirements while meeting corporate financial objectives. The program was on track, and in mid-2012 Jennifer was asked to be the chief engineer for the Chevrolet Bolt (Battery Electric Vehicle Gen 2).

She led the team to develop the Chevrolet Bolt, which was GM's first unique EV architecture intended to be sold nationwide and in many global markets. As the chief engineer, Jennifer was responsible for bridging the "voice of the customer" with technical execution of the Bolt while delivering a great customer experience. The Chevrolet Bolt set a new benchmark for affordable, long-range EV driving and went on to receive multiple awards, including the 2017 *Motor Trend* Car of the Year, the 2017 North American Car of the Year, and an *Automobile Magazine* 2017 All-Star, and was listed in *Time* magazine's Best 25 Inventions of 2016. It is now one of GM's most-awarded vehicles.

In 2014, Jennifer returned to the US to lead the Global Accessories team. She treated this role much like running a small business within the broader GM business. Jennifer was responsible for ensuring that GM Accessories meet all engineering, program, and financial objectives. She reported quarterly to a global governing board including the president of GM (Dan Ammann, who now leads Cruise), several functional vice presidents, and the regional

The first Spark EV was distributed in three states. *General Motors*

The Milford Proving Ground featured many surfaces. *General Motors*

managing directors. To better integrate the accessories team globally, she created the Accessory Global Summit to align all GM regions (Europe, South America, China, and International Operations) in growing the Accessory business. Under her leadership the Accessories team grew in head count, filed multiple patents, doubled their net sales, and significantly improved on-time accessory availability at the start of production for new programs.

In November 2016, Jennifer returned to the electrification team as the chief engineer for China Electrification. She rejoined the GM-Korea engineering team and was responsible for production execution of a new Buick Velite 7 (B121) for China and a Chevrolet Bolt EUV (C121) for the US and other global markets. In October 2018, she was assigned as chief engineer for the BEV3 (Battery Electric Vehicle Gen 3), a unique electric-vehicle architecture codeveloped with GM's joint venture partner in China, Pan Asia Technical Automotive Center (PATAC).

Jennifer made contributions to a number of programs: Saturn L Series (launch and midcycle), GMT800 full-size truck, GMT900 full-size truck, GMT900 full-size 2-Mode Utility, GMT900 full-size 2-Mode truck, Chevrolet Orlando (sold in Korea), Chevrolet Spark EV, Chevrolet Bolt EV, Chevrolet Bolt EUV, Buick Velite 7(Gen 2.5 China), to be announced, and several future electric vehicles based on the BEV3 architecture, to be announced.

In 2020, Jennifer returned to the US from China. She was promoted to executive director of global aftersales engineering and service operations in 2022 after serving 1.5 years as global aftersales director of mechanical engineering.

Until recently, Jennifer resided in Shanghai with her husband, Jeff, a GM retiree, and their daughter, Kathleen Claire ("K.C."). K.C. was born in Seoul, South Korea, in 2011, while Jennifer and Jeff were on assignment at GM-Korea. Jennifer enjoys traveling and has visited more than fifty countries. Since K.C. was born, they have visited more than nineteen countries and multiple states, including Alaska and Hawaii, as a family. In her spare time, Jennifer enjoys golfing, playing the piano, and scuba diving. She has logged more than two hundred dives and is a PADI-certified rescue diver.

Last, we commend Jennifer for her charitable activities. She notes, "My philanthropic values were directly influenced by the strong example set by my parents, Kurt and Maureen. They are lifelong volunteers within their community and continue to be great role models to me. No matter how busy they are, they always find the time to give back to the community through financial contributions and volunteerism."

Jennifer has been an active member of the SAE International, the SAE Detroit Section, and the SAE Foundation for more than twenty-five years. She has held multiple leadership positions, including Detroit Section chair and governing board member; SAE International Education Board chair; Pre-College Education Committee chair; Membership Board member; Fellows Nominating Committee member; and SAE Foundation Women's Giving Circle and Sustainer's Club. Jennifer continues sharing her love of STEM education with local elementary school students as an SAE International A World In Motion volunteer.

Jennifer has received several awards, including SAE International Distinguished Younger Member (2008), SAE International Significant Contributions to AWIM (2006), SAE Detroit Section Outstanding Younger Member (2007), SAE Detroit Section Outstanding AWIM Contributions (2006), and the Red Cross Certificate of Merit National Life Saving Award, signed by President George H. W. Bush (1988).

The Buick Velite 7 was developed at the GM Technical Development Center in South Korea. *GM Korea*

Jennifer has traveled extensively with the corporation; her daughter was born in South Korea. *Jennifer Goforth*

Courtesy Jessica Hettinger

JESSICA HETTINGER

My role at home is to be the mother of three children and inspire them to believe they can do anything they work hard to achieve. My role at General Motors is to be an inspiring leader and a change agent.

—Jessica Hettinger (b. 1978)

CAREER HIGHLIGHTS

Jessica Hettinger started her career with General Motors as a co-op student at the GM Metal Fabrication Plant in Parma, Ohio, in 1997. She started full time with GM at the Pontiac Center Point Engineering Campus in 2002 as a body structures validation engineer. She held various positions in the engineering organization, growing her technical and leadership skills.

Jessie co-owns and helps manage Hettinger Motorsports and Katie Hettinger Racing.

BIOGRAPHICAL NOTES

Jessie Hettinger was born and raised in Olmsted Falls, Ohio. She attended Fitch Elementary School and Olmsted Falls Middle and High Schools. Hettinger was a four-year letterman in women's soccer, played slow- and fast-pitch softball, and was also a black belt in karate.

Her job throughout high school was that of a karate instructor at New World Karate in Berea, Ohio. She trained under Jerry Roberts and competed in point-sparring events all over the United States with the NASKA and MBL sanctioning bodies. She was a member of the Five Knuckle Bullet point-fighting competition team. Hettinger was the women's advanced-belt national champion in 1994 and won the women's black-belt world title in sparring at the Arnold Classic in Columbus, Ohio, in 1999. Hettinger is a strong believer that sports are so important to help teach young people the value of hard work, leadership, and cooperation in a team atmosphere.

Her passion for engineering stemmed from two origins: her father, Jack Prest, and her great uncle, William Agnew. For most of her life, Hettinger's dad owned an auto body shop in North Olmsted, Ohio. It was a family business, with Jessie's mom, Terry Prest, working in the office. Jessie spent lots of time at the body shop and developed an appreciation for cars and all things mechanical.

When she was fourteen years old, the family made the trip from Ohio up to Romeo, Michigan, to visit her granduncle Bill Agnew and his family for Thanksgiving (Agnew worked at General Motors Research Laboratories for thirty-seven years as a researcher, department head, and technical director, and he died in 2020). During that visit, he took Jessie and her father on a tour of the General Motors R&D Center in Warren, Michigan. He also shared stories of work he had done for GM as well as the US Army. It was during that trip that Jessie knew she wanted to become an engineer. Jessie decided to attend GMI Engineering and Management Institute (Kettering University). As a co-op student, she started her career at the GM Metal Fabrication plant in Parma, Ohio. She worked at the plant for two years and then transferred to the General Motors Milford Proving Ground in Milford, Michigan, to pursue her passion in vehicle safety.

When she graduated in 2002 as a first-generation college grad, Jessie worked as a structures validation engineer. She continued her education and, in 2007, obtained her master's degree in mechanical engineering from Purdue University.

She subsequently moved about every two years to a different position, including CAE structures engineer, dimensional systems engineer, designing engineer, and engineering business manager for Structures and Exterior, supporting Jim Hentschel and John Calabrese.

Jessie had the prodigious opportunity to be the lead structures design release engineer for the ATS-V, CTS-V, and ATS Coupe. She led the structures development for those programs from the early stages of the program in the Advanced Vehicle Design space all the way through to the launch of the vehicles at the Lansing Grand River Plant in Lansing, Michigan. It was such a rewarding experience to be able to follow a program all the way through the development cycle. One of the most memorable experiences was being able to do back-to-back rides with the ride and handling engineer at Milford, comparing the base ATS with the ATS-V, which included the bracing package that Jessie developed. It was exhilarating to feel the difference the bracing package made on the ride and handling of the vehicle.

Jessie entered her first leadership position as the Engineering Group manager for sealers and adhesives in 2013, where her team was responsible for the structural adhesive and paint shop sealer applied to all vehicles worldwide. Her team worked to ensure that corrosion and sealing requirements were met. Jessie also led a work group focused on new joining methods for mixed-material vehicles such as the Cadillac CT6. She leaped at the chance to be the business planning manager for Ken Kelzer, the vice president of Global Vehicle Components and Sub-Systems. Among other assignments, Jessie helped lead the office transformation at the Warren Technical Center and facilitated the executive leadership move into an open office environment. It was a pivotal point in the transformation at GM. The company was initiating the Autonomous Vehicle programs; pursuing a vision of zero crashes, zero emissions, and zero congestion; and changing the culture of the company under CEO Mary Barra's leadership.

Hettinger was then promoted to senior manager of the interior design engineering organization, leading a team of interior designers. A year later, she also took over the senior managerial position for the chassis design engineering organization, leading a team of over five hundred designers. During that time, she was able to initiate a culture change in the organization and used design thinking to develop and implement a new work-remote policy, allowing employees to work remotely up to two days a week.

Her PRW Performance Center chassis with a Harrington Enforcer engine is good for about 425 hp. *Molly Helmuth / 9D Creative*

Hettinger was the recipient of GM's Working Mother of the Year Award for 2019. She attended *Working Mother* magazine's WorkBeyond Summit in New York City with her husband, Chris, and was honored at the gala.

Hettinger recently transitioned to the role of senior manager for body and exterior validation. She is getting back to her roots in the body structures area and is looking forward to learning and growing in her new role.

Hettinger met Chris while attending GMI. They were married in 2004 and reside in Dryden, Michigan. They have three children, Katelyn, Grace, and Keith. Together, they own and manage Hettinger Motorsports and Katie Hettinger Racing. Jessie is very involved with her children's extracurricular activities. She has coached travel softball and is the coleader for her younger daughter Grace's Girl Scout troop. She loves to teach the girls about STEM and has worked hard to instill in her girls the same things her parents instilled in her: girls can do anything they set their minds to!

Her daughter Katie is a third-generation race car driver and is currently part of the GMS Driver Development program, working her way up in the stock car world. Hettinger's father-in-law, Jim Hettinger, was a well-known Midget driver in the Midwest and was inducted into the Michigan Motorsports Hall of Fame in 1994. Hettinger spent many years helping her husband work on his race cars throughout his twenty-year-plus racing career. He raced Midgets, sprint cars, modifieds, and super-late models. Hettinger's daughter Katie started racing Quarter Midgets at the age of five. She would say, "When I turn five and become a boy, I'm going to race cars too." Hettinger quickly informed her that girls can race cars too!

"When I turn five and become a boy, I'm going to race cars too."

In 2016, the younger Hettinger daughter moved to Junior Sprints on dirt, racing in Indiana and Jackson, Michigan. In 2017–2018, she drove a 600 cc Micro Sprint on dirt and made the jump to a full-size stock car on pavement in 2019. In 2020 Katie became the first female champion in any CRA division by winning the Jr. Late Model Championship. The year 2021 will see Katie racing a full-size late-model stock and pro-late model in North Carolina, powered by a Chevy 602 and 604 Crate motor. The engines produce about 400–450 hp and reach top speeds around 100 mph. Jessie Hettinger's main focus on the team at this time is helping coach her young driver, guide her with social media engagement, do interviews, and sponsor interactions.

In addition, Jessie Hettinger has been the GM Women's Employee Resource Group president for the Global Product Development team for the past two years. In this role, she leads a group of women that facilitate events and activities to increase engagement and development for the women of General Motors.

Yan Huang sits conformably in the interior of Centieme show, which she designed. *PATAC / GM China*

YAN-HONG HUANG (YAN)

I always find my ability to adapt to different environments is the key to my success.[1]
—Yan Huang

CAREER HIGHLIGHTS

Yan Huang, a product of the Chinese school system, was largely trained as a fine artist before discovering the field of industrial design. When her talents were uncovered, her "accidental career" as a global automotive interior designer, which took her to Australia (Holden), the United States (the GM Technical Center), and Italy (Bertone), was launched.

Her portfolio includes numerous spectacular concept and production vehicles. Her design work for the experimental aXcess Australia and Razorback truck led to her contributions to the Daewoo Matiz and Indonesian Maleo for Millard Design.

Huang would later contribute to the Buick XP2000; the groundbreaking Chinese Qilin concept; an Australian version of the Buick Park Avenue designed for China; the Buick Centieme concept; the Buick Excelle concept; production Buick LaCrosse, Sail, and Lucerne cars; the Chevrolet Malibu; and the Cadillac XTS, among others.

After a nineteen-year stint in the automotive industry, Huang teaches part time in the industrial design program at RMIT. An entrepreneur, she has recently established Yandesign

with the support of her husband, to exhibit and sell her sculpture, jewelry, and glass collages. In 2017, her fine arts were featured at the Gallery in Australia. In recent times, she has created indoor gardens.

YAN HUANG'S JOURNEY

Born in Xiamen, China, Yan Huang is the daughter of Huang Da-fu (father) and Huang Shu-qin. She attributes her problem-solving skills to her father, who had served as a production plant manager of a large state-owned rubber manufacturer. He was the go-to person when there were any problems or issues at the plant. Even after retirement, he repaired bicycles, clocks, and even sophisticated electronics.

Huang's interests in art began early. While her parents worked, her grandmother looked on as she covered the walls with her drawings. She enjoyed creating things on paper. As a high school student, she had a clear vision of what she wanted to do, and trained in an after-school art class to prepare for the university entrance exam in 1985. She received the highest score, and this led to her acceptance to Xiamen University.

Huang notes that the four years of art education were the "best years of my life."[2] Majoring in oil painting, she painted day and night. She fell in love with the Dutch masters and the grand portraits of Rembrandt. Huang learned techniques from the impressionists. She also focused on the landscapes of Claude Monet and the vibrant-colored canvases of Alfred Sisley. When she completed her studies, Huang was invited to study English in Australia but had to forgo her graduation certificate in order to do so. Because the Chinese government had paid for her university education, she could not travel overseas unless she worked for them for five years first. She notes, "For me, coming to Australia was a bridge to see the Western world, a chance to see the original impressionists' work."[3]

Huang arrived at the Language Center at La Trobe University in January 1989 to pursue a six-month course in English. At the completion of her studies, she searched for a university with undergraduate fine-arts courses. She found some of the programs lacking and not worth the $14,000 she would have to pay per year of her hard-earned money.

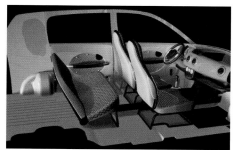
QiLin *Courtesy Yan-Hong Huang*

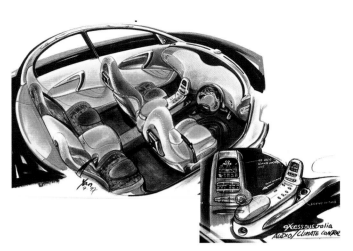

The Australian aXcess came complete with manufacturer's parts. *Yan Huang*

Ian Wong

As an alternative, Huang discovered an Industrial Design program offered by the public Royal Melbourne Institute of Technology (later, RMIT University, created from its 1992 merger with the Phillip Institute of Technology). While she was ahead of others with her drawing skills, she learned about creative thinking, materials, model making, and problem solving.

After her third semester, she met lecturer Wayne Draper, an ex-Ford design chief. He was a "great guy" and inspired her to take up automobile design in her final year as a major, emphasizing that women designers were needed. Under his guidance, Huang designed and made a full-size clay instrument panel with her classmates for her graduation project and received a BA in Industrial Design in 1994. She notes, "I won an internship with Ford and got a job with Millard Design as an automotive designer."

PURELY AUTOMOTIVE

Yan Huang has contributed to the design of concept and production cars, amassing a portfolio of significant designs before and after joining General Motors. As a principal designer for Millard Design, which GM later acquired, she contributed to the aXcess Australia concept car exhibited in 1998, the Daewoo Matiz, the Indonesian Maleo, and the VW Razorback drop-bed pickup truck.

AUSTRALIAN AXCESS

The Australian aXcess concept originated from an idea developed by Gary Millard in the early 1990s to produce a one-off custom motor car to showcase the skills and design of Australia's automotive industry. Huang worked on the design of the instrument panel and contributed to the innovative interior. The aXcess also introduced or featured an advanced orbital engine, sequentially electric interlocking clam shell doors, a carbon-fibre and magnesium frame, carbon fibre body panels, solar roof panels, Autoliv buckets, a unique VDO slim line steering column, airbags, satellite navigation, and so forth.

This was joint initiative of a group that included federal departments, state governments, and support from 130 independent components manufacturers and designers. The car later received rave reviews at the SAE (Society of Automotive Engineers) International Congress in Detroit and from critics in ten other countries. Along with the aXcess Hybrid Low Emission Vehicle, this concept was donated to the Museums Victoria.

DAEWOO MATIZ

The Matiz was a show car unveiled at the 1997 Seoul Automobile Show. Huang was part of the multi-disciplinary team responsible for the interior.

MALEO

Indonesia sought to have a national car of its own built from scratch. Utilizing a three-cylinder, 1200 cc engine likely from the Orbital Engine Corporation, the Maleo project was initiated in 1993. Millard Design was contracted to assist with the design.

Huang worked with a multi-disciplinary team to build six working prototypes for this production car which was made from 1997 to 1998.

The venture ended abruptly as funds were reassigned to another project.

VW RAZORBACK TRUCK

Huang also contributed to the design of the Razorback truck, a vehicle marketed to farmers. The Razorback pickup, a product of Australia's Razorback Vehicle Corporation, featured an innovative floor and tailgate that dropped down flat to the ground so loads and smaller vehicles could be loaded or driven right onto the floor. The truck incorporated a special rear axle and U-shaped chassis mounted behind a VW truck cab. The electro-hydraulic pumps built into the sides raised and lowered the floor. A disabling switch was incorporated to shut the system down when the load was too heavy.

JOINT VENTURE AT THE SHANGHAI-PAN ASIA TECHNICAL AUTOMOTIVE CENTER FOR GM CHINA

Huang worked at the PATAC design studio in 1998-1999; she was hired by GM as a design consultant, working for PATAC on an eight-month contract.

She was there supporting then Design Director Phillip Zmooth and worked on the first ever Chinese show car called Qilin which featured an all fiberglass body (B2B - back to basic vehicle). This was one of GM's advanced research projects and was used to train this newly established design and engineering team. Training on the job. Huang helped to guide the first car design team in China, of about 20 people. Many of them now are the design directors of major car companies in China including PATAC design director Min Cao and Huang Bin.

It should be noted that PATAC is a joint venture of General Motors with the former Shanghai Automotive Industry Corporation.

This entry level show car was designed to provide affordable basic transportation for the hip gearhead. In order to appeal to the emotional side, it was today's cool—fun and colorful.

With low labor costs in this era, the car was an experiment with the use of fiberglass. Of course, in the United States, the first series of fiberglass Corvette concepts was unveiled in 1952. Fiberglass parts, which were fabricated using a mold, allowed the designers to explore three-dimensionally. The instrument panel relied on basic shapes including round gauges and air vents. To make the vehicle even more versatile, a flat floor and foldable seats were included.

BUICK XP2000

The most famous Holden product to ever wear a Buick badge is the Chinese-market Park Avenue, a concept car never produced. In 1995, GM apparently planned to use the VT Commodore architecture as the basis for a new Buick sedan, previewed in the XP2000 concept.

Upon receiving her assignment, Huang noted, "It's intimidating to walk into a large design studio full of men. I was the only female in the design studio, but soon I forgot about the gender difference, I had so much fun creating the interior for my first project—the XP2000 show car."

Huang loved sketching, refining an idea, working to build a show car from a sketch, interfacing with engineers, clay sculptors, fabricators, etc. Huang had to prove she could give direction and

overcome an attempt to sabotage the progress of her project.

By 1999, Huang was offered a position at the GM Technical Center in Warren, Michigan.

ADVANCED DESIGN STUDIO

After the initial culture and weather shock, Huang joined 120 other designers at the GM Technical Center. She was assigned to the Advanced Design studio speed division. The chief designer, Ed Welburn, would later ascend to the position of VP of Design. The studio was equipped with the latest computer design technology, a huge screen to project the designer's work from their PC, a music sound system that played music selected by the designers. It was exciting to go to work daily in this great environment.

Huang worked on design concepts for all brands until she realized that these designs would never reach production. Not able to follow her designs into the final stages of preparation for production became unbearable. Huang made her move the Buick Brand studio.

BUICK CENTIEME

As early as 2001, Buick sought to attract younger customers which included those with families. This resulted in the introduction of the Buick Rendezvous in the spring of 2001 as a 2002. Sharing platforms or running gear with the Pontiac Aztek, Montana and Chevrolet Venture, the crossover came in all flavors from CX to CXL offering supple leather and mahogany along the way. This roomy family hauler was equipped with large commercial-like side view mirrors and other safety features attractive to drivers. A nicely loaded FWD Rendezvous (it also came in AWD) when Buick ended its manufacture in 2007 could be acquired for around $15,000—far less than its Japanese competitors.

While the Rendezvous sold well, by 2007, Buick followed up with its pricier and more luxurious Enclave with its standard mahogany trimmed instrument panel.

The Centieme concept car was futuristic. *Courtesy of Yan Huang*

When Buick's Anniversary centennial celebration was anticipated, it was decided that a special crossover, which would attract even more attention from younger customers, was to be designed in America and built by Style Bertone in Italy.

Whereas there was no Nuccio Bertone, Giorgetto Guigiaro, or Franco Scaglione on site, Gary War, the exterior designer whose design was selected to go forward, was likely familiar with the prize-winning Cistalia 202 GT (now owned by the MoMA), the Bertone BATS, and the Alfa Romeo 6C 2500 Grand Racer and their curvaceous fronts. His exceptional ideas for the Buick futuristic concept would roll out as the handsome Buick Centieme. Yan notes, "The project was a celebration of Buick 100 year's anniversary. It is one of the very first SUVs for Buick. A vision looks forward to the future with the awareness of its rich past."

In 2002, Huang's design won the competition for the interior of the Buick Centieme. Perhaps creating its "futuristic" inside was even more challenging than its exterior design. According to Huang, "a vision looks forward to the future with the awareness of its rich past." She designed the elegant interior "to have smooth soft overall flow lines incorporating a simple oval-shaped instrument panel, head up displays, jewelry-like gauges and controls, tailored soft leather trim, Buick branded purses on seatbacks, seating controls, sliding consoles and a drink holder. The full LED lit panel on the roof provided the feeling of openness".

Huang pointed out that all the competitors' vehicles and concept cars were showing a lot of buttons for the radio and climate control system, to make them appear high-tech. Given Buick's customer base (averaging over 70 years), she believed this brand should promote understated technology—a "quiet servant," where all the latest technology is logically designed and simplified so it is intuitive. Minimum switches—only the basics like sound, favorite stations, temperature, and fan speed—need control and should be big and easy to see. The three main knobs—temperature, volume, and radio station—were flush when pushed in and slid out for easy access. Safety features should be built in and automatic.

"I made the gauges look like fine classic watches with jewel like details, added Yan. "The instrument panel used dark color with contrast light stitching, large decorative brush stainless steel insert and nice sculptured walnut timber." The Centieme interior was designed for maximum comfort with luxurious touches; the four front seats all have lighter and softer colors, integrated armrests like sofas at home, and powered seating adjustment with memory.

In addition, Yan's vision included the backs of the two front seats held Buick brand tailor-made handbags which the customer could remove for shopping and clip back onto the seats afterward, 7" DVD displays with remove control under the armrests, a center console that moved forward and back with a push of button, built in wine and glass storage, a flat floor for easy movement between seats, and a headliner that lit up with soft ambient lighting.

The show car was well received at the 2003 Detroit Auto show. A milestone for the Buick centennial, the handsome Centieme set the design direction for the stunning production upscale Buick Enclave.

PARK AVENUE

As GM worked to better establish PATAC, Yan Huang was asked by Ed Welburn (or David Lyon under him) to oversee the design of a much larger Buick Park Avenue with a vendor—the Australian arm of Venture. Burt Wong was also on staff. While the upscale American version of the Buick Park Avenue measured 206 inches in length, it was not selected for use here. The Australian version of Commodore VE, which also led to a longer Park Avenue, was chosen for this project.

While the instrument panel and door structure of the Commodore VE was retained, the inside was retrimmed and the new rear seating structure was designed and built to create leg room. The responsibility and success for this design rested largely on Huang's shoulders.

The new instrument panel was luxurious and flowed into the door to create a feeling of roominess. Even today, Katherine Sirvio, a Chevrolet Executive, notes that the latest Spark relies on this integration to create a spacious feeling. The design provided closed storage.

The new seating structure addressed the need for extra space and comfort and featured heavily padded leather seats assembled with French or deck seams. The larger panels of leather added to the quality of the interior. The larger rear seats inclined and the added legroom a requirement. JCI—Johnson Controls International—the seating supplier was praised.

With close supervision from upper management, the designers provided a new Park Avenue for the elite in China in a very short period of time. However, this entry lost popularity in the marketplace when the Chinese Governments posed a price restriction on the allowance of official vehicles after the car was released. This made the car expensive to the very customer it sought to target.

LACROSSE

It was the end of the line for the mid-sized Buick Century and Regal. Huang was assigned to the Buick Lacrosse. Debuting in 2004, the first generation of the model was offered from 2005 to 2009 in CX, CXL and CXS levels. Buick marketers relied on coated steel—called Quiet Steel—which appeared to eliminate NVH (noise, vibration, and harshness).

GM China

GM China

LUCERNE

Huang was later appointed lead designer for the Buick Lucerne.

She is said to have drastically changed the face of Buick by introducing soft-touch materials and appealing to a younger customer.

From 2007 to 2010, she coordinated the design development of the Chevrolet Malibu across three global regions and delivered a vehicle that was designed and engineered to be sold in 100 countries.

By 2010, she was appointed Chief Designer for Interior Components at PATAC in Shanghai, China. By 2012, she accepted the position Design Manager of Holden's Advanced Design Department.

At Holden, Huang provided novel interior concepts for Buick, GMC and Cadillac. She contributed to the 2014 Buick Lacrosse interior, the 2014 Buick Excelle, the 2014 Cadillac STX rear infotainment system.

THE 2013 MALIBU

Through the years, there is no question that the handsome Chevrolet Malibu, introduced in 1964, has monopolized the mid-sized segment. The 7th generation Malibu was unveiled in 2008, and the 8th generation unveiled at automobile shows in New York and Shanghai in 2011 and offered for sale as a 2013. Perhaps this model and the Impala have received more accolades for both styling and design than any other Chevrolet offerings. The 2013 Malibu Eco was the most fuel-efficient ever, and all Malibus, equipped with 10 standard airbags and a rearview camera, were the first 2013 models to earn a 5-star rating from the National Highway Traffic Safety Administration. This 8th generation model was designed to be offered in nearly 100 countries and on six continents. This would mean that the cars would have to meet the needs of residents from Uzbekistan, Sydney, Sao Paulo, New York among others around the globe.

Yan Huang arrived in Michigan at the General Motors Technical Center in 1999 where she remained until 2012. It should be noted that she had other temporary assignments during this time period before being assigned to the Malibu project around 2007. When her design for the 8th generation Malibu was chosen to go forward, she was promoted to Design Manager under the supervision of Crystal Windham, director of mid-sized interior design. Ed Welburn was Vice President of Design at this time and has since retired. There is no question that the threat of bankruptcy at the end of the decade would eventually limit promotions and induce early retirements.

Before the Malibu was fully distributed, Huang joined GM's joint venture team (PATAC Shanghai) to manage the interior component design team in order to tweak elements in order to address Chinese market preferences.

HUANG FACES HER BIGGEST CHALLENGE

Huang notes that the design for the 8th generation Malibu was the biggest challenge she would ever face. Due in part to the requirement to include 10 air bags and the preference to include larger and larger touch screens, the design, and the manufacture of the interior of an automobile became far more complex than ever before.

There were many parameters which Huang had no control over affecting the project. Huang noted that as the competition between manufacturers became fierce, cost and manufacturing efficiency became even more important. A world car needed to be cost-effective wherever it was being manufactured.

Furthermore, it was not easy to get a consensus from around the world to be able to prioritize features. Whatever design she proposed had to work equally well for right-hand and left-hand drive. Global conferences almost daily could keep her busy 24 hours a day. Among other things, Huang learned the language of marketing, engineering, manufacturing, safety, cost, and finance. Perhaps nothing short of a miracle, after four years of development, she managed to preserve her initial design theme.

The spectacular interior features the duel cockpit that Chevrolet cars are noted for and that are standard in sports cars like the Corvette—perhaps this was the only given. In an early article posted by Holden, Huang explained, "The use of materials . . . plays an important role in delivering an interior with a premium feel."

As priorities fluctuated internationally, Huang designed the center console over and over. She would later return to China to make changes. The production design incorporated chrome and decorative wood accents around the shifter.

The 8th generation Malibu was wider than its predecessor offering nearly four cubic feet of interior space more. The interior featured a number of storage areas including—surprise—a radio face that lifted up to reveal a six-inch deep bin behind this seven-inch touch screen. There is a pocket to house a mobile phone, and cup holders on the doors, in the console and on the rear seat armrest.

It is also notable that the introduction of the Malibu Eco which relied on eAssist, a cut-off system and regenerative braking, delivered impressively high fuel mileage at less cost than hybrid power plants.

Huang's team designed everything. *GM China/PATAC*

THE SAIL

Huang went back to PATAC again from 2010 to 2012 to help set up the interior component design studio. The Sail was one of the small car interior projects her team was responsible for; they designed everything inside – the steering wheel, cluster gauge, center stack HVAC, audio and infotainment system and

seating. Most importantly, they set up the sharing strategy and did the design for all interior components to be used across different architectural platforms. The PATAC interior component team is responsible for all the GM and SGM interiors - Buick, Cadillac, Chevy, Sail and Rover.

GLOBAL CONFERENCING

The ultimate goal is to satisfy the customers; they want to see where their money is being spent. However, the decisions made must meet everyone's needs.

When it comes to globalization, it is important to note that

Huang's team designed everything. *GM China/PATAC*

collaboration between designers worldwide was made possible via telephone conferences. Huang notes, "For instance, if I was attending a global meeting at 5AM, there would be little disagreement between me and my counterparts in China. However, after the meeting, things were different and there was disagreement. My counterparts had to report to others above them. My Chinese colleagues also had concerns over their use of the language, security, and wanted more time to consider the solutions."

This being the case, a good designer needs to include all parties (designers, global design managers, engineering, marketing, finance, manufacturing) early in the decision-making process to make the proposals and end solutions visible.

YAN RETURNS TO FINE ARTS

When her simple sketches morphed into a production car, Yan Huang knew she made a difference. Eventually, it came the time for her to celebrate her success and be "joyous."

After finishing her assignment in China, Huang asked GM if she could return to Melbourne so her partner could be near his family. This was a lifestyle decision on her part. However, there were no managerial positons available at Holden and after an acceptable demotion she felt that her position duplicated one held by another. This led to her unplanned separation.

Yan Huang returned to her artistic roots remarking, "I thought it was about time for me to pursue my passion—create beautiful things for me." Yan believes that everyday objects should be both beautiful and useful. She believes designers have a responsibility to create timeless and enduring designs - art people will treasure and enjoy daily.

Her company, Yandesign, transcends the borders of art and design in her bold and expressive creations. In 2017, her fine arts were featured at The Gallery in Australia. She gives back to RMIT as a part-time college professor, inspiring future designers.

Marie Johnson

MARIE JOHNSON

The training I received at Kettering helped me become an inventor. The profs who taught our classes were hands-on with real engineering experience, which is different from other universities. You got the connection between theory, lab, and reduction to practice.[1]

—Marie Johnson (b. 1967)

CAREER HIGHLIGHTS

While a co-op student at General Motors, Marie Johnson (Cole) began her career at Delco Moraine in Dayton, Ohio, and later sharpened her engineering R&D skills at the New

Departure Hyatt facility in Sandusky, Ohio. She transferred to GM Service Parts Operations in Edina, Minnesota, to follow her husband to Minnesota, where they moved to pursue his master of divinity degree. GM tuition reimbursement opened the door for her to pursue postgraduate biomedical studies. Ultimately, she left GM to pursue full-time graduate research at the University of Minnesota. She completed a BS in mechanical engineering, an MS and PhD in biomedical engineering, and three postdoctoral fellowships.

In 2008, she was recruited to design and lead a medical device incubator at the University of Minnesota Medical Devices Center. She trained three classes of MD and postdoctoral-level engineers. In 2010, she received the Qualifying Therapeutic Delivery Project grant, which led to the establishment of her first company, AUM Cardiovascular, and first product, CADence. In 2017, CADence was cleared by the FDA as an advanced stethoscope, ECG, and software. To date, over 2,500 individuals have been tested with CADence, and over 150 asymptomatic patients have been diagnosed and successfully treated. Johnson seeks to reduce the death toll from cardiovascular disease by at least one million in her lifetime and is a vibrant and outspoken evangelist for cardiovascular health.

A fast, noninvasive, radiation-free, globally available and radically inexpensive device such as CADence can have a tremendous impact on cardiovascular disease, the number one killer worldwide. The World Health Organization reported that 30 percent of deaths worldwide were caused by cardiovascular disease.

In addition to receiving honors from others, Johnson continues to share her knowledge with the educational community as an adjunct professor of biomedical engineering at the University of Minnesota and as a guest speaker around the world. In 2014, she and her company were featured in *Fast Company*, and she was honored as one of the most creative people in business by the magazine. She has lectured and serves on Kettering University's board. Her TED Talk presentation, *Listening to the (Her) Heart*, is both informative and inspiring.

A JOURNEY WITH MANY TURNS

Marie Johnson, like some other bold women of her era, was part of the General Motors family since birth, and perhaps her paternal great-grandmother, who worked on the assembly line at Standard Aircraft (parent company GM) to support World War I efforts, was even more fearless. It is this ancestor who makes her a fourth-generationer. Her maternal grandfather was a machine operator for GM's Harrison Radiator. Her father worked for GM's Inland as a journeyman electrician. To continue this tradition, she felt that General Motors Institute (GMI), renamed Kettering in 1982, was the best place for her to study mechanical engineering. "I applied to one school, Kettering, and it was a great decision. My expectation was to work for GM someday."[2] Her daughter, Micahela (Mica) Guion Johnson, became a fifth-generation GM employee in fall 2021 as an engineer at the Jet Propulsion Lab in Pontiac.

After marrying GM New Departure Hyatt engineer Robert Guion, Marie followed him to his home state—Minnesota—when he sought a master of divinity degree. She spent several years working as a supervisor at a GM Service Parts Operations warehouse in Edina before joining the University of Minnesota as a full-time student. After completing a master of science with a focus on engineering hip replacement solutions alongside a prolific inventor and orthopedic surgeon, she moved on to a PhD degree focused on cardiovascular acoustics and was sponsored by the 3M Company.

During her studies, Rob died suddenly and unexpectedly from a heart attack caused by a blockage in his left anterior descending coronary artery, one of the vessels that vascularizes the heart. She decided it was providence and invented a solution, started a company, and led it through product development and regulatory clearance in and outside the United States, as well as early product commercialization in the United States and Europe.

She is an adjunct full professor in the Biomedical Engineering Department at the University of Minnesota and sits on several for-profit and not-for-profit boards. She has patents in the areas of stroke, maternal-fetal medicine, food science, cardiovascular medicine, pulmonology, neurology, and automotive-related technologies.

Recognizing her two decades of work and extraordinary achievements, Dr. Marie Johnson received the Engineering Achievement Award from her alma mater, Kettering University, in October 2020.

Kettering University was named General Motors Institute prior to 1982, and this is inscribed at the top of this campus building. *Constance Smith*

General Motors

JENNIFER KRASKA

There's something really amazing about not only coming up with an idea but seeing it through all its growing pains and being able to get behind the wheel and it's alive. It's amazing. I don't think it's ever going to get boring.[1]

—Jennifer Kraska (b. 1972)

CAREER HIGHLIGHTS

Jennifer Kraska currently serves as interior design manager. While her assignments have included both production and concept cars and trucks, she has also served as the strategic advanced design manager, GMC Exterior/Interior, from 2016 to 2018.

Prior to assuming this position, she worked as the interior design manager for Cadillac at the time when the Escala concept was under development—2014 to 2016. From 2013 to 2104, she also managed UX for Cadillac and Buick. In 2013, she was selected to lead Advanced User Experience Strategies.

Earlier, Jennifer led a team of designers, sculptors, and engineers through the early stages of development to final production release at Opel in Germany. She also guided interior design for the 2008 Cadillac CTS, named Car of the Year by *Motor Trend* magazine. As a representative of Oldsmobile, Kraska worked with Bertone in northern Italy on the design of the interior of the O4 concept car. Her drawing was featured in a press kit distributed at the 2001 New York International Automobile Show.

Kraska started her career as a creative designer in 1997 and was promoted to the interior design manager for Cadillac seven years later. Kraska has worked on Saturn models and spent a summer in Italy working on a show car for Oldsmobile.[2]

Jennifer's accomplishments include design for and management of the team creating the Pontiac G6.

In 2017, as interior design manager, Kraska was on hand at the North American International Auto Show at Cobo Center to accept the *Detroit News'* Reader's Choice Award with Taki Karras—the exterior design manager—when the Escala was voted the Best Future Concept by readers.

BIOGRAPHICAL NOTES

Kraska's earliest memories involve crayons and Matchbox cars; given her fascination with the toy cars' minute details, she says GM was a natural fit.[3] Like many of her colleagues, male and female, she would study at the College for Creative Studies. She received her bachelor of fine arts, focused in industrial design, in 1997 and joined General Motors Design the same year.

Around 2000, Kraska was assigned to Oldsmobile and worked with designers at Bertone in Turin, Italy, on the design of the interior for the O4 Concept. The "O" represented the symbol for oxygen, and the "4" signified that it was a four-seater. The vehicle was a convertible, however, and also featured rear access doors to provide entry and exit for rear-seat passengers. Smaller than the Alero, the car was designed for the college-aged customer.

Kraska's design, recorded in a computer drawing, featured an innovative interior that focused on ergonomics and incorporated a versatile liquid crystal display. An information ring around the steering wheel displayed data, and toggles operated by unseen touch switches 3 inches away.

On the outside, the narrow headlamps and taillamps were far ahead of their time and contributed to its sleekness.

In 2001, GM Design created a press kit for the New York International Auto show featuring computer drawings of the O4 as well as other concept cars created by each division.

The Oldsmobile 04 concept interior was ahead of its time. *General Motors*

Pontiac G6. *Constance Smith*

PONTIAC G6

There is no question that the Pontiac G6 was a game changer for the division. The model gained publicity when 276 cars were given away to preselected audience members at the televised *Oprah Winfrey Show*.

Inside and out, the G6 was a head turner. The cockpit featured a racing-inspired instrument cluster with analog gauges with chrome surrounds. Red numerals jumped out. The automatic climate control and a driver information system matched in color and style.

The interior design team consisted solely of women. Anne Asensio was the executive director of all interiors; Elizabeth Wetzel was the director for car interiors. Under them, Crystal Windham was working as the design manager, and Jennifer Kraska was the lead designer for the G6 interior. Kraska's theme that was used in the G6 show car interior was then transformed into the production design.

CADILLAC CTS

Kraska also contributed to the interior of the 2008 CTS, named Car of the Year by *Motor Trend* magazine.

OPEL

From 2010 to 2012, Kraska had an international assignment and joined Opel in Germany. As a lead designer, she contributed both to Opel and Vauxhall entries, which included the 2014 Chevy Cruze (the interior was designed in Europe; the exterior was done in North America).

CADILLAC ESCALA

The most significant concept car at this time was the Escala.

In the tradition of the 2011 Ciel and 2013 Elmiraj before it, the Escala concept, inside and out, takes your breath away. We continue to discover nuances from the styling of the Escala in production introductions.

The Escala received rave reviews and served as the basis for future Cadillac interiors, including that of the Escalade. *Constance Smith*

Kraska stresses that the Escala's interior was an exercise in simplicity, but the challenge was ensuring it did not come off as incomplete or gimmicky.[4] The selection of refined materials speaks to the intended audience. The elegantly designed seats and lack of a B pillar contribute to passenger comfort. Laetitia Lopez and Hannah Dunbar, Color and Trim designers, concentrated on the creation and selection of materials, which included leather and cloth. Somewhere along the line, designers created a piece of trim that transitions from metal to wood.

As the popularity of full-size automobile winds down in favor of the SUV, the curved OLED displays introduced here were exciting for designers to incorporate and are already featured on the 2021 Escalade and ES. The attention to color and multiple coats of paint contribute to Escala's exterior, and luxurious trim continues to appear across the Cadillac line.

The design was initiated in GM's Warren, Michigan, location studios, where Kraska was joined by Sharon Gauci, the director of Color and Trim, and Carrie Crowley, Cadillac's global strategic design manager, in making the car a reality.

Taki Karras served as the exterior design manager, and Frank Wu and Aaron Riggs collaborated on the exterior. The design teams created a concept that was nothing short of perfection.

FINE ARTIST

Jennifer, appreciative of the natural beauty around her, also paints sensitive watercolors of insects and animals, which she has exhibited in the building gallery where she works.

Courtesy of Stacey Marmara

STACEY MARMARA

Learn from everything in life because each moment is a precious opportunity to discover something valuable, and then continue to ask yourself: How can we do better?

—Stacey Marmara (b. March 14, 1975)

CAREER HIGHLIGHTS

Stacey Marmara worked at Delphi Chassis Group in Brighton, Michigan, formerly part of the General Motors Proving Ground, from 1999 to 2001. This assignment led to an opportunity with the General Motors Midsize and Luxury Car Group in Warren, Michigan, where she served as a chassis electronics resident engineer for W, U, and Y body programs (Chevrolet Impala, Monte Carlo, Venture, Corvette, and Pontiac Montana).

In 2001, Marmara transferred to General Motors of Canada to join a team of engineers working on a joint venture with Suzuki Motor Corporation toward successful launch of the 7L body program (Chevrolet Equinox, Pontiac Torrent, and Suzuki XL7). Marmara was awarded a patent for "Torque Steer Compensation Algorithm for Hydraulic Power Steering Vehicles." Marmara also served as a supervisor for the Pre-Production Operations Build Garage and Machine Shop.

Subsequently, from 2006 to 2011, Marmara decided to focus on family life in order to raise her then three children; she requested a temporary personal leave from employment with General Motors of Canada.

Under a part-time contract with General Motors of Canada, Marmara returned to the accessories team in 2011. She soon transitioned into work in advanced technology development.

From 2013 onward, Marmara has served in advanced technology engineering and was awarded a patent 9316278 for "Brake Pad Monitoring Sensor and System Configuration." She authored Defensive Publication GM P045686, *A System of Diagnosing Unintended Vehicle Motion Hazard and Providing Notification to the Surround Pedestrians*. Marmara and her teams filed two additional patents: P046128, "Self-Learning Algorithm for Brake Pad Life Determination Using Wireless Sensor Measurements," and P051800, "EMI Fault Detection for Brake Pad Wear Estimation Using Electric Park Brake." Work on trailer brake systems included patent filings P052031, "Current Management—Trailer Electromechanical Brakes," and P052033, "Trailer to Truck Integral Current Draw Management." This critical GM publication and Marmara's work resulting in additional patents related to brake life, wear, and systems contributed toward the proof of the GM Trailer Brake System Concept: Tow vehicle + trailer braking performance is equivalent to stopping distance of truck without trailer, thus bringing a new performance standard to the industry.

BIOGRAPHICAL NOTES

In the Greater Windsor area, the recession of the 1980s hit Marmara's family hard and involved the demise of the family construction business. Marmara's parents were determined to avoid disruption to their girls' lives and found a way to keep their peer circles intact by relocating within the community to ensure they would continue to attend the Sacred Heart Elementary School in LaSalle, Ontario.

In order to financially sustain the impact of the recession, Marmara's mother took on work with Bell Canada and worked for many years as an operator, where an aptitude for numbers applied to switchboard operation served her well. Technology worker demand in the automotive industry helped bring the economy back in Marmara's community, and her father, Roy, also happened to be skilled in automotive repair. He had a neighborhood reputation as a self-taught success at fixing most anything, which invited a socially busy garage where Stacey would often hang out during the summer. The LaSalle neighborhood was a great place to grow up with friendly families on Willow Drive, and many of these families spent time together boating on the Great Lakes. An inclination for technology brought Marmara's father into the auto industry, where he would ultimately retire from robotics controls at Chrysler Corporation. Marmara's grandfather, Joseph, who emigrated from Malta, had worked in the trades for FMC—his specialty was metalworking. Marmara's father taught her to learn from every encounter and especially to put focus to understanding the situations you disagree with! "Everyone has their perspective" is what he would say.

Marmara was an optimist who, by turning over stone after stone, explored new opportunities that arose in an effort to find out what she was good at and enjoyed. Marmara's mother, Cheryl, kept her and sister, Jaclyn, accountable to always work hard in school and attain their fullest potential. This strategy worked well, since it led Stacey to a career in engineering at General Motors, and Jaclyn to a career of legal practice with Export Development Canada. For Marmara, Cheryl was the loud and proud supporter on the sidelines of the figure-skating rink, basketball games, cross-country and track events, art project deadlines, piano recitals, and many other things Stacey would become involved with to find her pathway. Early on, Marmara enjoyed and found the subjects easy to breeze through included mathematics, art, and science. Early on, Mrs. Linda Ryan, her first- and third-grade teacher, noted Marmara's academic interests and looked to accelerate the workload for these subject areas. This resulted in participation with advanced-learning classes, where she met longtime friend John Morris.

At the high school level, Marmara continued to participate in sports at the Sandwich Secondary School. Sandwich Sabres teams included track and field, cross-country, and basketball, where a lifelong friendship with Jaimie (DiTomasso) Peltier developed. Jaimie was also very good at math, and her uncle was a math teacher at the school. Math was everywhere! Indeed, it helped that two of Stacey's favorite math teachers, Mr. Gomes and Mr. Yakopich, were also the basketball coaches. Marmara also participated in arts programs and student Parliament, which led to her attendance at the Hugh O'Brian Youth (HOBY) leadership program, focused on government-related career opportunities. Mrs. Daniel's sewing class was Marmara's secret hangout where she could let loose and just "use her hands to make stuff." At one time, Stacey owned four sewing machines, largely thanks to Grandmother Josephine. Marmara's successful experience with Mr. Palinaki's eleventh-grade physics class would prove to be the strong indication

to her guidance counsellor, Mr. Wright, that Marmara was a good candidate for engineering at the postsecondary level of study. In fact, Mr. Wright did well to promote engineering to his students, both male and female, including Brigitte Mora, Marianne Cmar, and Sheri Meek. Kettering University's ties to the automotive industry, and the ability to earn an income while studying there, were the core enablers for Marmara to accept an offer by the school to enroll in 1994.

During her time at Kettering, and when electrical engineering became the favored pathway, Marmara formed strong study habits and bonds with Rae (Montemayor) Klug, Lina (Dimitrov) Battestilli, Paul Shaub, and Edmund Tse. Through cooperative employment, these friends were with General Motors, and at the time Marmara was employed with Ford Electronics in Canada. Battestilli's parents were in fact math professors at the school, and strong mentors for Marmara's academic success. The camaraderie of this study group in part resulted in a capstone project to develop an electric go-kart, mentored by Professor Dr. Mohammad Torfeh. Marmara went on to graduate in December 1998 with a bachelor of science in electrical engineering, with a mathematics minor. Experience at Ford Electronics Manufacturing combined with strong academic performance at Kettering enabled Marmara's success in applying for a role with Delphi Chassis, which, at the time, was located at the General Motors Proving Ground in Milford, Michigan.

General Motors

Marmara accepted the position as an electrical systems, diagnostics, and communications engineer for Delphi Chassis Systems in Brighton, Michigan. The enthusiasm of this team inspired in Marmara what would be a lifelong interest in chassis electronics technology. When Marmara was twenty-four years of age, her first son arrived. At this time, she would begin to navigate a balance between work and life. As she started her family, she also assumed the responsibilities of a chassis electrical resident engineer at the General Motors Warren Technical Center for the midsize and luxury car group on U, W, and Y car programs (Chevrolet Impala, Monte Carlo, Venture, Corvette, and Pontiac Montana). Working alongside peers, Paul Shaub (also from Kettering) and David Kowal would provide a foundation for understanding the complexities in electrical-vehicle engineering and begin the road into deeper involvement with chassis-related electronics for many years to come.

In 2001, coinciding with Marmara's husband's career prospect in Toronto, the opportunity arose to transfer to General Motors of Canada to work on the Chevrolet Equinox and Pontiac Torrent (7L programs) chassis electronics, involving brake controls and steering-controls design and release engineering. This required a trip to Japan to support Suzuki Joint Ventures, including prototype build in Hamamatsu. Marmara was also the project lead in Canada for vehicle simulation bench builds to be used for serial data testing of the 7L programs. During this time, mentored by Norm Weigert, the engineering manager at the time and long-standing mentor, Marmara contributed to and demonstrated technology involving an awarded patent aimed at reduction of torque steer, utilizing hydraulic power-steering controls.

Returning from a second maternity leave after the birth of her second son, Marmara held a people leader role for the GM Canada Pre-Production Operations Garage, leading a skilled trades team of thirty technicians and machine shop professionals responsible for vehicle service, lab testing, and prototype builds for the 7L programs, including periodic 7L-program-based hydrogen fuel cell vehicle prototypes. Mentored by Karen Low, also of GM Canada, Marmara began work to support promotion of STEM educational outreach programs, coordinating field-of-play build for the FIRST Robotics Competition (FRC) team activity, and also serving as an FRC judge and mentor. This is where Marmara met the similarly STEM-ambitious-minded Stephanie Thompson of St. Catharines Manufacturing. Marmara began pursuit of a master's degree in engineering with Stanford University, interrupted by a third maternity leave. This resulted in an almost six-year opportunity to stay home until 2011, raising the three boys. During this time and for many years since, Marmara volunteered with the children's Markham, Ontario, community school.

In 2011, Marmara returned to work as a part-time employee under contract to GM Canada as an electronic accessories release engineer, specializing in the remote-start accessory product lineup as the work was being transitioned from a global operation ultimately centralized back to North America, where a vision for accessories was developing strongly.

Marmara continued FRC volunteering and work with her delivery partners and the SAE International (formerly the Society of Automotive Engineers) to bring A World in Motion (AWIM) curricula to teachers and students of the Toronto and Fort Frances areas. At this time, Marmara became involved with the SAE Central Ontario Section as AWIM chair and participated as a board member for SAE Foundation Canada, with a partner development focus to bring additional A World in Motion activity to over 2,000 teachers and students in the Toronto District, York Catholic District, Peel District, Durham District, and Halton District School Boards. This included multiple conferences with the Ontario Council for Technology Education and the Science Teachers Association of Ontario, where Marmara met Lisa Lim Cole, who shared the same passion for STEM outreach. The work continues today due to new and repeat customers, with strong support provided by the SAE International team led by Lori Gatmaitan, executive director. Marmara attended school with Gatmaitan at Kettering University.

By May 2015, Marmara rejoined GM full time and transitioned into advanced-technology work, involved with team activity in advanced transmission controls, and special brake-related exploratory projects. She also began supporting GM's vision toward zero crashes, zero emissions, and zero congestion. Here, efforts to back electrical-systems development of technology for brake pad wear estimation were led by Dave Antanaitis and Matt Robere of the chassis team in Michigan. A patent award was granted for resistive pad wear sensors and system, including diagnostics. Additional future versions of the system included work contributing toward two additional patent applications, including a method of EMI detection and mitigation for the system. Marmara is a recipient of the General Motors Production Use Award as a result of the feature being introduced into the GM product family for customers. The same feature received a rare annual nomination for the General Motors Boss Kettering award in the 2018–2019 period.

The STEM quest continued (never stopped!) in supporting mentor Regan Dixon's lead (also of GM Canada) in development of a formal STEM corporate social responsibility committee, and Marmara continued to be involved with community after-hours programming in STEM education outreach to over fifty newcomer-family students conducted in partnership with the Centre for Information and Community Services (CICS). Here at CICS, a not-for-profit organization, Marmara served two consecutive terms as volunteer board member, culminating in the receipt of the Province of Ontario Volunteer Service Award. Marmara continues to serve on the SAE Central Ontario Section Board as well as SAE Foundation Annual Giving Committee, aimed at thanking donors for their contributions to STEM education outreach. In 2016, Marmara also copartnered with other parents to coach a FIRST Lego League team at her children's local Markham school.

While on maternity leave from 2016 to 2017 with her fourth child, this time a daughter, Marmara trained with former vice president Al Gore in Denver, Colorado, to become a member of the Climate Reality Leadership Corps, supporting message delivery around the impacts of and solutions to climate change as part of the Climate Reality Project.

Returning to work from her final maternity leave, Marmara transitioned to the advanced-technology development for future chassis controls, involving steering and the next generations of pad-wear-related technology. She led the development of a defensible publication involving mitigation of a longitudinal roll hazard, utilizing electronic park brake controls and using external means of communication to reduce incidents. Marmara went on to successfully pursue a certificate in architecture and systems engineering with the Massachusetts Institute of Technology.

A proud moment in Marmara's career involved leading a truly capable team, mentored once again by chassis technical subject matter expert Dave Antanaitis. The team was responsible for delivering an advanced technology envisioned and commissioned by Truck Products chief engineer and now GM vice president Tim Herrick. Herrick challenged the US and Canada partnering team to improve trailer braking performance for trailer systems. As recently published by GM Media in early 2020, the proof of concept was a success and has resulted in a 40-foot stopping-distance reduction, drastically raising the bar on trailering-dynamics performance for the trailering-technology industry. This work has resulted in two additional patent applications involving charge management technologies.

Marmara is motivated by professional relationships that include mutual mentorship, resulting in career and personal growth for everyone involved. She is thankful to the leaders who enable an awesome workplace and team environment, including great projects with challenging goals. Marmara's relationships with her parents and family, notably her four children, and time spent engaged in sports, community activities, and outdoor walks provide high-quality time with loved ones. These are the sources that freshen her perspective to continue to get out there and to do better. She is proud of her children for each of their unique personalities and pathways, and they inspire her work and keep her moving forward targeting the best way, every day.

Bucket list mention: Marmara dreams of visiting the Cadillac V-Performance Academy and is especially looking to the horizon toward the arrival of an affordable 250 km range electric motorcycle that can charge over lunch hour!

Marmara's mantra is "INNOVATION, SAFETY, TEAMWORK, AND THINK CUSTOMER INTO EVERY WORKDAY."

Courtesy of Laryssa Hulcio, GM Canada

Brett Mountain

CHARON (MERUCCI) MORGAN

It was a truly great opportunity to be able to gain that theoretical and applied experience in parallel. The program offered by GM was exceptional.[1]

—Charon Morgan (b. ca. 1971)

Charon Morgan currently serves as vice president of North America Engineering, Crouse-Hinds, B-Line, and Oil and Gas Division for Eaton Corporation.

Morgan also serves the industry through service with the Society of Women Engineers, Automotive Women's Alliance Foundation, and SAE International (formerly the Society of Automotive Engineers). With SAE International, she serves on a number of boards and committees, including the Board of Directors, Technical Standards Board, Scholarship Advisory Committee, Executive Nominating Committee, and Motor Vehicle Council. Morgan has received multiple awards for her volunteer work, including SAE Distinguished Younger Member in 2008 and Member of the Year in 2010. Charon frequently speaks at technical conferences and guest-lectures in international business and STEM education, and she advocates for women in engineering, as demonstrated through her work with Ladies Who Tech (in Shanghai) and FIRST Robotics. In 2016, she became the chairwoman of the Automotive Committee at the American Chamber of Commerce in Shanghai.

Growing up just north of Detroit, Michigan, Charon was raised in a large family with a high regard for work ethic. Her parents were role models for her. When possible, her mother cared for the elderly in their home, while her father was a tool- and diemaker for Chrysler for over thirty-five years. Her father made it to the sixth grade before being forced to drop out to work three jobs to provide for his family after his father's death. With both parents born during the Great Depression era, Charon was brought up to be resilient to the unexpected and mindful of a thrifty lifestyle.

Charon was the first one in her family to go to college and earn a degree. She notes, "I had a group of friends who considered college the only option as a next step after high school. I was so thankful I had a good group of friends." Her family was not familiar with the benefits of college, and she saw her parents' struggles, so she knew she had to find a different path. Morgan enrolled at a local community college and waitressed to pay tuition. Charon recalls at one point working two full-time jobs waitressing at family restaurants and a part-time job as a banquet server. She saved money so she could offset the low pay she would earn to start at entry level in her field. She recalls, "It was hard to find a job to pay tuition and rent, car payment, and so on. I knew if I wanted it, I had to work hard to get it." She eventually transferred to Oakland University and worked at a company designing motor-operated doors in her last year of college, leading to her bachelor of science in mechanical engineering in 1996. Morgan joined General Motors for a year right after graduation as a contract employee. At that time, it was common for GM to bring in college graduates for a couple years to ensure it was a good fit for them culturally.

Morgan started with General Motors full time in 1998 as a test engineer for chassis components, working up to release engineer position suspensions and eventually moving into other areas of chassis systems. She spent a few years at the Milford Proving Ground while earning her master's degree through Purdue University, noting, "It was a truly great opportunity to be able to gain that theoretical and applied experience in parallel. The program offered by GM was exceptional." After she graduated from with a master of science in mechanical engineering, vehicle dynamics and chassis integration, from Purdue University, Morgan's career progressed with positions across multiple disciplines in Global Product Development at General Motors at the Technical Center in Warren, Michigan. This included assignments in Vehicle Dynamics at the Milford Proving Ground, and various special assignments, including management and leading special task forces for crisis situations. Morgan led the transition of thousands of components from troubled suppliers and was the lead for engineering during the Delphi bankruptcy filing in 2007. This was instrumental, in that GM would go on to file for bankruptcy the following year. Charon was moved into a management position leading cost for the automotive giant for all of chassis components globally. She then had a two-year stint as technical assistant to the global leader of testing and durability.

The running gear for the EN-V was based on the Segway, which is attributed to inventor Dean Kamen. *General Motors*

In 2006, Charon picked up a side assignment for an advanced-technology project that had been in development for over a decade but was not able to move to execution. Charon was a lead engineer for the next generation of full-size trucks and took the lead in a side project over the next two years, eventually bringing it to production on the Cadillac DTS. The technology resolved the industry's largest warranty issues by applying a ferritic nitrocarburizing process to brake rotors. Charon was honored with the prestigious "Boss" Kettering Award in 2010 for this first-to-market technology, which is now being widely used across the industry. Charon also holds a patent for "Brake Rotor with Intermediate Portion," US 9,127,734 B2.

As Charon's career progressed, she became involved in the advancement of women in engineering and STEM education. She became very actively involved in SAE International and locally in the Detroit Section. Morgan led programs for the industry, including new-vehicle introductions across the major OEMs and tiered suppliers to bridge the connection for education and profession with those more senior in the industry to college students and recent graduates. She eventually went on to serve on the SAE Detroit governing board in various positions, leading up to chairwoman in 2010. She was the sole recipient of the SAE Distinguished Younger Member Award in 2008 and SAE Member of the Year Award in 2011.

After gaining more experience with roles in increasing scope and responsibility, Morgan also expanded her role with

Super Cruise was explored globally. *General Motors*

SAE, serving on standards, scholarship, and nominating boards, to name a few, as well as the board of directors. She also served other professional associations, dedicating time to provide guest lectures promoting international business, advanced technologies, and women in STEM fields at universities both in the US and in China, as well as key notes in technical and career development consortiums.

She then moved into Program Operations and Management, in charge of GM's largest global architecture at the time, which spanned across most continents. This position allowed Charon to learn and understand how to run a business internationally, comprehending differences in culture and capability. Leading the technical aspects of the negotiations for engineering services with its joint ventures (JVs) in China, Charon then helped in transitioning business from the United States to China, with a key role at GM's largest JVs in China in 2013. Charon was the driver for capability growth by introducing a portfolio of processes and tools to the JVs to enable them to lead the first vehicle architecture consisting of small cars and crossovers for the global market.

While in China, Charon took on a new role leading the product engineering and supplier quality functions for GM China, while still working with GM's Joint Ventures. Charon aligned the wholly owned portion of GM in China to lead portions of global product development. She led the development and execution of key projects in China, such as the Urban Active all-electric-car-sharing platform, known as the EN-V 2.0. This electric-concept-vehicle fleet was the pilot program, with a fleet of sixteen vehicles at Shanghai Jiao Tong University that helped GM learn more about car sharing for the onset of Maven, which would launch in the United States in 2016.

Expanding her network in China, Charon became the first chairwoman to lead the automotive industry for the American Chamber of Commerce in Shanghai. While performing her duties, she helped drive collaboration across US regulators and Chinese ministries for synergetic strategic plans with growth in advanced automotive technologies, including electric vehicles and autonomous development. This would later become critical as she led the development of the first autonomous vehicle platform in China, Cadillac's Super Cruise, to execution at the conclusion of her five-year stint in China.

Charon Morgan returned to the States and joined Eaton in April 2020, after over twenty-two years with General Motors. She is currently the vice president of North America Engineering, in part responsible for its Crouse-Hinds series, B-Line solutions, and Oil and Gas Division.

FAMILY

Sharon has a twin sister and, like other twins, knows this runs in the family. She shares her time with her husband, Bob, and three sons; two are twins. All three are in college.

JENNY MORGAN

CAREER HIGHLIGHTS

The exciting thing about designing is that as each new project arises, it sets you off with the promise of what is to come, the process of discovery and exploration, as new ideas bubble up. Through collaboration and teamwork these ideas grow, always with surprises and challenges. They take time to develop, with experimentation and lots of communication, lasting over months or years. Always working toward a design that sparks an emotional response for the customer and brand, a design that is beautifully proportioned, harmonized with the form, has exceptional quality, and provides some intriguing details that reach beyond expectations.[2]

—Jenny Morgan (b. 1962)

Jenny Morgan served as a General Motors color and trim design manager from 2005 to 2020, after returning from maternity leave and welcoming a second child. Prior to this position, she served as a chief designer from 1995 to 2005 and design manager in 1993. She began work as a senior designer in 1991.

Before joining GM, Morgan served as an adjunct lecturer in textile design for Royal Melbourne Institute of Technology and spent two years as a designer in the Films and Fabrics Division of BTR Nylex.

During her tenure at GM, she contributed to a large range of concept and production vehicles.

On the production side, this includes the MY92-MY17 Holden Commodore (VR, VS, VT, VX, VY, VZ, VE, VF) and all related Statesman/Caprice, utility vehicles, wagon variants, and the Monaro coupe while working under the leadership of Phillip Zmood, Michael Simcoe, Anthony Stolfo, Andrew Smith, Richard Ferlazzo, and Sharon Gauci. This included designing their exterior paint ranges, with some very distinctly Australian sporty "hero" colors. Assigned to international products, she contributed to China's Malibu and Aveo and Buick Enclave for PATAC, as well as Buick Encore and Chevrolet Colorado, both targeted at global markets.

Her involvement in concept car and truck portfolio consists of the 1998 Holden Coupe (Australia), the 1999 Holden YGM-1 (Australia), the 2000 Holden Sandman (Australia), the 2004 Holden Torana TT6 (Australia), the 2011 Holden Colorado (Australia), the Chevrolet Adra (India), the award-winning 2015 Buick Avenir (NAIAS), the groundbreaking 2015 Bolt (NAIAS), the 2016 Colorado Extreme and Trailblazer (Bangkok and Australia), and the 2016 Chevrolet Niva (Russia).

Morgan's design work as a team member and manager was highly rewarded inside and outside Australia.

Holden Design captured the General Motors President's Council Honours' "Best of the Best" award for the 1998 VT Commodore, the 2001 Monaro Coupe, and the 2002 Malibu and Aveo Programs for PATAC.

Established in 1996 by the Victorian government, the Victorian Design Awards were notable: in 1997, in the industrial design category, the award went to Michael Simcoe and the Holden Design team for the VT Pontiac to the US, Chevrolet to the Middle East, and Vauxhall to the UK.

In 2002, in the industrial design category, awards went to

The award winning Avenir concept was a significant achievement for Morgan and GM. *Photo/John F. Martin.*

Buick Avenir concept vehicle. Elegant and inviting interior, trimmed in light, warm-colored Lyric aniline leather, contrasted against Coastal Mist. A flowing water motif on the seat stitching and the innovative 3-D decor. *Courtesy of Bandits and Company*

Holden VT Commodore, 1997 Colour & Trim display, Jenny Morgan and Marie Smyth. *Courtesy of GMA Design*

Holden Design for the Monaro Coupe (exported as GTO Pontiac to the US, Chevrolet to the Middle East, and Vauxhall to the UK).

In the textile design category, awards went to Autofab Australia (a textile manufacturer) for its mosaic fabric design, under Morgan's concept and design direction for the VX Commodore.

The 1993 VR Commodore, the 1997 VT Commodore, and the 2006 VE Commodore captured *Wheels* Car of the Year awards.

In America, Morgan was part of the GM Design team that was highly recognized at the EyesOn Design Awards at the North American International Auto Show (NAIAS) for the 2015 Buick Avenir, which won over popular entries in North America and Asia for both the Best Overall Concept and Best Colour and Trim.

MORGAN'S JOURNEY

Growing up in Melbourne, Australia, Jenny Morgan was lucky to have creative influences all around her. She recalls, "I was surrounded by a large garden and native bush. My mother was as an occupational therapist who kept my three sisters and me busy creating and making things, I remember the large kitchen table full of projects, sewing, textiles, pottery, painting, and cooking. I enjoyed ballet classes for many years and often visited galleries and the theater. I must have gained my more practical, analytical skills from my father, who was an engineer, managing Ford Australia's production plant facility." All the sisters worked in creative fields, and in the early 1990s there were a couple of years' overlap when Jenny and her next-eldest sister, Bronwyn, both were employed as C&T designers (GM and Nissan). Their father never expected to have two daughters in the automotive industry, and "it made for some rather interesting, noncommittal work conversations around the dinner table, avoiding confidential topics."

At Vermont Primary School, her clear and favorite memory was of the experimental art room. After completing her secondary school years at Methodist Ladies College, she did not know what career direction to take, but she naturally spent her spare time taking classes and continuing in drawing, weaving, and pattern-making, which ultimately lead her to study textile design at Royal Melbourne Institute of Technology, where she thrived, found her niche, and completed a bachelor of arts degree.

She notes, "At my first design job, at Nylex Films and Fabrics division, I gained experience designing commercial vinyl products, as well as understanding design for manufacture."

Unexpectedly entering the automotive designs industry after seeing a job advertisement, Morgan quickly found it was a surprisingly good, natural fit for her. She easily related to the creative application of color and materials to vehicle design and was comfortable with the technical challenges of implementing these ideas into mass production.

For many of her earlier years at GMA Design, she was primarily involved in the C&T design of the locally built Holden Commodore. During the 1990s, there was an increased focus and appreciation of C&T design at Holden, the C&T team grew, and improvements were made in research, creative exploration, design strategy, supplier engagement/development, and quality. As Jenny Morgan-Douralis, she initiated and managed the writing of the *Holden Appearance and Colour Manual*, a first for the Australian automotive industry.

Morgan notes that the Holden Commodore was highly popular and the bestselling car in Australia, where it was manufactured from 1978 to 2017. In New Zealand, the Commodore was sold from 1979 to 1990. Sales of the Commodore ended worldwide in 2020 with the discontinuation of the Holden brand, primarily

Bolt team collaboration, C&T and Interior designers working closely to integrate each other's ideas. *Left to right*: Frank Rudolph, Joe Rudolph, Krista Lindegger, Jenny Morgan, Harsha Ravi. *Courtesy of GMA Design*

Chevrolet EV Bolt concept vehicle, 2015. The highly chromatic "Red Fox" exterior. The fractal pattern on the printed glass roof and 3-D lamp lenses. *General Motors*

General Motors

bring, understanding the changing societal landscape, advanced technologies, and trends. She believes that we are living in a booming age of materials innovation that offers designers exciting opportunities in new aesthetics and more-sustainable solutions.

Of all the show vehicles, her two favorite experiences were both at the 2015 (NAIAS) Detroit Motor Show. There was great collaborative energy with the GMA team, which was under the direction of Michael Simcoe. Working most closely with her C&T colleague Krista Lindegger, they were able to incorporate some of their advanced C&T ideas with the help of interior designers.

PROMOTING THE FUTURE

Morgan is passionate about encouraging students to pursue automotive design as career—including providing interning opportunities. Over the years, Morgan has initiated and participated in many collaborative projects and guest-lectured to textiles and industrial design students.

FAMILY MATTERS

Jenny Morgan lives in Melbourne with her children, Lucas and Zoe.

caused by the loss of interest in cars due to the preference for SUVs and trucks and the highly competitive Australian market.

In 2005, Helen Emsley initiated a new global advance C&T design team, and, as a key member, Morgan began researching and developing some far-reaching projects. Morgan worked solely on advanced C&T from 2006 to 2013 and continued addressing advanced C&T projects on and off until 2020. She has always been energized by the possibilities of what the long-term future will

HOLDEN VE SSE *Bandits & Co.*

Monaro CV8 *Bandits & Co.*

TRICIA MORROW-GROUSTRA

With our new global economy and our new mobility space, I just really want to be part of bringing great technologies to our customers and really helping them be safe on the road. ... Any path that can help me do that, I'm all in.[1]

—Tricia Morrow-Groustra (b. 1976)

CAREER HIGHLIGHTS

Tricia Morrow-Groustra currently serves as a global vehicle strategy manager and is responsible for safety strategy, feature development/implementation, and biomechanical assessments. She is the single point for safety engineering technical communications for the VP of global vehicle safety.

Morrow-Groustra has over twenty years of experience at General Motors and has worked within a number of groups in a variety of roles: Global Vehicle Safety, Global Electrical Controls and Software, Global Product Planning, and Global Advanced Vehicle Development Innovation.

As a mother, the most significant accomplishments in her career are the Rear Seat Reminder and Buckle to Drive—which is the newest upgrade to Teen Driver.

In 2020, at forty-four years old, Morrow-Groustra was selected as a Rising Star by *Automotive News*.

BIOGRAPHICAL NOTES

Tricia Morrow-Groustra attended the Barnes Early Childhood Center, Parcells Middle School, and Our Lady Star of the Sea lower school, and Grosse Pointe North High School in Grosse Pointe, Michigan. In 1994, she graduated from Grosse Pointe North High School, located in a waterfront community on top of Lake Shore Drive.

In 1998, Morrow-Groustra was awarded the bachelor of science in mechanical engineering from Purdue University. Three years later, she earned a master's degree in biomedical engineering from Wayne State

Drawing by Constance Smith

University. She completed her formal education with an MBA from the University of Michigan in 2007.

Tricia joined GM as a safety project engineer (1999-2002) and an integration engineer from 2002-2007.

In 2016, Morrow-Groustra brought the Rear Seat Reminder from concept to fruition to life to prevent children and pets from heatstroke. Other manufacturers will offer similar devices by 2025. Rear Seat Reminder, which launched on the 2017 GMC Acadia, is the technology that can prevent child hot-car deaths. The concept became even more personal to her since she has two daughters.

In a recent interview, she notes, "This can happen to high-functioning, well-intentioned human beings. And at General Motors, we were searching for technology to try to prevent these hot-car deaths and protect kids in vehicles. The technology doesn't detect people or pets in the back seat. Instead, it registers that the rear door was opened within ten minutes before the car started or sometime after the car was already running. If you opened the rear door, odds are you put something it. It could be a bag of groceries or a briefcase, but it could also be a child."[2]

Morrow-Groustra was also influential in bringing Buckle to Drive technology to market. It has been added to GM's original Teen Driver software.

The device prevents teen drivers from shifting out of park until they buckle their seat belts. The feature arrived on Chevrolets in the summer of 2019 and is available on the 2020 Chevrolet Malibu, Traverse, Malibu, and Colorado and also on the associated GMC Canyon. Morrow explains how it works: "'Buckle to drive' is embedded in Chevrolet's Teen Driver System and is aimed at helping teens to buckle up every time they get behind the wheel."[3]

The initial Teen Driver product debuted in 2016 on the Chevrolet Malibu, under the direction of Mary Ann Beebe.

Malibu's Teen Driver can track distance driven, maximum speed traveled, overspeed warnings issued, stability control events, antilock-brake events, forward collision alerts, if equipped, and forward collision braking events, if equipped.[4]

When questioned about autonomous vehicles, Morrow-Groustra answered, "We've been working really hard to try to figure out what restraint technology looks like in an autonomous vehicle. It's really been part of our strategy to say, 'What do we need to do to ensure the safety of our customers in that vehicle?'"[5]

The first Rear Seat Reminder appeared on the 2017 Acadia.
Constance Smith

Courtesy of Brigid O'Kane

BRIGID O'KANE

At General Motors Design Center, I always thought of myself as a professional designer who happened to be a woman. I knew I had a lot to contribute, and that's what I did.[1]

Aztek was the peak of my career at GM. My aesthetic approach was bold, and when my design was selected to go into production, I was so thrilled. Colleagues gave me so many compliments. After that, it seemed like everyone wanted their hand in the design, which caused many design changes. Maintaining the integrity and essence of the original design aesthetic is the hardest part of being a creative designer.[2]

Brigid O'Kane (b. 1965)

CAREER HIGHLIGHTS

Brigid began her career at Pioneer Engineering, where she spent two years as a technical illustrator developing drawings for manuals that largely focused on military equipment and included the wiring systems of tanks.

She was an intern as a creative designer at Prince Corporation, where she developed and built automotive interior concepts, and at Cars and Concepts, where she contributed a design to the C&C Show Car that was a two-passenger, hardtop convertible.

O'Kane accepted a position at GM Design Center in 1990 as a lead creative designer, before leaving in 2000. She contributed to the exterior and interior of a number of award-winning designs for show cars and production vehicles.

More specifically, at the GM Design Center in Michigan she worked in many different brand centers, including Chevrolet, Pontiac, Cadillac, GMC, Oldsmobile, and Saturn, in addition to the Advanced Concept Studios. Her most-significant accomplishments include the 1995 Saturn S Series interior, the 1995 Oldsmobile Antares Concept Car (which was the prelude for the 1997 Oldsmobile Intrigue), and the controversial 2001 Pontiac Aztek. In 1994–1995 she transferred to the GM Advanced Concept Center in California, where she worked on radical vehicle prototypes for electric vehicles. O'Kane also led GM's Concept Cure project in 1998, a joint venture between GM brands and fashion designers in America.

O'Kane's design accomplishments at General Motors have been highly recognized. In 1998 she received the prestigious Award of Excellence for achieving extraordinary leadership accomplishments at the GM Technical Center. In 1998 she received the Most Outstanding Creativity and Leadership Award from the GM Design Center. She also received *Auto Week*'s Best Concept Award for the Oldsmobile Intrigue in 1993, and the Most Significant Design Award for the Oldsmobile Antares Show Car in 1995.

Although she loved her career at GM, in 2000 she decided to pursue a different creative path. GM awarded her a two-year leave of absence, and she moved back to California as a production set designer, creating a series of stunning illustrations for the movie industry.

She then secured a position as a professor of design at the University of Cincinnati and led the development of the transportation design curriculum. From 2013 to 2016 she was promoted as the interim director of the School of Design within the College of Design, Architecture, Art, and Planning (DAAP). Her tenure at the University of Cincinnati has lasted over two decades.

O'Kane is cofounder of a highly successful nonprofit arts organization called Manifest Creative Research Gallery and Drawing Center in Cincinnati, Ohio. From 2004 to the present, O'Kane has served on the board of directors for Manifest and continues to teach classes at the Drawing Center.

BIOGRAPHICAL NOTES

O'Kane's father, Jim O'Kane, worked at General Motors Design Center as a mechanical engineer in the truck interiors and exteriors studios for forty years before retiring in 1993. In 1990 he received the General Motors Research Award for Most Valuable Colleague for his visionary contributions in the evolution of Autoshape, a 3-D surfacing software. Brigid's mother, Virginia, was "an organized and creative artist." Most noteworthy among her creative endeavors were her quilts. Virginia also received her degree in accounting and opened her own business. Within the O'Kane household, numerous works of fine art were exhibited and appreciated by the entire family. Jim and Virginia O'Kane had nine children. Brigid was their seventh child and was born between two sets of twins in Royal Oak, Michigan—a town abutting Warren, Michigan, home to GM's elaborate Technical Center. When Brigid was three years old, the O'Kane family moved from Royal Oak to Almont; after another move to Warren, Michigan, she enrolled at and graduated from Cousino High School.

Brigid O'Kane notes that as a child, "everything I did was creative. I was self-taught for the most part. Drawing and painting never bored me. Every chance I got I was drawing. I would disappear for hours in the woods where we lived, so I could draw and study nature and how things grew. I would bring home interesting objects that I found, and then I would study and draw every detail. I also loved drawing people. At one point I drew portraits of everyone in my family." When Brigid was thirteen years old, her father recognized her extraordinary abilities and made her a drawing table, which she still cherishes today.

MACOMB COMMUNITY COLLEGE AND THE COLLEGE FOR CREATIVE STUDIES

After high school, Brigid enrolled in the Graphic Communication Design program at Macomb Community College. Macomb employed full-time faculty as well as adjuncts from the automotive industry in their evening programs. O'Kane gained extensive skill and knowledge from Professor George Hriczik, who graduated from Art Center College of Design and was a designer at Chrysler. Hriczik was a highly regarded realist painter as well as an accomplished automotive designer. After graduating from Macomb in 1986, Brigid visited the College for Creative Studies (CCS), since she planned to further her education in communication design. However, on her visit to the college, Brigid notes, "I stumbled upon a wall of futuristic car sketches and immediately wanted to switch my major, but at that time I didn't even know what industrial design was. I went home and told my dad, and he looked at me like I was out of my mind." Then he told her, "That's what I do at work!"

When Brigid entered CCS, Carl Olsen chaired the Industrial Design Department. O'Kane also studied with Bill Robinson, a noted Chrysler designer. Tim Gregg, a GM designer who also an instructor at CCS, taught her how to design automotive interiors and helped guide Brigid's career development. Russell Keeter was O'Kane's most influential professor at CCS. He was

an acclaimed painter and anatomist who would draw the human figure in accurate and invented ways. O'Kane was fascinated with figure drawing, and Keeter challenged her while he directed her creativity. Brigid's intense focus on figure drawing strongly influenced the forms she created as an automotive designer. This approach made her designs stand out.

O'kane's thesis model was refined. *Brigid O'Kane.*

"After my junior year at the College for Creative Studies, I had already worked thousands of hours studying and practicing design; my mind was wide open. I developed new creative strategies that embraced anomalies and different points of view that others would ignore. I became a conduit for creativity. This approach changed my life."[3]

When asked about her most memorable undergraduate project, O'Kane described her senior thesis: "It was very original design, a two-passenger Pontiac with an electric motor at each wheel. The batteries were distributed for a low center of gravity. The concept was similar to the 1996 EV1, only mine was a much-sleeker design. I painted the clay model a lush dark purple with teal accents. I developed an extensive interior for it as well. I love the process of priming and painting clay models." She received her bachelor of fine art in industrial design, focused on transportation, in 1990. Before graduation she had seven job offers.[4] Later she would earn a master of fine art in 2005, with an emphasis in drawing, from the University of Cincinnati.

Brigid's dad brought her to work one day. *Brigid O'Kane.*

O'KANE REPORTS TO WORK AT GM

Manager of GM Design Resources Sheryl Garrett coordinated the interview team that hired Brigid, which included Chuck Jordan, the vice president of GM Design, and Jerry Palmer, the director of GM Design, among others. O'Kane explained the progression of her career:

I went to GM because they had the broadest portfolio of vehicles, and I figured after five years I would have extensive experience and more career options. In 1990, my first year at Design Center, Chuck Jordan was active in all four of the studios I rotated through, which included production interiors, production exteriors, advanced, and truck. I was eventually assigned to Saturn Studio and worked with Art Pryde on the S Series interior. I gained an incredible amount of knowledge relating to interior design from Art.

Wayne Cherry rose to the position of vice president of Design in 1992; he had a very different perspective from his predecessors. He sought to increase the importance of design within the company by setting goals and new processes, with an emphasis on brand identity. O'Kane's design career matured under Cherry's leadership.

Cherry, who spent the majority of his career in Europe, established front-end design control, the Advanced Portfolio Expansion Group (APEx), brand centers, and computer technologies in Warren, Michigan.

Front-end design control allowed Cherry to supervise all advanced-design proposals for the corporation. These projects included future vehicles, concept options used to fill a space in the company portfolio, and vision models designed to establish design directions for the brands.[6]

Cherry adopted APEx to clarify and redefine the market and restructure the GM portfolio so that each brand hit a separate target. He sought to structure a large portfolio, eliminate overlaps, target divisions, and cover a broader market. Design teams should have expertise across the organization—marketing, retailing, engineering, and manufacturing—plus cultural knowledge such as social anthropology. His European colleague, John Taylor, mapped out two areas for research scenarios and trends.

Cherry eventually created brand character centers for each division, with their own individual environment, design philosophy, and signature.[7] O'Kane described this as a very exciting time at Design Center: "When you walked into any studio you automatically saw, felt, and sensed the essence of each individual brand identity. This was part of Wayne's legacy."

CAD BECOMES NORM WITH CHERRY

Early designers relied on pencil and marker to initiate designs and airbrush to refine them. For many, the pencil and some sculpted clay still provided the most spontaneous way to record an idea both two- and three-dimensionally. Not long ago, British designer Simon Cox initiated a sheer design style and the Cadillac Cien concept car three-dimensionally in clay.

However, the computer was Wayne Cherry's Zeus. In fact, Cherry would later note, "The transition to [the use of computers] has been the single biggest influence on the way automobiles are designed in the decade." He was said to have installed computer cables in the design studios, created a virtual-reality studio—the Cave—and run one program entirely by computer. The Chevrolet SSR, selected for the program, was a poster child for computers.[8]

Brigid O'Kane notes that the first software developed at GM was engineering oriented and was largely developed by her father. Jim O'Kane, chief engineer in Truck, started working on Autoshape in 1985. Although it was a Bezier-based surface software like Daussault's ICEM Surf, it functioned more as a tool to quickly convert point data from clay models into surface data to be shared with engineering. In that way, it was a precursor to software that converted cloud scan data into polygonal surfaces.

Dave Warn and Richard Bartles were the software developers for Autoshape. Jim O'Kane took on the task of incorporating its use into vehicle development at General Motors. A group of four surface specialists—Glen Skinner, Eric Beasley, Amy Dale, and Joel Bachler—worked under Jim O'Kane's leadership. Jim drove the vision of how Autoshape would be used in the design studios, helping Warn refine and improve the software. As Skinner describes it, "Back then a touch probe was used to capture point coordinates off the clay model in a grid pattern 100 millimeters apart. Typically, this would then be provided to the Surface and Prototype Engineering Department, who would use it as a template for developing a CAD surface model interpretation of the clay, using the "slab and fillet" method. This was a laborious process often taking a week or more. Using Autoshape, we could turn out a surface sometimes in just a couple of hours with some minor cleanup of the point data received from the touch probe. As we gained experience and improved the process, our output grew much more precise in accurately capturing the aesthetic of the clay models. Autoshape was developed at GM Research but relied on Jim O'Kane to show the studios how it could help them get fast, accurate CAD of their clay models. Jim played a key role in the development of the software, its application, and techniques, as well as navigating the politics of introducing a new technology that helped accelerate the vehicle development timeline."

By the time Brigid was transferred to California in 1995, CAD enabled designers and engineers to generate complex three-dimensional surfaces. However, more-sophisticated products arrived from Autodesk, an American company that provides software for designers, architects, and engineers. Later, Rhino could translate NURBS curves, surfaces, solids, polygon meshes, and clouds. Any geometry could be exported to laser cutters, milling machines, and 3-D printers. Brigid mentioned her use of Alias built momentum while she was in the Saturn studio working on interior components. She recalls that you could have parts back within the same day, which really accelerated the design process.

While it took expensive software to communicate with engineers and generate three-dimensional models during Cherry's tenure, today's designers generate models in their own homes and studios with commercially available software and 3-D printers.[9] With the proliferation of these devices, manufacturers fight for market share. However, manufacturers struggle with providing reasonably priced bigger printers for the production of large-scale models.

The Intrigue was a best seller. *General Motors*

The Concept Cure team consisted of Joe Boxer's Nick Graham, Dana Buchman, Karen Harman, and Max Azria. *BO and General Motors*

The Olds Team poses on the patio at Design. *Brigid O'Kane/General Motors*

CONCEPT:
CURE AND CARS & CONCEPTS, INC.

On being asked to be the lead designer for a program called Concept Cure, Brigid recalls, "I thoroughly enjoyed the experience. I was so lucky to be given the opportunity to work with so many distinguished designers. I traveled to each of the fashion designer's studios and then to California when they filmed and photographed the vehicles for the sweepstakes. It was amazing and all for a great cause."

O'Kane penned this design for the Escalade. *Brigid O'Kane and GM*

GM set up the Concept Cure program with the Council of Fashion Designers of America. A handful of iconic fashion designers made GM's most-significant vehicles their own. Joe Boxer's Nicholas Graham upgraded a Chevrolet Venture taxicab. Dana Buchman and Karen Harman outfitted a zebra-striped Pontiac Grand Am. Joseph Abboud transformed the rugged GMC Sierra, and Vivian Tan brought grace to an Oldsmobile

The Antares. *Brigid O'Kane*

Alero. Max Azria created a brushed-nickel Cavalier convertible. [Note: The concepts were exhibited at Music Hall in Detroit and the Chicago Automobile Show, and the program raised $2.6 million for breast cancer research over a three-year period.]

OLDS ANTARES CONCEPT CAR AND THE INTRIGUE

A website titled Outright Oldsmobile outlines the career of Ed Welburn. Welburn, who was appointed GM vice president of global design in 2005, moved from the Advanced Design Studio to the Oldsmobile Exterior Studio in 1975, where he contributed to the Cutlass Supreme and later the Ciera and Calais. He was appointed chief designer of Oldsmobile Exterior II in December 1989, prior to the Aerotech, Aurora, Antares, and Intrigue. Welburn received the EyesOn Design Award in 2018 after his retirement.

O'Kane worked closely with Welburn and designer Peter Lawlis on the Oldsmobile Intrigue. When the possibility of developing a show car became real, Welburn supported O'Kane's ideas for the Antares. O'Kane has enormous respect for Welburn, who was incredibly generous with sharing his knowledge. O'Kane described his leadership style: "He let designers and other team members have a say, and he listened. He didn't dictate. If things got hard, he would step in and either take control or guide us through it. That takes real wisdom. I learned a great deal about exceptional leadership from Ed Welburn."

The Oldsmobile Antares project, to which O'Kane was assigned in 1995, was a significant one. The Antares concept would win an award. The Antares was shown before the Intrigue; it was developed in the studios as the Intrigue was being released for production.

The Antares was a concept car created to generate excitement for the Oldsmobile Intrigue. The Intrigue was later selected by *Autoweek* as "The Most Significant Car" of the 1996 North American International Auto Show.

PONTIAC'S LYNN MYERS DEFINES PONTIAC STYLE

The Oakland Motor Car Company started producing Pontiacs on December 28, 1925, and in 2000, Pontiac Motor Division celebrated its seventy-fifth year. John Gunnell recorded Pontiac's history in *75 Years of Pontiac: The Official History* (Krause Publications, F&W Media, 2012).

In this historical encyclopedia of sorts, general manager Lynn C. Myers noted in its foreword: "As I write this at the start of the new millennium, I can only dream where Pontiac is headed in the next 100 years. I can say, however, that our mission will continue to be 'driving excitement' in whatever form future

drivers define it. It's safe to say that handling and performance will remain Pontiac's building blocks long into the future."

Myers further pinpoints the defining elements of Pontiacs: "Signature design cues like twin-port grilles, athletic forms, and cockpit styled interiors will continue to appear on next[-]generation Pontiacs."

O'Kane's original drawing for the Aztek was chosen for development, but she could not control those above her that greatly modified it. Collection of B.O. *General Motors*

AZTEK

Members of the Pontiac Studio received one of the greatest challenges of the decade when General Motors entered the race to introduce the first crossover/hybrid—the Aztek. Brigid noted that they called it a hybrid at the time because it combined two types of existing vehicles. The Aztek concept was unveiled at the 2000 North American Auto Show in Detroit, Michigan, as the first SRV—Sport Recreational Vehicle. This attempt to break new ground resulted in a controversial design.

This assignment was not an easy one. The vehicle would be built atop the van chassis developed for the Montana—Pontiac's sporty minivan, offered with a 112- and 120-inch wheelbase both in FWD and AWD. Aztek would be offered in front-wheel drive and Versatrak—an AWD system that automatically engaged all four wheels as needed.

Brigid O'Kane observed that the overall proportions of Aztek were most challenging. She recalls, "The small wheels were too far inboard and should have been pulled out for a wider stance. The vehicle required more ground clearance to hold the visual weight of the body; we should have utilized the platform of an off-road vehicle or at least designed it with bigger wheels and tires. The visual size of the body was so large, it made the wheels look smaller than they really were." The Aztek's track was only slightly wider than that of the Montana. However, to generate sales, advertisers would later note that Aztek had a low entry height, which made it easy to load child seats and gear.

While working on Aztek, Brigid worked with Joel Piaskowski and Eric Clough under the direction of chief designer Tom Peters. In the era in which the Aztek was designed, it was probably difficult for many men to accept Brigid because of her enormous talent. She was sometimes uncomfortable with communications in the studio and talked openly about this to get what she called "reality checks." It is important to her to see circumstances from different points of view. Brigid O'Kane has the passion, work ethics, and a drive to succeed. One of her strengths is she enjoys working in teams. She mentioned how she appreciated Eric Clough because of his sound approach and clarity of vision. "He did an impeccable job on the interior of Aztek."

When the exterior design was running behind schedule, several designers were brought into the studio to help "put out the fire." While her colleagues were given two modelers to help develop a three-dimensional design, Brigid was given only one: "It didn't matter, I just did the best job I could." The modeler who was assigned to work with O'Kane was in the throes of a divorce and not motivated to work. On the positive side, he committed to the project partly because Brigid enjoyed talking with him. Brigid noted, "We worked and worked at a steady pace and created a fantastic model." Years later, he thanked Brigid for her advice at that time, which he said saved his marriage.

During the final design selection process for Aztek, Jerry Palmer, executive director of Design, was praising Brigid's model, and Wayne Cherry, GM's vice president of Design, described it as a strong direction to move forward with. However, Tom Peters supported the other designers. After much deliberation, Palmer made his preference clear: "Why do you want to change this design completely when Brigid's design has it all right here?"

Brigid's design of the Aztek was chosen for production. However, Wayne Cherry advised Brigid, "We have to convince Peters not to change your design." Brigid notes that the hardest part of the design process is maintaining the essence of a two-dimensional design as it gets translated into a three-dimensional model for production. When politics are thrown into the mix, it gets even more difficult.

Once O'Kane's design was selected for production, six sculptors were assigned to develop her design as a full-size model. At that time, O'Kane applied the leadership skills she learned from Ed Welburn and her father. She gained intimate knowledge about the three-dimensional model that enabled her to incorporate good design input and deflect bad ideas. "I could reason through why some ideas worked and others didn't. When the focus is on what is best for the design, the vision comes into focus."

Brigid notes, "Aztek was the peak of my career at GM. My aesthetic approach was bold, and when my design was selected to go into production, I was so thrilled. Colleagues gave me so many compliments. However, once the full-size model was displayed and the process to get it ready for production had begun, it seemed like everyone wanted their hand on the design, which included people from marketing, Pontiac, engineering, and design leadership. Sometimes the input we got from one person was the complete opposite from someone else. This caused many design changes. Maintaining the integrity and essence of the original design aesthetic is the hardest part of being a creative designer."

The Aztek afforded space to travelers when equipped with a number of available accessories. *General Motors*

The Aztek remains an attractive leisure vehicle for some. *General Motors*

By the time the Aztek design was finalized and released for production, the design was altered. "The original design had crown with graceful transitions (crown in a panel is compound curvature, as opposed to simple curvature). Individual design elements lined up with a sense of unity. The production version was flattened, the transitions lacked grace, and the essence of the original design was altered."

While many refer to this as design by committee, Wayne Cherry, according to O'Kane, put it this way: "Death by a thousand cuts." Unfortunately, this happens often in the design process. O'Kane learned a great deal from the process. She firmly believes that there is always something to learn, even when things don't go as planned.

The front of the Aztek is characterized by a twin-port grille and ram air slots. These are heavy negative elements in a positive form. The front bore the aggressiveness of the Pontiac Firebird. Other jewelry included oversized fog lamps and cat's-eye lights. Aztek's heavy cladding was stylishly grooved to generate Pontiac excitement.

The so-called failure of the Aztek is described by Bob Lutz in his second book, *Car Guys vs. Bean Counters: The Battle for the Soul of America.* The press, as usual, sought to hold GM up to a higher standard. Bear in mind that while Lutz promoted design, he was never an automobile designer. He graduated from UC Berkeley in 1962 from what is now called the Haas School of Business, before beginning his career as an analyst in GM's Department of Overseas Operations. The vast majorities of the members of the press are not trained designers and never will be. Even designers themselves disagree on the definition of good design. When it comes to aesthetics, designers usually lead the general public. Lutz appears to have equated the failure of the Aztek with other financial failures caused by the economy and other factors. His description of the Aztek is informative:

"GM proudly launched the Pontiac Aztek, a minivan-based vehicle designed for a niche somewhere in the U.S. market. Since it was often displayed with a large tent deployed somewhere from the back end, one can only assume it was created for people to go camping or who over wise have no permanent dwelling. It was atrociously ugly, with featureless, flat body panels offset in front by what appeared to be one lower and one upper grille opening. I remember staring at it in disbelief the first time I saw it: I could not imagine that a group of automotive designers and executives had green-lighted this Quasimodo of crossovers."[10]

On the positive side, the design team devised a number of innovative features inside. Upon introduction, Aztek had a flat load floor and flip-fold removable seats. A portable console cooler came with the GT option. Utility packs that were included with the front doors were designed to house small electronic devices such as cell phones and cameras.

A clever fold-down tailgate incorporated two molded seating surfaces and cup holders. Upon seeing this depression, users knew the tailgate would support their body weight. The sliding rear cargo tray would have been appreciated on any vehicle. Pontiac also offered an optional cargo net system. Later, Aztek was featured as Walter White's daily driver in the acclaimed TV series *Breaking Bad*. O'Kane laughed out loud about this. "They had to pick Aztek for *Breaking Bad*. They even removed one of the wheel covers."

The Aztek was included in the major auto shows along with thirty-five unique and rare Pontiacs. One might think that because the press panned it, there would be no sales. However, over an eighteen-month period, 38,000 of them had been sold.[11]

In hindsight, retired GM VP of Design, Ed Welburn, noted in an interview that he felt design, engineering, and marketing had different visions for the Aztek. Design had their vision of what the car should look like, and wanted an off-road vehicle with a huge personality. Engineering required that the car use existing car architecture, and marketing wanted all kinds of things like camping and tents (Autoline *After Hours* online: "Ed Welburn: A Life in Design," January 31, 2019).

O'KANE DESIGNS SETS

After ten years at General Motors, O'Kane departed for California, where she worked as a production set designer for the film industry. "When I first voiced that I was leaving GM, Jerry Palmer tried to prevent me from leaving; he was very sweet about it." Palmer responded by offering her a two-year sabbatical with medical insurance and an open invitation to come back at any time.

Combining her extensive knowledge and training in design with her creative approach to fine arts, Brigid created her own technique to provide set design illustrations measuring 23 by 30 inches. Preliminary sketches were assembled to build rich compositions. The assemblage of final sketches was xeroxed on one large piece of paper, then she added value, color, and detail. She made her own large markers from the ink used for refilling markers and folded cloth up to 3 inches wide. After the value system was applied, she used mixed media to finish the illustrations, including chalk, pencil, marker, and gouache. Her illustrations captured a variety of subjects, including automobiles and buildings.

O'KANE AS EDUCATOR

Brigid joined the University of Cincinnati in 2000 as an associate professor within the College of Design, Architecture, Art, and Planning (DAAP). She held the position of interim director of the School of Design during a three-year period. She has lectured nationally and internationally on topics that include product design processes, systems thinking, and sustainable design.

As a professor, she has led sponsored studios, published peer-reviewed papers, written a chapter in a book titled "Design and Designing," and penned numerous other articles. She has given over thirty significant design presentations and keynote addresses globally in Germany, Belgium, Korea, Canada, China, India, Mexico, Brazil, and the United States. Today, she focuses her research on the design principles of visual organization and holistic design processes, which include systems thinking and ecologically conscious design solutions.

In academia, O'Kane has received numerous awards and honors.

O'Kane is a cofounder of the Manifest Creative Research Gallery and Drawing Center, a nonprofit arts organization that documents and presents visual art and design from around the world.

COLLABORATION IS KEY

In one of her many conversations with the author in 2021, Brigid O'Kane noted that "in the design of something as complicated as a vehicle, a collaborative effort is needed. This paradigm can be applied today, more than ever, as different disciplines must respect each other and each other's ideas. Interdisciplinary collaborative teams that embrace diverse perspectives will achieve broader ideals that can align with the challenges of our time. Designers, through their unique way of interpreting the world, are essential in developing creative results. Systems thinking and ecological design approaches are necessary for holistic solutions, which is critical for the future of design."

KRISTY RASBACH

Do it! It is not the easiest path, but it is incredibly rewarding. You will endure some adversity, but never give up.[1]

—Kristy Rasbach (b. ca. 1977), 2019

Courtesy of Kristy Rasbach

CAREER SUMMARY

Kristy Rasbach started at GM as an engineering co-op student and assumed her first full-time position in chassis validation in 1999. In 2002, she became a steering lead engineer, where she implemented Cadillac's first premium steering system. Throughout the next decade, Rasbach served in various roles, including specialty vehicle activity, global steering systems, advanced vehicle development, and computer-aided engineering.

After following a mechanical-centric path, she decided to switch over and learn about electric motors. Rasbach was named chief engineer of autonomous vehicles at General Motors in 2019. In this role, Rasbach is responsible for the development and execution of General Motors' first self-driving vehicles. Previously, Rasbach served as Engineering Group manager for the Vehicle Dynamics Center of Expertise and served as program engineering manager for electrified vehicles, where she led the nationwide launch of the 2017 Chevrolet Volt.[2] In 2022, Rasbach became Director of Global Safety Systems.

She is a passionate advocate for recruiting young women into STEM careers and was a founder of GM's annual chassis charity event for Lighthouse PATH, an Oakland County shelter designed to assist women and children with job training, education, and soft skills.

BIOGRAPHICAL NOTES

Kristy Rasbach graduated from Clarkston High School in 1995, and there is no question that she had both parents' support. Kristy notes, "Early on, my father was instrumental in encouraging me to pursue engineering. In high school, he convinced me to try courses like Basic Engineering (drafting) and Basic Automotive that were not traditional course selections for young women in the 1990s.[3]

"My mother has always been my biggest cheerleader, and unfortunately she passed away in 2019, just as I was beginning my role as chief engineer of autonomous vehicles. She became an amputee in 2010, which was a significant challenge for her. It changed her life in many ways, and I witnessed firsthand what it is like for a person to adjust to having a disability. I recognize the potential of autonomous vehicles to provide access to transportation for people with disabilities. Even in her death, my mother inspires me to be the first to bring autonomous technology to market, due to the positive impact can have on society. I know she would be proud of me."[4]

Kristy Rasbach began her engineering career as a co-op student from the University of Michigan at General Motors in 1995 at seventeen years of age. The co-op experience at UM allows students to work in the real world and get paid for their contributions. It is notable that in 1978, David Cole established the Office for the Study of Automotive Transportation at UM. This organization still exists as the Center for Automotive Research, and Cole is on the advisory board of the college. The wide range of studies performed by the group is significant. David is the son of Edward N. Cole, an innovative leader who served as president of GM from 1967 to 1974 and was inducted into the Automotive Hall of Fame. This family likely led to the school's association with GM. After finishing the co-op program, Rasbach earned a bachelor of science degree in mechanical engineering from the University of Michigan at Ann Arbor in 1999, and later a master of science in engineering from Purdue University in 2004.

Kristy is a third-generation General Motors employee; her grandfather and father both retired from the company. After four years rotating through various engineering roles, Rasbach was hired by the company full time as a chassis validation engineer. Early on, she contributed to the design of the 2004 Cadillac SRX and 2005 STS. In 2005, Rasbach became a GM steering lead engineer, where she led the implementation of Cadillac's first premium steering system. Throughout the next few years, she oversaw the engineering of Cadillac suspension systems, government programs in specialty vehicle activity, and global steering-systems quality, where she led a 50 percent reduction in North American steering-system warranties in one year.[5]

THE XLR

In 2013, Rasbach was named engineering business manager for Global Advanced Vehicle Development and Computer Aided Engineering. One of the standouts of the era was the one-of-a-kind XLR convertible.

The Cadillac Evoq reiterated a striking new design vocabulary that already had appeared on the production Escalade and CTS. They have all been described as innovative and striking or even chiseled. Designed on the outside by Kip Wasenko's team, which included Scott Wassell and Chip Thole, it was named the best concept car by *Autoweek* magazine. This design led to the production XLR roadster convertible.

THE VOLT

The original Volt Concept was introduced in 2007 at the Detroit Auto Show. This amazing vehicle was recognized nationally and internationally. In one of his books, Bob Lutz was sure to mention that it was a sequential hybrid, unlike the Toyota Prius it competed against. In 2015, it was time for a makeover, and Rasbach was named program engineering manager of electrified vehicles, where she led the nationwide launch of the 2017 Chevrolet Volt.

The Volt inspired Rasbach's passion for electrification, which, as a mechanical engineer, was something she did not anticipate earlier in her career. Two years later, Rasbach became engineering group manager for the Vehicle Dynamics Center of Expertise at the Milford Proving Ground, where she was responsible for developing strategy and best practices for road to lab to math. In 2019, she was named chief engineer for autonomous vehicles, leading the execution of GM's first autonomous vehicles.[6]

XLR instrument cluster. *Keith Furino*

CADILLAC ELR

Rasbach also served as program engineering manager (assistant chief engineer) for the 2016 Cadillac ELR.

The 2014 Cadillac ELR utilized almost the same power train as the 2011–2015 Chevrolet Volt. The stunning coupe was expensive and was discontinued for 2015. In 2016, the steering, suspension, and brakes were recalibrated to improve performance. The price was reduced to move cars.

Super Cruise was integrated into the steering wheel. *General Motors*

CADILLAC'S SUPER CRUISE

Super Cruise, a semiautonomous system for long-distance and daily highway travel, delivers comfort and convenience to the CT6 driver and will be available on all Cadillacs soon.

To add to its accuracy, Cadillac has mapped out all roads considered highways in the country, so that the system can take over reliably; no other manufacturer has gone to this extent.

Cruise is easy to engage. Once on the highway, an icon appears to signal that the system is available, and the driver pushes a button to activate it. A lighted green strip appears at the top of the steering wheel to indicate it is on. The original system shut off while the car was changing lanes, and the lighted strip turns blue. The system provides head-tracking software to track your eyes, which should remain focused on the road.

Always looking to make improvements, Cadillac has now introduced Super Cruise with a lane change feature.

The first autonomous vehicle concept is pictured here. It features LiDAR.

ENTER CRUISE AUTOMATION

Cruise Automation and Strobe were brought together to be able to deliver autonomous vehicles to the masses. GM was reported to have acquired Cruise, founded by Kyle Vogt, in 2016 for a sum of $1 million. Strobe, which initially included only a dozen employees, was founded in 2017. Its board member, John Bowers, is an engineering professor and researcher at UC in Santa Barbara. Bowers has spent years researching how to pack sensors onto a silicon chip. In a photograph posted online, Strobe's design is about the same length as a magic marker. In 2020, the company unveiled their newest vehicle, the Origin.

As time progressed, other investors came out of the woodwork, including Softbank Vision Fund and even Honda.

Autonomous vehicles need to sense, make decisions based on input, and activate in response. Today, our sensors include cameras, LiDAR, radar, ultrasonic, infrared, ultrasound, V2X, and GPS. We use 5C to communicate with the cloud. This electronics has matured over a number of years.

While we have available multiple technologies, the availability of LiDAR, because of its speed, has allowed GM to change the course of history. In simple terms, LiDAR uses laser pulses to project beams that when returned calculate the distance of objects or people in a vehicle's path. While early LiDAR units cost $80,000, newer ones are less expensive, since the key to success rests on reduction of cost.

LiDAR, short for light detection and ranging, made its appearance at MIT in 1962, was employed during the Apollo program, and was promoted by DARPA (US Defense Advanced Research Projects Agency) challenges sponsored by the US Department of Defense. Most early systems incorporated a large roof sensor that swept the field around a vehicle. Davis Hall, of Velodyne, is said to have set an industry standard by his entrance in DARPA's third competition. He mounted an array of lasers on a spinning gimbal in order to collect distance data.

DARPA (US Defense Advanced Research Projects Agency) created projects to further explore the use of LiDAR with college students. The Chevrolet Tahoe best suited their needs and this vehicle. The Carnegie Mellon entry is pictured. *General Motors*

However, in 2007, a Chevrolet Tahoe "Autonomy Boss" won the third Grand Challenge. GM collaborated with Carnegie Mellon University.

The 2015 paper emanating from Strobe researchers is titled *Fully Integrated Hybrid Silicon Two Dimensional Beam Scanner*, which describes MEMS-like scanning capabilities without using me-

chanical parts.[7] Advances in Strobe's LiDAR are projected.

In regard to other important research, we need to monitor the driver and explore machine vision, which incorporates rolling and global shutter imagers, wavelength selection, use of secondary optics, continuous versus pulsed IRED operation, thermal design, power consumption, eye safety certification, and HMI considerations. Our affiliated research needs to include iris recognition, cabin monitoring, and facial recognition.

In an interview, Kristy notes that after twenty years in a mechanical-centric position, a mentor challenged her to take something new on: electrification. She was stepping out of her comfort zone.

She notes that the chief engineer for any program is the chief decision maker. She is leading the GM team. With safety being a priority, the team makes sure all the critical systems have a backup. Cruise's expertise is in software, and marrying that with GM strengths makes great things happen.

The development of an autonomous vehicle is one of the major challenges to the automotive designer today and will be remembered well into the future.

The fully autonomous Bolt is one of the greatest engineering feats of our era. *General Motors*

FAMILY NOTES

In addition to her extensive engineering career, Rasbach is a passionate advocate for recruiting young women into STEM careers, and, presently, volunteers in Scouts BSA. In 2004 and 2012, Rasbach served as the chairwoman of GM's annual chassis charity event for Lighthouse PATH, an Oakland County shelter designed to assist women and children with job training, education, and soft skills. In 2009, she, along with the chassis planning team, was awarded the Lighthouse PATH "Beacon Award" for her efforts.[8]

Kristy married in 2002. Born in Clarkston, Michigan, she currently lives in Lake Orion with her husband and three children.[9] Like most kids, hers love Disney cruises, and she celebrated her fifteenth wedding anniversary in Greece. However, Yellowstone and the Grand Teton National Park were also on the agenda.

Drawing by Constance Smith

KRISTEN SIEMEN

As one of the world's largest automakers, we aim to set an example of responsible leadership; I am honored and humbled to have the opportunity to help lead GM in our plan to reach a zero-emissions future, and am excited for all we plan to accomplish in the coming years.

Kristen Siemen (b. 1971) and GM Corporate Newsroom

CAREER HIGHLIGHTS

Kristen Siemen, named GM vice president of sustainable workplaces as well as chief sustainability officer, replaced Dane Parker, who retired on May 1, 2021.

Before transitioning to her current position, Siemen served as executive director of Global Energy Strategy, Certification and Compliance, and Test Labs in the ongoing effort to set science-based targets for a net-zero carbon future (2020–2021).

Siemen previously held the positions of executive director, Global Functional Leader/Electrical Systems; executive director, Global Thermal/HVAC and Toluca Engineering Center; and global validation engineer (2010–2020).

Siemen was a founding member of GM's STEM Reentry Task Force, a paid, midcareer internship program for engineers returning from a multiyear career break. The GM Take 2 Program pilot initially had ten midcareer interns, all returning engineers in suburban Detroit. With Siemen acting as mentor, the majority of interns received job offers. GM is now greatly expanding the program.

Siemen has served on the Advisory Board of Oakland University's School of Engineering and Computer Science since 2014. She is also a member of the Board of Advisors for Catalyst, Inc., since 2016.

As executive director, Global Thermal/HVAC Engineering, General Motors, Siemen was the recipient of the Activist Award from *Working Mother*, which goes to a woman who has worked to improve policies or practices effecting change for women at her job or in her community.

KRISTEN SIEMEN'S JOURNEY

Kristen is a native of Warren, Michigan. Like a number of her colleagues across the corporation, Kristen grew up in an automotive-oriented family. Her father, her grandfather, and even her grandmother all worked in jobs that produced cars or car components.

Following a high school career evaluation, Siemen realized she wanted to study engineering. Growing up in Warren, one of her dreams was to work for GM. Earning her bachelor's in electrical engineering in 1992 put her closer to that goal.[1]

In 1992, she was awarded the bachelor of science degree in electrical and electronics and subsequently the master of science degree in electrical and electronics engineering from Oakland University in 1994. However, before proceeding to GM, she was recruited by Chrysler, where she spent two years while studying for her master's degree.

Chris Kobus, associate professor and OUSECS outreach director, knew Siemen from their time spent together in the organization Tau Beta Pi, in addition to serving as her teaching assistant for thermodynamics in 1992. Kobus said they both were very involved with TBP as students, and he saw she was always very driven and ambitious. "Kristen was driven not just as a student but as a leader," Kobus said. "She took naturally to leadership positions in her classes and in student orgs. It is those natural leadership skills in combination with her scholarship that makes for a potent combination qualifying her above many others for an executive position out in industry."[2]

She currently serves as a member of that institution's School of Engineering and Computer Science Advisory Board.

With her wide range of experience, however, she said one of her favorite assignments was leading the Safety Electronics team, which was responsible for technologies such as adaptive cruise control, side blind-zone detection, and park assist. This team also began, and continues, the work on GM's new semiautonomous driving feature known as "Super Cruise," which was planned for introduction in model year (MY) 2017. Siemen thoroughly enjoyed her experience working with the safety electronics area, which kept her feeling constantly connected to customers.[3]

The General Motors Newsroom posted that Kristen Siemen was named vice president of Sustainable Workplaces and chief sustainability officer, replacing Dane Parker, who had decided to retire effective May 1, 2021. "Dane has helped the company strengthen our work to address climate change, and efforts to realize a future with zero emissions, and we wish him every success," said GM chairman and CEO Mary Barra. "I look forward to Kristen's leadership in driving our ongoing actions to create a safer, more sustainable world."[4]

FAMILY MATTERS

Siemen is married and with her husband is raising three sons. It is no surprise that her family enjoys sports.

In 2017, with the introduction of the Chevrolet Bolt, GM began its quest to make its vehicles and facilities carbon neutral by 2035 and 2040.
Constance Smith

General Motors

KATHERINE SIRVIO

The opportunity to travel, work, and live in another culture has had a profound impact on me as a designer and a manager. I love working at a company that embraces and encourages diversity in culture, thought, and experience. In fact, some of my team hails from the jewelry, lighting fixtures, and footwear industries.[1]

—Katherine Sirvio (b. 1969)

CAREER HIGHLIGHTS[2]

Katherine Sirvio started her career with GG Warren Jewelers, repairing jewelry and creating beaded works for their display cases in 1987. During her college years, she interned at the Michigan Design Center's Harkema Associates, where she found her love of colors, materials, and finishes designing residential and commercial interiors. In the following years, Sirvio bolstered her creative endeavors with retail and business experience at the Detroit Artists Market and Coach House Art Gallery. There she not only worked the retail floor and set up displays to merchandise art but also exhibited her works and sold her first pieces outside school exhibits.

In 1990, she began an internship with General Motors Design, which quickly resulted in a job offer contingent upon her graduation. In 1992, Katherine began in the position of associate creative designer and was one of the first degree-holding color and material designers since the Damsels of Design. She worked creating hand renderings of fabrics and materials under multiple leaders.

Sirvio accepted her first overseas assignment at Adam Opel AG in Rüsselsheim, Germany, in 1994. She contributed to the production Opel Astra and traveled to Italy to work with Bertone on the Opel MAXX concept vehicle. Upon return to the United States and advancing consistently through the years, she became senior designer.

Sirvio's work then took her to Japan to be part of the team designing the original Chevrolet Colorado, led by Ken Parkinson. This earned her and the team the Harley Earl Award.

In 2004, Sirvio traveled to China for work with PATAC (Pan Asia Technical Automotive Center) to set up the new Color & Trim Studio in Shanghai. There she worked closely with the team, teaching, mentoring, and creating relationships that strengthened her global positioning and passion.

The following year, Sirvio was selected to participate in the first Color & Trim Global Face-to-Face meetings taking place in Brazil. There she became the champion under Helen Emsley to create a twice-yearly forum specializing in reducing and creating meaningful and globally manufacturable color and material commodities.

Sirvio went on to create the interior and exterior colors for the Chevrolet Nomad concept vehicle and the Chevrolet Trax concept vehicle and contributed toward the Chevrolet "Triplets" (Trax, Beat, and Groove), which foreshadowed her next overseas assignment in 2007, when she led Daewoo Color & Trim Design through bankruptcy and in fully joining the GM Company. She was now responsible for Chevrolet, Buick, and Opel designs, working closely with all seven design regions of the time. Some noted vehicles are the Chevrolet Spark, Sonic, Cruze, Orlando, and Trax; the Opel Mokka; and Buick Encore. Sirvio accepted awards for the Spark, Sonic, Malibu, and Equinox from WardsAuto and delivered a speech on small segment vehicles at the 20XX Conference.

In 2011, again back in North America, Sirvio became the Color & Trim design manager for Global Chevrolet and GMC Trucks. By this time, Sirvio had worked on all GM brands, including Cadillac, Hummer, Saturn, Oldsmobile, Pontiac, Saab, Holden, Vauxhall, and Joint Venture Isuzu. Sirvio had traveled to all the design regions and built relationships with the global color-and-trim community. She continued leading Global Chevrolet for the next decade, developing marketing concepts such as "Truth in Materials" and person-based trim levels through colors, materials, and finishes.

Katherine left Chevrolet only to join Cadillac as their global senior design manager in 2018. There she was integral in the color and material selection of China's Cadillac House, and her team was responsible for all Cadillac vehicles, including CT4, CT5, CT6, XT4, XT5, and XT6.

Sirvio served GM Design for twenty-nine years before retiring in June 2019 to pursue her own art and jewelry business interests. Today she also serves as vice president of Marketing and Design at SISU Print Solutions, which she began with her husband in 2007, and is the founder of Sirvio Design.

Sirvio attended the 2013 Javits New York International Auto Show reveal for the Spark. *Constance Smith*

BIOGRAPHICAL NOTES

Katherine hails from Lancaster, Pennsylvania. Graduating from the College for Creative Studies in 1992, she is unlike her colleagues who studied automotive or industrial design. Sirvio chose to study fine arts in the Crafts Department and majored in fiber—simply meaning weaving, silkscreening, jewelry making, and woodworking. She did a lot of hands on. After creating a student show, a GM educational representative caught her by surprise by buying a number of pieces. A struggling student at the time, she was delighted by the sale, since she needed the money. When she sat down with the buyer to suggest frames, she was recruited and later retained by General Motors. Had she ever thought about working in the automotive industry? No.

When asked to name one of GM's greatest competitive strengths, Sirvio points to the global footprint of its design organization at the top the list.

As a member of the first and largest OEM design function, with a network of ten design centers in seven countries, she knew firsthand how diversity brings new opportunity. After overseas assignments in Korea and Europe, and working with the global design studios, she filled her studio with designers from all over the world, including India, Australia, Vietnam, Brazil, Poland, Ukraine, and North America.

Many of these international designers bring unique skill sets and fresh perspectives from their hometowns that help shape a truly global Chevrolet. She shared with her team the same enthusiasm and courage that she felt as a GM new hire and the first art-degreed color-and-trim designer in North America.

"My job is to make sure our color and trim programs are progressive and that my team is continually reaching through fresh thinking and new technologies," said Sirvio. "The opportunity to travel, work, and live in another culture has had a profound impact on me as a designer and a manager. I love working at a company that embraces and encourages diversity in culture, thought, and experience. In fact, some of my team hails from the jewelry, lighting fixtures, and footwear industries."[3]

Perhaps Katherine Sirvio is a new breed of color-and-trim design manager—one who has earned street creds as a creative designer as well as a businesswoman. As the manager of GM's Global Chevrolet Color & Trim Design Studio, Sirvio had the ability to move conceptual ideas and designs into production-viable vehicle programs.

"The first fabric that I designed that made it into production was Saturn's SC2 in 1992, but our production work really took off after Helen Emsley arrived. That growth has continued under the leadership of Sharon Gauci. Having a combination of global experience and business acumen was pivotal to the growth of the Color & Trim Studio and to me."

"Today's color-and-trim designers wear a lot of different hats, understanding and working closely with engineering, purchasing, and cost balancing, all while creative design is our priority."

Kathy's portfolio includes a variety of concept and production vehicle programs and brands, including assignments for Cadillac, Saturn, and Chevrolet. Her recent work includes the new Chevrolet Bolt EV, Volt, Spark, Sonic, Cruze, and Malibu. In an interview, she notes the many colors, both trendy and traditional, that differentiate Sparks. In 2012, her fancifully painted Spark was selected as the pace car for the Color Run, a series of 5K races.

Sirvio's responsibilities extended to Chevrolet production interiors, concept vehicles, the brand's global color palette and material portfolio, and the articulation of a cohesive design strategy that is tailored to each region around the world, while maintaining a global focus and appearance.

Katherine left Chevrolet only to join Cadillac as its global senior design manager in 2018. There she was integral in the color and material selection of China's Cadillac House.

THE OUTSIDE WORLD

Katherine finds value in her hobbies, one of which is traveling near and far accompanied by her husband, Andy. Travel helps heighten her awareness, visual acuity, and appreciation for the colors, patterns, and textures of everyday objects; her greatest joy is still getting outdoors and experiencing the world with her husband on international vacations, riding motorcycles, and scuba diving.

She was inspired by a visit to the ice caves in northern Michigan and noted the effects of light on the surface and shadows. Perhaps the effect could be incorporated in an automotive material—a fabric or decorative plastic. She noted that sand dunes might lead to an automotive hue; possibly this influenced the simulated leather that appeared on the Spark.

Antiquing is her favorite hobby. She collects treasures from antique fairs, some destined for refurbishing. Color, material, texture, and feeling are what attract people.

Kathy realizes that the importance of making time for activities and artistic passions outside work is vital to her creativity during work.

Nick Hagen

SUSAN SKARSGARD

Susan Skarsgard's path to a design position at GM Design was fortuitous and unlikely. "I didn't have a linear career path like most folks here."[1]
—Susan Skarsgard (b. 1954)

CAREER HIGHLIGHTS

Susan Skarsgard started her artistic career as a calligrapher in 1994 and later as a GM designer/manager, creating graphics, nameplates, and emblems for vehicles. She worked in what came to be called the Brand Identity Studio. Her team worked on the development of graphics for the 2002 Buick Rendezvous, a vehicle designed inside and out by teams led by a woman. The designers explored new ground for the Buick Division. In 2006, she was asked to design a commemoration for the fiftieth anniversary of the General Motors Technical Center, which was created by the architectural team headed by Eliel and Eero Saarinen. At the opening of the General Motors Technical Center in 1956, the stage was crowded with male executives, and a large audience was on hand for a presentation made by President Dwight David Eisenhower. Perhaps it is ironic that a woman has dedicated and written about an event to which few or no women were in attendance.

In 2008, Susan founded the GM Design Archive and Special Collections, as we know it today, although GM had previously employed archivists. Skarsgard was on hand sometime later after a flood in a basement area to better organize and catalog the collection. Through the years, she has collected and exhibited artwork in the hands of retired employees and collectors. Exhibits in the archives gallery in the design center paid tribute to notable design VPs and retired designers; a portrait of Irv Ribicki, a VP of Design, was created for one show.

Skarsgard also created a handful of short self-published publications featuring the work of retired designers whose work was displayed in her exhibit area.

In 2016, Skarsgard lectured during the show *Michigan Modern* at the Cranbrook Museum. The exhibition included photos of the GM Technical Center, a model of the Firebird III concept, the work of Susan Vanderbilt, and other notable exhibits.

Skarsgard has written extensively about the GM Technical Center in articles and books and lectured about women designers and midcentury design. Other activities to which she has been assigned include special projects, speaking engagements, and the interviewing of employment applicants. After a twelve-year study of the architecture at the GMTC, Skarsgard's efforts came to fruition in the book *Where Today Meets Tomorrow: Eero Saarinen and the General Motors Technical Center*, published by the Princeton Architectural Press in 2019. This in-depth study documents the work of the Saarinen office and Smith, Hinchman & Grylls via drawings and photos, and their significant contributions to midcentury American architecture.

BIOGRAPHICAL NOTES

Susan was born in Detroit and graduated from Cody High School. She studied music.

An interviewer notes that after she finished college, it took some time for her to figure out what she wanted to do—first getting into Ann Arbor's baroque music scene, then working as a ward clerk at the University of Michigan Hospital. On a whim, she took up calligraphy and realized she had talent—and possibly a career.[2]

Skarsgard interviews and reviews drawings from the 1950s with H. Roy Jaffe. *Constance Smith*

From there, she was apprenticed in Austria and freelanced in the studio of commercial artist Jerry Campbell. On the basis of her accumulated portfolio, she eventually was offered a position at GM in 1994 as a lettering specialist designing graphics—emblems and nameplates—for cars and trucks. She later joined the Brand Identity Studio.

At first it was difficult for her to settle into corporate life, but one thing defining Skarsgard's career is the pursuit of her own interests. That eventually would lead to her carving out a niche archiving GM's illustrious design history.[3]

Susan"s skills at creating graphics would later lead to a promotion. In the late nineties, her department would be taxed to design the identity for the Buick Rendezvous. Elizabeth Wetzel was project head for this crossover, managing both interior and exterior designers. While the exterior form attracts the eye from afar, features such as nameplates keep the observer interested and promote the model and brand.

After serving on GM's workforce, Skarsgard went back to college and earned an MFA from the University of Michigan. In 2004, while studying fine arts. Skarsgard organized an art installation at the Nichols Arboretum. By planting a bed of 20,000 yellow daffodils a half mile long that blooms each spring, she brought emphasis to the nature of borders and the rhythm of the seasons.

In 2010, GM representatives presented "Designing Women," a lecture at the Museum of the City of New York. The presentation, by Teckla Rhoads, Susan Skarsgard, and Christine Park (Cheng), was a highlight at the time of the *Cars, Culture and the City* exhibit.

In 2016, the Cranbrook Museum mounted an exhibit titled *Michigan Modern: Design That Shaped America*. The show included many collections that had been stored and inaccessible for years; some of these included the work and photographs of women automotive artists. It also included images of the Technical Center, a Firebird concept model, and other automobilia. Skarsgard gave a lecture with colleague Christo Datini in conjunction with the *Michigan Modern: Design That Shaped America* book launch lecture series, Preserving Michigan Modern.

A book signing with the editors and authors of *Michigan Modern: Design That Shaped America* followed the lecture.

In 2019, Skarsgard's twelve-year study of the GM Technical Center concluded with the publication *of Where Today Meets Tomorrow: Eero Saarinen and the General Motors Technical Center*. While the book begins with the history of GM this definitive volume also documents the work of Eero and Eliel Saarinen, architects Kevin Roche and John Dinkeloo, and their colleagues from Smith, Hinchman & Grylls. The copyright of the book is held by GM LLC.

In 2019, customer preferences for SUVs over cars, union-negotiated salaries, and expenses for research into advanced technologies appear to have forced GM to consolidate and close factories in the US and Canada. GM employees, because of a possible change to retirement plans, were encouraged to retire early, and Skarsgard likely did. Her new freedom has perhaps changed due to her contributions as a grandparent.

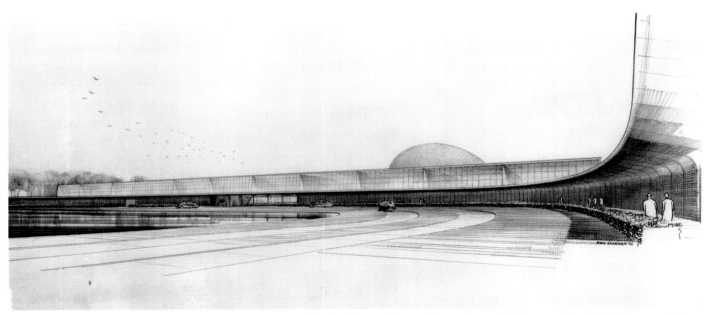

Eliel Saarinen received a commission for the design of GM's Technical Center. His son, Eero, who would take over after his death, penned this design in 1946. *Reprinted from* Damsels In Design

Courtesy of Terese Spafford

TERESA SPAFFORD

When I arrived at GM, I confronted the hierarchy. Exterior designers were considered "gods," interior designers couldn't make it into exteriors, and materials designers were dubbed "pillow tossers." This has to change. I have just as much training as these exterior designers. Why would my opinion be worth less? I needed to up the game plan and get respect.

—Teresa Spafford (b. 1971)

CAREER ABSTRACT

Teresa was born in Australia and studied industrial design at Brigham Young University in Provo, Utah. Around 1999, Spafford joined the Materials Studio upon her arrival at General Motors. She was subsequently invited to join the Pontiac Studio by management. At this time, the Pontiac team worked on developing Grand Prix derivatives and the Pontiac Vibe. The Vibe was a joint venture with Toyota and was manufactured in the NUMMI plant in California.

At the end of 2000, she was invited to join Mazda and was eventually promoted to Lead Design at Mazda's North America Operations. She was the only woman designer at its California location. Early in her career, Spafford contributed to the design of the 2005 Mazda Kabura concept and the Furai race car, built on a Lola chassis. Teresa later contributed to the first-generation RX-8 in 2003–2004, the Mazda3 RT (2004), the Mazda6 (2003), and a 2007 concept car that Mazda sponsored at ArtCenter. She

worked with Mark Jordan on this project. Later assignments included the 1-3 or 1-4 gens of the Mazda2, Mazda3, MX-5 Miata, Mazda6, MX-30, CX-5, CX7, CX-9, B-Series Truck, and so on

Other show cars she contributed to included Nagare, Ryuga, Furai, Shinari, and countless SEMA concepts and race cars. She also worked on Mazda Brand, Product Planning, and Sustainability. Throughout her career, she has influenced numerous vehicles as a designer or manager.

SPAFFORD'S JOURNEY

Spafford was born in Australia, and one of her grandfathers farmed the land before opening a butcher shop. Her other grandfather was a baker and a businessman. Her father, who resides in Australia, worked in banking, and her mother, who lives in the United States, practiced psychology. While neither was particularly creative artistically, she notes that Aussies are inventive by nature—they know how to figure things out. She was one of three girls. She attended several K–6 elementary schools as a youth in Darwin, Northern Territory. She focused on drawing animals, especially horses. One day, someone donated oodles of scantron cards, sparking her interest in 3-D design. She found she could use them to make clothes, shoes, and models of cities. She even wore the shoes she fashioned.

In the 1970s, Cyclone "Tracy" hit South Australia on Christmas Eve, leaving devastation everywhere. By the time she was eight, her parents divorced, and her mother, a devout Mormon, took her and her two sisters to Provo, Utah. Teresa enrolled in Provo High School, which houses grades seven to twelve, completing courses in AP art, photography, and ceramics. Her teacher, Verl Morgan, would go on to change her life.

During her teens, they took trips, camped out, and exhibited their art from outings on return. On one trip they visited ArtCenter in Southern California. She was thrilled by the work, fell in love with industrial design, and noted that this was not a typical college, since students did not have to take courses outside design to graduate. But ArtCenter was costly, and she knew her family was unable to afford it. She decided she would have to go elsewhere and make do—she found an excellent alternative path.

After graduation from high school, she enrolled in Utah Valley University—her mother's employer—to gain access to a free education. She was attracted to architecture until she found out that if there was a storm and lives were lost, she would be responsible—this was something she could not do. She received an associate's degree in commercial art and graphic design.

Though her Mormon connections, she was able to attend Brigham Young University in Utah, which had a considerable reputation; here, she chose to study industrial design. Although there was no transportation program, the school was able to arrange visitations to product design studios and automobile manufacturers. She completed visits to Nissan, Toyota, and

The 1994 Pontiac Grand Prix SE Coupe was a popular offering.
General Motors

Mazda before a bridge collapsed, canceling her tour of BMW and VW. While she had not expressed an interest in cars in general, the colors, materials, and finishes she had seen excited her. After her visit to Nissan, she contacted Brenda Parkin and arranged to spend a day with her. Brenda reviewed her portfolio, gave her some directions, and changed her life.

In 1999, after graduation, Teresa joined General Motors Design. During this time, materials designers were located in a separate studio and assigned to tasks as needed. She was elated when she was requested by Pontiac because of her avocations, noting, "I was extremely athletic. I lived and breathed it. I biked three to four times a week and loved snowboarding. There were pictures all over the wall of the studio of what could have been any of my friends. They thought it was great." However, she doesn't think that her colleagues understood how the brand was perceived outside the walls of the company. Compared to other areas, the brand was not huge, but she viewed it as a winnable division.

While she noted Pontiacs had a strong performance reputation, she thought that GM was trying to make as many cars as possible off one platform. Designing for cars with designations such as the J-car (Sunfire), the N-car (Grand Am), the F-body (Firebird), the W-body (Grand Prix), the H-body (Bonneville), and the U-car (Montana) was perhaps memorable. In comparison, up until 2008, Mazda, with whom Teresa would later join, had only one or two platforms that it shared with Ford. Today their platforms are similarly limited. At Pontiac, her assignments could have included the Montana and controversial Aztek as Pontiac moved forward.

Teresa was very knowledgeable about clothing construction, color material design, and finishes. When she was assigned to work with a less experienced person on a prototype, she became frustrated, and this led to her decision to leave.

At some point in time, Teresa had a daughter with her husband. She notes, however, that he is color blind. Trained as a music sound engineer, he worked as a roofer. Both athletic, they went rock climbing at Bald Mountain in Michigan.

Teresa subsequently joined Mazda and rose through the ranks. She observes that Mazda has four locations worldwide. Their headquarters in Hiroshima, Japan, is the largest, housing up to a hundred designers. Other small staffs are located in Yokahama, Japan, and Frankfort, Germany. Each location develops themes, but Hiroshima takes the lead more often than not.

Teresa's California studio, where she serves as lead designer, houses nine to ten designers and is under the direction of Derek Jenkins.

After two or three rounds of competition, the winning design is later engineered in Hiroshima, and if the design from America is chosen, they follow the trial to production.

Over the course of years, she contributed to a large number of vehicles as a designer or manager; some are more memorable than others. She notes that the 2005 Mazda Kabura concept car looked like the Veloster, which was manufactured by Hyundai. In 2007, she worked with Mark Jordan on a project with ArtCenter. The Furai (meaning "sound of the wind") race car, which utilized a Lola chassis, stands out. They designed race cars in their Irvine, California, studio.

With the display of Mazda convertibles at the New York International Auto Show at the Javits Convention Center a few years back, who could forget the MX-5—Spafford notes she also worked on the Club Sport, the first-generation RX-8, the Mazda3 (2003), and the Mazda6 (2003). Two concepts were more recently exhibited at the Javits. Of course, she contributed to the Mazda's mainstay—the CX series—over the years. In 2014, Teresa celebrated when the Mazda3 placed in the top three at the World Car Awards.

Although her older sister is creative, she was instead recognized for earning a PhD in biology and joining the University of Hawaii as an accomplished professor. Her younger sister traveled even farther, to Alaska, to work as a nurse practitioner and train others in surrounding villages.

When it comes to car talk, Teresa finds the Porsche 356 a classic beauty, and the Aston Martin, a manufacturer now under a female president, in good taste.

"Good design," she notes, "has to be exciting, have a stance and pleasing proportions, be in good taste without being overdone, and provide a positive emotional value."

Constance Smith

Nick Hagen

CRYSTAL WINDHAM

No matter what accomplishments you make, someone helped you.[1]

CAREER HIGHLIGHTS

Crystal Windham completed internships at Ford Motor Company in 1992 and General Motors in 1993 while a student at the College for Creative Studies. After receiving her bachelor's degree in 1994, she began her career at GM Design, addressing assignments in the Chevrolet, Oldsmobile, Pontiac, and Saturn brand studios. Following a production-oriented design project in 1997, she accepted a yearlong assignment at Adam Opel in Rüsselsheim, Germany, where she explored internal and external design elements.[2] Upon return to the States, she held the position of lead designer for the 2004 Malibu and Malibu Maxx.[3] In 2002, she was promoted to design manager for midsized interiors and contributed to the design of the 2006 Pontiac G6 coupe and hardtop convertible.[4] Following an auto show reveal, the original G6 had had an exciting introduction on TV thanks to Oprah Winfrey. Windham had numerous other diverse assignments—one working with exterior designers.

As manager of interior design for Chevrolet and Saturn passenger cars and small SUVs, Windham worked on the 2007 Saturn Aura and as director of design for the 2008 Malibu. The Aura won the North American Car of the Year Award in 2007, and the Chevrolet Malibu won the North American Car of the Year Award in 2008, making them memorable. Windham also contributed to the Equinox. In May 2007, she had moved to the position of design manager, advanced exteriors, for full-size trucks (working with Ped-pro) and later design manager, exteriors.[5] Windham's team also designed interiors for the 2012 Buick Verano and Chevrolet

Malibu. Her group contributed to the sporty 2014 Impala, perhaps Chevrolet's last full-size sedan as customers transitioned to SUVs and trucks. In 2016, she was appointed director of interior design for Cadillac, leading the design team for the luxury and sporty Cadillac CT5 and CT5-V passenger car and groundbreaking 2021 Escalade.

Windham directed the interior design for the Cadillac Lyriq, the first vehicle to use the Ultium battery technology.

In her spare time, Windham encourages others to follow their dreams. She mentors an event called the "You Make a Difference" Creative Arts Program, to acknowledge Detroit public school students who networked with professional mentors from GM Design. She is a mentor at University of Detroit Mercy, where she earned an MBA, and a member of its alumni board and board of advisors. Windham's work and community service have been widely recognized.

Her awards include the 2013 Urban Wheel Designer of the Year, as well as the Emerging Leader Award from the Rainbow PUSH Coalition's Global Automotive Summit, and inclusion in *Automotive News*' 100 Leading Women in the Automotive Industry. Windham notes on her own online post that she received numerous leadership accolades, including Designer of the Year and the *Michigan Chronicle* Women of Excellence Award. She appeared in a *New York Times* feature article about women in the automotive industry with two of her colleagues and was named one of *Automotive News*' "Top 100 Women."

BIOGRAPHICAL NOTES

Crystal Windham grew up in Detroit. Her tenth-grade art teacher Jim Jennings and first mentor advised her to investigate the College for Creative Studies (CCS), where she would learn about automotive design. Carl Olsen, Windham's professor, also chaired the transportation design department. Olsen had honed his own skills as the director of design at Ogle Design in England and director of style at Citroën. At one point, he set up a website to celebrate the accomplished women in automotive design passing through his program. He also assisted Crystal by arranging for a scholarship for her after her first year of study. In the immediate area of

This sporty Saturn SC coupe qualified for the AACA Grand Nationals in 2020. *Constance Smith*

The 2011 hybrid Volt, with incorporated state-of-the-art materials inside. *General Motors*

corporate design centers, most CCS professors came out of the auto industry themselves, including the renowned Homer LaGassey, who served GM, Ford, and Chrysler and also chaired or cochaired the Industrial Design Department. It is interesting that both Olsen and LaGassey were graduates of Pratt Institute in Brooklyn, New York, sometimes considered a competitor of CCS.

After finishing an internship at Ford after her sophomore year, she completed a second one at GM a year later and joined GM in 1994 with her industrial design degree in hand. After joining GM, she purchased a 1994 Saturn SC2.

CHEVROLET IMPALA

The all-new Chevrolet 2014 Impala was unveiled at the New York International Auto Show at the Javits Convention Center in 2012 to an excited audience with John Cafaro, who oversaw its exterior design, and Windham, director of Chevrolet Passenger Car Design at the time, in attendance to say a few words. In the past, Cafaro was feted for his design of the Fiero and Corvette, and Windham made her mark with the Malibu. The Impala, a sporty full-size sedan, captured the needs of the families of the future.

Windham's team was thorough in exploring the interior space. This kind of study is even more relevant today as driverless transportation reaches the market.

In 2013, GM staff noted, "The team used the spaciousness calculator—a General Motors exclusive tool—to analyze how customers perceive the vehicle's roominess, and virtual human models to make the most of vehicle interiors based on an extensive database of driver sizes and postures. The 3D CAVE helped in evaluating design concepts for blind spots, reflections, and visibility of objects inside and outside the car."[6]

Windham added, "Using various advanced technologies, we were able to make dimensional and design modifications in a virtual environment before locking down on a final architecture, These steps are necessary to develop a solid foundation to build on to achieve the best spaciousness, comfort, and overall design that will impress our customers."[7]

2016 CHEVROLET VOLT

In respect to the second-generation-model Volt, Windham noted, "The 2016 Volt maintains the high-tech interior design aesthetic of the first-generation Volt but has more user-friendly elements, creating an inviting balance between ambiance and functionality. The new interior will appeal to existing owners, but also to those who will be new to the Volt family because of its integrated yet familiar technology."[9]

Like the exterior, the Volt's cabin flows with sculpted cues, visual jewelry, and a greater emphasis on form. The instrument panel, for example, flows into the door panels. The center portion of the instrument panel flows almost seamlessly into a more ergonomic center console.

The Volt was one of three finalists nominated for a World Car Award.

THE 2020 CT5

On the heels of the Escala concept, Cadillac introduced the CT5 in New York in 2019 and the CT4 shortly thereafter. While crossovers rule for most, Cadillac has hopes that customers will remember the standard-bearers in earlier days—renowned for their power, opulence, and mechanical reliability.

Replacing the CTS, the car has simple, smooth lines, even though the grille pattern is reminiscent of a series of mini chevrons too, emulating the Cadillac crest.

THE 2021 ESCALADE AND ESV

The stunning Escalade serves as a portfolio piece for at least four women designers and an engineer. The crisp exterior was designed under the direction of Therese Pinazzo, who honed her skills guiding the design of Cadillac's smaller SUVs that proved popular. The exterior of the Escalade still pays allegiance to the "art and science" style, which relied on sharp edges and strong corners—cues that initially appeared on the 1999 Evoq concept initiated

The reveal for the Impala took place at New York's Javits Convention Center. *Constance Smith*

The interior of the 2021 Escalade, with its amazing curved OLED displays, is state of the art. *Constance Smith*

by Simon Cox. This style homage is also evident in an early Escalade drawn by Scott Wassell.

The 2021 Escalade balances vertical DRLs and horizontal headlamps in the front and two-stage vertical taillamps in the rear. All lamps seem to feature tiny decorations or etching up close, sometimes complicated for the eye to see. from afar. The rear decoration has been compared to a skyscraper.

There is always need for personalization. The latest offering will include the Onyx Package, complete with 22-inch, twelve-spoke, high-gloss-black alloys; a gloss-black nameplate; and monochromatic emblems.

Joanne L. Leddy served as program manager of the Entertainment and Displays. For the Cadillac Pressroom, this state-of-the-art design would monopolize their articles:

Escalade's industry-first curved OLED display offers more than 38 inches of total diagonal display area, with twice the pixel density of a 4K television. The technology delivers bold imagery, perfect blacks, and the largest color range of any automotive display in production today.[10]

The system includes three screens: a 7.2-inch-diagonal touch control panel driver information center, and to the driver's left, a 14.2-inch-diagonal cluster display behind the steering wheel and a 16.9-inch-diagonal Infotainment screen to the driver's right. The OLED is paper-thin, and its curvature positions the displays for optimal visibility.[11]

Rear seat passengers are treated to 12.9" screens offering three modes that can operate independently or together to view content.

The vivid color and visual quality of OLED technology also eliminates the need for the common "hood" shrouding many typical in-vehicle screens, creating a brighter and less cluttered environment.[12]

The real wood on the instrument panel and around the vehicle adds depth to the environment.

The addition of an all-new, available Augmented Reality–enabled navigation relies on live street views with directional overlays and more to enhance driving directions. The Cadillac Pressroom describes it on their current website: "A live street view in front of the vehicle is projected on the cluster display with turn indicators and other directional information overlaid on the scene. It includes features such as direction-based audio prompts. For example, a 'turn left' audio prompt comes through the left speakers to further emphasize the navigation instruction—with the volume increasing as the turn approaches."

This complements the popular Cruise technology—a reliable, semiautonomous system because of the premapping of many roads. A new feature is added: the Infotainment portion of the instrument panel can be operated as a touchscreen or manually with the use of a large dial on the center console.

It should be noted that the dramatic increases in passenger and cargo space are due primarily to the longer wheelbase and longer overall vehicle length, compared to the previous model, as well as a new independent rear suspension, which enables a lower interior floor, features that not only expand the Escalade's roominess but improve comfort by allowing easier access to the second and third rows, as well as creating a more natural seating position for third-row occupants.[13]

Cadillac has kept its promise to introduce a new model every six months. They have refined the CT4 and CT5 Blackwings, cars for the street and track, for production. The stunning 2021 Cadillac Escalade, with the contributions of five women designers, has raised the bar inside and out. Cadillac continues to prepare their electric offerings, including the Lyriq, a crossover using BEV3 technology, and the Celestiq, a luxurious sedan. At the reveal for the Lyriq (Cadillac Pressroom), Windham noted, "Every new entry for Cadillac is an opportunity for us to elevate the brand."

Women worked on the design and engineering of the Lyriq. *GM Book*

The interior of the Cadillac CT5-V Blackwing interior is dazzling. *General Motors*

PART IX.
2000–2010: GM SETS THE PACE FOR THE AUTOMOTIVE INDUSTRY

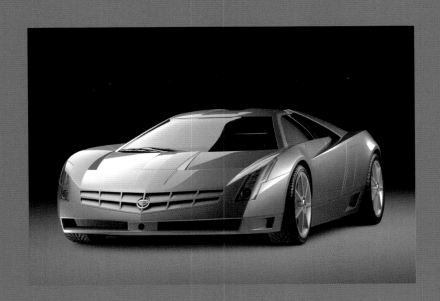

AUTOMOTIVE INDUSTRY

While the 9/11 attacks in 2001 interrupted our peace, General Motors was able to look forward to some of its most lucrative years. The reentrance of Bob Lutz as vice chairman of Product Design and later Global Product Design this year was significant. In 2002, Lutz eliminated the brand character studios and replaced them with five new areas: body-on-frame, unibody vehicles, advanced vehicles, character and interiors, and design center engineering. In 2003, Edward Welburn replaced Wayne Cherry as VP of Design. Lutz's support for design and new products is evident in the books he has written, and proved invaluable in this period of time.

In this decade, engineers made inroads exploring the future of fuel cell vehicles running on hydrogen from renewable sources. Researchers studied side airbags, which are effective in the space between the passenger and vehicle; they were not dictated by law at this time or as they are now. The relationship between night vision and low-beam halogen headlamps was explored.

In 2000, having been a 50 percent owner, GM completed its purchase of Saab and worked on alliances with Fiat for parts and a larger portion of Suzuki. However, GM would be restructured in 2009, and the new pared-down GM would consist of Buick, Cadillac, Chevrolet, Holden, Opel, Vauxhall, and the majority stake in Daewoo.

Buick finished 1999 after unveiling the Cielo, the LaCrosse, and the 2000 Blackhawk concept. In 2001, Buick revealed the Bengal roadster concept; in 2002 to 2003, the Centime, a show car, was designed on the inside by Yan Huang. Models included the most dependable car—the Le Sabre—and the smaller Century, with a more power. The Opel Insignia was labeled a Regal.

Completed in 2001, the 2003 Buick Rendezvous arrived in 2002 and was designed inside and out under the direction Elizabeth Wetzel.

In 2007, the introduction of the Enclave would further set the direction for the division, which continued to put its efforts into SUVs. The 2008 Beijing Auto Show included an Invicta (also the name for 1960s Buicks) concept with a waterfall grille. The production LaCrosse would arrive at the end of the decade.

At Cadillac, the 1999 Evoq concept was inspired by an exciting design style referred to as Art & Science. Elements of the style, which is muscular and crisp, would come alive in the Cadillac XLR convertible, the Escalade, and the CTS sedan. The Evoq would lead to the 2002 V-12 Cien Concept and Cadillac Sixteen.

When it came to production vehicles, the 2000 Cadillac DeVille combined the oldest and newest technology. Infrared night vision enables drivers to detect objects beyond the range of the headlights. In 2001, the navigation option included a touchscreen. In 2000, the midsized CTS replaced the Catera and had two engine offerings. The Cadillac Sixteen concept car, equipped with a thirty-two-valve V-16, would turn heads. The CTS's very

dominant horizontal grille with its eggcrate inserts attracted attention away from the stacked headlights on both sides. The CTS-V version, rated at 400 hp, competed in the SCCA's Speed World Challenge series. In 2004 (2003–2009), the rear-drive, two-seat XLR convertible arrived again, with the crisp style that was initially explored in the Simon Cox studio. In 2005 the STS replaced the Seville, and in 2006 the DTS replaced the DeVille.

The 2008 Denali XT concept was a hybrid. In 2009, the Converj Concept was designed to introduce customers to Cadillac's electric propulsion system called Voltec to provide emission-free driving. The Voltec propulsion system consisted of a 16 kWh T-shaped battery, an electric drive unit, and a four-cylinder engine-generator.

New Chevrolet products captured the market. Michael Simcoe and Liz Wetzel would compare notes to create a new grille with a line running horizontally across it. In 2000, Chevrolet replaced the Lumina with the front-wheel-drive Impala and updated the Monte Carlo. The Trailblazer, replacing the smaller S-10 Blazer, featured a 4.2-liter I-6 with a dual OHC engine and variable valve timing. In 2001, the Corvette Z06 arrived with fanfare: the LS6 engine replaced the LS1. In 2002 the versatile Avalanche, with its pass-through bed, was off and running. The thirty-fifth-anniversary package for the Camaro was available in a limited number of cars.

Six new vehicles mesmerized the buyers in 2005: the sixth-generation Corvette, the Malibu and later Malibu MAXX, a new SUV (the Equinox), the Cobalt (which replaced the Cavalier), the 2004 Colorado midsized pickup (which replaced the S-10 Blazer), and the Aveo (which arrived from Korea). Chevrolet teamed with Monroe Truck Equipment to offer the Chevrolet Kodiak (GMC Topkick) for fifth-wheel towing. The Uplander minivan was made from 2005 to 2009.

Also popular were the SSR (Super Sport Roadster) and the revolutionary 2006 HHR (Heritage High Roof). In 2005, the 2006 Camaro and the high-performance Trailblazer SS arrived; the TB was with a 6.0-liter Corvette LS2 small block, which developed 391 horsepower and 395 lb.-ft. of torque. Equipped with a 5300 V-8, built-in generator, and 42-volt hybrid VRLA-regulated battery pack, the hybrid Silverado was a first. This year, the Uplander LT was also of note.

In 2007, the Volt concept was unveiled, and this synchronous hybrid would meet the competition head on and monopolize one awards presentation after another. It would also fast-track the careers of Denise Gray, Anne Asensio, and Terese Tant Pinazzo.

The year 2008 brought the seventh-generation Malibu, which shared the Saturn platform and won a Car of the Year award. Following the success of the Bumblebee character in the film Transformers, a new Camaro arrived in 2009, and the COPO Camaro arrived in 2012.

In 2012, the Onix (a coupe was originally called the Prisma) arrived, by GM Brazil. By 2016, it was the bestselling car in Latin

America. In 2019, it was introduced in China and is now sold in about forty markets.

In 2017, the electric Bolt captured the 2017 Motor Trend Car of the Year Award. More specifics are presented elsewhere in this manuscript.

Holden in Australia offered an extensive range of products surpassing the competition in sales for many years, which included the following: in 2000, the Commodore VX, Ute VU, and Frontera UES; in 2001, the Zafira was added; in 2002, consumers relied on the Commodore VY, Monaro V2, Ute VY, and Cruze YG; in 2003, the Vectra VZ, Caprice/Statesman WK (from South Korea), Ute VZ, and Crewman VY arrived; in 2004, the Monaro VZ, Statesman/Caprice WL, Crewman VZ, and Adventra VY went forward; 2005 brought the Astra AH and Adventra VZ; and 2007 brought the Epica EP (a midsized sedan), Ute VE, and Captiva CG (a small SUV). Other recognizable Holden models, including the K8 Suburban, the Barina X, and the Buick Royaum (from China), made an entrance. By 2003, the Chevrolet Lumina coupe, Pontiac GTO, and Vauxhall Monaro were sold. In 2009, the Cruze JG was the last of the decade to be released.

Although the phaseout of Oldsmobile was within sight, it was delayed until 2004. A stunning redesigned Aurora arrived in 2001. Oldsmobile's last vehicles included the Silhouette, the Bravada, the Intrigue, and the Alero.

In 2000, Pontiac welcomed a redesigned Bonneville. In late 2001, the controversial Pontiac Aztek arrived with and without a tent. While sales were not as expected, they were not that bad either; it was canceled by 2005. In 2002, the Solstice convertible made an appearance at the auto show in NYC, but it would take forever to get one—only a manual was available for months. In 2003, the Pontiac Vibe, which shared running gear with the Toyota Matrix, did well in the marketplace. Pontiac offered a three-year warranty, and Toyota only two. In 2004, Bonneville customers could order a Northstar V-8. Likely in an effort to save money, from 200 to 2005 the new GTO was based on Holden's Monaro coupe, in an effort to deliver V-8 performance and European handling to Americas, or perhaps it was a cost-cutting measure. Many customers had to choose from cars that had already arrived, since a special order could take many months. While the GTO was offered in some interesting hues, some customers shopping for a GTO expected sunroofs, and Australian cars had none. Fortunately, by 2005 the GTO started looking more like a performance car, gaining a Corvette engine and the expected hood scoops, but 2006 was still its last year. In 2005, the Grand Prix GXP was upgraded. In 2003, Oprah Winfrey awarded 276 new G6s to deserving audience members, and in 2005 the car arrived for purchase. The G6 came in many flavors, including a four-door and a coupe, and later a convertible with a power hardtop arrived. The G6 was one of the first models designed primarily by a team of talented women. Exhibited at a 2002 auto show, the Solstice, a two-seat sports car, arrived in 2006 to an excited audience. A team of contestants on a television reality show, *The Apprentice*, were challenged to design its first brochure—its round shape had to be die-cut. Early on, some women were discouraged after discovering that for the first six months or more, the car came equipped with only a manual transmission. However, eager customers sought early cars, which were numbered and collectible. In 2008, the G8 replaced the Grand Prix, but the future was dim. Most of the last Pontiacs would be built in December 2009.

Saturn continued to do well and added a second product line—the midsized L—which was offered in a sedan and wagon. Carryovers were designated the S series. By 2003, Saturn replaced the S series with the Ion and offered the Red Line the following year. By 2006, Saturn models were rebadged as Opels. The new Saturn Aura was almost devoid of plastic but was offered in V-6s and even a hybrid. By 2007, the Saturn Sky convertible, the sister car to the Solstice, also arrived to adoring fans. Sadly, Saturn would be lost in the restructuring process in 2009.

General Motors' reach in this decade extended to Opel, GM of Canada, Wuling and Baojun in China, Daewoo in Korea, GM South Africa, and GM Brazil.

ANNE ASENSIO

I like explicit yet balanced design—to be able to read the design all at once—in one shot. If you get closer, you should have subtle surprises through the attention to details. Some people think design is ornament. Not to me; you need to read the purpose right away, a superb striking form to begin with.

—Anne Asensio (b. 1980)

CAREER HIGHLIGHTS

Anne Asensio, balancing the demands of work and family, is only one of a handful of women entrusted to refine both the interiors and exteriors of concept and production vehicles, some of which reached production.

Initially trained as an industrial designer in France and later at the College for Creative Studies (CCS) in Detroit, Anne Asensio started her career in the exterior design department at Renault before joining General Motors.

Asensio served as the brand character design director leading the eight North American Brand Character Centers from 2000 to 2002 and then went on to supervise the design of GM concept cars from 2002 to 2007.

As executive director of Design, Advanced Design, at the General Motors Design Center from 2000 to 2007, she was in charge of vehicle design at GM's Warren, Los Angeles, and Coventry Advanced Design studios. Asensio led the development of a number of auto show concepts, including the Cadillac Sixteen and the Hummer H3T. She played a major role in the development of the provocative Buick Velite concept, a stunning rear-wheel-drive convertible, revamping Buick's style for the following years. After designing the marked rebirth of the striking 2006 fifth-generation Chevrolet Camaro concept, and defining the future of fuel cell cars with the Sequel concept in 2006, Anne played a significant role in selecting and refining the design of the Chevrolet Volt, presented in 2007 in Detroit.

Asensio returned to France and now works for Dassault Systèmes as its vice president of design experience.

She currently serves on the board of the World Design Organization and several boards of schools of design, including Université de Nîmes and Strate School of Design, both in France, and Umeå Universitet in Sweden.

Over the years, Asensio had been recognized worldwide by her professors and by the automotive community. Carl Olsen, the former director of design at Citroën and the head of the Design Department at CCS, recommended her. She was included in the best twenty-five leaders in the car industry in Europe, as "A Rising Star" when she was under forty, and as a "Leading Woman in the Auto Industry." Perhaps more notably to some, the cars to which she has contributed have won numerous international awards for design and innovation.

BIOGRAPHICAL NOTES

Anne's grandfather was a marine. Her grandmother was related to the Farman family; Henri, Richard, and Maurice Farman were French aviation pioneers in the beginning of the twentieth century. These two adventurous domains inspired Anne profoundly. After a record granted of the "first 1-kilometer flight" by Henri in 1908, the brothers Farman built not only around two hundred types of aircraft, but also cars in 1931, during the great era of French bodyworks called "Carrosserie." Later, her grandmother bought and ran a restaurant serving aviation clientele, including mechanics and pilots.

Anne remembers this community very well. The women in the family were strong. When asked about their support or lack of it, Anne notes, "There was nothing there that stopped me." Her father was a salesman serving the Ferguson brand of tractors and later a French petroleum company. After a divorce, her mom worked in a fashion company, and, after working her way up to the executive suite, she created her own brand.

Anne grew up in Le Chesnay, near Versailles. She did moderately well at school but was already into dirt bikes and motorcycles. She was also a dreamer. At twelve years old, she saw a movie—a biography of Michelangelo—that changed her life. The artist fought the white marble to be able to release the form inside. She saw some rocks in her grandfather's yard and thought she might create something of her own. Her grandfather found some tools—a hammer and a chisel—and she began her own sculpture before realizing how hard it was to penetrate the rock. However, this stone was softer than marble, and she was able to chip at it over a number of days until a form started to emerge. Anne was carving a horse. Finally, she released the horse—it is still there.

She attended high school in Versailles and then the École des Beaux-Arts before qualifying for a national design school in Paris. The Beaux-Arts' program consisted of art and literature; the art projects were conceptual. She learned to look through the eyes of Matisse and impressionists such as such as Monet.

Asensio was thrilled when she used real clay at Beaux-Arts. One of her more progressive teachers, a mentor of sorts, advised her to pursue higher design education.

At the École National Supérieure des Arts Appliqués et des Métiers d'Art, she was able to study industrial design in the form of theory, geometry, and philosophy. In the pure tradition of French design, the school was established by Jacques Viénot in the 1940s, founder of "formes utiles" and today's World Design Organization. Her other influences include Roger Tallon and Raymond Loewy.

Anne met Carl Olsen, a design director in Paris, who suggested she take courses at the College of Creative Studies in Detroit. Following his advice, she attended CCS from 1986 to 1987.

Anne would later teach master classes in French schools to share her industrial experience.

Anne notes the popularity of design in France, which is renowned for its luxury goods. The French are not consummate car designers. They tell their story with luxury fashions.

RENAULT

Anne graduated at the top of her class, won her first-prize "Design Janus de l'Étudiant," and applied to Renault for a position in exterior design. At the time, Renault had one female designer in interiors, and Anne was invited to work there. When she mentioned she was applying to serve as an exterior designer, Gaston Juchet, the design director, reacted with surprise. Somewhere along the line, it was felt that women could not fill the exterior design position. Anne overcame the response in part due to the transportation design credentials acquired at CCS. She joined Renault in 1997 and then rose to the position of design director of midsize cars by 2000.

One of her first projects was to design a Renault concept car, the Renault Scénic. Renault had produced the first MPV ever with the Renault Espace in 1984. The Scénic was its continuation and met with great success in production, reportedly peaking at 2,500 units a day. Consumers were drawn to the new interior architecture, which Anne designed to accommodate new emerging behaviors in family travels, and innovative features such as storage compartments under the floor.

The Scénic was believed to be a woman's car, in the shape of an egg ... it was successful anyway.

As director of small and midsize cars, partnering with

Anne Asensio

Carlos Tavares, program director at the time, Anne developed the full Mégane II range, recognized as the European Car of the Year in 2003.

In 2001, Anne joined GM as executive director for Advanced Design. She was known to keep a model of the 1938 Buick Y-Job in her office—Buick's first convertible concept remains iconic. Concepts of the 1930s and 1950s were low slung. The Y-Job was followed by the 1951 LeSabre, which relied on aircraft forms and introduced a lot of futuristic technology, and the 1951 XP 300.

THE CHEVROLET SEQUEL CONCEPT

Touted as the world's most advanced automobile technologically, the Sequel was introduced at the 2005 Detroit Auto Show; drivable models followed in 2006.

Asensio headed Advanced Design for the Sequel. Anne's group created a movable center console accessible both by front and rear passengers, designed to deliver driver-oriented information or serve as a hub for shared communications. The seats were designed to rotate 180 degrees when the vehicle was stopped.

Designers and engineers successfully integrated a hydrogen fuel cell system with advanced technology, which included steer and brake-by-wire controls, wheel hub motors, and lithium-ion batteries. Two Sequels were successfully driven a distance of 300

The first hydrogen car—the Sequel—travels 300 miles on a fill-up. *General Motors*

miles and ended their journey at Niagara Falls. Hydrogen cars have zero emissions. The cars use only hydrogen and produce only water as a byproduct. GM VP John Burns noted, "It is our fuel cell team's tremendous record of success and absolute dedication to this tremendously important cause, which will ultimately enable our country, and our world, to diversify our energy sources and displace large amounts of petroleum."

The Buick Velite was praised for its European style. *General Motors*

THE BUICK VELITE

From 2001 to 2007, Anne served as an executive design director and, from 2002 to 2003, focused on interior design.

Anne became a force for Buick. She would be considered as bringing a European flair to the brand. Asensio was in charge of the Velite project—a four-seat convertible concept. Perhaps history repeats itself.

An elite team was organized to develop the new Buick Velite four-seat convertible, and, aside from vertical grille bars and the port holes from the Wildcat, the Velite borrows little from its predecessors.

In a corporate photo, Asensio is surrounded by the design team, consisting of Tom Peters (2014 Corvette), Sang Yup Lee,

Asensio joined engineer Renee Bryant to configure the Velite.

Orlo Reed, Bryan Priebe, David Snabes, and Tom Weeks—the last duo are sculptors.

Renee Bryant was the single voice for concept engineering in 2003 for the Velite. She spent seven months traveling back and forth to Turin, Italy, to oversee the engineering, design, and build of the Velite at Stile Bertone and did the best she could to learn Italian. The Velite was revealed at the 2004 Greater New

Velite styling would influence the Buicks of the future. *General Motors*

York Auto Show at New York's Javits Convention Center. Kelly Ripa, of the *Live! With Regis and Kelly* television talk show, was so impressed by the car that she had it brought onto the show.

The fresh convertible was anchored in the front by numerous vertical grille elements that bend slightly at the top. Instead of being heavy chrome, the surround is fine and thoughtfully shaped. As is to be expected, the Buick badge is dead center on the grille. Svelte side-view mirrors and huge-diameter chrome wheels dominate the sides of the Velite, which rises pleasantly near the rear like the Wildcat. The three portholes on each side, near the mirrors, appear less significant here than on earlier-production Buicks. The fall of 2004 also brought in the LaCrosse and the Terraza.

THE HUMMER HT3

The Hummer HT3 was unveiled at the 2004 Greater Los Angeles Auto Show as a tangible vision to extend the Hummer family by adding a smaller, sporty, and rugged yet versatile premium mid-sized truck, which would open a new niche for Hummer. Standing to express new cues and character design for the brand, it delivered rebellious traits for outdoor enthusiasts as well as a distinctive personal attitude for the urbanites; this uncompromised concept was designed for men or women drivers. Asensio notes that we at GM Design did collaborate with Nike Design to combine off-road capabilities, innovative features, lightweight materials, and characteristic Nike AG trail orange and black color breaks to finalize

The Hummer H3T would have been welcomed if the company wasn't forced to eliminate the division. *General Motors*

its unique appearance. Asensio was pleased with the dramatic proportions of the exterior and noted that it was her favorite part.

Under Asensio's direction, the design of Jelani Aliyu, a native of Nigeria, was chosen as the starting point for the new Volt. *General Motors*

THE VOLT

In 2006, it was Bob Lutz who promoted the idea of the Volt. He sought to transform GM from a laggard in technology to a leader, and he was successful. Lutz, with a marketing background, Ed Welburn, GM's global design director, and Anne Asensio, GM's advanced design chief, would choose an exterior design from across the design studios to develop. The chosen design was penned by Jelani Aliyu, a native of Nigeria who trained at CCS.

After the concept was finished in 2006, many refinements were made to reach the production design. For instance, Asensio, Young-Sun Kim, and Aliyu worked together to refine the grille. Just about everything was redesigned. The menacing aggressive design, which Aliyu based on lions, became more conventional, but still handsome. When it came to technology, everything was ground up. The idea of making a hybrid, in this case, ended up as a sequential hybrid and was much more difficult than creating an electric car. Pam Fletcher served as GM's global chief engineer for Voltec and the plug-in hybrid electric power train. Engineer Frank

Weber was tasked with making the production Volt from the concept car. Denise Gray led the battery development program.

The production Volt, sold globally, might have garnered more awards than any previous vehicle in GM's history. *General Motors*

DASSAULT SYSTÈMES

Anne Asensio joined Dassault Systèmes in 2008 as vice president of design experience. In this role, she launched Dassault Systèmes' Design Experience strategy, with the mission to define and implement "best in class" design solutions for enterprises, design studios, and individual designers, as well as to foster a Design Excellence culture within Dassault Systèmes.

Dassault Systèmes' strategy covers both technology innovation and business innovation with a single 3DEXPERIENCE platform that answers both of today's design trends for technology and user participation and inclusion, providing openness and emotional connection for designers and citizens.

Acculturation, visualization, and understanding design capacities trigger imagination and drive toward more-responsible ways of making and doing. This fundamental paradigm shift requires that we reconsider design in these new lights with a new set of values, practices, and approaches. Being and acting as a participant of all systems, immersed in the "perceived" sensibility at all scales, we will better comprehend and be able to tackle extremely important problems. Instead of designing other people's systems, we will redesign our way by shifting our thinking, affecting the world by first redesigning ourselves.

She captures our challenges to meet future needs in a 2019 article titled "Engaging Our World with Re-generative Design":

As in the original Renaissance, designers such as Anne Asensio can apply their art in an emerging "Industry Renaissance." If we disqualify design for technology, or art for science, as too often was done in the past, we disqualify an important part of ourselves, the human quest to redefine our place in the world. We can continue in old ways, or we can focus on changing ourselves and the way we do things in order to change the world.

Drawing by Constance Smith

JAMIE BREWER

Lyriq represents ingenuity; it's everything I went to engineering school for ... my ultimate goal was to make this the best hands-on Cadillac SUV that anyone has ever seen.

—Jamie Brewer (b. 1978), Cadillac Pressroom release

CAREER HIGHLIGHTS

Jamie Brewer serves as vehicle chief engineer for future electric vehicles (2018–present). Initially joining General Motors in 2000, she has held diverse positions, including vehicle performance engineer, lead design release engineer, Engineering Group manager, director and global BOM lead, and vehicle chief engineer for launch vehicle remediation, before her promotion to her current position.

BREWER'S JOURNEY

Raised in Farmington Hills, Michigan, Jamie was the first female high school student to win an annual state competition in drafting design. Later, she received a bachelor of science in mechanical engineering from the University of Michigan (2000) and a master of business administration from Oakland University in 2006. Going through college early on, she compared notes with her twin sister, Jacklyn McQuaid. McQuaid studied in the University of Michigan undergraduate and graduate engineering programs; in 2020, she was promoted to executive chief engineer for full-size trucks. To some degree, the sisters fulfilled the dream of their late father, George Lossia, whose plan to become an automotive engineer was derailed by the Vietnam War draft.

The design of the Cadillac Lyriq may be the most memorable one in Brewer's engineering career, since it brings the Cadillac marque into a new era, and it is its first all-electric vehicle. A Cadillac Press release described its introduction in June 2020: "Led by LYRIQ, Cadillac will redefine American luxury over the next decade with a new portfolio of transformative EVs," said Steve Carlisle, executive vice president and president, GM North America. "We will deliver experiences that engage the senses, anticipate desires, and enable our customers to go on extraordinary journeys."

Brewer notes that you spend years at drafting tables, in conference rooms, at computers, and modeling in clay to get the vehicle to the point where you actually sit behind the wheel and drive it (from Driving Electric Luxury / Cadillac Pressroom online).

The Lyriq is based on GM's next-generation, modular electric-vehicle platform and is driven by the Ultium propulsion system, allowing Cadillac to deliver to customers a variety of range and performance options. On the basis of internal testing, it will offer 300 miles of range on a full charge.

Ultium's state-of-the-art NCMA (nickel-cobalt-manganese-aluminum) chemistry uses aluminum in the cathode to help reduce the need for rare-earth materials such as cobalt. In fact, GM engineers reduced the cobalt content by more than 70 percent compared to earlier GM batteries.

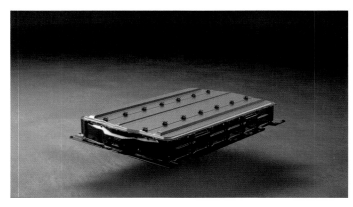

The Ultium pouch battery assemblage powers GM's electric vehicles. *General Motors*

258

GM Book

The advanced battery chemistry is packed in large, flat pouch cells that enable smart module construction to reduce complexity and simplify cooling needs. Additionally, the battery electronics are incorporated directly into the modules, eliminating nearly 90 percent of the battery pack wiring compared to GM's current electric vehicles.

Brewer also points out that since "the battery pack is tied into the underbody of the vehicle, it's going to help stiffen the vehicle, such that your handling and your steering, your responsiveness, are going to be light and they're going to be quick. That combined with the nice wide stance of the vehicle is going to give you a great road-hugging experience. We designed this vehicle to have nearly a 50/50 weight distribution. When you think about an EV and you think about driving dynamics, the first thing that comes to mind is the near-instantaneous torque that you get out of the electric drive motors" (from Cadillac Pressroom). Lyriq offers an AWD option that features a second drive unit in the front. Brewer explains that "not only are you getting power distribution to all four tires, but you are also increasing your horsepower. When the first preproductions came off our manufacturing line, and I had the time to drive it and I was able to feel the handling, able to feel that near-instantaneous torque, I was able to feel the ride control. In any vehicle

development, aerodynamics is critical, and in an EV, especially when you talk about things like range anxiety, aerodynamics becomes that much more critical."

Brewer points out that they have not reduced any of their noise abatement strategies; in fact they've added more in their new noise cancellation technology.

She predicts the range of anxieties that consumers may experience, and notes, "We also offer Level One and Level Two A/C chargers as well as a D/C dash charger capable of up to 150 kilowatts to make sure the concern of range and charge time is not something that will get in the way of the Cadillac customer enjoying the driving experience."

Other technologies featured on the Lyriq include Super Cruise with lane change on demand, remote self-parking, and an augmented-reality, head-up display.

With many introductions delayed due to the pandemic, many schedules have been reset. It is predicted that the Lyriq will reach the public by 2023.

FAMILY MATTERS

Married, Jamie Brewer is the mother of Connor and Lucia.

Courtesy of Laura Sipes Brown

LAURA SIPES BROWN

Our greatest fear should not be of failure but of succeeding at things in life that don't really matter.

—Francis Chan, author and teaching pastor

CAREER HIGHLIGHTS

Laura Sipes Brown is in the Appearance Definition Group, in collaboration with the interior and exterior design studios. Here, the materials and finishes are documented as they are designated for the content of the vehicle. In addition, verification with the materials and component engineers is made to ensure the information is provided correctly for sourcing and parts release. She worked with designers, suppliers, engineers, and program management to help carry out the first vehicles to have leather-wrapped instrument panels in the mid-2000s, including the Cadillac XTS and the 2008 Corvette.

Prior to joining the Appearance Team in 1995, Laura was a validation engineer for exterior bumpers and lighting, where she contributed to the first Cadillac to incorporate HID (high-intensity discharge) lighting. This new technology required the development of several new tests and procedures to ensure that all the components from each of the suppliers were rigorously evaluated, first individually and then as a system. The addition of several new electrical components to the trunk area of the 1994½ Cadillac DeVille (K-Special) required more new tests, and she developed new test procedures and helped conduct the tests.

Laura's first full-time position was with Cadillac Engineering on Scotten Avenue in Detroit, where she was assigned to the crashworthiness group in the body lab in 1989. She subsequently served as liaison between the interior engineering group and the crashworthiness group.

Brown started her career at the Chevrolet Engineering Center in 1982 as a co-op student. She rotated through many areas of the engineering center, following a pattern typical of the manufacture and testing of parts and then to the engineering of parts and vehicles. Chevrolet Engineering became the CPC (Chevrolet-Pontiac-GM of Canada) Engineering Center within her first year, and she learned then that change was constant and inevitable.

BROWN'S JOURNEY

Brown is the first of four children born to Leon and Rosemary Sipes.

She is grateful to have been blessed with parents who put a high priority on education, foregoing many creature comforts in order to provide all four of their children with amazing opportunities to learn. Brown's maternal grandmother, Helen Seaver, had been a school teacher in Detroit, and her mother was the owner and director of the Montessori school in Rochester, Michigan, for several years after seeing the value of the early education Laura received from the Montessori preschool curriculum.

Brown attended the Academy of the Sacred Heart for middle and high school. Early in high school, she was interested in pursuing medicine, but near the beginning of her junior year, her dad encouraged her to take an engineering aptitude test at Lawrence Institute of Technology. She scored well on the mechanical-engineering portion and decided to pursue an engineering degree instead. There were no engineering-type classes for her to take, but she took all the science classes offered, and audited the Calculus I class while taking precalculus. Laura later encouraged the school to at least offer a drafting class as an art class option.

Becoming a third-generation General Motors employee was a logical career choice because her father was an engineer at GM for years. He worked on the M1 tank and the Caprice (B-body) programs, among others. Her maternal grandfather, Glenn Seaver, retired from GM as a tool- and diemaker. He was always creating amazing contraptions! er favorite, a marble run, was enjoyed by her children and still delights her young niece and nephew.

One of Laura's lifelong mentors was her ballet teacher, Fern Beasley. Fern not only taught Laura ballet techniques from age three to twenty-one, she imparted life lessons. She encouraged Laura to go outside her comfort zone by dancing with a male counterpart in a different studio and taking the Cecchetti method of ballet certification exams, which she successfully completed through the first three levels. Later, Laura taught a ballet class for a young group of girls; she thoroughly enjoyed the experience, and it helped pay for her own lessons. Fern was strict about matters of technique and safety, not allowing Laura to get her first toe shoes until she was twelve or thirteen years old, but she was kind and encouraging in all matters, especially through the rough teenage years. Laura still keeps in touch with Fern and continues to realize the value of good mentors in the lives of young and older people alike.

Other mentors of Laura's were her high school youth group leader, Mary Cummings, and the retreat center director, Daniel Homan, OSB. Mary was just real. She was honest and blunt when necessary, but also one of the most understanding and encouraging people Laura has ever met. She was principled but fun, and extremely approachable. After Laura's first year of college, Mary taught her that her worth as a person did not come from her college or her job or her status in society.

Father Dan was sincere and humble, with a great sense of humor, but exhibited a remarkably quiet strength. He was one of the first people who made Laura realize that people are people regardless of their titles, roles, or status. He played hockey, wore plaid flannel shirts when he worked outside, and liked thin-crust pizza. When one of Laura's close high school friends committed suicide during her freshman year of college, Mary and Father Dan helped her and other close friends process and deal with the tragic loss. He performed the wedding ceremony when Laura and her husband, Patrick Brown, were married in 1992. Both of their sons had the good fortune to attend high school retreats at the same center with Mary and Father Dan as coleaders. Laura kept in touch with him through letters, phone calls, and the all-too-rare visit until his untimely death due to a heart attack.

Brown graduated from the University of Detroit (now the University of Detroit Mercy) with a bachelor of science in mechanical engineering. Her path to graduation was not an easy one. The beginning of her college career was rocky, but with the support of her parents, her mentors, and her co-op coordinator, she persevered. She changed schools and became much more successful in the new environment, making the dean's list her first semester there. She learned that following in her father's footsteps didn't mean the steps had to be the same. She could and did forge her own path to becoming an engineer. When people ask her if it was difficult being a woman engineer, she says she never really gave it much thought. Being a woman and an engineer didn't seem the least bit incongruous to her. "I am not an engineer because I'm a woman nor despite being a woman; I am a woman who is an engineer."

She credits the co-op program with keeping her on track in the engineering program. In fact, she encourages every young person she can to *try* the job he or she intends to make into a career, before graduating with the specific degree. Co-op experience provides a practical component that academics cannot. Brown stresses that in addition to making a little money and having experience for a résumé, doing the job can provide valuable insight to encourage or discourage a particular field. The encouraging helps when school is difficult or long; the discouraging allows a literal course correction before too much time and money are invested. Either way, it is a valuable experience.

Brown thoroughly enjoyed all of her co-op assignments. She liked the practical, hands-on nature of making tools or parts and then testing them. The exposure to all the shops and labs helped the processes and methods involved in developing the whole vehicle come together like pieces of a complicated puzzle.

Another mentor emerged from her co-op assignments—the technician in the vehicle-handling facility, Conrad Humphrey. They had many lengthy philosophical discussions during breaks. He reinforced the ideas that character matters and that being an engineer did not mean she had to give up being feminine. He taught her how to drive a stick shift and showed her how antilock brakes worked, by taking her onto the Tech Center test track, having her get the vehicle up to a healthy speed, then telling her to slam on the brakes. She thought he was crazy, but she trusted him. Wow! That was amazing!

When Conrad and his wife, Lynne, had children, Laura babysat for them. Conrad modeled the same strong family values that her own father exhibited and that Pat has demonstrated since before they were married. He modeled a work-life balance that impressed her. Although both families lost touch for several years, except for Christmas cards and the occasional sighting at the Auto Show, they reconnected a few years ago over dinner, and it was as if no time had passed at all—except that his mentee was grown up and was passing along words of wisdom of her own.

While not her first co-op assignment, her first assembly plant co-op assignment in the mid-1980s was for the purpose of helping determine body build variation on the Pontiac Fiero. She explained her proposal of an experiment to track at least one set of specific front, mid-, and rear body components through the entire build system, but she was told it would be impossible. She asked if she could at least try, and her supervisor agreed. Laura had to buy clothes to wear at an assembly plant, because skirts and heels, the standard "uniform" for women at the time, just weren't practical for what she wanted to do, but it never occurred to her that she *couldn't* do it. Before the plant started building the next day, she set to work tagging, moving parts on carts, and making sure the particular components were queued up to be assembled together. It worked! Laura didn't gloat or say, "I told you so." But she learned a valuable lesson: often, *not* having preconceived ideas about a particular process or project was often her most valuable tool.

That principle was extremely helpful when her first child was born—five and a half weeks early. She didn't know that others were concerned that her 4-pound, 4-ounce baby boy might not

Even with some modifications, the C4 Corvette still turns heads. *Constance Smith*

be healthy and strong. After all, she too was born five and a half weeks early by emergency C-section. She believed that her son would thrive almost from the beginning, and he did.

Another particularly interesting student assignment was to research the feasibility of a high-speed, limited-access road system that would allow people to drive a vehicle such as the concept Chevrolet Express. She researched the use of old railway beds, learned about the easement and other legal requirements, and researched the rules and benefits of the famed Autobahn and the efficiency of roundabouts, a fairly new idea in the US at the time. The road project never took off, but the vehicle was one of the very early autonomous vehicles.

Laura has worked in varying capacities as a student and then as a permanent employee on the C4, the C5, and the C6 Corvette programs, with four different chief engineers. The complexity of the programs and the need to figure out how to manage the immense number of trim combinations and options were part of the fascination of the project. Though challenging, it was extremely satisfying.

Brown has always focused on relationships and processes. She naturally asks questions with the intent of understanding the Why as well as the What about a particular project, which often led to reevaluating the How. These factors were the likely

catalysts for her involvement on every transition team in her given department at the time—when Cadillac Engineering joined Buick Engineering, when BOC (Buick-Olds-Cadillac) merged with CPC (Chevrolet-Pontiac-GM of Canada), and again when the Car Group merged with the Truck Group.

When Laura was expecting her first child, she was determined to work part-time after the baby was born. Not many people were doing that in the mid-1990s, but she would not be deterred. Her manager in the Validation Group knew of one position that might work, and encouraged her to reach out—which she did repeatedly. Whether just to get her to stop calling or because he thought it was a good idea, the manager agreed to have her transferred from the Validation Department to the Appearance Engineering Group. It was a great fit, and she has worked in that field in some capacity for most years since then.

Brown has always paid attention to vehicles and appreciated them for their qualities. Her first vehicle was a full-size 1975 Chevy Blazer 4×4. Her parents bought it new right before an epic snowstorm, and Laura remembers her dad driving nurses from the neighborhood to work at the local hospital. She fondly recalls sitting on the front fender with her feet inside the engine compartment so she could check the air filter or the oil. Changing the headlights was a simple task too! Her parents moved up to a

Suburban after her brother was born. She has preferred SUVs over cars since before it was cool.

But she cannot deny the "cool" factor of the silver SS Rally Sport Nova with black racing stripes that her grandmother bought at the age of seventy! That car holds a special place in her heart, and just maybe Laura will be as cool as her grandmother when she gets older.

And she definitely appreciated the comfort of her dad's Oldsmobile '98. That car was great to ride in but was so much more difficult for her to maneuver than the Suburban or the Blazer. At least with those vehicles she could see where the front ended.

Her favorite design features of most vehicles have always been the hood ornaments and the taillights. Perhaps for safety reasons, vehicles don't have hood ornaments anymore, but they were works of art in and of themselves. A visit to the GM Heritage Center educated her about the connections among train, airline, and automotive designs.

Laura has two sisters and a brother. Both her sisters were connected to the automotive industry after graduation. Alicia, a graduate of Michigan Technological University, was a technical writer at GM for several years, working mainly on owners' manuals. Elena worked for a French automotive component supplier after graduating from the University of Michigan. Her minor in French made her the perfect person to take engineers to the supplier's headquarters in France and to communicate with the French-speaking employees in Michigan. Her brother took a different route after graduating from high school; Tyler joined the US Marine Corps in 1998. Laura remembers writing letters to him every day he was in boot camp, except Sundays, and reading the book *Making the Corps* as he was going through the different stages of the grueling training. She has a much-greater respect for and appreciation of our military men and women since reading that book and hearing stories from various veterans.

Above all, Laura is grateful for the bond they share as siblings. Never was that more evident than during their father's illness and since his passing in 2017. Each of them did what they could, given their individual family responsibilities. There has never been any squabbling about who did or didn't do something or about material items. She understands that this is unusual and precious, and she does not take that for granted.

Her supportive husband, Pat, also a mechanical engineer, graduated from Michigan Tech. They were part of the same "hiring class" at Cadillac where they met. He has helped her every step of the way—often getting dragged into her projects. He was a committee chair for artist logistics with Art & Apples and was instrumental in the success of the Pinewood Derby for the Cub Scouts. Over the past nearly twenty-eight years he has often looked at her like she's daft, but he eventually catches a glimpse of her vision and jumps on board. This past summer he assembled seven hive boxes and nearly fifty-six beehive frames for her new passion and hobby: beekeeping. She supports his career and hobbies too, even though hunting means he's usually gone for her birthday and their actual anniversary. Launching several GM vehicles over his career meant Laura was home alone with their sons often over the years, but that is what teamwork is all about. Most things that they accomplish, they accomplish together. They have even worked successfully on the same vehicle programs (in nonreporting roles).

Pat and Laura have two sons. Their older son, Ethan, also graduated from Michigan Tech with a mechanical engineering degree and is working in the transportation field. He recently married his high school sweetheart, Faith. Younger son Logan graduated from Western Michigan University and is a pilot for a regional airline.

Laura was rehired to the GM Appearance group in 2015 after a few years' hiatus working at church, at her sons' high school as the assistant registrar, and then at an automotive interior supplier. She knows it is the people who make or break the success of every team and every project, and she was thrilled to be reunited with the amazing people in the Appearance Group.

Laura enjoys volunteering, Bible studies, family gatherings, gardening, beekeeping, doing puzzles, reading, needlecrafts such as crochet and cross-stitch, playing games, traveling, and just spending time with family and friends. She is also quite interested in family genealogy and will allow herself to spend time on that research in the future.

Courtesy of Teresa Cerbolles

TERESA L. CERBOLLES

From the farm in western New York to the General Motors Milford Proving Ground, I have followed my passion for customer voice to build a career utilizing data to drive the best decisions.

—Teresa L. Cerbolles (b. 1977)

CAREER SUMMARY

After completing a co-op assignment at Delphi Harrison Thermal Systems in Lockport, New York, Teresa L. Cerbolles fulfilled requirements for a bachelor of science in electrical and electronics engineering and a master of operations management from Kettering University. She has supplemented her education with other diverse training in her field and management throughout her career.

The completion of numerous assignments, sometimes outside her major, has contributed to Teresa's high level of expertise. Beginning in 2000, she provided calibration, electrical integration, and automatic climate control (ACC) development for Delphi Thermal Systems in Troy, Michigan. In 2006, she joined General Motors as an electronic climate control (ECC) and heating, ventilation, and air-conditioning (HVAC) hybrid development engineer in Milford, Michigan. In 2008, she arrived at General Motors Technical Center in Warren, Michigan, to serve as a design release engineer and controls lead. In 2011, she was promoted to global systems integration lead. Shortly thereafter, she became the advanced cabin engineering manager and was placed in charge of a newly established team. In 2014, she served as an HVAC duct and outlet engineering manager. From 2011 to 2015, she served as the customer voice specialist within HVAC. It should be noted that HVAC activities are usually assigned to mechanical engineers.

In 2015, Teresa was reassigned to Milford, home of GM's Proving Ground, as a systems engineering vehicle controls integration engineering manager and then took even more responsibilities as reflash service manager.

In 2017, Teresa was promoted to senior manager of the Global Human Factors Center—the position she currently holds. She currently leads numerous teams, examines and elevates customer-focused decisions, and maintains and improves relationships with multiple partners, including those associated with quality and design.

Teresa's research in the area of HVAC vents, engine temperature control, and exhaust heat recovery has been published and patented. She was the recipient of the BOM Leadership Excellence Award.

TERESA'S JOURNEY

Born in 1977, Cerbolles grew up in western New York on a farm, learning what responsibility is at a very young age. Her father worked as a UAW worker and retired from Delphi Automotive Systems. Her mother kept the family and farm running smoothly.

Cerbolles started working as a teen—she was just a junior in high school. She was selected to participate in a high school co-op program working with a GM components group in 1993. At that point, she left the Barker Central School District, where she attended from kindergarten onward, to attend Lockport High School with approximately twenty other students. Students rotated between work and school every other week. She notes, "I recall feeling scared and overwhelmed walking into my first role in Human Resources as a sixteen-year-old."

Prior to her experience in the high school co-op, Cerbolles had planned to pursue a career in accounting; this resulted from the skills gained by helping with the farm taxes. After being exposed to working with computers and product engineers, her career path shifted quickly to engineering. Her experience working with product designers to understand computer programs to calculate reliability exposed her to new paths. She had four different assignments in high school, and fantastic mentors who allowed her to build confidence and abilities beyond others her age.

Cerbolles continued in the path of engineering, applying to the GMI Engineering and Management Institute for a bachelor of science in electrical and electronics engineering. This was the most difficult major at school. She co-oped with Delphi Automotive Systems, officially moving to Michigan in 1998 to work in Systems Engineering and on her thesis, graduating in 1999. After officially starting in, she continued to work toward her master of business administration degree in operations management from Kettering University, via VHS tapes.

In her current position, she leads a team of many engineers, many in the field of industrial engineering.

Cerbolles's previous role was in the Thermal SMT as an EGM for HVAC and Outlets, where she led design, release, and execution, working in close collaboration with interior studios. She was also the "voice of the customer" specialist for HVAC (heat, ventilation, and air-conditioning), working with market research, usability, and human factors criteria development. In addition, she has held multiple other roles with GM, including reflash services manager, integration GSSLT lead, and both electrification DRE and development engineer.

Cerbolles's name appears on three US. patents. Perhaps her topic in 2014 has been made even more significant as we rely more and more on electric motors in hybrid or alone to power our vehicles and accessories: "Method and Apparatus for Controlling Hybrid Powertrain System in Response to Engine Temperature" (Assignee: GM Global Technology Operations, working in part with the US Department of Energy). In the abstract, the topic is delineated: "A method of controlling a hybrid powertrain system including an internal combustion engine includes controlling operation of the hybrid powertrain system in response to a preferred minimum coolant temperature trajectory for the IC engine."

In 2015, Cerbolles shifted in her career to take on the entire vehicle in the position of systems engineering vehicle controls integration engineering manager. In this role, she had responsibility for final software integration into the vehicle for all GM North America lead programs. Cerbolles's scope also included management of a large team of outside resources to enable vehicle software reflashing.

Continuing to follow her passion, she was promoted to the position of senior manager of the User Experience's Human Factors (HF) team for General Motors. Named to this position in July 2017, Cerbolles is responsible for four teams: Usability, Driver Distraction, Seat Comfort, and future Program HF assessments. <Cerbolles notes, "I have been married for nineteen years and have two wonderful children: a fourteen-year-old son named Ryan and an eleven-year-old daughter named Ally. They keep me very busy, but when I find time, I enjoy photography, especially capturing special moments for my family and friends." She enjoys spending high-quality time with her family, cheering them at sporting events, and horseback riding, as well as photography, reading, and camping with family and friends.

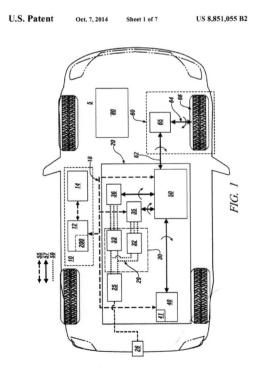

Courtesy of the US Patent and Trademark Office

Corvette Cruise. *Teresa Cerbolles*

General Motors

CHRISTINE PARK CHENG

During my first year at Art Center College of Design in Pasadena, California, I learned a valuable lesson that helped shape the mindset I have today. As one of the few female students studying automotive design, I naively felt the need to blend in with my male classmates. I contemplated signing all of my design sketches as Chris Park instead of Christine Park, but in the back of my mind I knew it didn't feel right. My professor, Richard Petruska, offered some great guidance by telling me, "Be who you are." I learned my unique perspective helps me become a better designer.

—Christine Park Cheng

CAREER HIGHLIGHTS

As a designer and manager, Christine Park Cheng has amassed a large portfolio of designs for concept and production vehicles. She is one of the small number of women who have contributed to both the interior and exterior design of vehicles.

BIOGRAPHICAL NOTES

Cheng graduated from Art Center College of Design and received a bachelor of science in transportation design in 2006. She joined the GM Advanced Concept Studio in January 2006 as an intern and was hired full time upon graduation.

From 2008 to 2010, Cheng designed interiors and exteriors for Cadillac, contributing to the 2010 XTS Platinum concept and the 2013 XTS production vehicle.

By 2011, she became the lead interior designer and contributed to the interior of the dramatic 2011 Ciel Concept.

From 2011 to 2014, Cheng served as lead exterior designer for Cadillac, working on various internal concept vehicles and the lamps of the 2017 XT-5.

From 2014 to 2015, Cheng worked as lead exterior designer for Chevrolet, contributing to the top-selling 2019 Chevrolet Blazer. At the time, the Chevrolet Press Room recorded some observations from the top. John Cafaro, the executive director of Chevrolet, noted, "The Blazer has attitude. It looks commanding on the road, while fulfilling the promise of versatility at the heart of every Chevy crossover and SUV."

In 2015, she was promoted to exterior design manager for GMC.

She led the design of the 2020 GMC Acadia and contributed to early foundation work for the 2021 GMC Yukon.

In 2017, she joined Buick as the advanced design manager, developing future design strategy for Global Buick.

Cheng subsequently served as the exterior design manager for the 2021 Buick Envision, and her team designed the exterior of the Buick Envision Plus for China.

She returned to GMC Design Studio in 2019. Cheng continues to lead in the creation of multiple future vehicles as exterior design manager at GMC.

The stunning XT5 preceded the smaller XT4. *Constance Smith*

MICHELLE CHRISTENSEN

In junior high, I learned about exterior car design; it was the perfect melding of my interests in design, cars, and working with my hands.

Michelle Christensen (b. ca. 1985)

The Acura NSX made its debut at the 2015 New York International Auto Show. *Constance Smith*

CAREER HIGHLIGHTS

During her final year at Art Center College of Design, Michelle Christensen designed a Chevrolet wagon for part of a General Motors–sponsored school project in which she participated—her first experience designing for GM!

After receiving her bachelor of science in industrial design in 2005, Christensen joined Honda Research and Development as a designer, where she worked on the design of the Acura ZDX crossover.

In 2010, she followed her manager to General Motors Design, where she worked as an exterior designer.

In 2011, they both returned to Honda R&D Americas; Christensen was later chosen as lead exterior designer for the 2016 Acura NSX. This is a 500-horsepower-plus exotic midengine car. She was heralded as the first woman to design the exterior of a limited-production car.

In April 2018, Christensen joined Faraday Future as its senior exterior design manager for a period of eight months. In November 2019, she joined Nissan Motor Company as a senior manager.

Articles about Christensen's work have appeared in numerous publications, from *Marie Claire* to the *New York Times*, and she has visited *Jay Leno's Garage* to talk cars.

CHRISTENSEN'S JOURNEY

Michelle grew in San Jose, California, a community steeped in car culture. It was no surprise, given her early exposure to stunning cars, that at De Anza College, a public college in nearby Cupertino, she went from sketching prom dresses to sketching cars and later compared her design of the Acura ZDX to a pair of Alexander McQueen shoes.

As a young girl Christensen worked on vintage cars with her father. "Northern California has a heavy muscle-car and hot-rod culture. I grew up around muscle cars and hot rods." She studied the bounty in her dad's garage. "He was a Mopar guy," she recalls. He cycled through a Plymouth GTX, a Dodge Super Bee, and a Dodge Dart. "When I was eleven or twelve, he got into hot rods, and he bought a '32 roadster." Christensen was immersed in the classic-car scene and found her personal favorite:

"My favorite car is the '67 Chevelle. It's simple, beautiful, and timeless."

She did not even realize that car design was a profession until junior high, when her father pointed out Chip Foose, an ArtCenter graduate at a car show. After that, she followed in his footsteps.

Like other women designers have noted, "I was the son my dad never had." That led her to the ArtCenter College of Design in Pasadena.

At ArtCenter, where she studied from 2001 to 2005, Christensen formulated what one might consider an ambiguous theme for her senior project—an experiment between Sacrilege and Heritage. The goal was to attract two generations with one vehicle. She appeared to be trying to integrate a sporty Barracuda with a modern attitude. However, the Cuda model on display, with its wedge-shaped windshield that rose up to accommodate the driver, was not practical and would make better sense if it were made as a toy.

In 2005, as noted earlier, Christensen designed a Chevrolet wagon for a GM-sponsored project. However, Christensen also delivered a notable rendering consisting of three versions of a vehicle (of which one of the cars was a rough future ZDX) below a Chevrolet bow tie. A second model was built. Both were featured in the ArtCenter College of Design 2005 Spring Show. The more interesting of the two was called the Chevrolet convertible delivery wagon, although the finesse of the rendering was totally lost in the model. Interesting features included small, creased bulges over the front wheels, and bulky fenders over the dual rear wheels, which were barely integrated. The windshield wrapped around to in front of the rear wheels. Perhaps the thick roof functioned as a carrier.

Constance Smith

In 2006, Acura challenged company designers to create a car that filled a hole in the market. Christensen notes, "My sketch for the exterior won—and became the blueprint for the ZDX, which went on the road in 2013." Features of this AWD were oriented toward a road trip and included expansive windows, a glass-covered roof, and a see-through hatch. The unusual slope of the roof of this unusual but attractive design affected visibility and limited the travel of the sunroof.

Christensen was later chosen as exterior lead designer for the 2016 Acura NSX.

The first woman to manage the design team for a supercar, she joined the NSX team after the midengined concept was introduced at the 2012 North American International Auto Show in Detroit; it replaced a V-10 concept. Christensen then led a crew through the rework of the exterior. The car was further defined after work in the wind tunnel and a switch to a midengine configuration. There is also a distinctive gap between the rear window and a floating C pillar. The final rendition was beefy, with better hood intakes and large side scoops that feed the intercooler on this limited-production exotic.

INFLUENCERS

In the past, Michelle Christensen credited her ArtCenter instructor Dave Marek, who was global creative director for Acura, for hiring her and her husband, Jason Wilbur, right out of school. When it comes to Jason, she noted, "We're always bouncing ideas off each other. He always questions everything and gets me to really think." But, certainly, General Motors and Michelle's talent provided her entrée to the automotive design industry.

ERIN CROSSLEY

I always loved cars. I just found them very cool—the design, the shape of the vehicle; I considered them works of art.

—GM Media (source)

CAREER SUMMARY

Erin Crossley is a design director for Global Cadillac.

BIOGRAPHICAL NOTES

Erin grew up in Saranac Lake, New York, and found a passion for cars very early on, thanks to her parents and the older cars they owned: a 1974 Corvette Stingray and a 1973 Chevy Caprice convertible.

Erin attended Syracuse University in 1995. After completing her first year of studies, she transferred from the Industrial Design Department to the Surface Pattern Design Department, which addressed the design of home furnishings, fashion, and paper products.

After graduation, Erin joined GM in 2000 as a color and trim designer, realizing her dream of working in automotive. Erin has worked on the Cadillac brand for the majority of her career thus far and has worked on nearly every Cadillac in some capacity since joining GM.

This has included multiple generations of the CTS and Escalade, as well as niche products such as the XLR and ELR. Most recently, Erin was appointed to the position of design director for the Celestiq.

Courtesy of Lee Anderson and Erin Crossley

The 2021 Escalade led the segment for its design and innovative engineering. *Constance Smith*

With the XTS, designers really looked for soft and supple leathers and used pops of color to add an element of contrast and drama. *Courtesy of GM China*

Cadillac CTS. *Constance Smith*

MANDI DAMMAN

What I have learned now is to be authentic, be you; it's the best way to go, and advice that serves both men and women well. Be yourself and learn everything you can. You'll need it later, and you'll be glad you have it. As you go through your education, being exposed to people, relationships, and teamwork, really immerse yourself and learn everything you can.

—Mandi Damman (b. ca. 1985)

CAREER HIGHLIGHTS

Mandi Damman, director of Vehicle Dynamics, HVAC, Noise, and Vibration, has and will continue to improve the way we interface with our transport and the very way we move.

After completing numerous work study assignments, Mandi Damman graduated with a bachelor of science degree in mechanical engineering from the esteemed Kettering University and began her career in an engineering position at the Milford Proving Ground. She also completed assignments exploring noise vibration harshness (NVH) and ride and handling. Simultaneously, she enrolled in the graduate program at the University of Michigan, where she completed studies for a master's degree in global automotive and manufacturing engineering. After filling a number of diverse positions at the Milford Proving Ground and in Warren, Michigan, she rose through the ranks and now serves as the director of Vehicle Dynamics, HVAC, and Noise and Vibration development, with the purpose of filling CEO Mary Barra's objective of creating a future with zero crashes, zero emissions, and zero congestion. Damman has also served as a mentor preparing women for engineering careers in the future.

BIOGRAPHICAL NOTES

Born in Michigan, Damman attended Seneca Middle School and Dakota High School, where innovative teachers had developed a state-of-the-art Design Technology, a CTE program sometimes referred to as an engineering program. The director of career and technical education at Dakota, Claire Brisson, notes in a Macomb Schools District newsletter that "for two decades, teaching it has been approached innovatively, including a heavy emphasis on projects, fabrication, and exposure to advanced manufacturing technologies. It's notable that 3-D printing has

been a part of this program for all that time." Damman learned how to use machine tools such as saws and drill presses and explored CAD—later found to be a necessity in the workplace. Damman notes that she wasn't denied any of this because she was a girl, and it was the CTE curriculum that piqued her interest in engineering. She finds it awesome that she knows her way around a machine shop. Today, even a course in design thinking has been added to the curriculum.

After graduating from Dakota High School, Damman and a handful of high school classmates qualified for entrance to Kettering University.

This being a work-study program, Damman would receive seven unique work assignments and started at Body Structures in Pontiac, Michigan; Concept Vehicle Integration at the Technical Center in Warren; and Interior Noise at the Milford Proving Ground. When she first started in the co-op program, her neighbor recommended that she meet a woman the neighbor knew who worked as a chief engineer at GM. Damman later noted, "There weren't many engineers that looked like me." Every time Damman returned from a co-op assignment, the seasoned engineer, perhaps her unofficial mentor, would buy her lunch and speak about her assignment. She taught Damman about networking, mentoring, and building relationships—that is, until she retired.

Another assignment included a return to Milford, this time experiencing the Structural Vibration Lab. She also managed stints in Vehicle Assembly Engineering in Morraine, Ohio, and Global Energy in Warren and completed her Kettering senior thesis project in the Noise & Vibration Lab in Milford, Michigan.

Perhaps with a future Opel assignment in mind, Kettering organizers sent Damman to Germany to study at Hochschule Konstanz für Technik, Wirtschaft und Gestaltung (HTWG), located on the shore of Lake Constance. HTWG is a major player in the scientific and economic development of the region. In 2007, she was awarded a bachelor of science in mechanical engineering. While she received various corporate placements, she also enrolled in the engineering program at the University of Michigan, where she completed the requirements for a master of engineering in global automotive and manufacturing engineering in 2012.

From 2007 to the present, Damman received ten more placements, many at the Milford Proving Ground, including engineering specialist in structural vibration (Milford) and engineering specialist in squeak and rattle (Milford). In 2010, she served as a critical launch team member as cochair of an issue resolution team (chassis and power train), and as a design release engineer for chassis, steering, and power train (Warren). In 2013, she developed Ride and Handling packages back in Milford. She spent a year as an engineering business manager for Global Vehicle Performance in Milford.

She advanced to lead development engineer for hybrid and electric vehicles by 2014, and in 2016 she became the program engineering manager for autonomous vehicles.

The amazing driverless Bolt AV was initially introduced in San Francisco for testing. *General Motors*

Damman previously served as the chief engineer for autonomous vehicles and was interviewed for *Automotive News*—her comments were disseminated in an attachment article financed by an advertiser, Deloitte. In the exposé, "Building a Driverless Future" by Darrin Kelley, Ryan Robinson, and Steve Schmith, the authors relate that Damman stresses that a driverless future beckons companies to build the most-effective and most-efficient autonomous cars.

Damman notes that autonomous vehicles should be electric vehicles, "so we built our own program off the zero-emissions Bolt EV platform, which is ideal for this application. In terms of zero congestion, deploying the first autonomous vehicles in a rideshare environment allows us to adjust to the times when vehicles are on the road. When cars aren't transporting rideshare passengers, we can use them to deliver packages in the middle of the night, to completely change the way mobility works. This is something we're doing to move humanity forward."

Success consists of working with a cross-functional team to create environmentally friendly autonomous cars. Damman also addresses her role and the role of women in this environment.

MENTORING

From 2006 to 2014, Damman assisted in the Smarter Girls Math & Science Camp, addressing the needs of eight-to-thirteen-year-olds. In 2016, she served as a mentor and host for the Inforum AutomotiveNEXT Cross-Company Mentoring Program (Inforum AutomotiveNEXT).

MAGALIE DEBELLIS

CAREER HIGHLIGHTS

In 2020, Magalie Debellis was Cadillac's lead exterior designer and on the design team for the groundbreaking Ultra Luxurious Cadillac Celestiq and Cadillac Lyriq. During her fifteen-year tenure with General Motors, she also contributed to the exterior design of the C7 Corvette under the leadership of Tom Peters, chief of design for its Chevrolet Division.

2014 Stingray. *General Motors*

DEBELLIS'S JOURNEY

Magalie holds a masters' degree in industrial design, with a specialty in automotive design, from Strate School of Design in Paris, France. She subsequently joined GM's design staff at the Warren Tech Center, Michigan; she refined her design skills in GM Australia and GM United Kingdom design studios.

THE AWARD-WINNING 2014 CORVETTE

Debellis's assignments included work on the award-winning Chevrolet C7 Corvette. In 2013, Chevrolet dominated the field on and off the track. The collection of winners was displayed at auto shows here and abroad. The stunning Corvette Coupe and Convertible Stingrays were later described as "it" cars by excited fans. In 2013, Chevrolet provided the winning ride for Jimmie Johnson and sponsored Danica Patrick—the first woman to win the pole position. Johnson also took home the Harley Earl Award Trophy, named for GM's first vice president of Design.

This seventh-generation model Corvette is also referred to as the Stingray; this designation is most significant. The original Stingray was an open race car secretly designed under the direction of Bill Mitchell, GM's second vice president of Design, as well as Larry Shinoda and Peter Brock, using a 1957 Corvette chassis. GM exhibited the original at the Atlanta Art Museum and in the lobby of GM's Design Building. A full-size illustration, painted by GM alumnus Peter Maier, was exhibited at the AACA Museum in Pennsylvania. From a short distance, you got the feel that the real car was just 15 feet away.

The 2014 Stingray renewed the tradition of the Sting Ray / Stingray heritage. It was fast (450 hp; 0–60 in under four seconds), handsome (clean and sophisticated inside and out), technologically innovative (rev management and driving modes), and impressive in terms of technology.

DEBELLIS JOINS CADILLAC

Shepherding the look of the new Cadillac EV program, Magalie worked with a team of designers and engineers to bring the vehicle's exterior design to life, from concept to production. She has over 15 years of automotive design experience and specializes in creating exterior design.

The design of the Cadillac Celestiq and Cadillac Lyriq may be the most memorable one in Debellis's career; the Cadillac SUV called the Lyriq brings Cadillac into a new era and is its first all-electric vehicle. The Cadillac Pressroom introduced it in June 2020: "Led by LYRIQ, Cadillac will redefine American luxury over the next decade with a new portfolio of transformative EVs," said Steve Carlisle, executive vice president and president, GM North America. "We will deliver experiences

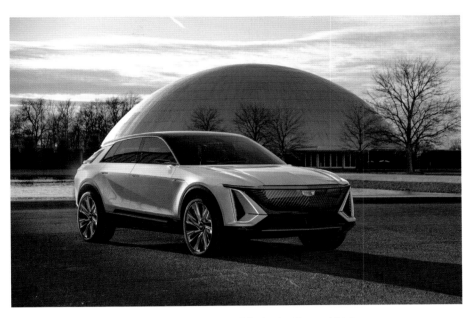

DeBellis worked on the design of the exterior of the Lyriq. *General Motors*

that engage the senses, anticipate desires, and enable our customers to go on extraordinary journeys.

In a virtual presentation hosted by CDN on December 3, 2020, called CD Dialogues, we meet the team that designed the Lyriq—both the concept and production model. Andrew Smith served as executive director of Cadillac's Global Design team, and Josh Thurber as exterior design manager. The exterior design director, Brian Smith, conversed with Magalie, the lead designer in the presentation.

The team brings a passion for developing how the brand will evolve for its electric future. When it comes to exterior design, there is a new freedom and a clean slate. While designers no longer have to design to contain a traditional power train, Andrew notes that this brings different problems to solve. There are a lot of new components and trays of batteries at the bottom of the vehicle. When Brian asks about innovation, Magalie cites many and begins with "I guess the inspiration started with a differed project called the Celestiq. This is the flagship of the brand, the most luxurious product in our future lineup. I looked at what we created, and evolved it into the Lyriq personality." She then mentions American architecture of the 1950s, its bold and dramatic presents, and fashion haute-couture when it comes to detail. Perhaps her French origins preside here.

Brian asks, "When you look at the Lyriq, what drives you most?" Magalie responds: "Well, first of all it has a very premium proportion. It's a very dramatic silhouette, and it's got a magnifique presence. When you look at the face, which features a new concept for Cadillac, the black crystal billet grille has a sculptural effect. The high-end technology with different radars is artfully integrated. The front of the grille remains very sculptural, expressive, and sophisticated."

Magalie is proud of the side view of the Lyriq, which is a

much-different silhouette than earlier SUVs, showcasing a very sporty and dynamic figure, while the newly designed Ultium battery architecture also enables a very roomy interior space.

She continues, "When we get to the rear, it has a unique split vertical taillamp design; this is very new and very distinctive as a Cadillac signature. Overall, the Cadillac Lyriq design is effortless, pure, and elegant."

The addition of the dramatic lighting choreography to the front of the car, designed by Candice Willett, reminds us of the lighting strips first added by Betty Oros to the hood of early 1940s Hudsons and the Pontiacs of the 1950s, which attracted attention with their lighted Indian chief mascots.

Willett can be described as lighting designer and choreographer. There is an order to the Cadillac Lyriq's beautiful light show up front. First the Cadillac emblem glows, then the numerous grille pinstripes illuminate from the center out—also called "precision pattern," followed by the vertical light strips on the sides. The animated lighting creates a distinct personality and creates a new language. The light travels back to the rear.

Crystal Windham, the interior design director, believes Lyriq is a leap forward. Under her, joining Cadillac in 2019 with nineteen years' experience elsewhere, Jennifer Widrick was placed in charge of color and materials.

Jamie Brewer, the engineer on the project, realizes that perhaps she has conquered her own most challenging assignment, and is profiled separately. Alexandra Dymowska works with photographer Michelle Watt to create a book comparing Lyriq's features to nature on the grounds of the GM Technical Center.

The Lyriq made its public debut in spring 2020 in the domed auditorium at the historic GM Technical Center in Warren, Michigan. However, because of disruptions, the Lyriq SUV may not be manufactured until later in 2022. This is the first electric SUV in the Cadillac portfolio, and other vehicles will follow.

MAGALIE DEBELLIS EXPLORES ABSTRACTION

Magalie Debellis is also an abstract painter and sculptor; she partners with Nicolas Rousselet. Nico hold a master's degree from Strate School of Design and works for GM as well as a designer. He also creates automotive art. They share a website and promote their art at Gallery Momentum.

Debellis is also a member of the group called GM Women in Design.

From 2007 to 2014, Dymowska served as a senior creative designer in the Cadillac Color and Materials Studio, moving over to the Cadillac Interiors Studio for two years. In 2016, she was promoted to lead designer, Brand Strategy, for Cadillac Design.

Dymowska inspires young designers. Like John Cafaro, a fellow Pratt Institute graduate (he attended three decades earlier) and Corvette designer who recruited her, she continues to visit her alma mater and works as a college relations representative.

BIOGRAPHICAL NOTES

Dymowska was born in communist Lodz, Poland, in the early 1980s, where ordinary citizens relied on public transportation, with taxis as a backup. Citizens would have been lucky to own a compact Fiat, which would serve an entire family.

When Dymowska was a child, one car—the Volga, a mainstay of the Soviet Union—stood out. It was very different than the boxy Fiats of the era; it was more solid and rounded and was easily identified by its hood ornament—a zinc die-cast, chrome-plated reindeer. When Dymowska thinks about it, she notes, "My first visual memory of a car is the famous Russian '60s Volga. On one occasion, I found myself getting into this oversized bulbous car at the taxi stand. I was fascinated because the look of the car was curvy—very different from the standard, boxy Fiat 125 taxi. It stood high and looked strong and heavy. The Volga had a presence, and owning one in the Soviet Union back then meant you made it. In terms of social status, it was the equivalent of a Cadillac."

At age fifteen, Dymowska immigrated with her family to the United States.

In 1996, she began studies at the Columbia College Chicago and, after completing thirty credits, applied for and won a Pougialis Fine Art Award. The award enabled her to study as an apprentice with an artist of national or international reputation for one semester. By the time the program ended, Dymowska would have also exhibited in the Arcade Gallery. Winners received scholarships to defray tuition costs. She received a bachelor of arts in art and design: fine art / art history in 2000.

After graduating, Dymowska was hired as a visual art consultant for the Chicago Department of Cultural Affairs.

In 2004, Dymowska applied for entrance to the graduate program at Pratt Institute after being awarded a Jack Kent Cooke Foundation grant. According to its website, the Jack Kent Cooke Foundation is "dedicated to advancing the education of exceptionally promising students who have financial need." Since 2000, the foundation has awarded over $200 million in scholarships to over 2,600 students from eighth grade through graduate school.

In addition, General Motors and Pratt's Department of Industrial Design were partnered to give talented underrepresented students at Pratt the opportunity to expand their automotive design skills and portfolios through scholarships in transportation design.

Drawing by Constance Smith

ALEXANDRA DYMOWSKA

It thrills me that I can design something that serves so many people.

—Alexandra Dymowska (b. ca. 1980)

CAREER HIGHLIGHTS

Alexandra Dymowska served as a visual arts consultant for the Chicago Department of Cultural Affairs from 2000 to 2003. Additionally, she consulted for contemporary art collections of Chicago's Department of Cultural Affairs, Arthur Andersen LLP, Columbia College Chicago, Fassbender Gallery, Oak Park Art League, and private collectors.

Dymowska was awarded artist residencies in painting, notably with the Ragdale Foundation and the University of Maryland. She has exhibited at the Polish Museum of America, at the South Bend Museum of Art, and in numerous galleries. In 2003, she worked with Archi-treasures, contributing to an award-winning model outdoor classroom integrated with a garden.

She notes, "I didn't decide to enter auto—it just happened. That's the story of a lot of women in the field. It thrills me that I can design something that serves so many people. Designing an interior is about humanizing technology, about taking new technology and interpreting it in an artistic, elegant way." Dymowska graduated with a master of industrial design from Pratt in 2007.

"I didn't decide to enter auto—it just happened. That's the story of a lot of women in the field. It thrills me that I can design something that serves so many people. Designing an interior is about humanizing technology, about taking new technology and interpreting it in an artistic, elegant way."

A perennial student, Dymowska studied automotive design at the College for Creative Studies from 2010 to 2013.

As noted previously, from 2007 to 2014, Dymowska served as a senior creative designer in the Cadillac Color and Materials Studio. Here, she created an outstanding implementation of a high-quality innovative interior and exterior production program for numerous vehicles, including the 2010 Urban Luxury Concept, the award-winning 2013 ATS, and the CT6.

From 2014 to 2016, she served as a senior interior designer in the Cadillac Interiors Studio. She notes that she was responsible for creating compelling design sketches and renderings for future world-class Cadillac interiors with consideration for form, function, and luxury. She influenced the evolution of an aesthetic vision of the brand's top-of-the-line products on the basis of the latest trend research and sensitivity to the luxury market form and execution cues. She designed brand-appropriate creative solutions of new technology integration. Interacting with internal and external cross-functional partners enabled Dymowska to develop and follow through on execution. During this time, she was featured in a National Geographic documentary film, *Driving America.*

Today, Alexandra serves as a lead brand strategy designer for Cadillac. In this position, she leads development of cross-disciplinary innovation initiatives. She also directs the evolution of design brand philosophy. Driving visual and conceptual design consistency, Dymowska strategizes the product portfolio and ensures brand identity focus. She also builds creative relationships between design and marketing/advertising to ensure brand alignment. In addition, she has contributed to the XT5 and the 2021 Escalade.

In her role as a "brand ambassador," Dymowska also identifies future brand opportunities, conceptualizes product media stories, and supports brand communication. She backs the luxury customer focus group research and delivers actionable insight. Last but not least, she inspires a team, fosters a stimulating work environment, and works as a liaison with executive design, research, and marketing leadership.

Research included visits to Lineapelle, a leather industry show, in Bologna, and the 2019 International Contemporary Furniture Fair at the Jacob K. Javits Convention Center in New York City.

Alexandra recently assisted in framing photos of the Lyriq at the Technical Center and creating material for the Lyriq book.

Alexandra Dymowska recalls her work at school being evaluated by John Cafaro, a prominent 1977 Pratt graduate: "Reviews by working professionals like John lent a new perspective on my work and its potential for application in the real world," says Dymowska. "I now attend Pratt's industrial design reviews to return the favor. I also draw inspiration from the creativity and purity of ideas produced at Pratt. This kind of interaction is invaluable for design professionals. It reminds us to dream again."

Cadillac Lyriq interior. *General Motors*

The Volga made an impression on Alexandra. *Constance Smith*

Drawing by Constance Smith

WULIN GAOWA

The China market is playing a dominant role both in Asia and globally, [and as] demand in China accounts for a bigger and bigger portion of GM's global sales, our success is critical. We need to closely monitor and predict Chinese customers' mobility behaviors, needs, and preferences to ensure we are bringing the right products to market. China's vast geography means that many current mobility solutions are necessary, and it seems logical to think that inventions here could have appeal in other markets with similar customers' needs and behaviors.

—Wulin Gaowa, interview published by General Motors in 2012

CAREER HIGHLIGHTS

Wulin Gaowa was named one of the best young designers of China 2010 by the China Industrial Design Association. She was appointed the first design director of the GM China Advanced Studio in September 2011. This coincided with being assigned to the new GM Advanced Technical Center in Shanghai.

Gaowa's international experience before joining General Motors included work for DaimlerChrysler in 2000 at the Mercedes-Benz Technology Center in Sindelfingen, Germany, as well as Italdesign Giugiaro in Moncalieri, Italy.

Other experience included work at BenQ-Siemens Mobile Phone Technical Development Center in Beijing. Before advancing to the director's position, she was an advanced design director at the Beijing Automotive Technology Center (BTAC). Gaowa also lectured in transportation design at the Central Academy of Fine Arts (from GM China Pressroom).

In 2016, she took on a new role for BAIC Group's EV brand. Gaowa became the design director of the BAIC (officially the Beijing Automotive Industry Holding Company) subsidiary Arcfox. Arcfox is the premium brand of BJEV (Beijing Electric Vehicle Company), a division of the BAIC Group dedicated to electric vehicles. In 2017, they unveiled two electrics at the Beijing Auto Show.

In 2018, it was reported that Wulin Gaowa, outgoing design manager of BAIC's Arcfox brand, made a surprising move to become responsible for the exterior design and brand image of an unmanned aerial vehicle (UAV) start-up called EFY Technology. As well as developing drones and their control systems, EFY has been working on a full-sized unmanned helicopter that can be adapted for different purposes. It boasts a longer range, greater speed, and greater load-carrying capacity than a drone.

GAOWA'S JOURNEY

Gaowa holds a bachelor's degree in industrial design from the Central Academy of Arts and Design in Beijing and a master's degree in transportation design from Pforzheim University in Germany.

By joining GM, Gaowa followed in the footsteps of Yan Huang; Yan was instrumental in establishing PATAC many years before. The Pan Asia Technical Automotive Center, a design and engineering facility, is GM's joint venture with SAIC Motor.

Gaowa was welcomed by her supervisor, Bryan Nesbitt, GM International Operations VP of Design, who had his own reputation as the designer of the Chevrolet HHR and the Chrysler PT Cruiser and experience as a manager for Cadillac.

Ed Welburn, global vice president of GM Design, was also pleased with her hire. In a Chevrolet Press release, Kevin Wale, president and managing director of the GM China Group, noted, "Having a person like Wulin who has an innate understanding of Chinese culture and market needs as well as a strong background in automotive design will ensure that our new organization fully addresses the needs of our local customers" (from GM Pressroom / China).

Around this time, the PACE program, headquartered at Wuhan University of Technology, made its debut; it was sponsored by a group of five companies, including GM and its affiliates, to set up research facilities and collaboratives for colleges. Wulin visited Monash University in Australia, whose program was under the direction of Ian Wong, to recognize student achievers.

In 2010, the podlike, two-passenger, electric-networked vehicle, incorporating the technology and gyroscopes from the Segway

Human Transporter (or Segway PT), was unveiled by GM at the Shanghai Auto Show. Three versions were developed internationally. The EN-V would later land on a college campus, where it was rented. In 2010, the electric SIAC Sail concept was also unveiled.

Subsequently, in 2011, GM and SAIC Motor Corporation agreed to develop electric-vehicle architecture together at PATAC.

By 2011, OnStar made its debut. GM and its joint ventures in China showcased fifty-three production and concept vehicles under six brands at Auto Shanghai 2013. Among the vehicles on display were the new Buick Riviera concept vehicle, which was making its global debut at the show, and the Chevrolet Cruze hatchback and Cadillac Escalade ESV, both of which were making their China debut.

The Buick Riviera concept vehicle was designed jointly by GM's Shanghai GM and PATAC. It offered a preview of Buick's future design trends through its elegant exterior and interior. Additionally, it featured a range of advanced technologies, including plug-in hybrid electric-vehicle propulsion technology.

The Chevrolet Cruze hatchback complemented the Cruze sedan, one of Chevrolet's most popular models. The domestic lineup was also displayed.

Cadillac had ten models on display, including the Escalade ESV; the brand's flagship SUV made its debut in China. The Escalade ESV introduced new technologies, design, premium equipment, powerful performance, advanced safety, and riding comfort.

Opel returned to Auto Shanghai with its full product lineup in China, led by its newly launched Insignia Sports Tourer, which went on sale at a price of between RMB 325,000 and RMB 375,000. Opel also introduced two new models—the Zafira Tourer and Astra GTC—together with its most popular model on the market, the Antara SUV.

The Baojun passenger car brand revealed the new 2013 Baojun 630, which was powered by 1.5-liter DVVT and 1.8-liter EcoTec engines and featured improvements from the original model in handling, interior styling and comfort, exterior styling, and safety. Accompanying the Baojun 630 was the Lechi, an iconic high-performance minicar that joined the brand's lineup in 2012.

Jiefang from FAW-GM displayed two models that went on sale later that year. The new Jiefang S230 and Jiefang F330 were important additions to the brand's growing light-duty truck family.

In 2015, the revolutionary Chevrolet FNR concept was unveiled. At the time, Chevrolet Authority online noted that the autonomous electric concept offered a glimpse of the future. It was developed in Shanghai by GM's Pan Asia Technical Automotive Center (PATAC) joint venture.

While we do not know when the idea was initially penned, the Chevrolet FNR-X Concept made its global debut at Auto Shanghai 2017. The plug-in hybrid electric vehicle offered two driving modes: V (Versatility) and S (Sport). The FNR-X can modify its suspension and handling profile thanks to an adaptive suspension that adjusts ground clearance on demand (from GM Corporate Newsroom online, 2017).

By 2016, Wulin Gaowa moved on to Arcfox and, in 2018, brought her expertise to EFY. At EFY, Gaowa is reportedly "focused on the front-end design, production, and corporate brand strategy reshaping" of the brand and its aircraft, according to weixin.qq (translated from Chinese).

Chevrolet's FNR concept was unveiled at the Chinese auto show. *GM China*

The Cruise hatchback made its debut in China. *General Motors*

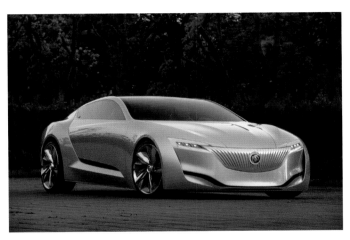

The Buick Riviera concept was a joint venture. *GM China*

Nick Hagen Photography

SHARON GAUCI

My design philosophy is fairly straightforward—beautiful, simple, refined, uncomplicated, clean surfaces, well executed, tailored, and coordinated. Synergize with the exterior form vocabulary. Know the personality of the vehicle you are designing for, understand the future landscape. Design with some "wins."

—Sharon Gauci (b. 1970)

CAREER HIGHLIGHTS

Over a twenty-seven-year span, Sharon Gauci has contributed to interior and exterior color and trim design for a groundbreaking concept car portfolio and numerous handsome production car offerings.

Starting as a Ford designer in Australia, Sharon later connected with BMW before joining GM's Australian design facility at Holden, Ltd. She relocated to Michigan in 2008. Her early design contributions included work for the Ford R7 SUV Concept and later the Territory—a la American Taurus.

Once at General Motors, she contributed to the WTCC Ultra concept, Efijy concept, GMC Denali XT concept, Ute concept, Cadillac Converj concept, Shanghai EN-V, Stingray concept, Miray concept, and Coupe 60. As a member of the production car team, she contributed to the Volt, ATS, Malibu, Cruze hatchback and notchback, Barina, Spark, Commodore, Statesman, Caprice, and Camaro.

Gauci served as global director of Color and Trim for GM North America. From 2003 to 2013, Sharon was the global design director for Color and Trim for Buick, contributing to the Cascada, the Avenir, and the Avenir packages available on luxury offerings. The stunning 2015 Avenir concept captured the award for interior design at NAIAS. In 2018, she assumed the position of executive director of Global Industrial Design. Her responsibilities include the supervision of User Experience, Design Archives and Special Collections, Brand Identity, Product Design–Experiential and Photographic, Animation, and Visualization.

In 2018, Sharon was the first woman to provide the keynote presentation for the WardsAuto Interiors Conference. The following year, she received the inaugural Women in Design Award at the sixty-first annual Australian Good Design Awards Ceremony.

As executive director of Global Industrial Design, Sharon's team was in charge of generating the stunning new logo corporate logo, which was unveiled in 2021 in an effort to promote electric vehicles and the Ultium battery. They also generated nameplates for the Hummer EV.

SHARON'S JOURNEY

Sharon's earliest memories of her childhood date back to 1971. She started ballet at just three years old and developed a love both for visual and performing arts that would last a lifetime. She

Gauci (*left*) and her colleagues accept the award for the interior design of the 2015 Buick Avenir. *Courtesy of John F. Martin Photography*

notes, "I remember the feeling of being completely content in art class. As a child at home, I 'coloured in' and drew, 'built' with Legos and boxes, and 'made' with plaster and odd bits. As I teenager, I continued to draw, found a passion for photography, interior design and merchandising. I would 'merchandise' my bedroom all of the time."

Gauci subsequently graduated from the Good Shepherd School and St. Columba's College, an all-girls Roman Catholic high school, both in Melbourne, Australia. Her high school teacher, Denise Bryant, was an inspiration and encouraged Sharon to push the boundaries. There were only two students in her high school in her last year.

After high school, Sharon sought to pursue something creative, but not fashion or graphic design—perhaps interior design or fashion photography. Instead of jumping right into college, she took a year off to practice and built a portfolio. She explored a number of creative mediums and techniques and also covered design foundation. "I discovered industrial design and pursued this avenue not with a view to becoming a designer in the automotive industry but a designer of interior design and product." Sharon completed the requirements for the bachelor in art (industrial design) in 1992 from Swinburne University of Technology in Melbourne. There were only two women in the industrial design program.

In 1993, she accepted an invitation to join the Ford Motor Company in Melbourne as designer for Colour & Trim. To be honest, Sharon had no idea what "Colour and Trim Design" was. She had learned about the "position vacancy" at the Ford studio in Melbourne after speaking to a designer at an auto show in 1992.

The Ford R7 concept Sharon contributed to was unveiled at the 2002 Melbourne Motor Show and reached production two years hence as the Ford Territory. Simon Butterworth had worked with his American counterpart—J. Mays—in styling the exterior of the Territory. Sharon worked with Marcus Hotblack and Graham Wadsworth on the interior of the BA Falcon range, FPV range, and Territory range. The car had flexible cup holders and a handbag holder to the side of the front seat for a female driver; Ford recognized that many SUV buyers were women.

In 2003, Sharon received the Design Institute Award for textile design for her fabric design for the Ford BA Falcon. In 2004, the Ford SX Territory, a crossover SUV, received the *Wheels* Car of the Year Award. The SX series was available in RWD or AWD and later was utilized for emergency services. From 2004 to 2011, FMC sold over one million Territory SUVs.

As the Territory hit the market in 2004, a friend dropped a copy of a help-wanted advertisement on Sharon's desk. Her colleague, Michael Simcoe, was on his way to the United States. Sharon interviewed with GM's Tony Stolfo; the rest is history.

In 2006, she accepted the addition of Asia Pacific C&T team before moving to Detroit two years later, where she was brought onto the Cadillac Converj concept team. For most of us, style and elegance are synonymous with Cadillac. Cadillac has progressed from the LaSalle series 303 to the Eldorados of the 1950s to the transcontinental partnerships negotiated with Pininfarina and others. However, the visions of the future are most evident in the concept cars of the past and present.

The Coupe 60 concept was a pleasant surprise when it arrived. *General Motors*

CADILLAC CONCEPTS

As noted earlier, Sharon was involved with the design of numerous concept cars at home and abroad. Perhaps the success of Cadillac rests on the development of concept cars exploring new styles and features throughout its history.

In 1905, founder Henry Leland ordered the two-seat Osceola, a closed-body car that led to the future. The 1933 Aerodynamic Coupe featured a new sloping tail and captured our imaginations at the 1933 Chicago World's Fair. In 1953, the LeMans, with its panoramic windshield and automatic roof—reminiscent of Earl's LeSabre concept—made its debut at a Motorama. In 1954, we welcomed the Park Avenue, La Espada, and El Camino. The Park Avenue, later the name of the premier Buick model, had a hand-brushed aluminum top and would lead to the Eldorado Brougham. The other models forecast a future with quad headlamps and towering tail fins. The sporty 1955 LaSalle led to the iconic 1955 Cyclone, which combined rocket-like fenders and a canopy fit for a fighter plane. The radar-sensing crash avoidance system heralded safety in the distant future. In 1956, Buick would try to compete with its own futuristic Centurion. In 1999, we welcomed the wedge-shaped Evoq, complete with keyless entry, voice-activated navigation, a heads-up display, and Night Vision infrared technology. These features would become commonplace soon afterward. The 2000 Imaj utilized an aluminum space frame and radar and sensors to monitor nearby objects. Three cameras replaced review mirrors.

In 2001, the Vizón was Cadillac's first hybrid. A Bulgari designer added his own vision to the instrument panel.

In 2002, we celebrated Cadillac's one hundredth birthday with the carbon-fiber midengine Cien powered by a V-12 engine. Its crisp edges and lines were contrasted by blue-tinted windows and headlamps.

In 2003, we would welcome the lengthy Cadillac Sixteen, identified from the side by a long hood and leading to a low cabin.

In 2004, Sharon started at GM Australia as chief designer in the Colour and Trim department, which included Asia Pacific from 2006 onward. She worked with GM Holden and Asia Pacific's studios overseeing the VE Commodore Range, WM Statesman, Caprice, Camaro, Cruze J300, Efijy concept, Chevrolet Cruze, WTCC Ultra, Coupe 60 concept, and Denali SUV concept. The Coupe 60 project was somewhat of a secret project generated by Michael Simcoe and was a surprise when it arrived at a show. Simcoe is VP of Design, following in the shoes of Ed Welburn.

Holden's innovative Coupe 60 concept graced the pages of magazines in 2008 on Holden's sixtieth birthday. The low-slung coupe arriving on stage for the unveiling featured a bold form, machined 21-inch rims, and Kumho semislicks. Its design cues seemed to appear in the Pontiac GTOs and G8s sold on American soil.

The one-off Efijy was a side project—a curvaceous hot rod that pays tribute to the 1953 Holden FJ, Holden's second production model. The design was the vision of and initiated on the outside by Richard Ferlazzo and the C&T by Sharon's team. They explored the latest mechanicals, electronics, and materials. Efijy incorporated a long list of suppliers and utilized a 6-liter V-8.

By 2009, Sharon was part of the design team assembled to develop the Converj electric concept destined for the 2009 North American International Auto Show in Detroit. The interior is memorable. Synthetic suede contrasts the black leather in the cabin; aluminum and wood trim, subsequently used very successfully in production models, contributes the required dose of elegance. The wool blend carpeting and silk headliner are top quality. The ubiquitous center console is attractively designed. White and blue lighting contribute to its high-tech ambiance.

Buick hadn't offered a convertible for about twenty-five years, and the Cascada was welcomed. *Constance Smith*

In January 2009, Sharon returned to her roots, joining Holden as chief designer of Color and Trim for both production cars, including the Holden VF Commodore and advanced concepts, and continued to lead the advanced groups at GM Asia Pacific, heading a team of creative designers at GM Holden to design visionary color, trim, texture, and materials design solutions and strategies for application on production and advanced design concepts in the auto industry, trend forecasting, and material innovation. She watched over GM Asia Pacific, Colour and Advanced Trim Design.

In 2013, when Sharon was the global design director for Color and Trim for Buick, Buick went on to produce its stunning Cascada convertible and other Avenir concept cars. The stunning Avenir concept went on to win two EyesOn Design Awards in its category. It was recognized inside and out.

From 2013 to 2018, Sharon served as global design director of Color and Trim. Perhaps the most notable concept of this time is the Cadillac Escala, which sports a stunning interior to which Jennifer Kraska contributed. It is this concept that leads Cadillac into the future, and the styling language continues to grace the

Sharon and team created color and trim for the Efigy. *General Motors*

The instrument panel of the Escala would lead to the design of the 2021 Escalade. *Constance Smith*

2019 and 2020 products introduced by Cadillac. The state-of-the-art OLED curved instrument panel served as the basis for the design of the 2021 Cadillac Escalade.

In January 2018, Sharon was promoted to the position of executive director of Global Industrial Design. Her keynote speech for the WardsAuto Interiors Conference likely incorporated her own thoughts and opinions with the corporate history provided by GM's Archives.

She described the changes in automotive design. Sharon noted that without having a driver, things will change. She referred to the current trend of soft materials inside as perhaps humanizing the vehicle. As we look into the future, things will change rapidly. Sharon believes, "Designing interiors won't be about space, shapes, textures, and color anymore. It will be just as much about the experience of being there, whether that means mobile phone use, navigating, shopping, watching films, whatever the experience is about that day—and that is what industrial designers do; just as in our past, we create products and experience—some that may surprise you, like the test tracks at EPCOT and Shanghai Disney, and of course the interiors of the next generation of EVs." Gauci advocated for mentoring activities for grade school, high school, and college students, ranging from five days to fifteen weeks. GM has established the You Make a Difference (YMAD) program for school-aged students, providing for activities for the Girl Scouts and running projects with the College for Creative Studies. These opportunities to engage and direct promising young people continue to this day and are challenging yet gratifying. In her presentation, Sharon also mentioned her teenage son, who has no interest in an automotive career and perhaps even appears to dismiss creativity—which is the lifeblood of our future. He will certainly pursue another path.

Gauci advises, "We have to dispel the myth of the starving artist. Moreover, we must convince young people and, most importantly, the people who influence them—parents, guardians, and teachers—to help them embrace the field, so that young artists who like cars aren't pushed into engineering, or kids who can draw well aren't told it's a nice hobby but to go to medical school first. There are so many creative opportunities in our field, where even if you never sketch a car, you will make a significant contribution to global products and brands" (*Innovation* 38, no. 4 [Summer 2019]).

In 2021, GM publicized the "Everybody In" new brand identity in GM's Exhibit 0 announcement.

GM notes, "As GM amplifies its EV message, it has also created a revitalized brand identity designed for a digital-first environment. The new logo builds on a strong heritage while bringing a more modern and vibrant look to GM's familiar blue square. The new brand identity extends to technology brands including Ultium. The team of GM designers tasked with creating the new logo considered how to balance the history and trust inherent to the existing design with GM's vision for the future."

Gauci describes the assignment: "This was a project our team took so personally, not just for ourselves but for the 164,000 employees this logo represents. At every step we wanted to be intentional and deliberate because this logo signifies creative and innovative thinking across the global General Motors family."

The new GM logo features a color gradient of vibrant blue tones, evoking the clean skies of a zero-emissions future and the energy of the Ultium platform. The rounded edges and lowercase font create a more modern, inclusive feel. The underline of the "m" connects to the previous GM logos as well as visually representing the Ultium platform. And within the negative space of the "m" is a nod to the shape of an electrical plug.

Sharon's team designed GM's handsome brand-new corporate logo. *General Motors*

The Buick Avenir (*avenir* meaning "future" in French) had a sweeping interior and seated four with a console resting in the center. *General Motors*

Karla Waterhouse, Waterhouse Photography

CECILE GIROUX

First, I try to learn who my customers are, and how they would use/enjoy the space I am envisioning for them. Second, I determine if there is a problem to solve, what could improve from the current condition. Last, it is about implementing the solution, encasing it in a beautiful and compelling package, with the appropriate materials (I geek out watching the sun track on a well-executed line/surface). It is about working with love and empathy. Understanding that it takes a community to develop complex products as vehicles that transport people and their goods.

It was like a lightbulb went off in my head. I could actually see what I wanted to draw in my head, and I could spin it around to see it from different angles. I fell in love with the idea of making things that people could use and enjoy!

—Cecile Giroux (b. 1964), who prioritizes the art of drawing, explains her technique.

CAREER HIGHLIGHTS

Cecile Giroux has contributed to the design of significant concept and production vehicles for each for each of the "Big 3" and their affiliates.

As a junior intern from the College for Creative Studies, Giroux joined an exhibit designer, a specialty auto builder, and Chrysler. In a transportation design class of eleven, she had a choice of full-time employers even before graduation and "on-boarded" to Ford (1998–2000), where she worked in the American and European advanced studios. Ford waited for her to start when the death of her father interrupted her schedule. She cherishes her work on the Ford GT 90 and Contour Show Car. She also contributed to the preproduction interior packaging for the Ford GT—the project was code-named Petunia.

In 2000, Giroux joined General Motor's Brand Character Center, and in 2001 she was promoted to lead interior designer, sketching the style for appearance.

In 2001, she was tasked with developing strategies to freshen the line. She spent two and a half years in the Cadillac Character Center, working to enhance the product via interior design and materials to target youthful affluent customers.

Giroux was behind the interior design of the sleek Cadillac Sixteen concept car, which required collaboration with Steuben Studios in Elmira, New York.

She was awarded a US patent with GM for the cluster, which emulates the feel of jewelry—it is stunning even today. The Sixteen went on to win multiple awards.

In 2003, she worked as an exterior designer for the Saab-branded truck. In 2005, she contributed to the GM Lambda Mid-Size Saturn Branded Truck Studio (Interior Design). Working in the midsize truck studio from 2004 to 2005, Giroux supported the build of the Saab-branded 9X exterior design and also various SEMA (Specialty Equipment Market Association) vehicles.

In 2007, she led the Large Truck Interior Studio–Hummer H2 (midcycle action). The H2 concept car was jettisoned when Hummer was eliminated, but the interior design work generated a Saturn-branded midsized truck. When Saturn wound down, the design was resurrected as a Chevrolet midsized truck.

Waylaid by department changes and moves at GM in 2008, Giroux moved to Fiat Chrysler Automobiles, serving in brand definition. In 2013, she contributed to the SD truck, in 2015 to the RU platform minivan, in 2017 to the Pegasus and Fiat Doblò Brasil, and in 2019 to the global Jeep interior.

During these assignments, she designed a curved touchscreen for the Chrysler 200C show car. Her design work for the Rotary e-Shifter and transfer case identification is protected by patent. The Ram 1500 and the Jeep received WardAuto's awards for Best Interiors. In 2019, her designs for minivan consoles were also awarded patents.

In 2014, Giroux joined the adjunct faculty of the College for Creative Studies.

GIROUX'S JOURNEY

Cecile Giroux and a slightly older brother were born in Buenos Aires, Argentina, to Ita Donnelly de Carey. Although a fashion designer, her mother also worked as a stewardess for Pan American Airways in South America. Tragically, Cecile lost her mother at age three.

Her father, a mechanical engineer, worked as general plant manager for Chrysler. She used to call him their "heavy-metal Daddy." He set up tooling and staffed manufacturing operations for the Latin American plant facilities for Chrysler's partner, Fevre and Basset Ltd.—the San Justo Complex in Buenos Aires, Argentina—in their stamping, motor, transmissions, painting, and assembly sectors, as well as at Mexico's Toluca Plant.

On occasion, her dad brought her to work. The AutoMex facilities in Toluca de Lerdo, Mexico, had some architectural masterpieces on the grounds that she found inspiring even as a child. While her father did the best he could to parent the children and never remarried, he relied on relatives to help out. Two uncles on her mother's side took care of the family's religious needs throughout their lives; both were ordained priests, and one was Argentina's representative at the Vatican.

Giroux attended school at Mexico City's prestigious American School Foundation. She learned Spanish in the morning and English after lunch. She loved art and notes that "Art Every Day! Mexico is where I learned to LOVE art, architecture, and the art of drawing."

Once the family relocated to the Detroit area, where she had an aunt, she enrolled in the College for Creative Studies. This was a life-changing event.

In her freshman year, she studied advertising in the Graphic Arts Department. She enjoyed the curriculum but was not fulfilled. She recalls, "I really wanted to learn how to draw

The interior of the Cadillac Sixteen was painstakingly made by hand. *General Motors*

well." She decided to switch departments, to the Industrial Design Department, chaired by Carl Olsen, where the craft of drawing was prioritized. "It was like a lightbulb went off in my head. I could actually see what I wanted to draw in my head, and I could spin it around to see it from different angles. I fell in love with the idea of making things that people could use and enjoy!" Giroux started working after her sophomore year at school. She interned at an exhibit design company, a specialty automotive builder, and finally at Chrysler Corporation. At Chrysler, she was assigned to work on the second-generation minivan. She continues, "It was a very interesting time to work there, because the studio was busy developing the strategy for the front-wheel-drive platforms that would set up the success of Chrysler through the nineties. I felt privileged to behold the creation of a long-term strategy for such a large company. I was able to meet and work with the design team that realized those projects. As interns we were able to meet with Lee Iacocca that summer. I was one of eleven graduates in the transportation department that year."

Having had multiple offers for full-time employment the year of graduation, Giroux was lucky. "I was onboarded to Ford Motor, two weeks after graduation," she explains. "My father had died when I was a sophomore. I had to liquidate the contents my dad's home and move out, two weeks after graduation, so the estate could be settled, as it was in probate. Ford was very understanding and forwarded me my first paycheck so I could have money for fuel to drive to work. This was humbling for me, and an amazing gesture of kindness on their part." She remembers, "While employed by Ford, I worked mostly in packaging, platform strategy, in the advanced studios in Dearborn, Turin, England, including time at the Jaguar Studio. I had two favorite projects there: the Ford GT90 and the Contour show cars. I also did a lot of work for the preproduction interior packaging Ford GT (a.k.a. Petunia)."

GENERAL MOTORS BRANDS

Giroux comments, "While at General Motors, I worked on various strategies of the brand-freshening projects. I spent two and a half years at the Cadillac Brand Character Center, focusing on freshening the brand, and making it more attractive to a younger, more affluent customer by focusing on the interior design and materials strategy."

This work culminated in a concept car, the Cadillac Sixteen, intended to launch Cadillac into a new era with a fresh product. The Sixteen launched at the Opera House in Detroit. It was embellished with unique walnut burl veneer inserts, custom silk blend carpeting, and crystal pieces cast and hand-finished by Steuben Glass Works, just to name a few opulent details. The Cadillac Sixteen received the Best Concept award at the North American International Auto Show in 2002. As the lead interior

person, Giroux art-directed the interior design's early concept and content story, collaborating with artisans in Elmira, New York, and Steuben Glass Works.

Giroux received a US patent for the Cadillac Sixteen Cluster Gauge Design and Function (2003).

She also led a similar project for a new Hummer H2 interior, which was never realized since the brand was discontinued before the project was finished (2008.3). Giroux notes, "I generated a Saturn-branded midsize truck interior, which was well received, but, alas, Saturn was sundowned as a brand too. The design was later resurrected to become a Chevrolet midsized truck interior" (2006). During her tenure, Giroux's artwork was selected by GM to be featured in various publications, including *Time, Architectural Digest, Robb Report, Car Design News, Car & Driver, Autoweek,* and the *Detroit News.*

FCA

At GM, people and departments were being moved around, and Giroux felt uncomfortable and unsure if there was a place for her; this led to her move to Fiat Chrysler. At FCA, her innovative work was protected by patent. Fiat Chrysler vehicles to which she contributed design won industry-wide awards. This included the 200C show car interior and curved touchscreen, a Rotary e-Shifter for Truck MCA, interior packaging for the Ram truck, and similar ventures. Defining moments for her and the company were the repeat awards won by the Ram 1500 and Minivan midcycle action. In 2008. Giroux worked on a minivan freshening, in 2011–13 the new minivan Pacifica, and in 2018 the Pacifica freshening. The 1500 Ram truck won a Best Interiors award from WardsAuto, and the Jeep Compass placed in the top ten. In 2019, her series of minivan consoles were patented. Giroux recently severed her relationship with FCA to pursue other opportunities.

GIROUX JOINS CCS TO GIVE BACK

Cecile Giroux is currently teaching the craft of creating artistic, fresh innovative design to a new generation of aspiring designers. She summarizes, "Primarily I teach my students how to draw well, technically and artistically, to visualize their ideas and concepts. I help them organize their thoughts and synthesize them into a plausible idea/proposal that solves a problem and delights their customer. In 2018, four of my eight students received awards for their interior designs. They traveled to Shanghai to participate in the awards ceremony. One of my students won best interior. I am well liked by the student body and the faculty in my department."

AMANDA KALHOUS

Innovation is bringing forward new ideas, whether that's a new invention or a new business process. I think that we innovate when we look for change.

—Amanda Kalhous (b. 1972)

Courtesy of Amanda Kalhous

CAREER HIGHLIGHTS

Amanda Kalhous is an accomplished engineer and leader with a background in electrical engineering. With twenty-five years of experience, she has spent her career in the transportation industry; she began her ascent in aviation. She served as an officer in the Royal Canadian Air Force and subsequently with an aerospace supplier before moving on to Line Haul Trucking with Purolator Courier.

Kalhous finally landed in automotive at GM Canada in 2005. She served as an Engineering Group leader in the Active Safety & Autonomous team at General Motors of Canada.

Kalhous moved to the Global Innovation team as a technical product manager in December 2019 and now serves as the portfolio manager across all product for a new internal start-up within GM called BrightDrop.

Kalhous is a leading innovator, with twenty-eight patents to her credit, most of which are in the areas of infotainment and communication. She is an inspiring role model for engineering professionals and young people interested in pursuing careers in engineering. Kalhous was recognized in 2017 by Women of Innovation as one of twenty leading female engineers influencing innovation in Canada, and by GM in 2019 as a Boss Kettering Award winner.

AMANDA'S JOURNEY

Born in Donaghadee, Northern Ireland, approximately 30 kilometers (19 miles) east of Belfast, Amanda immigrated to Canada with her family just shy of her eighth birthday.

Her mother worked in a doctor's office in Northern Ireland before having children. She stayed home to raise Amanda and her two siblings and returned to work part time once her children were in school. Amanda's father was a service technician for Hobart Canada, the worldwide supplier of equipment, systems, and service for the food industry. He later started his own business for commercial kitchen equipment repair, serving hotels and restaurants primarily in the Toronto area.

Amanda's parents did not demand that their children pursue higher education, but they supported it. It was the guidance of her teachers, particularly her math and science teachers, that influenced Amanda's decision to go to university and ultimately to enter engineering. After hearing a presentation by recruiters from the Royal Canadian Air Force (RCAF), Amanda decided to enroll in the Regular Officer Training Plan (ROTP) at the Royal Military College of Canada (RMC). Under the ROTP program, in exchange for serving a minimum of five years with the Canadian Armed Forces (CAF) following graduation, tuition and other costs for accepted candidates were paid for by the Department of National Defence. Officer cadets also received a monthly stipend.

Courtesy of Amanda Kalhous

Oshawa is a sprawling facility. *General Motors*

EARLY CAREER

Amanda was one of only two women in her electrical engineering class at RMC, but she did not feel out of place. The initial recruit term of basic officer training, she recalls, helped the cadets bond. Amanda graduated with her bachelor's degree in engineering in 1994 and was commissioned as a second lieutenant in the CAF. From 1995 to 1997, she served as a technical maintenance officer for the 726 Communications Squadron of the RCAF in Halifax, Nova Scotia. In 1997, she was promoted to captain and took over as wing telecommunications officer for the 12 Wing Shearwater. After completing her five years of obligatory service, and intent upon pursuing her master of engineering degree full time at Dalhousie University, Amanda made the difficult decision to leave the RCAF. Her nine years with the Air Force exposed her to focused leadership training. This training helped her develop leadership qualities that transferred well to the civilian workforce, helping Amanda advance and become a widely respected engineering professional.

Amanda completed her master's degree in engineering in 2000. In October of that year, she joined Litton Systems Canada, a large defense contractor, as a junior engineer. After only six months, she was promoted to systems engineer. Her strong technical and collaborative skills did not go unnoticed, and she was selected by the business development team as the lead project engineer for a proposal on a communication management system for government aircraft.

In 2000, Amanda got married, and she moved to Toronto, Ontario, the following year. Together with her husband, Tom, she traveled around the world for ten weeks and then began looking for work. With only eight months of work experience outside the military and no industry contacts in the city, it took Amanda eight months to find a position. She ultimately secured a contract with an independent consultant to work on a project to design and implement an onboard computer system for bulk pickup and delivery for Purolator Courier. Amanda was subsequently hired on contract by the supplier to complete the implementation of a transportation management system (TMS) for the ground transportation fleet. She successfully transitioned the TMS to the in-house project management office at the end of the contract.

The arrival of Amanda's first child coincided with the end of her work for Purolator. After six months being home with her daughter, she resumed her work search. Her friend had recently secured a position working as a production supervisor at GM of Canada in Oshawa through a contract agency. He suggested she contact the recruiter. Amanda interviewed and was offered a position as a design release engineer. She held this role for three years, working on the original navigation (nav) radio for the 2007 Chevrolet Equinox and Pontiac Torrent. For the 2009 model year, the nav radio was being updated for GM's 2-Mode Hybrid program, the Saturn Vue 2MH. It was an interesting project that required interacting with GM's design studio on the new displays to show customers how the system performed (by flowing from the battery pack to the wheels, for instance). Amanda left for a one-year maternity leave after the birth of her second child in 2007.

Upon her return in 2008, Kalhous was named vehicle software integration engineer for the Saturn Vue 2MH program. The program was being built at GM's facility in Ramos, Mexico, and when her youngest was eleven months old, Amanda left for a week at the plant to oversee the vehicle integration and help with any software issues that came up. This was a fantastic opportunity and learning experience. Seeing how the multiple systems came together to make a complete vehicle, then having the software installed and finally tested as the vehicle approached the end of the assembly line, as you waited with bated breath for the successful test and first ignition start-up, is truly rewarding. It still amazes her when it works the first time, and that is when you can truly appreciate all the elements that it takes—suppliers, designers, engineering teams, manufacturing teams, and others—to get the product to that end point. Unfortunately, the Saturn Vue 2MH never made it to a dealership, since the brand did not make it out of bankruptcy protection, but much of what was learned was carried into other programs.

In that same time frame, Amanda was offered the opportunity to become a GM mentor for the US Department of Energy's

Select universities in the US and Canada participated in the EcoCar Program. *General Motors*

three-year EcoCar: The NeXt Challenge program. With three of the teams coming from Canadian Universities, three mentors were selected from GM of Canada. Amanda became the mentor for the University of Ontario Institute of Technology (UOIT; now known as Ontario Tech University), which is located twenty minutes north of the Canadian Technical Centre's Oshawa Campus. For EcoCar 2: Driving into the Future, Amanda took the opportunity to mentor students from the University of Victoria from 2011 to 2014. The experience with EcoCar was mutually enriching not only for the students, but also the mentor. Since Amanda had spent her time primarily on infotainment-related areas thus far, the exposure to the rest of the vehicle and supporting the teams through the entire (albeit shortened) Global Vehicle Development Process was an invaluable experience.

AMANDA ENCOURAGES INNOVATION

In late 2008, Amanda became a project lead for advanced technology work. In this role, she managed projects in multiple innovation areas, including infotainment, human machine interface, and vehicle access and starting security. She was also responsible for conducting proof-of-concept demonstrations to program teams, global engineering teams, executives, and research and development. In 2014, Amanda became the Bluetooth low-energy (BLE) subsystem lead engineer. She led the design team developing the first introduction of BLE technology in vehicles. She also holds a patent for the concept of a BLE-based passive-entry and passive-start system.

From 2015 to 2017, Amanda served as the Engineering Group manager of propulsion systems integration controls and onboard diagnostics. The position was new for her, and the opportunity resulted from significant company growth, particularly in the area of controls. She managed a team of twenty-one employees across three domains: calibration, controls and software, and systems engineering. She says she was thrilled to be in a leadership role.

With the growth of the Canadian Technical Centre and the goal of reaching 1,000 engineers in July 2017, Amanda transitioned to a new role as the Engineering Group manager for active safety controls and began to grow a new team to take on the lateral controls for GM's Active Safety systems; namely, Lane Keeping Assist (LKA), Lane Departure Warning (LDW), Adaptive Cruise Control, and Super Cruise, which had previously been handled by a team from Opel in Germany. When proliferation of the LKA features caused the team size to grow significantly, Amanda split the team and continued to lead the Controller System team for the front camera module, a role she held until November 2019.

In the fall of 2019, Amanda interviewed and was ultimately selected to take on a new role within the Global Innovation team, led by Pam Fletcher, as product manager for a new start-up that had recently graduated from the incubation phase. In that role, Amanda led customer-focused design and empathy activities to develop the product requirements and continued to grow the product management team as the portfolio manager within the broader Strategy & Operations team within BrightDrop. Currently, Amanda leads a team of product managers across the portfolio of products that BrightDrop offers.

In April 2018, Amanda volunteered for a judging opportunity at the AutoDrive Challenge, cosponsored by SAE International (formerly the Society of Automotive Engineers) and GM. Getting back into the student design competition space as a judge was a great experience, and Amanda particularly enjoyed connecting with students who are passionate about creating autonomous vehicles of the future. Helping General Motors identify future employees is one of the most successful outcomes of these competitions.

Amanda exemplifies what it means to be an innovator in her industry. When the GM Oshawa facility moved into advanced technology in 2009, Amanda says she was initially pushed to work outside her comfort zone. She nonetheless quickly adapted, and the change ultimately revealed her capacity for innovation and invention. Amanda received her first two patents in 2011, one for a carbon dioxide feedback system and the other for a vehicle communication method that receives, transmits, and manages wireless communication over a vehicle network. She has filed thirty-two inventions with the United States Patent and Trademark Office (USPTO) since 2010 and now holds twenty-eight (and counting) patents.

As previously noted, during her time in Advanced Technology, Kalhous and her colleagues developed a Bluetooth low-energy system for locking, unlocking, and starting a vehicle with a smartphone. The first adoption of this technology was in the 2017 Chevrolet Bolt, which permits lock, unlock, and cabin preconditioning as well as providing welcome lighting on the vehicle when the phone is within proximity of the vehicle.

CANADIAN WOMEN OF INNOVATION

In August 2017, Amanda attended the Women of Innovation symposium as one of twenty leading female engineers influencing innovation in Canada. Anne Millar, a postdoctoral fellow, and Mary Wells, a professor, both from the Department of Engineering at the University of Waterloo (now Dean of Engineering at University of Waterloo), penned *Women of Innovation* in an effort to highlight the contributions and careers of Canadian women engineers. Their goal was to reverse the difficulties of recruiting and retaining women in STEM careers by highlighting female role models. Amanda Kalhous embodies the ideals of this honored group.

General Motors

MIN YOUNG KANG

I always think about becoming a designer. I have passion.
—Min Young Kang

CAREER HIGHLIGHTS

After graduating from the College for Creative Studies like many of her colleagues, Min Young Kang arrived at General Motors Design at a time when Ed Welburn, GM's vice president of Design, sought to give young designers the opportunity to grow and to establish themselves. She joined others chosen to bring Hummer back to the forefront.

The design of the small Hummer HX Concept hit the bull's-eye, but it was too late to reverse the downtrend for the division due to fiscal problems across the industry.

BIOGRAPHICAL NOTES

Min Young Kang grew up in South Korea and earned a degree in economics. This led her to pursue a career in investment banking. At some point in time, she fell in love with design and was accepted by the entrance committee of the College For Creative Studies (CCS). She was a little older than the other students, but she looked young and declined to reveal her age. Talented, passionate, and highly trained, she got what she came for and was offered a position at GM Design.

Welburn assigned a trio of its newest designers to develop the HX concept. Min was selected, along with Robert Jablonski and David Rojas from Peru, to work on the Hummer HX concept, which was unveiled at the 2008 North American Auto Show.

Before her arrival, a number of Hummer concepts were unveiled. An illustration of the Hummer H2 Sport Utility truck (SUT) concept was included in a press kit for the 2001 New York International Auto Show. Derived from the production intent 2003 H2, the SUT, which was later produced, was touted as functional, versatile, and almost endlessly configurable. Its wide stance and long wheelbase continued a tradition. This AWD truck featured GM's 6-liter Vortec V-8 mated with an HD five-speed transmission. Terry Henline, the designer of the H2, noted in the special press kit guide that "extreme functionality was the over-riding objective in designing the H2 SUT concept, and this quality is apparent in every detail of the truck." Designed with a short overhand and exceptional ground clearance, it was ready for trails. Massive tow hooks and receiver hooks were included, and a winch was optional. The SUT would preserve the reputation of the H1.

The Hummer H3T, designed under the direction of Anne Asensio, was unveiled at the 2004 Greater Los Angeles Auto Show as a tangible vision to extend the Hummer family by adding a smaller, sporty, and rugged yet versatile premium midsized truck that would open a new niche for Hummer. Standing to express new cues and character design for the brand, it delivered rebellious traits for outdoor enthusiasts, as well as a distinctive personal attitude for the urbanites; this uncompromised concept was designed for men or women drivers. Anne Asensio, who managed the project, noted that those at GM Design collaborated with Nike Design to combine off-road capabilities, innovative features, and lightweight materials with characteristic Nike AG trail orange and black color breaks to finalize its unique appearance. Asensio was especially pleased with the dramatic proportions of the exterior.

However, it would be a challenge and an opportunity for Kang to design a new version for Hummer, designated HX. While Kang and her colleagues initially penned three designs, once the design was chosen, all contributed.

In reviewing her input, Min noted that her inspiration came from toys that she could transform. She notes that the HX, which was unveiled in 2008 at the North American International Auto Show, incorporated a number of sophisticated features. She thought that they were pushed to find things they were unfamiliar

Hummer HX concept. *Courtesy of Alan Vanderkaay and General Motors*

with. Davis Rojas, the lead designer, noted that it was fun to come in and get inspired by other designers that you looked upon in school as really, really good (from gmnext.com).

The three designers were led by Carl Zipfel, exterior director of Design and a professional motocross racer, and Steve Kim, design manager. Stuart Norris headed interior design.

This AWD vehicle, powered by a 3.6-liter V-6 mated to a six-speed automatic was simply described as a two-door, four-passenger SUV with extreme off-road capability. The engine also ran on E85 ethanol, part of Hummer's push to make all of its offerings biofuel-ready.

The exterior was more reconfigurable than anything else on planet Earth at the time and set a new direction. The HX measured 170 inches in length and had a wheelbase of 103 inches. The front and rear overhangs were ideal for off-road assignments. There was literally nothing in front of the tires, and the SUV had an approach angle of just 46 degrees; this almost matched the largest Hummer. When it came to reconstructing the exterior, it put the Jeep Wrangler in its place. The rear quarters, the fenders, and the roof were removable. One could change a slant-sloping-back vehicle, a la British Leyland, to a wagon back or leave the back off altogether. The panels were easily moved using Zeus fasteners. The LED lights were kept small. Of course, Zipfel noted that this vehicle that was angular, stealthy, armor-like, and futuristic. It had attitude.

In a KBB interview at the Auto Show, Carl Zipfel, exterior director of design for the HX, noted that this vehicle had to attract rock crawlers, cool urbanites, and public servants.

Stuart Norris noted the functionality inside. Like some others, it had a fold-flat rear seat. However, the helicopter seats up front had their own suspension—looking like someone brought their

Erector Set to work. It is noteworthy that the seats were covered with a digitized-looking camouflage material, combining the requisite with the future.

As usual in a Hummer, there was an oversized center console, a shifter, and an engine starter built in, and a huge rubber bank encircled the steering wheel.

More than anything else, the instrument panel surpassed all expectations. The three large gauge areas offered information depending on the mode. The displays can show a navigation system, a trail camera feed, vehicle speed, engine rpm, and wheel angle information. After all, an off-road user might need an altitude reading.

The round knob to adjust the rebound on the shocks was a nice touch. Naturally, this vehicle had the essential D rings needed for recovery and an integrated winch.

The Hummer HX had it all, but it was just a little too late for the party. However, it will never be forgotten.

The 2022 GMC Hummer EV pickup was revealed in the fourth quarter of 2020, two later. The pickup will be followed by a 2024 Hummer EV EUV. The Hummer EV PU, which is powered by electric motors and is equipped with the Ultium battery pack, is touted as the world's first all-electric super truck. The truck is fast and versatile. With up to 1000 hp, the truck moves from 0 to 60 mph in about three seconds in Extract Mode—this lowers the truck 6 inches. In the Crab Walk Mode, it can move diagonally. Its four roof panels stow in the rear compartment. Hummers are slated to be built in Factory Zero along with an electric Silverado in the newly refurbished Hamtramck plant in Michigan.

Thus, while Min Young Kang has moved on, the Hummer look and nameplate have been resurrected, and Hummer enjoys a new popularity.

General Motors

MICHELLE KILLEN

I consider my career to be my greatest professional accomplishment. It's allowed me to grow both personally and professionally.

—Michelle Killen (b. 1980)

CAREER HIGHLIGHTS

From 2018 to the present, Michelle Killen has served as the design manager in the Color and Trim Department, where she has recently addressed the needs of the Cadillac Division of General Motors. From 2006 to the present, she has also held the position of creative design lead.

Killen and her team specified or designed the color and trim for the stunning all-new 2021 Cadillac Escalade, which went on sale in 2020.

Previously, in 2016, she had the opportunity to contribute to the interior design of the trendsetting Escala concept, which has influenced the design of all Cadillacs since.

Since joining GM in 2006, she has also worked on Buick, Chevrolet, GMC, the older Hummer Division, and Opel. At the very beginning of her career, she spent eight years exploring and specifying exterior paint.

KILLEN'S JOURNEY

Killen graduated from Rochester High School in Michigan in 1998. She began her career after earning a bachelor's degree in interior design from the College for Creative Studies, unlike most of her colleagues at GM, who majored in transportation design studies. In the early days, she was particularly proud of the pink-and-white motorcycle she decorated for racing at Grattan Raceway. In a recent interview she noted, "Those are race plastics; I designed the paint colors myself with a custom painter. I wouldn't have it any other way!"

Her assignments included the early Hummer, the three-row

Surfaces and materials are rich in the Escalade and highlight the curved 30-inch OLED instrument panel. *Constance Smith*

Chevrolet Traverse, and a global color initiative supporting Buick, GMC, Chevy, and Opel. She did an eight-year stint supporting every facet of exterior paint.

However, everyone contributing to the Escala concept unveiled in 2016 has made their mark in a significant way. This includes the design team under Andrew Smith, lead designer Jen Kraska, and, of course, Michelle Killen. The Escala was the third Cadillac concept unveiled at Pebble Beach, following the Ciel in 2011 and the Elmiraj in 2013.

"We wanted the design for the Escala to show the industry where the direction of Cadillac is going," Killen explained on the College for Creative Studies website dedicated to alumni. "Designing a show car allows a designer to think outside the box. This can sometimes be a struggle on production programs where we have budgets. We wanted the design for the Escala to show the industry where the direction of Cadillac is going."

This four-door sedan, a bit larger than the CT-6, was sweetened with the edition of hand-cut and hand-sewn cashmere-colored seats and matching door trim. The contrasting brushed aluminum and America walnut make it all the more fashionable. The curved OLED (organic light-emitting diode) instrument panel is one of the first of its kind and found its way into the 2021 Cadillac Escalade.

THE CADILLAC ESCALADE

It appears that Killen is one of a handful women who designed the all-new 2021 Escalade. Crystal Windham holds the position of Cadillac interior design manager, Joanne Leddy holds the title of program manager for Infotainment, and Therese Tant Pinazzo headed exterior design, a role assumed almost entirely by men before Anne Asensio and Liz Wetzel followed in the footsteps of Bonnie Lemm to break the barrier. Jaclyn McQuaid signed on as chief engineer.

Killen and her team design every detail that customers see on a vehicle. This includes color, wood finish, fabric patterns, and seating. They have designed and provided nine interiors, four customer inserts, and seven hand-selected woods for the Escalade.

FAMILY MATTERS

Married to Kris Killen since 2006, Michelle Killen is the mother of a daughter and a younger son.

CHRISTINE KIRBITZ

It's a very exciting time in the automotive industry with the push toward electrification and autonomous vehicles. As a motorsports enthusiast, it's important for me that as we make this industry shift, we don't leave behind the gear heads that will still want to drag-race and autocross.

—Christine Kirbitz (b. 1990)

Courtesy of Christine Kirbitz

CAREER HIGHLIGHTS

After earning a bachelor of science in engineering from the University of Michigan, Christine Kirbitz joined Chrysler in 2012, where she worked as a suspension design release engineer. In late 2013, she joined General Motors. Participating in the Kettering University Program from 2014 to 2017, she also earned a master of science in engineering. As a compartment integration designing engineer, she led a diverse, cross-functional team of more than fifty engineers to develop balanced manufacturing and engineering criteria in support of creative surface design for the interior console on the 2018 Chevrolet Equinox and the 2018 GMC Terrain. This included the physical integration of GM's first execution of push-button ETRS (electronic transmission range select) shifters. Christine has also held multiple roles in support of vehicle performance. Currently, she is a vehicle performance engineer, responsible for ride and handling performance of the next generation of full-size utilities.

Kirbitz contributed to the design and engineering of the 2021 Yukon AT4, which won the Truck of the Year Award from *Four Wheeler Magazine*.

Kirbitz is in her thirteenth year of racing at US 131 Motorsports Park in Martin, Michigan, and drives a Chevy big-block-powered 2012 Mullis rear-engine dragster. Her on-track accomplishments include being the 2016 US 131 Motorsports Park Top Eliminator Summit Super Series points champion, 2017 IHRA (International Hot Rod Association) Division 5 Top Eliminator runner-up, and 2018 IHRA Division 5 Top Eliminator Runner semifinalist.

In early 2021, Kirbitz started a new role as a lead development engineer, in which she has the responsibility for vehicle performance for all GM Defense programs.

BIOGRAPHICAL NOTES

Born (née VanderSloot) and raised in Kalamazoo, Michigan, Kirbitz grew up in a family that loved cars and motorsports.

Spending weekends at the local drag strip, she doesn't remember a time when she didn't long to get behind the wheel! Graduating from Parchment High School in 2008, Christine has spent her life immersed in car culture.

She remembers counting down to her eighth birthday—the year she would be eligible to drive a junior dragster. She was crushed when her local track decided to discontinue a junior drag-racing class the year she turned eight, and so the countdown began for her sixteenth birthday. While waiting for her time in the driver's seat, Christine crewed for family members studying the sport so she was ready when her time finally came.

During her senior year studying biomedical engineering at the University of Michigan, Christine participated in the school's first ever Formula Hybrid Team. She met her husband, Michael, through their racing-team collaborations.

Kirbitz joined Fiat Chrysler Automobiles (FCA) in 2012 after graduation. At FCA, she worked as a suspension design release engineer supporting multiple product programs, including the Grand Cherokee, Dodge Durango, and Ram 2500.

Kirbitz poses with helmet. *Courtesy of Christine Kirbitz*

GM's first electronic transmission range selector was introduced. *General Motors*

The SLT is a high-end Terrain. *General Motors*

Christine got her start at General Motors after hearing about the company from her father-in-law, Kevin Kirbitz, who managed the Factory One facility in Flint at the time: "He told me these great things about working at GM, and I have always really identified with the product. It's the cars that I really loved. I decided to apply, and the rest is history."

In late 2013, she joined General Motors as a compartment integration designing engineer, where she led a diverse, cross-functional team of over fifty engineers to develop balanced manufacturing and engineering criteria in support of creative surface design for the interior console on the 2018 Chevrolet Equinox and the 2018 GMC Terrain. This included the physical integration of GM's first execution of push-button ETRS.

In 2015, she moved over to the vehicle performance organization, where she has made her home. When first joining vehicle performance, Christine served as a noise and vibration engineer on full-size-truck programs, with her key contribution as developing a package to improve vehicle-level low-frequency noise sensitivity in full-size utilities. She also served as the Vehicle Performance Team chair, where she was able to hone vehicle evaluation skills while gaining an understanding of the big picture of the automotive industry and how GM does business. The most important, and also Christine's favorite, aspect of this role was managing the "Knothole Rides." During these rides, GM senior leaders would regularly evaluate upcoming products against the outgoing model and the competition. Kirbitz would have the opportunity to ride with the executives and hear their perspectives on the vehicles' performances in real time. My time in that role and getting to learn from those people was invaluable and has provided me with insight and perspective that will carry me through the rest of my career." Christine was now a vehicle performance engineer responsible for the ride and handling and vehicle dynamics of the next generation of full-size SUVs.

Kirbitz notes, "It's a very exciting time in the automotive industry with the push toward electrification and autonomous vehicles. As a motorsports enthusiast, it's important for me that as we make this industry shift, we don't leave behind the gear heads that will still want to drag-race and autocross. It's my hope to be involved in a way that we can continue to push toward our mission of zero crashes and zero emissions, while maintaining the ability for grassroots racers to do what they love."

Kirbitz was assigned to the development of the 2021 Yukon AT4. After competing in four areas, the vehicle captured the Truck of the Year Award from *Four Wheeler Magazine*: Trail Performance, Empirical (acceleration, braking, price), On Pavement, Interior, and Exterior.

According GMC's online post, the all-new available Active Response 4WD™ System on the AT4 provides greater confidence in slick or off-road conditions, so it automatically and seamlessly detects the wheels with the most grip and then sends the torque to where it's needed most. For descending steep grades, Yukon AT4 features Hill Descent Control. This leverages antilock braking technology to assist with a smoother, controlled descent on uneven terrain to help the driver with not needing to repeatedly push the brake pedal.

To help give greater ground clearance and keep you moving, GM will be adding the first-in-class available four-corner Air Ride Adaptive Suspension, which has variable-rate air springs that allow you to select the ride height. While engaged, Yukon AT4 can be raised by 1 inch in "Increased Ground Clearance" mode or 2 inches when in "Maximum Ground Clearance" mode. The underside is offered further protection by skid plates to help shield components from debris.

Finally, adding refinement to the driving experience is the Magnetic Ride Control®, which not only has been enhanced to provide greater performance but is tuned to complement the Air Ride Adaptive Suspension. So even while the system is engaged for greater ground clearance, Magnetic Ride Control is reading the surface of the road every millisecond to adapt and adjust the suspension and damper settings in real time. These enhancements mean Yukon AT4 delivers a smooth and refined ride whether you're on- or off-road.

In early 2021, Kirbitz started a new role as a lead development engineer, in which she has the responsibility for vehicle performance, with a focus on ride and handling, of all GM Defense programs.

Kirbitz spends her weekends at the drag strip with Mike, their dogs (Luke and Tadge), and their extended family competing in the Lane Automotive Points Series at US 131 Motorsports Park in Martin, Michigan, and other races around the state. She is looking forward to adding to her impressive on-track record as an integral part of VanderSloot Motorsports.

MAGDALENA KOKOSZYNSKA

As a passionate artist and someone who loved to draw, I was enthralled by the fact I could sketch, use form, color, and incorporate pattern all in a career as a GM auto designer. — Magdalena Kokoszynska (b. 1985), gm.com/ our-stories/culture/automotive-designer-car-innovaton.html

Drawing by Constance Smith

CAREER SUMMARY

Magdalena Kokoszynska joined General Motors in 2007 as a Buick color and trim designer. Her early contributions in color and trim were evident in the LaCrosse GL concept exhibited at the Los Angeles Auto Show in 2011—the car that set the direction for future Buicks. In 2012, she continued in the Buick Interiors Studio, and by 2014 she was promoted to lead designer for Chevrolet color and trim. The 2017 Tahoe, Suburban, and Traverse, to which she contributed, are the mainstays of the truck market. After an almost six-year stint at Chevrolet, she became the lead designer for Cadillac. At the current time, she also assists with collegiate relations.

BIOGRAPHICAL NOTES

Magdalena emigrated from Poland to the United States as a six-year-old. In the GM.com interview, she recalls that as a resident of Queens, New York, her family struggled and overcame a lot of obstacles, "We had a really small apartment. We were thankful for the opportunity to start a new life."

She adds, "When I entered junior high school, I remember doing this pastel drawing of this girl in a garden, and she's sitting among these flowers; the colors are so vibrant they almost are being illuminated by the sunlight. That's when I started to grapple with the idea of art and design as a potential future path for myself. I grappled with what I wanted to do, whether I wanted to go into fashion design or graphics, or whether I wanted to do traditional illustration. My parents were a little apprehensive because at this point they didn't know what to do with me. From a family perspective, you have no future; you're never going to make a career out of this. You're never going to have money; your parents are going to be in the same situation you are now, but even worse. It was a lot of weight that was put on my shoulders. I wanted to develop my technical skills, so I started to dive deeper into illustration and drawing and sketching. I would go to sketch dinosaur bones. I love the detail and the intricacy in the bones and the crevices—all the lights and the darks, the shadows, the dynamism of the structure of the bones, the drama surrounding it."

Magdalena attended Fiorello H. LaGuardia High School of Music & Art and Performing Arts in Manhattan, where she majored in art. Upon graduation, she was accepted by Pratt Institute in Brooklyn, New York. After a diverse first year, she chose to major in industrial design. At Pratt, there is a heavy emphasis on abstract three-dimensional design, which relies on the curriculum created by Rowena Reed Kostellow—who started in 1938 and taught 3-D Design for over fifty years. Kostellow's husband, Alexander, was one of the founders of the department and also taught. All Pratt industrial design students complete a series of assignments that include the study of line, plane, and form as single elements, as well as designing environments with interrelated parts. Starting with a rectilinear form assignment, they move on to curvilinear form, lines in space, fragmented form, concavity, convexity, planar construction, and special design. These studies culminate in subsequent courses, one of which was transportation design.

For more than a decade, GM and Pratt's Industrial Design Department had partnered to give talented underrepresented students at Pratt the opportunity to expand their automotive design skills and portfolios in transportation design. Magdalena was among the award recipients.

Magdalena notes, "I was first introduced to automotive design after taking a transportation design class as a studio elective in my junior year. In the spring 2011 issue of *Prattfolio*, she explains that "this methodology allows designers to bring sculptural form to life and to truly understand how color and pattern interact on different three-dimensional surfaces. Reviews by professionals like John Carfaro lent a new perspective." Alumna John Carfaro, designer of the Corvette C5, returned to campus annually to review student work.

According to Kokoszynska, "The class, being very conceptual, focused on designing far-reaching vehicles and concepts through the process of abstraction, three-dimensional form ideation, and pattern and color exploration" (Nicole Ziza Bauer for *Darling* magazine, online: "Why STEM and Design Careers Aren't Mutually Exclusive," June 2, 2017). She graduated in 2007.

Early in her career, Magdalena contributed to the color and trim for the 2011 Buick LaCrosse GL concept, which was revealed at the Los Angeles Auto Show. Nick Palermo in *Autotrader* quotes her description that "every surface in the interior of the LaCrosse GL has been crafted with the knowledge that Buick customers enjoy the finer things in life but don't need to flaunt it." The rich metallic cabernet exterior is in contrast to the elegant, posh interior. The seats, adorned with contrasting leathers consisting of dark cocoa brown and a much-lighter caramel choccachino, are beautiful, subtle, and elegant. Creamy caramel and tinted trim appear on the instrument cluster and center console.

Magdalena subsequently contributed to the color and trim for the 2017 Chevrolet Tahoe, Suburban, and Traverse.

She was one of the members of the 2018 Traverse team who celebrated after winning the Best Production Vehicle Award for 2017. The EyesOn Design honor was presented at the North American International Auto Show in Detroit, Michigan. Tom Greig and Mike Simcoe, GM's VP of Design, were also on hand.

Magdalena was later promoted to lead designer for Global Cadillac as well as collegiate relations lead.

The Tahoe was featured in the Greater New York International Auto Show. *Constance Smith*

KAYLA MCDONELL

I can recall at least a half-dozen times in my life when others told me what I wasn't capable of achieving. They said I wasn't smart enough, I didn't possess the traits of a leader, and I lacked the focus and drive to be successful. Well, I don't like being told what I'm capable of doing, and I love a good challenge.

—Kayla McDonell (b. 1990)

Courtesy of Chuck Cloud; collection of Kayla McDonell

CAREER SUMMARY

Kayla McDonell graduated from the Mechanical Engineering program at Kettering University. Early in her career, McDonell held engineering positions with Altair, Calsonic Kansei, and Mubea. In 2014, she was invited to join General Motors, first as a contractor and then offered a permanent position. Her team worked on the exterior lighting for the second-generation Chevrolet Cruze and Cadillac XT6. She has already received notable recognition for her tremendous efforts and work ethic. In September 2016, Kayla was recommended for and selected to be part of the Chevrolet Cruze Innovators marketing team. Assigned to the Spring Hill facility, she served as the design release engineer for rear lighting for the 2020 XT6. She was later promoted to the issue resolutions team for the entirety of the exterior, working in plant to find and resolve any and all issues that touched her parts before vehicles shipped to customers.

In December 2018, McDonell was selected to be a board member on the Kettering University Alumni Association Board of Directors. She currently serves on three different subcommittees.

In December 2019, Kayla was invited to serve on Kettering University's College of Science and Liberal Arts Advisory Cabinet as part of a key group of alumni to support the mission and vision of the college.

While continuing to grow her career and expand her volunteer outreach, McDonell is attending the University of Michigan, Ann Arbor, to complete requirements for her master of engineering degree in global automotive and manufacturing engineering. She expects to graduate in spring 2021 and hopes to earn a second master's degree in business.

McDonell is included in *Forbes'* "30 Under 30," and her accomplishments will serve to motivate others of her generation.

MCDONELL'S JOURNEY

Kayla McDonell was born into a village; her grandparents, aunts, uncles, and parents all contributed significantly to her upbringing. She was born in Flint, Michigan; coincidently, Buick, which served as the basis of General Motors, was also established here by founders Durant and Dort. The properties have been restored. Flint is also the home of a Chevrolet truck factory and the Sloan Museum. Alfred P. Sloan served as president, CEO, and chairman of GM long before Kayla came along. At age four, she moved with her father a few miles down the road to Davison. Her grandfather was a retired Air Force officer, working for the US Customs and Border Protection, and her grandmother was a registered nurse. Kayla spent a lot of time as a child with her grandparents, who taught her how to take pride in her accomplishments and be proud of the life she had. McDonell's father was a Home Depot store manager, and her stepmother worked as a teacher but then became a stay-at-home mom once Kayla's brother and sisters were born. Her parents were the most influential in her upbringing, always supporting and encouraging her to have confidence in herself and strive for better things; to work hard and believe she could accomplish anything. They pushed her to step outside her comfort zone and cheered her on every step of the way. Despite the large age gap, Kayla's siblings unknowingly also encouraged Kayla to be her best self, wanting to serve as a role model for them and be the best version of herself. Despite the love and support Kayla received from her home life throughout her adolescence, she did not have the confidence in herself for many years to come.

In 2003, as Kayla was going into the seventh grade, she was offered the opportunity to test into all honors courses for middle school. She doubted herself and her abilities and pleaded with her parents to let her remain in the general education classes, but they insisted she challenge herself and accept the placement.

Kayla poses with Cruise. *Kayla McDonell*

She reluctantly joined the Davison Middle School honors program and remained in the program, welcoming the challenge, throughout high school. She notes, "This was the first time I can remember taking such a big step outside my comfort zone and, more importantly, feeling successful. It was my first encounter with self-confidence."

During her years at Davison High School, Kayla was recognized for her leadership and her community service efforts. In 2006, with the encouragement from her parents and through a series of interviews, she was selected as the participant from Davison High School for the Michigan Youth Leadership Conference (MYLead) at Concordia University. Kayla left the conference feeling, for the first time, like she had the potential and desire to be a leader. In the summer of 2007, Kayla was one of three students selected for the Odd Fellows United Nations Pilgrimage for Youth, a unique opportunity to travel and learn some of our country's history with students from across the globe. This trip opened Kayla's eyes to the different cultures, ideals, and possibilities around her. At an early age, she recognized the benefits of collaborating with individuals from different backgrounds and upbringings and the diversity it offered.

When Kayla first began thinking about attending college, she wanted to major in writing. She had received various recognitions and one *Flint Journal* publication for her school writing projects and loved the creative outlet. However, every aptitude test she took resulted in being recommended to be an engineer or an auditor, neither of which she knew anything about or had been exposed to. The engineering and computer classes in high school were mostly male and not often recommended to females. In addition, her family did not have experience in engineering or computer sciences. Kayla loved math and science and scored very well in both subjects but never considered a career in either. Luckily, she received a flyer in the mail in fall 2007 from Kettering University in Flint, Michigan, inviting her to spend a weekend with the Society of Women Engineers (SWE) to learn about engineering and the university. Although Kayla was hesitant to

attend, again doubting her abilities to be successful at a prestigious university or having a career in a male-dominated field, her father insisted she go to at least get an idea of what college life would be like. That weekend was life changing for Kayla, and by the time she came home from the visit, she knew she wanted to be an engineer and was going to apply to Kettering University. She knew she wanted to be a positive role model for other young ladies who enjoyed math and science and wanted to pursue an engineering degree. She wanted to be at the forefront of change in the industry. In early 2008 she received her acceptance letter from Kettering and was awarded the Presidential Trustee scholarship.

Kayla joined the national sorority Alpha Sigma Alpha, Delta Nu-A chapter, in 2009 at Kettering University. This organization enabled Kayla to further develop her leadership and communication skills, continue building her confidence, and provide both personal and professional networking opportunities. The women she met through the sisterhood supported and enabled her growth into a successful, confident, and intelligent engineer. She held various positions during her collegiate years, including secretary, social chair, and vice president of public relations and recruitment, which gave her leadership experience and responsibilities. During her year as vice president, Kayla learned how to work with and manage various types of personalities to achieve a common goal—recruiting the best and brightest female students on campus to join the sorority. Her year as VP was considered successful and further established her foundation of self-confidence. Through the sisterhood she participated in multiple philanthropic and community service events, including demonstrating science experiments at the Flint Children's Museum, volunteering for the Smarter Girls' Day Camp, being a representative on the Flint Historical Neighborhood beautification committee, and assisting at Flint's Coolest Race in Michigan (CRIM). She learned the importance of giving back at an early age and made it a priority in her life. She often took on a leadership position for each volunteer event and gained valuable experience motivating and inspiring others to do their best.

In 2008, as a participant in Kettering's co-op program majoring in mechanical engineering, Kayla experienced life as a professional engineer at just seventeen. She subsequently joined the SHW Group, an architecture firm based in southeastern Michigan that designed school buildings to house grades K–12 and older students pursuing a higher education. On her first day of work, she notes, "I was so nervous that I locked my lunch and my keys in the car and was too embarrassed to tell anyone, especially since I was the same age as most of my coworkers' children. I went my first day without eating during my lunch period and after work walked around downtown Berkley looking for a locksmith to open my vehicle. It was a dreadful first day, but she immediately liked the atmosphere of a professional engineering office."

She stayed with the company for one year, soaking up everything she could. Her first taste of career success was the honorable mention she received in the annual company newsletter for her contributions to the Jackson Community College project, routing ductwork and calculating required airflow to meet legal building standards. However, due to the downturn in the US economy, her co-op career took a turn into the engineering consulting world in 2009. McDonell began working at Altair, in the Product Design Division, assisting with the construction of and procuring materials for the world's first series hybrid hydraulic mass transportation bus. She reported to Jeffrey Hopkins, a Kettering University (GMI) alum, who quickly became her mentor and role model. He assigned her tasks to help her grow as a professional and a leader. She learned how to procure materials, winterize a vehicle structure, and then teach the shop team how to do this. This gave her the opportunity to earn the respect of a team roughly three times her age and to encourage them to achieve a common goal successfully. While it was terrifying at the time, Kayla learned that "respect is earned by proving yourself as a contributing team member, regardless of age." She remained with Altair through her college years, learning from her mentor, and earned Kettering's University's Outstanding Thesis Award for her work on the bus project.

After graduation from Kettering, Kayla accepted her first full-time position at Calsonic Kansei, where she worked on the Infiniti JX35 interior cockpit design and implementation. She took the lead on cost-reduction efforts in collaboration with Nissan to improve the market price for the target customer. After a short time with the company, she moved on in 2013 to work with a different commodity at Mubea. As a suspension project engineer, she assisted the lead validation engineer with testing coil springs and stabilizer bars for General Motors and Chrysler vehicles. Although her time with the company was short, she enjoyed working for a German supplier and learning about their business culture. She had the opportunity to spend three weeks in Germany for company training and almost didn't return to the United States because she loved the experience so much. In 2014, a recruiter reached out to Kayla with the opportunity to interview with General Motors for an exterior-lighting position as a contract employee. She was reluctant to accept the invitation for the interview because she didn't want to leave a full-time position for a contract position, but she decided to utilize this interview for practice. To her surprise, Kayla was enthralled with the two exterior-lighting managers she met with during her interview, and the prospect of the design release engineering position. While walking through the parking lot back to her vehicle after the interview, she received a phone call from the recruiter who had offered her the position. Kayla spent the next several hours evaluating whether or not she should take such a big risk to accept a contract position. Her father was the one to give her career-changing advice: "Take a chance on yourself and prove to GM why they need to hire you as a full-time employee. Prove your worth to them and show them the value you can add to their company." Less than twenty minutes after accepting the position as a contract employee, she was offered the opportunity to interview with General Motors for a full-time position. In less than two months, Kayla was hired directly as an exterior-lighting design release engineer. By happenstance, her fiancé was given the opportunity to work for General Motors as an industrial engineer and started on the same day. Both were thrilled to work for a company leading in automotive technology.

In September 2016, Kayla was recommended for and selected to be part of the Chevrolet Cruze Innovators marketing team. The team consisted of seven GM employees who significantly contributed to the success of the second-generation Chevy Cruze and would help market the vehicle to its target customers.

She joined cross-functional team to implement the exterior lights on the second-generation Chevrolet Cruze and the lighting for the 2020 Cadillac XT-6. These designs are highly decorative and complicated. She notes, "I worked on both the front and rear lights and was the design release engineer solely for the rear lighting on the vehicle. I was then promoted to the issue resolution team member for the entirety of the exterior of the XT6, working in the plant to find and resolve any and all issues that touched my parts before the vehicles shipped to the customer."

On her first day, she was assigned to work with a senior exterior-lighting engineer, Nick Egli, who befriended her and grew to be a valued mentor. The best piece of advice she received from him was not to take work too personally. When meetings get tense and people get passionate during discussions, it's easy to get caught up in the emotions and take the stress home. But when you remember that all employees are there to achieve a common goal, to do what's best for the company, it's easier to keep the bigger picture in perspective and realize that business decisions are not personal attacks. Kayla was assigned to the Spring Hill, Tennessee, assembly plant to assist the plant team in resolving launch build issues in the general assembly area. She aspires to be a people leader within General Motors to encourage and inspire her fellow employees to enjoy their work and take pride in their contributions to the company.

Kayla is currently assigned as a vehicle systems engineer for Body and Exterior, working out of the Warren Technical Center. She is responsible for balancing the budget and meeting program deliverables on six upcoming vehicles. Kayla looks forward to the next challenges in her career, including learning moments and triumphs.

Kayla also remains a servant of the community by contributing time to various organizations. Since 2010, she has volunteered for the Smarter Girls' Day Camp. This organization encourages young girls to explore career possibilities in STEM-related fields and provides positive female role models in the workforce. Through the TutorMate program promoted by General Motors, she has served as a reading tutor for first graders in the Detroit Public School system since 2015. Her favorite part about being a reading tutor is the amount of progress her students make from the first tutoring session to the last tutoring session. The children's perseverance and determination to improve their reading abilities is inspiring. Through GM's Engineering Resource Group, GM–Women, Kayla also volunteered in 2018 and 2019 as a mentoring coach to four female coworkers. They met biweekly to discuss career ambitions, work-life balance concerns, and personal struggles. She has been the recruitment lead for A World in Motion (AWIM), a joint effort between the Society of Automotive Engineers (SAE) and General Motors, since 2016. Through AWIM, Kayla has had the opportunity to see the positive and lasting impact that volunteers can have on a young child's life. Also, since 2016, she is a member of GM's Recruitment and Engagement Team for Kettering University, serving on the Candidate Care committee. This allows her to mentor and guide co-op students who are in the same position she once was into the workplace, as they adjust from college life to professional life. She is a regular volunteer for Detroit's Junior Achievement program since 2017, and she volunteered as a soccer coach through the Warren Youth Soccer League for children ages four to six in 2018. Most recently, Kayla became a TryEngineering Together eMentor, mentoring a young girl from Arizona to create a safe and powerful STEM learning experience through online communication. Working with children and encouraging them to follow their passion and pursue their dreams gives Kayla a sense of purpose. It keeps her humble and hungry for success.

In January 2017, Kayla was recognized globally by *Forbes* as one of their "30 Under 30" for Manufacturing and Industry, the only female noted in the automotive industry. This prestigious award led to local news channel appearances, newspaper interviews, and a guest blog post on HelloGiggles. Later that year, in October, Kayla was awarded the Young Alumni Award from the Kettering University Alumni Association. She had the opportunity to meet with outstanding alumni who were positively changing the world. This fueled her passion for inspiring others in the STEM industry and renewed her confidence to continue striving for greatness in her career. In March 2018, Kayla was honored by the Alpha Sigma Alpha National Sorority with the "30 Under 30" award, a similar recognition to *Forbes*', for her outstanding professional achievements and dedication to community service. In fall 2018 Kayla was approached with another Chevrolet marketing opportunity: to star in a series called "Unlocked," which aimed to highlight the incredible members on the Chevrolet design and development team. Kayla's episode was released in November.

FAMILY MATTERS

Kayla's life changed dramatically following her graduation from Kettering. First, she started dating Josh McDonell, a fellow Kettering graduate, who would later become her husband and biggest fan. Josh and Kayla met in the summer of 2010 in West Virginia as part of Kettering University's Outdoors Club. Kayla noticed Josh immediately as someone she had not seen around campus before, so she walked right up and introduced herself. The two were good friends for the remaining years of their college careers and began dating immediately after Kayla graduated in September 2012. Josh said he knew after three months that Kayla was the one he wanted to spend the rest of his life with, and the couple wed in May 2015. Since their very first date, Josh has given his unwavering support of Kayla's ambitious personal and professional aspirations.

Kayla's family photo includes Don McDonell, Cheryl McDonell, Josh McDonell, Kayla, Sarah Petrach, and Ron Petrach. *Courtesy of Kayla McDonell*

JACLYN MCQUAID

We set out to make the best HD trucks on the market, bar none. We increased towing capabilities across the line, not just for dually buyers. We added class-leading towing technologies, such as 15 available camera views,[1] to make trailering more convenient, whether pulling a large cargo trailer or fifth-wheel camper. And we made a host of changes to make tasks easier.

—Jaclyn McQuaid (b. 1978), Chevrolet Media Release

Jaclyn McQuaid

CAREER HIGHLIGHTS

Jaclyn McQuaid was promoted to the position of executive chief engineer for full-size trucks in 2020. She previously served as executive chief engineer for Global Mid-Size Truck and Medium Duty Truck & Van at General Motors.

During her more than twenty-one years with the company, she has rotated through a number of roles. McQuaid joined GM in 1999 as a road load data acquisition engineer. She subsequently worked as a handling engineer, NV engineer, exhaust design release engineer, lab supervisor, group manager, and commodities manager.

MCQUAID'S JOURNEY

Jaclyn McQuaid is one of four girls born and raised by Linda and George Lossia in Farmington Hills, Michigan. The girls were taught from an early age that anything was possible. Her father studied automotive engineering, but his education was interrupted when he was drafted into the Army to serve in the Vietnam War. Having to care for family, his formal education was cut short.

From an early age, Jaclyn planned to work for GM and enjoyed driving her Chevy Suburban as a teenager.

McQuaid received her bachelor's and master's degrees in mechanical engineering from the University of Michigan in 2000 and 2004, respectively. The first leg of her higher education was shared with her twin sister, Jamie Brewer. Brewer serves as chief engineer for the Cadillac Lyriq and likely fully understands and appreciates her sister's accomplishments.

McQuaid gained expertise in a variety of positions in over two decades with GM, including exhaust design, vehicle handling, brake systems, and program purchasing. From 1999 to 2005,

McQuaid was assigned to the Milford Proving Ground. From 2005 to 2007, McQuaid notes that she served as exhaust design release engineer in Warren, Michigan.

In 2007, assumed the position of AWIM manager, and she reported to the GM Technical Center in Warren, Michigan. In 2008, she returned to Milford to work as the tire wheel systems lab manager, later moving to other challenging assignments back in Warren. In 2020, she was promoted to executive chief engineer for full-size trucks.

Jaclyn served as chief engineer for the heavy-duty 2020 Chevrolet Silverado and GMC Sierra. Used by many to trailer, the new GM 2500 and 3500 HDs will deservedly dominate the

McQuaid presents at the reveal for the Silverado HD 2500/3500. John F. Martin Photography. *Courtesy of General Motors*

market. In addition to a new 6.6-liter gas engine (401 hp) and six-speed transmission, the 6.6-liter Duramax turbo diesel (445 hp) is equipped with a ten-speed Allison transmission. This combination delivers a whopping 910 lb.-ft. of torque.

Chassis and suspension enhancements contribute to an incredible 35,500 pounds of maximum towing rate.

The transparent trailer is a first-in-class feature. The surround camera system can show the view behind the trailer when pulling a big cargo trailer or fifth-wheel camper. The truck features eight cameras that deliver fifteen exterior views, including a surround-view monitor, a view that peers directly into the bed, and a brilliant transparent trailer that uses the images from two exterior cameras through the trailer to see what's behind it.

CHEVROLET SILVERADO HD

With Chevrolet offering five models—Work Truck, Custom, LT, LTZ, and High Country, the most dramatic inside and out—be assured that Chevrolet did its homework.

Chevrolet did not stop here. Exterior features include chrome assist steps, bed and corner steps, a spray-in liner (DuraBed), and a rear power-sliding window. In addition, the High Country Deluxe adds a host of safety features: a HUD, Bed View Camera, Forward Collision Alert, Lane Departure Warning, Automatic Emergency Braking, Following Distance Indicator, and gooseneck / fifth-wheel package.

Chevrolet Pressroom releases on the truck also describe the power-up/power-down tailgate. It has the only available PTO (power takeoff). VIN-specific trailering data is posted right on the truck, something that no competitors have, but it comes in handy for those speccing a truck and consumers. Chevrolet notes

that this consists of the truck's specific trailering metrics, including curb weight, gross vehicle weight rating (GVWR), gross combined weight rating (GCWR), max payload, max tongue weight, gross axle weight rating (GAWR), and fifth-wheel and gooseneck ratings. The production of the HD Silverado will add many jobs to the Flint assembly plant.

SIERRA HD FROM GMC

The GMC HD Sierra was also all new for 2020. The low-end work truck that featured vinyl seats stood in stark contrast to the high-end Sierra HD Denali, which dominated sales in the previous year. For those looking to take refined capability off-road, GMC fortified the new AT4 brand with an all-new Sierra AT4 Heavy Duty, available for crew cab configurations as both a 2500 and 3500 single-rear-wheel-drive offering.

While interiors are similar in nature depending on version, the distinct exteriors compete—with some observers commenting that the grill on the GMC had more-rugged appearance. Somewhere along the line, Helen Emsley, GMC's design director, noted that once someone on the road saw your GMC truck in their rearview mirror, it would leave an impression—and this was important. Accommodating the same payload, offering the same power train, and providing the same hauling capabilities, the HD Silverado and Sierras are considered mechanically identical.

However, this being the first year out, GMC offered one more option that Chevrolet buyers might not be able to resist: the world's first six-function MultiPro tailgate was available on all trims and standard on SLT, AT4, and Denali. The six functions are described as the primary tailgate, the primary gate load stop, easy access, full-width step, inner gate load stop, and inner gate with work surface. Of course, it was only a matter of time until Chevrolet offered this option.

Both the Chevrolet and GMC trucks are still the most capable haulers on the market today.

FAMILY MATTERS

Married, Jaclyn McQuaid is the mother of Josephine and Nicholas.

The Sierra truck offered the first Multi-Pro tailgate as Chevrolet customers waited another year for a similar option.

CHRISTINA MICHAEL-SHENOUDA

I can do all things through Christ who strengthens me.

—*Christina Michael-Shenouda (b. 1981)*
Bible quote, Philippians 4:13

Christina Michael-Shenouda

CAREER SUMMARY

Dr. Christina Michael-Shenouda received a bachelor of science in civil engineering from Wayne State University in 2005.

Early in her career, Michael-Shenouda held the position of roadway design engineer for the Mannik and Smith Group and the Genesee County Road Commission.

She was inspired by the different technology used to design intersections. During this time, Christina pursued her master's degree at Lawrence Technological University, receiving a master of science in engineering management in 2008.

Desiring to be part of the automotive environment, she joined General Motors in 2013 as a contract design release engineer on the accessories team. She enjoyed working on new projects and endeavored to find new ways for customers to be pleased with the vehicles they purchased. She was with the accessories team for six months before she was hired by GM and joined the switches team. Working closely with suppliers, Christina strove to ensure that the parts released met all the quality requirements and specifications for the customers.

In this vein of thought, Christina dedicated her doctoral studies to focus on quality assurance along the supply chain, so as to ensure a smoother and more predictable manufacturing process.

As she completed her doctor of engineering in manufacturing systems in 2017 from Lawrence Technological University, Michael-Shenouda wanted to continue learning by taking on different positions at GM. She became the cochair of the Electrical Issue Resolution Team (IRT), working on autonomous vehicles. In this position, she worked hard to ensure that issues were addressed and closed out properly in order to ship vehicles out of the plant for further testing. Christina enjoyed identifying concerns and working with the plant quality team to address and solve them with the engineering team right away; there was no time to be wasted! She likened it to an operating room: "You think of the car just like the human body, with all of the wires running down representing the veins and all of the modules are the organs." For her, it was such a great feeling just to see the cars get off the End-of-Line and go to Lab Check, and move on to the next vehicle.

She developed a great relationship with the core team to find better ways to catch errors before they even get on the line.

Michael-Shenouda is currently working as an electrical vehicle system engineer (VSE) on future midsize trucks. Here, she deals with budgetary considerations and the challenges of working with her team to stay on target.

While engaged in a successful career, Christina also volunteers with her Coptic Orthodox Church.

MICHAEL-SHENOUDA'S JOURNEY

Christina was born in Cairo, Egypt, and lived there until the end of middle school before moving to the United States. During elementary and middle school, Christina was an honor student and eager to grow and learn.

As a top student, she was rewarded with field trips to the zoo and the pyramids. When she moved to the States, it was very hard at the beginning, but she was motivated to earn high grades and assimilate into a new culture. Christina recalls that she spent a lot of time with her grandfather, who taught her to follow her dreams and believe in herself. Likewise, her parents, Adel and Arleet, always encouraged her and her three siblings to be ambitious, and pushed them to complete college. When Christina went to high school, she was so inspired by AutoCAD and Drafting classes that she enrolled in as many of these male-dominated courses as she could. She wanted to be an engineer even though she was the only girl in most of those classes. During this time, competing against college students, she won several AutoCAD and design contests, cementing her desire to become an engineer.

Michael-Shenouda started school at Wayne State University in 2000 in the Mechanical Engineering program. During college, she served as the vice president of the American Society of Engineering for the WSU Chapter. While exploring different engineering classes and co-op programs, she became interested in the Civil Engineering program. She held the position of social coordinator of the American Society of Civil Engineers and was an active member serving the community and young engineers. Joining the Society of Women Engineers (SWE) afforded Christina the opportunity to encourage other women to study engineering. She extended her outreach to middle schools through the Young Engineers and Scientists Program. In this program, she mentored students building projects for competitions. In turn, this experience enabled Christina to help advisors at WSU recommend appropriate courses for incoming students She received her bachelor of science degree in 2005.

When Christina started working as a roadway design engineer, she decided to pursue her master's degree in engineering management from Lawrence Technological University. She focused her engineering portion on manufacturing systems, during which she relished the idea of getting manufacturing systems up and running without wasting time; she earned her master of science in 2008.

In 2012, Christina and her husband, Michael, welcomed their first child, Jacob. It was difficult trying to achieve a life balance of bonding with her new baby while working full time an hour away from home. As difficult as it was, she accepted a voluntary layoff and decided to return to postgraduate studies in mechanical engineering while caring for her son.

Christina applied for the master's in mechanical engineering at Lawrence Tech and did well in the first two classes. However, a call from the department's chairman caused her to reevaluate her path; she was offered the opportunity to apply for a doctorate in manufacturing systems. Initially, this posed a conundrum; she feared she would be overqualified for a future job. However, her husband, echoing her parents and grandfather, supported her dreams. At the same time, Michael-Shenouda started working at GM as a contract employee. Juggling school, work, and a toddler was real life, but it was good ... she felt alive! When she was halfway through her classes, she was surprised to learn that she was expecting her second child. She considered dropping out of school and just focusing on her job and family. Mike kept supporting her aspirations, freeing her up to focus on her classes so she could start working on her doctoral dissertation. Baby Joshua arrived; by that time, she viewed her life as "three shifts"—work, family, and school. While dealing with a challenging assignment in Mexico, Christina was able to pull it together and complete her dissertation and present it in March 2017.

Christina did not just stop at publishing her dissertation. She has also coauthored two papers: "Enhanced Process to Improve Supplier's Quality and Reduce Warranty" in *SAE International* (2017), and "Enhanced Production Process to Reduce Warranty" in *ASME* (2018). In 2017, she also learned that her dissertation was selected for the Library of Congress. In early 2020, Michael-Shenouda began teaching at Lawrence Technological University as an adjunct professor. This fulfilled another one of her dreams: to impart the true values of engineering to the next generation in her role as an educator.

As noted earlier, Christina is involved in her church's activities. She helps run a diocese-level competition run smoothly both for the children and the church. Another program currently running is the "Fun Wednesday Classes," which focuses on making programming, coding, art, cooking, etc. enjoyable for kids. Most importantly, she strives to keep the kids involved with STEM projects to familiarize them with engineering and technology—perhaps she is inspiring the next great innovator right now.

Christina joined the faculty at Lawrence Technological University. *Constance Smith*

Christina enjoys spending time with family. *Courtesy of Robert Monsour Photography*

THERESE TANT PINAZZO

GM's really, really looking into the future. Where is transportation going? What do our customers need just to get around? The landscape is going to be completely different soon ... obviously, autonomy is one piece of it. Electric vehicles are another piece of it. We've formulated groups that have end user interfaces happening at the time.
—Therese Tant Pinazzo (b. ca. 1972)

General Motors

CAREER HIGHLIGHTS

Therese Tant Pinazzo served the Ford Motor Company from 1994 to 2000 before joining General Motors and advancing to manager of Advanced Design Interiors in 2006. She contributed to the interior design of the 2007 Volt Concept and the production interior of the 2007 Escalade and managed the Advanced Eco Vehicle Project. In 2009, GM formed the new Product Design Studio, encouraging the design of consumer products offered to build individual brand equity.

From 2010 to 2011, Tant Pinazzo subsequently served Buick and Cadillac as color and trim manager and managed the Cadillac Interiors Studio. In 2014, she was appointed design manager of the Cadillac Exterior Studio, which shaped the 2019 XT4—a significant entry designed to attract the younger customer. Most recently, as design manager, she led the design team responsible for the exterior of the groundbreaking 2021 Cadillac Escalade and slightly longer Escalade ESV.

A FAMILY TRADITION

Tant came from Detroit and grew up in its suburbs. Her father worked for Ford and spent many hours with her two brothers in the garage. Her enrollment in the College for Creative Studies (the automotive design program was chaired by Carl Olsen) would set the direction of her career for the rest of her life after her 1994 graduation. It is no surprise that she would spend the first six years of her career in auto at Ford.

THE CHEVROLET VOLT CONCEPT

A highlight of her career, Therese's design work for the interior or the 2007 Volt Concept car was also significant for the corporation. She served as lead designer under Wade Bryant, the interior design manager. At one point, Tim Greig and Theresa Priebe held the same positions, but for the production version of the car.

The Volt's design theme appears to have originated in GM's British studio. A compact disc, part of a press kit, described the interior. The Volt's roof and side glass and even its beltline were constructed of a transparent, glazed polycarbonate material that provided a shiny glass-like surface. As a result, the Volt provides the driver and occupants with exceptional visibility, enabling a "City Light" theme in which the outside world passes through to the interior of the vehicle.

Bryant describes the instrumentation at length. He notes that the display of information, beginning with analog technology, progressed to incorporate LEDs and even holographic readouts. Designers used LEDs to display fuel level, battery level, speedometer, odometer, and transmission positions. An additional screen added to the base of the windshield displayed holographic-style, color-animated data related to the advanced-propulsion system. This system used visible fluorescent inks printed on a transparent screen. When lit by an ultraviolet laser projector from behind the cluster, the inks provide four-color animation and illumination.

The bottom of the instrument panel, the lower trim on the bottom of the door, and the trim on the quarter panels consisted of compression molded foam with a textile-patterned surface. This material is used on some luggage.

Be reminded that the seasoned Anne Asensio, executive director for Advanced Vehicle Design, would work with Jelani Aliyu in the refinement of the exterior design; the final design seemed to have lost some of its aggressiveness in preparation for the manufacturing process but remained remarkable.

The Volt concept was introduced at the North American International Auto Show in Detroit in 2007. Even Bob Lutz, vice chairman, noted that this was the most exciting project he had been involved with in his entire career. Unlike the Prius, where gas and electric motors ran at the same time, the Volt would rely on a sequential hybrid engine.

THE CADILLAC XT4

The Cadillac Pressroom appears to have introduced the Cadillac XT4 and Pinazzo at the same time in 2018. "The XT4 has a great presence that is confident and poised. It exudes Cadillac's DNA, but with a new boldness that speaks of the youthfulness of its team and its customers. At Cadillac House in Manhattan, Cadillac unveiled the first-ever XT4, an all-new compact luxury SUV with the customer in mind. Exterior Design Manager, Therese Pinazzo, is a youthful designer, representing the demographic GM hopes to attract. Pinazzo noted, "The XT4 has a great presence that is confident and poised. It exudes Cadillac's DNA, but with a new boldness that speaks of the youthfulness of its team and its customers." (Cadillac Pressroom online posts when new products are introduced.)

The exterior appointments differ within the three trim levels: Luxury, Premium Luxury, and Sport. The Luxury and Premium Luxury feature grilles with bright metallic accents, satin aluminum window moldings, and satin chrome-accented door handles. The Sport features a glossy-black mesh grille, glossy-black window moldings, and a choice of wheels.

LED lighting technology appears front and rear, with front LED low and high beams and LED-illuminated light blade for the DRLs. Cadillac's vertical, L-shaped lights signature is stretched horizontally, contributing to a wide and confident stance. In the rear, LED taillights are housed in red lenses on Luxury models, while the Sport features clear lenses that work well with darker shades of color. There were eight colors at launch.

CADILLAC ESCALADE

The Cadillac Escalade, utilizing Chevrolet Tahoe and GMC platforms, burst out of the gate in 1999. Equipped with the venerable 6.2-liter engine, still a mainstay today, the Escalade had plenty of creature comfort features. It was more than ready to compete with other luxury offerings. In 2002, a new model arrived, and in 2003 the ESV (Escalade Stretch Vehicle), being a tad bigger vehicle, was appreciated by limousine drivers and those with plenty to haul. A gas-electric hybrid was added in 2009. In 2015, a new Escalade and ESV arrived.

The corporation appears to have put many of its eggs in the Cadillac basket as sales continued to blossom. The motoring world, consumed by the introduction of the midengine Corvette until recently, is now taken by surprise by the 2021 Escalade and the 15.9-inch longer ESV.

Much of the design and engineering is due to the efforts of the women designers and engineers at Cadillac. With the success of the XT4, it is no surprise Pinazzo would "pass go" and continue to dictate the exterior design of this fifth-generation Escalade.

Pinazzo notes the intricacies of the design: "Escalade has always made a bold statement that says you've arrived. We have updated that statement for a new era, adding layers of sophistication. The goal was to create a new Escalade that is unmistakable at a glance and then rewards you with greater details on the second or even third read." The added layers of detail extend to unique

The 2021 Escalade, built longer than its predecessor, commands respect. *Constance Smith*

trim elements and grille textures. Escalade will offer Cadillac's Sport trim for the first time, featuring a black mesh grille and black trim across the exterior. Luxury and Premium Luxury models showcase a bright Galvano finish, while Platinum models top the range, with unique interior and exterior details.

The short and longer model both sit comfortably atop 22-inch wheels. In this day and age, there is an overwhelming emphasis on lighting, and recent Cadillacs rely on vertical additions to headlights and taillights to set them apart, particularly after dark. Escalade maintains Cadillac's signature vertical lighting element, but the new interpretation adds a sleek, horizontal headlamp to reinforce a broad, confident stance. The tall, vertical, rear light signature continues but adds deep three-dimensional layers and finishes with detailed etching.

The intricately designed chrome grille of the Luxury Package model attracts more attention up front than the blacked-out mesh on the Sport. The windshield, roof, and basic door panels are shared with the other variants. Design cues were incorporated merely to reduce the size visually: the massive sides are hollowed; a depression around the wheel wells, common in many GM trucks, breaks up the front and back sides; a decorative chrome strip at the bottom of the door draws attention just above the rocker panel; and a slight jump in the sheet metal just behind the C-pillar deemphasizes the length. From the back, the towering vertical lights attract the eye, and a large multicolor Cadillac ornament is mounted on the hatch where it meets the window. Backup lights sit just above the chromed exhaust vents, and the chrome strip over the license plate has become traditional.

This masterpiece also features state-of-the art technology, notably the first curved OLED (organic light-emitting diode) display and a sumptuous interior also designed by women on the Cadillac team.

Therese Pinazzo continues to lead Cadillac into a bright future around the world.

FAMILY MATTERS

Married to Nicholas Pinazzo in 2014, Pinazzo also has a daughter.

HEATHER SCALF

As a designer, you want to create beautiful color combinations. We look to the future trends in fashion, interior design, [and] architecture, and we come up with several ideas and proposals of color combinations, variance of hue, and saturation of color that we explore.

—Heather Scalf (b. 1975)

Heather Scalf

CAREER HIGHLIGHTS

As a Lawrence Technical University intern, Heather Scalf joined Rossetti Architects. Upon graduation, she discovered career opportunities at GM and joined the Chevrolet and Buick teams in 2003.

This afforded Scalf the opportunity to contribute to a number of significant production entries, with teams in Michigan as well as internationally. Perhaps the most memorable assignment included work for the 2008 Chevrolet Malibu, which captured the Car of the Year Award and met every success in the marketplace.

Scalf also contributed to the midsize 2010 Lacrosse, a mainstay for Buick and 2013 Regal, which was in part based on Europe's award-winning Opel Insignia.

In 2013, Scalf assisted the Korean team in supplying research material for the design of the Buick Encore, which continues to set sales records for the division as Buick introduces models and recently added a new power plant.

Around 2018, Scalf's position transitioned from lead designer, Color and Trim, Strategic Global Commodities, to include Advanced Innovation and Technologies. The team's current objective is to focus on developing responsible materials, keeping sustainability a priority in an effort to maintain and protect our natural resources.

BIOGRAPHICAL NOTES

The son of a truck driver and nurse, Heather's father, Detroiter Ron Downs, received a bachelor of science degree in civil engineering from Lawrence Tech. The daughter of a lumberjack and then machinist in Sault Ste. Marie, her mother, Annette, was one of nine children; her family resided on Sugar Island. In addition to her household duties, she also pursued a career in the restaurant industry to supplement their income. Heather is an only child.

Heather was born at the height of a gas crisis in December 1975. Designers in the Advanced Studio designed gauges to track the gas mileage of automobiles, which would, it was hoped, influence driving habits. While never manufactured in the mid-1970s and not needed now, its timeliness varies.

At Chevrolet, the 1975 Vega replaced an earlier 1971 model. It was advertised as "a lot of car for such a little car." A wagon and lightweight delivery truck were also added to the offerings. Having won the *Motor Trend* Car of the Year Award, the Monza hatchback coupe was even more of a success story. Inside, the sporty 2+2 featured a speedometer, tachometer, and gauge package surrounded by simulated maple in a tight cluster. Sue Vanderbilt, who held a building-level position at this time, assisted with the interior color and trim. The Monza was equipped with an available 4.3-liter, 262-cubic-inch engine in Michigan, but in California, an even-larger 5.7-liter V-8, although safety and emissions continued to become concerns. With 15 more horsepower, the 5.7-liter engine was crammed into the same car in an attempt to make it fly. Some of the designers, however, would soon have to decide whether to invest in a place to live or in a new Corvette Stingray coupe. At this time, the Advanced Concepts Group was preoccupied with designing new instrument panels to incorporate airbags to comply with anticipated government regulations. General Motors was the first manufacturer to introduce airbags.

In the 1980s, Heather fondly recalls her visits to the North American International Auto Show in Detroit. In this era, Chevrolet overhauled its car and truck line and introduced front-wheel drive. In 1982, the first Cavalier debuted; it later led to the hotter Z24 and RS models. In 1982, Chevrolet ended an era with the sophisticated silver-beige 1982 Collector's Edition Corvette, and it seems we waited forever for a completely new, more angular body style to debut in 1984. The C4 Corvette featured the first full cluster with TN LCDs, as did its Opel and Cadillac counterparts. Six years before the introduction of the 1984

Corvette, we built and designed the first LCDs, which were installed in a Monte Carlo prototype. The 1984 Corvette captured *Motor Trend*'s Car of the Year Award. In the late 1980s, the Beretta GTZ, with 175 horsepower, raced past competitors. This was a new era for reclining buckets, full consoles, cup holders, and Scotchgard™ fabric protector.

By the early 1990s, Detroit's Cobo Hall exhibit had perhaps the most Chevrolets ever—Caprices, Luminas, APVs, Corsicas, Cavaliers, Camaros, and Corvettes.

In high school in 1993, Heather acquired her first car, a sporty red 1984 Fiero. It is likely that chair and CEO Mary Barra worked in the factory when it was manufactured. After graduating from Waterford Mott High School in 1994, Heather later spent a year or two at Oakland Community College and Western University before transferring to Lawrence Tech—her dad's alma mater and favorite school. Lawrence is located locally on a sprawling campus in Southfield, Michigan. Heather majored in interior architecture and graduated in 2001 with a bachelor of science degree. In an alumni publication, Heather noted, "LTU created a solid foundation of creative problem-solving, critical thinking, and teamwork that I use every day."

Today, Lawrence is home to other carefully selected aspiring automotive designers. At a recent annual open house, sponsored by Dassault Systèmes, Lawrence welcomed Bob Lutz and Ann Asensio as guest lecturers. In 2014, Dassault introduced its new MCAD mechanical software. Lutz, one of the founders and ardent supporter of the new Lawrence transportation program, started his career at GM in 1963 and later served as vice chairman of product development, chairman of GM North America, and interim president of GM Europe. In his book *Car Guys vs. Bean Counters: The Battle for the Soul of American Business*, Lutz notes the importance of automobile designers in an environment perhaps monopolized by accountants. His newest book at this time, *Icons and Idiots: Straight Talk on Leadership*, records his experiences as an executive at GM, Chrysler, BMW, and Ford.

After graduating from Lawrence Tech, Scalf worked as an assistant for a residential interior design firm, where she learned about opportunities in the Color and Trim Studio at GM.

Heather met her husband, Jason, during the summer after both had graduated from Waterford Mott High School and started college. Jason initially worked as a project engineer—working with plastic injection molds and tooling—in the automotive industry. He transitioned to a global company specializing in coal-fired power-plant optimization and supplying engineering services to the mining industry. With his real estate license in hand, he now is following his passion for real estate with an agency in Birmingham.

As a designer and lead designer, Heather Scalf has promoted the aesthetic vision of both the Chevrolet and Buick Divisions. From 2003 to 2009, Heather served as creative designer in the

The attractive 2014 Buick Encore, smaller than the Enclave, becomes the vehicle of choice for many—setting sales records starting in 2013. Exterior colors are developed to complement the interior offerings. *Constance Smith*

Designers work closely with their UX partners to place elements in convenient locations. *Constance Smith*

Color and Trim Studio. There is no question that the 2008 Chevrolet Malibu, which captured the North American Car of the Year Award, had everything anyone ever wanted in an automobile—it was stylish, affordable, and well made. The hybrid and 3.5 SFI V-6 flex-fuel engine offerings were even more fuel efficient than the base engine.

With her knowledge of architecture and inspired by the fashion industry, Heather notes that the handsome interior incorporated state-of-the-art materials. Her duties included the development of comprehensive strategies and proposals for interior and exterior color and trim design. The jet-black/brick-red interior for the 2008 Malibu is fashionable and contemporary. Premium tinted chrome accents and tipped-leather seating inserts add an air of luxury to a reasonably priced offering.

In 2010, Heather was promoted to Buick lead color and trim designer, serving as lead color and trim proxy during her supervisor's absence.

After meeting with her counterparts in Germany, China, and Korea, Heather's other assignments included the implementation of color and trim strategies for the 2010 Buick Lacrosse and 2012 Buick Regal. The 2013 Buick Encore, an exquisite luxury crossover introduced at the 2012 Detroit Auto Show, is even more desirable than vehicles costing considerably more. This small SUV continues to gain supporters. Heather served as lead color and trim designer for the GMNA region at the time the Encore was developed. Heather currently serves as senior color and trim designer, global commodity lead, for GM North America. Heather notes that she enjoys traveling and studying cultural and regional differences.

In 2013, she assumed the position of global commodities lead, senior color and trim designer, for GM North America. She currently "creates strategic solutions for materials, finishes, and color that enable great color and trim design."

Heather's latest design efforts make the 2013 Buick Encore notable—the interior is truly special. GM Korea was homeroom and lead for the Encore; this global program had several variants that added interest. The complete interior incorporated a number of notable features. The saddle and cocoa leather seats are lush and inviting, with just the perfect amount of contrast between hues. Heather points out the carefully planned French stitching on the insert and surround of the seating surface. These colors will change, she notes, with the fashions of the times. The simulated burled wood trim begins at the center console, wraps across the lower face of the instrument panel, and melds across the door panel; it downplays the ubiquitous chrome-plated door handle. The combination of wood and leather is something we would expect in a full-size Cadillac Escalade and is even more welcome in this smaller crossover. Other interior color options that complement exterior colors are also available.

As in the past, Heather relied on current fashion design for inspiration—from Target to Tory Burch. She combines classic timeless pieces with eclectic yet stylish clothing. She also looks to online websites to keep abreast of trends. We look forward to new designs as new products are released.

Heather's strategic global commodity role evolved to include advanced innovation technologies.

In the area of strategic solutions for materials, she prioritizes sustainability in an effort to protect our natural resources.

Courtesy of Brigid O'Kane

MIRANDA STEINHAUSER

CAREER HIGHLIGHTS

Enrollment as a student in the industrial design co-op program at the University of Cincinnati gave Miranda Steinhauser the opportunity to serve a number of companies in what would be described in industry as agile half-year sprints.

In her 2011 co-op assignment, she designed accessories for electronics for Speck Products. In her subsequent assignment, she designed footwear for Under Armour. She worked at Motorola (a Google company) in 2012, followed by Priority Designs in 2013.

Her co-op assignments enabled her to work on the design of products for numerous brands, including Coca-Cola, Nike Golf, Radio Flyer, Frontgate Furniture, and similar.

From 2014 to 2016, she joined ARĪV eBikes as an associate creative designer, a brand being established in the marketplace by GM's Advanced Design Team, begun under director Clay Dean and design manager

Wade Bryant and completed under director Sharon Gauci and design manager Stuart Cooper. Steinhauser and a colleague were tasked with developing the ARIV Merge and Meld e-Bike models initially marketed and sold in Europe. From 2016 to 2019, she was promoted to creative designer for ARĪV eBike. Her work selected for manufacture was patented or is pending. The sale of the e-Bike was suspended in 2020, in part due to the COVID-19 coronavirus pandemic.

In 2016, she and her partner joined forces to restore three floors of a 1927 Tudor Revival home from the ground up. This required her design expertise, light construction, maintenance, and, later, management of this rental property.

From 2019 to 2020, she served as a creative designer in Advanced Interiors–Human Machine Interface, and then Advanced UI/UX, where she worked with UI/UX in the development of future products.

Steinhauser currently works as a creative designer in Advanced User Interface and User Experience (UI/UX).

Over many years, Steinhauser has entered a number of competitions in which she has received a Director's Choice Award or placed near the top in the rankings.

She also has participated in the Detroit Public School's You Make a Difference Program as a mentor.

A DIVERSE JOURNEY

As a high school student, Miranda Steinhauser elected to study math, science, art, and journalism courses at Gahanna Lincoln

When it came to Steinhauser's thesis, she designed a moped. *Courtesy of Brigid O'Kane*

The innovative eBike came in two models—the second folded. *General Motors*

High School in Gahanna, Ohio. During the last two years of high school, she enrolled in courses in math, art, design, and advanced calculus at the Ohio State University. She graduated at the top of her high school class in 2009.

From 2009 to 2014, Steinhauser was enrolled in the Industrial Design: Transportation Track program at the University of Cincinnati and studied under the direction of Brigid O'Kane and Raphael Zammit. O'Kane had built her own diverse portfolio, started her own career at General Motors, and received an award for a Pontiac concept car at a major auto show. Raphael Zammit also began his career at General Motors in Design.

Perhaps her restoration of a 1957 DKW Hummel Type 101 bike would prove fortuitous.

Steinhauser joined GM as an associate designer of the ARIV eBike and later codesigned the eBike.

In 2019, GM announced the new ARĪV e-Bike, which included two innovative, integrated, and connected eBikes. At this time, Hannah Parish served as the global director of this unit of GM, establishing its presence. The name ARĪV was selected as part of a global crowdsourcing campaign announced in 2018.

The eBike—electric bike—was a byproduct of GM's groundbreaking research into electric vehicles through the years. Referring to this innovative product, GM used the term "micro-mobility."

The Meld was a traditional compact eBike, and the Merge was an ingenious folding eBike. Both versions were introduced in three European countries: ARĪV eBikes launched in Germany, Belgium, and the Netherlands. The eBikes enable speeds up to 15.5 mph with four levels of pedal-assisted power, fully charge in 3.5 hours, and run about 40 miles (64 kilometers) per charge.

In 2019, Steinhauser held the position creative designer, Advanced Interior HMI, where she noted that she led two engineering teams focused on advanced vehicle technology integration for future production and developed UI/UX and HMI for future vehicle programs and concepts. In 2020, she continued work in a similar position, creative designer for Advanced UI/UX.

AWARDS

While attending the University of Cincinnati, Steinhauser placed third in a tire competition in which she designed her Tessela Tires with removable tread located with aluminum bands. Removing and replacing the tread would eliminate the problem of disposing of tires and the fee added to vehicle sales for this disposal. Hankook featured student tire designs at a SEMA show.

Also while attending the University of Cincinnati, Steinhauser was a 2014 Lelo Undesign Award winner for her work on a smart kitchen island design called Google Home. This work was created while on co-op with Motorola (a Google company).

In 2019, ARĪV eBikes won the Good Design Australia Gold Award.

Kevin Unger

STEPHANIE THOMPSON

I am a passionate engineer and community leader who actively pursues new and innovative ways of promoting science, technology, and learning to General Motors and in my community. I credit GM's community investment focus on STEM with starting me down the path of mentoring the FIRST robotics program. This sparked a way for me to ignite a passion for community outreach and helped me enhance my career goals by leading volunteer projects that encourage more young girls and women to participate in STEM. My personal motto is to "Be a ladder, be a lamp, or be a lifeboat" to those who come after me.

—Stephanie Thompson (b. 1977)

CAREER HIGHLIGHTS

In 2020, Stephanie Thompson was included on Canada's Most Powerful Women's 100 Award Winners list. To receive this honor, it was noted that Thompson had provided learning opportunities in technology geared toward girls and women, in an effort to inspire and empower them.

Stephanie joined General Motors of Canada in 2001 as a process engineer for the launch of the High Feature V-6 Engine program. Over the past eighteen years, she has held a variety of roles on St. Catharines and Tonawanda manufacturing teams, including production group leader, block machining engineer, and lead launch engineer for the revamped Camaro and Gen V

engine platforms. From 2013 to 2017, she worked in New and Major Programs. She is currently assigned to the GF6 transmission line as the Engineering Team leader for prismatics and gear machining—she leads the process, controls, and tooling engineers in manufacturing of six-speed transmissions.

Stephanie Thompson, a professional engineer, is a Women in STEM volunteer and serves in the GM of St. Catharines Propulsion Plant.

STEPHANIE'S JOURNEY

Growing up in Ottawa, Ontario, Canada, the oldest of four children, one of Stephanie's fondest memories is of her dad teaching her not to be afraid of bugs. "I remember him being really proud of me for letting spiders crawl on my hands; from spiders and bugs we moved to snakes, and there was a sense of pride in me in trying something that other people were afraid to do.

"But it was my mom who really ensured that I had the right foundations at home to gain the confidence needed to take part in a future in STEM—she always supported any project I wanted to tackle, and there was never a time when I felt I couldn't do something. I like to say that I didn't have to worry about failing, because I always knew she would be there to catch me if I fell. This helped me always be someone who tries new things and to be a risk taker.

"When I was in the eleventh grade, I had an amazing chemistry teacher, who selected me to participate in a three-day overnight conference for students at Chalk River, a research nuclear power plant near Ottawa, Canada. It was an opportunity that sparked my interest and curiosity about the research scientists and nuclear engineers I shadowed that week. An interview by local papers after the event allowed me to reflect and talk about the experience. In hindsight, I can remember that early on, there was a sense of learning about an experience and wanting to communicate and share that experience with others, which I now consider one of my mother's strengths. This opportunity, along with several other confidence boosters, helped her believe that there was no reason I couldn't pursue a STEM career in engineering."

Stephanie received a scholarship from her high school for being the only girl to apply to an engineering program. She notes, "I debated going into chemistry or chemical engineering, as I admired the chemistry teacher who selected me for the outreach program. Practicality won out when I learned of the positive job opportunities that an engineering degree afforded."

Stephanie attended the University of Waterloo, in the Bachelor of Applied Science, Chemical Engineering program. In 2006, she was accredited as a professional engineer in the province of Ontario. "I didn't think there was anything particularly brave about applying to the university program—approximately 43 percent of my class was female—even if the remainder of the disciplines were not as balanced. It was only when I was out in the workforce that I was able to see the true minority that women engineers, particularly ones in technical roles, represent."

Stephanie moved to southern Ontario, assuming a role on the engineering launch team at General Motors in St. Catharines, Canada, after graduation in 2001. She remembers, "I had no idea what an opportunity this was—right place, right time, and right team! I can reflect back on this experience years later for the opportunity it afforded a young engineer to learn an engine assembly process from the ground up. It built my confidence in a way that would serve to strengthen my resolve as I pursued other roles in my career."

INTERNATIONAL ROLE

In 2008, Stephanie applied for a six-month international assignment at GM in Qingdao, China. "I was set to take a Quality Engineering role in a newly launched plant, when my then boss called me and told me of a promotion opportunity in the small-block-engine assembly department. It was not an opportunity I could miss out on, so an international assignment was on the back burner." Stephanie was promoted to Engineering Technical Team leader of the Gen IV assembly area. "This was a very high-volume, high-production line—probably something I'll never see again in my career. My first week, our piston-stuffing team stuffed over 1,000 engines in one eight-hour shift, one every twenty seconds!

In 2012, GM announced the introduction of a replacement small-block engine to replace the Gen IV—the Gen V Engine. Stephanie was selected to be the lead launch process engineer and left the St. Catharines organization for a short stint. She notes, "The Tonawanda Propulsion Plant (USA), St. Catharines (Canada), and Ramos (Mexico) were selected as the three sites for the new production lines. Due to its closeness, I was able to maintain my living situation in Canada and travel to the US to work on the launch of the Tonawanda plant's Gen V line. Over the next six months, I was able to consult and bring lessons learned from the Gen IV manufacturing insights to the Tonawanda staff and take back valuable training and insights from their launch. This allowed me to install my line in record-breaking time later the next year. I was able to capitalize on improvements and make the equipment installation ramp more efficient. But the real value gain was the friendships and trust I created with my counterparts in the USA—being there during their tough timelines created relationships and ensured GM benefited from a sharing of technical knowledge between our two sites."

BALANCING FAMILY AND CAREER

Stephanie and her husband, Richard Vernon, were also married in 2012. She jokes about the circumstances: "It was a real test of

my project management skills. Originally, my GM project launch deadlines were in October, so I planned my wedding in August. Imagine my surprise when with the accelerated timing, the production timing was moved to the week before the wedding date. It meant being really, really organized, but I was able to pull off the two most significant events in my life in the same month, rather successfully."

One of Thompson's mentoring teams includes M. Middlestadt, D. Burgess, L. Woodward, and S. Cameron. *Stephanie Thompson*

At the same time, her work assignment afforded Stephanie the opportunity to come full circle in her manufacturing career. "I was hired on as a launch engineer on a team of excellent engineers, and ten years later I was able to take the lead role on a similar team. We even worked with the same equipment supplier, and some of the junior engineers for that company were now the engineering leaders that I worked with to deliver the line. There is something serendipitous about being part of two similar engine assembly launches, and I was able to juxtapose the experiences to understand changes in our manufacturing organizations of the last decade."

In 2016, Stephanie and Richard had their first child, Amelia. "As a woman in STEM, having a girl makes you really reflect on the state of the world, and how you can impact the world that will be her future. It's really important to me to make my mark in this area as a part of my career path."

Over the last fourteen years, Stephanie has been heavily involved in mentoring FIRST robotics programs as well as other STEM community outreach projects. As lead mentor, Stephanie's protégées have captured FIRST competition awards at local elementary and high schools. Her focus is on the empowerment of female students on the team in leadership and technical roles. She continues to reach out to former students in a mentoring capacity. She was recognized by the robotics community with the Woodie Flowers Finalist Award, which celebrates the effective communication of mentors in the art and science of engineering and design.

In 2017, the FIRST Canada organization asked Stephanie to join their Girls in STEM Executive Advisory Council, representing GM. This group seeks to collaborate with corporate executives,

St. Catherines power train plant is harnessing the pure energy of water from the Welland Canal to cool processes in its operations. Its microhydro system marked GM Canada's first use of renewable energy. *General Motors*

Stephanie Thompson joins Cassandra Tom, a co-op student. *Stephanie Thompson*

educational institutional leaders, and passionate individuals who all believe in success for, and inclusion and acceptance of, girls and young women in science, technology, engineering, and mathematics (STEM).

"The Girls in STEM Executive Advisory Council offers insight and oversight that will help us break down the barriers of girls." Stephanie has participated as the keynote speaker, a career mentor, and, in 2021, set up a General Motors Design workshop to help students see the possibility of a career at GM. "There are so many aspects to a career at GM; with the change in technologies, even a manufacturing engineer like me finds it difficult staying up to date on the latest collaboration techniques.

"By engaging my peers from the Canadian Technical Centre, we were able to run a workshop connecting the robotics students to a design ideation process that would benefit those in future robotic competitions and see what design thinking looked like. It was also a great opportunity to introduce them to our female engineers and the variety of engineering roles that exist at General Motors, from manufacturing of existing products to dreaming up the future of mobility."

Stephanie is also a member of the Canadian GM STEM Corporate Social Responsibility team. She is part of a small committee that determines allocation of GM of Canada STEM funding in the community. "This is a phenomenal opportunity to see the world beyond the four walls of the workday and to make a long-term impact that will affect STEM opportunities for thousands of young Canadian girls. Perhaps the organizations I help select will help ignite the spark in the girls like the teacher who helped me to see engineering as a specific career path."

Thompson also participates on the GM of Canada Women's Council to help engage and retain women across the organization, and is the founder of the General Motors St. Catharines Women in Leadership and Manufacturing Group. She notes, "I get teased a lot about my extracurricular activities, but I love being involved in all aspects of our business, in particular trying to engage and retain the female voice. It helps us see the bigger picture of who we are as an organization and the overall value set that we want to adhere to."

In the last few years, Stephanie has taken on leading roles in the Industrial Engineering Department. She was the St. Catharines plant planner and is now currently leading the Process and Controls Engineering teams in the GF6 Transmission Prismatics and Gears teams.

She notes, "These last few assignments were a real stretch for me professionally, each one with a unique set of technical attributes that were very different than the ones I grew up learning in the organization. It caused me to definitely put aside any preconceived notions of my talent and skill set and allowed me to really work on trusting the talented people who work around me and seeking to draw out and support them to the best of my ability."

"I am only about halfway through my career, but I feel that I've seen so much and had such a wonderful set of experiences both in the engineering and community aspects of my job. I've always been a big believer of learning everything I can in a role, and I always feel challenged by the expectations needed to run a world-class engineering department to the best of my ability. I hope for my future that I will continue to have a positive impact on my part of the business and seek to be someone who can inspire others."

In 2018, Stephanie was honored by the Greater Niagara Chamber of Commerce with the "Women in Niagara–Science and Technology Award" for her contributions to the STEM community. "It feels great to take everything that I've learned and share it with others—knowledge is a powerful thing. I love the saying that says 'Be a ladder, be a lifeboat, or be a lamp' to those around you. I strive to be that for the women at General Motors, and those in my community."

She concludes, "GM is well into a corporate transformation. It's hard to imagine what the future will bring. But I know that I've been able to develop a unique set of skills over the course of my manufacturing engineering career that will help me thrive through the change over the next few years."

FAMILY MATTERS

Thompson is a dedicated mom. Married to Richard, she enjoys bringing daughter Amelia Skye to many events.

SABRINA RASO (VAUGHN)

The boundaries between sketching and modeling are blurred. Sketching is most important for ideation and must progress to three-dimensional modeling.

—Sabrina Raso Vaughn (b. 1980)

Constance Smith

CAREER HIGHLIGHTS

While enrolled in the Master in Transportation Design program at Instituto Europeo di Design in Turin, Italy, Sabrina worked as an interior and exterior designer with Lancia on the Haizea Project, which resulted in the production of a full-size model. After receiving her master's degree in 2006, she joined the Volkswagen Design Center in Brazil as an intern in 2007. Sabrina subsequently joined General Motors of Brazil as a creative designer focused on interiors. She also designed exteriors. Around 2010, she joined Ryan Vaughn, her future husband, and moved to the United States. In 2013, Sabrina enrolled at the College for Creative Studies to supplement her education, enabling her to join Fiat Chrysler Automobiles (FCA) as an exterior designer. During this assignment, the Dodge Challenger, Jeep, and Alpha Romeo Giulia were under development. After becoming a mother, she joined her husband in China, where Ryan holds an executive position at the Pan Asia Technical Automotive Center (PATAC). In 2011, she founded SR Design LLC/NA, where she serves as the product design manager. The firm handles product design development, including photography, graphic design, and textile and fabric design. In her spare time, Sabrina exhibits her own photographs in hotels.

BIOGRAPHICAL NOTES

Sabrina Maria Raso Vaughn was born in São Paulo, Brazil. After earning a bachelor's degree, she enrolled in a master's degree program in Turin, Italy.

Sabrina notes that her grandmother was the first woman to own and drive a car—a Chevy—in São Paulo. Her grandfather drove a Suburban. But it was her grandmother who later gave Sabrina a C4 Corvette. Interestingly, the Corvette was not scheduled for production in 2003 as Chevrolet prepared for the new 2004. However, a small number were assembled, one of which is or was on view in the Corvette Museum.

The 2004 C4 still seems to have appeared in early 2003.

While the family had some smaller cars in the sixties and seventies, perhaps a Mazda or Toyota, she also remembers a 2008 Opel being among them.

Sabrina was born to two physicians. However, when her father passed away prematurely, her mother managed a construction business.

The Raso Family all together. *Sabrina Raso Vaughn*

The Astra was a mainstay in more than one country. *General Motors*

Sabrina is an accomplished exterior designer. *Sabrina Raso*

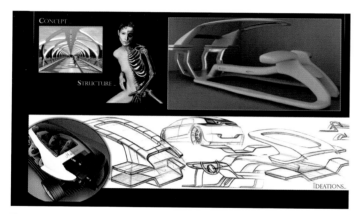

This was drawn in connection with the Lancia student project. *Sabrina Raso Vaughn*

Sabrina was drawn to cars early on. As a student at the Colégio Agostiniano São José, she drew cars in its elementary, middle, and high schools. She also experimented with watercolor, like our elementary school students do here in the US, and built tree houses of dried clay. In high school, she enrolled in the History of Art and Graphic Design—there was an optional corporate identity program.

Her mother, who was knowledgeable when it came to construction, tried to steer her to architecture, but industrial design was related. In 2004, she was the recipient of a bachelor of industrial and product design from the Centro Universitério de Belas Artes de São Paulo. As noted earlier, Sabrina graduated with a master's degree in transportation design from IED (Instituto Europeo di Design).

In 2007, Raso was a design intern at Volkswagen do Brasil before accepting a position at General Motors in Brazil, where she remained for almost three years. Sabrina was the only women of the thirty-to-forty-person staff at GM and started in the exterior studio. Their assignments included work on the interiors of the Trailblazer, Blazer with Isuzu, and GMi700 pickup.

After meeting and marrying a colleague, Ryan Vaughn, who

was assigned to Brazil, Sabrina moved to the US and enrolled at the College of Creative Studies to learn Alias digital modeling and Catia. She was recruited by Ralph Gilles from FCA.

Joining FCA as an exterior designer in 2014, Sabrina worked on 3-D surface development for Chrysler, Dodge, Jeep, and Ram. She also worked on the 3-D lizard shaping trim for the Jeep.

Noting the popularity of large wheels and tires to buyers in this day and age, Sabrina penned designs for the 2017 Dodge Challenger 19X7.5s and Mopars and for the Wrangler 17X8.5.

As a Chrysler designer, she has supported many STEAM (science, technology, engineering, arts, and mathematics) events held at Macomb Community College, Roosevelt Elementary School, and Rochester High School.

A highly trained photographer, Sabrina had set up shows in Europe and Brazil and exhibited at Industry Day at CCS. It is no surprise that most of the time, her subject matter—Corvettes—coincides with the work of her husband, who contributed to the design of the 2014 Corvette interior. From 2011 and later, she served as a photojournalist for the Corvette team. Under her own name, she has worked in other industries as well.

When asked about her favorite designers and designs, Sabrina mentions Raul Pires, the former head of exterior design at Bentley. It is not surprising that he comes from São Paulo and also worked at VW. She mentions the 2004 GT, which is similar to the Mulsanne; from the front, the cars are dominated by four large, intricate lights in two sizes, and a grille slighted rounded at the top atop a repetitious wire insert.

Then she mentions Flavio Monsoni, of Ferrari, who also worked on Lancias.

She begins to praise her husband, Ryan, who contributed to the 2014 Corvette instrument panel and the new C8 midengine Corvette. He says no—use someone else. She smiles and then she mentions Larry Shinoda, the designer of the C2 split-window Corvette—the most noteworthy Corvette for many.

Ryan continues to impress. In 2018, he was promoted to executive director for design at PATAC in Shanghai City, China, and in 2021, head of full-size truck interiors in Warren, Michigan.

Ryan headed the design team for the 2024 electric Silverado EV, a strong, handsome truck delivering 664 hp and 400 miles on a charge. He presented the truck at the 2022 CES.

Sabrina and Ryan are the proud parents of a young son, Hugo. The future is bright for the talented Vaughn family.

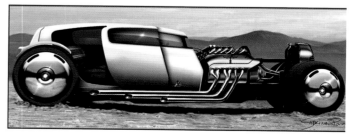

Raso penned this super rod. *Sabrina Raso Vaughn*

VICKI VLACHAKIS (VON HOLZHAUSEN)

General Motors

I've got to say there's never an ideal place to begin the learning experience; you just jump right in. I think with any good designer who's interested and motivated, they'll learn it on the go.'

—Vicki Vlachakis

CAREER HIGHLIGHTS

After advancing to the position of design manager in the GM Advanced Studio in Hollywood, California, Vlachakis joined a team of designers, digital sculptors, and engineers to design vehicles for all GM brands. The studio designed the Chevrolet Borrego and SS concepts, and she was a member of the team credited with the production Pontiac, Solstice, Solstice GXP and GXP Drift, and Saturn Sky.

After leaving GM, Vicki worked with two European car companies and later started her own business, using her married name—von Holzhausen—to sell bags and later offer Apple watch-bands with carrying cases. Instead of real leather, her products are produced from what she terms Technik-Leather. Through the years, many attractive imitation leathers and suedes have appeared in vehicles as some have sought to replace the use of animal hides. Vlachakis capitalizes on the advances in technology.

BIOGRAPHICAL NOTES

Vicki grew up in the Pasadena area of California, not far from ArtCenter College of Design. At age twelve, she was socially popular and began sketching automobiles on the back of note-books. Living in the area gave her access to select courses offered to high school students by the staff of ArtCenter College. By the time she graduated from high school, she headed to ArtCenter to continue her studies. She notes, "I knew I was going to be a designer; I just didn't know where the energy was going to be directed. And then I became totally attracted to industrial design—especially automotive because it was this thing that embodied the latest trend, technology, and exciting artwork." Vicki received her BS degree but also notes, "I studied at ArtCenter, branching out to their campus in Switzerland, which is where I became really intrigued with the European direction in design. That experience changed my direction entirely." She was the only girl in her graduating class.

ADVANCED DESIGN STUDIO

In 2000, the *Los Angeles Times* reported that GM would reinvent its Advanced Design Studio in Southern California and hired Frank Saucedo back again to run it. This meant he would have his own design studio without relocating. The idea was for GM designers to create cars and trucks of the future instead of relying on cars of the past and customer loyalty for sales. Saucedo, who began his career at GM, had joined VW when they closed the California studio in 1966. He relied on the success of the New Beetle to make the argument that GM was falling behind others in creating new products. Saucedo wanted to work with the best and hired Franz von Holzhausen, who headed Mazda Design. Franz was also credited with the Audi TT and is the driving force behind Tesla design. Saucedo also hired Rob McCann from Porsche. One man headed the analog area, and the other the digital arm.

At some point in time, Vicki joined the team as an interior designer both for concept and production cars.

In 2001, the idea for a two-seat crossover with a small storage area in the back was proposed, and the Chevrolet Borrego was born. Chevrolet marketers described the Borrego as a concept combing the road-taming agility of a rally car with the traditional rock-hard toughness of a Chevy. The AWD addressed the commute during the week and the need to let off a little steam on the weekends. The concept—inside and out—was captured in computer-generated images distributed on a disk in a 2001 GM Design press kit at the New York International Auto Show.

Saucedo noted, "The Borrego has the agility of a rally car and the influence of a Baja racer." The concept appears in a GM Design press kit in 2001 as a computer illustration. According to marketers, "The vehicle's sporty swept-back look and athletic stance take their inspiration from international rally cars and pre-runner trucks—spare customized pickups that were part of the California scene." According to Saucedo, "We see it here every day, a younger buyer moving out of a sport coupe and getting into a tricked-up little truck—or in this case a crossover vehicle." Ron McCann, the chief designer, described the interior as a dual cockpit design: "It looks like you could rattle around and get banged up."[5]

The Borrego concept was metallic blue and measured just 168.2 inches in length and 71.6 inches in width and was 61 inches high. The power train was based on Subaru's longitudinal AWD system, which allowed Subaru to take the world rally circuit by storm and win acclaim, and consisted of a 2.5-liter, horizontally opposed, SOHC four-cylinder turbocharged engine to ensure a low center of gravity, as well as a five-speed manual transmission. GM leveraged the international network of alliances to expand the range of this and other concepts.

The vehicle's midgate slid to provide two extra seats instead of storage. Borrego's midgate relied on solenoid pins and remote control. The rear window retracted into the midgate, and the roof panel could be stowed under the cargo bed. Vicki likely contributed to the design of the instrument panel and interior. Some think this vehicle led to the successful Avalanche, which used a versatile Convert-a-Cab system, which allowed one person to reconfigure the cargo area in seconds without tools to create a 4-by-8-foot area to transport large cargo, but also led to the less-than-expected sale of the GMC Envoy XUV, in which a storage area was created from a passenger area.

THE SOLSTICE CONVERTIBLE

Bob Lutz, whose vision led to the development of the Pontiac Solstice, was instrumental in promoting and initiating the project.

The curvaceous exterior of the Pontiac Solstice was easily identified by two carefully rounded grille elements, topped in the center with a Pontiac emblem set flush with the front. This car

The Solstice concept was featured at the EyesOn Design Show. *Constance Smith*

was decidedly low slung, with carefully shaped halogen headlamps below the sheet metal leading the way. The rear deck consisted of engineered plastic. The manually operated Hartz canvas top could be released by using the key fob or from a button in the glove box. The base model led to more-powerful convertibles such as the GXP that were sometimes sought for sale overseas.

Vicki's design, sketched in marker, was chosen for the interior. The motorcycle-inspired cluster featured a large, round speedometer and tachometer in deep circles, with a small fuel gauge dropped in the center. The striking red italic numerals, printed on a light-and-dark-gray ground in the cluster, were surrounded by chrome bezels. The simple hood over the cluster was later elongated to wrap around in one continuous piece over the center console in production. The simple steering wheel was jettisoned and replaced by a more substantial unit. Perhaps the replacement was shared with another car or incorporated other safety features.

The console between the seats was home to the gear shift assembly. In the original drawing, the assembly was undersized; in the production car, it took almost the full width of the console between the seats.

The first round of deliveries featured the Asian red five-speed manual gearbox, causing the earliest of women buyers to cancel what would become a highly collectible car. It took close to a year for the optional five-speed 5L4DE electronic automatic to arrive at New York dealers.

While there were a few seating options, the stunning steel-and-sand seats, or black ebony option, provided the needed lateral support for aggressive cornering. To ensure safety, the convertible incorporated retractor seat belts, head restraints, and a passenger seat sensor that detected the weight of the occupant to turn the air bag on or off.

The convertible debuted in 2002 at the North American International Auto Show in Detroit and was introduced on *The Apprentice*, a TV show created with Donald Trump, in the spring before 2006. His aspiring contestants designed the first brochure—an unusual die-cut round book. Pontiac dealers had a limited number of the first brochure before the traditional rectangular books arrived.

Sometime later, Vicki and Franz von Holzhausen married and had two children.

The exterior of the Solstice was designed by Franz von Holzhausen; the couple likely met at GM before he was retained by Tesla as their head of design. *Constance Smith*

REBECCA L. WALDMEIR

As designers we are constantly and consistently inspired by our surroundings.

—Rebecca L. Waldmeir (b. 1982)

John F. Martin Photography

CAREER HIGHLIGHTS

Rebecca Waldmeir was promoted to the position of Digital Experience Manager in 2022. As a color and trim manager, she had directed the design of concept and production vehicles. Her portfolio includes the 2015 Avenir concept car, which captured the EyesOn Design Award for Best Overall Concept.

Her contributions to the interior of the 2019 Chevrolet Silverado stand out. Chevrolet offered eight different levels of trim—from work trucks to LT to High Country. The High Country featured the most sophisticated interior design ever. Waldmeir was also entrusted with the interiors for GMC, including the Acadia and Sierra. The division introduced the new "Black Editions," which were developed for more than one model.

WALDMEIR'S JOURNEY

Having shown an early interest in the elements of art and design, Waldmeir started CCS in 2001. That year, the Center for Creative Studies–College of Art and Design changed its name to the College for Creative Studies to better reflect the mission of the college to educate and inspire talented students to become artists, designers, and leaders in their fields. In the fall of 2001, CCS inaugurated the new Walter B. Ford II Building and renovated historic homes nearby for their use. This was prior to the redevelopment of the Argonaut Building in 2008 (a.k.a. the Taubman Center) for a second campus. Waldmeir graduated with a bachelor of fine arts in interior design in 2005.

Joining General Motors upon graduation, Waldmeir worked as a lead creative designer. In 2014, she was appointed color and trim manager, Advanced & Global Exterior Color, her current position.

Her contributions to Buick concepts are notable.

In 2015, the stunning Buick Avenir concept attracted attention at the Detroit Auto Show. It was easily identified as a Buick by its waterfall grille, which featured a thin, winglike horizontal bar running across it behind the tricolor emblem, and LED headlights. The boat tail rear reminded some of the early 1930s Auburns and, later, the special Riviera that Bill Mitchell chose to drive.

While designers drew inspiration from nature—specifically water washing upon a shoreline—when shaping the graceful lines within Avenir's interior, the color-and-trim team worked to find the right materials to add a dynamic flair. The Buick Pressroom currently features the Avenir concept on its website. "With Avenir's interior, we really wanted to select materials

From the front, the waterfall grille symbolizes Buick, and the winglike creation keeps our attention. *General Motors*

This handsome Chevrolet Silverado LTZ made its debut before throngs of attendees at the Greater New York International Auto Show in New York City. *Constance Smith*

that would complement the surfaces within," Waldmeir notes. "Using a distinctive combination of premium leather, suede, wood, chrome, and acrylic, we were able to design elements that flow seamlessly throughout the interior."

Avenir's designers even put a new twist on wood trim, a traditional Buick element. Not only are wood accents featured on the door panels, but the wood itself provides a more luxurious and natural appearance that adds to the airiness of the interior.

Waldmeir adds, "We've used open-pore wood in a modern way, much like what you'll find in high-end furniture. It's an oiled, low-gloss execution that contrasts beautifully with other interior decor."

The 2015 Buick Avenir won the EyesOn Design award for Best Overall Concept at the 2015 North American International Auto Show over some exceptional competitors, and this reinforced the fact that Buick could not only compete but win.

After the introduction of the Silverado High Country, Waldmeir described some of her motivations: "As designers, we are constantly and consistently inspired just by our surrounding. I could be walking down the street and someone could have on a really cool pair of shoes or a backpack that has some sort of detail, and some stitching and some perforation, and look at that and say that there was something we could use, the stitching detail, the color that we could interpret [for use] into the vehicle. Scale it up and see if that's right for Chevy."

The Chevrolet Suburban has eight trim levels, with black being the perennial favorite of consumers in clinics. She explains that her two-tone jet-black-and-umber interior was inspired by nature, with a hint of the desert. The small nuances include

touches of satin chrome on the steering wheel as well as on the grille and around the touchscreen. The textured and perforated leather has contrasting stitching and is durable and made to last.

Waldmeir collaborated with her design colleagues to make the High Country edition of the Chevrolet Suburban a reality, but it is the color and trim that make this truck notable.

The mother of two young children, Rebecca Waldmeir considers practicality as she continues to add her design expertise to new products.

The stunning High Country interior, in a Chevrolet truck, was an attraction at the 2020 Philadelphia Auto Show. *Constance Smith*

PART X.
OTHER EXTRAORDINARY WOMEN

PART X.
OTHER EXTRAORDINARY WOMEN

This section includes biographies of women designers and engineers who have in the past made, or continue to make, significant contributions.

> *Note: As indicated, material for these memoirs was provided by the women themselves or reviewed by them; was recorded during interviews or is firsthand (FH); was posted by GM Media, the GM Newsroom, or Archives (GM); was extracted from Car Design News (CDN) presentations online; was featured in online Automotive News (AN) posts; or was taken from the public domain and noted. Some data were extracted directly from the women's own business or social media posts, such as LinkedIn (LI), from 2010 to the present.*

ALEX ARCHER

Archer graduated in 2015 with a BS degree in engineering and product design from Stanford University. She started work as an intern in the Stanford Athletics Media and Communications Department in 2013. In 2014, she interned for physical therapist Marc Guillet, with whom she modified the design of a new medical device—LeverUp—designed for caretakers to move patients. From 2015 to 2016, Archer served as an interior studio designing engineer and from 2016 to 2017 as an interiors design release engineer for floor consoles. From 2016 to 2018, she led the solar car project for GM at Stanford. Perhaps it is fortuitous that Archer is restoring a 1955 Packard Clipper, a car that features Torsion Level Ride, which incorporates an electric motor. In her position as lead design release engineer, she was instrumental in developing a movable center console powered by electric with three others for the 2021 GMC Yukon. Archer has also contributed as a mentor and coach. On behalf of GM, she has worked and continues her association with high school students at Detroit FIRST Robotics, located at the Hispanic Development Center. Archer has recently accepted a position with Rivian as a design release engineer for the Rivian Amazon van. *[Taken from GM Media Post online/email communication, August 23, 2020]*

MICHELE ASSAD

From 2020 to the present, Michele Assad has served in the position of business development manager for Rightsize Facility. Just prior, Michele served as a project leader for CMF (2019–2020).

From 1999 to 2019, Michele provided a diverse range of services for GM in the position of senior creative design project leader of Architectural Interiors. Assad posted that during her tenure, she directed the aesthetic design of all GM Design operations and facility projects and crafted conceptual and strategic visualization to specify and procure workspace furniture, specialty furniture, materials, finishes, artwork, graphics, and applications, providing the environment with a strong, specific, and consistent brand message. She additionally served as the creative liaison between General Motors Design and architectural firms, contractors, vendors, internal partners, and teams to provide solutions that met timing and budget, and instituted the preservation and restoration of historical furniture and spaces. Assad also directed and maintained GM corporate and executive artwork and procurement/appraisal programs on personal collections and artwork curation. Last, she designed, directed, and executed special events for Design VPs, VIPs, senior GM executives, and GM Board of Directors members to promote GM Design brand, GM philanthropic events, and so on. Assad graduated with a BFA from the University of Michigan. *[LI]*

DARBY JEAN BARBER

Barber earned a BFA in 2015, majoring in automotive design at the College for Creative Studies. In 2014, she interned in Chevrolet Truck Exteriors and in 2015 with Honda R&D. She joined GM as a creative designer in 2016 and serves at the Warren Technical Center. Barber's student project is displayed at the Henry Ford Museum of American Innovation with other designs made by CCS students. *[LI/FH]*

SHARON BASEL

A 1981 graduate of Purdue University with a bachelor's degree in engineering and industrial management, Basel served in the position of communications manager from 1981 to 2010. In 2010, she added sustainability to her GM assignments. In 2016, she rose to senior manager, Sustainability & ESG. *[LI]*

ANNA BECHTEL

While attending the University of Cincinnati for transportation design, Anna Bechtel (she/her) interned at various product design companies, including Fisher Price, TOMY International, William McDonough + Partners, LG electronics, and Weltech Centre (UX/UI) in Wellington, New Zealand. During her time at Cincinnati, Bechtel was also an active member for the school's Formula Society of Automotive Engineers (FSAE) student team, a student engineering-design competition. After graduating in 2013 with a bachelor of science, she carried on this involvement in FSAE, joining the staff at Formula North Inc., the Canadian competition, as their art director. In 2015, Bechtel joined General Motors on the creative-sculpting team, working both in the clay and digital workspaces. She is currently employed by GM in the position of creative sculptor. *[AB]*

GABRIELA BELINI

Belini joined GM Brazil in 2003 and rose to design assistant program manager in 2009. In 2015, she was promoted to design manager, Color & Trim, CDI, and Brand. She received a bachelor's degree from Universidade Presbiteriana Mackenzie in 2003 before continuing her education at Universidade Belas Artes. *[LI]*

TERESA BIANCO

Bianco joined GM as a designer in 1996; she continues to serve in this position in Michigan. She has noted that she is an interior unigraphics designer in Advanced Vehicle Design, with a focus on carpets and acoustics. *[LI]*

JUDY BRENNAN

Judy Brennan is currently (2020) North America director of Exterior Lighting, Wipers, and Glass. She previously served as chief engineer for Buick's 2016 Envision and the 2020 Buick Enclave and Chevrolet Blazer in China. Prior to that, she was a vehicle line director in Shanghai, China, and beforehand the first female engineering director at GM Holden in Melbourne, Australia. Judy joined GM in 1981 as a cooperative education student from Michigan State University, where she earned a BSME. She holds an MS in management from MIT, where she attended the Sloan School of Management as a GM Fellow. *[JB]*

MELISSA BYLE

Byle attended the College for Creative Studies on a partial scholarship, earning a BFA in 2010. She joined GM in 2015 as an appearance definition lead for Global Color & Trim. She has her BFA in interior design from CCS and an AA in liberal arts. *[MB]*

KEYSHA CAMPS

Camps currently serves as an Engineering Group manager. She graduated with a bachelor's degree in mechanical engineering from the University of Puerto Rico–Mayaguez in 2013 and earned a master's degree in global automotive and manufacturing engineering from the University of Michigan in 2019. She interned with Lockheed Martin and GM before rejoining GM as a full-time employee. *[LI]*

SHELLEY CHILDS

Childs holds a BS in biology and a minored in advertising and marketing at Central Michigan University. After graduating in 1985, Childs went to work for GM Cadillac Motor Car on Clark Street in Detroit. She spent two years as a production supervisor on the chassis line. Two years later, with the plant closing, she moved into Facilities Engineering as an environmental engineer, coordinating the Hazardous Materials Control for four GM plants. Three years later, she was promoted as the first on-site senior environmental engineer at the GM Powertrain Livonia Engine Plant. During her two years at Powertrain, she installed and managed environmental programs, maintaining regulatory compliance during the multimillion-dollar Northstar Engine construction project. A couple of years later, USPCI, a division of Union Pacific, recruited her from GM to lead the largest hazardous-waste contract to date. Having production and engineering experience, she was assigned to GM plants outside metro Detroit. Two years later, she was recruited by Earth Tech, to serve as their senior sales representative in the auto industry. Returning after three years in technical sales to GM Worldwide Facilities, she joined the new group called Plant Closures. She specialized in the remediation and cleanup of many facilities around the country. A few years later, she joined GM HQ's Chemical Risk Management Group to set up a new centralized approval and data management center servicing North America. Winding her career down in 2009, she was assigned to the Lordstown Assembly Plant to finish production and close the facility. Unfortunately, shortly afterward she was forced to retire due to rheumatoid arthritis. During her career, she put a spouse through medical school and raised four successful adults. [Author interview and SC]

DANIELLE CORY

Cory graduated with a BS in mechanical engineering from Kettering University and an MS from Central Michigan University. She started her career in Milford, Michigan, where she worked as a project engineer. Cory has served the company for over twenty years. In 2014, she was promoted to the position of Engineering Group manager of electrification driver data; from there she became the Engineering Group manager of Next Generation Controls. [DC]

JENNIFER DANESHGARI

Daneshgari was awarded the J. Cordell Breed Award for Women Leaders by the SAE International in 2018. She also rose to the position of global chief engineer of Engines the same year. She joined GM full time in 2004 and has held engineering and managerial positions for a period of more than twenty-six years. She has also been self-employed in a private management company since 2006. She holds a BS in electrical engineering from Kettering University, an MBA from the University of Michigan, and a JD from Western Michigan University Cooley Law School. [LI]

KIMBERLY (DUDA) GONDEK

Gondek holds bachelor's and master's degrees in mechanical engineering from Wayne State University and an MBA from Indiana University. She has over twenty-one years of experience at GM. Early in her career, she worked on midsize truck rear suspension systems, as well as suspension/steering warranty, and was the chassis/power train integration issue resolution lead for the launch of full-size SUV at Janesville, Wisconsin; Sialo, Mexico; and Arlington, Texas. In 2006, she was the lead engineer for midsized car suspension systems and leads a motivated team to package a new power cube on the 2008 Malibu. She then worked on the first global launch team as the chassis/power train/thermal resolution lead for the Epsilon programs. She lived in Shanghai, China; Russelsheim, Germany; and Fairfax, Kansas, leading global

issue resolution for that team. She has progressed through the roles as a global thermal warranty manager, manufacturing engineering quality manager, and an Engineering Group manager for suspension/structure. In 2016 she led the Global B Super Cruise team through initial inception, strategic rollout, and feature planning. In October 2018, she moved to Shanghai, China, as the vehicle chief engineer for the Buick Velite7, Lacrosse, and Regal. In 2020, she repatriated back to the US and is now leading next-generation autonomous-vehicle development. [KG]

YELENA GONOPOLSKAYA

Yelena graduated from the College for Creative Studies in 2000 and joined Visteon upon graduation, where she spent six years as an industrial designer and account manager. From 2006 to 2010, she worked for the Faurecia Group in the color and trim area. After a four-year stint at Ford, she joined GM in 2014, where she contributed to the design of the Chevrolet Malibu. She serves as a color and materials designer. [LI]

MEINAN HE

Dr. Meinan He received her bachelor's degree in materials science from Beijing University of Technology in 2010 and her PhD in materials engineering from Worcester Polytechnic Institute in 2016. From 2014 to 2017, she worked at Argonne National Laboratory as visiting student and postdoctoral appointee, conducting research for battery electrolyte and electrode materials. After joining GM in 2018 as a researcher, Dr. He has been focusing on the validation and development of advanced ultrahigh-energy battery materials. Lately, Dr. He was promoted to senior researcher and is now focusing on the underlying chemistry and the design principle of high-energy lithium batteries. Dr. He is also the author or coauthor of articles in over fifty refereed journals. Currently, Dr. He holds seven awarded US patents and has over ten patent applications pending.

KELLY HELFRICH

Helfrich is manager of electric vehicles (EVs) and charging infrastructure. Previously, she oversaw creating the blueprint for EV-centric mobility solutions and informing investments in charging infrastructure for Maven, General Motors' urban mobility group. Since joining GM, Kelly has overseen the deployment of hundreds of electric vehicles across major US cities. In evaluating how the cars function within each landscape, she partners with cities, utilities, and charging companies to craft strategies to optimize further growth. Prior to General Motors, Kelly worked at Evercar, a start-up that applied the solar power purchase agreement model to transportation electrification by renting electric vehicles to municipalities and rideshare drivers on a total-cost-of-ownership basis. Kelly is also cofounder and president of a nonprofit established in 2007 that is focused on youth education and development in Detroit and East Africa. Kelly studied economics and business at Central Michigan University and received a master's from Indiana University in Bloomington. *[GM Corporate Newsroom]*

JIWON HWANG

Serving as a design program manager, Jiwon Hwang worked with designers, engineers, and fabrication teams for the introduction and presentations of show cars to promote GM's Korean interests (2004–2018). From 2004 to 2005, she served as the Lean Vehicle Developing Process coordinator. From 2005 to 2012, as Show Vehicle Design Program manager, she created a single communication channel to resolve issues identified by a global team. Her duties included providing for the debut of the Miray concept car launched at the Seoul International Motor Show in 2011, the Sonic concept car launched at NAIAS (Detroit) in 2010, the Orlando concept car launched at the Paris Motor Show in 2008, the Mini Triplet concept cars launched at the Greater New York International Auto show in 2007, the WTCC ULTRA concept car launched at the Paris Motor Show in 2006, and the T2X Concept car launched at Seoul Motor Show in 2005. Prior to this assignment, from 2004 to 2005, she served as the representative program manager to create a communication channel for the global GMNA team.

Jiwon Hwang holds a bachelor of art and design degree from Sookmyung Women's University (2000–2004) and an MBA from Yonsei University (2010–2012). *[FH and JH]*

EUN KANG

Kang received a BFA in industrial design from Hongik University in Seoul, Korea, and completed her education at ArtCenter. She served as a creative designer in GM's Advanced UX studio. *[LI]*

SHARON KEMP

Kemp graduated with a BFA degree in sculpture in 1987 from Alfred University. She joined GM in 1991 as a creative sculptor and in 2001 was promoted to manager of creative sculpting. In 2005, she served as a manager for global digital design processes and training, which included a one-year oversees assignment with GM's Asia Pacific Design studios. From 2009 to the present, she has served as group and senior manager. *[SK]*

JUNGHYUN KIM

Kim graduated from Hongik University in 2011 and interned at Toshiba Samsung Storage Technology Corporation. From 2011 to 2016, she served as a power train mount design engineer and as a suspension design engineer. In 2016, she was retained as a body and exterior validation engineer . *[LI]*

LAURA (WONTROP) KLAUSER

Klauser holds a bachelor's degree in mechanical engineering from Rensselaer Polytechnic Institute and master's degree in automotive engineering from the University of Michigan. Early in her career, she served as an RPI admissions ambassador and team manager for the RPI Formula SAE Team. She joined GM's co-op program in 2006 and rose through the ranks, serving as a vehicle definition engineer, Advanced Operations engineer, suspension engineer, integration engineer, and Cadillac Racing Program manager. At the beginning of 2021, Klauser was promoted to Sports Car Racing Program manager, overseeing the Cadillac, Corvette, and Camaro GT4 programs. Cadillac won the Rolex 24 race in 2017, 2018, 2019, and 2020 and achieved the manufacturers' overall Endurance Cup Championship in 2017 and 2018. Corvette won the Rolex 24 in 2021. As a volunteer, Klauser had served as the dynamic events coordinator for the Formula SAE Michigan competition, chaired the SAE's Detroit Section in 2018, and sits on the Detroit Section Board. *[LK]*

ANNA KRETZ

Kretz holds a BS in engineering from Oakland University and an MBA in industrial management from Central Michigan University. She started with Buick in 1992 and served as chief engineer for electrical and electronics for Saturn in 1985. She subsequently held a director's position before serving as a vehicle line executive. She retired after a thirty-six-year career. [*AN, September 26, 2005*]

STACY KUCHLBAUER

Kuchlbauer graduated from Eastern Michigan University in 2012 with a BS in apparel and textiles. After a four-month internship, she joined Faurecia as a trim engineer. In 2016, she joined GM as a trim specialist. Currently, Kuchlbauer serves as a seat trim BOM family owner. [*LI*]

MARY ALICE KURTZ

Since 2009, Kurtz has served as a Global Sustainability Initiatives Program manager. During an affiliation lasting thirty-seven years, she previously held positions as the director of facility operations for Opel Vauxhall, director of Energy and Utilities Services for GM North America, Regulatory Energy and Utilities manager, GM North America site utilities manager for GM Powertrain, and mechanical engineer in facilities operations. Having graduated from Michigan State in 1983 with a bachelor's degree in mechanical engineering and an MBA from Wayne State University, she also holds energy and sustainability licenses and a PE license in the state of Michigan. [*LI*]

CRISTI LANDY

Landy holds a BE in electrical and electronics engineering and an MBA from the University of Michigan. After spending almost eight years at Saturn, she served as a planning manager for Future Programs at GM from 1997 to 2002. From 2004 to 2017, she held diverse positions with Chevrolet, rising to director of Global Chevrolet Product Strategy. After this lengthy association with GM, she joined Waymo. [*LI*]

JUNIA MARTIN LAPP

Lapp graduated from the Universidade do Estado de Minas Gerais–Escola de Design (UEMG Brazil) with a bachelor's degree, with a concentration in industrial and product design, in 2003. From 2003 to 2008, she served as a creative designer for Fiat Chrysler Auto (FCA). In 2008, she joined GM as a creative designer and remains in that position at this time. [*LI*]

SARA LEBLANC

Sara LeBlanc began her career at GM in 1990 as a floor supervisor in a manufacturing plant and, over her career, held many cross-functional positions at GM within Engineering, Quality, Finance, and Program Management before becoming managing director of electric engineering at the GM Korea Technical Center. In 2019, she was appointed director of Canadian Technical Centers and is currently the director of connectivity engineering. She holds a bachelor of science in mechanical engineering from Michigan State University and a master of business administration from the New York Institute of Technology. [*SL*]

JOANNE L. LEDDY

Joanne Leddy is an Engineering Group manager for the Infotainment and Connectivity organization at General Motors (2016–present). She has responsibility for the infotainment strategy across the Cadillac brand and served as the program manager for the new 2021 Cadillac Escalade. Joining GM in 1987 as a consultant until 1993, Leddy went on to hold positions both in Planning and Project Management. Her assignments have included Lambda, Hummer (original), and Cadillac. She holds a BS in mechanical engineering from Michigan Technological University. [*JL*]

KIRSTY LINDSAY

A graduate in textile design from RMIT University, Lindsay joined GM Australia and served as a lead designer from 2005 to 2008. From 2008 to 2013, she worked as the design manager of Colour and Trim and, in 2013, was appointed chief designer. [*LI*]

LAETITIA LOPEZ

After serving Faurecia, Laetitia joined Opel in 2014 and Cadillac Color and Trim in Michigan in 2016. She worked on grains development for the 2014 Opel Corsa. She received a master's degree from CREAPOLE, a French design school, in 2012. [*LI*]

MARYBETH MACDONALD

MacDonald received a BS in mechanical engineering from Lawrence Technological University in 1990 and a master's degree in mechanical engineering from the University of Michigan in 1993. She has held numerous positions over a thirty-five-year period, including OBD II engineer, design responsible engineer, engine application engineer, total validation engineer, power train vehicle systems engineer, Engineering Group manager, global engine sector integration engineer, and engineering business manager. In 2019 she was promoted to global program manager of Electrification Propulsion. *[LI]*

ELIZABETH MACK

A graduate of Michigan State University and the College for Creative Studies, Mack also holds a bachelor's degree in visual art education from Madonna University. Joining GM Design Center in 1989, she enjoyed a twenty-year career. She is currently a visual art teacher in the Dearborn Public School District. *[LI and email communication]*

ALISYN MALEK

Malek studied at the University of Michigan and Indiana University, where she received bachelor's and master's degrees, respectively. Malek started as an investment manager at GM Ventures, her engineering study, most of it completed at the University of Michigan, seems to have dictated her future. She led a global team assembled to develop advanced charging technology for the Chevrolet Spark and Bolt EV. At GM, she led their investment in the autonomous space, including early negotiations with Cruise Automation, helping investigate GM's Autonomous strategy (taken from Carla Bailo and Terry Barclay, *The Road to the Top Is Not on the Map: Conversations with Top Women of the Automotive Industry* [Warrendale, PA: SAE International, 2019]). In 2017, Malek, a former Ford autonomous head, co-founded May Mobility with Toyota Institute codirector Edwin Olsen and Steve Vozar, who previously oversaw the University of Michigan's robotics laboratory. Its six-seat electric shuttle was launched in a handful of states across the Midwest, with plans for nationwide expansion. In 2021, Malek was listed as the executive director for the Commission on Future of Mobility. *[VB, February 13, 2020, venturebeat.com/2020/02/13 online]* In 2022, Malek recorded her position as Executive Director, Coalition for Reimagined Mobility.

DARCI MARCUM

Marcum serves as plant director in Lansing, Michigan, a position she has held for a little over two years. She joined GM in 1994 as a group leader, rising up through the ranks to assistant plant director before assuming her current position. Marcum received a BS in industrial management and engineering in 1993 and an MBA from the University of Dayton in 2000 and has supplemented her education with other coursework. *[DM]*

FIONA MEYER-TERUEL

Joining GM's electrification team in 2018, Fiona currently serves as a lead technology development engineer and is tasked with releasing the first wireless battery management system, which will serve as the brain of products such as the GMC Hummer pickup and Cadillac Lyriq. Meyer-Teruel has prepared to focus on the future. She holds a bachelor of science degree in mechanical engineering from Stanford University (2016) and a master's degree in computer science from the Georgia Institute of Technology (2019). Stanford's extensive initiatives across industries enabled her to work at various engineering internships before she joined GM in 2016 as a shifter controls engineer. She subsequently served as an autonomous software research engineer before tackling her current assignment. *[AN, November 16, 2020, MT]*

NAKAGOME (FUKUSAKI), TAEKO

Nakagome is described as Opel's First Lady of Design in a PSA newsletter. She contributed to the interior of the Opel Commodore. She currently lives in Japan. *[PSA Group newsletter]*

INGRID NIELSON

Nielson worked as an automotive interior designer in the mid-1960s. *[GM Archives]*

SEUNGHEE OH

Oh was awarded a BA in industrial design from Hongik University in 2007. While she began her career as a GM CMF intern and Hanssen furniture design intern, she later served as an exterior designer both for Hyundai (2007–2011) and GM (2011–2013). Additionally, she designed exhibits for Steelhead Products (2013–2015). She currently serves as a senior design manager for Fisker. *[LI]*

KANA OKADA

Kana Okada currently holds the position of cell technical specialist with Advanced Li-ion Battery. Assigned to GM's Warren, Michigan, Technical Center, she is responsible for the development of new cell materials, design, and technology for the fuel cell system for next-gen batteries and propulsion systems. She previously served in the position of senior materials engineer, fuel cell systems and battery (2018–2020), From 2016 to 2018, Okada worked on the development of polymeric materials for automotive interiors and exteriors. Her previous experience and diverse education are worth noting. From 2014 to 2016, she worked on materials development for manufacturing for Toyota Boshokov America. Previously, she served as a research assistant and postdoctoral researcher at the University of Michigan (2007–2014). Before conducting research at UM, she spent three years as a materials engineer at Nissan in Kanagawana, Japan. With a colleague, Okada worked with on the development of polymeric materials that resulted in the issuance of four US patents. Okada earned her bachelor of engineering degree in chemistry from Nagoya University, an MS degree in earth and environmental engineering from Columbia University in New York City, and a PhD in chemical engineering from the University of Michigan. In her spare time, Okada seems to have also mastered the art of photography.

BARBARA PERLUKE (DERONDE)

Perluke studied chemistry before graduating with a BID from Pratt Institute in 1972. She later earned an MBA in Finance, MS in Clinical Psychology, MA in Psychology, and a Masters in Religious Studies. After working as a designer in the Frigidaire Studio, she moved to New York to marry and joined IBM where she held a number of diverse positions over a sixteen-year period. She was tasked with making the Company's interiors handicapped accessible, designed a cafeteria interior, assisted with site space planning, tracked finances, and so on. [FH]

TECKLA RHOADS

Teckla Rhoads is a graduate of the Center for Creative Studies. Raised in Birmingham and Rochester Hills, Michigan, she was the oldest of four children in a family with a long automotive history. Her father, Otto Rosenbusch, started out as a designer at American Motors and Chrysler Corporation, eventually becoming manager of special events at Chrysler during the Lee Iacocca years.

After her graduation from CCS, Rhoads was hired at GM as a calligrapher and lettering-design specialist. She eventually rose to the position of director of Global Industrial Design. Now retired, she devotes herself to various charitable pursuits. [TR]

SABRINA RIDENOUR

Sabrina Ridenour is a 2017 graduate of West Virginia University with a BS in mechanical engineering and a minor certificate in vocal performance; she is originally from Frostburg, Maryland. Currently, she is employed as a controls design engineer at General Motors while pursuing her master of engineering in energy systems engineering at the University of Michigan.

As a controls design engineer, Ridenour works on developing the charging software for GM's entire electric and autonomous vehicle lineup. She has owned five different charging features, including location-based charging, which allows the customer to save their home charger settings via their phone app or dashboard. She participates in company culture initiatives, including a reverse mentoring program to mentor an executive, and is one of three representatives of her controls organization on her vice president's inclusion advisory board. Her cross-functional work both on the future of electric vehicles and diversity and inclusion efforts has been highlighted numerous times by General Motors, the Society of Women Engineers (SWE), and her alma mater.

Prior to her current role, Ridenour had extensive experience across the company. She got her foot in the door of the automotive industry with a summer internship as a manufacturing engineer at GM Arlington Assembly in Texas. Following that internship, she served as the system safety lead and mechanical team member for WVU's EcoCAR3 design competition team, in which sixteen universities competed to integrate a 2016 Chevrolet Camaro into a hybrid-electric vehicle. Her leadership contributed to WVU's second-place finish in the competition, which is primarily sponsored by General Motors and the US Department of Energy. This continued experience led Ridenour to pursue the Technical Rotation and Career Knowledge (TRACK) entry-level program at GM, where she would experience six four-month rotations throughout the Global Propulsion Systems organization. She completed rotations in transmission development and validation, power train noise and vibration, electrification charging controls algorithm design development, engine platform calibration testing, autonomous-vehicle integration controls, and calibration of a small gas engine.

Ridenour has actively advocated for women in STEM through both SWE and the American Association of University Women (AAUW) in various positions throughout the last eight years. Most notably, Ridenour was selected as one of ten students from around the country to serve on the 2016–2017 AAUW National Student Advisory Council in Washington, DC, publishing an article in *USA Today* titled "We Need to Be the Engineers of Feminism," and has served as a featured guest speaker for numerous conferences, including the TechConnect WV "Women & Technology Conference" in West Virginia's state capital. She has served in numerous leadership capacities with SWE, including serving as cochair with both WVU's and SWE-Detroit's largest outreach events of the year, inviting over three hundred local middle-school girls and their parents for a day to explore STEM careers. Ridenour has represented WVU SWE at two regional and two national SWE conferences, where WVU SWE has been awarded 2015 Silver Level and 2016 Gold Level awards for "Outstanding Collegiate Section." She also was the runner-up in SWE's inaugural "Sing It to Begin It" singing competition that kicked off WE15 in Nashville, Tennessee. Drawing from her background in engineering, noise and vibration, and professional singing, Ridenour was selected to present her session, "'Is This Thing On?': The Science behind Public Speaking," at WE19 in Anaheim, California, to hundreds of conference attendees.

Ridenour hopes to continue inspiring the next generation of female engineers in many years to come, just as her mom, also a mechanical engineer (like mother, like daughter), has done for her.

SONIA RIEF

Rief holds a bachelor's degree in mechanical engineering from North Carolina State University and an MBA from the University of Michigan. She began her career serving GM as a durability test engineer. Later, she joined Renault-Nissan in Japan. She currently works for Nissan as VP of Program Management. (Source: Carla Bailo and Terry Barclay, *The Road to the Top Is Not on the Map: Conversations with Top Women of the Automotive Industry* [Warrendale, PA: SAE International, 2019]).

BETTY ROMSEK

Romsek graduated from Kettering University with a bachelor's degree in industrial administration in 1982 and an MBA from Michigan State University in 1985. From 1977 to 1982, she had a diverse range of co-op assignments that prepared her for a number of challenging positions, which included plant and area manager, production supervisor, and similar. She served the corporation for over forty-two years, retiring six years after being promoted to executive director of Global Pre-Production Operations. *[LI]*

CHELSEY SEMIDEY

Chelsey Semidey attended Ringling College of Art and Design, where she received a BFA degree in computer animation in 2007. She started her career with General Motors Design in 2007, where she was hired as a digital sculptor. Initially assigned to the Chevrolet Performance interiors group, she had the opportunity to work on the 2014 C7 Corvette Stingray interior. After several years in the Michigan design studios working on production vehicles, Chelsey moved to GM's advanced design studio in North Hollywood, California. There she has worked on several Cadillac show cars, including the 2010 Cadillac ULC and 2013 Cadillac Elmiraj. Soon

promoted to lead digital sculptor, she led the sculpting of the 2011 Cadillac Ciel Interior, the 2016 Chevrolet Colorado ZH2 hydrogen fuel cell vehicle, the 2021 Cadillac eVtol interior, and the 2021 Cadillac PAV interior. Chelsey was promoted to digital design and visualization manager of the California Advanced Studio in 2019, where she manages a team of digital sculptors as well as animation/visualization artists. *[CS; Photo courtesy of CS]*

CAMILA SERAFIM

Camila Serafim currently serves GM of South America as a lead design release engineer for after-treatment and monitors the effectiveness of catalytic converters and related components to meet emissions standards for gasoline vehicles. She joined GM as a junior designer in 2006 after leaving Affinia. She holds a Bachelor of Engineering/Mechanical Production Engineering Degree (Universidade do Grande ABC) and, in 2021, graduated with an MBA (Universidade de São Paulo). She also has Black Belt Certification in Lean Six Sigma, Kaizen Blitz, and 8S Methodology. In 2015, she received an EC Award after the implementation in Brazil of the process of virtual bucks and kits. At the end of 2021, she was appointed to be part of the Women in Action group in South America.

MAUREEN SHORT

Dr. Maureen Short is a human factors expert for General Motors. She graduated from the US Military Academy at West Point and served in the position of engineer officer in the US Army.

She has deployed to Nicaragua for hurricane recovery and commanded a company in Iraq. After leaving the army, Maureen worked in the position of senior systems engineer, developing the Joint Test and Evaluation Methodology for Joint Forces Command. Before moving to General Motors, Maureen served as director of curriculum for the army's Comprehensive Soldier and Family Fitness Program. In this capacity, she was responsible for the education and training of soldiers across the army, focused on performance, energy management, and resilience. Mrs. Short was also selected for the position of program manager for the Special Operations Cognitive Enhancement and Performance Program, which adopts the principles of sports and performance psychology to provide mental-skills training for Special Operations Forces. These skills focused on teaching human biorhythms, sleep science, energy management, attention control, and memory improvement. This training was critical for elite soldiers to remain adaptive and ready during high-stress training and deployments. Maureen holds an MS in engineering management from Missouri S&T, and an ME in systems engineering from the University of Virginia, and completed her PhD in systems and engineering management education at Texas Tech University. *[MS]*

BIANCA SKELTON (IACOPELLI)

Skelton graduated with a BFA degree in graphic design from the College for Creative Studies in 2013, and an MA in sustainable design from the Minneapolis College of Art and Design in 2020. In her own online posts, she calls herself a creative problem solver. From 2014 to the present, she has worked as a creative designer in GM's corporate ID and graphics studio. In this capacity, she has contributed to the development and design of the GMC Hummer's identification. Logos and identification graphics are part of or appear on the grille, tailgate, and accessories including the bed liner, railings, and mud flaps. Skelton and her team recently gave a virtual presentation in the *Car Design Dialogues* presented by CDN, where she noted that the letter forms for the logo reflect the proportions of the vehicle. *[LI, CDN]*

JEEHEE SONG

Song graduated from Konkuk University with a BE in mechanical and aerospace engineering in 2007. She subsequently received a BFA from the College for Creative Studies. In 2009, she worked for the L-F Co., Ltd., located in Korea, as a product designer. In 2012, she worked at GM as a creative sculptor. In 2013, she accepted the position of digital designer and continues in this position. *[LI]*

PADMA SUNDARAM

Sundaram earned her bachelor's degree in electrical and electronics engineering from Jawaharlal Nehru Technological University, India, in 1992 and subsequently earned two master's degrees: the first in computer science and engineering from Oakland University, in Rochester, Michigan, and the second in systems architecting and engineering from the University of Southern California, Los Angeles. Before joining GM, she worked for Hughes Aircraft / Raytheon and Delphi. Sundaram has over twenty-two years of experience in engineering safety-critical automotive systems and working with complex software intensive embedded controls. Sundaram was honored as the GM technical fellow in 2014. In 2019, Sundaram, who holds fourteen patents and has published numerous publications, was promoted to chief architect of Autonomous Vehicles: Safety and Systems Engineering. Sundaram is a strategic thought leader who loves to innovate and is not afraid to challenge the status quo. She enjoys being herself and leads from within. *[PS]*

SIMONE THOMPSON

Thompson started her engineering education at the Borough Manhattan Community College and completed it with an MS in manufacturing operations at Kettering University in 2003. From 2000 to the present, she has served as senior process engineer of Heads and Blocks (GM Powertrain). *[ST]*

NELLY TOLEDO (MALDONADO)

Toledo holds a BFA from the University of Puerto Rico, a master's degree in industrial design from Wayne State University, and an MBA from Michigan State University. She worked in interiors at GM for about ten years, beginning in the late 1970s. In 1988, she left for FMC to be able to design exteriors, notably the Aerostar minivan and the 1998 Mercury Cougar. Toledo, a skilled painter, later established a fine-arts business. *[NT, online post]*

JAN TRIBBEY

Tribbey, with a BS in industrial design from the University of Cincinnati, joined GM in the early to mid-1970s as an interior designer in a production automotive studio. She experimented with tie-dying. After resigning to get married, she later served as a staff designer for JC Penney in New York City. *[FH]*

MONICA VAUGHN

After earning a bachelor's degree in electrical and electronics engineering in the co-op program at Kettering University in 1990, Vaughn went on to earn a master's degree in applied mathematics at Purdue in 1992. Beginning in 1985, she served as a maintenance supervisor, project controls engineer, facilities manager, business planning manager, and engineering manager at GM. In 2018, Vaughn was promoted to Technical Group manager, a position she still holds. *[LI]*

CATHERINE WAGNER (CATHERINE KASCUR, CATHERINE DENEK, CATHERINE GRIDLEY)

Wagner graduated from Pratt Institute with a BID in 1965 and spent her entire career at GM Design. Wagner frequently teamed with Suzanne Vanderbilt on special projects until Vanderbilt was forced to retire prematurely because of health issues. Cathy spent a portion of her career designing interiors for Cadillac. She was also chosen as a model from time to time and was featured in print with early GM cars. At the time of her retirement, Wagner—pictured on the right here in this GM photo—held the position of senior interior lead designer. *[FH]*

PAMELA WATERS

Waters joined GM in the mid-1960s and served in the Cadillac Interiors Studio for a short time before opening a design consultancy. An industrial design graduate of Pratt Institute, she tried her hand at teaching for a short period of time recently at the school. In past years, she also lent a hand during annual student reviews. *[FH]*

LIZ BERMEA WILKINS

A communication design graduate from the Cleveland Institute of Art, Wilkins was retained as a Chevrolet color-and-trim designer at the GM Technical Center in Warren in 2013 and as a Chevrolet and GMC color-and-trim designer in 2018. *[LBW]*

CANDICE WILLETT

Candice Willett is the lead designer for choreographed experiences and lighting at Cadillac. In her role, she works with Cadillac's advanced engineering and design groups to identify technologies for the brand. She is also key in business strategy development, bringing innovation to the production teams she supports. Known for her work across GM's brand portfolio, Willett's most recent project was the Cadillac LYRIQ. For this vehicle, she challenged conventional technologies to create and leverage features to enable a choreographed lit grille and true vertical lighting, redefining the brand signatures to create a welcoming experience for customers as they approach and enter the vehicle. Having joined the GM Creative Design team ten years ago, she began her career working on Cadillac lighting and was also instrumental in building the lighting studio as the Cadillac designer. She now leads exterior and interior lighting strategy for the Cadillac brand while incorporating meaningful, customer-focused experiences throughout. Prior to her current role, Willett worked as a GM contract employee in the Accessory Studio, leading HUMMER-branded accessories and licensed content. Willett received her bachelor's degree in fine arts in industrial design, with a transportation focus, from the Cleveland Institute of Art in 2003. *[CW]*

JENNIFER WIDRICK

Recently contributing to the color and trim design of the stunning Cadillac Lyriq, Widrick was promoted to the position of director, Global Color and Trim. After graduating from the College For Creative Studies, she spent eighteen years with the Ford Motor Company before joining GM in 2019. Widrick and Crystal Windham recently presented the design features of the Lyriq with colleagues in a virtual event, *Design Dialogues*—a CDN program held on December 3, 2020. *[CDN and LI]*

NOTES

PART I

1. Louis F. Fourie, *On a Global Mission: The Automobiles of General Motors International* (Victoria, BC: FreisenPress, 2016), 6.
2. Ibid., 730.
3. Ibid.
4. Ibid., 598.

MARY T. BARRA

1. Laura Colby, *Road to Power* (Hoboken, NJ: John Wiley and Sons, 2015), 140.
2. Online: gm.com/our-company/leadership/mary-t-barra.html.
3. Laura Zarrow and Adam Grant, *Women at Work* radio recording (Philadelphia: Wharton Business Radio, 2019).
4. Tim Tankersley, "What Drives Mary Barra," *Stanford Magazine*, September–October 2019.
5. Colby, *Road to Power*, 10.
6. Troupe Noonan, *GMI Kettering University at 100* (Chapel Hill, NC: Heritage Histories, 2019), 179.
7. Ibid.
8. Colby, *Road to Power*, 17.
9. Ibid., 18.
10. Ibid.
11. Ibid., 27.
12. Ibid., 53.
13. Ibid., 67.
14. Tankersley, "What Drives Mary Barra," 12.

MARISSA WEST

1. https://www.designnews.com/electronics-test/14-engineers-who-are-transforming-auto-industry/14406628658912#West
2. Ibid.
3. Ibid.
4. Ibid.
5. gm.com/gmc-life/trucks-interviews-with Sierra-hd-chief engineer.

PAMELA FLETCHER

1. Pardeep Toor, "Kettering Graduate Leading GM's Electric Vehicle Efforts," *Kettering Magazine*, Spring 2017.
2. Larry Edsall, *Chevrolet Volt: Charging into the Future* (Minneapolis: MBI Publications, 2010), 133–135.
3. Ibid.
4. GM Heritage Center, Electric Vehicles, online post at GM Heritage Center.com.
5. Ibid.
6. Ibid.
7. Edsall, *Chevy Volt*, 33.

PART II

BONNIE EVA LEMM

1. Michael Lamb and Dave Holls, *A Century of Automotive Style* (Stockton, CA: Lamm-Morada, 2015), 88.
2. Arthur Pound, *The Turning Wheel* (Garden City, NY: Doubleday, Doran, 1934), 179.
3. Lamb and Holls, *A Century of Automotive Style*, 90.
4. Ibid.
5. Pound, *The Turning Wheel*, 295.
6. Ibid., 135.

HELEN BLAIR BARLETT

1. Pound, *The Turning Wheel*, appendix IV.
2. Ibid.
3. Karl Schwartzwalder, "The Memorial of Helen Blair Barlett," *American Mineralogist* 56 (March–April 1971).
4. Ibid.
5. Ibid.

PART III

HELENE ROTHER ACKERNECHT

1. Mary Morris, women's ed., "Woman Scores in Automotive Design," *Detroit News*, 1949.
2. Interviews with Ina Rother by author in Michigan, 2011.
3. Ingrid Bieber and Katharina Walch, *Leipzig und seine Geschichte* (Leipzig: I. P. Verlagsgesellschaft, 1991), 21–23.
4. Richard M. Langworth, *GM: 100 Years* (Lincolnwood, IL: Publications International, 2008), 120–122.
5. Morris, "Woman Scores in Automotive Design."
6. Charles K. Hyde, *Storied Independent Automakers: Nash Hudson and AMC* (Detroit: Wayne State University Press, 2009), 40–63.
7. Ibid.
8. Ibid.

AMY JEANETTE STANLEY (AMY LIGHT)

1. Interview of Elizabeth Williams (deceased sister of Amy Light) by author, 2012.
2. Ibid.
3. Interview of Robin Montgomery by author, 2013 and August 2020.
4. Ric Morgan, *The Train of Tomorrow* (Bloomington: Indiana University Press, 2007), 8–18.
5. Ibid.
6. Telephone conversation between Todd Light and author, August 13, 2020.

MARY VIRGINIA LORING

1. Phone conversations between Martha Loring and author, 2010–2014 and July 27, 2020. All quotes are from these conversations.

2. Conversations between H. Roy Jaffe and author at his home, 2012–2014.

3. Phone conversations between Martha Loring and author, 2010–2014 and July 27, 2020.

PART IV

MARYELLEN GREEN (DOHRS)

1. Author conversations with MaryEllen Green Dohrs (2018–2020).

2. Ibid.

3. Ibid.

4. Ibid.

5. Ibid.

6. Ibid.

7. Ibid.

RUTH GLENNIE (PETERSEN)

1. Interviews by author with Ruth Glennie and members of the Glennie family, including Ruth, her two sisters, and her son, in person, on the telephone, via email, and via US mail, 2011–2020.

2. Ibid.

3. In-person conversation between Charles R. Pollock and author in Queens, New York, June 2012. Mr. Pollock's executive chair, manufactured by Knoll, is in the collection of the Louvre, the Metropolitan Museum of Art, and the Smithsonian. Pollock, who died in 2013 in an accidental fire, is also recognized as an outstanding student at Pratt at the same time as Ruth Glennie.

GERE KAVANAUGH

1. Steven Kurutz, "If It Has a Shape," *New York Times*, May 8, 2013.

2. Gere Kavanaugh, presentation at Carnegie Mellon, posted online, vimeoco>cmudesign, October 9, 2012.

3. Ibid.

4. Ibid.

5. Ibid.

6. Robert Judson Clark, Andrea Belloli, Joan Marter, et al., *Design in America: The Cranbrook Vision, 1925–1950* (New York: Abrams, 1983).

7. Ibid.

8. Ibid.

9. Author conversations with Kavanaugh, 2013.

10. Thesis project excerpt, unpublished, Cranbrook Collection.

JEANETTE KREBS (LAPINE)

1. Author email communications with Marc Chabot, MC Fine Arts, 2019 and July 2020.

2. Author telephone interviews, 2011–2014.

MAJORIE FORD POHLMANN

1. In-person conversations between Peter Brock and author in New York and Las Vegas and online, 2019–2020.

HELENE POLLINS

1. Interviews with Helene Pollins by author on June 26 and 29, 2020.

2. Interviews with Helene Pollins by author in 2013 and 2014. The information presented in this chapter primarily consists of data recorded from conversations at Pollins's New Jersey residence.

3. Interview with Helene Pollins by author on June 29. 2020.

SANDRA LONGYEAR RICHARDSON

1. Conversations with Sandra Longyear Richardson by author from 2010 to 2014 and in 2028.

2. Ibid.

3. Ibid.

4. Ibid.

5. Ibid.

JEANETTE (FIORAVERA) LINDER ROBERTS

1. All Peter Linder quotes are from conversations with author, 2012–1014.

2. All quotes from Jeanette Linder are from conversations with author, 2012–2014.

MARTHA JAYNE VAN ALSTYNE

1. Firsthand interviews between M. J. Van Alstyne and author, 2011–2012.

2. Ibid.

3. Ibid.

4. Ibid.

5. Ibid.

6. Ibid.

SUZANNE E. VANDERBILT

1. Association of Women Industrial Designers, *Goddess in the Details: Product Design by Women*, exhibit guide (New York: AWID, 1994).

2. Ibid.

3. David Crippen, interviewer, Suzanne Vanderbilt Oral History Project, unpublished (Dearborn, MI: Henry Ford Collection, 1988).

4. Ibid.

5. Ibid.

6. Ibid.

7. Ibid.

8. Ibid.

9. Ibid.

10. Ibid.

11. Ibid.

DAGMAR ARNOLD-WAHLFORSS

1. Association of Women Industrial Designers, *Goddess in the Details.* This guide to the show in Pratt's Manhattan Gallery was produced in conjunction with Pratt Institute's Exhibition Department.

2. Communication with Norm James by author, 2012.

3. Association of Women Industrial Designers, *Goddess in the Details.*

4. John K. Diveny, "Designing Woman," *IBM San Jose News,* June 21, 1961, 3.

5. IBM, "D. L. Arnold 1st IBM Woman Employee to Receive Patent," *IBM Research News,* March 1963.

6. IBM, "Two Get Special Awards," *IBM San Jose News,* June 1, 1962, 3.

7. Op. Cit., "Designing Woman."

8. Ibid.

PART V

JOAN KLATIL (CREAMER)

1–5. All quotes are from author communications over many years.

PART VI

JACQUELINE "JACQUI" DRURY DEDO

1. Pardeep Toor, "Kettering Provided 'Foundation Knowledge' for Graduate Auto Industry Career," *Kettering Magazine,* Spring 2014.

2. Ibid.

3. "100 Leading Women," *Automotive News,* 2010, http://autonews.com/awards/2010-leading-women-jaqui-dedo-dana-holding-corp.

4. Ibid.

5. *Washington Post,* washingtonpost.com/archives/local/1978/09/14.

6. Bloomberg.com/profile/company/VAS/A:US.

ELIZABETH GRIFFITH

1. Carla Bailo and Terry Barclay, *The Road to the Top Is Not on the Map: Conversations with Top Women of the Automotive Industry* (Warrendale, PA: SAE International, 2019), 75.

2. *Auto News* 100 Leading Women in the NA Auto Industry, https:www.autonews.com/static/section/1001w-landing.

GRACE (LARRINUA) LIEBLEIN

1. "Top 100 Leading Women in the North American Auto Industry," *Automotive News,* 2015.

2. Ibid.

3. Noonan, *GMI Kettering University at 100.*

4. Ibid.

5. Great Minds in Stem, 2014 Engineer of the Year: Grace Lieblein, Technica, Fall 2014 (online).

6. Ibid.

7. Ibid.

8. Ibid.

9. Ibid.

BARBARA MUNGER

1. Conversations with Barbara Munger by author, February 1–7, 2014.

2. Henry Adams, *Viktor Schreckengost and 20th-Century Design* (Cleveland, OH: Cleveland Museum of Art, 2000).

3. Conversations with Barbara Munger by author, February 1–7, 2014.

4. Ibid.

5. Conversation with Jerry Hirshberg by author in 2012. Hirshberg hired accomplished women automotive designers while serving as director of NDI. He is the author of *The Creative Priority,* published by Harper Collins, and exhibits his fine arts at a New York City gallery.

6. Conversations with Barbara Munger by author, February 1–7, 2014.

7. General Motors, *Chevrolet Passenger Car Product Guide* (Detroit: General Motors, 1993). This guide was published for confidential use by employees of Chevrolet franchises.

8. Ibid.

9. Ibid.

CAROL PERELLI

1. The author interviewed Carol Perelli in her Michigan apartment in 2015.

2. Ibid.

VIRGINIA (GINNI) ROMETTY

1. Karis Hustad, "How Ginni Rometty's Childhood in Chicago Influenced Her Path to CEO of IBM," bizjournals.com/Chicago/inno/stories/new/2016, October 21, 2016.

2. "Ginni Rometty: How Purpose Helps Innovation," interview by Chana R. Schoenberger, *Insights by Stanford Business,* April 23, 2018.

3. Ibid.

4. Ibid.

5. Ibid.

6. IBM Newsroom, "Executive Biographies of Senior Executives and Former CEOs," posted March 16, 2021.

7. Ibid.

8. Ibid.

9. Hustad, "How Ginni Rometty's Childhood in Chicago Influenced Her Path to CEO of IBM."

10. IBM Newsroom, "Executive Biographies of Senior Executives and Former CEOs."

11. Ibid.

12. Ibid.

13. Ibid.

14. IBM.org, P-TECH, posted April 4, 2021.

15. Ibid.

16. Ibid.

PART VII

CARLA (DISBROW) BAILO

1. Christina Selter, "Carla Bailo at NAIAS," *HerHighway*, 2020.

2. Ibid.

3. Noonan, *GMI Kettering University at 100*, 204.

4. Ibid.

5. Ibid., 169.

6. Selter, "Carla Bailo at NAIAS."

7. Ibid.

HELEN EMSLEY

1. "100 Leading Women in the Auto Industry," *Automotive News*, 2000.

2. Nick Gibbs, "Meet the Brit Who Designs GM Pick-Ups," *Autocar*, August 20, 2016.

3. Ibid.

4. "100 Leading Women in the Auto Industry."

5. Ibid.

6. Dave McLellan, *Corvette from the Inside* (Cambridge, MA: Bentley, 2002), 27–35.

7. Ibid.

DENISE GRAY

1. Denise Gray, panel discussion, 2018 CTI Auto Week in Novi, Michigan, May 16, 2018.

2. Phoebe Wall Howard, "A Daughter of Detroit Defies Odds, Takes Car Industry into the Future," *Detroit Free Press*, July 13, 2018.

3. Ibid.

4. Ibid.

5. "LG Chem Power's Denise Gray on Everything Batteries," *Shift* (podcast), November 25, 2019.

6. Howard, "A Daughter of Detroit Defies Odds, Takes Car Industry into the Future."

7. Ibid.

MARY GUSTANSKI

1. Bailo and Barclay, *The Road to the Top Is Not on the Map*, 83.

2. Ibid., 82.

3. Center for Automotive Research (Ann Arbor, MI), online post, 2017.

4. Ibid.

5. "Top 100 Leading Women in the North American Auto Industry."

MARIETTA L. KEARNEY (ELLIS)

1. "Marietta Kearney," *City Magazine*, March 1988, 18–20.

2. Ibid.

DIANA (WERRELL) TREMBLAY

1. Gabe Nelson, "100 Leading Women in the North American Auto Industry," *Automotive News*, June 4, 2020.

2. Wallmine.com/people/13497/diana-d-tremblay.

3. Diana D. Tremblay, LinkedIn, June 4, 2020.

4. Nelson, "100 Leading Women in the North American Auto Industry."

5. Noonan, *GMI Kettering University at 100*, 179–180.

6. Ibid., 168.

7. Ibid., 179–190.

8. Nelson, "100 Leading Women in the North American Auto Industry."

9. Ibid.

PART VIII

SANGYEON CHO

1. Daewoo Design History, ItalDesign Giugiaro S.p.A., Torino, Italy (website), 2016.

2. Ibid.

3. Online post: http://www.designersparty.com/entry/Chevrolet-Trax-Concept-Taewan-Kim.

4. Ibid.

ALICIA BOLER-DAVIS

1. Mike Colias, "100 Leading Women in the NA Automotive Industry," *Auto News*, May 31, 2020, www.autonews.com/article/20151109.

2, Laura Colby, *Road to Power* (Hoboken, NJ: John Wiley and Sons, 2015), 18.

3. Colias, "100 Leading Women in the NA Automotive Industry."

4. Colby, *Road to Power*, 74.

4. Ibid., 75.

5. Colias, "100 Leading Women in the NA Automotive Industry."

YAN-HONG HUANG (YAN)

1–3. Conversations and commutations by Yan Huang with the author from 2015 to present.

MARIE JOHNSON

1. "Academia to Entrepreneurship," *Kettering Magazine*, 2020.
2. "Johnson Named Minnesota CEO of the Month," *C-Level Magazine*, online edition, July 13, 2016.
3. "Academia to Entrepreneurship."
4. Ibid.
5. "Johnson Named Minnesota CEO of the Month."

JENNIFER KRASKA

1. "Jennifer Kraska, Interior Design Manager, Cadillac Design Studio," *Crain's Business News*, May 11, 2008.
2. Ibid.
3. Ibid.
4. Michael Accordi, "The Escala Will Be the Face of Cadillac by 2018," *GM Inside News*, 2018.

CHARON (MERUCCI) MORGAN

1. Charon Morgan, all quoted material was excerpted from email communications with the author in 2020.

JENNY MORGAN

1–2. All quotes and related material are from author communications with Jenny Morgan.

TRICIA MORROW-GROUSTRA

1. Tricia Morrow, interview by Hannah Lutz, *Auto News Rising Stars*, *Auto News*, July 2020.
2. Ibid.
3. Chevrolet Pressroom, "Chevrolet's Industry-First Buckle to Drive Feature Reminds Teen Driver to Buckle Up," online post, May 21, 2019.
4. Ibid.
5. Chevrolet Pressroom, "New Malibu Tech Helps Parents Teach Kids Safe Driving, 2016 Chevy Midsize Sedan Offers New Drivers Feature to Promote Safe Driving Habits," online post, March 20, 2020.
6. Ibid.

BRIGID O'KANE

1–5. Author interviews with Brigid O'Kane, 2014–2016.
6. C. Edson Armi, *American Car Design Now* (New York: Rizzoli International, 2003), 131–156.
7. Ibid.
8. Ibid.
9. Ibid.
10. Helen Jones Earley and James R. Walkinshaw, *Setting the Pace: Oldsmobile's First 100 Years* (Lansing, MI: Public Relations Department, Oldsmobile Division, 1996), 449.
11. Bob Lutz, *Car Guys vs. Bean Counters: The Battle for the Soul of American Business* (New York: Portfolio/Penguin, 2011).
12. Langworth, *GM: 100 Years*, 401.

KRISTY RASBACH

1. Kristy D. Rasbach, EngineerGirl (online), National Academy of Engineering, ca. 2003–2020, and National Academy of Sciences.
2. Kristy Rasbach and GM Communications, 2019.
3. Rasbach, EngineerGirl.
4. Ibid.
5. Kristy Rasbach and GM Communications, 2019.
6. Ibid.
7. Timothy B. Lee, arstechnica online 10/11/2017 arstechnica.com/cars/2017.
8. Rasbach, EngineerGirl.

KRISTEN SIEMEN

1–3. Stephanie Sokol, "ECE Alum Uses OU Experience to Change the World of Engineering," Oakland University post, November 13, 2014.
4. GM Pressroom online, March 10, 2021.

SUSAN SKARSGARD

1–3. Aaron Monday, *Metromode* (online digital magazine), October 25, 2015.

CRYSTAL WINDHAM

1. "Crystal Windham of General Motors," SimplyRides, 2014, simplyrides.com/profile-crystal-windham-of general-motors.
2. Madelyn Miller, ed., *Travel Lady* magazine, online post, www.travellady.com/Issue07/4505DesigningWomen.html.
3. Ibid.
4. Ibid.
5. Crystal Windham, LinkedIn, 2020.
6. "Virtual Reality Helps Make Impala Roomier for Real," GM Corporate Newsroom online, April 4, 2020.
7. Ibid.
8. Ibid.
9. Ibid.
10. Cadillac Pressroom Online, April 23, 2020.
11. Ibid.
12. Ibid.
13. Ibid.

PART IX

ANNE ASENSIO

1. Author conversations with Anne Asensio, 2012–2016.
2. "Chevrolet Sequel 300-Mile Zero Emissions Fuel Cell

Drive," *My Chevrolet* (GM blog), September 28, 2007.

CHRISTINE PARK CHENG

1. Communications by Christine Park Cheng with author.

MICHELLE CHRISTENSEN

1. Sophie Moura, "Michelle Christensen," marie claire, online post, February 15, 2014, http://www.marieclaire.com/career-money/advice/michelle-christensen.

2. Michelle Christensen, email to author on December 7, 2010.

3. Tamara Warren, "Acura NSX Designer Michelle Christensen," *Car & Driver*, March 20, 2015.

4. Ibid.

5. Moura, "Michelle Christensen."

6. Ibid.

7. Ibid.

8. "Rising Stars," *Automotive News*, April 20, 2015, 47.

MANDI DAMMAN

1. Deloitte Insights, *Automotive News*, ca. 2019, Deloitte Development, member of Deloitte Touche Tohmatsu, 10–13.

2. Claire Brisson, "Making the Connection to Career Technical Education (CTE)," CTE Program, MISD Macomb Intermediate School District, Clinton Township, Michigan, March 29, 2018.

3. Deloitte Insights.

ALEXANDRA DYMOWSKA

1. Aaron Monry, Metromode / Issue Media Group online.

2. Trendline.com/all-in-the-details (Trendline and Cadillac, June 13, 2020).

3. Office of Communication, Pratt Institute, *Prattfolio*, Spring/Summer 2011.

WULIN GAOWA

1. "Interview with Wulin Gaowa," *car body design*, January 10, 2012.

2. Michael Gooderham, "Wulin Gaowa Moves to UAV Startup," *car design news*, August 13, 2018.

SHARON GAUCI

1. Sharon Gauci, various email communications with author in 2012.

2. Ibid.

3. Ibid.

4. Sharon Gauci, keynote speech, "Design Studios Must Diversify for Future," WardsAuto, June 1, 2018, www.Wardsauto.com.

CECILE GIROUX

1. All quotes were provided by Cecile Giroux to the author in email during numerous communications from 2019 to July 31, 2020.

MICHELLE KILLEN

1. 2006 Alumni Notes, 2021, CCS online.

2. Jake Lingman, "Is the 2021 Escalade New King of the Road?" *Autoweek*, April 15, 2020.

3. Ibid.

4. 2006 Alumni Notes, 2021.

CHRISTINE KIRBITZ

1–2. Personal communication between the author and Christine Kirbitz between 2018 and 2020.

THERESE TANT PINAZZO

1. John McElroy, interviewer, *Tomorrow's Auto Designs*, Autoline TV, Blue Sky Productions, 2018, http://www.autoline.tv/journal/?p=54656.

2. Edsall, *Chevrolet Volt*, 78–81.

3. Ibid.

4. Cadillac Pressroom, "2021 Cadillac Escalade Elevates the Extraordinary," online post, 2020.

5. Ibid.

HEATHER SCALF

1. Conversations with Heather Scalf by author, February 9, 2014–March 7, 2016, and July 24–30, 2020.

2. "Chevy's New Car Is Open for Business," Vega brochure, collection of C. Smith.

3. "The New Towne Coupe and the 2+2 (1975 Car of the Year)," Monza brochure, collection of C. Smith.

4. Conversations with Heather Scalf by author.

MIRANDA STEINHAUSER

1. Lelo Undesign award finalist, https://www.wishpond.com/vc/296575?scid=205677&type=Merchant.

2. Good design award source: https//good-design.org/projects/general-motors-ar%E1%BF91v-e-bikes/.

VICKI VLACHAKIS (VON HOLZHAUSEN)

1. Jerome Miller, "It Shows in the Solstice," *Pontiac Performance*, Spring 2005, 14–17.

2. Ibid.

3. Ibid.

4. Ibid.

5 "Press Kit," GM Design, (2001).

INDEX

THE WOMEN OF GENERAL MOTORS
A Century of Art and Engineering

ERRATA

PAGE 3
Credit for top right photo: *Holden Effigy/GMA Design and Bandits & Co.*

PAGE 7
Photo credit: *Courtesy of Anne Asensio*

PAGE 16
Photo caption: The wireless Ultium battery pack sits below the passenger compartment in the Hummer. *Constance Smith*

PAGE 17
Photo credit: *General Motors*

PAGE 29
The first sentence under MARY MAKELA'S FIRST RIDES:
While Makela had savings from a part-time job, she found that the price of a Firebird, the sister to the Camaro, was over her head, and she had to settle for a 1970 red Chevette without power accessories and with a lack of trunk space for her needs.

PAGE 41
Caption of photo at bottom right: The exterior of the Bolt was designed in Korea. *General Motors*

PAGE 45
Credit for photo at left: *GM Book*

PAGE 61
Photo credit for image at left: *Helene Rother Collection*

PAGE 65
Caption for top photo: In 1948, Cadillac received all-new styling. Rother designed and/or managed the design for the interior. While the original fabric was broadcloth or Bedford Cord, she also selected leathers herself. *Courtesy of J. X. McCarty/National Cadillac Club*

PAGE 75
Photo credit: *General Motors*

PAGE 92
Caption for top photo: Peter Brock made this stunning drawing for the C3 Corvette in 1957. *Courtesy of Peter Brock*

PAGE 93
Photo credit: *Courtesy of Elena Kondracki/Helene Pollins*

PAGE 116
Photo credit: *General Motors*

PAGE 125
Caption: Klatil's design was configured three-dimensionally in clay. *Joan Klatil*

PAGE 128
Photo credit: *General Motors*

PAGE 149
Caption for top photo: Smith illustrated one of her earlier designs using airbrush. *Constance Smith*

PAGE 155
Missing text at the bottom of the first column:
…Buick Quester. Some prototypes appeared after they were approved for production, but before production. The new Pontiac Transport concept would not continue until 1990 as the new APV minivan. It was considered a truck as it featured a space frame. A Buick Lucerne concept also appeared. In 1985, the first HUD which used a vacuums fluorescent display and production windshield, reminiscent of the one proposed by Ruth Glennie in the 1950s, was featured on the 1988 Olds Cutlass Supreme driven in the Indy Pace car parade.
Saturn was established, but cars would not be offered until 1990.
Let us not forget the contributions made by Opel and Vauxhall,…

PAGE 188
Photo credit: *Lucerne/GM China*

PAGE 228
Caption for center photo: In addition to the Red Fox exterior, the 2015 EV concept incorporated a contemporary interior, a fractal pattern on the printed glass roof, and 3D lamp lenses. *General Motors*

PAGE 242
Photo credit: *Courtesy of Constance Smith*

PAGE 246
Photo credit: *Courtesy of Teresa Spafford*

PAGE 251
Photo credit: *General Motors*

PAGE 290
Caption for photo at right: Surfaces and materials are rich in the Escalade and highlight 38-inch OLED instrument panel display which consists of three screens. *Constance Smith*

PAGE 299
Photo credit: *John F. Martin Photography*

PAGE 331
Notes
SANDRA LONGYEAR RICHARDSON
1. Conversations with Sandra Longyear Richardson by author from 2010 to 2014 and in 2021.

JACKET, FRONT FLAP
New text:
…Suzanne Vanderbilt, the holder of numerous engineering patents and the designer of the first adjustable lumbar seat supports;…

COVER IMAGE CREDITS:
Front: *GM*: Lyriq, Mary Barra, Barbara Munger; *Julie Sabit*: Margaret Sauer; *Nick Hagen*: D.J. Barber; *Petersen Family*: Ruth Glennie; *Constance Smith*: Helene Rother, Mei Cai, Renee Bryant. **Back:** *GM*: Denise Gray (jacket), Mei Cai; *Christine Kirbitz*: C. Kirbitz; *Yan Huang*: Yan-Hong Huang; *S. Fecht*: Magalie Debellis; *John F. Martin*: Rebecca Waldmeir. **Back Flap:** *Dominic Peluso*: Constance Smith